The Windows 95 Book

The Windows 95 Book

The Definitive Desktop Reference for Windows 95

Richard Mansfield & Charles Brannon

VENTANA

The Windows 95 Book: The Definitive Desktop Reference for Windows 95
Copyright ©1995 by Richard Mansfield & Charles Brannon

Library of Congress Cataloging-in-Publication Data

Mansfield, Richard.
    The Windows 95 book / Richard Mansfield & Charles Brannon.
        p.   cm.
    Includes index.
    ISBN 1-56604-154-6
    1. Operating systems (Computers) 2. Microsoft Windows 95.
    I. Brannon, Charles.   II. Title.
    QA76.76.O63M354   1995
    005.4'469--dc20   95-1390
                                                                          CIP

Book design: Marcia Webb
Vice President, Ventana Press: Walter R. Bruce III
Art Director: Marcia Webb
Design staff: Bradley King, Dawne Sherman, Charles Overbeck
Editorial Manager: Pam Richardson
Editorial staff: Angela Anderson, Beth Snowberger
CD Product Manager: Neweleen Trebnik
CD Technical Director: Eric Knisley
Project Editor: Jessica Ryan
Print Department: Kristen DeQuattro, Dan Koeller, Wendy Bernhardt
Production Manager: John Cotterman
Production staff: Patrick Berry, Scott Hosa, Lance Kozlowski, Jaimie Livingston
Index service: Richard T. Evans, Infodex
Proofreader: Sue Versenyi, Vicky Wells
Technical review: George Moore, William R. Stott III

First Edition 9 8 7 6 5 4 3 2 1
Printed in the United States of America

Ventana Communication Group, Inc.
P.O. Box 13964
Research Triangle Park, NC 27709-3964
919/544-9404
FAX 919/544-9472

Limits of Liability and Disclaimer of Warranty

Trademarks

Trademarked names appear throughout this book. Rather than list the names and entities that own the trademarks or insert a trademark symbol with each mention of the trademarked name, the publisher states that it is using the names only for editorial purposes and to the benefit of the trademark owner with no intention of infringing upon that trademark.

About the Authors

Charles Brannon was Program Editor for *Compute Publications* from 1980 to 1986, where he developed numerous ground-breaking programs, including SpeedScript, the best-selling word processor for home computers. In his hundreds of magazine articles and columns, Charles has taught millions of computer owners how to get the most out of their machines. Charles was a Project Manager for Epyx, Inc., from 1986 to 1988, where he developed leading productivity and entertainment software. He is currently a computer consultant, shareware programmer, network administrator and freelance author.

Richard Mansfield's books have sold over 350,000 copies worldwide and have been translated into six other languages. He was editor-in-chief of *Compute Magazine* for seven years. His published work includes 15 books, magazine columns, numerous articles and several short stories. He is author of several bestsellers, including *The Visual Guide to Visual Basic* and *The Visual Basic Power Toolkit* (both published by Ventana) and *Machine Language for Beginners*. The Software Publishers Association gave him its award for special contributions to the industry. He is currently a full-time writer.

Acknowledgments

Our gratitude to the talented and thoughtful staff at Ventana Communications, particularly Joe and Liz Woodman for their vision; Jessica Ryan for her patience, editing and calm; Marcia Webb for her designs; Pam Richardson for her several contributions; John Cotterman for managing production; and Neweleen Trebnik for organizing the CD. Special thanks go to George Moore and Wolliam Stott for their many helpful technical suggestions. Charles also wishes to thank the friends, relatives and colleagues who supported and encouraged him during this effort, including Marty Beste, Bill Brannon, Michael Brannon, Joel Diamond and the Powered by Windows 95 Advisors, Randy Fosner, Lori Herron, Wendy McChesney and all the Windows 95 beta testers on the WINBTU forum on CompuServe.

Dedication

Charles Brannon dedicates this book to his mother, Suzanne Brannon Ramsey.

Richard Mansfield dedicates this book to Jim Coward.

Contents

Section III   Interacting With Windows

Section IV   Focus on Software

Section V Focus on Hardware

Section VI Getting Connected

Section VII   Expert Windows

Chapter 20   **Multimedia** **965**

Chapter 21   **Optimization: Expert Memory Management** **1013**

Introduction

Nearly two years ago—when we first started using Windows 95 on a daily basis—we set ourselves the goal of writing the definitive book on this exceptional operating system. How close we've come to succeeding, we'll leave for you to decide. But if effort counts, we've spent more time researching and writing this book than any of the other 17 computer books we've written over the past 12 years.

We were particularly fortunate to have received ongoing and in-depth technical advice from several of the top people on the Windows 95 team at Microsoft. And the entire book was read and commented by a senior Windows 95 software engineer (George Moore). Even though it's written for the average computer user, we nonetheless wanted technical depth in this book. We wanted to explain, for example, how to use advanced features like the Windows 95 Registry to remove all icons from the desktop or to locate a forgotten password. But we wanted these explanations to be so clear and easily understood that anyone, even someone entirely new to computing, could follow the steps and achieve results.

We've covered virtually every aspect of Windows 95—from elementary topics like new mouse techniques to advanced subjects like setting up a network. But above all we've attempted to make every topic *clear*. We didn't avoid technical issues in the service of clarity; we just wrote and rewrote until we and the editors were satisfied that anyone could easily understand and use the information.

What's the Plan?

The book is divided into seven sections, progressing from the simpler subjects covered in the early chapters to more demanding topics later in the book. However, this isn't *Gone With the Wind*. We expect that few readers will move sequentially from Chapter 1 through 23. Therefore you'll find frequent cross-references in each chapter, suggesting where to look elsewhere in the book for additional or related information. And, of course, the Index provides the precise locations of any topic, anywhere in the book.

We've tried to make the book a useful and durable reference for all aspects of Windows 95, so in that sense the book is exhaustive in its coverage. But we've also organized individual chapters so they present information in a tutorial fashion. There are many ways to use Windows 95 to become more productive and to make your computing more enjoyable. This is an operating system with a deceptively simple surface concealing a powerful and highly configurable engine underneath. We're still finding new techniques and shortcuts—even after having used Windows 95 daily for 19 months.

It's our hope that you'll find in this book many helpful techniques and suggestions, along with answers to any questions you might have about Windows 95. And that you'll find those answers and techniques both useful and understandable.

What's Inside

Section 1, "Welcome to Windows 95," covers the basics of Windows 95.

The first half of *Chapter 1* is for readers who have never been exposed to Windows at all—even in its earlier incarnations as Windows 3.0 or 3.1. We introduce the elements of a graphical user interface—the mouse, windows and so on. The second half of Chapter 1 is an overview of what's new in Windows 95—the convergence of Program Manager and File Manager into the Explorer; novel elements like *shortcuts*, right-clicking and the taskbar; and the overall integration into the operating system of such utilities as disk compression, backup, multimedia and so on.

Chapter 2 explains why you're unlikely to see desktop add-ons like Symantic's Norton Desktop or Hewlett-Packard's Dashboard designed for Windows 95. The Windows 95 approach to launching programs—the Start button and it's many features—is so well-conceived and accessible that there's not much left for third-party products to improve on.

Chapter 3 covers the Windows 95 taskbar. It works harmoniously with the Start button to help you switch between running programs and take full advantage of multitasking, organizing open windows, changing the volume of sound effects or music, and showing you the time and date. For all its power, the taskbar is uniquely simple and easy to operate. We'll show you how to customize the taskbar, too.

Section 2, "Getting Organized," explores the Windows 95 approach to arranging and locating files on disk drives; how to customize the desktop; and using Control Panel to solve hardware conflicts, change fonts and so on.

Chapter 4 presents useful file management techniques and teaches you how to take full advantage of the Windows 95 Explorer, a powerful replacement for the Windows 3.1 file manager. You'll find out how to organize your hard drive and learn the lay of the land: what *are* all those folders Windows installs on your hard drive?

Chapter 5 takes a step back and examines the fundamentals of your computer's filing system. We answer the basic question, "What are files?" and follow that with thorough explanations of how your file system works. We also include detailed steps showing you how to optimize, defragment, scan and backup your hard drive.

Chapter 6 delves into the many and various ways you can design your desktop—choosing backgrounds and wallpaper; using screen savers; adjusting the size, color and fonts of menus, windows and buttons; and changing video resolution.

Chapter 7 describes every element of the Control Panel. You'll learn how to use the new Wizards to follow along step-by-step as a Wizard assists you in fixing a conflict between your new sound card and your modem. The Control Panel is also where you can change options and settings for all peripherals—from mouse to multimedia devices. It's the master control center where you set up, configure, troubleshoot and customize your computer. Here you'll find a description of every control panel icon and function.

Section 3, "Interacting with Windows," tells you everything you could possibly want to know about the keyboard and mouse.

Chapter 8 covers the keyboard—the various models, shortcut techniques, new Windows 95 "hot keys" and so on.

Chapter 9 forced itself into being. We had originally intended to discuss the mouse at the end of the chapter on the keyboard, but the little critter surprised us. There's a chapter's worth of information to convey about this seemingly uncomplicated device. For one thing, Windows 95 makes much more use of the right button and also introduces several new mouse techniques including ultra-slow double-clicking (use it to change a filename of an icon on the desktop, in a folder, or in the Explorer). You'll also learn how to customize your mouse pointer with colorful shapes and animations.

Section 4, "Focus on Software," includes the largest chapter in the book—an in-depth description of how to use all the accessories and applets bundled with Windows 95. You'll also find many tips and techniques for using new OLE technologies and getting the most out of desktop publishing.

Chapter 10 explores the generous set of accessories that Windows provides as part of the package. We cover WordPad, Notepad, Calculator, Paint, the games and all the other "freebie" applications in Windows 95. Some of these applets and utilities, however, are covered elsewhere in the book. Multimedia accessories (the CD and Multimedia Players, Sound Recorder) are covered in Chapter 20, and system tools (Backup, Defragmenter, DriveSpace and ScanDisk) are covered in Chapter 5.

Chapter 11 looks at several new and related techniques. OLE, Object Linking and Embedding is the technical term. We show how to work with compound documents—disk files that contain more than one kind of document. For example, you can embed a picture that you've created in Paint into e-mail you're sending over The Microsoft Network online service. We also look at the Windows Object Packager utility; in-place editing; the new Paste Special feature; and the differences between linking and embedding.

If you're at all interested in one of the most valuable, enjoyable and popular personal computer activities—desktop publishing—*Chapter 12* is for you. It's for anyone interested in producing ads, business cards, flyers, manuals, or any printed document. To achieve professional-looking results, you'll want to understand the basics of design and that's the focus in Chapter 12. It's packed with examples, before-and-after designs and tips to help you create commercial-quality documents.

Section 5, "Focus on Hardware," looks at how Windows 95 interacts with your system—your printer, the computer itself and other peripherals.

Chapter 13 covers the new, more efficient print spooling in Windows 95, how to install a printer, set it up, adjust its properties, control print jobs and, in general, get the most out of what is perhaps your most useful peripheral.

Chapter 14 goes "deep inside the machine" to explain everything you ever wanted to know about how a computer works—buses, microprocessors, RISCs and the rest. You might find this discussion a solid background for optimizing your computer or adding new equipment, which is covered in later chapters.

Chapter 15 is all about adding peripherals—devices like CD-ROMs and scanners—to expand the capabilities of your machine. You'll learn how to safely and effectively open your case and upgrade your machine. We look at how Windows 95 intelligently tries to assist in resolving mysterious conflicts with names like DMA and IRQ—and why in the future these headaches should become a bad memory.

Section 6, "Getting Connected," tells you how to expand your computer's potential by connecting it to another computer in your office, across the country, or even on the other side of the world.

Chapter 16, "The Communicating Computer," tells you how to connect via modem to online information and other resources. You'll learn all you ever wanted to know about modems and BBS services. You'll get online with Hyperterminal and understand how to use Microsoft Fax.

Chapter 17 is all about the Internet, probably the most active zone and hottest topic in computing today. We show you how to shop for an Internet provider, how to set up Internet access and ways to take advantage of your newfound connectivity to browse the Web, participate in newsgroups, retrieve new software and keep in contact with global electronic mail.

We waited until the last minute, only a few weeks before this book went to the printer, to write *Chapter 18*. The Microsoft Network is exploding internally—continually adding new services, sections, features and structures. Although this ferment will doubtless decrease somewhat over time, the content of MSN—like shows on TV or bestselling books—will always change. We cover content of course, but focus on technique: How do you navigate within this virtual world?

Chapter 19 shows you how to set up a business or personal network. Fortunately, Windows 95 contains sophisticated and extensive networking support. Networking is, of course, easily a book-length topic. However, in Chapter 19 we provide the basics and beyond, guiding you through the steps to connect together and work cooperatively, sharing files and printers to cut costs and coordinate teamwork.

Section 7, "Expert Windows," focuses on topics generally considered cutting-edge or advanced: multimedia, memory management, DOS 7, automation and programming.

Chapter 20 looks at Windows 95's improved multimedia support—both the tweaking "under the hood" and special features like self-starting CD's. We also explore improved caches, compression, MIDI "polymessage" technology and the like. And, of course, there's in-depth coverage of things like creating playlists for audio CDs; video playback and recording; and other multimedia features.

Chapter 21 demonstrates that managing your computer's memory will always be important. Sure, it was essential in DOS. If you wanted to play that game, you had to remove some TSRs and fiddle with AUTOEXEC.BAT and CONFIG.SYS. It was still important in Windows 3.1 and it remains important in Windows 95. In this chapter we tell you what you need to know to maximize the efficiency of your machine and its operating system. We cover how to take advantage of all the memory you have and how to let Windows create additional memory using virtual memory technology. We also see how to optimize memory for DOS and Windows applications.

Chapter 22 is retrogressive, but necessary. It's about DOS. Although DOS programs are fast going the way of the dinosaur, DOS isn't going to disappear overnight. In this chapter we describe how to efficiently use DOS programs within the Windows 95 environment and examine the most useful DOS commands, in case you find yourself atavistically drawn to that old command line.

There are useful techniques, such as the macro languages built into Windows applications, that can be used to customize most anything. *Chapter 23* shows anyone, step-by-step, how to make things happen the way you want them to happen. Write "scripts" that do 15 things with a click on a button. Make your applications work together, sharing data, exchanging data, even controlling each other's behavior. This stuff is advanced, but our challenge was to make it usable and clear to everyone. Through macros and other techniques such as OLE automation, you can make your Windows applications dance to your tune. If you want things to work a special way, or you want to automate a complicated, frequently required task—you'll find out how to do it here.

Conventions Used in this Book

There are only two things that might throw you: our format that indicates menus and their submenus and our way of indicating text that appears on a window. Let's resort to pictures to clarify this, as we do often throughout the book.

Vertical Lines Indicate Menu Items

You'll see vertical lines separating words—not a traditional punctuation. It looks like this: To reduce the size of the icons in a folder, click on **View | Small Icons**. That translates: click on the View menu and then click on the Small Icons option.

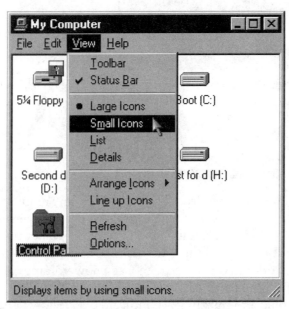

Figure 1: *We use the punctuation **View | Small Icons** to mean click on the View menu, then the Small Icons option.*

Sometimes you'll see multiple vertical lines to indicate submenus. The navigation illustrated in Figure 2 would be described like this: **View | Arrange Icons | Auto Arrange**.

Figure 2: *When you see **View | Arrange Icons | Auto Arrange** in this book, click on the View menu, then move down to the Arrange Icons submenu to pop out the final set of options. Then click on Auto Arrange.*

Dialog Descriptions are Italicized

We've striven to eliminate, or at least greatly reduce, any ambiguity in this book. So how do we punctuate text that appears in property sheet windows (or *dialog boxes*) ? We don't want it to blend in with the rest of the sentence. Here's an example. Do you find the next sentence easily comprehensible? When you want to add it to the taskbar, choose Show volume control on the taskbar from the Multimedia property sheet.

Rather cumbersome and puzzling. To indicate that "Show volume control on the taskbar" is a label in a property sheet—something you should look for within Windows 95—we *italicize* it:

When you want to add it to the taskbar, choose *Show volume control on the taskbar* from the Multimedia property sheet.

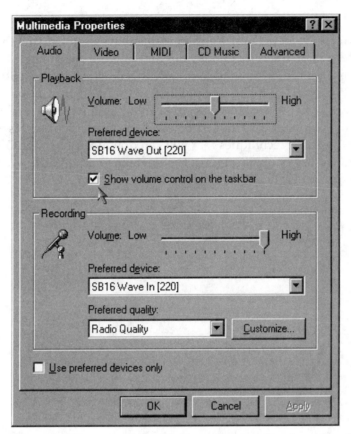

Figure 3: *When we refer to labels, captions or other descriptive text within Windows 95—like* Show volume control on the taskbar *here—we italicize them.*

Into the Future

Traditionally, you could expect a new version of a computer program or operating system every year or two. Windows 3 came out in 1990 and Windows 3.1 followed in 1992, then Windows 95 in—you guessed it—1995.

We don't think that Windows 95 will reappear like this, in new discrete versions as quantum packets in the coming years. Instead, we expect Windows 95 will be continually refined rather than revised all at once. It will likely undergo a steady process of improvement, and those small adjustments might be offered to us users continually. There probably won't be a series of major revisions, except for once every few years. You'll probably use your modem to download the latest fixes, changes and refinements perhaps monthly or quarterly. We don't have any inside word on this from

Microsoft, but we nonetheless expect Windows from now on to undergo ceaseless improvement. And we users will always be able to get the most up-to-date version over the phone lines and into our machines.

With this in mind, we intend to update this book in parallel with Windows 95. We expect to follow the publishing tradition of printing major new editions every year or so. However, in keeping with what we expect will be a constant adjustment of Windows 95, we'll also provide rewrites and updates, new tips and techniques that you can download from the Online Companion to our book, located on the Ventana Online World Wide Web Server (http://vmedia.com/win95.html).

Richard Mansfield
Charles Brannon

Welcome to Windows 95

Chapter 1

Up & Running

Part I: Graphical Computing

If you want a general overview of Windows 95, this chapter's for you. We'll start at ground zero. We've divided this chapter into two parts. In the first part we'll look at Windows 95 from the point of view of a person who's never used a computer before or someone who's coming to Windows 95 from DOS. So, if you're moving from Windows 3.1 to Windows 95 and you're familiar with the basics of "graphical computing," you might want to skip ahead to Part II of this chapter, "Windows 95: an Overview" on page 22.

Part II is for everybody. There we'll tour the main features of Windows 95, consider various ways you can organize your visual "desktop" and look at valuable techniques to help you get the most out of Windows 95.

The taskbar, docucentricity, 3D visuals, enhanced drag and drop, the Explorer and many other new or improved features combine to make Windows 95 a quantum leap forward from earlier Windows versions. You might not notice the depth of the changes immediately, but as the days and weeks go by, you'll likely find yourself increasingly impressed with new discoveries, new ways of doing things and the intuitiveness and essential *logic* of the behaviors of Windows 95.

We've been working with Windows 95 for nearly two years. And we're still discovering things it can do! We hope the illustrations, tips, step-by-step descriptions and in-depth discussions in this book will help you feel comfortable and confident about using this impressive new operating system.

Your First Day

Every year millions of people around the world learn to use a computer. Fifty million new computers will be sold during 1995 alone. Those starting now are lucky—computers are getting easier to use all the time. So, turn it on and let it "get itself together" for 20 to 30 seconds. When it's first turned on, the computer has to do some housekeeping—check its memory, remind itself what disk drives you have attached, and so on.

After this "initialization" process, the computer is ready to do what you ask it to do. In Windows 95 you'll see a screen that looks something like Figure 1-1:

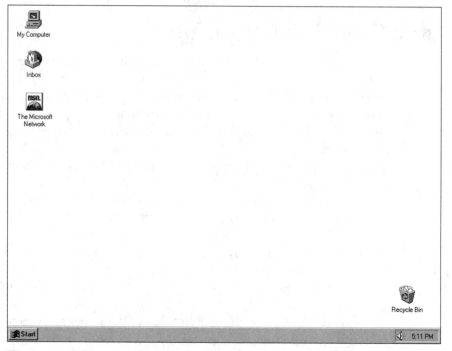

Figure 1-1: *When you first turn on a Windows 95 computer, you'll see something like this. It's your video "desktop."*

Don't worry if your screen looks somewhat different. Windows 95 is marvelously customizable. Everybody can personalize their own desktop, so few look exactly alike. The "desktop" is that vacant space around any opened folders or windows.

Notice that pointer arrow on the screen. That's your computer's mouse pointer. Try moving your mouse around a little and watch the pointer mimic your movements. The pointer is your representative on the Windows

95 desktop, you can use it to draw or paint or point to things, to open and close things, to save and print things, and much more. It's like a little hand that you can use inside the computer to manipulate things in the "virtual reality" of this "desktop." (For much more on the mouse, see Chapter 9.)

Figure 1-2: *The mouse pointer is a substitute "hand" you use to manipulate things on your video desktop.*

In the lower left corner there's a button labeled "Start." Move the pointer down there, then press and release ("click," it's called) the left button on your mouse. The Start button looks like it has been depressed. A "menu" pops up. This is a list of options. On top are some programs you can run by clicking on their name, or "folders" you can open.

Windows is extremely flexible. There are often two or three ways to do something. Why? Because people have different preferences and like to work different ways. Here's one example. Some people work a lot with graphics—designing books or newsletters, retouching photos, creating art. The mouse is especially useful for moving images around, trimming them, and so forth. Therefore, a person working in graphics usually has the mouse in hand. Clicking on a menu option is often their preferred way of maneuvering around Windows—choosing options, saving files and all the other things you can do with a computer.

But writers, editors and others who work with words usually have both hands on the keyboard. So, for many of these people it's easier to maneuver by using keys on the keyboard rather than reaching for the mouse. That's why Windows makes provisions for both preferences: you can do almost anything with *either* the mouse or the keyboard.

Most of us do various things with our computers, so sometimes a mouse click is fastest and other times a keyboard shortcut is fastest. You'll quickly learn many of your favorite ways to work the computer. For instance, you can also pop up the Start menu any time by pressing Ctrl+Esc. (This means hold down the key labeled Ctrl while also pressing the key labeled Esc.) This key combination might seem awkward at first, especially if you have to hunt for these keys. But eventually it will be second nature if you use it often enough. And there's an even easier way to pop up the Start menu if you have a new-style keyboard (like the Microsoft Natural Keyboard). There's a special "Windows" key—it has the Windows logo on it. When pressed, up pops the Start menu.

Now back to the Start menu. Notice that the menu is divided into three sections by two horizontal lines. The top section lists programs or folders. (You can easily add or remove these, but when you first install Windows 95 there won't be anything listed here. To add your favorite programs to the convenient Start menu, see Chapter 2.)

The middle section contains *categories* such as Programs, Settings and Help. The bottom section is where you click when you want to stop using the computer. This allows Windows to do some housekeeping before it gives you permission to turn off the power.

Try moving your mouse pointer onto the word *Programs*, but don't click it. (You can click if you want to, but you don't have to.) Another menu pops out. These selections include programs grouped together, categories called *folders* or, in earlier terminology, *directories* or *Program Groups*. For instance, if you use WordPerfect as a word processor, you might see the WordPerfect program there, as well as a couple of support programs supplied with WordPerfect. These categories are created by Windows if you installed Windows 95 over an earlier version of Windows. In other words, it takes your program groups and puts them on this menu.

Some of these folders (program groups) will have black wedge-shaped arrows pointing to the right—showing that there are additional menus that will become visible if you move your pointer onto the folder's name.

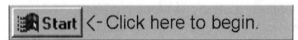

Figure 1-3: *The Start button. Here you can launch applications, change settings, search for files and accomplish many other common tasks.*

Getting Help

Let's briefly look at the rest of the categories in the Start Menu. For a thorough discussion of all the options and features of this important Windows tool, see Chapter 2.

Next, beneath Programs on the Start menu, is Documents—the most recent 15 files of text or graphics that you've worked on. They're sitting there ready to be clicked on (they'll automatically load the program in which you edited them previously). Next on the Start menu is Settings, where you can specify how your screen looks, how your printer prints and so on. Next is Find, where you can locate any folder, file, document, content in the Microsoft Network or even a specific piece of text on your hard drive. Click on the Help option (or press F1) and you'll see Windows 95's "electronic

manual" where you can get information on how to accomplish almost anything Windows 95 can do. Figure 1-4 shows the Contents options, where
answers and advice are located under general headings like the table of
contents of a book.

Figure 1-4: *One way to get help is to work your way down from a general
category like "Tour: Ten minutes to using Windows" to lists of more specific topics.*

A "window" is any framed piece of information; there can be several
open windows at any given time on your Windows desktop. In the window
shown in Figure 1-4, you can *double-click* (press and release your left mouse
button twice in rapid succession) and you'll see a list of other, more specific,
topics under the general heading you've clicked on.

Another way to use Help is to click on the "tab" at the top labeled Index
and you can look up information by typing in the topic you're interested in.
As you might guess, this Index is the equivalent of an index in the back of a
book. Far more detailed than a table of contents, but it does take a little
longer to research a topic in an index. In Figure 1-5, we typed in **CD** and
found that several entries related to CD-ROM drives are listed. To see one of
them, double-click on it.

Figure 1-5: *The other main way into Help: just type in a subject you're interested in and you'll see a list of related topics.*

Help also includes a *really* thorough way to explore an idea—there's no equivalent to the Find option in the world of books, other than reading the whole book. When you select Find, Windows will search *every word* in the entire Help "book," if that's what you want. In other words, you get more than an index, more even than a concordance—you get a cross-reference of everything.

Choose the Find option only if you haven't been able to locate what you're after via Contents or Index. Find can give you a fairly large list to look through—unless of course you ask it to find something that's not even in the huge Windows Help texts, like *Brad Pitt* or *peaches*.

The collection of information that makes up Windows 95 Help is about twice the size of an ordinary book. So don't ask Find to locate all instances of the word *mouse* unless you're prepared to deal with 65 hits.

When you select Find, you get into one of Windows's "Wizards" that steps you through a process until you've achieved your goal. First you're asked just how deeply you want to search Help. The Minimize Database Size option attempts to cut down on the time, and the resulting hits, by avoiding apparently useless hits. Maximize Database Size is the full treatment—you'll get a list of *everything* that matches your search criterion. Customize Search Capabilities displays a list of the seven help categories that

Windows clusters into its main Help engine. This way, if you know your query doesn't involve, say, networks, you can at least eliminate that area, thereby speeding up the search process and reducing the size of the list of hits that you'll eventually be shown.

Run

Finally, below Help at the bottom of the list of choices under the Start button, you'll see Run, which is yet another way to start applications running. Following that is Shut Down, which turns off Windows 95 in an orderly fashion.

 TIP When you're finished using the computer, instead of just turning off the power, you should click on "Shut Down." This way, Windows 95 will check to see if there are any unsaved documents or other information that should be sent to the hard drive (for permanent storage). For example, if you've been typing in a letter and turn off the power to your computer, it's likely that what you've written will not be available the next time you turn on the computer. Your work will have disappeared!

The reason for this unhappy prospect is that the computer keeps current work in its internal RAM memory (which is quicker to access). However, this kind of memory goes blank each time power is turned off. Therefore, you should save your writing (or other work) to your hard drive from time to time, and especially before you shut down a writing application such as Word for Windows, or before turning off power to your computer. Most applications, though, and Windows 95 itself, will remind you if you forget to save something that needs to be saved. A little window like the one shown in Figure 1-6 will appear. (This reminder, however, *will not appear if you just turn off the power.*)

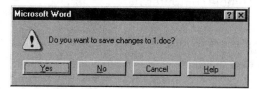

Figure 1-6: *Before allowing you to shut down, most applications will remind you that they contain unsaved work.*

TIP   You can almost always get Help by pressing the F1 key, no matter what else is happening in the computer, or where you "are" on the desktop or within a running program.

"My Computer"

There's one symbol on your desktop that never goes away. You can delete any desktop icons you create (you'll see how to do this later), but the icon labeled *My Computer* can't be removed.

 TIP   You can change the label on the My Computer icon. Just click on the label, pause a second or two, then click again. Now you can type in a new name, like "Fred" or whatever. Note that this slow double-click is uniquely used to change the names of files and folders. It's not the same as the common double-click where the second click is made quite rapidly.

My Computer

Figure 1-7: *The My Computer icon is always on your desktop. It can be moved around but can't be deleted. (There is, though, a way to hide it. See Chapter 6.)*

Double-click on My Computer and you'll see a window like that shown in Figure 1-8. (Precisely which icons you see, and their names, depends on what disk drives or CD-ROMs you have attached to your machine. However, the My Computer window is a bird's-eye view of all the drives and top-level folders for your whole computer.)

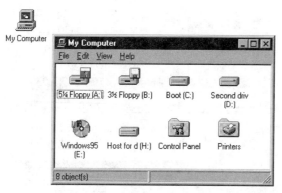

Figure 1-8: *Double-clicking on My Computer displays the highest level of your computer.*

If you now double-click on, say, the icon of your C:\ drive (that's the main hard drive in most people's computer), you'll see folders and icons like those shown in Figure 1-9.

Figure 1-9: *Double-clicking on the C:\drive icon displays the folders and files on your hard drive.*

Double-click on a folder and you'll see icons for documents (like pictures you've drawn or letters you've written) along with, possibly, other folders. Figure 1-10 is the result of clicking on the WinVideo folder in the StartUp(C:) window behind it.

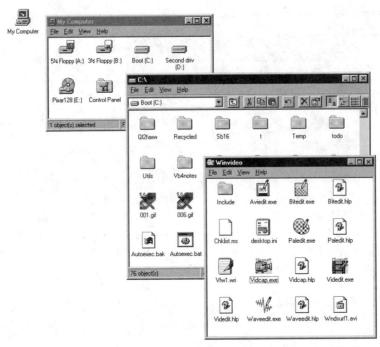

Figure 1-10: *Near the lowest level, we're now seeing mostly files (programs and documents) and only one folder.*

Common Questions

All beginners learn to use computers the same way—by trial and error. It's like finding your way around a new town; in this case, it's finding out how to communicate with their new machine.

However, all beginners mess up in unique ways—there's so much variety in computers, so many things you can do. If you get stuck, the first thing to do is click on the Start button, then click on Help Topics (or just press the F1 key). If you can't find an answer there (or don't understand the answer), try looking in the Index of this book.

There are, however, typical questions that most beginners ask during their first few days of communicating with their machines. What follows is a compendium of these questions, and the answers.

How do I install a new application?

When you buy a new piece of software—a game, a word processor, whatever—before you can use it you must first install it, or, as Microsoft prefers to call the process, *setup*. This means copying to your hard drive the software from the floppy disks or CD(s) that come in the software package. CD units and floppy disk drives don't run as fast as a hard drive, so you will normally want to put software on your hard drive.

Almost all software is installed into Windows 95 in the same way, so let's go through the process step-by-step:

1. In the software manual (or sometimes in a separate booklet) you'll find a section called "INSTALLATION" or "SETUP." Generally, this section describes how much space you'll need on your hard drive to hold the software, any special requirements (a sound card, for instance), and the steps necessary to install the new program.

2. Put the first floppy disk (it will be labeled #1 or 1 of 5 or SETUP or something like that) in your floppy drive. You'll find a program on the first floppy disk. This program is nearly always called SETUP.EXE. (A very few applications still use the term INSTALL.EXE or something else, but most use SETUP.EXE.)

3. Click on the Start button on your Windows 95 desktop, then move up and click on Run. See Figure 1-11.

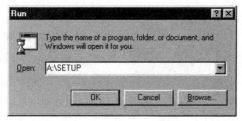

Figure 1-11: *Here's how you install a new application.*

 TIP   If you are installing from a CD drive, it will probably be drive E: or F: or some letter higher in the alphabet than A, B or C. The process is the same as for floppies, except that you initially specify E:\SETUP or whatever your CD-ROM's drive letter is. If you don't know, just click on the Browse button shown in Figure 1-11. Then click on the list box at the top (see Figure 1-12) and you'll see a list of your drives—the floppy(s), hard drive(s) and CD-ROM. You can click on any one of these drives to then see a list of the files on it. Finally, click on SETUP.EXE and you're off and running.

4. Type in A:\SETUP (or perhaps B:\SETUP if you put the floppy disk in drive B:). Then click on the OK button and follow the instructions that appear on your screen. When one floppy has been transferred to your hard drive, a message will appear asking you to "Put Disk #2 in your A: drive" or something similar.

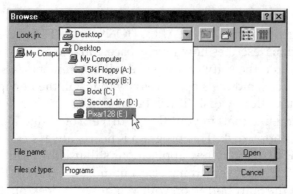

Figure 1-12: *Browsing a CD for the SETUP installation program.*

 TIP The Browse button allows you to locate SETUP.EXE the same way you'd use Windows 95's Explorer to locate any file you want to run.

How do I run an application?

Before you can write a letter or draw a picture, you must first start an application *running*. Applications like Word for Windows or Paintbrush have tools that are optimized for the task you plan to accomplish. For example, Paintbrush *does* let you type in text, but Word has all kinds of helpful additional tools like a built-in spelling checker, a Thesaurus, a word counter and so on. Put another way, Word is *optimized* to be a toolbox for writing text. Paintbrush, CorelDRAW!, Photoshop and other such applications have all kinds of features to help you create graphics; but to them, text is mainly just another set of shapes.

There are many ways in Windows 95 to start an application running. The simplest way is to double-click on the name of a text document or painting that's listed on your screen in Explorer or in another window.

TIP   You don't actually need to double-click. You can simply click on an icon and press Enter, or click on an icon, and choose Open from the File menu of the window. But you'll find that double-click is the most useful way to start programs and open objects.

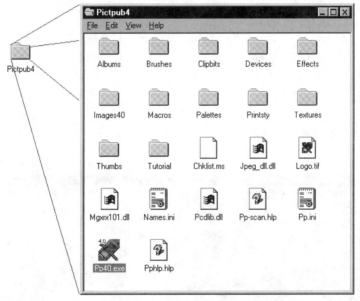

Figure 1-13: *Double-click on a folder to open the documents and applications collected inside the folder. Here we open the Picture Publisher graphics application's folder.*

Figure 1-14: *The quickest way to start an application running is to double-click on a document that you created in that application. Here we're clicking on a picture called seapples.*

Figure 1-15: *The application blooms open, containing the document you double-clicked on.*

Notice in Figure 1-14 that the *document* (the data, the graphic image you previously created) is not the same thing as the *application* with which you created the document (Picture Publisher in this case). However, as you can see, they both have the same icon, though the document's icon is smaller. Clicking on either of these icons will start Picture Publisher running, but clicking on the document also loads that particular document. This way, you're ready to start working immediately (without having to select Load from the File menu, then bringing in the document you're after).

There are many other ways to launch applications. See Chapter 2 for an in-depth discussion of how to run programs. In that chapter you're sure to find one or two techniques that fit best with the way you like to work.

How do I save my work?

Whether you're writing a letter, composing music, creating an animation or drawing a greeting card—you must *save your work*. Computers have two kinds of memory, just like people: short-term memory (RAM) and long-term memory (your hard drive, or a tape drive, or floppy disk).

Short-term RAM memory is very fast, but it's on silicon chips inside the computer and depends on a constant flow of electricity. Long-term memory is like a cassette tape: it contains patterns of magnetized iron filings and doesn't need any electricity to retain its information. (In fact, electromagnetism can *destroy* the information on magnetic long-term media like floppy disks. Hold one quite near a running electrical appliance like a TV screen and you run the risk of losing information stored on the disk. You will likely have disturbed the magnetic patterns that store the information.)

All applications will remind you to save your work, if you try to exit the application without first saving to the hard drive (or a floppy disk). If you're writing a letter in Microsoft's word processor, Word for Windows, then try to exit by pressing the X button at the top right of the window—Word will pop up the message shown in Figure 1-16.

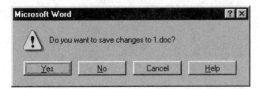

Figure 1-16: *If you try to exit a program without storing your work on the hard drive, the application will remind you to save your work.*

However, there are two situations where an application cannot warn you: If the power goes out, shutting down the computer suddenly along with all your lights and other electrical appliances; or you, or some imp in your house, shuts off the power to the computer.

Therefore, it's always good to get into the habit of saving your work every ten minutes or so when you're using the computer. It's easy to do. Just click on the File menu, then click on Save. (Alternatively, you can use a keyboard shortcut: press Alt+F, S. Hold down the Alt key while you press F, then release the Alt key and press S. This does the same thing, but you don't have to take your hands off the keyboard to reach for the mouse.)

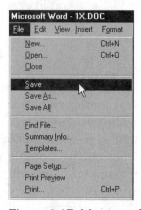

Figure 1-17: *Many people make it a habit to save their work every ten minutes or so.*

 Many applications have an automatic "backup" (or "autosave") feature. This feature will keep track of the time and save your work to disk at a regular interval. You'll usually find this option in the File menu under "Preferences" or possibly in a menu called *Tools* under "Options." In Word for Windows, press Alt+T, O to go to find it in Tools/Options. You'll see one of the new Windows 95–style "cardfile" windows, as shown in Figure 1-18:

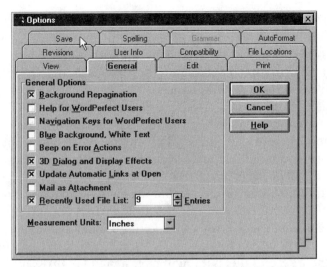

Figure 1-18: *When you have many options, it's Windows 95–style to present you with an organized, tabbed card-file metaphor.*

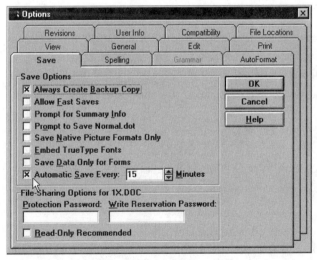

Figure 1-19: *Clicking on the Save tab offers you two ways to safeguard your work: automatic backup and automatic saving.*

Protecting your work

Notice in Figure 1-19 that Word for Windows has two ways to help you prevent losing your work. Many people use both, for extra protection. The Always Create Backup Copy option will make a separate .DOC file on your disk when you exit Word. This file is *in addition to the .DOC file that you origi-nally named and saved as the primary document.* Put another way, you'll have *two* copies of this document on disk. If anything should corrupt one of those files (disks do get corrupted sometimes) or if you accidentally delete one of the files, you'll still have the other one.

Word adds the tag ".DOC" to your documents, attaching onto whatever name you give a document. When you first save a new document, Word asks you where on your hard drive you want to save it, and what name you want to give it. You might name it *Harry*, if it's a letter to your uncle Harry. On the disk, it will be saved as HARRY.DOC. (If you've selected to save documents in some other format, similar tags will be attached, such as .TXT for unformatted text documents or .RFT for Rich Text Format styles. How-ever, most people just stick with .DOC, letting Word save in its native .DOC format.) If you have clicked on the Always Create Backup Copy option, you'll also find a second file, but it will have a tag like .BAK, for backup. So, if you use Explorer to look at the files on your disk drive, you'll see HARRY.DOC and HARRY.BAK. They're identical, but it's nice to know that you've got an extra copy just in case.

TIP   Windows 95 and most new applications written for it will suppress these "file extensions" such as .DOC, .TXT, .BAK and .BMP. In other words, the default will be "no extensions" and you'll have to specifically request to see extensions (by changing a setting in an "Options" or "Preferences" window). Instead of extensions, you're expected to identify the nature of a file by its icon or by its longer filenames: for example, "PICTURE OF PARIS." For instance, any document created in WordPerfect will be tagged with a WordPer-fect icon by default.

You can, however, change the icon that's "associated" with a particular program if you wish. To create a new association, or modify an existing one, double-click the My Computer icon (or run Explorer if you prefer). Then, from its View menu, select Options, then select the File Types tab. If you want to make a new association, choose New Type. To change an already associated file type, click on the type, and then select Edit. Another way to associate a *new* file type is to just double-click on the file itself in Explorer or a Folder view. The Open As dialog box appears, giving you a choice of programs to open the file with. If the program you want to use is not on the list, use the Browse button to locate it. You can also name the file type, and choose whether to always use this program for opening that file type.

The second option, shown in Figure 1-19, *Automatic Save Every* allows you to tell Word how often it should interrupt what you're doing to store the document. You'll be writing along, creating new paragraphs, and each time the document is saved you're keeping the latest version (the previous version is being overwritten and no longer exists). On most computers, there's no penalty when you use automatic save—the amount of time it takes to store even a large document onto disk is so brief that you'll hardly notice it.

Unfortunately, at this time word processors (and some database, spreadsheet and other applications) are one of the few kinds of programs that feature automatic saving. One reason is that automatically saving drawings, or other visual work, such as animation, *would* be intrusive. Graphics files are much, much larger, on average, than text files—so it would be an annoying interruption to automatically save while you're drawing a line or something. (Saving to or loading from the hard drive are two of the few operations that force the computer to pause until they are finished.) However, when you get up for a break, press Alt+F, S to let the computer store any improvements you've made to a drawing. In the worst case, it shouldn't take more than a few seconds.

 If your work is critical, and very difficult to re-create, be sure to implement a backup strategy. In Chapter 5, you'll learn how to backup your system to a tape drive (since backup to floppies is impractical). Also consider the purchase of a Uninterruptible Power Supply, a battery device that powers your computer for ten minutes or so if the power goes out, giving you a crucial opportunity to save your work and shut down gracefully.

How do I shut down an application?

There are four ways to shut down a running application. You can click just once on the X button at the top right of the application's window. Or you can double-click on the application's small icon at the top left of the window. (This is called the Control Icon, since it opens the Control Menu.)

Figure 1-20: *You can instantly shut down applications by clicking in either of the upper corners.*

Or you can close an application with a *single*-click on the application's small icon at the top left of the window. Then click on Close in the menu that drops down (the Control Menu).

Figure 1-21: *A third way to exit a program: click on the icon at the top left, then click on Close.*

A very fast way to exit is to press Alt+F4 (hold down the Alt key while pressing the F4 function key). If there is any unsaved work, the application will prompt you with a message asking if you want to save your work before exiting.

TIP You can repeatedly press Alt+F4 to shut down all running applications in turn. When there are no applications running, you'll shut down Windows 95 itself the final time you press Alt+F4.

The fourth way to exit is via the Exit option in the File menu of every application. Press Alt+F, X. Or click on the File menu, then click on Exit.

How do I remove an application?

Why remove an application? Perhaps you have a newer version, or you're switching from WordPerfect to Microsoft Word and you don't need two word processors. Whatever reason, you'll save space on your hard drive if you don't keep *everything* you ever used on the drive. (After all, if you change your mind, you can always re-install the application.)

Although it's possible to manually delete all the files used by an application, it's difficult to cleanly uninstall a program automatically. Software written for Windows 95 will always provide an automatic way to uninstall it, however. First, press Start, then choose the Settings menu. From Settings, choose Control Panel. When Control Panel starts and displays all the Control Panel icons, double-click the icon for Add/Remove Programs. Now choose the heading Install/Uninstall to see a list of applications that Windows 95 can uninstall for you.

If you need to manually remove an application, first read Chapter 5, which walks you through the issues involved in removing an application safely from your hard drive.

Part II: What's New

Now that we've covered the basics, let's see what's new in Windows 95. In the last half of this chapter we'll take a tour of the high points of Windows 95. The following general overview should be particularly interesting to anyone familiar with Windows 3.1 (or OS/2 or the Mac, for that matter). In other words, we'll assume that you know in general how a computer with a graphical user interface works, but that you're interested in an overview of Windows 95 in particular. While we cover all these topics in more detail in the following chapters, what follows should get you up and running under this exciting new operating system in short order.

Windows 95: an Overview

It's been years now since, in May 1990, Windows 3 took the computing world by storm. It's now by far the dominant way that people interact with computers. Estimates place its nearest rival, the Macintosh, at 10 percent market share, with other miscellaneous systems like UNIX and OS/2 in the single-digits. This means that Windows is *the* operating system for more than eight out of ten computers.

There are, of course, good reasons why Windows has been so overwhelmingly popular. But something good can always be improved, and the artists, programmers and designers at Microsoft haven't been idle for the past seven years.

There are many enhancements, both visible and invisible. We'll cover the main points briefly here; for greater detail, look in the Index for deeper coverage elsewhere in the book.

The New Look

The first thing most people notice is that Windows 95 is more attractive than earlier graphical user interfaces (GUI), such as Windows 3.1. The primary enhancement is added depth; a 3D, sculpted look has been added to virtually all the features and elements within Windows 95. Compare Figure 1-22 with Figure 1-23.

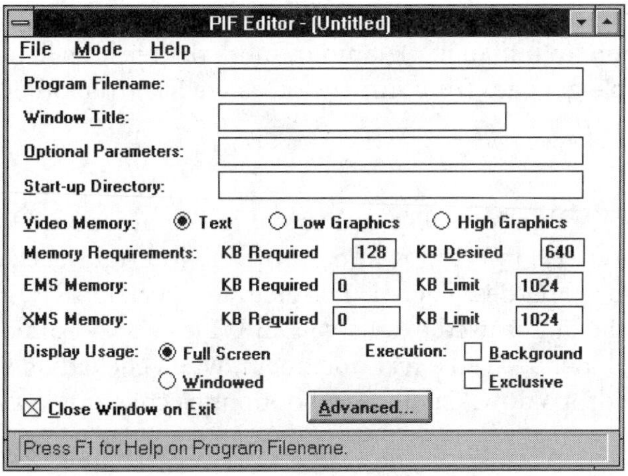

Figure 1-22: *Windows 3.1 is essentially* flat *looking—there's little highlighting or shading.*

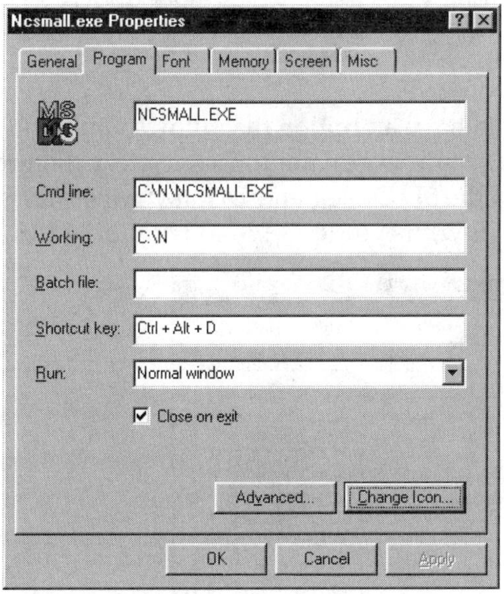

Figure 1-23: *Windows 95 appears etched, embossed and otherwise* dimensional—*more like objects in real life.*

As you can see in the two figures above, the Windows 3.1 look is essentially two-color, rather like a simple text document. Windows 95, by contrast, has several layers and is superimposed with 3D visual cues. This new look is the result of considerable usability testing and many focus groups. And there's more to it than just glamour, more than just its handsome appearance. People get cues from dimension as well as from other visual cues.

A New PIF Editor

Figure 1-23 shows Windows 95's equivalent to Windows 3.1's PIF Editor shown in Figure 1-22. In Windows 95, however, you right-click on any .PIF file to access its properties. There is no separate, special PIF Editor anymore. Indeed, right-clicking is used extensively in Windows 95—almost any object reveals a useful menu. Even a text document, when clicked on with the right mouse button, drops down such useful options as cut, copy, paste, font, etc.

 TIP   A PIF Editor is a place you can adjust a file that ends in .PIF—in other words, a special file that runs old-style DOS programs. However, in Windows 95, you generally don't have to do anything to make DOS programs run smoothly. For more about configuring MS-DOS applications, see Chapter 22.

Some applications even have an option that allows you to turn off 3D effects, though why you would ever want to is a mystery. Figure 1-24 shows Word for Windows with the 3D Dialog and Display Effects turned off. Figure 1-25 shows the default with Windows 95–style shading turned back on.

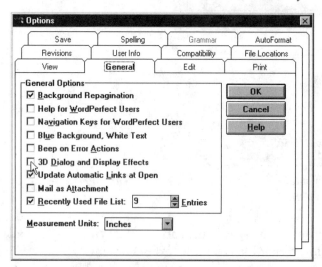

Figure 1-24: *You can, in some applications, choose the option of turning off 3D shading.*

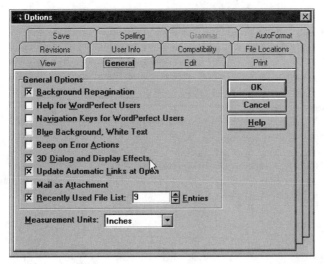

Figure 1-25: *Three-dimensional shading is so much better looking (as well as more efficient) that nearly everyone will likely leave it on.*

The User Interface

When you look at Windows 95, you're seeing a completely redesigned surface. Figure 1-26 illustrates several of the features that make Windows 95 both new and novel as well as effective.

Mini icons. As you can see in Figure 1-26, there are many new graphics techniques at work in Windows 95. Here's an overview, starting from the top left and moving clockwise around Figure 1-26. In several areas, Windows 95 uses small icons (25 percent as large as normal icons). Each opened window contains a small icon, a reduced version of its normal icon (in addition to its normal title). In the case of a folder, the icon is a tiny folder. Likewise, you can select to view these small icons rather than the normal-size icons inside your folder windows, thereby displaying more icons onscreen at one time.

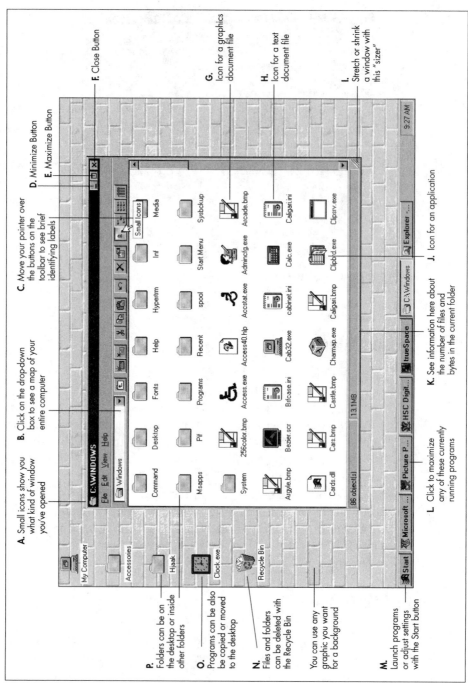

Figure 1-26: *Windows 95's new interface features.*

Figure 1-26 (facing page): *Many of Windows 95's new interface features: A. Small icons show you what kind of window you've opened. B. Click on this drop-down box to see a map of your entire computer. C. Move your pointer over a button on the toolbar to see a brief identifying label. D. Minimize button. E. Maximize button. F. Close button. G. Icon for a graphics document file. H. Icon for a text document file. I. Stretch or shrink a window using this Sizer. J. Icon for an application or program you can run. K.See information here about the number of files and bytes in the current folder. L. Click to restore any of these currently running programs. M. Launch programs, adjust settings or get help with the Start button. N. Safely delete files or folders with the Recycle Bin. O. Programs can also be moved to the desktop. P. Folders can be on the desktop, or inside other folders.*

For the purpose of this discussion, we will use examples from an Explorer window.

Toolbar. If you select Toolbar from the View menu (on any folder or Explorer window) you'll see both a set of quick-access buttons, as well as a drop-down list showing your current general location. You can click on this drop-down list to see the major drives, control panel, printer and other primary elements of your machine to which you can click on, and then view. (This list is essentially identical to what you see when you click on the My Computer icon.) If you want to view a list of the contents of one of these items, just click on its name in the drop-down list.

 Some windows might not be wide enough on your screen to display all the icons. To see them, drag on the frame of the window (or click on the Maximize button at the top right of the window) to enlarge it.

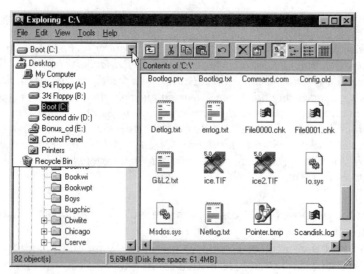

Figure 1-27: *Click on the drop-down list on the toolbar and you'll see a general map of your computer.*

Hovering your mouse pointer (without clicking it) over a Toolbar button displays a tool tip, a little label describing what each button does. The buttons across the toolbar are, in order

■ **Up one level**—takes you back up one level in the hierarchy of folders (some folders can be inside other folders). For instance, you might have created a folder called "Art" and created two other folders within it: "Modern" and "Classical." If you are currently looking at the folder named *Modern*, clicking on this Up one level button will open the "Art" folder.

■ **Cut**—allows you to move a file from one folder to another. Click on this button, and the current file (highlighted because it was the last one clicked on) will turn gray, indicating it's ready to be moved. Then click on the folder where you want to move the cut file. Now click on the fourth button, Paste, to move the file. You can also move whole folders to new locations this same way.

■ **Copy**—similar to Cut, described above. However, when you Paste, the original file or folder stays in its original location, and a new copy is pasted into the target location.

■ **Paste**—moves or copies a file or folder to a new location. See Cut and Copy above.

■ **Undo**—allows you to undo a mistake. If you decide that you made a mistake moving, copying or deleting a file or folder, click on this and the action you just took is now undone.

■ **Delete**—removes a file or folder. However, it is merely moved to a special holding area called the "Recycle Bin." If you decide you made a mistake deleting it, just click on the Undo button. Or, if you decide days or weeks later that you want to recover the file or folder, you can still open the Recycle Bin by just clicking on it, then move or copy the item back to its original location. However, every so often you should clean out the Recycle Bin so it doesn't take up too much room on your disk drive. You do this by either moving the contents from the Bin to a floppy disk, for example, where you can still keep them. Or, to delete them forever, click on the Empty Recycle Bin option in the Recycle Bin's File menu.

■ **Properties**—displays information about the currently selected item (the highlighted file or folder). This is the same as right-clicking (clicking on an item with the right button) on an item, then selecting Properties from the drop-down menu.

■ **Large Icons**—displays each folder, program or document as a normal size icon.

■ **Small Icons**—displays each folder, program or document as a small icon (25 percent as big as the Large Icon).

■ **List**—similar to Small Icons, except all items are displayed in columns. (Small Icons are displayed from left to right.) Also, you cannot permanently rearrange the icons in List view, as you can with Small Icons view.

■ **Details**—adds descriptions of the size, type and exact time of the most recent modification to the Small Icons and titles of each item.

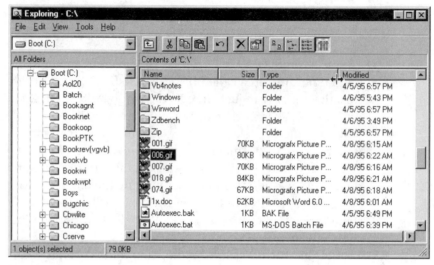

Figure 1-28: *Clicking on the Details button reveals statistics about each item.*

Seeing the details is useful in several situations. For example, if your disk is getting full, you can see how large your various files are to decide which to remove from the hard drive and store on floppy disks or to a tape backup system, or even delete. Or, if you have two versions of the same document, you can look at "last modified" to find out which one is the more current and delete the older one.

While in detail view, you can quickly sort the list by any detail header, such as by Name, Type, Size or Date. You can also get the same sorting options from the View menu.

TIP If you decide to view your files and folders in the Details mode, try moving your pointer to the headings above the listed files and folders. When the pointer is near one of the vertical separator lines, it changes to a cross-arrow. If you now *drag* the mouse horizontally (hold down the left button while moving the mouse), you can adjust the width of the various columns of information displayed by the Details option. Note in Figure 1-28 that we are about to adjust the size of the Type and Modified columns. The easiest way to adjust this spacing so everything shows up onscreen is to start by making enough space for the Name field. Then make enough space for the Size, Type and Modified fields in that order. If you try to work from the right side (Modified) or just randomly try to adjust the spacing, you'll find that it takes quite a bit longer.

Three Important Buttons

Minimize, Maximize and *Close buttons*. These buttons aren't on the toolbar. In the upper right corner of every window in Windows 95, you'll find these three buttons. The left button shrinks the window down to a small square on the taskbar. This is called *minimizing* the window. The program and whatever document you might be working on remain active, they are merely temporarily invisible. This is where you can park programs that you plan to use again soon but don't want taking up space on the screen just now.

The middle button changes, depending on the current size of the window. In a normal window (one that's not filling the entire screen, but also isn't minimized), you'll notice that the icon is a box with a dark line at the top. Clicking on it will *maximize* the window—make it fill the screen. However, when maximized, this button changes to an image of two windows superimposed (see Figure 1-29). Click on it now and the window will be reduced to whatever size it normally is—or whatever size you last adjusted it. (When a window isn't filling the whole screen, you can adjust its size by dragging anywhere on the frame around the window. Move your mouse to the outer edge of the window until it changes to a two-sided arrow. Then press and hold the left mouse button as you move the mouse.)

Figure 1-29: *This button changes its appearance. When it looks like the one on the left, clicking will reduce the size of the window. On the right, it fills the screen with the window.*

The right button of the three, the X, shuts down the window. If the window is a running program, it stops the program.

The Sizer

The rippled tab in the lower right of windows that are not filling the screen (not maximized) allows you to stretch or shrink the window. (Not all applications have a sizer zone, but you can usually resize them by dragging the window border.) Move your pointer onto the sizer. It will turn into a diagonal double-arrow. Now you can drag the window two ways at once (horizontally and vertically at the same time). If a window doesn't have a sizer, you can still move your pointer to the lower right corner and resize them anyway, by dragging the same way. Also, a sizer won't appear on the various folder windows unless you've selected the Status Bar option on the View menu at the top of the window, although you can still drag the window border to change its size.

The status bar displays context-sensitive descriptions as well as the Sizer.

The Status Bar

Along the bottom of some windows you'll find a status bar, with enough space to display a single line of helpful information. Aside from displaying a Sizer, this line can contain descriptions of what's currently happening in an application or a window. For instance, in a word processor it can display the current page number, the total number of pages, the line and column, the time, and so on. In an Explorer window like the one shown in Figure 1-30, it will describe the purpose of the various menu items as you move your mouse pointer over each item.

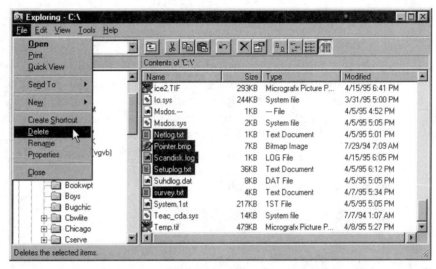

Figure 1-30: *With the status bar visible, fuller descriptions of menu items are displayed as you move your mouse over them. Notice the comment "Delete the selected items" on the status bar here.*

The Taskbar

The taskbar displays all currently running programs (you just single-click on its name and the application blows back up to visibility and usability). Optionally, it displays the time as well. Perhaps most useful is the Start button, which launches programs, changes settings, and is generally customizable to suit your individual preferences. Best of all, it can remain hidden unless you move the mouse pointer down to the bottom of the screen, thereby revealing it. (Click on Start, then Settings, then Taskbar. Under Taskbar Options, choose Auto hide.)

General Improvements

The single most valuable improvement regarding disk files is that you can now give them intelligible, *long* names. For over a decade DOS and Windows 3 users have struggled to overcome the limitation of 8.3 filenames. Filenames were limited to eight characters, plus a three-character "extension." The extension was usually an identifier, which by custom described the type of file: text files were .TXT, temporary files .TMP, backups .BAK, "executable" programs that *run* as opposed to documents that are loaded into those programs to be worked on were .EXE files, Word saved files with a .DOC extension and Paintbrush and other graphics programs added .BMP (for "Bitmapped Picture").

These extensions are still added, but you can ignore them. Windows 95 will use them to identify the program that's used to open a document, if you double-click on that document's icon or title in a folder. However, you won't even see the extensions unless you specifically click to deselect the option "Hide MS-DOS file extensions for files types that are registered" in an Explorer window's View/Options menu (see Figure 1-31). This option is selected by default when you first install Windows 95. So you won't see them unless you specifically ask to.

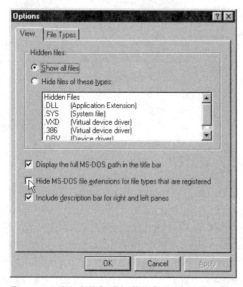

Figure 1-31: *With this "Hide MS-DOS file extensions" box clicked on, most of the titles of your files will have no extension. Also note the option above "Hide files of these types."*

So now you can identify your various files by giving them meaningful, descriptive file names. When you first create a new document, you have to save it to disk to keep it between sessions. Recall that turning off the computer destroys anything that hasn't been saved to disk. When you save a new document, you can give it a name by which you can later load it back into the word processor and work on it again. In DOS and earlier Windows, you were limited to 8 plus 3 characters—you had to call a file "BILLYRY1.DOC." Abbreviations were the order of the day. Now, though, you can call it "First warning letter to Billy Ray Bob Jones." You can use spaces. You can create a name up to 256 characters long if you wish, but that might be overkill.

TIP   A filename also includes its path, so you have to take into account a disk drive identifier (like C:\) as well as any folder names (like "TODO"). In other words, if your file is located in "C:\TODO," the path is 7 characters long. The maximum path\filename length is 260 characters.

Docucentricity: A Natural Way to Work

If you're working on something, building a birdhouse say, your tools, such as the saw and workbench, are likely in your workshop. So is the birdhouse. Knitting needles are stuck right into a sweater-in-progress. In the real world, tools are often right there with the materials they are used on.

Until Windows 95, however, this logical approach was rarely possible with a computer. Here's what you used to have to do to write a letter. In DOS and earlier Windows versions, you would first double-click on a *program*. A program is a tool—it *does something to* raw material. A word processor, for instance, is your tool for doing something to words. Then, when that program was running in the computer, you could "open" a previously written letter (a *document* or the *data* as it's called) that you wanted to finish into the program.

This loading involved clicking on the File menu inside the program, then clicking on the Open option. At this point, you were shown a list of disk drives, directories, subdirectories and the documents (files) within them. You searched around until you found the document you were interested in working on, then double-clicked on its filename and, finally, you were ready to start working on your letter. Whew!

Now, with Windows 95, you can directly double-click on a *document*, not the program that created it. Windows 95 looks at the extension (the three-letter ID tacked onto most filenames discussed above). If it's a .DOC extension, Windows 95 knows that you want it loaded into your word processor and fires up the word processor with the document right there ready for you to start writing. So, in any Explorer or folder window, just double-click on a document and you're off and running.

(Although Windows 3.1 also lets you double-click on a document to start the program that edits it, you could only do this with File Manager. Now files are integrated into desktop folders, so it's much easier and more natural to work directly with documents in folders.)

In-place Editing

A second major feature of *docucentricity* (working directly with documents and letting Windows 95 provide the correct tools) is "in-place editing." Let's try an example using Microsoft Word for Windows.

If your word processor is relatively new, it will have a way of inserting objects into documents. In Word, click on the Insert menu, then select Picture. Choose a file with a .BMP or .TIF extension, or some other graphics file to embed within your document. (You can find some sample .BMP files in your Windows directory.)

The picture is now in your text document. But you're in a word processor. What if you want to make some changes to this image? Word processors aren't much in the way of graphics tools. There's no "fill with color" tool, no "paintbrush" either. Why should you have to exit Word, load Paintbrush or some other graphics program, load in the picture, work on it, save the picture, close the graphics program, open Word, then reload the picture?

Well, with Windows 95, you don't have to. (This particular feature foreshadowed Windows 95, appearing late in Windows 3.1 in a few applications.) Now, as shown in Figure 1-32, you can just double-click on the picture and, temporarily, *Word itself changes*.

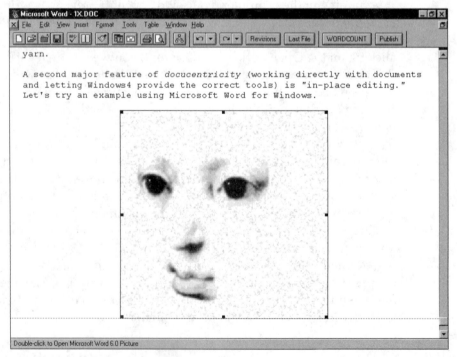

Figure 1-32: *Adding a picture to a text document is now easy. Best of all, you can edit this picture* without leaving Word.

Notice in Figure 1-33 that a whole new row of buttons has been added to Word, after we double-clicked on the picture. With these you can add various kinds of captions, colors, shapes, or, as we did, a double frame.

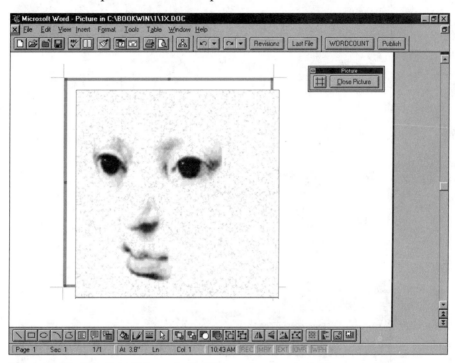

Figure 1-33: *What could be easier? All your drawing tools show up right there in Word.*

You're still "inside" Word—with all its text-editing specialized tools. However, you now also have a set of graphics tools with which to work on the picture. Click on the Close Picture button and Word returns to its normal state—but the changes you've made are now part of the picture.

Open a window anywhere, anywhere

Here are a couple more docucentric features of Windows 95. You open folders by double-clicking on them. *Any* folder you open *anywhere* in Windows 95 becomes a window. The title of this window is the same as the title of the folder.

Figure 1-34: *Double-click on any folder or icon and a window opens up,*
or at least displays new information.

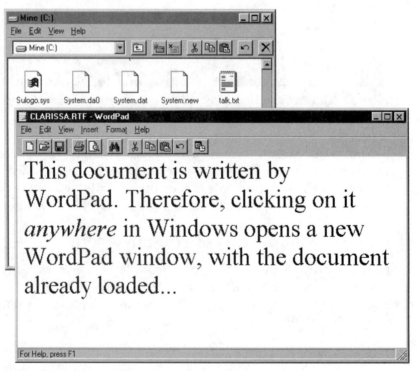

Figure 1-35: *After double-clicking on the WordPad document in Figure 1-34, the*
document and *the WordPad program open into a window.*

New anywhere

You can edit an existing document by double-clicking on it. But how do you make a new text, drawing, animation, music or whatever other kind of document? The easiest way is to just right-click on the desktop. You'll see the menu shown in Figure 1-36, which includes a New option. Move your mouse pointer to New and you'll see the various kinds of documents available on your system. What's listed is a catalog of the applications that you've installed (or those, like WinPad, that come with Windows 95 itself). Each application registers itself, like a new guest in a hotel. This is how Windows 95 knows which kind of documents you can create. Windows 95 then brings up the program with a blank sheet of paper ready for you to start designing, writing, composing or whatever.

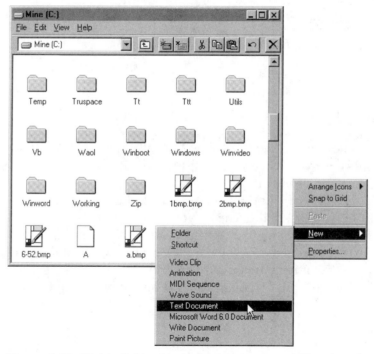

Figure 1-36: *Right-clicking between documents or folders (see the pointer) brings up a menu including the New option. Select New to create a new document or other kind of file.*

However, if you already have an application running that will do what you're looking to do, you can click on its File menu and select the New option there. The opportunities for choosing the nature of this new document will depend on the application. Graphics programs create graphics, but there can be subcategories, like color or grayscale. Figure 1-37 shows the response when you select File/New in Micrografx Picture Publisher.

Figure 1-37: *Select New from within a graphics application and you'll see options like these.*

Help Four Ways

Help is now just a keypress away. Virtually any aspect of Windows 95 is described for you when you press F1, even down to the details of specific options within something's properties.

For example, if you right-click on the desktop, then select the properties of the desktop itself (the screen), you'll see options such as those shown in Figure 1-38. If you don't know the meaning of an option, click on it (to "select" it) then press the F1 key. You'll see a box with a full explanation of the purpose of that item. If you right-click on an item, you'll see a small button saying "What's this?" Clicking on that button brings up the same help box.

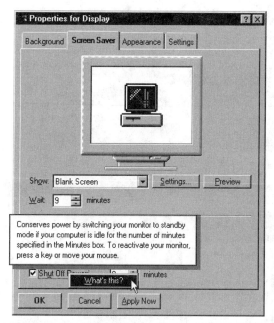

Figure 1-38: *Virtually anywhere in Windows 95 you can press F1 to get helpful information.*

Of course, there's also the general Help and Indexed Help mentioned above, available by pressing F1 when something *isn't* selected or when you click on a window's Help menu. We've also discussed the tiny help boxes above, which appear when you move your mouse pointer across a button bar. We've mentioned messages that appear in status bars when you move your mouse through menus. Then there are Wizards.

Wizards

Beyond all the other paths to help in Windows 95, there are the new Wizards. These are step-by-step, graphic instructions that ask you questions until a task is complete. Most Microsoft applications have Wizards, some non-Microsoft applications have them, and some Windows 95 features utilize them as well. (Add Printer in the Printers Folder, and Add/Remove Programs New Device in the Control Panel, are both Wizards.) Figure 1-39 shows one of the many Wizards in Word for Windows—this one creates calendars.

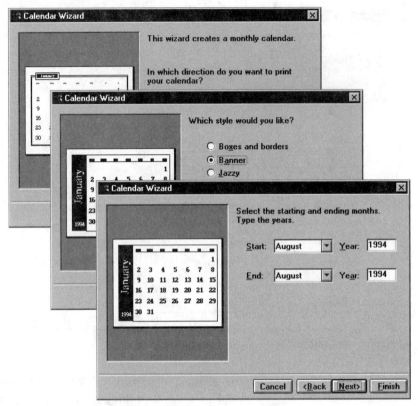

Figure 1-39: *Word's calendar Wizard leads you through various styles of calendars you can print out.*

The Explorer

Program Manager and File Manager, those two semi-redundant and somewhat confusing relics of Windows 3, are gone. In their place is Explorer, a full-featured, powerful file-management system. It has so much power and variety it can seem overwhelming at first.

You can start Explorer by clicking on the Start button, then selecting Programs, then Windows Explorer. (Explorer is covered extensively in Chapter 4.)

Shortcuts

You can create a special kind of icon that launches any program or document—even a network folder or a particular disk drive. A Shortcut icon doesn't actually represent the item itself—deleting a Shortcut doesn't delete the actual file from the disk. Moving the Shortcut doesn't move the file to a different location on the disk, and so on. Instead, a Shortcut is just a simple way of accessing items on your hard drive. You can create a Shortcut by right-clicking on a regular icon. You can tell which icons are Shortcuts, because they have a tiny twisted arrow in their lower left corner.

Aawin.exe   Shortcut to
Aawin.lnk

Figure 1-40: *A Shortcut icon is easy to recognize—there's a twisted arrow in the corner.*

 Windows 3 included a similar distinction between *the real file* and *a mere pointer to that file.* In the File Manager, you could copy, delete, move and otherwise *really* effect the files stored on your disk. However, Program Manager contained only pointers, "shortcuts" like the Shortcuts in Windows 95 (you could delete them, etc. without affecting the actual files on the disk drive).

Uses for shortcuts

■ Shortcuts are *persistent.* That is, once you create a shortcut that points to a particular file, the shortcut remembers how to start that file *even if the file is renamed.* Obviously this is quite useful in network environments where other people have access to files that you, too, use. Once a shortcut is created, it continues to work no matter what somebody renames the disk file. If the original file is deleted, the shortcut becomes invalid. On the other hand, if the original file was moved to a different location on the same disk drive, Windows searches the hard drive for the new location of the Shortcut and can usually repair the link.

■ Shortcuts simplify networked computing. Instead of having to search the network for a particular item or program, you can reference a program or document on another computer as a Shortcut icon, making it appear to be a local document on your own computer. You could also create a shortcut to a favorite network folder on your desktop that could then be accessed very quickly without having to take the trouble to re-establish the connection each time by accessing the network.

- Shortcuts can be embedded. For example, when you want to send a large file to someone else on your network, just drag the Shortcut icon into the mail message. This technique has two benefits. First, the shortcut is merely an address, a brief description of the real location of the file. So the shortcut uses up much less room in the mail message than actually embedding the real file. Second, when the mail recipient clicks on the Shortcut icon to look at the file you've sent, he or she will be working with the *original* file. This avoids creating two copies of that file that will be floating around on the network. This eliminates a major problem when more than one person works on a document: which version of the document is the current one? With a shortcut, there is only one version of the document in existence.
- Shortcuts can store objects. You can create a shortcut to some text in a Word document or a cell in a spreadsheet and use it as a convenient "object" in other documents. These type of shortcuts are also called *scraps*.
- Shortcuts can point to currently nonexistent network resources on a dialup network machine. (If the connection isn't already established, Windows dials the number for you, logs in and then accesses the target of the shortcut.)
- Shortcuts can point to areas or services on the new Microsoft Network or to the Internet. Click on the shortcut and Windows 95 dials and maneuvers you to the target—all automatically. This way, you could create a folder and put shortcuts there for all your favorite e-mail targets, forums, Internet locations and so on.

Find Anything

Even if you're not on a network, the new Find utility is useful. With disk drives now commonly 400 megabytes and growing larger, you can store thousands of different files on them. Keeping track of thousands of documents challenges even specialists—librarians go to school to learn how to do it. However, with the Find utility you can have Windows 95 quickly search your entire hard drive for any particular folder or document.

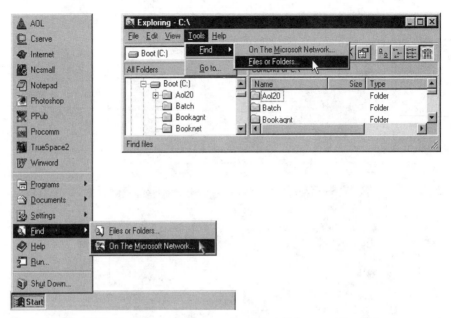

Figure 1-41: *With the Find tool, you can locate anything on your disk, or on a network.*

Find is available in the Tools menu of the Explorer, and also on the Start button menu. If you choose Find "On the Microsoft Network," you'll be able to locate forums, topics and so on on Microsoft's new online service. If you choose "Find Files or Folders," you'll discover a fast and extremely powerful searching tool—it can even look for specific text *within* files. You can also specify many qualities to help narrow the search.

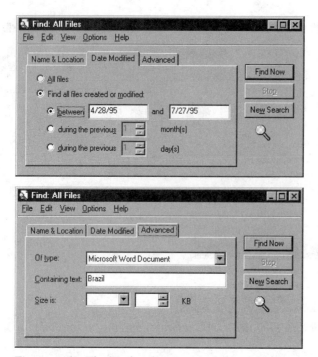

Figure 1-42: *The Find utility is quite powerful—you can specify many search criteria.*

We'll take another look at Find in Chapter 2, but here's a brief example. Say that a couple of months ago you wrote some notes for a trip you're taking to Brazil. Now you can't recall where you stored that file, or the name of the file either. However, you know that you wrote it in Notepad, so it has a .TXT extension, and that it was written in 1994, and that it contains the word "Brazil." Easy, tell Find the details you do remember, then click on the Find Now button. All files matching your criteria will be displayed in a typical Windows 95 list. Double-click in that list on the one you want and you've got it—ready to read or edit or whatever you want to do with it. In fact, it would probably be enough to just search for any file with the word "Brazil" in it.

Press Ctrl+F to bring up the Find utility instantly. If you have a new-style keyboard, like the Microsoft Natural Keyboard, you can also bring up the Find utility by holding down the Window key while pressing F.

Extended Dragging

In earlier Windows you could rearrange icons *within* Program Manager, but this was purely a visual reorganization (the file didn't move). You could also drag (press the left mouse button and hold it down while moving the mouse) a file from File Manager to the Printer icon. If the printer was activated (its icon was on the desktop, minimized) a document could be printed this way. Likewise, you could drag and drop a filename from File Manager to a running application (for instance a text document file could be dragged, then dropped, onto a running word processor).

However, this was a rather limited implementation of the concept of drag-and-drop. Windows 95 now takes dragging into more useful territory. You can still do what you could do in Windows 3, but now you can drag and drop things all over the place. Drag a file from Explorer or a folder window onto the desktop for quick access. Drag a document onto the Printer icon (which you can leave permanently on your desktop) to print the document. Even select some text in a document (by dragging the mouse along it to highlight it), then drag the selection onto the desktop to create a "scrap."

Figures 1-43 and 1-44 show how you can drag a graphic file (CARDS.BMP) from one open folder to a graphics program, PaintShop Pro (PSP.EXE). When you drop the graphic onto PSP, wham, PSP starts running and the CARD graphic is loaded and ready to work on. (In Windows 3, PSP would have to be already running—in which case loading in CARD would be just about as easy from the File/Load menu.)

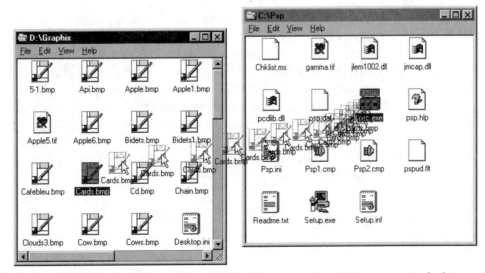

Figure 1-43: *When you drag an icon, a ghostly gray version of it appears attached to your mouse pointer.*

Figure 1-44: *Dropping the dragged icon in Figure 1-43 instantly opens the PaintShop application with the CARD graphic already loaded into it.*

Right-mouse dragging

If you drag an icon with the *right mouse button* pressed, you can choose between moving, copying or creating a shortcut. Normal dragging with the left button pressed always *moves* any item that's dropped on an empty space into a Folder window, onto the desktop, or into the Explorer. (Technically, normal dragging will move an item only if the target location is within the same disk drive, or same "volume" on a drive that's been partitioned. However, if you're sending the item to a *different* hard drive, such as between the floppy drive A:\ and the hard drive, it will be copied.) Copying creates two instances of an item; moving, by contrast, transfers the item to a different physical location on the hard drive.

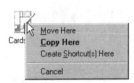

Figure 1-45: *Right-button dragging allows you to make a new copy, move an item or make a shortcut for it.*

 It's best to avoid *moving* programs around on your hard drive. (You *could* copy programs, but why would you? They usually take up a lot of room. And you have a copy already in the box that the program came in when you bought it.)

Word processors, faxing programs and most other programs create special subdirectories (folders) when you first install them. These subdirectories often contain essential support files that the program expects to find when you start it running. Many programs simply look in whatever directory they are started in, and, not finding the support files (because you moved the program), they refuse to run. Moral: Move or copy documents to your heart's content, but leave programs alone.

Quick View

In the File menu of Explorer, or a folder window, you'll find an option called Quick View—*if* you have selected a document's icon (single-clicked on the icon turning it darker). (**Note:** If you choose the Laptop installation option when setting up Windows 95, you don't get the quick viewers. Likewise, a system administrator of a network could also have chosen to set up your machine without the Quick View feature installed, in order to save space.)

In any case, Quick View depends on the fact that Windows 95 knows the difference between runnable programs like WordPerfect, and documents created by those programs. Knowing this difference, Windows 95 quickly displays a selected document. (Remember that documents can be music, art, animations, etc., as well as text.)

 Right-click on any document and then see it by clicking on Quick View in the drop-down menu.

 There are several ways to install Windows 95—Custom, Complete, etc. If you don't see Quick View as an option on the pop-up menu when you right-click a document, or on the File menu of Explorer, that means it wasn't installed when you first put Windows 95 on your hard drive. No problem. To add Quick View (or any of the 19 other free accessories that come with Windows 95), just click the Start button, then Settings, then Control Panel. In the Control Panel, click on Add/Remove Programs. Select the Windows Setup tab. Double-click on Accessories. You'll see a list of all 19 accessories—the ones that have check marks are already installed. Click in the box next to Quick View, then click the OK button, and click a second OK button to install Quick View.

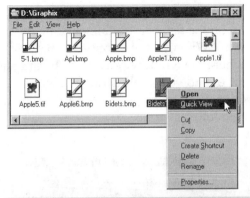

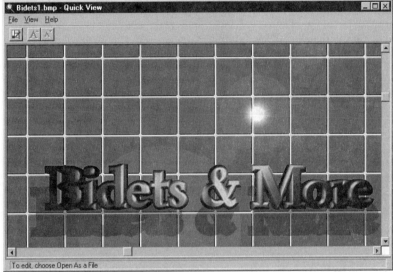

Figure 1-46: *Quick View shows you a graphic or text document, but to edit that document, you must open the document.*

Animation

Individual windows can be moved around and also resized on the desktop. Old hands understand this intuitively. But to make the idea of resizing (maximizing, minimizing and normalizing) more easily grasped by beginners, a window is now animated as it takes up the whole screen (maximizes), shrinks to an icon (minimizes) or opens to fill part of the screen ("normal" size).

Many actions resize a window (clicking on one of the buttons at the top right of a window; clicking on the taskbar; double-clicking on an icon to open the window; and so on). When you open, close or resize a window, Windows 95 shows you where the window came from by animating the explosion (or implosion) of the title bar to illustrate the window's new position and its previous position (see Figure 1-47). This animation assists new users, but is also attractive to most anyone.

Figure 1-47: *Animated title bars display a window in motion. Here, we've clicked on a taskbar to explode an Explorer window.*

The Recycle Bin

This is a trash can into which you can drag programs or documents you no longer want. (Or you can highlight a program's or document's icon and press the Del key.) In any case, Windows 95 removes the file from its current location, but keeps it in a special folder named "Recycled." Should you change your mind after deleting a file, you know where you can find it and restore it. Just click on the Recycle icon, or look for the Recycled folder on the same hard drive where your Windows folder is located.

Remember to open the Recycle Bin every few weeks and see if you can free up some disk space by deleting unneeded files. You can right-click on the Recycler and choose Empty Recycle Bin to free up all the space it's using for deleted files. To set limits on how big the Recycler can grow, and change other properties, right-click on the recycle bin icon, then choose Properties.

The Microsoft Network

We've left one of the best new features for last: The Microsoft Network (MSN). Deeply integrated into Windows 95 itself, the Microsoft Network has all the elements of a great online service (forums, news, Internet, e-mail, etc.) as well as several significant and unique improvements. For one thing, the Microsoft Network is splendidly easy to use. The elements of Windows 95 that you already know how to use (the Find tool, the Explorer and its buttons, familiar menus) are identical in the Network. In a way, The Microsoft Network isn't really a separate program with a separate set of tools, like all the other online services and telecommunication software. Instead, MSN is simply part of Windows 95.

This integration has tremendous benefits for us, the users. It greatly simplifies access to, and use of, The Microsoft Network. The e-mail system alone illustrates this—you can send messages to The Microsoft Network as easily as you can to your co-worker on your local network. And the multimedia features of The Microsoft Network are considerably more powerful than in other online services. A few examples: You can use italics, boldface, color and various typefaces in your e-mail messages. You can embed sounds or graphics. You can create shortcuts that take you directly to a particular part of the Network (or even the Internet) right from your desktop. The list goes on. In fact, it goes on so long that we've devoted all of Chapter 18 to The Microsoft Network.

Technology Update

The new Windows 95 user interface is the fruit of years of usability testing and careful design. And the more you use it, the more you're likely to appreciate all the care and thought that went into it. But, not as easily visible are the many core technology improvements to Windows 95. There's the 32-bit flat memory model, which makes for efficient, fast and reliable applications that you can *multitask*, so you can run many programs at the same time and even format a disk while simultaneously scrolling through a document. Windows 95 is also more dependable than earlier versions of Windows—it will lock up or "freeze" the computer much less often.

Graphics and multimedia have been accelerated. Windows 3.1 limitations, such as meager "system resources," have been almost entirely eliminated. We mentioned long filenames, but there are also numerous performance enhancements for the file system, which no longer relies directly on MS-DOS as did earlier versions of Windows. Don't worry if you don't yet appreciate what these things mean. Throughout this book we'll examine many of these new technologies, and how they can make you more productive, while making computing easier and more fun than ever before.

Moving On

Now that we've flown over Windows 95, looking at the highlights, novelties and main features, it's time to come in for a landing and explore things in more detail. In Chapter 2, "A Fine Place to Start," we'll take a look at the main door into Windows 95: the Start button. Chapter 2 explores how to launch programs and documents, along with an overview of all the other Start menu options. We'll see how installing new software creates new menu items and folders; how to customize the Start button; pitfalls to avoid; and how to get the most out of this useful new super-launcher.

Chapter 2

A Fine Place to Start

Roll up your sleeves, grab your mouse, head straight for the Start button, and give it a good thump. The Start button shouldn't be new to you: it's hard to ignore, since, apart from a few desktop items, it's the most prominent and unique object on the screen, and it's marked with the Windows logo. The first time you start Windows, a message box appears telling you to press Start.

In Windows 3.1 and earlier GUI's (Graphical User Interfaces), new computer users were often left wondering what to do first—where to *start*. The screen was cluttered with icons, menu choices, buttons and other symbols, symbols which made perfect sense to the initiated but were confusing and distracting to a beginner. Now, the "Where do I start?" question is answered immediately with a button marked "Start."

Windows's new minimalist approach to launching your applications is simple and elegant, but it's also flexible and customizable. Instead of being overwhelmed by a profusion of choices, you'll find it quick and easy to navigate through the menu to get where you want to go. We'll show you how to create your own Start menu items, and how to further personalize Start and the taskbar it lives on.

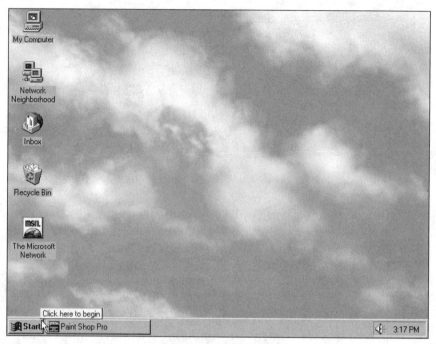

Figure 2-1: *You can "auto-hide" the taskbar and, hence, the Start button; but even if you do, the taskbar and Start button reappear if you move the mouse to the bottom of the screen.*

The Start Button

No matter how you've otherwise customized your desktop, there will always be a Start button. The Start button is an integral part of the Windows 95 taskbar. The taskbar shows you which programs are currently running, and gives you one-click access to each one. When a taskbar button is "depressed" (recessed), it indicates that program is the current one. The current window is on top; it's the one that overlaps any and all other open windows on your desktop. More important, if you type something on the keyboard, the current window is where your input shows up.

Also, the current window's title bar has a distinctive color (blue, unless you've already customized your color settings with the Control Panel). The title bar is always the top line of any window; it displays the name of the window and, sometimes, the contents of the window—for example: Microsoft Word-Police Letter.

Windows lets you run more than one program at the same time. Unlike DOS, you don't have to exit or close a program before you're allowed to start another one. The taskbar lets you see every program you're running, and easily switch between them with a mouse click.

To switch to another program, previously opened, just click on its button on the taskbar. The previous program's button pops out and the one you clicked on is now depressed. The selected program zooms open to the size it was when you left it.

The Start Menu

Of course, before you can try out the taskbar, you have to launch a couple of programs, and that's where the Start button comes into play. When you press the Start button, the first level of the Start menu pops up.

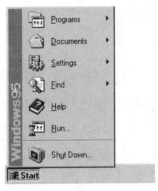

Figure 2-2: *The first click pops up the first level of the menu.*

There are three ways to access the Start menu. You can simply click once on the button, release the button, and move the mouse to the desired choice. The selected menu item is highlighted with a solid bar (cursor), which moves with the mouse. Then click the button again to choose it. (This "sticky" menu behavior is new to Windows 95.)

Or you can click and drag (hold down the mouse button while you move the mouse), move to the item, then release the button to choose it. On the keyboard, press Ctrl+Esc to activate the Start button, then use the Up arrow or Down arrow key to move to a menu item, then press Enter to choose it.

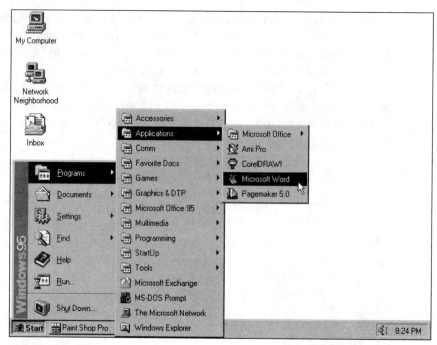

Figure 2-3: *Moving to a submenu choice displays the second level of the menu, which can itself contain a submenu.*

Submenus

A Start menu item can branch off to another menu, or *submenu*. An item with a submenu is marked with a right-pointing wedge. A submenu is sometimes called a *nested* menu, since it's "inside" the main menu; or it could be called a *child menu*, since it belongs to its *parent* (higher-level) *menu*. No matter what the terminology, the Start menu does a good job of visually representing this treelike branching structure, the *hierarchy*.

With Windows 95, the Start button brings up some main choices, such as Programs, Documents and Settings. A Programs submenu lists all the categories of program files you have on your computer (Applications, Accessories, etc.). Then each of those menus has a submenu listing the actual programs (Calculator, Character Map, Paint). Although navigating the submenus can seem a little tricky at first, it is a very compact way of organizing your entire computer.

To navigate to a submenu, just click the Start button, release it, move to the submenu item, and rest the cursor for a half-second. After the brief delay, the submenu pops up, and you can simply move the cursor into it. (If you're impatient, you don't have to wait: go ahead and click on the submenu choice to instantly pop up the submenu.) If there are more submenus, you can continue to follow the branch. Otherwise, just click the mouse on a menu choice instead of a submenu to choose that item.

If you click and drag, the method is similar. Click on Start, keep the mouse button depressed, move to a submenu choice, pause, move into the submenu, move to the menu item, and release the mouse button.

Due to a built-in delay, you can actually move the mouse diagonally to a menu item on a submenu, rather than having to first move horizontally into the submenu then vertically down to the item you want. If there was no delay, when you started moving the mouse diagonally Windows would see you moving the mouse down, cancel the submenu, and highlight the next main menu item.

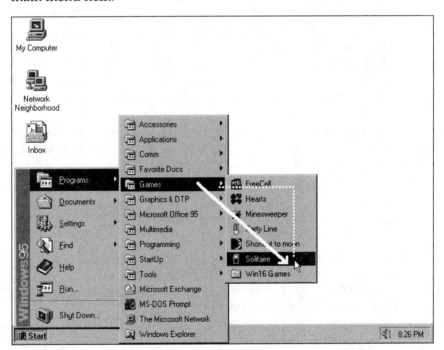

Figure 2-4: *You can move the mouse diagonally (the bold path shown in this figure), rather than orthogonally (the dashed path) to more quickly choose a menu item.*

Using the keyboard, press Ctrl+Esc, move the cursor up to the submenu choice, then press the Right arrow key to pop up the submenu. You can now move the cursor up and down within the submenu. To "back out" of a submenu, press Esc or the Left arrow key. You can press Enter to open a submenu, and you can also use Enter to choose an item.

Try each method to see which you like best. When you're busy typing, you may prefer the keyboard method. Click-and-drag is direct and familiar if you upgraded from Windows 3.1. The one-click method feels more effort-less, and you work hard enough with your computer as it is. Plus, if you're impatient, you can speed up submenus with a second click.

Start Button Overview

Let's take another look at Figure 2-3 and examine the menu selections:

Programs is your doorway to all the applications and tools that have been installed into your system. It is the Windows 95 replacement for Program Manager. If you upgraded a previous version of Windows, the Programs menu contains a submenu for each original Program Manager Group. If you installed Windows 95 for the first time, it will start off with only the Acces-sories and StartUp items. The Accessories submenu has two submenus of its own: System Tools and Games. (You may see others, too, depending on which options you installed when you ran Windows 95 Setup.)

Documents is a quick-access list of the files you've most recently used. Just clicking on one of them automatically opens the document using the appro-priate application.

Settings (shown in Figure 2-3) lets you customize the taskbar and other parts of your computer system. It normally has three choices: Control Panel, Printers and taskbar. Notice that the taskbar item is followed by an ellipsis (...), which means that choosing it causes another window to pop up, usually called a dialog box (or sometimes called a message box). These choices will be covered in detail in upcoming chapters.

Find, the next top-level menu option, lets you search for files by name, and/or look for a key phrase within the contents of the files you select. We'll discuss Find in detail later in this chapter. You can also use Find to locate a computer or file server if your computer is connected to a network. (We'll focus on networks in Chapter 19.)

Help Topics is always on hand to offer direction when you get stuck. You can quickly find the answer to whatever's troubling you. Some help topics even let you jump directly to the relevant program. For example, if you choose help for setting up a printer, you get a help message like that shown in Figure 2-6. When you click on the jump arrow ▣, the Printers folder opens so you can set up a new printer.

Figure 2-5: *Help is just a click away. First choose a topic from the table of contents.*

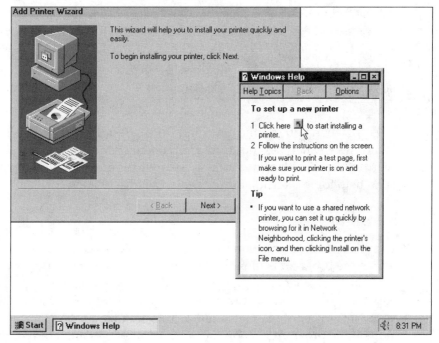

Figure 2-6: *After choosing a topic, you get the details, and you can often jump right to a solution to your question or problem, such as starting the Add Printer Wizard.*

The Help window floats "on top" of all other windows, so you can keep it in view while you follow the directions it offers. Use the Options | Keep Help On Top menu choice from the Help window if you want to prevent it from staying on top.

You'll find a wealth of information in the Windows 95 help system. Turn to it often when questions arise. There are many new features in Windows 95 Help. For example, you can now select text from a Help screen by dragging the mouse across text and using the Edit menu to copy the text into the Windows Clipboard. You can now use Paste from the Edit menu of another program, such as a word processor, to insert the Help text into that document.

 You can also run the Online Manual if you install Windows 95 from the compact disc. It includes lots of introductory material and lessons on using the mouse and performing common Windows desktop operations. While the book you're reading is designed to be complete and helpful to readers of all skill levels, it's still a good idea to run through the Online Manual if you have it, to get more familiar with Windows 95. (If the Online Manual is missing, try using Add/Remove Programs from the Control Panel, and use the Windows Setup tab to add any options that you didn't originally install.)

Also, when you use the new Find feature (Figure 2-6) with a Help file, Windows 95 analyzes the entire Help file to create an instant index to every word in the file. It's a great way to find what you're looking for, even if there is no help topic set aside for the subject you're looking for.

Up & Running

Use *Run* to start a program by its *filename*. The filename is the name by which the program is identified on the hard drive or floppy disk; it's not necessarily the name you have in mind. For example, to run the Paint accessory using Run, you have to use the filename MSPAINT.EXE. It's much easier just to choose Paint from the Program menu's Accessories submenu. What if the program isn't on the Start menu? Try using Find—covered a little later in this chapter—instead. If you use Find to search for Paint, you'll have more success than using Run.

So why bother with Run? Because it can be a convenience if you have memorized the filenames of certain commands, so it's kind of a power user's tool. For most of us, we'll mainly use Run to install software. Stick the install disk in the floppy drive, click on Run and type in A:SETUP (or A:INSTALL).

TIP You can also RUN a document file, as nonsensical as that may seem. For example, if you use Start|Run and enter \excel\data\spread95.xls, this makes Microsoft Excel start and open the spread95 spreadsheet file. This works because the filename *extension, xls,* is *associated* with Microsoft Excel. Most applications automatically create an association between themselves and their data files, so you can double-click on a document icon to run the program that's used to edit the document.

There are better ways than Run to start programs from your hard disk. We'll learn to use the My Computer folder or Windows Explorer to see what's on your hard drive and run programs directly from their home folders.

TIP You can run most MS-DOS programs using Run, but to run a DOS command like COPY, you'll have to use something like COMMAND /C COPY SAMPLE.DOC SAMPLE.BAK as the name of the program you want to run. That's because commands like COPY, DIR, ERASE, etc. are *internal* DOS commands, part of the COMMAND program. The easiest way to run DOS programs and issue DOS commands is to use the MS-DOS Prompt option from the Programs submenu of the Start menu. It starts an MS-DOS session in a window. See Chapter 22 to learn more about how to use DOS programs with Windows 95.

■ ■

A Concise Convention
In the rest of this book, we'll use a common Windows documentation convention when referring to menu choices. Instead of "choose MS-DOS Prompt from the Start Button's Programs menu," we'll tell you that you can use Start|Programs|MS-DOS Prompt. Each vertical bar represents the next sublevel of the menu.

■ ■

Press Start to Shut Down?

Shut Down lets you safely "get out of Windows" before you turn off your computer. By shutting down, you're informing Windows that you plan to turn your computer off or reboot it. Windows, in turn, prompts you if you have any unsaved work in any application, and gives you a chance to save it before you shut down. We strongly recommend that you Shut Down before you turn off your computer or press the Reset button. (Yes, it does seem a little nonsensical to click on Start when what you actually want to do is stop, but it does make this choice easy to find.)

If your computer supports power-saving features like APM (Advanced Power Management), there may be an additional choice above Shut Down called Suspend. This lets you put your computer to sleep instead of completely shutting down and powering off. Laptop and notebook computers, as well as the new "Green PCs," already power down computer components when they're idle, to save battery time or just save electricity. You can use Suspend whenever you want to force the computer to go into power-saving mode. Since many laptops and notebooks can save the contents of their memory even when shut off (a feature sometimes called *auto-resume*), Suspend is a good way to prepare the notebook computer to be shut off—but not shut down. (If you do use Shut Down prior to powering off an auto-resume notebook, you'll have to reboot the computer when you power it back on.)

 TIP If you don't see a suspend choice on the Start menu, and you'd like to have it, look at "Power" in Chapter 7.

An involuntary shut down

Occasionally, a misbehaving program can *lock up* or *crash* your computer. No harm is done to the machine, but it may appear to be frozen. You can't type, and you may not even be able to move the mouse. In the worst case, you may lose whatever work you were doing in any active application, which is why it's a good idea to save your work frequently. But when your computer freezes up, there's no way to use Shut Down so that you can safely power off your computer and restart Windows.

First, try pressing Ctrl+Alt+Del all at the same time. This may bring up a window that shows you which programs are running and if any of them are "Not Responding." If a program is not responding (hung up), you can terminate it and possibly unfreeze your computer. Then you can save your work in your other programs and gracefully restart your computer.

If Ctrl+Alt+Del doesn't help, then you've got a more stubborn crash; the only solution is to turn off the power then turn it back on to restart your computer. (Some computers have a reset button on the front that you can use instead of cycling the power.)

Starting Programs

If you upgraded a previous version of Windows, you can start running your familiar programs right away, and, after a little adjustment, you won't even miss Program Manager.

 TIP   Program Manager is still there, if you want it. Just select Run from the Start menu, type in **PROGMAN**, then press Enter. But we think you'll quickly see that Program Manager is just too limiting once you've spent some time learning a new way of running Windows. Choose Start|Run and type WINFILE if you want to run the old Program Manager.

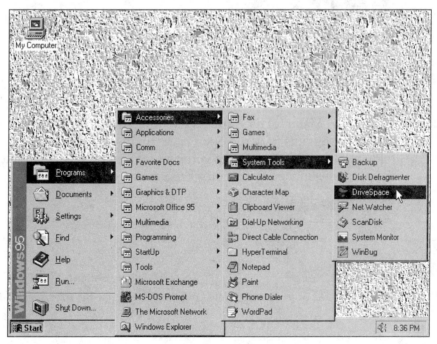

Figure 2-7: *There can be many folders in the Programs menu.*

Figure 2-7 shows an example of the Programs submenu off the Start button menu. All former (Windows 3.1) program groups have been converted into folders. We've rearranged the folders, and placed some folders inside other folders, to enhance the organization of its programs. On the Start menu, each folder calls up a submenu containing programs and shortcut items (you first encountered shortcuts in Chapter 1, and we'll create a shortcut later in this chapter). Each subfolder can pop up its own list of submenus. When you learn how to customize your Start menu, you'll probably want to limit your nesting of subfolders so that it isn't so awkward to "snake" your way to them. On the other hand, making all your folders first-level menu items can lead to an unwieldy Programs menu that takes up the whole screen from top to bottom.

In the next chapter, we'll learn about a possibly easier way to customize the Start menu, but we'll first do it "the hard way" (which is still quite easy) so that you can see what's going on.

Let's see how to customize the Programs menu. We'll look behind the "façade" of the Start menu, and see what's really happening. To do this, use the *right* mouse button to click on the Start button, then choose Open from the menu that pops up (Figure 2-8).

Figure 2-8: *Right-click on the Start button to open the Start Menu folder.*

The Start Menu folder contains the Programs folder (Figure 2-9). Double-click the Programs folder to open it. A window pops up with icons and folders (Figure 2-10), showing you another way of looking at and running the programs in the Start menu's Program menu.

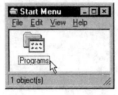

Figure 2-9: *The Start menu's folder contains the icon for the Programs folder.*

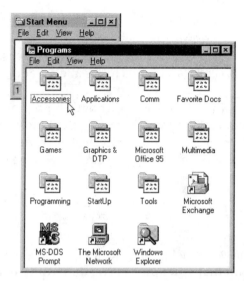

Figure 2-10: *The contents of my Programs folder contains other folders (which become submenus on the Start Menu), and those folders contain shortcuts to programs.*

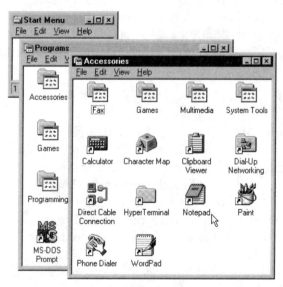

Figure 2-11: *Opening a Programs folder reveals a view of shortcut icons that is actually very similar to a Program Manager "group."*

What you're looking at now is neither Program Manager nor File Manager. It's a view of a *folder* on your hard disk. Actually it is a little more like File Manager than Program Manager, since this window, this folder, is a direct representation of a directory on the hard disk. (Assuming you installed Windows 95 in C:\Windows, this view shows you C:\Windows\Start Menu. Chapter 5 includes an in-depth discussion of the file system, and explains directories, subdirectories and what the colons and slashes mean.)

As shown in Figure 2-11, the icons clearly distinguish programs from folders, data files and documents. Again, these are actual directories on the hard disk, not an abstract "group" as in Program Manager. Any changes you make to the Start menu folder or to the Programs folder will be immediately reflected by the Start menu.

> **WARNING!** *While it's pretty safe to experiment with the Start menu folder, other folders on your hard disk are not fair game. If you copy, move, or delete a folder or application, you are modifying the actual contents of your hard disk. These are not just icons, as you may be used to with Program Manager in Windows 3.1.* **We recommend that you never move, delete or rename an application or that application's folder, at least while you're still learning your way around.**

Fortunately, Windows will try to protect you from making this kind of mistake. If you attempt to delete, move or rename a folder that contains an EXE or COM file within it, Windows asks you to confirm this action by warning you that some of your applications may not run after this action, then asks if you're sure you wish to continue.

The Start Menu Folder

The Start Menu folder holds the items that will appear on the first menu you see when you press Start. Note, however, that it only shows you the Programs folder. There is no folder for the other first-level menu choices, such as Documents, Settings and Find. So the first thing you'll do to customize your Programs menu is to open the Programs folder that's inside the Start menu folder. To do this, click once on the Programs folder, and press Enter. Or just double-click on the Programs folder icon (click twice in rapid succession).

When you open the Programs folder, you see the icons for each category of programs, which correspond to Program groups in Program Manager. In fact, the Programs folder has a lot in common with Program Manager. To see what's inside any of the subfolders, such as Accessories, just double-click on one of them. In Figure 2-11, we've done just that, and you can see that Accessories contains icons for the desktop applets like Calculator, Character Map, Paint, etc. Don't be concerned if you're missing any of these. Character

Map, for example, is not installed by Windows 95 Setup unless you use Custom Setup. In Chapter 7 ("The Control Panel") we'll show you how to add any missing Windows components. See Chapter 10 for more about these accessories.

Shortcuts: Virtual Icons

Like Program Manager icons, these icons are not the actual programs. For example, the Calculator program is a program named CALC.EXE in the C:\Windows folder. But this is the C:\Windows\Start Menu\Programs\Accessories folder. How can the same program be in two places? The answer is that the Calculator icon you see here is actually a file named Calculator.lnk, and it's a *shortcut* to the real CALC.EXE file. A short-cut is a convenience, a kind of alias, or shadow of the real thing.

A shortcut is analogous to a Program item in Program Manager: it is a reference, or a pointer, to the original file—a synonym, if you will. Windows 95 distinguishes a shortcut by adding a tiny little arrow at the lower left of the icon. A shortcut can also "point to" a folder. If the shortcut is in one of the Programs folders, then it appears conveniently on the Start menu.

Using a shortcut is easy: you just double-click on it like any other icon.

The easiest way to create a shortcut is to use the mouse to "drag and drop" the original program file into one of the Programs folders. Here's a step-by-step guide to creating a shortcut for WordPad.

Hands-On: Creating a Shortcut

Since you'll be creating a Shortcut, you'll first have to make a home for it. First, open the Programs folder by right-clicking on the Start button and choosing Open. Then double-click on the Programs folder that's in the Start menu folder. If you create your shortcut directly in the Programs folder, it will be at the top of the menu that appears when you press Start | Programs. (If you put it in the Start Menu folder, it will appear at the top of the Start menu itself.) Or you can add the shortcut to an existing Programs folder by first double-clicking on that folder.

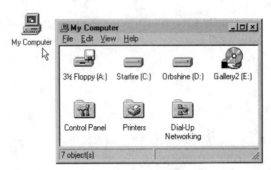

Figure 2-12: *My Computer contains folders for each drive.*

Double-click on My Computer. You'll see more folders, one for each drive and also some for the Control Panel and Printers folder.

Double-click on your hard drive (usually C:). Another window opens, showing all the folders on that hard drive. From that window, double-click the one named Program Files. Now double-click on the folder named Accessories.

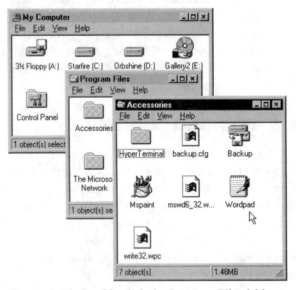

Figure 2-13: *Double-click the Program Files folder to view its contents.*

Wordpad

Figure 2-14: *Here's a closeup of the WordPad icon.*

Look for an icon called WordPad (it has a picture of a fountain pen). You may need to use the scroll bars on the side of the window to move to the bottom of the window.

Note that there is no shortcut arrow on the WordPad icon, so you know it's the original.

WARNING! *This is the actual WordPad program.* **Do not delete or move this icon, or you will have to reinstall Windows to restore WordPad.**

You can copy WordPad . . .

You can safely *copy* WordPad to the Programs folder. There are several ways to copy a file. Make sure you have both windows open on the desktop (the Programs folder and the Windows folder).

Figure 2-15: *Click the right mouse button to pop up the Edit menu.*

Quick and Easy: You've already learned that the Clipboard is a simple way to transfer information between applications, and now you know you can apply it to copying and moving files, too. Click on WordPad, and then choose Copy from the Edit menu of the window containing WordPad. Now click on the Programs folder, and choose Paste from the Edit menu of the Programs folder.

 A quick way to get to the Copy and Paste commands is to click the right mouse button when the mouse cursor is pointing to a filename or icon. You'll learn many more "right-click" tips and tricks in this book, but for now, try right-clicking on *everything* to see the options you get.

Advanced copy with drag and drop: Hold down the Ctrl key as you click on WordPad, and continue to hold down the mouse button. Move the mouse toward the Programs folder and release the mouse button. You'll want to use this drag-and-drop technique quite a bit in Windows. **Note:** If you forget to hold down Ctrl while dragging the icon, you'll get a shortcut to WordPad instead of an actual copy of WordPad, and you'll find the WordPad icon has disappeared from the Windows folder. If you held down Shift instead of Ctrl, then you'll know that WordPad was *moved* to the Programs folder. Drag and drop to put it back.

 TIP If you make a mistake when moving a file, you can choose Undo from the Edit menu to "Undo Move." You can usually reverse the most recent file action you've performed.

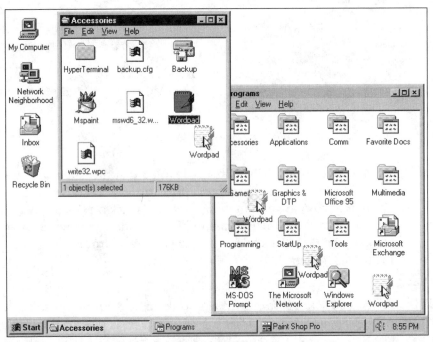

Figure 2-16: *Drag, drop and copy.*

Drag and drop II: Use the right mouse button to click on WordPad, and while holding the button down (don't let go yet), move the mouse and drag the icon toward the Programs folder. When you get there, let go. A new menu pops up. Choose Copy Here.

... But copying can be wasteful

The disadvantage of copying WordPad is that you've now got two copies of the file on your hard disk. Keep it up and you'll eventually run out of disk space. If you create a shortcut, you've got the *effect* of an extra copy of WordPad, but all you're really copying is the icon and a reference to the original location and filename. It's like a hologram: it looks the same as the original but has no substance.

To create a shortcut for WordPad, click on the WordPad icon, then do one of the following:

■ Choose Create Shortcut from the File menu and point to the WordPad icon, press the right mouse button and choose Create Shortcut from the pop-up menu, or use the right mouse button to click on WordPad, and while holding the button down (don't let go yet), move the mouse and drag the icon toward the Programs folder. When you get there, let go. A new menu pops up. Choose *Create Shortcut Here.*

Figure 2-17: *Choose Create Shortcut from the right mouse pop-up menu.*

A new icon appears, titled *Shortcut to WordPad,* with the characteristic shortcut arrow in the icon. You can now use Edit | Cut, then click on the Programs folder and use Edit | Paste. That removes it from the Windows folder. (Or you can drag and drop, *without* holding down the Ctrl key, since this time you want to move the icon, not just copy it.)

You can use this trick whenever you want to create an extra icon for an application. The advantage is that you can organize your program items conveniently in the \Windows\Start Menu\Programs folder, which makes them appear on the Start menu | Programs menu. The actual programs are stored in individual folders (directories) elsewhere on the disk. In Chapter 5, we'll go into more detail on how files are stored on your computer.

Hands-On: Renaming a File

You may decide that the arrow symbol is enough to remind you that an icon is for a shortcut, so you can routinely remove "Shortcut to" from the icon's name. Here's how:

■ Click on Shortcut to WordPad.

■ To rename the file, just click on it again. (The filename is highlighted, and the text cursor is poised at the end of the line, ready for you to make your change. If you just begin typing, you'll replace the old name completely. If you want to edit the name, press the left arrow key first.)

■ It's all too easy to double-click if you click on the file again too quickly, so you may prefer to choose Rename from the File menu (or use the right mouse button to pop up the menu and choose Rename).

Figure 2-18: *Right-click to rename (filename: rename1.bmp).*

■ Retype: **WordPad** (or edit the filename with the cursor arrow keys).

■ Be sure to press Enter to seal the change. To cancel, just click somewhere outside the filename or press the Esc key. You can also use Edit | Undo to change the filename back to the original if you made a mistake. Thanks to the Windows 95 long filename feature, you are creating the actual filename of the icon, not just a description.

 The keyboard "hotkey" for Rename is function key F2. Use the arrow keys to move to the file you want to rename, then press F2. You can now type the new name.

Now that you know how to rename files, be careful. You don't want to rename the original file if it's a program file or other file that you didn't create yourself. But you can feel free to rename the desktop icons such as My Computer and Network Neighborhood. Just click on the icon title once to select it, then click it again to rename it.

 Windows watches you work and tries to adapt to your way of working. If you routinely remove the *Shortcut to* syntax from newly created shortcuts, Windows 95 will eventually take note and stop adding it in the first place. This is just a hint of the kind of "intelligence" that will increasingly be built into the operating system and other software in the future.

To see what you've accomplished, click on the Start button then the Programs menu. You should now see that WordPad has been added to the Programs menu. You've created a custom Start menu entry! You've also learned how to use drag and drop, how to copy and move items between folders, when to use the secondary (right) mouse button for pop-up options and how to rename files.

 You can use Alt+Backspace or Ctrl+Z as a keyboard hotkey for Undo.

Note: *Since Microsoft has coopted the term* shortcut *as a specific term for a link to another file (as we mentioned above), we'll have to change some terminology elsewhere to avoid confusion. For example, we would normally call keystrokes such as Alt+F (which opens the File menu)* keyboard shortcuts. *So instead we'll use the term* hotkey, *the other common term for these time-saving alternatives. You probably already know some of these, such as F1 for Help, but you can find a list of these common hotkeys in Chapter 8.*

More Uses for Drag and Drop

As we mentioned, you'll use the drag-and-drop method often to manipulate files and folders. In effect, your files, documents and folders have become *objects*, almost tangibly. Just as you can reach out with your hand and arrange "real world" objects like the calculator, telephone and papers on your desk, you can use the mouse to arrange the tools and documents of the virtual reality world on your computer desktop. Be sure to experiment (we'll point out any potential problems, but don't be afraid to try new things). Try clicking the right mouse button on everything to see what kind of menu you get.

Here are some more uses for drag and drop:

- Rearrange the Programs menu layout by moving objects into folders, creating new folders, or even moving folders around into other folders. Just right-click on the Start menu, choose Open to reveal the Programs folder, and use drag and drop to move the objects. For example, if you want to move Games out of the Accessories group, just open the Accessories folder, drag the Games folder and drop it on the main Programs folder.

 We'll tell you all about how to manage your files in Chapter 5, but if you want to get started, here are a few pointers.

- Right-click on the icon to get a list of choices, including Rename, Copy and Cut.
- Right-click on an empty spot in a folder (or on the desktop) to get a list of choices that include New, which lets you create an empty folder or an empty document.
- Drag and drop icons between folders to rearrange their locations. (Avoid doing this except with the files you create yourself; don't move program icons or other program components from their folders.)
- Remember to use the right mouse button when dragging a file (icon) if you want a list of choices (Copy, Move, Create Shortcut) when you drop the object.

- You can drag and drop objects onto the desktop itself. Typically, these items are copied to the Desktop folder, found in C:\Windows\Desktop. To avoid wasting disk space, use shortcuts (instead of the original document or program) on the desktop. On the other hand, the desktop makes a convenient storage place for temporary documents. It also can make copying between different folders or drives easier. Just drag a document from its folder to the desktop, then open the folder you want to put it in and drag the document from the desktop to the target folder.

■ You can drag a document's icon and drop it on a program's icon, then edit the document. See Chapter 3 for a hands-on tutorial on drag-and-drop document editing.

■ If a program is already open, you can't just drag and drop a file onto the taskbar icon. In the next chapter, we'll see that you can drag a file, hold it over the taskbar icon (but not drop it), and wait briefly. When the application's window then appears on top of any other windows, you can move it to drop the object onto the application itself.

■ If the Printers folder is open (Start | Settings | Printers), you can drag a document's icon and drop it on the icon for the printer you want to use for printing it. If you do this a lot, consider dragging the printer icon onto the desktop to create a shortcut to it.

■ For the utmost in Start button customization, you can actually drag and drop a file or shortcut directly on top of the Start button. Open the Programs folder and try dragging WordPad or Explorer (use the right mouse button to create a shortcut) and drop one of them onto the Start button. Now click on the Start button and there it is, right on the top of the menu!

Getting it off the Start button is a little trickier. It's stored in C:\Windows\Start Menu. As you know, to open this folder, just right-click on the Start menu and choose Open (see Figures 2-8, 2-9). Then you can simply delete the shortcut icon for the item you want to re-move from the Start menu. You can't delete other menus from the Start menu, such as the Documents folder. We'll see in a moment how to clear the Documents menu (which is located in \Windows\Recent).

Finding a Mystery File

You've already discovered how to use My Computer to navigate to a de-sired folder and browse that folder for a particular file. It can be tedious to manually search for files. Worse yet, you may have forgotten where you put a file. Worst of all, you may have forgotten what you named the file! The Start button's Find command comes to your rescue.

As we saw earlier, if you click on Start | Find | Files or Folders (Figure 2-19), you'll get the Find Files dialog box as shown in Figure 2-20.

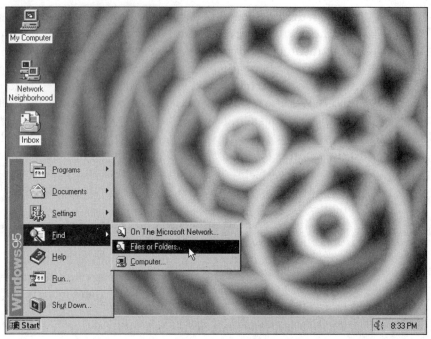

Figure 2-19: *Choose Find | Files or Folders from the Start menu to begin your search.*

 TIP If you have a Microsoft Natural Keyboard or other 104-key compatible keyboard, you can press Win+F to open up the Find program.

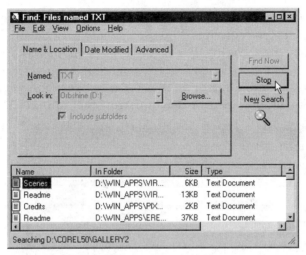

Figure 2-20: *The Find program makes it easy to locate your files.*

In Figure 2-20, we entered **TXT** in the Named box, and chose the name of the hard drive by clicking the down arrow next to the Look in box. (The down arrow next to Named lets you recall previous searches.) We then clicked Find Now. Find quickly inventoried the hard drive, giving us a complete list of all the text files (those ending with .TXT).

The search specification is magical, or at least surprisingly sophisticated. It will find anything close to what you're searching for. You don't need to use wildcard characters like * as you do in DOS, although they are supported. For example, in the search above, Find locates not only README.TXT but it would also find a file called TXT Editor. By using wildcards, and searching for *.TXT, you can refine your search to be more specific, and only look for files ending with .TXT. The * means: match anything up to the following. More about these wildcards in Chapter 5.

TIP You can specify multiple search criteria. Separate each one with a semicolon. Example: .TXT;.DOC;.PRN will find all files ending with .TXT, .DOC and .PRN.

The files displayed are *live*, just like in any folder view. You can open a document or run a program from the Find list just by double-clicking. You can drag and drop the items, or right-click on them to rename them or change their properties. You can cut and paste them to a new folder.

Also, the headings above the columns, describing the files, are "hot." They don't just label the columns. You can actually click on any heading to reorder the list by that heading. For example, click on the Modified heading to sort the list by date (see Figure 2-21). If a column is too narrow to read fully, you can position the cursor on the border between the column headings and drag it horizontally to widen or narrow the column.

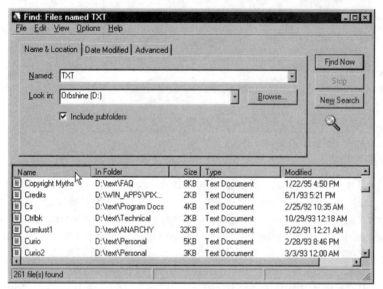

Figure 2-21: *These column headings aren't just words, they're also "hot"—you can click on them to rearrange things. Here, we've clicked on Name to sort the list alphabetically by filename.*

If you're sure that the file you're looking for is in a certain folder, you can save time by not searching the entire hard drive. Enter the name of the folder in the Look in box, and turn off the Include subfolders check box if you want to restrict the search to only the chosen folder. Leave the check box turned on if you want to search the chosen folder and look in any subfolders contained within it (and any subfolders contained in those subfolders, and so on). If you want to search the entire drive for a file, change the Look in entry to something like C:\ if that's the drive letter of your hard drive. Or choose My Computer from the Look in list to search all drives on your computer. If you're on a network, you can search the Network Neighborhood to include all the networked drives.

Instead of manually entering the name of the folder, use the Browse button. It pops up a "tree" browser like that shown in Figure 2-22. Click once on the ⊞ symbol next to My Computer, and it expands to show the drives on your computer. Click on the ⊞ symbol for a drive, and it shows you all the folders on that drive. Click on the ⊞ symbol for a folder, and it shows you the subfolders for that drive. (To *collapse* a folder's contents, click on the ⊟ symbol next to the folder.) Finally, click on the folder you want to search, and click OK (Figure 2-23).

Figure 2-22: *Choosing the ⊞ symbol next to Projects "drills down" to subfolders within it.*

Figure 2-23: *After clicking ⊞, you now see the subfolders contained within Projects.*

Advanced Find

What if you don't remember the name of a file? Click on the Advanced tab. Try to think of some text that would be in the file, and enter that in the Containing text box, and click Find. Remember that all the settings are relevant, so it will search in the folders you specified in the Name & Location section, and can be limited to search for the search phrase only in files that are a similar match to the name you entered in Named in the Name & Location section (Figure 2-21).

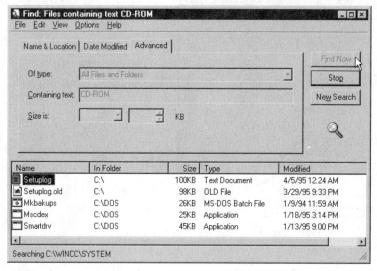

Figure 2-24: *Search for text.*

You can really get specific here. With the Of type box (click the down arrow for choices), you can restrict the search to only certain types of files, such as Microsoft Word documents. Or you can look for files within a certain range of sizes (click on the down arrow next to the Size is option to choose between At Least or At Most, and try to guess how big the file is in the box marked KB—kilobytes). Using Date Modified, you can home in on the date range to search. If you know you created the file this week, there's no reason to find every file on the disk.

In Figure 2-25, we used Date Modified to show all the files I created or changed in the previous 3 days. You'll get a good idea of how busy you've been!

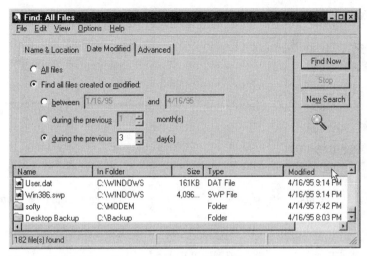

Figure 2-25: *Have I been a busy boy? You bet!*

The key to using Find is to fill out anything you know about the file so you can guess at what you don't know. Don't fill in fields that you don't have a good idea about. If you get a list that's too large, try narrowing the search using another option.

If you've spent a lot of time crafting a custom search, you'll be glad to know that you can save your search specification. After defining your search by filling in the various boxes, choose Save Search from the File menu. This saves your search as an icon on the desktop automatically, which you can retrieve just by double-clicking on it.

Shut Down

When you choose Shut Down, you're letting Windows know that you're about to turn the computer off, or that you want to restart the computer (sometimes called "rebooting"). Restarting resets Windows and lets you start over as if you had just turned the power on to start a new computing session. You should choose Shut Down before you turn off your computer (instead of just turning off the power switch on your computer) for these important reasons:

Figure 2-26: *Choose Start | Shut Down to prepare your computer to be powered off.*

■ You may have applications open, with unsaved files. Shut Down prompts you to save your changes.

■ You may have DOS applications still running, and they may have files open too. Aborting some DOS applications can lead to data loss.

■ Recently saved information is kept in memory (in a cache) and slipstreamed onto the hard disk during idle moments. Although waiting a few seconds before turn off your computer is enough to make sure this data is committed to disk, Shut Down performs an orderly "flush" of the cache. (More on the disk cache in Chapter 5.)

■ Certain changes to your system are not actually saved until you Shut Down. Rebooting without Shut Down (as happens when you suffer a complete system crash) may cause some of your customizations to be reset.

 If you've just rearranged your desktop and don't want to wait until you Shut Down to save your changes, go ahead and Shut Down anyway, but answer "No" when you're asked "Are you sure?" to cancel the Shut Down. Even though you've cancelled it, the Shut Down command still saves the state of the desktop.

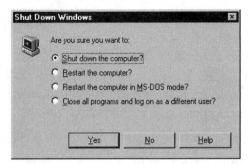

Figure 2-27: *You can also use Shut Down to restart Windows, or if you're on a network, you can reset your computer to allow a login by another user.*

Other Reasons to Use Shut Down

■ Shut Down is a convenient way to restart Windows. If you suffer less serious errors, such as a halted program (see Appendix C, Trouble-shooting), it's wise to re-initialize Windows to a clean state. It can also free up resources that some older Windows applications eat up, even after they're closed. (New 32-bit Windows applications always free up their resources when closed.)

Some people like to restart Windows occasionally even when it's not necessary, kind of like a preemptive strike against being forced to reboot due to system crashes. Actually, this habit is a carryover from Windows 3.1. Windows 95 is now so stable, and has so much in the way of free resources, that you may find you never need to routinely restart your computer.

■ Shut Down is a security measure. Why leave your files and programs vulnerable to others? When you leave for lunch, use "Close all programs and logon as a different user." When you return, just enter your password and pick up where you left off. Intruders can't access your files without the password, and it saves you the time it would take to restart your computer. (You don't have to log on as a different user. When you come back to your computer, just log in as yourself again.) This menu option appears only if you're connected to a network.

Note: *This kind of password protection safeguards only files stored on a Novell or Windows NT server. A knowledgeable user can simply press Esc to bypass the login prompt and still have full access to all the files on your local computer's hard drive.*

TIP If you leave any folders open when you shut down (even if the folders are minimized on the taskbar), they will be automatically reopened the next time Windows 95 starts. This can be very convenient if you always like to have a view of certain folders on your computer. Another way to have quick access to a certain folder is to create a shortcut to that folder, and leave the shortcut icon on the desktop. (Read Chapter 4 for more information on creating shortcuts.)

A Blast From the Past

You'll also see another choice on the Shut Down Windows dialog box, a choice to "Restart the computer in MS-DOS mode." This is a holdover from Windows 3.1, where it was sometimes necessary to shut down Windows and exit to MS-DOS. Because Windows 95 supports most programs in a DOS session, you will only rarely need to use this option, which has the effect of unloading Windows and putting you in plain MS-DOS 7.

Any devices supported by Windows 95 won't be available from MS-DOS. For example, if Windows 95 supports your CD-ROM with 32-bit drivers, you won't have drivers in your CONFIG.SYS file for your CD-ROM (because those drivers are now in Windows). When you restart your computer in MS-DOS mode, Windows is absent, so you don't get access to your CD-ROM in DOS. Before crying foul, turn to Chapter 22, where we'll show you how to have your cake and eat it too, so to speak.

Moving On

If you're getting curious about the other menu options offered by the folders, you may want to skip ahead to Chapter 4, where we cover file manipulation in detail, and introduce Explorer, a more powerful version of the folder viewer/browser. Explorer adds more file management features and new ways to view the folders.

In the next chapter, we'll discuss the taskbar in more detail, and we'll also examine the special buttons on the title bar (introduced in Chapter 1), and see how to neatly arrange windows and folders on the desktop. In Chapter 6, we'll present a variety of custom designs for laying out your desktop.

Chapter 3

The Taskbar
& Programs

We've touched on the taskbar in previous chapters, but it's so central to Windows 95 that it deserves a chapter of its own. The taskbar lives at the bottom of your screen and lets you see at a glance what programs you're running.

You can *minimize* a running program to free space on your screen. Minimizing means that you click on the first (left most) of the three buttons in the upper right corner of a window (it looks like an underline symbol). This collapses the window down to an icon. The program is still running, but it's no longer taking up much room on the screen. In effect, you've temporarily "parked" the program on the taskbar. However, if you give the application a job to perform, it can continue to work "in the background." So, minimizing doesn't shut down a program, nor does it even freeze a program that's supposed to be doing something.

Figure 3-1: *Click on the "underline" button at the top right of any application to minimize the program's window.*

You can instantly restore any program to visibility. Move your mouse to the taskbar and click on the button representing the program you want to revive.

It's too bad Microsoft calls it the *taskbar*—that makes it sound more like work than fun. However, the term *task* has a special meaning in computer science. Back in the days when hundreds of users had to share time on a single computer, each program was a task for the mainframe to perform. The word is still used that way today. A *process* is another computer term that means much the same thing. We prefer to call them *programs, tools* or *applications* (or simply "apps"; small utility programs are "applets"). A program on disk is sometimes called an *executable file*; since it's a special type of file that can be executed, its instructions run through the computer and acted on.

More than a launchpad

The Start button is the primary feature of the taskbar. It pops up the Start menu. You can launch programs from the Start menu or run them directly from their folders when you open the My Computer folder. (We'll discuss the more powerful Explorer option in Chapter 4.) But the taskbar does more than just host the Start menu.

Figure 3-2: *The taskbar lives at the bottom of the screen.*

Normally, the taskbar occupies a strip along the bottom of the screen (Figure 3-1). Open programs or folders can't overlap the taskbar, so you'll always see what programs you're running.

Sometimes you need to cut and paste between two programs, like a spreadsheet and a word processor. It's very convenient to simply click on the spreadsheet and drag your mouse to "select" a range of cells, copy the range of cells to the Clipboard (Edit | Copy, Ctrl+C), then click on the taskbar button for the word processor, and paste the cells into place (Edit | Paste, Ctrl+V).

The taskbar isn't the only way to switch between open windows. If both windows are visible, you can simply click anywhere on the visible part of an overlapped window to bring it to the top and make it the "current" program. (The current program is the one that will respond to anything you type on the keyboard.)

But if one window completely covers another one, the only way to get at the hidden one is to get rid of the program on top. Many users are accustomed to closing one program before starting another one, or closing a window to get at one that's been overlapped. But that's slow and inefficient, and you lose the advantages of a multitasking operating system.

What is Multitasking?

Windows 95 can make it appear that more than one program is running at the same time. In principle, you could be sending a fax, recalculating a spreadsheet, rendering a graphic, printing a letter, and copying files—all at the same time. Of course, you'd have to be pretty busy to get all that happening at once, but with multitasking, Windows can keep up with it all.

A computer can't *really* do more than one thing at a time. Instead, it divides time into tiny slices, measured in thousandths of a second (milliseconds). Every 20 milliseconds, Windows lets one of your programs run for an instant, then gives the next one a time slice, and so on. By switching in this round-robin style, extremely quickly, Windows gives you the illusion that the programs are running simultaneously.

In Windows 3.1, a program had to voluntarily surrender its control to the next program in the chain, so multitasking was only partially effective. Fortunately, with Windows 95 programs, Windows itself makes these multitasking decisions, *preemptively* switching between running programs. However, if you run old Windows 3.1 software (also called 16-bit software), those programs will multitask the old way. Buy all new 32-bit versions of your software if you want smooth, efficient multitasking.

In Windows 95, an application can spin off pieces of itself, called *threads*. Each thread can run independently and simultaneously with the main program. A word processor would create a thread to manage printing so that you can continue to type and edit while printing. A spreadsheet would perform its recalculation using a separate thread.

With Windows NT, and in future versions of Windows 95, it's possible to carry multitasking one step further: you can buy a computer with more than one central processing unit (CPU)—a second microprocessor. (The 486 or Pentium chip in your computer is your CPU/microprocessor.)

With symmetric multitasking, multiple program threads can be split between the microprocessors. In effect, you're running multiple programs on multiple computers, all in the same box. That's true multitasking. In the not-too-distant future, systems will feature as many as 64 Pentium processors running in parallel. Even home systems will probably benefit from multiple processors some day.

Figure 3-3: *The Control Menu in Windows 3.1 and Windows 95.*

In Windows 3.1, you may have used the Control button in the upper left corner of a window. The Control button looks like a box with a line through it (Figure 3-3). (That symbol was chosen because you can use Alt+Spacebar as a keyboard shortcut for the Control button, but that technique never really caught on with many users.) When you click on the Control button, it pops up the Control menu, which lets you Restore, Move, Size, Minimize, Maximize or Close the windows, or switch to another window. You can also double-click the button to close the window. But if you close a window, it's removed from memory, and to get it back, you have to open the program from the hard drive again, which can slow you down.

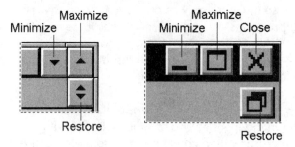

Figure 3-4: *Window control buttons in Windows 3.1 compared to Windows 95's buttons.*

Instead, to temporarily remove a program from the screen but not from memory, use the Minimize option from the Control menu. More typically, you press the minimize *button* (shown with its cousins in Figure 3-4 along with the Windows 95 equivalents). In Windows 3.1, a minimized program turned into a little icon at the bottom of the screen, but this icon *was still on the desktop.* Since there is no taskbar in Windows 3.1, the miniature icon squats at the bottom of the screen. It looks exactly like a Program Manager icon, leading to some confusion.

Windows 3.1 used the Task Manager similarly to the way we use the taskbar. In Windows 3.1, you could double-click on any "empty" part of the desktop background to open Task Manager, which lets you switch between running windows. Task Manager still exists: Try using Start I Run and typing in **TASKMAN** to run it. Although it has been souped up a little bit in Windows 95, the Task Manager is nonetheless a pale substitute for the real taskbar.

A source of confusion

Say you're working with Ami Pro (Lotus's word processor) with Windows 3.1, and you minimize it. When you want to get it back on the screen, do you double-click the Ami Pro icon in Program Manager or the one at the bottom of the screen? After all, they look the same. But if you run Ami Pro from Program Manager, you'd get a second copy of the same program. You'd be running two word processors at the same time!

You'll run out of memory if you always work this way—cloning new copies of programs that are already running. Windows will slow down considerably. Although it's not intuitively obvious, if you double-click the Ami Pro at the bottom of the Windows 3.1 desktop, you're doing what you intend to do—simply re-opening the document you were previously working with.

 Because most large applications allow you to have many documents open at the same time, it's not necessary to run more than one copy of a program. You don't need two copies of Ami Pro to work on two documents at once: just open more than one document at the same time in the original Ami Pro program. (Some programs, such as Ami Pro, require you to enable this Multiple Document Interface—MDI. In Ami Pro, there's an option on the Open dialog box called "Close Current Document." Turn this off when you want to open several documents at the same time.)

Another problem with Windows 3.1's icons at the bottom of the screen was that they were often hidden behind other windows, making it tricky to find them and restore the applications to windows on the desktop.

With Windows 3.1, if you could find the minimized icon, you could click on it once to display its control menu and choose Restore to reveal the formerly minimized window. Of course, you probably just double-clicked on the icon to restore it, instead of using the control menu. (Some people have difficulty with double-clicking, especially at first, so you may have developed a habit of always using the Control menu. No problem, but this can slow you down.)

Top of the Heap

Windows 95 has a superior solution to all those problems—the taskbar. The taskbar takes up very little screen space, so you can keep it visible all the time (we'll see how to hide it when you want to have all the screen space to yourself).

To get at a window that's been covered, you don't have to close, move or minimize the window on top. Just click on the taskbar button for the item you want to see. This puts it on top and makes it the current application.

The "Cool Switch"

In Windows 3.1, you may have learned about the Alt+Tab keyboard accelerator. If you press Alt and the Tab key together, you switch to the last window you were using. If you hold down Alt and press Tab several times, you'll cycle through all the open windows. Alt+Tab has been improved in Windows 95. Instead of displaying only the next application, it now shows a row of icons, representing all the applications currently running. That way you can see how many times you need to press Tab to get to the window you want (Figure 3-5).

 TIP   Use Alt+Shift+Tab to move backward through the Alt+Tab tasklist.

Figure 3-5: *Alt-Tab lets you cycle through your open windows.*

Using Alt+Tab to switch between running applications works quite well. It's particularly useful when you're typing, because you don't have to remove your hands from the keyboard to move the mouse down to the taskbar. Still, the taskbar can be both simpler and more convenient if your hand is already on the mouse. (The majority of Windows 3.1 users never used Alt+Tab because you had to read the manual to find out about it. It wasn't "discoverable," even by trial and error. Now, many techniques are easily discovered by just working within the Windows 95 environment. You can learn many things just by experimenting. However, there are still lots of undocumented or undiscoverable tricks in Windows 95. Readers of this book will learn many of those secrets.)

 Alt+Tab won't reveal every window you have running. There are some Windows "system properties" windows that aren't shown in the Alt+Tab list, nor are they on the taskbar. But you can use Alt+Esc instead of Alt+Tab if you want to sequentially switch between *all* open windows on your desktop, even if they're layered on top of each other.

It's Your Choice

There are usually several ways to accomplish anything in Windows 95. Some people like to click on the taskbar, others prefer Alt+Tab. The techniques you use are always up to you. Do what makes you comfortable.

Instead of the generic Control button (of Windows 3.1), each Windows 95 application displays its unique icon (shrunk down) at the far left of its title bar, followed by the name of the application, which is usually followed by the name of the open file. Even though it doesn't look like the Windows 3.1 control bar, it works the same way.

Other window control buttons also don't look the same in Windows 3.1 and Windows 95 (see Figure 3-4). The Minimize button looked like a downward-pointing triangle, to remind you that the program becomes an icon at the bottom of the screen. Windows 95 changes that button to a box with a line at the bottom, representing the position and shape of the taskbar.

In Windows 3.1, you may have used the Maximize button, which looked like an upward-pointing triangle, to make an application fill the entire screen. That was useful when you needed a lot of screen space to see your work clearly. Maximizing also helped you focus on your current project without the distraction of other windows.

However, usability research showed that some Windows 3.1 symbols were confusing to some people, so Microsoft replaced the "up wedge" symbol with a box that has a heavy line across the top. This indicates that the application fills the screen. The heavy line on top is supposed to remind you of the solid title bar of a maximized application.

After you maximize an application, you can either minimize it to the taskbar or restore it to its previous size. Restoring a maximized window is the same as "un-maximizing" it. Instead of filling the whole screen, restoring returns the window to its previous position, size and shape.

The Windows 3.1 twin-arrow symbol for Restore was ambiguous, and people would often click on it when they had intended to minimize the window. Worse still, when you had a window inside another window (this is the Multiple Document Interface, or MDI Window), you couldn't always figure out which button controlled each window.

It's a little bit clearer in Windows 95.

The Restore button now looks like two overlapping squares, to remind you that a restored window no longer steals the whole screen, but shares it with other windows, and therefore can overlap or be overlapped.

New in Windows 95 is a Close button that you can activate with a single click. It looks like an "X". If you used Windows 3.1, you'll probably click the Close button by mistake for a few days when you're reaching for Minimize or Maximize.

A maximized window is supposed to use only the screen space above the taskbar, but a few Windows applications aren't so well-behaved.

If an application covers the taskbar, you can manually resize the window. Just turn off Maximize (click on the restore symbol; see Figure 3-4), and drag the Sizer icon in the lower right-hand corner of the window. Only programs written for Windows 95 actually use a sizer icon, but you can also position the mouse on any border of the window—the cursor changes to a sizer symbol (a two-headed arrow)—and drag the window border to resize it.

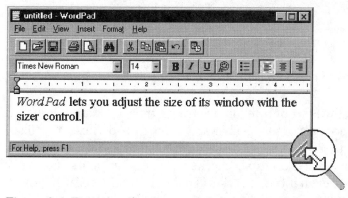

Figure 3-6: *Dragging the sizer symbol shrinks or enlarges a window.*

Sometimes you'll wish there were a way to hide the taskbar. Some people always want their current application full size. And maximizing is especially important when you're running a program that needs the whole screen, such as a slide show, or when previewing full-screen graphics. Windows 95 usually detects when you're running a program full-screen and lets the program cover the taskbar. Although you can't see the taskbar, you can press Ctrl+Esc to reveal it and pop open the Start menu. If you simply prefer not to have the taskbar visible all the time, there's a way to hide it.

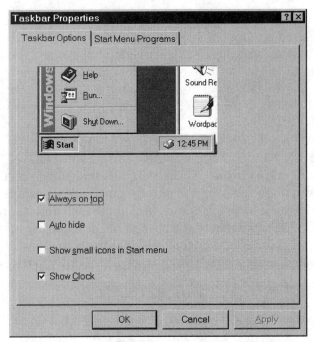

Figure 3-7: *Taskbar Properties, Taskbar Options.*

Click the Start button, then Settings, then Taskbar. (Or just right-click on any empty part of the taskbar and choose Properties.) You'll see a dialog box like Figure 3-7.

When Always on top is checked, the taskbar floats on top of all other windows, even if they overlap. This is desirable, because otherwise you wouldn't have one-click access to the taskbar buttons, you'd have to resort to the less friendly Alt+Tab keyboard sequence to switch among programs.

AutoHide is the power user's favorite. It allows the taskbar to disappear, leaving only a hair-thin gray line at the bottom of the screen to indicate its presence. This frees screen space to let you run a screen-hungry program full size. (Even the gray line would be disconcerting if you were running a full-screen slide show presentation, but Windows usually lets the presentation application take over the whole screen, hiding the taskbar. If you still have a problem with the visible part of the AutoHidden taskbar, turn off Always on top to make the taskbar disappear completely when covered by another window.)

Even with the taskbar set to AutoHide, you can still use it to switch between programs using the mouse. Just move the mouse pointer to the very bottom of the screen to instantly pop the taskbar into view. You can click on it as usual now. As soon as you move the mouse off the top edge of the taskbar—zip!—it disappears again.

You might prefer to keep the taskbar in view all the time, because it's a constant reminder of what programs you're running, and it offers convenient access to the Start button. Hiding the taskbar means an extra half-second to reveal it when you to use it. But, again, the decision is yours.

 To make more room on the Start Menu for shortcuts, right-click on the taskbar, choose Properties, then on the "Start Menu Programs" page, enable the check box for "Show small icons in Start menu".

Customing Start

In Chapter 2, we discussed a straightforward way to open the folder that holds the Start menu's Programs menu. Just right-click on the Start button and choose Open. The other way to customize Start is to right-click on the taskbar and choose Properties. Or, press the Start button, click on Settings, then click on Taskbar.

Once you've displayed the taskbar's properties (as in Figure 3-7), click on the tab heading for Start Menu Programs to see the view shown in Figure 3-8.

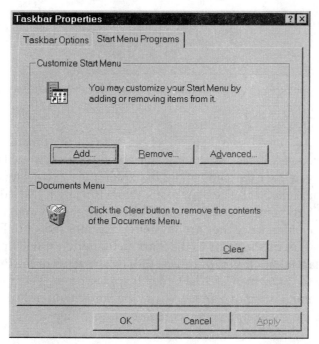

Figure 3-8: *Use the Taskbar Properties to change the Start Menu.*

The easiest way to add an item to your Start menu is to click on the Add button. This opens up the New Shortcut Wizard. You can now type the complete *path* to the program you're running or choose Browse to look for the program on your hard drive or network.

To remove a Start menu icon, click on the Remove button shown in Figure 3-8. This opens up a "tree" or hierarchical view of the Start menu, as shown in Figure 3-9. You can now easily find the icon you want to remove, and click Remove again to delete it.

Figure 3-9: *Browse through all the icons on the Start Menu, deleting ones you no longer use.*

If you click Advanced, you'll get direct access to the Start menu folder. Instead of the open-folder view you see when you right-click on Start and choose Open, you'll see the same folder in Explorer view (we'll focus on Explorer in the next chapter). The Start menu folder directly reflects the organization of the Start menu. (Actually, some Start menu choices aren't shown in the Start menu folder, since they are "system" functions like Shut Down.)

If you copy files or shortcuts to the Start menu folder, it will appear as an icon on the Start menu. If you put these files or shortcuts in the Programs folder (inside the Start menu folder), they'll appear on the Programs menu of the Start menu. To remove an icon from the Start menu or Programs menu, just delete the icon from the corresponding folder.

For Neat Freaks Only?

While you're looking at the Start menu options, consider the area labeled "Documents Menu." Clicking on the Clear button "empties" the Start menu's Documents folder, which shows you the most recent files that you've worked with. What's the use of clearing this menu? One reason is to keep your menus uncluttered, another is to keep other users who share your computer from seeing the files you're working with.

 TIP   In Chapter 17, we'll see how to let multiple users share the same machine using individual settings. If you use multiple logins, each person will have a separate Documents list.

Other Taskbar Tricks

There's usually plenty of room on the taskbar for more applications. The more windows you open, the narrower the taskbar entries become, until finally you'll see only each application's icon and a few characters of its title. To see the whole title, just hold the mouse pointer over any taskbar button for about half a second. A tiny white box with the full name of the taskbar item will pop up. Once the first help box has been displayed, there's no further delay—you can just slide the mouse across all the buttons to identify them quickly.

If you have a truly phenomenal number of open windows and applications, the taskbar can get so crowded that it simply can't hold all the buttons for the open windows. When this happens, a tiny up/down scroller appears on the taskbar to let you see all the buttons.

Figure 3-10: *Resizing the taskbar.*

Another way to accommodate many taskbar buttons is to make the taskbar bigger. Position the mouse pointer on the top edge of the taskbar until the pointer changes to a double-arrow (Figure 3-10). Now click the left button, and without letting go, drag the mouse up until you've enlarged the taskbar. Then release the mouse button.

A large taskbar may start to get in your way, so it's a good candidate for the Hide feature we just discussed.

TIP The taskbar can disappear. If you position the mouse pointer on the top edge of the taskbar until the pointer changes to a double arrow, then drag the taskbar *down* toward the bottom of the screen, it will never pop up or become visible. Even moving your mouse pointer on top of the thin line that was the taskbar now merely changes the pointer into the double arrow, but doesn't reveal the taskbar itself. If you "lose" your taskbar this way, just drag it back up by pressing the left mouse button, then pull the mouse pointer up the screen to restore the taskbar. You can also use Ctrl+Esc to access the Start button, even when the taskbar is invisible.

You can also reveal the taskbar's evil twin, or alter ego. Right-click the mouse somewhere in the unused part of the taskbar (where there are no application buttons). Without letting go, drag the mouse up and to the left or up and to the right (diagonally). Instantly, the taskbar stands at attention, becoming a vertical taskbar.

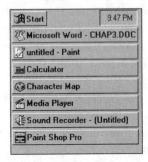

Figure 3-11: *The taskbar's vertical alter ego.*

Many people find a vertical taskbar ugly. Horizontal taskbar items display more information more naturally. You need to widen a vertical taskbar just to read the application descriptions. Of course, if you like the look of a vertical button bar, you can make the taskbar so narrow that it only has room for the miniature icons. In that case, there's won't be enough room to display the clock, so you might as well turn the clock off with Taskbar Options (discussed below). The Start button also appears to be cut off, but you can still click on the Windows logo icon to get to it.

Figure 3-12: *Resize the vertical taskbar to make it a "toolbar."*

For some applications, you may prefer to reorient the taskbar rather than hide it. Say your favorite modem communications software needs the full height of the screen to make room for 32 lines of terminal emulation, plus a status bar. But it doesn't need the full width of the screen. So instead of hiding the taskbar, you could just pull it to the right of the screen whenever you run the terminal program.

There's another cool trick you can use with the taskbar: if you have WordPad minimized on the taskbar and find a file in a folder that you want to edit or view, just drag the file from the folder's window and, in effect, drop it on the Wordpad icon in the taskbar. Here's a step-by-step tutorial for doing that.

 If you're getting ahead of our discussion, note that you can't simply drag an icon onto a taskbar button. Instead, drag the icon and hover it over the taskbar button for a moment. This causes that window to float to the top of all other windows and restore itself if it was minimized. Now you can drop the icon in the "workspace" of the open application. Use this tip to expose a hidden window that you're dragging to. Just dip the icon you're dragging to the taskbar to pop up the obscured target window, then move it up to that window and drop it. You can drag any OLE object (such as a paragraph of text) to another application's button on the taskbar to bring that application to the foreground.

Hands-On: Drag-and-Drop Documents

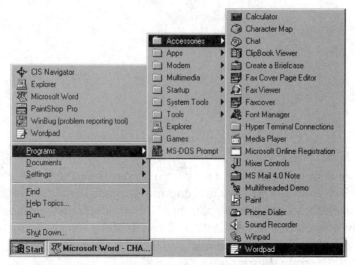

Figure 3-13: *Launching WordPad from the Start menu.*

- Press Start | Programs | Accessories | WordPad to launch WordPad.
- We need to create a sample file for this example, so just type a few lines, such as your name and address, or that infamous line about the quick brown fox. Use Save from the File menu to save the file to C:\EXAMPLE.DOC.
- Now "empty" WordPad by choosing New, and Formatted file again. We'll see how to use drag-and-drop to open the example file instead of using Open from the File menu.
- Minimize WordPad by clicking on the ▬ symbol in the upper right corner of the WordPad toolbar. It's now waiting for you on the taskbar.

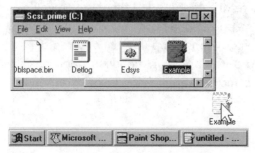

Figure 3-14: *Drag the document from My Computer to WordPad on the taskbar.*

▓ Open My Computer, then open your C: drive. You should see a WordPad document labeled Example. Click on it, and without releasing the mouse, drag it all the way to the bottom of the screen. While you're dragging, the mouse is moving a ghostly, transparent copy of the icon.

▓ When you get to the taskbar, let the mouse cursor (which is still "holding" the Example document as long as you keep the mouse button down) hover over the WordPad button. After a brief delay, WordPad zooms open, waiting for you to release the mouse button to drop the document into it.

Figure 3-15: The "yes-drop" and "no-drop" symbols let you know when it's okay to drop an object.

▓ When WordPad opens, the mouse pointer changes to either the universal "no" symbol (a circle with a line through it) or to a tiny picture of a page with a + symbol. The "no" symbol means "you can't drop *that* here," and the document symbol means "yes, you can drop that here." It should show the document symbol when held over a WordPad document, so release the mouse button when you get there to drop it.

▓ As soon as you drop the document, WordPad opens the document you created. Pretty handy!

If you drag a document to an inappropriate program (a text document to a photo-editing application, for example), it's not a problem. Usually nothing happens (that's why the "no drop" symbol appears). Some programs may attempt to open the object anyway, and display meaningless "garbage." As long as you don't re-save the document (which may alter it), no harm is done—just close it.

You can drag and drop a variety of documents onto application buttons on the taskbar. Drag-and-drop is just another tool in your bag of tricks. (Sometimes, of course, it's more convenient just to open a document from an application's File menu, or double-click on the document's icon in a folder window.)

You can often drag and drop text or graphics documents directly between applications. If you have your Printers folder open and have opened the icon for your printer, you can drag documents and drop them on the printer icon to print them on demand. (For more on drag-and-drop techniques, see Chapter 2.)

The Taskbar Notification Area

Another use of the taskbar is to display the status of certain system programs, along with the time of day. When you receive new mail in Exchange, an envelope symbol appears on the taskbar. A fax machine icon appears if you're using Microsoft at Work Fax (discussed in Chapter 16). A printer icon appears when you're printing. The MSN icon tells you that you're connected to The Microsoft Network. There's also a little "modem" icon that appears whenever you're connected via modem to another computer. Double-click the modem icon to see how many characters have been sent or received while you've been online. If you have a notebook computer, there's a battery meter on the taskbar. Other programs can create status icons, but we hope this practice doesn't get out of hand: imagine a row of a dozen or more status icons.

A Sound Idea

If you have a sound card, you probably have a wee speaker icon on the taskbar. Just click on it to pop up a slider that lets you adjust your master volume control. **Warning:** the higher range of the slider gives you a very loud volume that may damage your speakers (or even your hearing) if you play loud sounds. To disable sound, just click on the Mute button.

 To enable the volume control, see Chapter 7. Run Multimedia from the Control panel, and turn on the check box for *Show volume control on the taskbar.*

You can make other volume adjustments, such as setting the volume independently for sound effects, CD Audio, Microphone input, and so on. Just right-click on the volume control icon and choose Volume Control.

If you choose Adjust Audio Properties when you right-click on the volume control, you can adjust other default settings for your sound card. Chapter 17 tells you more about adjustments and the sound mixer, but you can turn off the check box for *Show volume control on the taskbar* if you don't want it on your screen.

Time Tools

Normally, Windows 95 displays the time in the notification area. If you don't see a time display, you may have turned it off. To turn on the time display, right-click the taskbar, choose Properties, and on the taskbar Options page, make sure "Show Clock" is checked. To remove the clock, simply un-check the box.

Here's how to set your clock:

Double-click the clock on the taskbar to open the Date & Time Properties box. Now you can set the date and time conveniently, without opening the Control Panel folder.

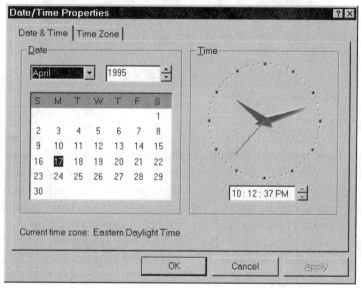

Figure 3-16: *Date and Time settings.*

The quick way to set the date is just to click on the correct day in the calendar. To change months, click on the arrow next to the month above the calendar. To change the year, click on the up and down arrows next to the year. (You can also type directly into the year box.)

To change the time, click on any digit of the time, and click the up and down arrows next to the time to increase or decrease the hour, minute or second. Or, you can highlight part of the time and just type your change. You can't simply drag on the hands of the clock to set the time, though. Maybe this will be supported in a future version of Windows.

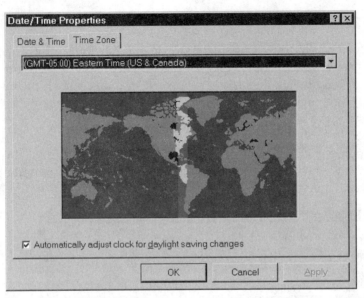

Figure 3-17: *Set Time Zone.*

To tell Windows what time zone you live in, click on the Time Zone tab button. Time zones are reckoned relative to "Greenwich Mean Time" (also known as "universal coordinated time") as kept in Greenwich, England. Midnight in Britain is zero o'clock GMT around the world. United States Eastern time is five hours behind GMT (or six hours during daylight savings time, since GMT ignores such artificial conventions), so you would click on the arrow next to "Greenwich Mean Time" to drop down a list of worldwide time zones, and scroll down to "(GMT -5:00) Eastern Time (US & Canada)." Of course, you'll choose whatever time zone is relevant to the area of the world you live in, and you can simply click on your location on the world map to quickly set your time zone.

It may seem unnecessary to use the Time Zone window, because your clock will keep the correct time no matter what time zone you choose. It's provided for compatibility with international applications that use your time zone to coordinate your activities with a machine or person in other zones and countries.We're living in an increasingly global community, with services like The Microsoft Network and the Internet connecting computers around the world, so it's a good idea to set your time zone correctly.

Windows NT and Windows 95 always pass file date/time stamps on the network wire as UTC time so that if you have a Windows NT or Windows 95 server in New York and two clients in Dallas and Denver who are editing the files on that server, all of the file times will be kept straight, and no one will see files that appear to have been edited hours ahead of their local time (this is a very common scenario, especially with Dial-Up Networking when you're on the road).

You also need to set your Time Zone correctly to tell Windows 95 exactly when to switch between Daylight Savings Time and Standard Time, especially if you're in Arizona, Indiana or Saskatchewan, where they don't switch to Daylight Savings Time in the summer (or in Europe, where the DST changeover happens on different dates than in the US).

The Time Zone setting is also necessary for Briefcase reconciliation between two parties in different time zones. (We'll talk more about the Briefcase in Chapter 19.)

You can also click on "Adjust for Daylight Savings Time" to let your clock automatically spring forward or fall back at the appropriate the times of the year (and automatically adjust relative to GMT).

 The clock only shows the current time of day, but if you let the mouse hover over the time, a *tooltip* pops up giving you the date and day of the week.

More Taskbar Tricks

Use the right mouse button to click on an empty part of the taskbar to find some useful taskbar tools. Except for the Properties choice (discussed above), these options affect any open windows on the desktop.

Figure 3-18: *The taskbar menu let you rearrange your windows.*

Cascade arranges all your windows so that they overlap, and neatly arranges them "front to back." See Figure 3-19.

Figure 3-19: *Cascade arranges your windows so they overlap neatly.*

Tile Horizontally stacks the windows from top to bottom without overlapping them. The current window becomes the topmost one in the stack.

Figure 3-20: *Tile Horizontally stacks your windows from top to bottom.*

Tile Vertically lines up your windows from left to right without overlapping them. The current window becomes the leftmost one in the stack.

 TIP There is no difference between tiling horizontally and vertically if you have more than three windows open.

Figure 3-21: *Tile Vertically lays out your windows from left to right.*

Be aware that many programs remember the size and position of their windows, so tiling or cascading can upset the customary size and position you prefer for your windows. Tile and Cascade are really provided as a last resort if you've managed to massively clutter the desktop with piles of overlapping windows.

Finally, the Minimize All Windows menu item becomes available when you right-click on the taskbar. This is probably the best way to wipe your desktop clean. It minimizes all windows into buttons on the taskbar to reveal the desktop, so you can easily click on any desktop icons, or otherwise get things together.

When you're finished with the desktop, just right-click on the taskbar again and choose Undo Minimize All, and you're back to work with your open windows, just as you left them.

 If you have a Microsoft Natural Keyboard or other 104-key compatible keyboard, you can press the ⊞+M sequence to minimize all open windows. Use Shift+ ⊞+M to reverse this, restoring all minimized windows.

If you right-click on an icon on the taskbar, you can view that program's System menu (also called the Control menu, the same one that appears when you click on that program's Control icon). From the System menu, you can quickly close an application without having to restore it to the desktop and click on its X (Close) box.

Moving On

In Chapter 4, we'll look at Explorer, a powerful file browser, organizer, launcher and viewer. If you've ever used File Manager in Windows 3.1, you'll find Explorer instantly familiar, though more thoughtfully designed and considerably easier to use. We'll discuss routine file maintenance procedures, such as copying, moving, renaming, deleting and opening files. We'll also examine how Windows's own folders are organized. Then, in Chapter 5, we'll see how the disk drive and its file system work together, how to keep them running reliably, and how to optimize their performance.

Getting Organized

Chapter 4

Exploring Your Computer

By now, you're getting comfortable with the Windows 95 methods for opening and managing windows. We'll now begin to study the file system and see how Windows manages your hard drive.

We'll begin our expedition at the source: Look for an icon called My Computer on your desktop, and double-click it to open its window. (You can create your own desktop icons, but Windows provides some "system" desktop items that you can't remove, including My Computer, Network Neighborhood and Info Center.)

Figure 4-1: *The My Computer icon is always available on your desktop.*

Inside the My Computer folder, you'll see more icons, one for each floppy drive, hard drive and CD-ROM drive on your machine. You'll also see icons for Control Panel and Printers. You can access both Control Panel and Printers by choosing Settings from the Start menu, but they're also directly available by double-clicking their icons inside My Computer.

My Computer is a container for your whole computer, at least for its local resources. Another container, called Network Neighborhood, holds all the drives and resources for the entire network, if your computer is attached to one (either by cable or via modem). See Chapter 19 for more information about networking.

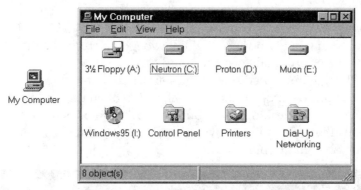

Figure 4-2: Inside the My Computer folder, you'll find the main avenues to your disk drives, printers and the Control Panel.

By convention, disk drives are "named" according to letters of the alphabet. Drive A: is always a floppy disk drive, and may be either a 3.5-inch drive or a 5.25-inch size. Your system may also have a B: drive, which is also always a floppy drive. Next comes drive C:, which is the first (and often only) hard drive. It's called a *hard* drive, since unlike the flexible magnetic media in a floppy drive, a hard drive employs a rigid metal or glass platter coated with the same type of brown magnetic material. Sometimes it's called a *fixed drive*, since the disk platter is not removable. However, some hard drives use removable media, including drives from Bernoulli, Iomega and SyQuest. Other variations include optical and magneto-optical drives, which take advantage of the short wavelength of light (as opposed to magnetic waves) to pack more data into less space. Removable and optical drives are also assigned drive letters such as D:.

(Note that Windows 95 will automatically assign these drive letter names. These *volume names* were created when the drive was originally formatted. However, you can change the descriptive name that follows the drive letter, as you'll learn later in this chapter.)

When you attach to a network, the distant hard drives on the network servers or the shared hard drives on your peers' computers can also appear in My Computer as a drive letter. (In Chapter 19, we'll also see how to access shared or network drives without having to *map* a drive letter to them.)

To complicate matters, there is another type of *virtual* hard drive. When you compress a drive with DoubleSpace or DriveSpace, or a third-party tool like Stacker, your original hard drive is often renamed to a new drive letter, such as D: or H:. A huge file is created on this *host drive*, and special software makes this file (which holds compressed data) appear to look and act exactly like a hard drive; it is usually named drive C:. The only time you need to distinguish the virtual vs. the real hard drive is when you remember that most of the space is used up on the host drive, so you usually don't use it to store files (use the compressed drive C: for that). We'll examine these issues in detail in Chapter 5.

However, most computers have at least one traditional fixed hard drive, known as C:. Before we examine what's on your drive, let's learn more about it. Click once (don't double-click) on drive C: in your opened My Computer window, and choose Properties from the File menu. You'll see something similar to Figure 4-3 (although your drive will have different properties).

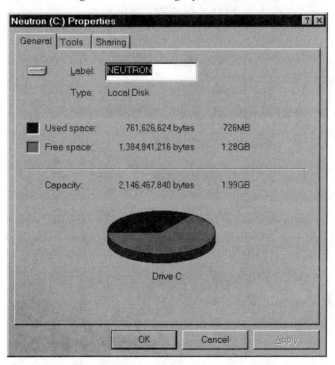

Figure 4-3: *Right-click on a drive icon in My Computer and choose Properties to find out more about the drive.*

You'll first notice a tab heading marked General. If your computer is on a network (and your network administrator permits *peer-to-peer* networking), you'll also see a tab heading for Sharing. If you click on Sharing, you'll see a new view that lets you decide if you want to share your hard drive with others in your networked workgroup. We'll save consideration of this for the chapter on networking, Chapter 19.

On the General page of the drive's properties sheet, you can get, at a glance, an idea of how much disk space you have left, shown in bytes, megabytes (millions) or gigabytes (billions), and the proportion of used space to empty space is illustrated in a pie chart.

Disk space is of course the most precious resource for a computer, since every new application you install can consume many megabytes. You can upgrade to a new hard drive if you run out of space, but many computers are limited to two hard drives. When buying or upgrading, try to buy the biggest hard drive you can afford. No matter how big your hard drive is, it's important to manage it wisely, or it will fill up. We'll discuss some techniques for deleting files and uninstalling applications, and just as important, how to back up your critical data in case of catastrophic drive failure.

You'll also notice that the label for the drive, shown at the top of the General page, is editable, so feel free to give it a descriptive name to go with its otherwise meaningless moniker, perhaps as a reminder of what type of drive it is. For removable media, you are naming whatever disk is in the drive, not the drive itself, and you can't change the name of a CD-ROM, of course.

If your drive C: is currently named STARTUP, you could type over that and change it to MAIN or MINE or whatever you want. You could also change the name by slowly clicking twice (not double-clicking, but two single-clicks with some delay between them) on the label underneath the drive's icon inside the My Computer window. Then just type in the new name.

Taking a Dip

Let's wade right in. Close Properties and double-click on the icon for drive C: in My Computer to open its window. Drive C:'s window shows you icons for every file and folder, and there are often too many to fit in the window. You can either resize or maximize the window to see more items, or just use the horizontal and vertical scroll bars to shift your view.

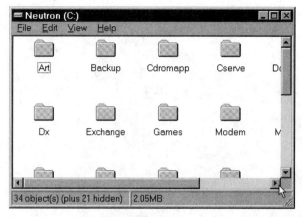

Figure 4-4: *Use the scrollbars to move around within a window.*

Another way to get a wider view is to shrink the icons. Choose Small Icons from the View menu. You can use View I Large Icons to go back to the big icons that are easy on the eyes. Go ahead and try out List and Details if you like, which we'll discuss a little later.

As you double-click to open My Computer, then a drive and then double-click a folder, you're drilling down deeper in the directory structure. Remember that files are organized on your disk drives in a hierarchy, like having several file cabinets (the drives) each containing many *folders* (the subdirectories), which in turn contain more folders and/or individual files (applications and documents).

You're also opening up a lot of windows, possibly cluttering your desktop. On the one hand, it's useful to open a new window for each view, since it's simple and obvious, and makes it easy to back up to the previous view: you just close the current window, or click on the window of the previous view to bring it to the top of the pile.

However, it's possible to use the same window (container) for all your views. Let's try it. From any open view, choose Options from the View menu, to get a dialog box like the one shown in Figure 4-5.

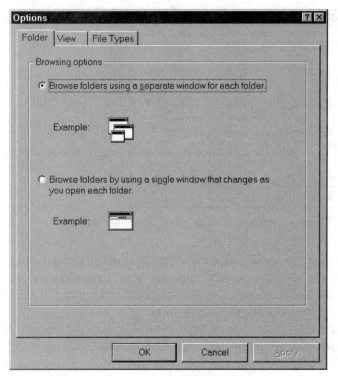

Figure 4-5: *Use View | Options to change the appearance of open folders.*

Try clicking on the box next to the second choice, *Browse folders by using a single window that changes as you open each folder* (what a mouthful—some simply call it Single Browse Mode), and then click on OK. Don't worry, if you prefer to have new windows pop up each time, it's easy to go back by clicking on the first choice, *Browse folders using a separate window for each folder* (a.k.a. Multiple Browse Mode).

 TIP If you're using Single Browse Mode, you can force Windows to open a separate window for a folder by holding down either Ctrl key while you double-click the folder's icon. When using Multiple Browse Mode, the Ctrl key has the reverse effect, forcing the folder to open using the current window as the container.

Now, when you open a folder, it stays in the same window. But how do you back up to the previous (parent) folder? You can't just close the window, or you would close My Computer altogether. The keyboard hotkey for backing up is Backspace, but that's not always easy to remember.

It's time to add another level of control. Choose Toolbar from the View menu, and a new set of controls is overlaid at the top of the toolbar (see Figure 4-6). If the toolbar seems to be cut off, resize the window so that it's wide enough.

Now there's a simple way to back up to the previous window. Just click on the  symbol.

Figure 4-6: *Use the View menu to enable the toolbar.*

From left to right, let's tour the toolbar. At the left of the toolbar is a *control* called a drop-down list box. (A control is an element of the user interface, such as a button, an icon or an edit box.) The drop-down list box shows you the names of the drives and folders, and it lets you jump directly to any drive or object in My Computer. Next is the "back up" button we just mentioned. The next two symbols concern networks (the first lets you attach to a shared or network drive, and the second lets you disconnect a shared drive; we explore these buttons in Chapter 19). Next, you have icons for Cut, Copy, Paste, Undo, Delete and Properties. The remaining four toolbar icons are equivalent to the Large Icons, Small Icons, List and Detail options of the View menu.

Toolbars are convenient, but the symbols are not very meaningful until you've learned to associate them with the actions they perform. To find out what a toolbar icon does, point to it with the mouse pointer (but don't click). If you pause over the icon for about a second, a pop-up help bar appears, giving you the name of the icon. You first encountered pop-up tool help with the taskbar in Chapter 2. (A more detailed description of each button's purpose will appear at the bottom of the window, on the *status bar* if you've opted to have it visible. You make the status bar visible by selecting Status Bar in the window's View menu. The status bar displays the complete action performed by any menu item, or when you click on a toolbar button.)

 TIP   If you click on an icon or other control but wish you hadn't, just move the mouse pointer away from the icon before you let go of the mouse button.

The buttons make the window more complex, but more informative and convenient, too. Instead of choosing Small Icons from the View menu, you can just click on the toolbar icon for Small Icons.

Figure 4-7: *Small Icons let you fit more files in the same space.*

At first glance, the List view looks the same as Small Icons, but Small Icons are ordered from left to right, they way you'd read a page in a book. List view is ordered by column, top to bottom, the way you'd read a phone book. With Small Icons, you can rearrange the initially orderly position of the icons to your heart's content, whereas the List view always preserves the columnar structure.

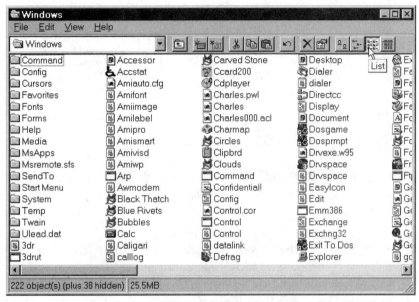

Figure 4-8: *The List view is automatically organized in columns.*

 TIP Unless you have Auto Arrange turned on (see below), you can freely reposition icons using Small Icons and Large Icons view. Both List and Details view force the icons into neat columns, but when you return to Small or Large Icons, the positions of your icons are restored.

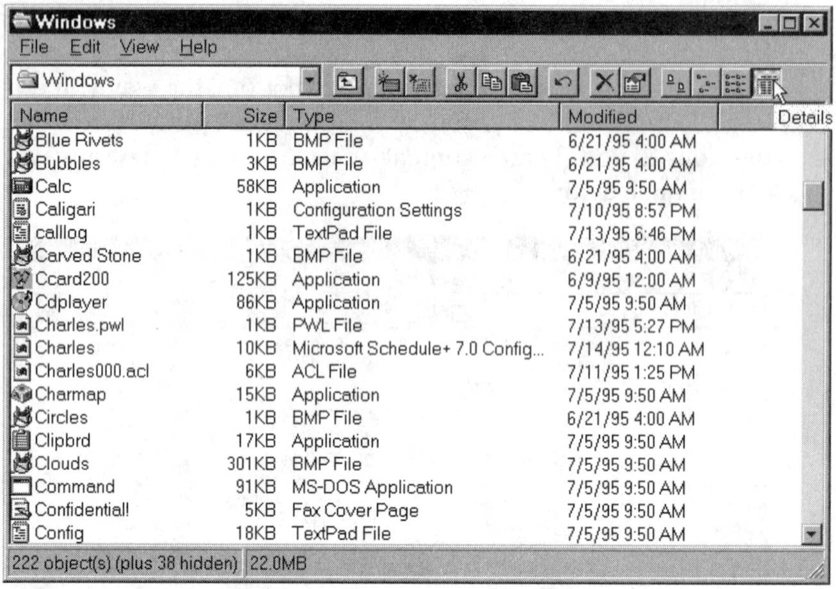

Figure 4-9: *Click on any heading using Details view to quickly sort the files by that category.*

The Details view (Figure 4-9) also shows small icons but displays them in a single column, with additional columns for Size, Type and Modified. You can reorder the list by clicking on these column headings, as if they were buttons. For example, you can click on Type to sort the list by file type, which groups together the related files. The Modified heading is useful when you have two versions of a file, and you're trying to figure out which one is more recent. Sort by Modified, and you have a chronological list of files, like those layers of strata that archeologists dig through to find buried civilizations.

> **(TIP** Click once on a column heading to sort the list according to Name, Type or Date Modified. Click on the same heading again to reverse the order of the sort. For example, click once on Name to sort the files alphabetically [A to Z] by their filenames. Click on Name again to sort in reverse alphabetical order [Z to A]. Reverse order is actually more practical when sorting by date or size.

Every file has a type, which tells Windows what program is used to create or edit it. We'll discuss file types completely in Chapter 5 and show you how to associate files with the proper programs.

It's handy to sort the list by Size when you're hunting for files to delete and free up disk space. No sense wasting time on small fry when you can go to the end of the list and get rid of the big boys!

As long as you have the toolbar turned on, go ahead and enable the status bar from the View menu, too (unless the status bar is already visible). Sure, the status bar takes up some screen space, but it provides handy one-line help for each menu command.

For even more detail, click on a file and choose Properties from the File menu or click on the Properties toolbar icon (the one that looks like a hand holding a page). Or you can right-click on the file and choose Properties from the context menu. You get a display similar to Figure 4-10.

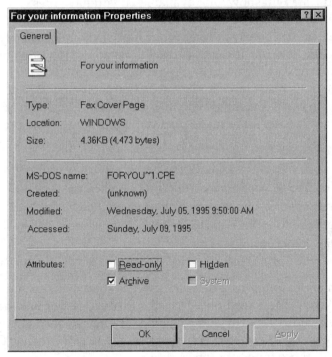

Figure 4-10: *File Properties gives you the straight scoop, including the actual MS-DOS name of the file.*

The properties sheet gives you all the facts about a file, all in one place. Notice the line MS-DOS Name. Although you can use virtually any filename you like when saving or renaming a file, Windows always invents a standard filename that's compatible with DOS and Windows 3.1. So you could call a file "Letter to Mom," and Windows will save it as "LETTER~1.DOC." The rest of the file is still there, but it's stored in a separate location. If you need to open a Windows file with a DOS program or with an earlier 3.1 version of a Windows program, you'll need to use the shorter MS-DOS name. (When using Windows 3.1 programs that haven't been updated for Windows 95, you'll still be limited to eight-character filenames anyway.)

In addition to the Changed Date (same as Modified in the Details view), Windows now tracks two other dates for a file. It knows when a file was created and when it was last accessed, even if the file was only opened but not changed. Windows 95 can provide these dates only for files it creates, so the Created Data will show "not available" if you have files created by DOS or older versions of Windows.

You can use Attributes to protect your file. Click on Read Only, and you've "frozen" the file. It can't be deleted, renamed, modified or moved (but you can copy it). If you have any problem deleting a file, check its Properties to see if it's read-only. But be aware that there may be a good reason it's difficult to erase. Deleting some files can "break" an application program, so they're sometimes made read-only to provide some protection.

TIP When you copy files from a CD-ROM, they are still marked read-only when copied to your hard drive. You can select all the files and choose Properties and then turn off read-only for all the files at once by unchecking the Read Only box. You can apply other file properties to groups of files the same way.

Often an entire folder on a network drive is shown as read-only. You can also make your folders read-only by using Properties, but unless you have read/write/modify security authorization, granted by the network supervisor or the owner of the shared network folder, you can't change the read-only status of those types of protected files.

For even more protection, you can make your files invisible by clicking on Hidden on the Attributes page. Under normal circumstances, this file won't appear in folder view. It's not really secure protection, though, since we'll show you how to enable the display of hidden files in Chapter 5, and you can assume others know about this technique, too.

If you choose Properties for a folder, you'll see another tab marked Sharing (if your computer is part of a network). On a network, you can allow others to read and/or write files to your hard drive. Rather than making your entire drive public property, you can choose to share only selected directories. We'll cover file and folder sharing in Chapter 19.

When you choose File Properties for a DOS program or batch file, you'll get a much more complete set of properties to let you control how Windows should emulate DOS for that program. These settings were formerly called .PIF settings in Windows 3.1 (for Program Information File). We present an extensive discussion of DOS program properties in Chapter 22.

Interior Design

You've already learned that you can drag and drop icons between folders to move and copy objects, and create shortcuts (we first discussed file shortcuts in Chapter 2). You can also move icons within a folder to customize their position. Some people like to set up a custom layout, but if you're trying for a neat and orderly look, it can be frustrating to try to manually line up your icons. And if you're not using Detail view, how to you order the icons alphabetically or by type? Do you have to manually rearrange them too?

Fortunately, we can find a way out of this chaos. Choose Arrange Icons from the View menu (as shown in Figure 4-11) and then choose one of the arrangement options from the submenu to sort the icons and neatly arrange them. If you want to have your icons automatically arrange themselves when you add or remove icons to a folder, choose Auto Arrange. Auto Arrange is also convenient because it rearranges any icons when you resize a window.

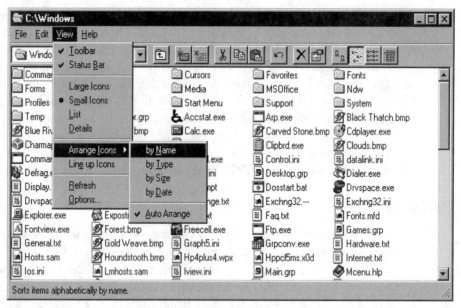

Figure 4-11: *Arrange your icons in any order.*

Another way to help you align your icons is to choose View | Line Up Icons. It neatly arranges all your icons, as if you chose one of the Arrange Icons options—but without changing their order.

Each folder remembers its own information about the icons' positions, the order in which they were last sorted, and whether the toolbar, status line and Auto Arrange are turned on.

Actually, there is a limitation on how well this works with the current version of Windows 95. Although ideally all folder attributes should be preserved, currently only the last 50 or so folders are "remembered" by Windows 95, and some operations, like installing new software, can reset all your folders back to their default view (large icons, no Auto Arrange, no sort order, status bar enabled and so on). This limitation (arguably a feature designed to prevent the user profiles from filling up with folder settings) will hopefully be fixed in a future version of Windows 95.

There's no simple way to select Auto Arrange for the entire disk, and perhaps that's best. If you were able to Auto Arrange every folder on your drive with a single click, what if you chose it by mistake and scuttled the custom layout of all your carefully designed folders?

There's no way to set the default folder properties for folders you haven't "visited" yet. Or is there? We've discovered a technique that does the trick, sort of. Arrange any folder the way you'd like new folders to appear. If you prefer small icons, choose the Small Icons view. Turn the toolbar or status bar on or off to suit. To force Windows to memorize your preference, hold down the Ctrl key as you click the close box (the "X" in the upper right corner of the window). Now, before you do anything else, use Start I Shut Down and shut down Windows. When you restart your computer, your preferences will be honored, but only for windows that you haven't opened yet. Also, this trick doesn't seem to memorize Auto Arrange. Too bad. That's one we'd especially like to set as the default.

Explorer View

If you've been trying out these various techniques as we've been looking at them, your drive folder has come a long way from its original simple layout. Perhaps you prefer this simple layout for some purposes, such as launching applications. You may want all these extra controls and small icons only when you're engaged in file-management chores.

 Hold down either Shift key while double-clicking a folder or drive icon to open it using Explorer view. You can even do this while you're already in Explorer view if you want to quickly open another Explorer. If you have multiple folders selected, they will all open up in Explorer view, which may not be what you had intended, so you may want to single-click on the folder before using Shift+double-click to prevent a range of files from being Explored. If Alt+double-click gets tiresome, just right-click on an icon and choose Explore.

Figure 4-12: *Use the right mouse button to switch to Explorer view.*

One way to instantly transform a plain folder view into a power tool is to click the right mouse button on the control icon (the folder icon in the upper-left corner of the folder windows) and choose Explore (see Figure 4-12).

As you can see in Figure 4-13, not only do you get all the controls and a status bar, the file window is now split into two *panes:* the folders pane and the files pane. The files pane is normally the same as choosing List view, but you can click on the toolbar to choose any other view (if you don't see the toolbar, use the View menu to turn it back on).

 TIP Normally, when you double-click on a folder, it opens using folder view. If you prefer to *always* use Explorer view, follow these steps:

1. Open any folder
2. Choose View | Options, and click on the tab for File Types.
3. Look for an entry named *Folder* and double-click on it. (Ignore the one named *File Folder*.)
4. You'll be taken to the Edit File Type dialog box. In it, you'll see that there are two actions for folders, *explore* and *open.* Normally, *open* is in boldface, meaning it is the default action. Explore is only an option if you right-click on the folder.

5. To reverse this behavior, simply click on the *Explore* action, then press the Set Default button.
6. To restore the normal Windows behavior, click the *Open* action, and press Set Default.

Figure 4-13: *Explorer View shows you more information about your files and makes it easier to manage them.*

 TIP   If you have a Microsoft Natural Keyboard or other 104-key compatible keyboard, press ⊞+E to pop up an Explorer view of My Computer. You can then view any other drive or folder from its list of drives.

Rather than transform a standard view into Explorer view, you can also run Explorer directly, as if it were a program. You can find it on the Programs submenu of the Start button menu.

TIP You may also want to create a desktop shortcut for an Explorer view of your hard drive. Right-click on the Start button and choose Open. Then open the Programs folder to find the Explorer Shortcut. Now you can use the right mouse button to drag it to the desktop, choosing the Copy option, so that it isn't moved out of the Start menu.

The folders pane on the left (also called the *tree pane*) shows you every folder on your hard drive. It's a *hierarchical*, or tree view. When you run Explorer, the folders pane shows you the "top level" drives and folders. Each folder can branch to a list of subfolders, which in turn can each branch to their subfolders. Rather than deal with only one view at a time, as you normally get with My Computer's view of your files, Explorer shows you the entire tree.

If the tree were fully expanded, it could be hard to comprehend amongst all the clutter, so the branches are usually collapsed, except for the current folder. Each folder that contains other folders is marked with a tiny ⊞ symbol. You can expand a collapsed view by clicking on the ⊞ symbol for that folder. Figure 4-14 shows Figure 4-13 with the Programs folder expanded to show its subfolders. To back up and collapse a branch, just click on its ⊟ symbol.

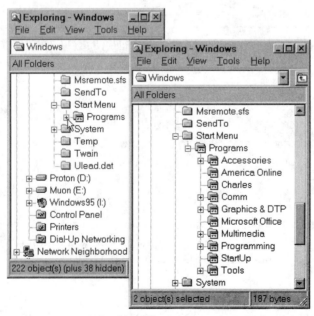

Figure 4-14: *Click on the ⊞ symbol to expand a branch.*

This capability makes it easy to compactly organize your files into folders and subfolders. If you're experienced with MS-DOS, you instantly recognize them as directories and subdirectories, but they've never been so easy to access.

The file pane is independent but linked to the folders pane. You can expand or collapse branches of the tree, even on different drives, without affecting the contents the file pane, as long as you click only on the ⊞ and ⊟ symbols. To see "inside" a folder, click on the folder name shown in the folder pane on the left. Now you see the contents of that folder in the file pane on the right.

Navigating With the Explorer

You'll want to get comfortable locating files using the folder pane. This procedure is known as *navigating* with the Explorer. Here's how:

- To navigate to a folder, first find the drive it's on by scrolling up and down through the folders pane. Or choose the drive directly from the drop-down list box on the toolbar.
- If the drive is collapsed, click on the ⊞ symbol next to it to show all its folders.
- If you don't see the subfolder you're looking for, it's probably in one of the collapsed folders. Click on the ⊞ symbol for the parent folder to reveal it.
- Once you've navigated to the proper folder, click on the folder name to reveal its contents, which appear in the file pane.
- An alternative to using the folders pane is to double-click on folder names in the file pane to "drill down," using Backspace or the 🗐 toolbar icon to back up to a previous directory. You use this method with My Computer folders, since they normally lack the Explorer folders pane.
- Once you've found the folder you're looking for, just click on the name of the file you're interested in and choose an option from the File menu or the Edit menu (or click the right mouse button for the context menu). The idea here is that you first choose the subject (the file) and then the verb (the menu command) to tell the computer what you want to do.

If you're still having trouble finding the file or subfolder you're looking for, turn to the Find tool on the Start menu (covered in Chapter 2). You can also access Find from Explorer's Tools menu. Or to search from the current folder, just press the F3 function key.

TIP Instead of searching through your hard drive, you can open a folder immediately if you know its exact path and filename. Choose Go To from the Tools menu or click on Start | Run, and type in the folder name to open it on the desktop.

Managing Your Files

You can launch programs from either Explorer or My Computer (or from the Start button directly). But Explorer excels when it comes to managing your files. Let's review how to copy, move, rename and delete files and folders. We'll also discuss some other common file-management tasks.

Copying & Pasting a File

First, let's learn how to copy a file.

■ In the file pane, click on the name of the file you want to copy and choose Copy from the Edit menu or click the Copy button on the toolbar. Or you can click on the filename with the right mouse button to open the pop-up menu and choose Copy. (This places the filename and its location in the Clipboard, not the file itself.) Note that this procedure does not work like Copy in File Manager: it doesn't start the copying right away—that doesn't happen until you use Paste.

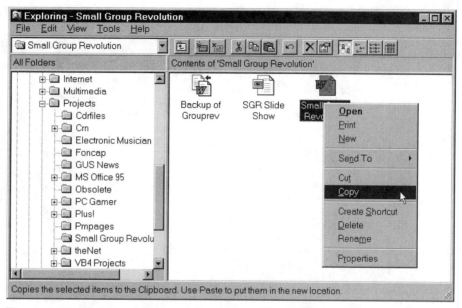

Figure 4-15: *Click the right mouse button on a file and choose Copy from the pop-up menu.*

▓ Now find the folder you want to copy to, the destination folder, by scrolling the folders pane up and down, and if necessary, clicking on ⊞ to expand a drive to show its folders. Click on the destination folder to display it in the file pane on the right.

▓ Click anywhere in the file pane and choose Edit | Paste (or choose Paste from the right-click context menu).

▓ If you paste the file into the original file pane, it's saved as the same filename, starting with "Copy of." If the original file is named Readme.doc, the copy would be "Copy of Readme.doc." If you paste it again, you'll get "Copy #2 of Readme.doc."

Moving a File

Now let's learn how to move a file.

▓ In the file pane, click on the name of the file you want to copy and choose Cut from the Edit menu or click on the Cut button on the toolbar. Or you can click on the filename with the right mouse button to open the context menu and choose Cut. Again, this doesn't move the file when you choose it—that doesn't happen until you use Paste. Don't worry, the file is not actually deleted until you paste it.

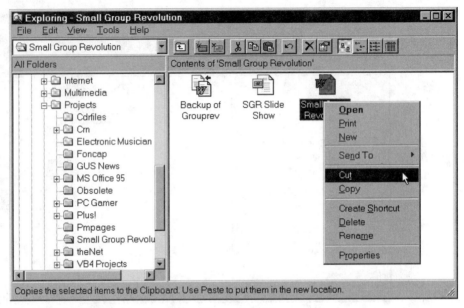

Figure 4-16: *Use Cut to choose the file you want to move.*

■ Now find the folder you want to copy to, the destination folder, by scrolling up and down the folders pane, and if necessary, clicking on ⊞ to expand a drive to show its folders. Click on the destination folder to display it in the file pane.

■ Click anywhere in the file pane, and choose Edit I Paste (or choose Paste from the right-click context menu). The file is copied to the destination folder and then deleted from the original folder.

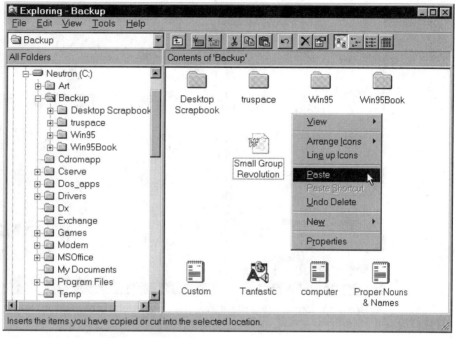

Figure 4-17: *Use Paste to move the file to its new location.*

■ Pasting back to the original folder has no net effect, except that it cancels the Cut (but leaves the filename in the Clipboard in case you want to paste it somewhere else).

■ If you paste the file into the original file pane again, it's saved as the same filename, starting with "Copy of." If the original file is named Readme.doc, the copy would be "Copy of Readme.doc." If you paste it again, you'll get "Copy #2 of Readme.doc."

Changing the Name of a File

Next, we're ready to learn how to change the filename.

■ In the file pane, click on the filename and choose Rename from the File menu, or click on the filename with the right mouse button and choose Rename from the pop-up menu.

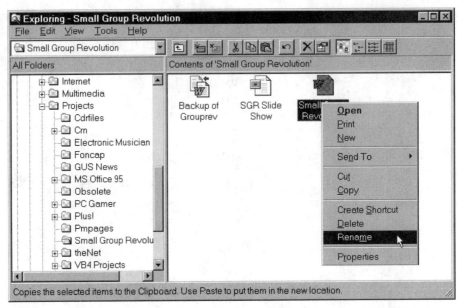

Figure 4-18: *Renaming a file is easy with the right-button pop-up menu.*

■ A seemingly simpler but actually trickier method is to click on the filename once, pause a half a second, and click on it again. You pause to prevent an accidental double-click. If you double-click while trying to rename a file, the file is opened instead, and this wastes time.

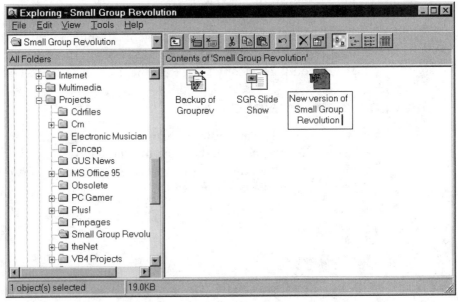

Figure 4-19: *Use the cursor (arrow) keys to edit the filename.*

- A box appears around the filename, and you can use the left and right arrow keys to move within the filename and edit it. Notice that the entire filename is highlighted at first. If you simply start typing, the selected filename is cleared and replaced by your new keystrokes. When typing a new filename, you're free to use up to 250 characters or so. (The entire pathname, including the drive letter and slashes, can't exceed 255 characters, so you're limited to fewer characters for the filename itself.) You can use almost any character on the keyboard for the filename, except for these characters, which have a special meaning in the file system: * ? / | \ : < " >

- Press Enter to seal the change. To cancel the name change, press Ctrl+Z, select Undo from the Edit menu (or from the right-button pop-up menu), press the Esc key, or just click anywhere outside the filename. You can also click on the Undo button on the toolbar. When renaming, you must press Enter to make the change "stick." Even after you finish the renaming, you can still revert to the original name by choosing Undo.

Caution: *Feel free to change the names of files you create with Windows 95 applications or to change the name of new folders you create, but avoid renaming folders or files that you use with Windows 3.1 applications (ones that haven't been updated for Windows 95). Here's why:*

When you create a long filename, Windows actually creates two filenames. It remembers the long, meaningful filename, but the file is also stored in a way that's compatible with the eight-character limit on MS-DOS filenames. If you rename a file from README.TXT to "My readme file," it will change the MS-DOS name to MYREAD~1.TXT. (If you have two similar filenames, Windows adds special characters to make sure the MS-DOS filenames are different.) If you need to open this file in a DOS or Windows 3.1 application, use the Properties command from the File menu or the right-button context menu to see the true MS-DOS filename.

In general, avoid renaming application folders (the directories created when you install a new program) or any files within them. It's always safe to rename or move shortcuts, but the original programs often look for specific directory (folder) names and specific program names when they run and will fail if you've renamed them. (It's okay to rename or move documents—but the actual programs that create those documents should be left on your hard disk where the programs were originally installed during their setup.)

Opening a File, Launching an Application

The fastest way to open a file is to double-click the filename. Or you can right-click on it and choose Open from the right-click context menu, or click on it and choose Open from the File menu. Assuming that the file type is associated with an installed application, the application starts and automatically opens the file. Another way of opening a file is to drag the filename and drop it onto an application icon in a folder.

If the file is a program (application) file, opening it has the effect of starting the program with an empty document.

Another way to accomplish this is to use New from the File menu or right-button context menu. It lets you create a new folder or a new document in any format that has been registered with Windows. When you install applications, they register the file types they support, so you can create a blank document or spreadsheet in one step by selecting File | New.

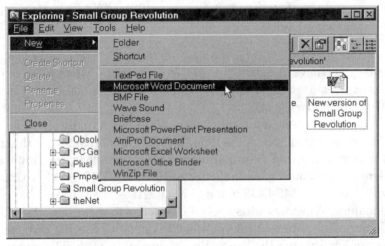

Figure 4-20: *Create a blank document by using New from the File menu. The options shown on your New menu will vary, depending on what applications you've installed.*

Viewing a File

It can take anywhere from a few seconds to a few minutes to start an application and view a file after that application finally opens and is ready to display a document. Your wait time depends on the speed of your computer and its drives, as well as the application's inherent launching speed (some application's are notoriously slow to get themselves together when you run them). Windows 95 lets you more quickly take a peek at a file, if it's one of the supported file types, by using Quick View from the File menu of a folder or Explorer, or by clicking the mouse's right button on any document's icon to reveal the context menu. **Note:** Quick View, as handy as it is, is not installed by default during Setup. We'll show you how to add optional components in Chapter 7, "The Control Panel."

Currently, Windows Quick View can show you a preview of a file in many file types: pictures (.BMP, .WMF); documents (.DOC and .RTF); Excel, Lotus and Borland spreadsheets, word processing files from Microsoft, Lotus and WordPerfect. The complete list of extensions and file types you can view in Quick View is shown in Table 4-1.

Extension	File Types
.ASC	ASCII files
.BMP	Windows Bitmap Graphics files
.CDR	CorelDRAW up to Version 4.0 files
.DIB	Windows Bitmap Graphics files
.DLL	Dynamic Link Library files
.DOC	Any of a number of word processing file formats
.DRW	Micrographx Draw files, all versions
.EPS	Encapsulated PostScript files
.EXE	Executable files
.GIF	CompuServe GIF files
.INF	Files used by the setup program
.INI	Configuration files
.MOD	Multiplan Version 3, 4.0 and 4.1 files
.PPT	PowerPoint Version 4 files
.PRE	Freelance for Windows Version 2.0
.REG	Registation Entries
.RLE	Bitmap files (RunLengthEncoding)
.RTF	Rich Text Format files
.SAM	AMI and AMI Pro files
.TIF	TIFF files
.TXT	Text files
.WB1	Quattro Pro for Windows Version 5 files
.WDB	Works Version 3 database files
.WK1	Lotus 1-2-3 Version 1 and 2 files
.WK3	Lotus 1-2-3 Version 3 files
.WK4	Lotus 1-2-3 Version 4 files
.WKS	Lotus 1-2-3 files or MS Works Version 3 spreadsheet files
.WMF	Windows Metafiles

Extension	File Types
.WPD	WordPerfect Version 5.x for MS-DOS and WordPerfect for Windows Version 6 document files
.WPS	Works word processing files
.WQ1	Quattro Pro Version 1 through 4 for MS-DOS files
.WQ2	Quattro Pro Version 5 for MS-DOS files
.WRI	Windows 3.x WRITE files
.XLC	Excel 4 chart files
.XLS	Excel 4 and 5 spreadsheet files

Table 4-1: *Quick Viewers provided by Microsoft. (**Note:** Some Quick Viewers, such as the .GIF and .TIF viewers, were removed from Windows 95 by Microsoft as this book went to press. We expect that they'll be added back in a future version of Windows 95.)*

If no Quick View option appears on either the File menu or the right-click context menu, that means no Quick Viewer is installed for that file type.

The viewer is *extensible*, so you'll be able to buy commercial or shareware add-ons to let you view more file types. It's anticipated that Windows 95 programs will install their own Quick Viewers for the file types they support or even replace the default Quick Viewers with enhanced or updated versions.

Each Quick Viewer has its own toolbar options. For example, the Quick Viewer for text files and documents lets you change the font size (see Figure 4-21). One toolbar button also lets you launch the associated application, since you can't edit the file with Quick View. Quick View is especially handy for previewing graphics, such as wallpaper, and it's a lot faster than starting a paint program. Normally, a separate Quick View window opens each time you use it. If you'd prefer to use a single window for viewing files, just choose *Reuse Window* from Quick View's *View* menu. You'll have to keep the Quick View window open on your desktop to take advantage of this feature

 TIP   You can greatly improve Quick View by purchasing Quick View Plus from Inso Corporation (developed by System Compatibility Corporation, that created the original Quick View for Microsoft). Quick View Plus adds 175 more viewer formats, with higher fidelity preview (formatting, graphics, embedded objects, and tables are all intact). You can also print files with Quick View Plus, and use the Clipboard to copy from the Quick View window and paste into any Windows application. Call (312) 329-0700 for more information or send Internet mail to support@syscomp.com.

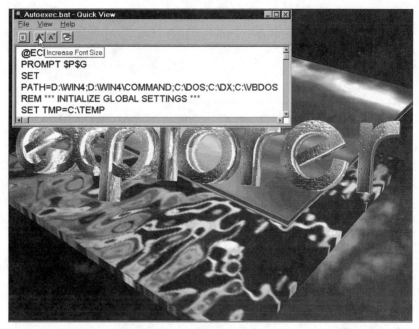

Figure 4-21: *The Quick View can be the fastest way to read a text file. Use the arrow button to change the text size.*

Figure 4-22: *You can swiftly view many kinds of documents using Quick View.*

You can also get version information on a program file by choosing Properties from the File menu, and clicking on the Version tab in Properties View.

Printing a File

It's easy to print a file from a folder. Click on it and choose Print from the File menu, or right-click on it and choose Print from the pop-up menu. The associated application starts up, opens the file, prints it and then closes, all automatically. Some files without associations will print from WordPad. We'll learn more about file associations in Chapter 5.

Another way to print a file is to open the Printers folder first, then drag the file you want to print and drop it on the icon for the printer you want to use. It also invokes the associated application to print the document. If you use this trick a lot, consider placing a shortcut to your printer on the desktop itself.

Deleting a File

To delete a file, simply click on the name of the file you want to delete and press the Del key. A message box pops up to confirm the deletion (Figure 4-23). You can also choose Delete from the File menu, or right-click on a filename and choose Delete from the context menu.

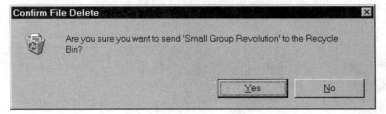

Figure 4-23: *You get a chance to change your mind before deleting a file.*

A deleted file is not gone forever; it's moved to a special folder called the Recycle Bin, which resembles a wastebasket on the desktop. You can easily open the wastebasket icon and retrieve deleted items, even move them back to where they came from.

Deleting files to the Trashcan takes longer than just deleting the file, since the file must be copied to the Recycle Bin. One way to avoid the delay (and immediately free the disk space) is to hold down the Shift key when you select Delete or press the Del key. Shift+Del removes a file permanently, bypassing the Recycle Bin.

If you decide you don't need to be able to restore deleted files, right-click on the Recycle Bin and choose Properties. From the Recycle Bin Properties, turn on the *Do not move files to the recycle bin* check box. If you don't want a confirmation message each time you delete files, you can also take the opportunity to turn off the *Display delete confirmation dialog* check box.

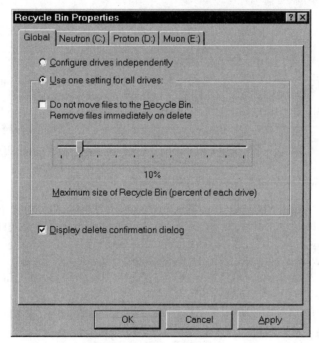

Figure 4-24: *Recycle Bin Properties gives you a choice of how deleted files are handled.*

As shown in Figure 4-24, you can also control how much disk space to allow for deleted files. Each drive contains a special Recycled folder, which holds the files deleted from the rest of the drive. You can set how much disk space, as a percentage of total disk space, to allow for recycled files. You can assign a separate percentage for each drive or use the same percentage for all your hard drives.

If the Recycle Bin grows beyond this limit, the files in it are automatically "emptied"—deleted permanently. For that reason, you may choose not to set a limit, or at least give the Recycle Bin a generous allocation and manually empty the Recycle Bin to free up space when necessary. To empty the Recycle Bin, right-click on it and choose Empty Recycle Bin.

TIP   The Recycle Bin only "catches" files that you delete yourself from a folder or from Explorer. It does not save files that are deleted from DOS or from within an application. However, the enhanced Recycle Bin (SmartCan) provided by Symantec's Norton Utilities for Windows 95 does this and more. See Appendix B for more information on third-party Windows 95 tools.

Even though the Recycle Bin gives you a margin of safety, you still have to be careful with Delete. Never delete application programs unless you intend to uninstall the software. Also, before manually deleting anything, check to see if the software has an Uninstall feature already built in. Keep in mind that only the files you delete manually are moved into the Recycle Bin. Files deleted within an application program or from DOS are not moved to the Recycle Bin. Another limitation of the Recycle Bin is that it does not store files that you delete from a floppy disk or a network drive.

Here are the files that are usually safe to delete:

- Files ending with .BKP or .BAK are backup copies of a document that are created by some applications when you resave a document. The previous version of the document is saved with the .BAK extension and after a while is just wasting disk space.
- Files ending with .TMP, especially if they *start* (not end) with the ~ symbol. These temporary files are used as "scratchpad" space for an application that needs a little disk space to store items that won't fit in memory. Normally, they are deleted automatically when you exit the application.
- Temporary files are usually stored in your TEMP folder, so you can clean out this folder from time to time, but only if you're sure that no applications are running. The TEMP folder is usually defined by the statement SET TEMP=C:\TEMP in your AUTOEXEC.BAT file.

  If you don't have a TEMP folder defined in AUTOEXEC.BAT, then DOS programs will use the DOS directory for temporary files. Windows programs will put their temporary files into \Windows\Temp, unless you have defined a separate TEMP folder using something like SET TEMP=C:\TEMP in your AUTOEXEC.BAT file.
- You can also delete shortcuts for files and applications, since they're easy to re-create anyway! (Each shortcut [.LNK file] uses only a few hundred bytes, but due to the way files are stored, a file has to use at least one cluster. The average cluster size is over 8,000 bytes, so lots of shortcuts can take their toll. Chapter 5 explains more about clusters and the way files can waste disk space.)

▓ It's also safe to delete a file if you have a backup copy of it on a floppy disk or other backup medium, like tape. But remember that even good archival material degrades over time (optical media like recordable CD has the longest life), so don't trust a single backup as your only source for an important file.

▓ You can usually delete .HLP files if you're critically low on disk space and no longer need the Windows Help files for those programs. The applications usually don't need the .HLP files to run, but your brain might miss them.

▓ Information files ending with an extension of .TXT or .DOC can also be safely deleted. You may want to print these files for reference before you delete them.

When you intend to uninstall an application, first check to see if its setup program has an Uninstall option. This feature will more completely and safely uninstall an application than deleting files manually. Another way to uninstall is to use a commercial uninstall program. Shareware uninstaller programs are also available. These utilities can monitor the installation of a program to keep track of which files are added or changed, and intelligently reverse this operation.

New to Windows 95 is a way for applications to add themselves to the Control Panel's Add/Remove Programs applet. Only new Windows 95 software can support this, but when it's commonplace, it will be easy and safe to remove unneeded programs. See Chapter 7 for more about this Control Panel option.

■ ■

Manual Uninstalling

For Experienced Users Only: Uninstalling Windows application files manually is tricky. It's best to back up any files you change or delete in case you change your mind. First delete the folder containing the application. Then look in the Windows folder for any .INI files with similar names to the application files. You'll also look for .DLL, .OCX, .VBX, .386 and .DRV files in the Windows\System folder that have names that appear to be specific to that application. Another way to tell if these files are related is to see if they have the same date and time (use the Details view in Explorer to see the date and time). Some .DLL files are shared by many applications, so don't delete them unless you're sure they are idiosyncratic to the application you're removing. Examples of shared .DLLs include VBRUN300.DLL (for Visual BASIC), COMMDLG.DLL, BWCC.DLL, CTL3D.DLL and the files used for drivers like Video for Windows. Even if you think you know which files to delete, you may still do more harm than good. In Windows 95, applications that use shared DLLs register a usage count in the registry so that the system (and other apps) can determine that when no applications use the .DLL anymore, the .DLL is safe to remove. "Nuking" these shared files without changing the share count in the registry is not a good idea.

You can then edit AUTOEXEC.BAT, CONFIG.SYS, SYSTEM.INI and WIN.INI to remove references to the application. You may also need to run the RegEdit program to remove registration entries for the program. Be sure to make backup copies of any files you change in case you make a mistake. Rather than delete any files, you should move them to a temporary directory. If you removed a necessary file, you can easily restore it.

As you can tell, manually uninstalling software is not for everyone. So vote with your wallet; insist on buying software that has an Uninstall option built in. Fortunately, Microsoft now requires that Windows 95 applications support automatic uninstallation—if they want to earn a Windows logo, that is.

Creating a Shortcut

A *shortcut* is a "dummy" file that can launch the original. The shortcut file itself uses very little disk space, but it pretends to be the actual file it is linked to. (**Note:** This is not actually the same kind of linking that occurs when you use Object Linking and Embedding, or OLE, to embed an object into another document, although from a programmer's perspective, shortcuts are stored using OLE style links.) To open the original file, you can double-click on the shortcut or apply any other file command to it. However, if you copy, move, rename or delete the shortcut, it has no effect on the original file.

A shortcut is provided mainly for convenience. It's used primarily for applications, so you can create folders analogous to Program Manager groups. The Programs folder in the C:\Windows\Start Menu folder holds the programs that appear on the Start menu.

It's usually impossible or impractical to move or copy the actual program file to the Programs folder (or one of its subfolders), since a program file usually expects to find other program resources, such as graphics, configuration files and program libraries in its home folder. A shortcut lets you transcend the disk structure required for applications and create your own organizational structure for programs and documents.

Many programs also store their documents in their own folders, but this structure can seem artificial. When you're working on a sales presentation, why keep all the files for that project in different folders? Instead, create a Sales Presentation folder and copy the files (or create shortcuts for them) you use for your presentation to keep related documents together, even if they are created in different programs. You have your documents, spreadsheets, clip art, slide show, media clips, all in one place. You can even copy shortcuts for the programs you use for your project into the folder for quick launching.

 TIP Microsoft Office for Windows 95 extends this technique even further. You can create an Office Binder to store related files. The Binder is convenient, because it actually stores related files as OLE objects. You can open, save, print, and distribute the Binder as a single file, which contains all the documents, spreadsheets, presentations, and graphics for a project.

Shortcuts can be very powerful. A shortcut copied from a network drive automatically connects to that network resource when you try to open it, even if it requires a telephone call, as in the case of a shortcut copied from The Microsoft Network. You can embed shortcuts in mail messages sent with Microsoft Exchange, so the recipient can run the program just by double-clicking on the embedded Shortcut icon. You can even establish a shortcut to a single paragraph in a word processing document or a range of cells in a spreadsheet (these are also called *scraps*).

 TIP The easiest way to create a *scrap* is to select a range of text, spreadsheet cells, or graphics, then drag the selection out of the application and drop it onto the desktop. It appears on the desktop as an icon. You can then drag this *scrap* icon into any other program that can accept OLE objects, where it's displayed as the original text, graphics, or spreadsheet range. See Chapter 23 for more about OLE Automation.

Figure 4-25: *A Sales Presentation folder made from shortcuts.*

To create a shortcut, click on the original file and choose Create Shortcut from the File menu. Or click the right mouse button on the file and choose Create Shortcut from the pop-up menu. (These pop-up *context* menus are sometimes called shortcut menus, but they don't really have anything to do with shortcut files.)

A new file appears in the file pane, identical except that it starts with "Shortcut for" and includes the shortcut symbol (a little arrow) in the icon. You can now cut and paste this file like any other, or drag and drop it to a new folder. If you drag and drop the shortcut onto the desktop, you've created a convenient desktop icon for the shortcut.

You can also create a shortcut from scratch. Select File | New | Shortcut to start the Create Shortcut Wizard. Now you can fill in the Command line field with the path and filename for the original copy of the file you want to create a shortcut to. You have to know the path, the exact drive and subdirectory, of the original file (see Chapter 5 for more information on paths and filenames). In Figure 4-26, we've created a shortcut to WordPad, which is on drive C: in the Windows folder, hence the link is to C:\WINDOWS\WORDPAD.EXE.

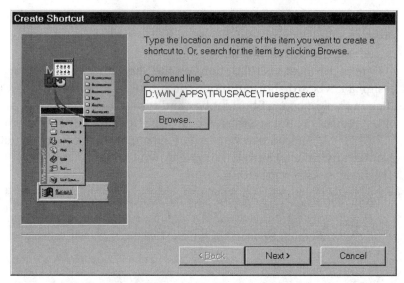

Figure 4-26: *Define the shortcut by filling in the Command line.*

If you don't know the exact location and name of the file you want to create a shortcut to, choose the Browse button to look for it on your hard drive. Navigating with Browse is similar to using Explorer or a folder view. When you find what you're looking for, double-click on it, and you'll see that the location (path) and filename are filled in for you in the Create Shortcut Wizard's Command line.

You may find that it's easier simply to find the original file with Explorer, and use the right mouse button to drag the file to its destination in Explorer, to the desktop or into a folder. When you release the right mouse button, choose Create Shortcut from the context menu.

Shortcut Properties

When you choose Properties for a shortcut, you don't see the actual properties of the original file. All you see is the name of the shortcut file (which has the extension .LNK, a vestige of the term *link* originally proposed but dropped in favor of *shortcut*). If you choose the Shortcut tab heading, you can see where the shortcut is "pointing to." By choosing the Find Original button, you can actually open this folder and reveal the original file. You can also choose the Change Icon button if you want to assign a different file as the source of the icon for the shortcut, but usually you'll accept the icon chosen for you when you create the shortcut. (If you do want to choose from alternate icons, some good files to use for icons are SHELL32.DLL, EXPLORER.EXE, PROGMAN.EXE and MORICONS.DLL.)

Another choice on the Shortcut Properties page (if the shortcut is to a program file) lets you control how the program starts when it opens: minimized, maximized or normal.

One of the most useful options on the Shortcut Properties page lets you assign a keyboard shortcut (not to be confused with the shortcut itself). Just click in the Keyboard Shortcut box and type a letter of the alphabet or any other symbol. You'll see the keyboard shortcut appear as something like "Ctrl+Alt+A" (if you pressed "A"). This means that you can run this program at any time by simply holding down Ctrl and Alt while you press A (then release Ctrl and Alt).

Note: *Although the Keyboard Shortcut box can be edited for any shortcut item, the keyboard shortcut is honored only if the shortcut itself is contained within the Start menu or any subfolder of the Start menu, such as Programs and its subfolders.*

Some shortcuts are special. If you create a shortcut to a floppy drive, for example, the Format option appears when you right-click on the Shortcut icon, just as it does when you choose the context menu for the floppy drive in My Computer. Similarly, a shortcut to a CD-ROM will have Eject as an option when you right-click on it. This lets you use desktop shortcuts to your favorite drives, without giving up handy features like Format or Copy Disk.

Explorer Tricks

Some people believe that Explorer is a limited tool compared to File Manager, and indeed, it's not a high-end power user utility. On the other hand, it does pack a lot of features into a program that's easy to use and understand.

You can select Start | Run and then enter **WINFILE** to run the old File Manager. Because File Manager does not support long filenames, it's better to avoid it, since renaming a short filename can remove the long filename from the file.

For example, some people liked File Manager's capability to select a range of files, such as *.TXT. You can get a similar feature by using Explorer's Find command and searching for *.TXT. This gives you a separate window with just the .TXT files for the current folder. (Use the F3 key to trigger a Find from the current folder.) You can also select files by date/time, size and so on using Find. Perhaps the easiest way to group files by their extension is to select View | Arrange By Type. Now all files with identical extensions are arranged next to each other in the file list.

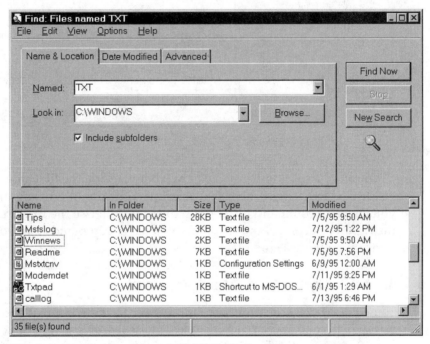

Figure 4-27: *Find has selected all .TXT files in the current folder.*

Another way to select more than one file is to click on the first filename you want to select and then Shift+Click (hold the Shift key on the keyboard while clicking) to choose a range of files. Or you can use Ctrl+Click to select individual files without unselecting anything. (You can also use Ctrl+Shift+Click to define a subrange, even if you already have a range selected.) Perhaps the easiest way to select files is to simply hold down the mouse button over an empty part of the screen and drag the mouse to display a "rubber band" rectangle. Anything you touch with the rectangle becomes selected. (You can even use Ctrl+Drag to define additional ranges without unselecting an existing range.)

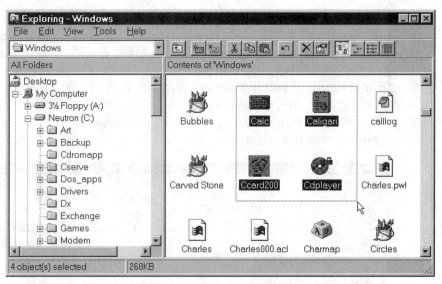

Figure 4-28: *Drag the mouse to "lasso" icons.*

To cancel a selection, just click anywhere outside the filenames you've already selected. Remember that selecting a file doesn't do anything until you choose a command to act upon the selection. Use the Explorer menus or the right-click context menu to pop up a list of commands that you can perform on the selected files.

You Can't Always Get What You Want

Some File Manager features are simply not supported in Explorer, such as using F7 to copy and F8 to move files. These features would be confused with the new method of Edit I Copy and Edit I Paste for copying and pasting files, but it would still be convenient to be able to fill in the destination of a file directly. (But see the Tip following the section "The Most Powerful Windows 95 Secret," later in this chapter.)

But Sometimes You Get What You Need

On the other hand, Explorer lets you expand the folder panes on the left without changing the file pane on the right, so it's easier to copy files now with Drag and Drop than it is with File Manager.

TIP As an alternative to using Edit|Copy and Edit|Paste to copy and paste a file, try just dragging the file to the desktop. Now open the destination folder and drag the file's icon from the desktop to that folder.

Some other File Manager commands are supported, but not via a menu item. The Disk menu in File Manager contains choices for Copy Disk, Label Disk, Format Disk and Make System Disk. Table 4-2 shows how to do the same things with Windows 95.

File Manager's Disk Menu	Explorer Equivalent
Copy Disk	Right-click on a floppy drive and then choose Copy Disk from the pop-up menu.
Label Disk	Click once on a floppy from My Computer and then click again to rename disk label.
Format Disk	Right-click on a floppy drive and then choose Format from the context menu.
Make System Disk	Right-click on floppy drive and then choose Format from the context menu. Choose Copy System Files Only from the Format page. Or use Add/Remove Programs from Control Panel and go to the Startup Disk property sheet.

Table 4-2: File Manager commands and their Explorer equivalents.

Another thing that's missing is a way to open up more than one drive window at the same time. This is actually intentional. Microsoft is moving away from the Multiple Document Interface (MDI) that File Manager and other Windows 3.1 applications use. Instead, just open a separate Explorer for each drive. (Remember that you can hold down Shift while double-clicking a folder to open an additional Explorer view of that folder.) This is especially easy if you've created desktop shortcuts for Explorer and edited them to open up specific drives or locations.

Hands-On: Creating Desktop Drive Shortcuts

Here's how you can create desktop shortcuts to specific drives:

1. Right-click on the desktop and choose New | Shortcut.
2. Type the following line in the Create Shortcut Wizard's Command line box (you may have to adjust the command line if you installed Windows somewhere else than C:\WINDOWS):

   C:\WINDOWS\EXPLORER.EXE /n,/e,C:\

   Then press Enter. If you want the drive Shortcut to show only the contents of that drive, use

   C:\WINDOWS\EXPLORER.EXE /root,/n,/e,C:\

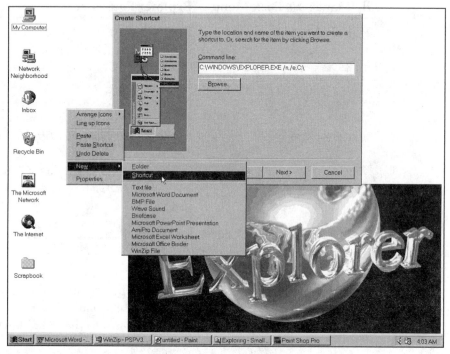

Figure 4-29: *Creating a custom drive shortcut.*

3. When asked to choose a name for the shortcut, type in something like **C** or **Drive C**.
4. You now have an Explorer shortcut. If you want to create one for another drive, change the C:\ in the Command line (Step 2) to the drive letter you want to use and set the shortcut's name accordingly. You can also change the C:\ in the Command line to some-

thing like C:\Projects if you want to have an Explorer shortcut to that folder. Combine it with the /root switch, and the Explorer view will show only that folder.

5. Optionally, right-click on the shortcut and choose Properties. (You'll see the command line there again, in case you want to change it.) Choose the Change Icon button and choose a "drive" icon from SHELL32.DLL. This makes it look just like an on-desktop hard drive.

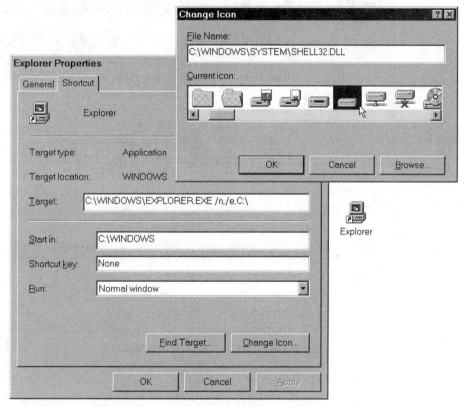

Figure 4-30: *Choose an icon that looks like your hard drive.*

6. Arrange your drive shortcuts horizontally or vertically on your desktop so you can get to them conveniently. (Right-click on the desktop and choose Line Up Icons to help you keep them neat.)

The Most Powerful Explorer Secret

You may have discovered the Send To menu option while clicking the right mouse button on files in Explorer. Using Send To lets you "send" a file to one of your floppy drives, to a Briefcase, or lets you send one as a fax. (The file isn't removed; it is simply passed on—copied—so it's not truly "sent" away. If you want to actually move the file, hold down Shift when you click the Send To "target.")

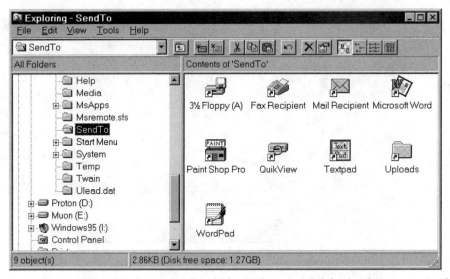

Figure 4-31: *The \Windows\SendTo folder is the source of the Send To menu on the right-click pop-up menu.*

This is handy, but did you know you can create your own custom SendTo items? Just copy a shortcut to the \Windows\SendTo folder, and it will appear on the Send To menu. For example, copy the shortcut for Notepad out of the \Start Menu\Programs\Accessories folder and into the \Windows\SendTo folder. Or just use New Shortcut and the command line NOTEPAD.EXE to create a new Notepad Shortcut in that folder.

If you want to view a text file, just right-click on it and choose Send To | Notepad. This procedure works even if the file is not associated with Notepad. (Normally, files ending with .TXT are associated with Notepad, but the .DOC extension is associated with WordPad or Microsoft Word. Using Send To lets you bypass that default association.)

As this book went to press, Microsoft released a collection of handy tools written by staff programmers, dubbed "Power Toys." These add-ons include a nifty "Send To Any Folder" shell extension. When you install it, you can right-click on a file, choose SendTo|Any Folder, and a box pops up that lets you type in the destination for the file, and whether you'd like to copy or move it. It's slick, and restores the "missing" F7 (copy) and F8 (move) features that you may have relied on with File Manager.

There are other goodies in the Add-On kit, including a convenient viewer for CAB (Microsoft Cabinet) files, a way to view the contents of a folder without opening it, a Quick CD player that lives on the Taskbar notification area, and a special version of the Clock accessory that can be displayed using a unique round window. The programmers are also working on other nifty enhancements for Windows 95.

Microsoft hasn't announced formal plans for how it will distribute the Power Toys. Officially, they don't even support it. But look for a file called ADDON.ZIP from Microsoft's FTP server at ftp.microsoft.com. You can also log into The Microsoft Network and use MSN's Find feature to search for ADDON.ZIP. Happy hunting!

You may also want to put shortcuts to a graphics viewer (like the shareware program Paint Shop Pro), WordPad, and other tools and accessories you use a lot. You can also drag a shortcut to your printer from the Printers folder (available from My Computer or Start | Settings | Printers) to the \Windows\SendTo folder. When you click on a filename and choose Send To and then your printer, the file is automatically opened by the program that created it and is printed. It's also convenient to place shortcuts to folders on the Send To folder, so you can copy or move a file to your favorite folders with just a few clicks.

 For added versatility in viewing files, create a shortcut to \Windows\System\Viewers\quikview.exe in your \Windows\SendTo folder. Now you can use Send To|Quick View to try the Quick Viewer on any file, even one that normally isn't supported by the Quick Viewer.

Note: *You may have problems using Send To if you've selected more than one file. It works with some applications, but usually you're limited to sending just one file at a time.*

Expert Exploration

Let's use the Explorer to examine the Windows folders and get the lay of the land. In this example, Windows is stored in C:\WINDOWS (your drive and directory may be different, such as D:\WIN95 or something).

First, run Explorer from the Start | Programs menu. When you run Explorer this way, the C: drive is automatically displayed. Change drives with the toolbar if necessary so that you can display the Windows folder.

The following sections provide a rundown of some of the special folders Windows uses. (We don't cover *every* folder in the Windows directory, since it will vary depending on which applications you're using with Windows. For example, if you use Microsoft Plus! or Microsoft Office for Windows 95, you'll see a \Windows\Favorite folder that holds your "favorite" files and shortcuts. We also ignore the "propeller-head" folders that are only of interest to programmers.) Note that some of these folders are normally hidden, unless you use View | Options and choose *Show All Files.*

⊞ 📁 Windows

The Windows home directory (C:\WINDOWS in Figure 4-32) holds some of the Windows accessories (applets) and their help files (many other accessories are stored in C:\Program Files), configuration (user settings) files, wallpaper, screen savers and some other odd bits. It's a good idea not to save files or install programs to the Windows folder, since the names may conflict with existing or future Windows files. It's better to install new programs to their own folder, which also makes it easier to delete them if you want to uninstall them later.

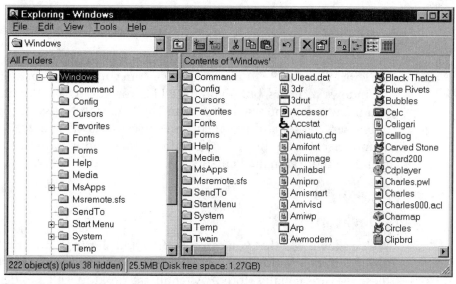

Figure 4-32: *Windows directory in the Explorer.*

⊞▢ Program Files

In addition to \Windows, another folder created on the same drive is called
\Program Files. (It's a folder in the *root* directory, not a subdirectory of
\Windows.) The larger accessories such as WordPad and Backup are stored
there, along with folders for HyperTerminal and The Microsoft Network.
\Program Files is provided so that new applications have a place to store
their folders, rather than cluttering up the \Windows folder, as was all too
common with Windows 3.1.

⊟▢ Windows
▢ Command

The \Windows\Command folder holds the Windows equivalents of the
DOS command-line utilities. (DOS stands for Disk Operating System. An
operating system is the critical software that manages the low-level and
routine operations of your computer. MS-DOS is a primitive precursor to
modern operating systems like Windows 95.) If you want to learn more
about MS-DOS compatibility, see Chapter 22. In practice, you'll never need
to use MS-DOS or DOS commands if you only run Windows software.

Windows
Cursors

In Chapter 9, we'll show you how to use animated and colored mouse pointers with Windows 95. A meager few custom cursors are stored in \Windows\Cursors, but if you install Microsoft Plus! for Windows 95, you'll find many more here. Look on The Microsoft Network and other online services for additional custom cursors—just as with wallpaper and sound effects, we anticipate a booming cottage industry to support the demand for more animated cursors.

Windows
Desktop

We've shown you that you can copy files and shortcuts directly to the background of the Windows screen—the desktop. Have you wondered where these files are actually stored? After all, the desktop isn't a folder in the normal sense—or is it? In fact, any files you store on the desktop are actually kept in the \Windows\Desktop folder. However, certain desktop icons simply exist on the desktop, such as My Computer, and aren't actually stored in \Windows\Desktop. Also, the Recycle bin corresponds to the Recycled folder on your hard drive. It's not a subfolder of \Windows\Desktop as you might have guessed.

Windows does something curious: it pretends that the Desktop folder is at the "root" of the file system. So often when you open a file in an application, the Open dialog box (covered in Chapter 5) starts at the Desktop folder, where you can open My Computer or any other desktop object for browsing. It does this because people frequently store files on the desktop, and treating the desktop as the root of the file system makes it easy to find the files. This is also necessary because the \Windows\Desktop folder is normally hidden—you won't see it if you open the Windows folder unless you have View | Options set to *Show all files*.

Windows
Fonts

The \Windows\Fonts folder contains the Windows system fonts and any TrueType fonts you've installed. This is an improvement over Windows 3.1, which stored all fonts in the Windows system folder, making it large and cluttered. (Since the entire directory must be searched when looking for certain system files, a large System directory can also slow down Windows.)

Windows
Help

The \Windows\Help folder organizes help files and their contents files. Not all help files are stored here, but more and more applications will choose to install their help files in the Windows\Help folder.

Windows
Media

Use the \Windows\Media folder to organize your .WAV (sound), .MID (MIDI music) and .AVI (videos). Windows stores its own sound schemes here, too.

Windows
MsApps

If you have installed any Microsoft software, the \Windows\Msapps folder contains the shared applets, such as Microsoft Word Art, that can be used with Microsoft Office applications. Other applications may also install parts of themselves into folders under Windows, even though this practice is frowned on by Microsoft, since it can conflict with future plans for Windows. (In the future, applications are supposed to use the \Program Files folder, not \Windows, to store these kinds of folders. In fact, Microsoft Office for Windows 95 uses the \Program Files\Common Files folder to store the files that used to be kept in \Windows\Msapps.)

⊟ 🗀 Windows
🗀 Pif

The \Windows\Pif folder holds custom options for DOS programs you run. PIF stands for Program Information File. In Windows 3.1, you used the PIF Editor to tell Windows how to configure custom DOS sessions and stored these files as .PIF files, usually in the Windows directory. Rather than clutter up Windows, they are now kept in their own folder. You don't need a PIF editor in Windows 95; the Properties setting for a DOS program lets you customize these settings directly. And many more DOS programs will run compatibly with Windows 95, without any tinkering required.

⊟ 🗀 Windows
🗀 Recent

Here you'll find shortcuts to all the documents on the Start | Documents menu. Instead of deleting them from this folder, you can use Start | Settings | Taskbar, and click on the Start Menu Programs tab heading. Click the Clear button (under the Documents section) to empty the Recent folder. This of course has no effect on your original files. This folder is normally hidden.

⊟ 🗀 Windows
🗀 SendTo

We covered this folder earlier in this chapter. It holds any shortcuts you'd like to appear when you right-click on a file and choose Send To from the pop-up menu.

⊟ 🗀 Windows
🗀 ShellNew

Windows stores empty document objects here for all the types of documents it can create. You create a blank document by choosing New from the File menu of any folder or from Explorer. You can also right-click on any empty part of a folder and choose New to create a new file (which we discussed earlier in this chapter).

⊟ 🗀 Windows
⊞ 🗀 Start Menu

The \Windows\Start Menu folder holds shortcuts that appear on the Start menu, as well as the Programs folder, which holds shortcuts for programs that appear on the Start | Programs menu.

Your Start Menu folder holds any programs that you may have added to your Start button menu. You can drag and drop shortcuts for programs directly onto the Start menu, and they'll appear at the top of the Start menu when you click on the Start button. You can also drag shortcuts into the Start Menu folder to accomplish the same effect, and it's the easiest way to remove items you've manually added to the Start menu. Just open the Start Menu folder, click on a shortcut, and press the Del key (or select File | Delete) to remove it. (Don't mistake the Start Menu folder for the StartUp folder that's in the Programs folder.)

 TIP The fastest way to open the Start Menu folder is to right-click on the Start button, and choose Open from the pop-up menu.

The \Windows\Start Menu\Programs folder holds all the application icons, usually shortcuts, that you've installed. If you upgraded from Windows 3.1, it contains equivalents to your Program Manager groups. Each former group is now a subfolder under Windows\Start Menu\Programs. Any changes you make to the Programs folder are reflected in the Start button menu, too.

The StartUp subfolder in the Programs folder is special. Anything you put in the StartUp folder will run automatically the next time you start Windows. It's like the "AUTOEXEC.BAT" for Windows 95, and is equivalent to the StartUp group in Program Manager. For example, if you always use the same program, like your word processor, when you turn on your computer, you can create a shortcut for it in the StartUp folder, so your word processor will be fired up and ready to go whenever you turn on your computer.

You can even place shortcuts for folders in StartUp, and those folders will open in the same place every time you start Windows. For example, if you drag a shortcut for the Programs folder into the StartUp folder, then every time Windows starts, it displays the Programs folder, which is great if you miss the convenience of Program Manager's obvious onscreen icons.

> **TIP**   While the Startup folder is convenient, sometimes you'll want to skip it when you start Windows. Just hold down the Shift key while Windows starts to bypass your Startup group.

Windows
Spool

When you print from your applications, the documents are not usually sent directly to the printer. That ties up the computer and slows it down. Your application can create the file it sends to the printer much faster than the printer can accept it, so the spooler lets your application go ahead and create the file it intends to print, storing it as a temporary file in the Windows\Spool folder. When it finishes printing to disk, it's freed up to let you continue typing or whatever. Meanwhile, the Windows printer spooler continues to feed the printer characters from the spool file, invisibly and "in the background," even while you continue to type. When the file has finished *spooling*, it's deleted to free up space.

The Spool folder holds waiting print jobs. A new feature in Windows 95 allows you to "print" even if you don't have a printer. Perhaps you're on the road with your notebook computer. You can print your documents, and they will wait in the Spool folder until you return to the office and dock your notebook (or attach a printer). Windows notices that the printer has become available and will ask you if you want it to start printing the held documents.

If for some reason Windows itself crashes (shuts down due to a fatal error) while printing, you might want to check the Spool folder and delete leftover spool files.

Windows
System

The guts of Windows is stored in the \Windows\System folder. Here you'll find all the inscrutable files such as .DLLs (dynamic link libraries), Virtual Device Drivers (.VXDs and .386 files), font resources (.FOT), device drivers (.DRV), and some control panel applets (.CPL). You will fortunately never need to manipulate any of these files; they're taken care of for you by Windows. These files are critical for the operation of Windows, and if you accidentally move or delete any of them, you may need to reinstall Windows or your applications to restore them.

The System folder contains a few other folders, too. The System\Iosubsys folder contains additional virtual device drivers and other input/output subsystem files. The System\Viewers folder contains the files used for the Quick View feature (see explanation earlier in this chapter). Again, you'll never need to worry about the System folders or subfolders, but now you know what they're for.

🗀 **Windows**
🗀 **Sysbckup**

Finally, there is a Windows\Sysbckup folder. Windows 95 contains special system files that are new and specific to Windows 95. If you install a program that doesn't know about Windows 95 (an older application that was created while "Chicago" was still a twinkle in Bill Gates's eyes), it may assume that you need the latest version of some Windows 3.1 system files and cheerfully replace what you have, sometimes without even checking to see if your current versions of these files are actually more up-to-date. This can be annoying and troublesome in Windows 3.1, but it's disastrous to replace certain Windows 95 system files with their 3.1 equivalents.

Fortunately, when you start Windows (or after running any program named "setup" or "install"), it can detect that these files have been modified, and it can restore the Windows 95 files, which are preserved in the Windows\Sysbckup folder.

Moving On

The Explorer is a powerful tool that gives you full control of your file system. Using the techniques in this chapter, you're well on your way to mastery of your computer's files. In the next chapter, we'll examine the file system in more detail. We'll consider fundamental issues like "what are files?"; how to safeguard your drives; how to optimize disk performance using DriveSpace to double the size of your drive; and we'll show you how to back up your hard drive, for goodness sake.

Chapter 5

Inside the File System

In Chapter 4, you learned how Explorer can be a powerful tool for managing your hard disk. You can move, copy, delete, rename and launch files. Now let's step back a bit and consider what we're dealing with, what files are and how they're handled in Windows 95.

Windows 95, even more so than earlier versions of Windows, is *object oriented*. If there ever was a buzzword to replace *user-friendly* as most-cliched, *object oriented* would win the prize. Yet such a popular phrase must have something going for it.

The word *object* generally means something particular and solid, something with clearly defined boundaries in the material world. In other words, the color red would not be an object, but a particular car would be an object. Things that drift or fade—such as smoke and fog—aren't objects. Things that you can use or move—like a pencil on your desk or your chair—are objects. A rainbow falls between object and non-object; it's something individual, but yet it also has no defined edges or even an independent existence (it is really a quality of mist, something that happens to water suspended in air). You get the idea—objects are *material* and *particular*.

In a graphical user interface (GUI, pronounced *gooey*) like Windows, objects are a natural. Icons are the most obvious candidates to be called objects, and since they can be grabbed, moved and rearranged almost tangibly with your hand (via the mouse), they do behave something like real-world objects.

A Windows 95 object is usually a document, but it can also be a component of a document, like an embedded picture. A program, or application, is also an object (which contains other objects, such as documents, icons, buttons and so on). Objects can contain other objects: a folder object can contain document objects and even other folder objects.

You can apply consistent actions to an object, no matter what it contains. For example, almost all objects in folders can be printed, and all objects can be opened (double-clicked). Opening a folder displays a subfolder. Opening a document launches the associated application. Opening an application icon starts a program.

Most objects are *files*. There are two fundamental classes of things (objects) on your hard drive: programs, like Word for Windows, and documents, like letters and reports that you wrote in Word. The terms we use to describe our document objects hark from 1950s offices with file cabinets, folders, even wastebaskets. Indeed, many computer metaphors are still rooted in old-fashioned office technology, from word processors with typewriter-like controls to telephone switchboard analogies for networks; even electronic mail resembles the conventional letters we send off with a stamp. The only concession to modern office life is that Windows's wastebasket is now labeled with a recycling logo.

The File Cabinet Metaphor

My Computer (the desktop icon and the folder that opens when you double-click on it) is like a master filing cabinet containing folders. Consider a traditional vertical file. You have multiple drawers in a filing cabinet, corresponding to the drives in your computer. Each drawer contains expandable vertical file folders, which are like your primary (root) directories (C:\ , D:\ and so on). Each vertical file folder contains other folders, which in turn contain sheets of papers, or files. The only difference with computers is that it is common to continue to put computer folders within other folders, sometimes down to three or four levels, whereas in an office you usually have only three levels: file cabinet, vertical file, folder and then file.

Figure 5-1: *A computer file system has a lot in common with a traditional filing cabinet.*

Some other objects on your desktop aren't files. They are components of the *user interface*. (User interface is computerese for the various ways that you and the computer communicate with each other.) These objects include the Start button and the clock on the taskbar; OK and Cancel buttons; drop-down list boxes; edit fields (text boxes); scroll bars; thumbs (the slider you can move inside a scroll bar); check boxes; Close, Minimize and Maximize buttons; and so on. Some of these GUI elements are shown in Figure 5-2.

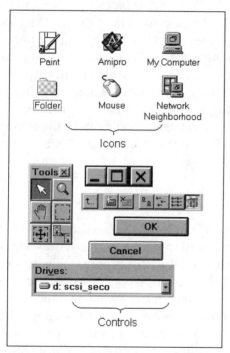

Figure 5-2: *A motley collection of objects.*

You might suppose that an object can be defined as any graphical element that can be manipulated in some way with the mouse, and you would be nearly right. Windows 95 takes the idea of *object orientation* much deeper though, down to the level of the system used by programmers who create applications. Parts of a program, called *subroutines* (or *functions, subprograms, procedures*) can be designed to be modular, even reusable between different projects, and the Windows operating system was built one piece at a time in the same building-block fashion.

The advantage of modularity is that you can build a program from the "top down," implement one feature at a time and test it separately, allowing you to focus on one small part of the complete, complex design. Programmers don't have to "reinvent the wheel" when designing a project. Instead they can take advantage of these shared libraries of program objects in the Windows application programming interface, or API.

Building a program is similar to how you put together a plastic model car. First, you glue the two halves of the engine block together and then glue on the other engine parts such as the radiator. Having completed the engine, you set it aside and craft the other parts, such as gluing the parts of the door together, setting it aside, fusing together the parts of a bucket seat, setting it aside, fitting the chrome hubcap onto the wheel, then inserting it into the rubber tire, until you've built each component separately. Then you can complete the project by gluing each separate part (engine, seat, door, chassis, hood, lamps, wheels) to create a finished model car. In the same way, the operating system (Windows 95 itself) supplies many "parts" that a programmer can use to put together a project.

Anatomy of a File

Returning to the most common Windows object—the file—let's consider for a moment what a file is. A file holds a document (text, drawing, whatever) on your disk, so you can later open it with a program where you can edit it, print it and so on. The file "holds" the document on disk because you can't preserve things inside the computer's memory; the memory goes blank every time you turn off the power. Technically, the contents of a file are made up of a sequence of bytes (characters, dots in a picture, numbers describing a sound) that tell an application (a program, like a word processor) what to put into the computer's memory when the document is "opened" (loaded in from disk). Physically, a file is a series of magnetic impulses, changes in the magnetic orientation of iron oxide atoms, on the surface of one of the platters of your hard disk. This process isn't that different from the way a movie is stored on a videotape. Of course, the technology used has no bearing on the contents of the file. CD-ROMs store data not magnetically, but as pits and shiny surfaces. In the future, a computer file might exist as a waveform diffraction pattern in a holographic memory crystal.

Whatever the medium, a file is a sequence of ones and zeros, which can be used to encode numbers, and numbers can in turn represent characters (using a code like A=65, B=66, C=67, ... , Z=90), and characters are grouped together into character *strings* that spell out words, or contain symbols such as the name of a font or a spreadsheet formula or a .WAV file's sounds.

A file can be a word processing document, a graphic picture, a database, a spreadsheet or a sound effect. These files are used by the application programs to store your typing, drawings, data, figures or recordings. For example, a file containing a graphic image of a circle inside a box might be represented in this kind of format:

```
[circle1]
CenterX=40
CenterY=40
Radius=30
Outline=None
Fill=Yellow

[rectangle1]
From X=10, Y=10 to X=90,Y=90
Outline=Red

[order]
rectangle1,circle1
```

Just Add Water...

In effect, a document on disk is a recipe for reconstructing your document, or it at least lists the ingredients used so that the "recipe" in the application program can reconstitute the original document from the dehydrated essence of the file. Not often is a document stored as actual words you could read in English (even word processor documents are often peppered with binary gibberish). The actual structure of a file is usually complex and indecipherable without the original program that created it or a Quick Viewer designed to read it. (For more information on Quick View, see Chapter 4.)

The applications themselves are also stored on disk as files. When you open an application, the numbers in the files are piped into the central processing unit (the CPU, which is the chip in the computer, a 386, 486 or Pentium). The numbers in a file are mostly *commands* that when strung together form more complex instructions and behaviors. For example, a series of simple MOVE instructions, repeating in a loop, can be used to transfer a word you just copied into the Clipboard. A different sequence of MOVE instructions is used when you later paste the word into another file. Modern programming languages automatically convert (compile) high-level, English-like commands into the pea-brained (but extremely fast) binary number language of your CPU.

What's Inside?

A simple text file is composed of a sequence of numbers. Each number represents one of the letters or symbols. It could use 1 through 26 for the letters of the alphabet, but so many other symbols are used in text, such as punctuation marks, that the alphabet is usually offset to positions 65 through 95 in the ASCII code used for characters. Table 5-1 shows how characters "map" to numbers in the ANSI code, an extension of ASCII that includes definitions for international, mathematical and typesetting symbols using character numbers 128 to 255. The ANSI code is used by Windows.

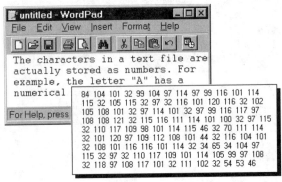

Figure 5-3: *A text file is really stored as a series of numbers.*

You can type any of the ANSI characters from 32 to 127 directly from the keyboard (letters like *a*, *b* and so on), but how do you type *extended* ANSI characters, such as the copyright symbol (©), which aren't available on the keyboard? You can use a special keyboard trick that's universal to all Windows programs. To get the © symbol, hold down the Alt key, and without letting go of Alt, enter **0 1 6 9** on the numeric keypad (not the numbers on the top row of the keyboard). Then release Alt and the character appears. Remember that you must precede the three-digit extended code (see Table 5-1) with the 0 key for this tip to work.

ANSI Character Set

32		64	@	96	'	128	_	160		192	À	224	à
33	!	65	A	97	a	129	_	161	¡	193	Á	225	á
34	"	66	B	98	b	130	_	162	¢	194	Â	226	â
35	#	67	C	99	c	131	_	163	£	195	Ã	227	ã
36	$	68	D	100	d	132	_	164	¤	196	Ä	228	ä
37	%	69	E	101	e	133	_	165	¥	197	Å	229	å
38	&	70	F	102	f	134	_	166	¦	198	Æ	230	æ
39	'	71	G	103	g	135	_	167	§	199	Ç	231	ç
40	(	72	H	104	h	136	_	168	¨	200	È	232	è
41	)	73	I	105	i	137	_	169	©	201	É	233	é
42	*	74	J	106	j	138	_	170	ª	202	Ê	234	ê
43	+	75	K	107	k	139	_	171	«	203	Ë	235	è
44	,	76	L	108	l	140	Î	172	¬	204	Ì	236	ì
45	-	77	M	109	m	141		173	–	205	Í	237	í
46	.	78	N	110	n	142		174	®	206	Î	238	î
47	/	79	O	111	o	143		175	¯	207	Ï	239	ï
48	0	80	P	112	p	144		176	°	208	_	240	_
49	1	81	Q	113	q	145	'	177	±	209	Ñ	241	ñ
50	2	82	R	114	r	146	'	178	2	210	Ò	242	ò
51	3	83	S	115	s	147	"	179	3	211	Ó	243	ó
52	4	84	T	116	t	148	"	180	´	212	Ô	244	ô
53	5	85	U	117	u	149	•	181	µ	213	Õ	245	õ
54	6	86	V	118	v	150	–	182	¶	214	Ö	246	ö
55	7	87	W	119	w	151	-	183	_	215	x	247	÷
56	8	88	X	120	x	152	_	184	_	216	Ø	248	ø
57	9	89	Y	121	y	153	_	185	1	217	_	249	ù
58	:	90	Z	122	z	154	_	186	º	218	Ú	250	ú
59	;	91	[	123	{	155	_	187	»	219	Û	251	û
60	<	92	\	124	|	156	Ï	188	_	220	Ü	252	ü
61	=	93	]	125	}	157	_	189	_	221	Y	253	y
62	>	94	^	126	~	158	_	190	_	222		254	_
63	?	95	_	127	_	159	_	191	¿	223	ß	255	ÿ

Table 5-1: *American National Standards Institute Character Set.*

If you don't have a chart like the above handy, you can use the Windows Character Map accessory, which is described in Chapter 10.

(If you're in DOS rather than Windows, use Alt and the three-digit code without the leading zero to get special characters. Instead of standard international characters, the DOS (IBM) character set includes many graphic line-drawing symbols that are somewhat obsolete in Windows. You can get these symbols in Windows documents, though, by opening the Control Panel, double-clicking on the Fonts icon and installing TERMINAL.FON, VGAOEM.FON, 8514OEM.FON or DOSAPP.FON (usually found in \WINDOWS\SYSTEM) into the Fonts folder. If you prefer TrueType fonts, look for a font named MS Line Draw or Lotus Line Draw (installed by either Word or Ami Pro).

A Sample File

Let's look at another example of how a file stores an object, such as a sound effect. A sound object, or Wave file, is composed of a sequence of numbers too. In its simplest form, each number represents a sample of the volume level of the sound, as measured over brief intervals. When the speaker cone pushes air in or out, reproducing these volume level changes at the same rapid rate, the digitized sound is re-created for your ears. So a sine wave representing a tone (Figure 5-4) would be stored as a "graphic" representation of the wave, using a number for each sample of the wave.

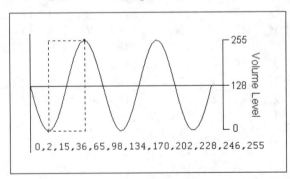

0,2,15,36,65,98,134,170,202,228,246,255

Figure 5-4: *A sine wave tone can be converted into numbers.*

What's In a Name?

DOS and Windows 3.1 were limited to filenames with eight characters plus a three-character *extension* (hence the term "8.3" filename). The basic eight-character filename was followed by a period and then the extension, as shown in Figure 5-5.

Figure 5-5: *The composition of an 8.3 filename.*

By convention, the last three letters (the extension) are used to specify what kind of file is stored by the filename. Ordinary text files usually use the extensions .TXT (text) or .DOC (document). Applications (programs) have the extension .EXE. (Some DOS programs use .COM, for *command.*) Other extensions are defined by the applications, such as .XLS for Excel spreadsheets, .BMP for Windows bitmap files or .SAM for Ami Pro word processing documents. (Microsoft Word co-opted the .DOC format for its word processing documents, so you can't be sure if a .DOC file is a simple text file or a Word document. The .DOC format is intended as a universal word processing file format, however, and will be supported by future versions of Lotus Word Pro, Novell's WordPerfect, and of course Microsoft Word.)

Strictly speaking, the period preceding an extension is not actually part of the filename. It's a punctuation used to separate the first eight characters from the three in the extension, but the period itself is not stored in the filename on disk.

The discussion on Quick Viewers in Chapter 4 includes a table (Table 4-1) that summarizes the most common and useful file types.

Extensions Revealed

Normally, Windows hides the file extensions and represents them visually as icons. (If you're using small icons in Explorer view, they appear to the left of each filename.) These icons are usually the program icons for the application that's associated with the file type. For example, a text file like README.TXT uses the WordPad icon. (If a file extension is not associated with anything, it shows up as part of the filename and uses a generic icon that looks like a little window.)

The first thing many Windows 3.1 or DOS users look for is a way to turn back on the file extensions. You can do this by selecting View | Options from the folder's menu. The Explorer Options dialog box then appears. If it is not already shown, click on the View tab to get Figure 5-6.

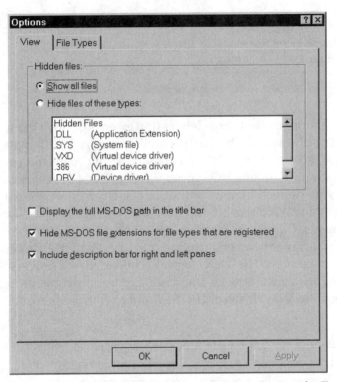

Figure 5-6: *Click the View tab to get the View Options for Explorer.*

The section we're looking for is *Hide MS-DOS file extensions for file types that are registered*. By default (when first installed), Windows leaves this box turned on (checked). That way, your Explorer views won't be cluttered up with the three-character filename extensions. It's thought that the icon symbol (and the File Type column if you're using Detailed view) make the file type obvious enough, so you'll probably leave *Hide MS-DOS file extensions* turned on for the sake of simplicity. Sometimes though, you want to see everything about a file, so you can enable the display of file extensions. If a file extension is not associated with any application, it appears regardless of the setting of this check box.

One disadvantage of viewing file extensions is that it makes some extensions visible in icons on your desktop or in folders, which spoils their elegance.

Let's look at the other options in Figure 5-6. The system files are usually hidden, since they need to be protected from accidental file operations with Explorer, and because there's nothing useful you can do with them in Explorer. (These files are Windows's "under the hood" objects, specialized system files.) So normally you'd keep *Hide files of these types enabled*. Only click on *Show all files* if you want to display these arcana in your Explorer views.

Another power-user option is to turn on the check box for Display the full MS-DOS path in the title bar. Normally, this box would be turned off, so only the folder's name appears in the title bar of the folder window. Turning it on puts the entire pathname for that folder on the title bar, so you'd see "C:\Windows\Programs\Accessories" instead of just "Accessories." It's a matter of personal preference and aesthetics.

In Explorer view, you get both the drives/folders pane on the left and the files/folders view pane on the right. Normally, the left pane includes the title "All folders" at the top, and the right pane lists a description of the name of the folder. If you turn off *Include description bar for right and left panes*, the only thing that happens is that the *All folders* description bar disappears from the left pane, and *Contents of* disappears from the right pane, freeing up an extra line for the display of drives and folders. (But this can make it more difficult to keep track of where you are in the file system.)

There's another reason you may need to display the file extensions. Normally, when extensions are not displayed, you can't change the extension of a file when you rename it. That can be a good thing, because when you're focused on your work, you don't want to forget to add the .DOC when you're renaming "Letter to Sales" to "Letter to Marketing." If you've set Explorer to display extensions, you have to remember to include the .DOC when you rename the file; otherwise, the file will no longer be associated with Microsoft Word or WordPad. (Windows will warn you if you try to rename a file's extension and thereby "break" the association.)

Erroneous Extensions

On the other hand, if you intend to change the file type by changing the extension and rename README to README.TXT, you may actually wind up with README.DOC.TXT. When file types are not shown, you can't change the "real" extension, so you're free to use periods in filenames without changing the file type. If you need to change README.DOC to README.TXT, and thereby change the association from Microsoft Word to WordPad, you need to make extensions visible first by turning off the check box for *Hide MS-DOS file extensions for files that are registered* in Explorer View Options, as we discussed in the preceding section.

 TIP   Use Alt+Enter or Alt+double-click as a shorthand method for viewing an object's Properties.

One trick to view a file's extension, without changing the Explorer View properties, is to right-click on the file to view its own properties. This includes a line for MS-DOS name, and any extension, if used, will appear in the MS-DOS filename. (More about the MS-DOS filename in the following sections.)

Built by Association

As we've mentioned several times, Windows uses the extension to automatically associate a file with its parent application. If you double-click on a .TXT file, Windows knows to start WordPad, since .TXT files are associated with WordPad. The list of associations is stored in the system registry, and the best way you can change the associations is by using Explorer's Tools menu.

 TIP   You may have used WIN.INI with Windows 3.1 to customize your extensions. While an [Extensions] section may still exist in your Windows 95 version of WIN.INI, it's there only because some programs still try to put entries there.

For compatibility reasons, Windows reads the [Extensions] section each time the system boots and adds those entries to the registry. However, the only component under Windows 3.1 that even used the [Extensions] section was the File Manager.

To access your registry, click Start | Run and then enter REGEDIT. When REGEDIT starts, click on the ⊞ symbol next to HKEY_CLASSES_ROOT. You'll see a list of all your extensions appear. Click on an extension, and you'll usually see that it's assigned a more meaningful name. Then, lower down in the list, you'll see these names. Click again on the ⊞ symbol to expand these names, and you'll see entries for variations methods (such as OPEN) supported by that "object."

Sometimes you can modify these settings, such as changing the Shell\Open\Command entry to use a different program to open the object, but this kind of direct tinkering with the registry can be risky and confusingly complicated. Instead, see below for an easier-to-use graphical method of changing your file types.

Windows creates default associations for many files. For example, .TXT files are associated with WordPad, so you can simply double-click on a text file and open it into WordPad. You may wish to create new associations for

WordPad, so you can double-click on other file types, too. For example, many disks come with a file called READ.ME or README.1ST that contains important notes about the application. You want to associate .ME and .1ST files with WordPad (or your favorite word processor).

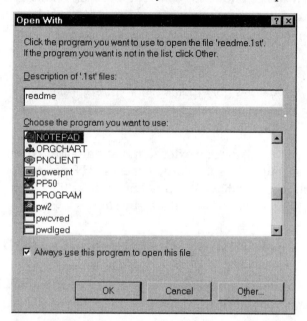

Figure 5-7: *Double-click on a file without an assigned extension, and Windows doesn't know what to do with it, unless you tell it which program to use.*

If no association exists for a file type, just double-click the file in an attempt to open it. Since Windows doesn't know how to open the file, it pops up a dialog box, as shown in Figure 5-7, asking you which program you want to use to open the file. The list of programs includes only those programs that Windows already "knows" about (*registered* applications). If the program you want to use isn't on the list, click on Other to locate the folder the program is in. If you want to always use the same program to open the file, leave on the check box for *Always use this program to open this file*. You can also fill in the Description box with a plain-English (or plain-Swahili, if that's your native tongue) explanation of this file type. (If you don't do this, then the file extension will be used as the file type.)

The Description is used in Explorer when you are viewing files in the Details mode, to show the file type. This description doesn't actually match the file extension, which explains why .INI files are shown in Detail view as Configuration Settings.

> **TIP** After you've assigned an extension (and turned on the check box for *Always use this program to open this file*), you can't get back to the Open With choice again. Or can you? The trick is to hold down the Shift key while you right-click on the file. This trick adds the choice Open With to the pop-up menu, which lets you choose which program to use to open the file, instead of the default choice, Open, which uses the program associated with the type of file. You always get Open With if you right-click on a file that lacks an association.

What if you want to change an extension that's already assigned? For example, if you install Microsoft Word, it causes .RTF files to open with Word. You might prefer to have WordPad open these files. This procedure is a little bit tricky, so let's go through it step by step.

Hands-On: Changing a File Association

1. Open any folder or run Explorer (select Start | Programs | Explorer).
2. Select View | Options.

Figure 5-8: *From the View menu, choose Options.*

3. If the View Options dialog box doesn't already show the File Types page, click the File Types tab heading.

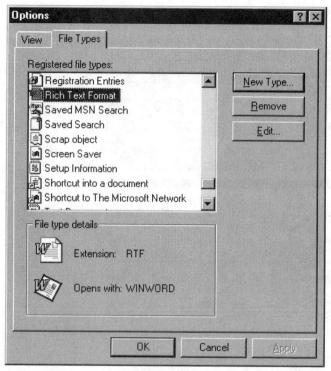

Figure 5-9: *Click the File Types tab heading so you can view the extensions.*

4. You'll see a list of all file types, sorted alphabetically by their description. If a file type has no description, its naked extension is used as the file type. In Figure 5-9, we're going to edit the .RTF file type. When we click on it, the dialog box shows us the extension of the file and which program is currently associated with it.

5. Scroll through the list to find the file type you want to change and click the Edit button.

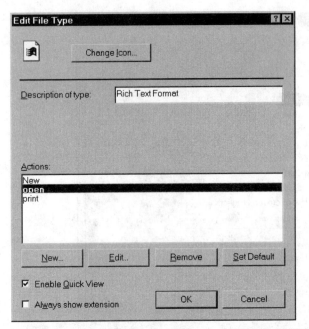

Figure 5-10: *A plethora of options are available from Edit File Type, but you'll want to focus on the Open action.*

6. The box in the center of the Edit File Type dialog box shows all the actions that can be performed on a file. Most files support at least the Open action, and Open is usually the default action (you can use the Set Default button if you know you want to use a different action, like Print, as the default when you double-click a file of this type). Double-click on the Open entry to edit it.

7. You can now edit the command line (the Open action) that points to the location of the program you want to use to open .RTF files. We changed the command line from C:\WINWORD\WINWORD.EXE to C:\Program Files\Accessories\WordPad.exe (the name and location of the WordPad applet).

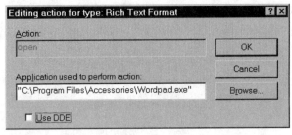

Figure 5-11: *Edit the command line to change which program is used to open this file type.*

8. That's it! You may also want to use the Change Icon button to assign an icon to the file type. This icon is displayed with the file
when you view it in a folder or in Explorer.

If you're curious, you might want to explore some of the other options in
the Edit File Type dialog box, such as turning on the check box for *Always
show extension*, if you want a particular file type to reveal its filename extension, even if you have Explorer set to hide extensions, as it does normally.
For example, if you assign a program to open READ.ME files, you may want
to keep the .ME part visible. You can also turn on the option for Enable
Quick View if you know that this file type is one that Quick View can display (for example, Quick View can display all plain text files, not just those
ending in .TXT).

In addition to the Open action, some file types have a Print action, which
is used when you click on the file and choose File | Print (or right-click and
choose Print from the pop-up context menu). For text files, the Print action
uses NOTEPAD.EXE /P. The /P *switch* tells Notepad to open the file, print it
and then close. You may need to research what command-line options are
supported by your favorite programs if you want to create custom actions of
your own.

 TIP It's easy to add your own custom actions. For example, you
know that a file ending with the extension .DOC is not always a
Microsoft Word document. Frequently, plain text (Notepad) files
are also saved with .DOC extensions. Yet when you double-click
a .DOC file, Word starts up, which takes a lot longer than opening the file in Notepad. One solution is to add a Shortcut to
Notepad to your \Windows\Send To folder. You can then right-
click on a file, then the Send To menu choice and then Notepad.
We explain more about this Send To trick below.

Or you can edit the Microsoft Word Document file type, and
add a custom action named "Notepad." From Explorer's
View | Properties | File Types dialog, scroll down to Microsoft
Word Document and double-click on it. Then click the New
button to add a new action. Name the action Notepad, and
assign the filename C:\Program Files\Accessories\Notepad.exe
(assuming you installed Windows to drive C:).

Now when you right-click on a .DOC file, a new Notepad menu choice appears on the pop-up context menu. Click on it to open the file in Notepad instead of Word. (If you don't have Word installed, .DOC files will be linked to WordPad, so you may have to follow different steps than the above. But you get the idea.)

When you close the Edit File Type dialog box, you're returned to the previous View Options dialog box. Here, you can also eliminate a file type association by using the Remove button. When you eliminate an association, double-clicking on that file type no longer launches a program automatically. But perhaps this method is an even easier way to reassign an association. First, use Remove to get rid of the old association, and then when you double-click on the file, the Open With box pops up, letting you easily assign a program to that file (and all other files with the same extension).

In some ways, using Open With is the easiest way to add a new extension, but you can also use the New Type button on the File Types panel of the View Options property sheets. Clicking on this button pops up the same dialog box we already examined for Edit Type, but of course, it's now empty. You'll want to fill it in with a description, an extension and at least an Open action.

 TIP   You aren't limited to three-character extensions anymore. You can create new associations for any named extension.

Even if you customize a file association, the change won't always stick. Some programs automatically "take over" the extensions that they work with, merely by running that program. One of these culprits is Corel PhotoPaint. Merely running PhotoPaint causes it to assign common bitmap extensions like .BMP, .GIF, .PCX and so on to always use PhotoPaint to open them. You can reassign these extensions using the File Types page of View Options, but the next time you open PhotoPaint, they're reassigned to Corel again. We can only hope that future versions of software allow you to disable this kind of "feature."

Long Filenames Set You Free

Windows 95 breaks free of the 8.3 filename limitation that forced a generation of computer users to stretch their ingenuity. It's no longer necessary to pretend that you're composing a message to squeeze onto a license plate. Instead of 1STQTRFC, or LTR2VNDR, we're free to name our files "First Quarter Forecast" or "Letter to Vendors." Any name is allowed, up to 255 characters long, including both upper and lowercase letters, and most symbols and punctuation. You are also allowed to use spaces in a filename. All of this was impossible with Windows 3.1 and MS-DOS.

 You are typically limited to filenames with about 245 characters or fewer. The extra ten characters or so are reserved for the drive letter and path, since the total length of a pathname also can't exceed 255 characters. For this reason, you may want to avoid getting carried away with long folder names, especially if you like to nest one folder inside another.

Although you can revel in long filenames like "Call of the Wild; An Examination of Primeval Yearnings," most of us will use far shorter names, just to save all that typing.

 Select Start | Find to help you track down a file that you've misplaced, since long filenames can actually be harder to remember accurately. First, check the Start | Documents list if you edited the file recently. (For the Microsoft Natural Keyboard or other 104-key compatible, use ⊞+F.)

The Mechanics of Long Filenames

Windows 95 implements long filenames in a way that preserves compatibility with existing Windows 3.x programs and doesn't require changing the way files are stored on the hard drive. Windows NT, which also uses long filenames, includes an entirely new file system called NTFS (New Technology File System) to support long filenames, but until the Windows NT 3.5 upgrade, it couldn't support long filenames on a standard FAT hard drive. (FAT is the type of file system used for MS-DOS files.) Now Windows NT version 3.5 (and higher) and Windows 95 both know how to support long filenames while preserving compatibility.

The secret is that Windows 95 always creates a standard "8.3" MS-DOS filename and uses that short filename to actually store the file. Essentially, the short MS-DOS filename is the "real" filename. The long filename, although fully supported by Windows 95, is a kind of cosmetic tag, although it's treated as a legitimate filename by all 32-bit software.

DOS and Windows 3.1 programs don't know about the long filename, but they can open the file using the short version.

Windows ensures that each short filename is unique, even if the original long filenames are similar. For example, documents titled "September Sales Figures" and "September Sales Forecast" would have the same first eight characters. Windows 95 solves this problem by naming the first one something like "SEPTEM~1.DOC" and uses "SEPTEM~2.DOC" for the second one. If you have many similar files, Windows may resort to increasingly meaningless variations, so some MS-DOS filenames may become nearly incomprehensible.

You can access a "friendly" variation of short filename composition that simply truncates (shortens) a long filename to the first eight characters, without the squiggly (tilde) character. You'll have to "hack the registry." Select Start | Run and then enter **REGEDIT**.

Now use the ⊞ symbols to "drill down" to the following registry location

HKEY_LOCAL_MACHINE\System\CurrentControlSet\Control\FileSystem

Use the New | Binary Value menu option and add NameNumericalTail to the FileSystem. Now you can double-click on NameNumericalTail and enter a value of **00**. (Enter **01** to go back to the old, "unfriendly" method.)

Now restart your computer, and from that point on, short filenames will be formed the friendly way. **Note:** Windows NT does not use the friendly method, so if you use both Windows NT and Windows 95 on the same computer, you may run into incompatibilities. We've also seen Windows setup get confused when you use friendly filenames, so reset NameNumericalTail to 01 before you reinstall Windows.

Seeing Both Sides

To view the MS-DOS filename for a Windows 95 document, just right-click on the filename and choose Properties from the pop-up menu. You'll get a properties sheet similar to the one shown in Figure 5-12. Here you can find out what filename to use to open it in an earlier Windows 3 application.

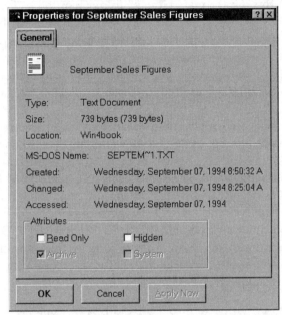

Figure 5-12: *Use File | Properties to view the MS-DOS filename.*

You'll have to buy new Windows 95 versions of all your favorite applications to take full advantage of long filenames. In the meantime, as long as the filename is kept to eight characters or fewer, the Windows 95 filename will be the same as the MS-DOS filename.

While viewing a file's properties (click on the file with the right mouse and choose Properties), you can move the mouse to the Location entry to pop up a tooltip that shows the full pathname to that file.

File Geography

A filename by itself, even a long one, is rather naked. The complete specification for a file must include the name of the hard drive where it's stored and any folders and subfolders that have to be navigated to reach the file. A file on your C: hard drive called "Red Riding Hood" stored in the "Wolf's Belly" subfolder of the "Grandma's House" folder would be "C:\Grandma's House\Wolf's Belly\Red Riding Hood" as a complete file specification.

A complete file specification, then, includes two parts: the pathname and the filename. In the preceding example, the pathname is "C:\Grandma's House\Wolf's Belly\" and the filename is just "Red Riding Hood." (The term *file specification* is often shortened to *filespec*, and *pathname* is sometimes just called *path*.)

The quotation marks are for clarity in this discussion; they are not part of the filename or the path name. In fact, you are not allowed to use quotation marks in filenames. (In MS-DOS, spaces are used to separate commands, such as DIR from filenames and command options. So DIR RED RIDING HOOD would request the RED directory using unrecognized, illegal command-line options RIDING and HOOD. The workaround is to enclose the entire name in quotation marks, as in DIR "RED RIDING HOOD". Windows 95, although it does not rely on DOS, inherits some of the same characteristics, so it needs to use quotation marks internally when defining a filename.

A command-line option, supported from a DOS box or from the Start I Run menu option, can also be used in Windows 95, for example, to open your word processor and immediately run a macro. If you specify WINWORD /MBIG, then Word for Windows will trigger a macro called BIG if you have defined such a macro. The /M command-line option tells Word to run a macro when Word first starts running. A command line like NOTEPAD C:\AUTOEXEC.BAT /P would open the AUTOEXEC.BAT file, print it and then close Notepad.

That's why you can't use quotation marks inside the filename itself; otherwise, the file system could get confused. Other illegal characters are *, ? and the backslash itself, since they are used as *wildcard* characters that allow you to partially specify a filename. We'll see an example of this later in this chapter.

Another meaning of the term *path* refers to the order in which directories are searched when you enter the name of a program at the MS-DOS prompt. A typical MS-DOS PATH (usually one of the first few lines in your AUTOEXEC.BAT startup file) might read as follows:

PATH=C:\WINDOWS;C:\DOS;C:\BATCH;C:\UTILS

So no matter which directory is current, you can run a program found in any of the directories in the path without having to precede the program with its full pathname specification. You probably have an AUTOEXEC.BAT file if you upgraded from a previous version of Windows, but Windows 95 does not require it. Instead, the path can be defined in the system registry. In fact, each Windows 95 application can define its own custom path.

The backslash (\ ) is not interchangeable with the forward slash (/) on the ? key. The backslash is usually located above the Enter key on most keyboards. In a filespec, each backslash specifies the next, deeper level of nested folder. It also separates the drive letter from the first folder. If a file is stored in the root directory, such as AUTOEXEC.BAT, there is no folder name, just the backslash, as in C:\AUTOEXEC.BAT. So the path to AUTOEXEC.BAT is C:\.

(You'll notice that we sometimes use the term *directory* instead of *folder*; these terms are interchangeable, and many of us still use the term *directory* for a folder name.)

If you have only one hard drive, you can usually leave off the drive designation and use pathnames by themselves. So you can just use \LETTERS\MORTAGE\Final Notice unless you need to save the file to a different drive, such as A:\.

The first backslash in a pathname is important. It makes sure that any folder names are referenced relative to the root (top) of the directory structure. If you saved the same file to MORTAGE\Final Notice, it would work only if the current directory was C:\LETTERS. The use of *current directory* can be a little hazy in Windows, since you can be running many programs at the same time, and each one of them may be using a different current directory. It's best to use the full specification when you specify a path.

With networks, you can use a *mapped* network drive. A mapped drive seems to be a new drive letter, such as F:, on your computer, when in fact it is actually stored on another computer, such as a networked file server. Windows allows the use of named resources, though, so if the file server is named MASTER, you could reference a file using the Universal Naming Convention (UNC) in the form: \\MASTER\DOCUMENTS\MYDOC.DOC. The use of twin backslashes is special: it tells Windows that what follows is the name of a resource, usually a network drive. When you share your hard drive with others, you give it a name that can be used by others in their UNC filenames. That way, the drive doesn't even have to be mapped to a drive letter. Chapter 19, "Wired: Getting Started With Networking," includes more information on UNC naming.

 TIP   Some older Windows programs and most DOS programs can't cope with UNC filenames. So you'll need to use drive mapping sometimes, so these fragile old programs can still find the file.

Common Commands

A complete pathname can get long and complicated. Fortunately, Windows rarely requires you to specify a full pathname in your file specifications. Instead, the Open and Save common dialog boxes let you navigate to the desired subfolders and either choose an existing file or type a new filename. You probably already know how to use the Windows 3.1 common dialog box, but the following sections contain some guidelines.

Windows 16-bit Open dialog box

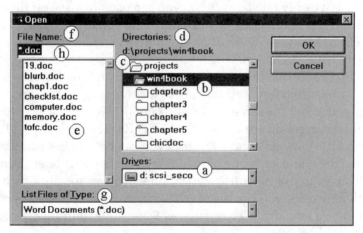

Figure 5-13: *The Open dialog box offers a consistent way to specify filenames.*

a. First, choose the drive name, if necessary, by clicking on the Drive drop-down list box and clicking on the drive letter. If you have only one hard drive, you won't need to change this setting unless you need to use a floppy drive.

b. The current directory is graphically represented using folders. The open folder at the bottom of the list is the current directory. To move up a level, just double-click any folder above the open folder.

c. To choose a new folder altogether, first move to the root by double-clicking the topmost folder marked with the drive letter (C:\). Then scroll through the list to find the folder you're looking for, and double-click on it to make it current.

d. As you change folders, the full path specification is shown above the list of directories (on the right).

e. The list of files is shown in the list box on the left side of the dialog box.

f. When opening a file or replacing an existing file, you can simply click on one of the files shown in the list. That name is automatically copied to the File Name edit field (text box). You can use the cursor keys to edit the filename in the edit field, or you can just type a new name.

g. Often only certain files are shown in the filename list box. You can change the files shown by choosing another drop-down list box and choosing another file type.

h. Another way to choose which files are displayed is to enter a wildcard specification in the File Name box. For example, *.TXT makes it show only files with the .TXT extension. Or use A*.* to show all files beginning with A. Use *.* to show all files of all types. The ? can be used to match one character at a time: ?O?E.TXT would match SOME.TXT, NONE.TXT, BONE.TXT and so on.

You can often leave off the extension when saving files. Some applications won't add the extension for you when you save a file, so you may need to add it to the filename yourself. To find out, save a sample file without the extension, then open Explorer and choose Properties for a file, so you can see if the filename includes the extension.

Windows 32-bit Open dialog box

The new Open/Save dialog box looks a lot like an open folder or an Explorer view. In fact, it's almost identical. Everything you can do with Explorer, including renaming, moving, dragging and dropping, even launching programs, can be performed from the new Open dialog box. This feature adds full file-management capabilities to any program that uses this standard dialog box. If, while opening a document, you run across a file you'd like to delete or rename, go ahead and do it from the Open dialog box rather than opening up Explorer and finding the file. (Some programs, like Microsoft Word 7.0, use a custom version of this box that is less flexible but specialized to support additional word processing features.)

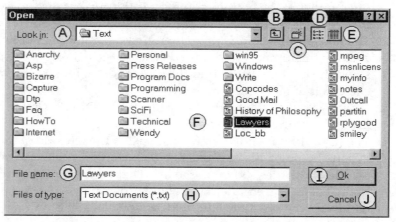

Figure 5-14: *The new Open dialog box looks very different but accomplishes the same goal, with new features.*

a. Click here to choose which drive to use to look for folders. Or choose My Computer to see icons for all your drives.

b. Use this toolbar button to back up to the previous folder.

c. Use this button to create a new folder. You can also create a new folder or other object by right-clicking within the folder view (F). You'll probably do this when using the Save version of this dialog box rather than when opening a file.

d. Use this button to view just the names and icons in the folder view.

e. Use this button to see details, such as date/time and size of each item in the folder view.

f. The folder view shows you all the files in the current folder and all the subfolders in that folder. You can double-click on any subfolder to replace the folder view with a view of that folder's contents. Try right-clicking on a file here to see even more powerful options.

g. When you find the file you want to open, just click on it to transfer its name to the File name text box. Or you can type the filename yourself. (You can even type a folder name to jump directly to that folder. Typing **Projects** by itself won't open a file but will switch to a view of the \\Projects folder. Typing has the same effect as clicking the Up One Level button.

h. Click here if you want to limit the files shown in the folder view to just certain types of files. Each application normally shows only the type of file it uses, but you can click here to choose All Files. Or you can type a wildcard specification, such as *.TXT, into the File name box, just as we discussed earlier with the 16-bit Open dialog box in step h.

i. Click OK when you've chosen the file you want to open. Or just double-click on the file you want to open.

j. Click Cancel if you change your mind and don't want to open a file after all.

When you're creating long file and folder names, keep in mind that the total length of a path, such as C:\Windows\Documents\Personal Letters\Letter To Mom, is also limited to 255 characters (or fewer), so you'll have to use shorter folder and filenames, in practice.

Inside the Drive

When you're learning about the file system, it's worthwhile to consider how the technology works. Of course, one of the great things about Windows is that you don't have to understand what goes on under the hood. You can just drive. A simplified diagram of a hard drive is shown in Figure 5-15. (Most hard drives actually employ multiple platters in a stack, with a read-write head for each platter.)

Figure 5-15: *A simplified diagram of a hard drive.*

The *platter*, a rigid metal (or sometimes glass) disc, spins at incredibly high speed (3,000 RPM or more). In fact, it spins so fast that it creates its own microweather. The read-write head (kind of like the tone arm on a record player) floats on the air stream above the spinning disc. The head can't actually touch the disc, or it would gouge the rigid platter, plowing up thousands of bits of data. This is the dreaded *head crash*.

Consider the scale: The gap between the head and the disk surface is so small, a human hair is like a log; a dust speck, a boulder. That's why hard drives are hermetically sealed to keep out all outside air and are manufactured in clean rooms where the air is highly filtered and workers wear space-suit smocks.

To keep the read-write head from crashing, a drive is buffered with its own shock absorbers. It's a testament to modern storage technology that hard drives can now be found in even notebook or laptop computers. Another safety measure is the *landing zone*: an unused part of the platter that the head can touch down upon and rest when the power is shut off. Many drives also auto-park the head to this landing zone when the drive is left idle for a period of time. (You may wonder how a drive can move the head to the landing zone once it's already lost power. Ingeniously, as the spin of the powerless drive coasts and slows, the leftover energy in the spinning platter is converted into the power needed to park the head in the landing zone.)

The surface of the platter is divided up into hundreds of concentric rings, called *tracks*. (A phonograph record uses spiraling tracks, as do compact discs.) A stepper motor moves the read-write heads from track to track, and always moves in a straight line from the center of the disc out to the edge. This works kind of like the arm on a record player (the record player metaphor, though apt, is fast becoming obsolete due to the ascendance of the CD).

TIP Is *disk* or *disc* the correct term? Although disc comes to us from geometry, somewhere along the way it was Americanized as disk, and is considered the correct term for describing hard drives and floppies. The newer Compact Disc technology restores the classic spelling.

When writing (storing something on the disk), the stepper motor first moves the head to the correct track, and then the drive waits until the sector in question rotates to the position of the head. At that instant, the drive head energizes to magnetize or demagnetize spots along the track, for the length of the sector. Each spot stores a binary one or zero, which is how information is stored digitally. When you open a file, the reading part of the head senses the magnetic patterns and converts the pulses back into ones and zeros.

A floppy disk works in a similar way, but the head touches the media, so it must be flexible, hence *floppy*. A CD-ROM drive uses a laser to detect pits burned into the incredibly fine tracks, as narrow as a bacterium. Magneto-optical drives use a laser to confine the otherwise broadly indiscriminate magnetic field of the write head to just the hot spot illuminated by the beam, packing much more data than magnetic techniques alone.

How do removable drives work? Some drives, such as Bernoulli hard drives, reverse the technology. The spinning platter hovers like a helicopter blade, floating up toward the head using the same Bernoulli principle that makes possible heavier-than-air flight using wings. The advantage: If power is lost, the platter simply falls back from the head so a head crash is nearly impossible, making them ideal for transportable drives. Some other removable drives simply encase the entire drive, heads and all, in an airtight package. When you switch cartridges, you are literally replacing the entire hard drive (except for the power supply and input/output interface).

How Are Files Written to Disk?

Just as the platter is divided into concentric tracks, each track on the platter is divided into segments in the shape of arcs. Each segment holds one *sector* of data. A typical sector holds 512 bytes of data, and a typical track holds 17 sectors. (A *sector* is also frequently called a *block*, but we prefer the more technically accurate term *sector*.)

When writing a file, the File Allocation Table, or FAT, tells the file system where free (unused or reusable) sectors are located. The FAT is a map to all the tracks and sectors of the disk, and is stored on the directory track. The directory track is usually in the middle, to minimize excess head movement.

The FAT actually keeps track of *clusters* of sectors. (Tech trivia: A cluster is also called an *allocation unit*.) The FAT has only enough room for up to 65,535 entries, which would limit a hard drive to 32 megabytes if each cluster was a single 512-byte sector. Instead, sectors are grouped together into logical clusters. Since the number of entries in the FAT can't grow, the size of the cluster has to change to allow the FAT to keep track of a large hard drive. Table 5-2 shows how the size of the hard drive determines how big a cluster can be.

Hard Drive (Volume) Size	Cluster Size
16 megabytes to 127 megabytes	2,048
128 megabytes to 255 megabytes	4,096
256 megabytes to 511 megabytes	8,192
512 megabytes to 1,023 megabytes	16,384
1,024 megabytes (1gigabyte) to 2 gigabytes	32,768

Table 5-2: *Cluster Sizes for Various Hard Drive Sizes.*

Even if a file contains only a single character (byte), it would still have to use an entire cluster. If the cluster size is 8,192 bytes, and you store a file with 8,193 bytes, it has to use two full clusters. The 8,193 byte file is actually taking up 16,384 bytes of disk space. This *slack space* can really add up, wasting hundreds of megabytes on large gigabyte drives.

One solution is to use DriveSpace, which still uses clusters but packs them completely. (In other words, the beginning of file #2 would be stuffed into the leftover space at the end of file #1's final cluster.) We'll discuss DriveSpace later in this chapter.

The best way to prevent slack space is to partition (divide) your physical hard drive into several logical drives, or volumes. Each volume will have a separate drive letter. For example, a 1.2 gigabyte drive uses wasteful 32k clusters. By partitioning the drive into two 511 megabyte drives and putting the leftover amount into a 128k partition, then all volumes will use the more efficient 8,192 byte cluster size. Of course, this process creates additional drive letters, which some people find distracting. See the FDISK command in Chapter 22, "The Other Face: DOS 7," for more information on partitioning your hard drive.

Note that the FAT system also limits the total size of a single drive to just under 2,048 megabytes (two gigabytes). While this amount once seemed plenty, you can now buy a four-gigabyte drive for under $1,500. Clearly, FAT has seen the end of its days, but it's retained for compatibility.

Future versions of Windows NT will feature the Object File System, a major upgrade to Object Linking and Embedding. OFS replaces the FAT file system with a database-like disk operating system that is much more efficient. Eventually, OFS will migrate its way to a future version of Windows 95.

Fear of Fragmentation

Creating a file involves writing new clusters, using FAT to find an empty space. Ideally, the drive can simply continue to write subsequent clusters of sectors to the same track in a continuous stream, so all the sectors in the file are *contiguous* (physically next to each other). Writing contiguous files is not always possible. When you delete a file, the clusters formerly allocated for the dead file are freed up and added to the list of available clusters in the FAT. That way, they can be reused.

But let's say you've written three files in a row, and each one uses 10 clusters. When you add new information (5 more clusters, say) to file #2, it can't fit all 15 clusters into the 10-cluster "hole" between file #1 and file #3. It has to skip over the 10 clusters in file #3 to finish the 5 remaining clusters. Such a file is said to be *fragmented*. Worse, even if you delete file #3, freeing up 10 clusters and then add a new file #4, file #4 doesn't try to reuse the open space, even if it would fit. Instead, it just moves to the end of the list to add its file. Only when the drive starts to get full does it then go back and try to fill in the holes, piecemeal.

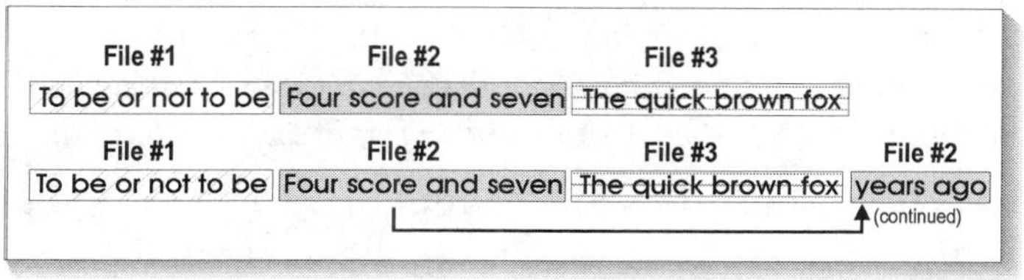

File #1	File #2	File #3	
To be or not to be	Four score and seven	The quick brown fox	

File #1	File #2	File #3	File #2
To be or not to be	Four score and seven	The quick brown fox	years ago

(continued)

Figure 5-16: *Fragmentation occurs when a file can't find enough contiguous space to store the entire file.*

A heavily used disk will get quite fragmented over time, since the file system puts new files in every little hole it can find, even if these free spots are scattered all over the disk. It begins to look like a crazy quilt.

In the best case scenario, when reading a contiguous file, the hard drive can simply find the starting cluster and read the track continuously. If the file is larger than one track, it can then smoothly switch to the adjacent track and continue feeding clusters. But with a fragmented file, the head must read a few clusters, skip to a different track, read a few more clusters, move again to another track, read more clusters, finally getting tired from running all around the disk. Each time the head changes tracks, it has to wait for the next cluster to rotate into view. All this waiting and reading takes time. Fragmentation can seriously slow down the speed of your hard drive.

Fragmentation Fix-It-Upper

Fortunately, Windows provides a means to *defragment* your hard drive, optimizing the layout of the files so that whenever possible, files are made contiguous and can be read and rewritten with a minimum of track switching. A freshly sorted and optimized disk can be significantly faster than a heavily fragmented one. However, defragmenting a disk can sometimes take a long time, especially on compressed drives, so you'll probably want to defragment your drive every few weeks or months (depending on how large the drive is) instead of every day.

WARNING! Only use Windows 95's own Disk Defragmenter or one written specifically for Windows 95 (such as the Speed Disk, which is part of Norton Utilities for Windows 95). Using older DOS-based defragmenters or optimizers will destroy the long filenames on your hard drive. While the files themselves will be okay, the long filenames will be converted into the cryptic short versions, replete with squigglies. Don't even run these defragmenters from MS-DOS mode, since they just aren't aware of the new rules of the game. This warning also applies to many other older DOS utilities that manipulate the hard drive directly. Fortunately, Windows 95 blocks any attempt by an older utility to directly access the hard drive. Also, during Setup, Windows 95 looks for and deletes any such old utilities from your hard drive (or disables them). It's still possible to run such a tool from disk, especially if you have a boot disk for DOS 6.22 or earlier, but you must avoid running these utilities if you want to retain all your long filenames.

It couldn't be easier to defragment your drive. Just run Disk Defragmenter from the System Tools folder, usually found in the Accessories folder. Or right-click on a drive shown in My Computer, choose Properties, and click on the Tools tab. (The advantage of doing it this way is that you can see how long it's been since you last optimized your drives.) From Tools, click Defragment Now.

Figure 5-17: *Choose Properties for a drive in My Computer and click on the Tools tab heading to view this page.*

When running Defragmenter from the System Tools folder, the only choice you need to make is which drive you want it to repair (or you can choose All Hard Drives). If you run it from the Tools page of the drive's Properties sheet, you don't need to even make this choice.

Of course, if your files aren't very fragmented in the first place, you won't get much benefit from defragmentation. That's why Windows asks you to make sure you really want to proceed if your drive doesn't really need it (Figure 5-18). Or you can choose the Advanced button to customize how the Defragmenter works (Figure 5-19).

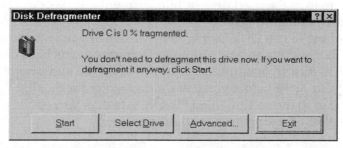

Figure 5-18: *You don't have to defragment your drive unless it really needs it.*

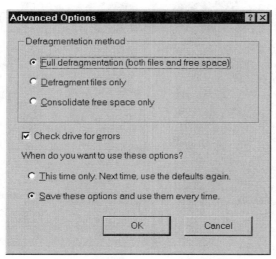

Figure 5-19: *Advanced Options let you choose how to apply defragmentation.*

In Figure 5-19, you can choose Full Defragmentation, which completely rewrites all the files so that they're not only defragmented, but also packed together to move all the free disk space to one area of the disk. For fastest operation, choose *Defragment files only*. Or if you want to get a large block of free space to store new files, affecting existing files the least, choose *Consolidate free space only*.

To let Disk Defragmenter remember these settings and use them in the future, choose *Save these options and use them every time*. Or choose *This time only* to keep the default Windows 95 settings (full defragmentation, no defragmentation of hidden or compressed volume files).

It can sometimes take a long time to defragment your drive, and it can really slow things down if you continue to use your computer while it works. If you want some entertainment, click the Show Details button to see a graphical map of the hard drive while Defragmenter works. (The detailed view is shown in Figure 5-20.)

The best time to run Disk Defragmenter is when you're away from your computer, like overnight. And although Defragment has been exhaustively tested, it does directly manipulate your drive, so you may want to have a backup of your drive before you use Defragmenter for the first time. You can skip ahead to the section titled "Better Safe than Sorry..." if you want to learn more about backing up your hard drive now.

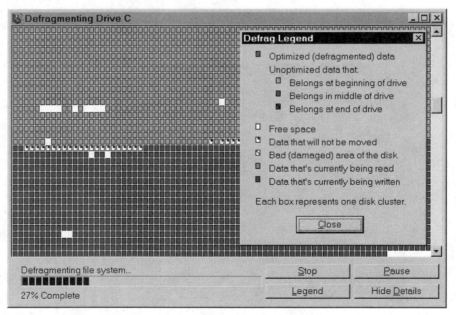

Figure 5-20: *Defragmentation is underway...*

With Microsoft Plus! for Windows 95 (an add-on utility kit from Microsoft), you can use the System Agent to automatically schedule disk maintenance (such as defragmentation, virus checking, ScanDisk, backup, and so on) overnight or when the system is idle.

Optimizing Disk Access

Hard drives have gotten pretty fast over the last few years, but you can speed them up further. Although your hard drive may be 170, 250 even 540 megabytes, it spends a lot of time rereading just a few files. If you used a font in one document, you've likely used it again in a different document. Why reread the hard drive a second time to load the font into memory?

Windows keeps a copy of the most frequently accessed data inside the computer, in ultra-fast Random-Access Memory, or RAM. RAM is solid-state and extremely efficient memory. Your hard drive also serves as mass memory but is hundreds of thousands of times slower than RAM, since the hard drive relies upon moving parts rather than moving electrons. Although your hard drive holds more information than RAM, keeping even a small amount of the most frequently accessed data in RAM prevents rereading the same information from the hard drive.

The area of RAM used to hold the frequently accessed data is called a *cache*. (A pool of memory is often called a *buffer*, so the part of memory holding the disk cache is often called the *cache buffer*.) The term *cache* comes from warfare, where armies would strategically place stores of arms and supplies across the countryside so that these goods would be at hand immediately in case of mobilization for war. Similar, a hard disk cache keeps the goodies (frequently accessed files) conveniently at hand.

Another example of a cache would be your refrigerator. You could go to the market every time you want a soda or a slice of cheese, but how much more convenient to keep your refrigerator stocked with your favorite foods, and it saves you the travel time of getting in your car whenever you want to get a drink of milk.

How Caching Speeds Disk Access

As you read files from the hard drive, your file access patterns are being statistically profiled by Windows. The more often a file is read, the more likely it is to remain in the cache. As you perform different tasks, lesser used files are discarded from RAM to make room for new cache data.

A cache can also speed up writing to a drive. When you save a file, instead of replacing the file on the hard drive, it can simply *write-back* to the same file in the cache memory, and that file in the cache is marked as "dirty." At regular intervals, whenever Windows has a moment to catch its breath, dirty files in the cache are streamed out to the hard drive. That way, you don't have to wait so long to start typing again when you save a file, and multiple writes can be coordinated smoothly.

Caching caveats

The only danger of write-back caching is that a power failure or system crash could occur in the brief interval between the time the file is written to the cache and the moment that the file is actually updated on the disk. If you experience such a failure, your most recent changes may be lost, since they never got a chance to make it to the disk.

This type of failure is actually quite rare, so Windows takes advantage of write-back caching to boost your hard drive's performance as much as possible. Write caching is also known as lazy writing, since Windows doesn't immediately write changes but waits for an idle moment. With Windows 95's improved multitasking capabilities, it is much easier to integrate file operations with other tasks, so lazy writing is actually much safer than in earlier versions of Windows or MS-DOS.

If you have a flaky computer or an unstable power source, you may decide it's important to disable write caching. To do so, right-click on My Computer on your desktop and choose Properties, or open the System icon from the Control Panel. Click on the Performance tab and then click the File System button. From the File System dialog box, click on the Troubleshooting tab.

Now you're deep into one of the most sensitive areas of Windows 95, where you can choose to disable some of the advanced file system features. One of them is *Disable write-behind caching for all drives*. Turn on the check box to turn off write-back caching. The penalty will be a noticeable drop in overall file system performance. There's little reason to change any of the other settings, unless you have a very unusual situation. We recommend leaving all these options alone.

Caching is especially important in a multitasking system such as Windows 95. If you are running multiple programs at the same time, and they are each reading and writing data, the hard drive can no longer read any one file continuously. It has to skip around getting a block of data for Program #1, then switch to a different sector to get the next block of data for Program #2, go back and read the next block for Program #1, then go back to Program #2, only to discover that now Program #3 needs to write to the hard drive. The file system attempts to interleave all these program requests so that they can all appear to be happening simultaneously, but it's inefficient and slow.

Fortunately, the cache can be used to sort these read/write requests into a coordinated sequence of track changes and keep frequently used data in memory instead of having to search the disk for them every time.

Another benefit of caching is that it saves wear and tear on your hard drive, since the head performs fewer and more coordinated track changes. (Of course, the platter spins continuously as long as your computer is turned on, but fewer track changes mean less wear on the stepper motor.)

Windows 95 performs its caching miracles automatically. Unlike the earlier MS-DOS SmartDrive cache, Windows 95 does not use a fixed buffer in memory for the cache. Instead, the entire amount of free memory is available for caching. As your memory fills up (when working on huge graphics files, running many programs simultaneously and so on), hard drive access slows down somewhat, since less free memory is available for the cache.

Note that the separate CD-ROM cache is *pageable*; that is, it can be stored temporarily on the hard drive when memory needs to be freed up. It's actually faster to page out portions of the CD-ROM cache and reread them from the disk than to reread them from the much slower CD-ROM drive. This capability gives Windows 95 unprecedented fast CD-ROM access. The CD File System also can read ahead of the location currently being accessed, to have data ready, allowing the computer to process the CD data at top speed.

Windows 95 now caches data from all sources, including hard drives, floppy drives, CD-ROMs, even network files. Lazy writing is not used with CD-ROMs, of course, because they cannot be written to, just read from. But lazy writing also can't be used with networks, since Windows doesn't directly control the hard drive on the network file server. If there was any delay between changes made to a networked file in a multiuser system, another user might end up reading a less recent version of that file, since his or her cache won't contain the updated version of the file that's still in your cache. Nevertheless, even read-only caching can really speed up networks and cut down on constant retransmission of data over the network cabling. Reducing network traffic speeds up network access for everybody and reduces wear and tear on the file server or shared hard drive.

TIP Windows 95 normally removes any DOS-based disk caching commands, including SMARTDRV, from your C:\AUTOEXEC.BAT file, since they only waste memory and actually interfere with Windows 95 automatic disk caching. Some Windows 3.1 programs may claim to improve your hard drive or CD-ROM speed, but avoid them—they're not useful or even desirable with Windows 95.

Swap Files as Virtual Memory

Ironically and paradoxically, just as memory is used to buffer the hard drive, Windows uses the hard drive to *buffer memory*. When memory starts to fill up, Windows swaps programs from memory onto a special *swap file* on the hard drive. When memory is later freed up, Windows can reread the swap file and quickly restore those programs to memory.

Consider this illustration (the specifics are actually more complicated): If you start the Excel spreadsheet program from within Microsoft Word, Windows temporarily "throws away" idle parts of the word processor, like the spelling checker, to make room for Excel. The discarded data is saved on the hard drive swap file. But when you later need to check the spelling, Windows discards parts of Excel, like its graphics package, so it can reload the spelling checker from the swap file. If you later need to graph a chart in Excel, the swaperoo continues. There is no really better compromise: when you don't have much RAM, something needs to go. Generally, the only programs that need to be kept in memory are those that are actively running. The rest can be swapped to disk until they're needed later.

But if memory starts to get really tight, this constant disk access, known as *paging*, can really slow down your computer. Although Windows 95 will run with only 4mb of RAM, you will avoid much of this paging by upgrading to at least 8mb. A faster hard drive also makes a big difference.

Since Windows needs all the memory it can get, there is no justification for using a RAM Disk, as you may have used in MS-DOS. A RAM Disk is a "virtual" hard drive created out of spare RAM and is lightning fast, although the data in it is wiped out if you don't transfer it to a real hard drive before you power off. The RAMDRIVE.SYS program still exists for compatibility with some MS-DOS applications that depend on a RAM drive, but you'll find that Windows new caching system gives you nearly all the benefits of a RAM drive, since most files can fit in the cache, which acts like a recycling RAM drive.

Paging is a way to make the most out of the memory you have. Since a swap file has no fixed size, your hard drive becomes an extension of your system memory. The extra "memory" on the hard drive is known as *virtual memory*. Unfortunately, it's so slow that it's a substitute of last resort. Still, it's better to have a slow computer than one that won't run large programs at all. Fortunately, you can avoid a lot of paging and run Windows 95 much faster if you have at least 8 megabytes of RAM. Less than that and you can still run many programs, but much more slowly due to the more frequent access to the swap file on the hard drive.

The universal swap file

In earlier versions of Windows, you had to choose between a temporary versus a permanent swap file. In Windows 3.1, Windows would build a large temporary swap file when you started it, so it had room to store the paged information. For faster paging, you had the option of creating a *permanent swap file* that was stored contiguously on the drive, with no fragmentation. Windows 95 now always uses the equivalent of a temporary swap file, but instead of a fixed size, it starts out small and only grows larger when necessary.

If you upgraded from a previous version of Windows, Windows 95 will reuse your existing permanent swap file, so you don't have to worry about reclaiming that disk space. However, once Windows 95 takes over the permanent swap file, your old version of Windows 3.1 (if it's still on your hard drive) may become confused, and if you try to run it, it may fail. We offer a solution in Chapter 21, "Optimization: Expert Memory Management."

You'll rarely need to alter the configuration of your swap file, but if you want to review the settings, run Control Panel and select the System icon (or choose Properties for My Computer). Click on the Performance tab and then click the Virtual Memory button to open the dialog box shown in Figure 5-21.

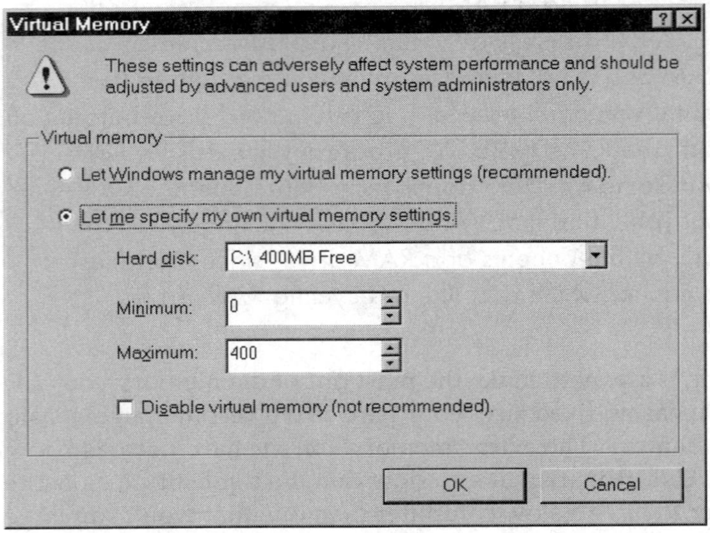

Figure 5-21: *Virtual memory settings from System Properties.*

Normally, the *Let Windows manage my virtual memory settings* box is checked (turned on). This option allows Windows to use its best judgment when creating virtual memory on the hard disk. Windows 95 uses a sophisticated technique for dynamically growing and shrinking the swap file, so you'll often get best results by leaving this option turned on. However, if you have special requirements, such as limited disk space, you may want to restrain the swap file. In this case, click on the *Let me specify my own virtual memory settings* option button. When you choose this option, Windows warns you that changes to virtual memory may degrade your computer's performance, and this is especially true when you have less than 8mb of RAM.

If you decide to customize your virtual memory, make sure that the *Disable virtual memory box* is not checked. If you have tons of memory (over 16mb), you might think you would actually get better performance by checking this box and turning off virtual memory, since it prevents slow hard disk paging; but since it effectively disables advanced memory management, overall performance will actually suffer. But if you have large amounts of memory, it's probably because you frequently work with large files, such as huge photographs, so you too will probably need extra virtual memory.

Other reasons you might want to disable paging are if you're low on hard disk space or if you are using a *diskless workstation*, a networked computer without a built-in hard drive. Even on a diskless workstation, you can store the swap file on a network drive, but doing so can be slow and create too much network traffic.

Nevertheless, you may want to choose where the swap file is kept. You can choose the drive by clicking on a drive in the Hard disk drop-down list in the Virtual Memory dialog box. Ideally, you should use the fastest hard disk on your system for the swap file, yet Windows always chooses its own directory to store the swap file. If you use DoubleSpace or DriveSpace, note that you don't have to put the swap file on the uncompressed host volume. Windows 95 can still put the swap file on the compressed drive. It simply marks the file as incompressible.

Another option if you're low on disk space is to limit the size of the swap file. By entering a value for Maximum, you can prevent the swap file from growing larger than a set size. You'll often want the swap file to be at least as large as the amount of physical memory you have, so you can specify this in the Minimum box.

If you have two SCSI hard drives, locate the swap file on the drive that does not hold Windows or the most common applications you run. That way, with SCSI disconnection enabled (see your host adapter manual), swap file access can occur simultaneously with access to the other drive. The advantage is not as clear with IDE or EIDE drives, although it can help minimize track switching and speed things up slightly.

Protecting Your Drive's Data

You might think that your computer never makes mistakes, but alas, nothing's perfect, even silicon. Sometimes the FAT is damaged, due to a disk error, a power surge, a buggy program, even a cosmic ray from outer space (really!). The FAT is the master list of all clusters used or free. It's a map to the layout of all files on the disk. If the FAT is damaged, then it's telling lies. The next time a file is written, the computer may be led to believe that clusters are free when they aren't, and intermingle its data with existing files. When that happens, the two files are said to be *crosslinked*. Only one file, the recent interloper, contains all its data. The second file is now partially corrupt, having been trampled on by the new file. What's worse, if you delete the damaged file, the FAT reports that all the clusters in that file are now freed up, including the clusters previously overwritten by the other file. Now when you write a third file to the disk, it's free to overwrite the part of the second file that originally overlapped the first file, since when you deleted the original file, it innocently released all its clusters, including the ones corrupted by the second file. So the crosslinking spreads, like an infection. (No computer virus is involved here, just a cascading series of errors.)

Another disk error can happen when you delete a file; for some reason, not all the clusters might be marked as free. Or a corrupted FAT can simulate this condition, since bad bits in the FAT can make it seem that clusters are in use when they really aren't. Sometimes a file's size is misreported in the FAT, again generally due to corruption of the FAT. These errors are more benign, but it still wastes disk space.

Since early versions of MS-DOS, the CHKDSK command has been available to help solve some of these problems. It traces each file on the disk to see which clusters are actually in use. Each sector contains a pointer to the next sector in the chain, so it's possible to reconstruct the FAT by analyzing each file. This command won't correct for crosslinked files, but CHKDSK reports the crosslinks, so you can manually check each one, delete the ones that are scrambled and rerun CHKDSK.

CHKDSK can therefore verify the validity of the FAT. After tracing each file, it may notice some clusters marked as in use that were not part of any of the files. It offers to free up this disk space and can reconstruct this orphaned data as a series of temporary files that it writes into the root directory.

ScanDisk to the Rescue

We mention CHKDSK because of its historical value and because it is still part of some old MS-DOS applications. CHKDSK has been supplanted by the ScanDisk utility since version 6.2 of MS-DOS, and ScanDisk has now been redesigned for Windows 95 (for example, it now can detect and correct errors in Windows 95's long filenames).

ScanDisk is smarter than CHKDSK was. ScanDisk tries to automatically repair crosslinked files by separating them into separate files, copying the overlapped data to a separate part of the disk. One or both of the files may still be corrupted, but you have a chance of preserving the most recent one, and by correcting the crosslink, ScanDisk also prevents further damage.

ScanDisk can automatically repair other problems too, such as misreported file sizes, bad dates and times, even orphaned data that was never marked as reusable in the FAT. If necessary, ScanDisk allows you to undo its fixes, because in some rare cases, the cure is worse than the disease.

ScanDisk can also perform a deeper diagnosis of your hard drive, by testing the integrity of each sector (block) of your hard drive. It does this by saving the sector to memory, writing a series of test patterns to the sector and then rereading them to verify the data. Then it restores the original data. If ScanDisk has trouble reading a sector, it will repeatedly reread the sector in hopes of recovering the data. If successful, it marks the sector as permanently bad, which prevents the FAT from reusing it, and relocates the data from that sector to a fresh, clean one. If you are getting frequent bad clusters, it's a sign your hard disk is on the verge of complete failure. Time to back up that hard drive and buy a new one. (Most hard drives are designed to last only about five years on average.)

It's especially important to use ScanDisk before you compress a drive, since errors buried within the host drive can make correcting a problem in the compressed drive notoriously difficult. That's why ScanDisk was included with MS-DOS 6.2 to help solve the problems some users were having with DoubleSpace. We'll discuss compression issues and the compression schemes DoubleSpace, DriveSpace and Stacker toward the end of this chapter.

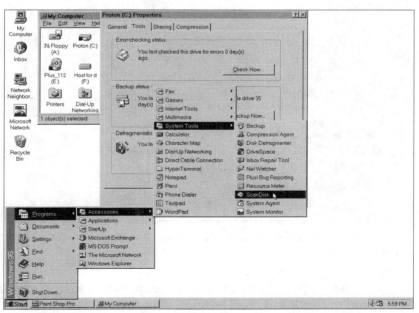

Figure 5-22: *You can open ScanDisk in two different ways.*

Windows Disk Fix-It-Upper

The Windows 95 ScanDisk tool is a graphical version of the DOS ScanDisk that was introduced with DOS 6.2. You can use it to simply check for errors, or you can let it automatically make the repairs. The easiest way to check a drive is to open My Computer, click on a drive, and choose File | Properties (or right-click on the drive and choose Properties). From the drive's Properties sheet, click on the Tools tab, and in the Error checking status section, click on Check Now.

Another way to check your drive is to run ScanDisk from the System Tools folder (a subfolder of the Accessories folder) by selecting Start | Programs | Accessories | System Tools | ScanDisk.

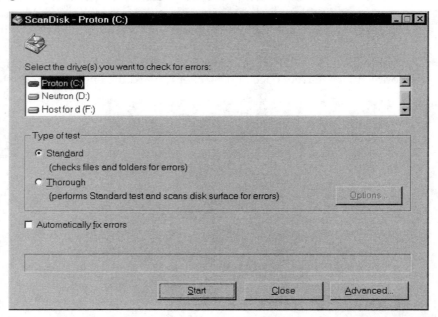

Figure 5-23: *Here's the ScanDisk main dialog box, useful for changing the behavior of ScanDisk.*

For most purposes, ScanDisk is very easy to use. Just select the drive(s) you want to check and click on Start. (Not the Start menu button, but the Start button on the ScanDisk dialog box. Confusing? Yes.)

When ScanDisk finds errors, it asks your permission before making a correction and gives you the option to create an Undo disk that you can use to reverse the correction if it caused more problems than it solved. ScanDisk rarely creates more problems, though, and reversing corrections can be tedious if there are many errors, so you may want to enable the check box (as shown in Figure 5-23).

Tradeoffs

In the main ScanDisk dialog box, you can also choose between speed (Standard testing) and completeness (Thorough). The Standard test is ideal for routine testing. Every once in a while, especially if you have known problems with your hard drive (maybe it's getting old), you should use the Thorough test. With Thorough testing, each sector of your hard drive is individually tested to see that it can reliably hold data. If it has any trouble reading or writing to a sector, ScanDisk attempts to relocate the data in this sector to a known good sector, which can help you recover from minor hard drive crashes.

Ideally, you'll have the System Agent installed from the Microsoft Plus! package. It regularly runs ScanDisk to keep hard disk problems from ever getting out of hand.

You can copy a shortcut to ScanDisk and place it in your \Windows\Start Menu\Programs\Startup folder to have ScanDisk check your drive automatically every time you start your computer. Or you could add a line like this one to your C:\AUTOEXEC.BAT file to run the DOS version of ScanDisk (which is somewhat faster).

SCANDISK /ALL /AUTOFIX /NOSAVE /NOSUMMARY

Surface testing can be invaluable, but it can take a long time, depending on how big your hard drive is and how fast your computer is. One way to speed up this testing is to customize how the test is performed by clicking on the Options button to view the Surface Scan Options.

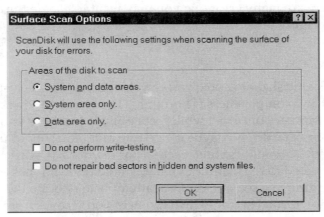

Figure 5-24: *The Surface Scan Options can speed up routine surface testing.*

For fastest use, you may want to choose *System area only* under the *Areas of the disk to scan* heading to have it check the FAT and directory tracks. Or you can have it check only the part of the drive that actually contains data. Still, for thorough checking, you want it to examine the entire drive (System and data areas), so you'll know ahead of time if there are problems when you create future files.

You can turn on the option for *Do not perform write testing* to speed up the scan. The surface scan still checks to see if the disk surface is readable, but the more exhaustive read/write/compare test is skipped.

Finally, you can turn on the option for *Do not repair bad sectors in hidden or system files* in case you have files with sectors that should not be relocated, such as a Windows 3.1 permanent swap file or the master DoubleSpace compressed volume file. Some older methods of copy protection, used to limit software piracy, also rely on intentionally created bad sectors in hidden files. This type of draconian enforcement is fortunately a thing of the past, but if you still have one of these dinosaurs on your drive, you may need this option to preserve the copy protection.

Advanced ScanDisk

By clicking the Advanced button in the main ScanDisk dialog box, you can customize the behavior of ScanDisk.

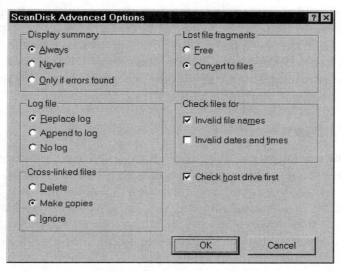

Figure 5-25: *You can leave alone most advanced ScanDisk options, but you might want to change some of them after you understand the implications.*

Under the *Display summary* heading of the ScanDisk Advanced Options dialog box, you can decide if you want a report when ScanDisk finishes its checkup. Use the log options to control how this report gets saved to disk, if at all.

When ScanDisk encounters crosslinked files, it can either delete the files (since one or both of them are probably corrupt), or it can unentangle them by creating new copies of the two files. Nevertheless, it can't recover the parts of a file that have been snarled up with another. By default, under the *Crosslinked files* heading, ScanDisk will make copies of the bad files.

You will usually want ScanDisk to free up lost clusters (file fragments), which are clusters that are marked as "in use," even though no file appears to use them. On the other hand, sometimes missing data can be found in the lost clusters, so you can choose to convert them to files (stored in the root directory as .CHK files) that you can examine later. You'll discover that these lost clusters almost never have any useful data, so you may want to choose the *Free* option to spare you the trouble.

ScanDisk also checks to see that the link between long filenames and short filenames is valid. There's no good reason to disable the option for *Invalid file names* (under the heading for *Check files*). You can also search for invalid dates and times in files, which isn't very important, and can slow down the check but may be useful for the sake of completeness.

If you use disk compression such as DoubleSpace, DriveSpace or Stacker, ScanDisk should check the host drive before checking the compressed drive, since any errors on the host drive must be corrected before any problems on the compressed drive can be resolved. That's why *Check host drive first* is normally enabled. If, for some reason, you're positive that the host drive is fine (perhaps you never store any other files there), you can turn off this option to speed up ScanDisk slightly.

What About Viruses?

The current version of Windows 95 doesn't have virus protection built in, and that has some people worried. Over the years, a number of malicious computer viruses have appeared, including the self-mutating *polymorphic* virus. Hackers create these parasitic programs, which are designed to glom onto existing files or weasel their way into your boot sector. When you save your files to another drive or format a floppy disk, the virus gets a free ride to a new destination. In this way, a computer virus simulates life by its most fundamental aspect of reproduction. A virus can also reproduce within your computer, adding itself to more and more files, eating up disk space (at its most benign) or waiting for some cue (like a date) to emerge from its nest and destroy data or cause random errors. Indeed, many a confusing bug in a program has been misidentified by novices as a virus infection.

Computer viruses are actually still rare, nonetheless, and you can take steps to protect your computer. First of all, it's wise to avoid participation in computer piracy, the unauthorized copying of computer software, also known affectionately as "sharing" software. Some bulletin board systems even specialize in publishing pirated software. These can be a great way to "catch" a virus. Indeed, some of these BBSs (or Internet FTP sites) actually make viruses available for your own nefarious purposes, in case you want to infect an enemy.

Even legitimate network sites can have viruses, although all the major online services and most local BBSs run virus scans on all software they make available for downloading. Some Internet sites are still unsafe, though, so the only way to be truly safe is not to participate in online file exchange.

Short of that, you can purchase a virus scanner. At the time of this writing, few Windows 95-specific virus scanners are available. Look for new versions of established scanning software, such as the McAffee anti-virus suite, and Norton Anti-Virus. Also look for ThunderByte Anti-Virus, the first virus scanner that uses heuristic techniques to catch even unknown viruses that aren't in its database.

Ironically, even shrink-wrapped computer software can sometimes contain a virus, one that wasn't caught at the duplicator. Some retailers accept returns of software and re-shrink-wrap the package and put it back on the shelf, even though the installation disks could have been infected by someone's virus-laden computer. It's difficult to tell for sure if you're the victim of this practice (some boxes sport a "tamper evident" sticker), so a virus scanner is still very useful.

But Windows 95 users actually have less to fear from most garden-variety DOS viruses because Windows 95 doesn't allow direct disk access to your hard drive by DOS programs. If a DOS program installs itself to intercept hard disk commands (prior to the startup of Windows 95, while Windows is allowing DOS drivers to load), Windows 95 warns you if it detects this type of tomfoolery (unless it recognizes the program as a legitimate device driver) and keeps the virus disabled.

True Windows-specific viruses are still extremely rare (in fact, we have never even heard of one), and Windows can use certain methods to protect itself more completely than DOS. One day, however, when the hackers set their sights on the conquest of Windows 95, we'll have more thorny virus problems to deal with, and a virus scanner will continue to be good insurance, along with frequent backups. Always keep more than one backup set, in case you discover you've backed up the viruses along with your other files. That way, you can often recover files from an earlier (pre-virus) backup set. Some anti-virus software can also "clean" viruses from your computer.

Better Safe than Sorry...

Even ScanDisk can't save you from every problem. There's no substitute for having a recent, complete backup of your entire hard disk. You'll hear this advice a lot from other computer users who have learned the hard way, and although there's no substitute for experience, we hope you never have to find out for yourself how horrible it can be to lose everything you've ever created or installed on your computer, and have to start over again at ground zero.

Forewarned is forearmed, so let's discuss some backup strategies. One technique is to *back up* (copy and save) all your data to floppy disks, which can be stored in a safe location, perhaps even in another building to protect against loss by fire. But with the size of today's hard disks, it would take a mountain of floppies to back up a large hard drive. Although a floppy disk can hold up to two megabytes using data compression, you'd still need over 85 disks to back up a 170mb hard drive. And it's not uncommon these days to own a computer with a 540mb or even a 1gb hard drive.

If you must use floppies, you could choose to back up only the actual documents, graphics or spreadsheets you create. After all, you can always reinstall your software applications from the original installation disks or CD-ROMs you got when you bought the applications. (However, some computers come with preinstalled software and don't include separate installation software. Look for a folder or utility that can create these disks for you, which can actually be a better choice than just backing up the original applications to floppy disk.)

Lazy Backups

An easy backup strategy is to leave a floppy disk in your drive at all times. Whenever you save a file to the hard disk, also save it to the floppy. When the floppy fills up, throw it in a box and put in a new one. When you run out of floppies, buy some more, or reuse the oldest ones in the box. Hopefully, you'll never need this insurance, because if you do, you'll have to search all those floppies for the file you lost. And it's a mess if you have to re-create your entire hard drive.

 On the other hand, here's one reason *not* to leave a floppy disk in your drive: Some computer viruses can be spread by floppy disk and sneak onto a floppy when inserted into a computer. They then "jump ship" onto your system if you accidentally boot your computer from this disk, which can happen if the disk is left in the drive when you power up. Granted, computer virus infections are still rare, and you can often set up your computer to boot only from the hard drive, but many computer experts advise against ever leaving a floppy inserted in your disk drive when it's not in use.

Microsoft Backup

Fortunately, Microsoft kindly provides us with the versatile Microsoft Backup program, found in the Accessories folder. It makes floppy-based backup easier and more organized, but it's really designed to take advantage of inexpensive tape drives.

Microsoft Backup is smart enough to properly back up and restore long filenames, something that earlier Windows 3.1 backup utilities can't get right. Although you can use the LFNBK utility described in Chapter 22 to manually back up and restore long filenames, we recommend that you get an updated version of your tape backup software if you don't want to use Microsoft Backup.

Choosing Files to Back Up

The main part of the Microsoft's Backup window resembles Explorer. It is divided into the left drives/folders pane and the right-hand files pane. You choose which files to back up by clicking on the check box next to the folder, drive or file you want to select for backup. (This procedure is called *tagging* the files.) If the box is not checked, the folder, drive or file won't be backed up. This way, you can separate your data files from your applications and shorten the time it takes to back up.

Figure 5-26 shows the Backup program getting ready to back up a hard drive. We've clicked on the C: drive to get a list of top-level folders on C: and also clicked on a few folders that we want to back up.

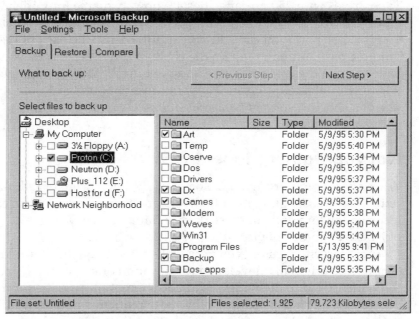

Figure 5-26: *Click the check boxes for the files and folders you want to back up.*

If you perform the same backup regularly, you can save your selections as a File Set by selecting File | Save. Backing up this way saves you time, since tagging all the files on a drive can take a while.

Windows creates a special File Set for you. It selects all files and folders on your computer, and it's the only way to safely back up all Windows files, including critical system files like your registry. Keep in mind that a Full Backup Set is intended only as a way to recover from a total hard drive failure; it's not a good way to restore individual files, since it will attempt to restore the registry, even if it's an outdated copy. You have to reinstall Windows to get the Backup program that's used to restore Windows, a kind of Catch-22 that makes this option nearly useless anyway.

After you've tagged the files or folders you want to back up in the Microsoft Backup window, click on the Next Step button so that you can choose where to back up. You then can choose the way you want to save these files, either on another hard drive, a network drive or to a floppy. Or you can back up to a tape.

Tape Drives

Tape drives with 250mb capacities are now available for under $150 and are relatively easy to install, especially if you choose a model that plugs into your printer port (you can still plug a printer into the back of the tape drive or into a pass-through plug on the cable). With these drives, you don't even have to open the computer case and plug in a board. You just plug it in where your printer plugs in. These lightweight outboard units are half the size of a shoebox so they're also useful as a way of taking mass storage along with a portable computer.

Not your father's tape drive

Years ago, computers (even the original IBM PC) used an ordinary audiocassette tape and a slightly modified version of an ordinary audio cassette recorder to store data. In those days, a floppy drive was an expensive, sophisticated storage device.

Audiocassettes aren't even very well-suited to quality sound recording. (They were originally developed for dictation only, but their small size and convenience led to the widespread adoption of the cassette for music, boosted by technologies like Dolby noise reduction and high-tech tape formulation.) It's not a surprise, then, that the first PC tape drives were slow, limited in capacity and more or less stupid.

QIC & Easy

QIC (Quarter Inch Cartridge) tapes are designed especially for computer data storage. The most common tape backup uses a QIC-80 tape in the DC-2120 or 2120XL format. These tapes, commonly available at computer and office supply stores, are designed especially for data recording and fast access to data.

Just like a floppy disk or hard drive, a tape has to be formatted before use, to lay down a pattern of timing signals used to keep track of the layout of data.

You can save the two hours it takes to format a tape by purchasing a preformatted tape, but for best results you'll want to format your own tapes, since tape formats can vary slightly between different brands. Each tape costs between $10 and $15.

A DC-2120 tape actually holds only 120mb, but by using data compression, you can store between 200 and 250mb of data on these tapes, depending on the type of files you're backing up. Microsoft Backup (and most 250mb tape drives) also support the new 2120XL format to fit up to 350mb of compressed data on a tape.

However, the Microsoft Backup program does not support some tape formats, including the new QIC Wide tapes with compressed capacities of 420 and 850mb. For these and other formats such as the HP/Colorado Travan and Digital Audio Tape (DAT) backup, you'll have to look for Windows 95 versions of third-party backup software. One such product is Arcada Backup for Windows 95, a full-featured package that supports nearly every type of backup device.

Compression emptor

Some files are already well-compressed, especially graphics files such as .GIF or .PCX graphics. A tape full of these files would probably only fit about 120mb. (We talk more about the benefits and limits of data compression below.)

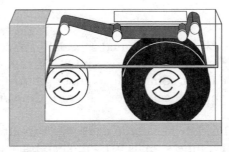

Figure 5-27: *A simplified diagram of a typical 250mb QIC-80 tape. It's not too different functionally than a cassette tape or even the big reel-to-reel tape drives you see in those old computer movies (and still used today by mainframe computers).*

QIC Alternatives
For larger hard drives, the 8mm videotape format or the 4mm DAT (Digital Audio Tape) formats will save you time, since you won't have to use multiple QIC-80 tapes to back up. Fast DAT drives can be used to store data that needs to be retrieved on demand, whereas the QIC-80 format can take several minutes per megabyte. Another advantage of DAT is that the tapes themselves are extremely inexpensive—$11 for a tape—and each tape holds two to four gigabytes, i.e., two to four thousand megabytes, depending on the DAT drive you buy. Ironically, DAT is also an audio tape technology adapted to computer use, but it's a good mate because DAT is inherently a digital format. Tapes can also be a handy way to copy large numbers of files between computers, and as such, they're an economical alternative to removable hard drives.

Another increasingly popular format is the removable hard drive, the least expensive of which is the Iomega Zip drive, which stores 100mb of data (uncompressed) on a single cartridge just a little larger than a 3.5" disk. These drives compare favorably with the 120mb (uncompressed) capacity of a typical QIC-80 tape drive, yet the Zip drives are nearly as fast as a hard drive and can be used as online storage. In late 1995, Iomega is expected to introduce the Jaz drive, with a 1 gigabyte removable disk cartridge.

Conversely, you can use software such as TapeDisk to access a SCSI-based tape drive, such as a 4mm DAT tape drive, and actually read and write to files on the tape as if the tape were a removable hard drive.

After you've chosen your backup destination from the Backup program, you can click on the Start Backup button. You can continue to work with

Windows while the backup runs "in the background," but keep in mind that any files you have opened won't be backed up, since the Backup program can't get exclusive access to them. Also, since some tape backup units use the floppy disk controller, you won't be able to access disks while the backup runs.

Customizing Backup Options

Use Microsoft Backup's Settings menu to choose backup options. For example, you can choose File Filtering, which lets you define criteria for the backup, such as files older than a certain date or whether to back up read-only or system files. You can also customize Backup by selecting the Settings | Options menu choice. The Backup page of the Settings | Options window contains the most useful options when you're backing up the data, shown in Figure 5-28.

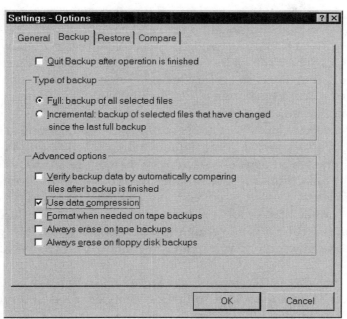

Figure 5-28: *On the Backup page, you can turn on or off data compression, among other things.*

The *Quit Backup after operation is finished* option is self-explanatory; it is useful if you want the Backup program out of your way when it completes.

Under the *Type of backup* heading on the Backup page, you can choose how complete the backup will be. The *Full* option backs up all the files you've selected and marks each file as having been backed up. If you later change a file, this mark is removed. The *Incremental* backup looks at these marks to see which files have changed since the last backup and backs up only those files, which saves you a lot of time.

You should use Full and Incremental backups together. Once a week (or once a month), do a Full backup. Then every day (or once a week), follow up with an Incremental backup to catch the changes. That way, you have on tape (or disks) a complete set that's never more than a day (or a week) out of date. If you delete a file by mistake, first check to see if it's on any of the incremental backups; it takes less time to search them since they're shorter.

You should rotate the tapes (or sets of disks) you use, in case the backup should fail. That way, you still have your old set of backups to fall back on, instead of a set that is only halfway complete. Rotating also helps you distribute the wear and tear of repeated backups across a set of tapes.

The Advanced Options round out your choices in the Settings | Options window. For ultimate security, turn on *Verify backup data*. When the backup completes, the tape or disks are reread and compared with the original files to make sure the backup succeeded. This capability is especially helpful with tape backup, which can be less reliable than other mass storage. A certain number of errors are correctable, since tape storage is redundant and includes Error Correction Coding (ECC), but if you find too many errors, you can try another tape or reformat it.

The *Use data compression* option not only lets you fit the most data on tape or disk, but also saves you time. It takes half as long to write a file that's been compressed 50 percent, which more than offsets the time needed to crunch the data. Similarly, this option saves you time when restoring.

The choice for *Format when needed on tape backups* is only necessary if you forgot to format a tape and want to let the format and backup occur together when you're letting it run overnight. Or you may prefer to always format for safety's sake, since reformatting can sometimes fix problems with an old tape.

If you turn on the *Always erase on tape backups* option, the tape is rewound and erased before the backup, so there's plenty of space for a full backup. On the other hand, if the tape has leftover space, you don't want to erase the tape before performing an incremental backup. Often you can fit the full backup and a few sets of incremental backups all on the same tape.

You normally want to keep the *Always erase on floppy disk backups* option turned on, since floppies usually don't have enough space left over on them to bother trying to append backup sets.

Restoring From Backup

Hopefully, you'll never need to restore from backup, unless you're installing a new hard drive or have bought a new computer. Of course, if you use tapes for transporting data between computers, you'll use this capability all the time. Click on the Restore tab in the Microsoft Backup window to switch your display to the Restore options, shown in Figure 5-29.

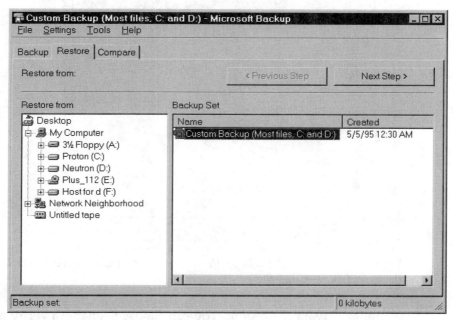

Figure 5-29: *Restore from Backup lets you choose which files and folders to restore.*

The Restore page also looks similar to Explorer, but here you are locating the backup set on the backup media. After you've found the backup set, you can choose which files you want to restore by clicking on the Files to Restore button. It recovers the list of files you selected when you first backed up the data set and lets you click on the files you want to copy from tape. When you're ready, click Start Restore.

In Figure 5-30, we selected Settings | Options and then clicked on the Restore tab heading. When you restore files, you may want to choose a different location than where the files were originally gathered. Normally, you'd leave the *Original locations* option turned on in the Restore page, but if you're copying files between different computers, you may need to specify an *Alternate location* (a different drive and folder). If you want to restore all the files from all the different folders to just a single folder, choose *Alternate location, single directory*. If you chose an alternate location, when the backup begins, you'll be prompted to specify the location.

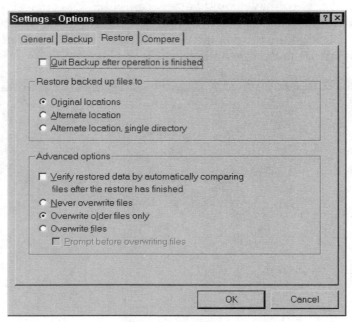

Figure 5-30: *Microsoft Backup's Restore Options let you customize the behavior of Backup when restoring files*

Under Advanced Options, you can choose to enable a verify pass. Here, the data on the hard drive is compared with the data on the tape to make sure the restore succeeded. It's rarely used with restore, since hard drives are much more reliable, but it also makes sure that the tape was not read incorrectly the first time by essentially restoring the file again if necessary.

The default choice, *Never Overwrite on destination device*, prevents the restored data, which may be older than the current data, from replacing the current files. It's a safety measure. Of course, you can just click on *Overwrite older files only* to have the same sense of security. If you don't care if files are overwritten, choose *Overwrite files*. But if you want the ultimate sense of control, turn on both the *Overwrite files* option and the check box for *Prompt before overwriting files*, and you can decide on a case-by-case basis.

Comparison Options

When backing up files to tape, it's a good idea to run a Compare operation to confirm that the files were stored properly. Or when you restore files, you can use Compare to verify that the files on the hard disk match the files on a tape. (Use *Verify Backup* from the Backup Options tab heading to automatically run a file compare operation after every backup.)

Before comparing files, you can use the Settings | Options choice and click on the tab heading for Compare Options. This lets you specify a different location for the Compare than the original location where the files were backed up. You might do this when you're comparing two different directories on different computers.

Miscellaneous Backup Tools

While most operations are performed automatically with Backup, you can use the Tools menu when you want to manually format a tape, erase a tape or reread (re-detect) a tape's header. You cannot manually format a disk using Microsoft Backup, but it's easy enough to format a disk. Just open My Computer from the desktop, right-click on the disk drive's icon, and choose Format.

DriveSpace Data Compression

When your hard drive starts to fill up, it's time to buy a new hard drive or find a way to squeeze more data into less space. Regular purging of old or duplicated files can help you stave off this eventuality, but you will eventually run out of disk space. Many Windows applications use 5 to 15mb, so each new program hogs up another big chunk of disk space. Some large packages, such as Microsoft Office or CorelDRAW, can use 50 to 70mb or more.

In Chapter 15, you'll learn how to add a second hard drive, but there's an easier way, if not as ideal. *Data compression* is a software technology that removes the "dead space" that is found in most files, kind of like squeezing a sponge, to fit the file into less space.

Stand-alone compressors such as PKZIP, LHA, ARC and ARJ have been used for years to compress a file or groups of files into a single *archive* file. These compressors are especially popular with modems and telecommunications, since it's more convenient to transmit the one archive file instead of a number of separate ones, and the compression cuts down the time it takes to transmit the data.

A graphics file or a text document can compress by as much as 90 percent, reducing a one megabyte file down to a 100k file. When you receive an archive program, you reverse the process and decompress the single file into a series of individual files, expanding them to their original size. (Compression programs like PKZIP/PKUNZIP both compress and decompress.)

The shareware program WinZip is one of the most popular utilities for compressing and decompressing archives, without requiring the PKZIP/ PKUNZIP programs, which have to be run from MS-DOS.

What if you could compress all the files on a hard drive into a single archive file? Wouldn't it be great to be able to let the file system do this automatically so that, when you save a file, it's compressed, and when you open it, it's automatically decompressed?

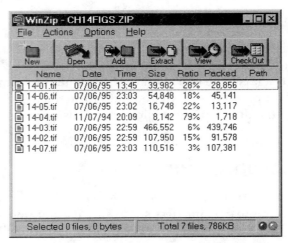

Figure 5-31: *WinZip lets you treat a .ZIP archive file like a hard drive volume. DriveSpace works somewhat similarly but on a more fundamental level.*

That's what the leading hard drive compression products do. Stac Technology's Stacker has been the leader for years in this category, and they established the utility and reliability of compressed drive technology.

Microsoft provided DoubleSpace to all PC users with the introduction of MS-DOS 6.0, and took steps to protect users from possible failures with MS-DOS 6.2, which added extra precautions. During a spat between Microsoft and Stacker, Microsoft had to temporarily remove DoubleSpace from MS-DOS 6.2.1. Then they created a new version called DriveSpace, introduced in MS-DOS 6.22. Finally, Stac and Microsoft "kissed and made up," and cross-licensed each other's technology. So it doesn't matter if you already use DoubleSpace or DriveSpace; both work the same way, and Windows 95 supports either type.

Compression Deception

A compressed drive is an illusion: your real hard drive is "renamed" to another drive letter, so your original C: drive might become drive D:. A huge, single file is created on the host drive (now drive D:), and MS-DOS or Windows is fooled into believing that this single file is really a complete hard drive. Whenever MS-DOS attempts to read a block of data, DriveSpace intercepts the read, finds the block in the compressed file and delivers it, as if it was read directly from the platter. When saving a file, DoubleSpace intercepts these writes, compresses them into blocks and stashes them away in the compressed file.

How does compression work, anyway? The simplest way, used most often with graphics, is to notice whenever there are runs (series) of the same data in a row. This is common with solid backgrounds in a painting. Instead of storing 100 red pixels, you could just store the number 100 and the fact that they're red. You've compressed 100 bytes into just a few. This compression is called *run length encoding* (RLE), which is used to compress bitmaps for wallpaper.

This type of compression doesn't work too well with text, and even less well with application files (programs). With text one trick is to reduce common phrases and pronouns into single character *tokens*. A single, unique character could be substituted for the most common words such as *the, and, but, he, she, or* and so on. Decompression simply reverses the substitution.

Codebreakers, trying to analyze encrypted documents, have studied the frequencies of letters, syllables and whole words in typical English language messages. They have found that the word *the* appears 6.5 percent of the time; *of*, 4 percent; *and*, 3.1 percent; *to*, 2.3 percent; and *a*, 2 percent. Merely tokenizing these five common words would shrink a typical text file over 15 percent.

DoubleSpace and Stacker use a similar but more clever method, which analyzes a stream of data and replaces redundant, commonly used strings of characters with a reference to the first occurrence of that string. So a phrase like "The creatures love to eat meat" could become "The creatures love to {7,3} m{7,3}." The compressor substitutes the reference {7,3} to mean "reuse the three characters at position seven" as an instruction to the decompressor when it later expands the file. While this example sentence isn't compressed very much, if you had a whole paragraph or page to scan, you'd find many more redundancies to take advantage of.

Compression Everywhere

Compression/*decompression* programs, also called *codecs*, are essential for large multimedia files. Videos are stored by comparing each frame with the previous frame, and only storing the parts that have changed. The wide range of colors in a movie are also compressed into a smaller *palette* of colors that approximate the original colors, so that smaller numbers can be used for each pixel. Redundant data is compressed using run length encoding. Sound files are analyzed to remove sound that isn't heard, such as when a trumpet blares out loud enough to drown the woodwinds. Speech sounds can be especially compromised by removing the high end and very low end frequencies, and other sound components that aren't necessary for intelligibility.

Compression is vital in these days of ever-growing data-storage needs and the demand for more and more data, especially given the limits of current communications technology. We further discuss the importance of data compression in Chapter 16, "The Communicating Computer."

DoubleSpace and Stacker compress files on average about 50 percent—a *compression ratio* of 2:1 (read as "two to one"). Some files compress extremely well. Text files, for example, can often be compressed at 10:1 or better. But files that are already compressed by another scheme can't usually be compressed any further. In fact, attempting to compress some files can actually make them a little larger. If your drive is filled mostly with programs, compressed graphics, .ZIP files and video files, you may not benefit much from software data compression. See the "Compression Ratios" section later in this chapter.

The Cost of Compression

You aren't aware of the compression process; it's transparent to the user, except that a compressed drive is usually somewhat slower. Saving files takes longer because of the extra step of compression, but when you open a file, the time it takes to decompress is offset by the fact that the file, being smaller in its compressed form, takes less time to read from the drive. The only applications that are noticeably slower on a compressed drive are databases that frequently read and write to the same file.

Some people view compression as inherently unsafe, since your entire hard drive is stored in a single file. If that file gets corrupted, your entire hard drive is lost. But numerous safeguards, including backup copies of the FAT and tests that verify the integrity of the cache, help ensure safety of your files. Besides, even an uncompressed drive can be rendered useless by damage to the relatively small part of the drive holding the FAT and directories.

We have used compression for years without having any major problems, although we still prefer to add more physical disk space whenever possible. Not because compression is overly risky, but because uncompressed hard drives can communicate with the computer more rapidly. Compression and decompression are rapid but do slow things up a bit. (However, with a Pentium processor, you don't really notice a speed penalty for using a compressed drive.)

Windows 95 is compatible with existing compressed drives, including Stacker and other third-party methods, but it includes all-new support for highly optimized DriveSpace compression, which can use existing DoubleSpace or DriveSpace volumes as is. The Windows 95 DriveSpace driver doesn't use up any DOS (conventional) memory in a DOS session and is even more tightly integrated into the file system. (Stacker and other companies are also expected to release Windows 95 optimized drivers, which were not available for evaluation when this book went to press.)

DriveSpace Explained

Before we discuss DriveSpace, let's look at the technology. To "double" hard disk space, you need to create a new virtual hard drive. This hard drive is actually a single, huge file—called a CVF, or Compressed Volume File—on the original hard drive.

The original hard drive is called the Host drive (or host volume) since it holds (hosts) the actual contents of the compressed drive. A new drive letter is created for the compressed drive, and the DriveSpace software manages all access to the compressed drive, translating file requests to automatically store or retrieve from the master compressed file.

A DriveSpace or DoubleSpace drive can be created out of the empty space on a host drive, in which case you have both your original (C:) drive and your new (F:) drive. (You can change the drive letter of the new drive if you like.) Or you can compress the existing files on the host drive. These files are moved to the new compressed drive, which is created initially out of the empty space on the host drive and then grows dynamically as space is freed by compressing the original files. When the compression transfer is complete, the original drive letter gets changed, and the new drive inherits the original drive letter. This means that the compressed drive now masquerades as the original C: drive, and your original (host) drive now sports the new drive letter (F:, for example).

TIP It's a good idea to use a drive letter such as F:, G: or H: for a new compressed drive or host drive. That way, you can easily add a new (physical) hard drive as drive D: without "bumping" the drive letters for any software you have already installed on the compressed drives. (It also leaves E: available for your CD-ROM drive.)

DriveSpace grows up

A higher level of compression, called DriveSpace 3.0, is offered in the optional Microsoft Plus! Companion for Windows 95. The DriveSpace built into Windows 95 (DriveSpace 2.0) can create drives only up to 512mb, based on 256mb of host disk space. With today's larger hard drives, this restriction (inherited from DOS 6) has become limiting, so DriveSpace 3.0 lets you have compressed drives up to 2.0gb (using about 1.0gb of host space).

DriveSpace 3.0 also offers three levels of compression for files stored on a compressed drive. You can choose not to compress files when you create them, or you can choose to HiPack the files (which is the default for DriveSpace 3.0), or you can even use UltraPack for the ultimate in file compression, at the cost of some speed.

The System Agent built into Microsoft Plus! works in tandem with DriveSpace 3.0 to allow you to schedule Compression Agent to run automatically when you are not using your computer. During idle times (after a set time of day), System Agent will proactively start Compression Agent to recompress files on the DriveSpace drive. That way, if you have a slower computer, you can choose not to compress your files routinely yet have System Agent compress the files when you're not using your computer. It's like having your cake and eating it too.

Setting Up DriveSpace

If you already have a DoubleSpace or DriveSpace drive, Windows 95 DriveSpace is installed automatically. You can compress an existing uncompressed drive or manage your existing compressed volume with enhanced Windows 95 tools. No longer do you have to use DOS to set up or maintain a DoubleSpace drive.

As with other Windows 95 tools, Microsoft provided redundant paths to accessing DriveSpace. The most straightforward method is to simply select Start I Programs I Accessories I System Tools I DriveSpace. You can also open My Computer or navigate to the top of an Explorer drive list and right-click on the icon for your hard drive, and then choose Properties. From the Properties sheet, click on the Compression tab.

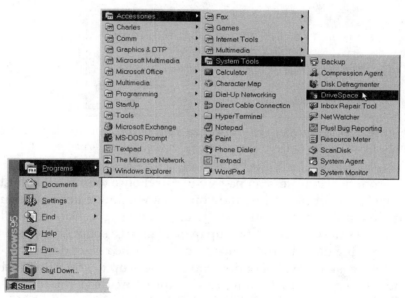

Figure 5-32: *Use the Start button to navigate to DriveSpace.*

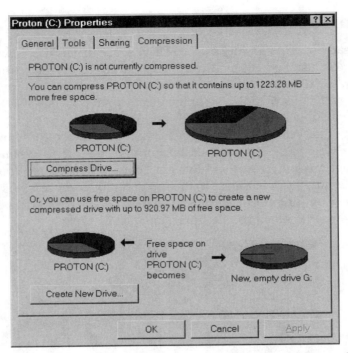

Figure 5-33: *Right-click your hard drive icon, choose Properties and click on the Compression tab to get to DriveSpace options for that drive (DriveSpace 3.0).*

From the Compression page, you can choose to immediately start DriveSpace for that drive, and you're shown how much space can be freed up. In our illustration, since we're using DriveSpace 3.0, we're allowed to compress the C: drive to free up over 1.0gb free space or create a new G: drive using only the free space on drive C: (the rest of drive C: is left uncompressed). Which option you choose is up to you. Ultimately, you'll get more free disk space by compressing the entire drive (up to the 1.0gb limit). (Remember that with the standard DriveSpace shipped with Windows 95, you can compress only up to 256mb of disk space, creating a drive up to 512mb in size.)

If you choose Properties for a drive that's already compressed (or for the host volume), you see a different page under the Compression heading, which graphically illustrates how your hard disk is being used (see Figure 5-34). The pie chart shows those files that are UltraPacked, HiPacked, compressed using standard compression, and files that are left uncompressed. Statistics are also available on the compression ratio for each file type and for the drive as a whole, which is used to estimate how much free space is left on the drive. Expect the display to take some time to calculate updated figures for these statistics, since it has to examine the drive to sniff out these facts. (If you are using standard DriveSpace compression, you won't get all these details; instead you'll see something similar to Figure 5-35.)

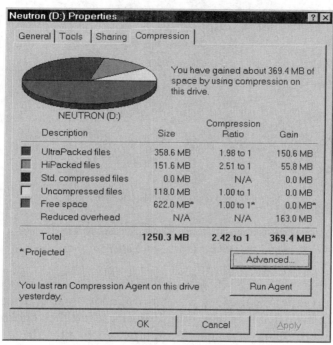

Figure 5-34: *The Compression Properties for a compressed drive offer a full set of facts and figures about your compressed drive (DriveSpace 3.0).*

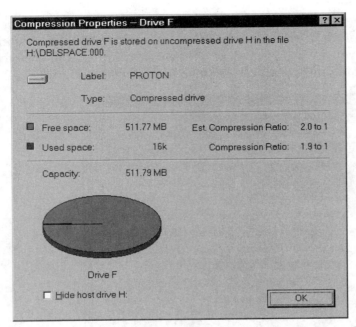

Figure 5-35: *Windows 95's standard DriveSpace offers a simpler view of your compressed drive.*

Finally, you can view the Compression page for the host drive (again, by right-clicking the drive icon, choosing Properties and then clicking on the Compression tab). This page shows you how much of the drive is devoted to compression; it also gives you a chance to run DriveSpace to reallocate space between the host and compressed drive, or use the other DriveSpace management options, such as defragmentation. You can also choose to Hide the host drive. (It actually hides the drive letter. If you have a compressed drive C: and a host drive of F:, you can hide drive F: so you seem to have only your original drive, yet twice as large.

Hiding the host drive is useful if you have used the entire host drive to create a compressed drive. In that case, the host drive has no free space left on it, and might as well be hidden so that it doesn't clutter up your Explorer drive lists or appear in My Computer. If you compress very large drives (1.0gb or larger), however, you'll have a big chunk of leftover space, and you probably don't want to hide the drive letter and waste the space.

One of the benefits of compression is that it doesn't waste space left over at the end of each cluster. DriveSpace compresses clusters to use even multiples of 512 bytes, so much less hard disk space is wasted, especially on large volumes, which normally have a minimum disk usage of 16k or 32k per file. This way, you save space even if you don't actually compress the files.

Taking the plunge

If you want to try out DriveSpace without committing to it, you can create a small "scratch" drive, useful for storing documents. Or you can take the plunge and compress your entire drive to get the maximum disk space savings. In either case, you'll want to back up your critical files at least, if not your entire hard drive, before you use compression for the first time.

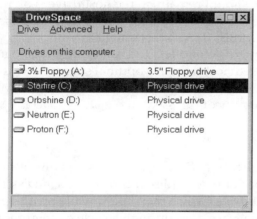

Figure 5-36: *Running DriveSpace from the Start button lets you pick which drive(s) you want to work with.*

When you start DriveSpace, you can choose which drive to work with by clicking its drive letter in the list and then choosing a menu option from the Drive menu (Figure 5-37). If you choose Drive | Compress, you'll see a preview of how DriveSpace intends to compress your drive. Click the Start button to begin the creation and compression of your new drive.

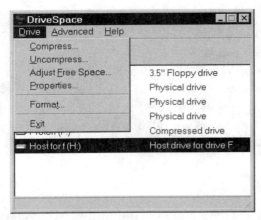

Figure 5-37: *The Drive menu lets you manage your hard drive compression.*

You can change the compression plan using the Options button. This way, you can choose which drive letter to use for the host drive and how much free uncompressed space should remain on the host drive. You may want to leave some uncompressed space set aside for your TEMP directory (the directory pointed to by the SET TEMP= statement in your C:\AUTOEXEC.BAT configuration file). You can change this to use a directory on your uncompressed host drive for optimal speed. (This isn't necessary with DriveSpace 3.0. If you like, you can tell Compression Manager to keep your TEMP directory uncompressed on the DriveSpace 3.0 volume.)

Let 'er rip

Immediately before compressing, DriveSpace gives you one last chance to change your mind and back up your files. It then runs ScanDisk to verify the integrity of the host hard drive (which may take a while on a large or slow hard drive). Finally, DriveSpace goes through a cycle of compressing and resizing the files, creating a Compressed Volume File on the host drive. When it's done, it restarts your computer and mounts (enables) the compressed drive.

 While compressing, DriveSpace uses a special "mini" version of Windows 3.1, which explains why some of the windows and dialog boxes still have the "old" look and feel.

Keep in mind that compressing a drive is an intensive process. You should not use your computer while it's compressing. In fact, it's a good idea to run compression overnight, or while you're away for lunch or running errands, since your computer could be busy for anywhere from 30 minutes to 3 hours (or more), depending on how large and how fast your hard drive is.

A fresh new one

Instead of compressing an existing drive, you can select Advanced | Create Empty to simply create a new drive out of the raw, uncompressed space on a host drive. Remember, in this case, the drive letter of the host drive remains the same, and you add a new drive letter for the compressed drive. Creating a new drive presents you with the options shown in Figure 5-38.

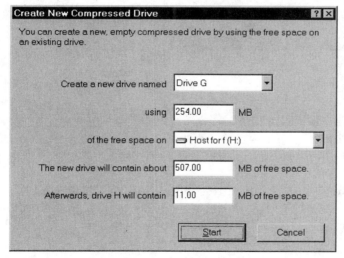

Figure 5-38: *Creating a new compressed drive out of existing space is easy and straight-forward.*

Here's one great use for creating a new drive: format a floppy disk; then compress the free space to create a doubled floppy with close to 3mb of free space. (Keep in mind that when you share this disk with others, they also need to have Windows 95 DriveSpace installed on their computer in order to read the floppy.)

Managing Compression

Once you have a shiny new compressed drive, you can use it just like any other hard drive. Microsoft's ScanDisk and Defrag programs work fine with compressed drives, although we recommend that you do not use earlier DOS or Windows utility programs. These programs can wipe out your long filenames and possibly wreak havoc with the compressed drive. However, the newest disk tools such as Symantec's Norton Utilities for Windows 95 work just fine.

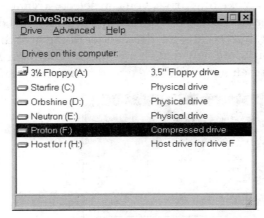

Figure 5-39: *When compression is complete, your new drive is available for DriveSpace to work with.*

Even after compressing a drive, you'll still use DriveSpace to work with your compressed drive. You can use the Adjust Free Space option from the Drive menu if you want to reallocate space between the host and compressed drive (Figure 5-40).

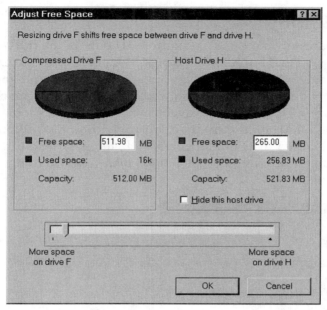

Figure 5-40: *Changing the ratio can be useful if you need to free up some more uncompressed space on the host drive, or if you want to increase the size of your compressed drive.*

In the Adjust Free Space window, shown in Figure 5-40, making this adjustment is as easy as moving a slider toward *More space on drive F:* to increase the size of the compressed drive (making the host drive smaller), or toward *More space on drive H:* to make the host drive have more uncompressed space (making the compressed drive smaller). In this figure, drive F: is the compressed drive, and drive H: is the host drive.

From the DriveSpace's Drive menu, you can also choose to uncompress a drive. You can only use the Uncompress option if there's enough free space on the uncompressed drive to hold all your uncompressed files. Once you start using DriveSpace, you pass a point of no return after you've used over half the space on the compressed drive. At that point, there's usually no way to fit all those files on the original drive anymore, unless you delete some of them.

More drastically, you can select Advanced | Delete to delete a compressed drive entirely. It removes the drive letter, erases the compressed volume file and frees up uncompressed space on the host drive. Only use this option if you have a full backup of the files on the compressed drive that you're removing (or if you simply don't care if they're permanently lost).

If you select Drive | Properties for a drive, you'll see the same type of windows we reviewed earlier, the windows you get when you right-click on drive icon and view the Compression Properties page.

Advanced DriveSpace

The DriveSpace Advanced menu (Figure 5-41) puts you in full control of your compressed and host drives. Use the Mount command to enable a compressed drive. This capability is normally automatic, even for compressed floppy disks. If you select Advanced | Settings, you can change this default (Figure 5-42) so that you have to explicitly use the Mount command to see the files on a compressed drive, including compressed floppies. You can select Advanced | Unmount if you need to temporarily disable (and hide) a compressed drive, although not too many reasons come to mind for why you would.

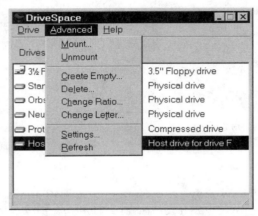

Figure 5-41: *You won't use the Advanced DriveSpace options very often.*

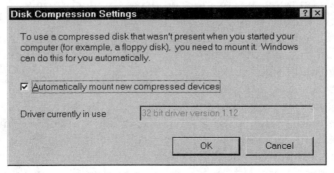

Figure 5-42: *We don't know why you'd want to turn off the automounting of compressed drives, but it's one of your Advanced menu choices. (The only advantage we know of is that disabling automounting can free up a small amount of conventional memory.)*

Compression Ratios

DriveSpace can't tell you exactly how much free space is left on a compressed drive because different kinds of files compress at different *ratios*. As we said earlier, a text file might compress to six times smaller than the original file (6:1), a spreadsheet might compress to a third of its size (3:1), but a program file might allow only 1.5:1 compression. Some files can't be compressed any more (they're already compressed internally). An .AVI video or .ZIP archive would probably compress only 1:1.

On average, files can be compressed at a 2:1 ratio. DriveSpace keeps track of the actual average for your drive and uses it to estimate how much free space is available. For example, if your existing files are stored at a ratio of 1.8:1, you might assume that all your future files will also compress at about this ratio. Consequently, 100mb of unused space in the Compressed Volume File would yield 180mb of DriveSpace free space.

 TIP Watch for low hard disk space. Many programs will simply crash (stop responding and lose data) if you run out of hard disk space unexpectedly. With no free disk space, Windows also can't store an updated version of the system registry when you shut down, and this can lead to serious problems. Since DriveSpace can only estimate free space, take its measure with a grain of salt when disk space starts to run low. You might not have as much usable space as it seems if you're storing poorly compressible files.

The Change Ratio command can override the "typical" compression ratio that DriveSpace anticipates. For example, if you're certain that any new files you're adding will compress better than the average, or if you know you're going to be adding files that compress poorly, you may want to tweak the ratio to get a more accurate estimate of the free space on your DriveSpace drive.

You can select Advanced | Change Letter to reassign a drive letter to the host file of a compressed drive or to hide the file. The same option is available if you right-click on a drive icon in My Computer and select Properties | Compression. On a typical system, where you've compressed the original drive, swapping its drive letter to make the compressed drive pretend to be your primary drive, you can change the drive letter only of the host drive. The compressed drive still has to be called drive C:. But if you use Advanced | Create Empty instead to carve a new compressed drive out of free space on a normal drive, the original drive keeps its drive letter, and you can change the drive letter of the compressed drive, in this case.

DriveSpace 3.0 Compression Agent

If you have Microsoft Plus! for Windows, you can use the Compression Agent, along with DriveSpace, to work with your compressed volumes. Compression Agent is designed to *recompress* an existing drive. You can also choose which files to UltraPack, HiPack or leave uncompressed. Compression Manager can be launched automatically by System Agent so that it works in the background during idle times when you aren't typing or moving the mouse.

Figure 5-43 shows the Compression Agent's Settings dialog box, which lets you choose these options as well as set exceptions.

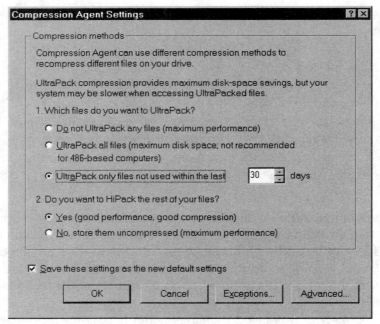

Figure 5-43: *Compression Agent lets you control what level of disk compression to apply to your files when they are recompressed. Note that these settings have no effect on real-time compression. Use the DriveSpace's Drive | Settings option to control that.*

Moving On

You now have all the tools you need to take control of the file system, optimize speed and free space, and keep it safe and secure. In the next chapter, you'll learn how to customize and personalize your desktop, and make it a comfortable, convenient, even attractive place to do your work, and to have fun with, too.

Chapter 6

Customizing the Desktop

The Windows desktop might seem like formless empty space, but you can do much with it. What you do is up to you. In this chapter, we'll explore all that can be done.

Some people prefer a smooth, clean desktop. Others like to work among piles of documents, folders, family photos, mementos, paperweights, what have you. How you organize your Windows desktop is a personal decision. Make it Spartan or Egyptian. Suit yourself.

The "desktop" is anywhere on your screen where you don't have any icons or folders—it's the space between objects and windows. Right-click and you'll see a pop-up menu. Now from this menu, select Properties to view the various ways you can adjust the "look" of Windows 95. The first and most obvious choice is whether or not you decorate the desktop with a picture. Windows 95 has a provision for *wallpaper*, displaying a photo or texture on your screen, "behind" all other windows and graphics.

Figure 6-1: *You can put any picture on your Windows desktop.*

In Figure 6-1, you can see a background that fills the entire screen (it was created in Caligari's trueSpace, a 3D modeling program). You can put any .BMP (graphics) file that you want on the desktop. For example, Figure 6-2 shows another .BMP file, a scanned Van Gogh painting. (You can find zillions of .BMP files on The Microsoft Network, CompuServe, bulletin board systems, or for sale in computer magazines or on CD at computer stores. For more on sources for computer graphics, see Chapter 12. Also, we've included some nice .BMP files on this book's CD.)

Figure 6-2: *Change your desktop graphics anytime you want.*

Figure 6-3: *Installing a new desktop graphic is easy—just right-click anywhere on the desktop and you'll see this menu. Then click on Properties.*

To display a new .BMP graphic, right-click anywhere on the desktop (not on an open folder or icon). You'll see the pop-up menu shown in Figure 6-3. Then click on Properties, and you'll see the dialog box shown in Figure 6-4.

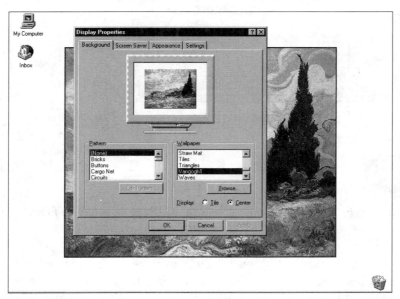

Figure 6-4: *Here you change the graphic file that's displayed on your desktop.*

Interior Decoration

In Figure 6-4, notice that Windows 95 provides you with a list of .BMP files in the File list box under Wallpaper. (Assuming you chose to install wallpaper when you ran Windows 95 Setup.) From this list, you select the picture that will appear on your desktop. Windows 95 (like Windows 3) includes a set of small .BMP files with such names as TILES, EGYPT, BLACK THATCH and so on. These files are found in your Windows directory, but they are automatically listed when you request to see the Desktop properties. Click on BUBBLES, as shown in Figure 6-5, and your screen will look something like Figure 6-7.

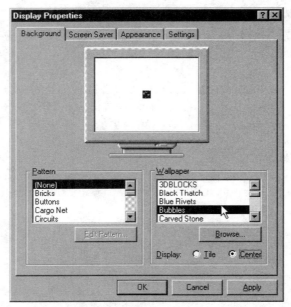

Figure 6-5: *Windows 95 supplies a dozen graphics files like this one.*

Figure 6-6: *This close-up shows the tiny .BMP file displayed in Figure 6-5. When these bubbles are combined, they'll form a seamless background texture.*

Notice the two option buttons in Figure 6-5: Tile and Center. If you want to wallpaper your desktop with a .BMP file that isn't as big as your screen, click on Tile. In Figure 6-7, the entire screen is full of bubbles after we selected the BUBBLES file, clicked on Tile and then clicked on the Apply button.

The Microsoft Plus! utilities for Windows 95 include a number of excellent "Desktop Themes"—Dangerous Creatures, Moderne, Leonardo DaVinci and so on—that not only feature high-quality wallpaper, but also change the sounds, desktop icons and cursors in keeping with each theme. Plus! also includes useful options. One of them automatically stretches any wallpaper to fit the size of your screen. Another maximizes the color quality of any icon. Yet another provides the first truly useful anti-aliasing of fonts (see Chapter 12 for more on this "font smoothing" utility).

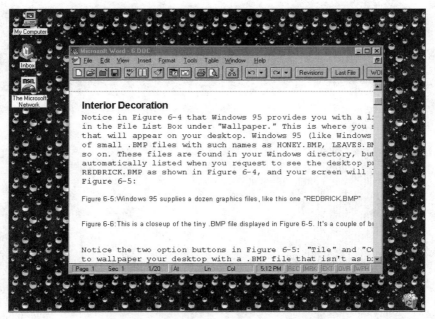

Figure 6-7: *The Tile option fills the screen with a small graphic, repeating it as often as necessary.*

To change one of these tiny Windows 95-supplied .BMP files, just click on the filename displayed in the File list box under Wallpaper; then click on the OK button or the Apply Now button. Either button does the same thing (but the OK button also shuts down the Desktop Properties window). Figures 6-8 through 6-11 show samples of some of the .BMP textures that Windows 95 provides.

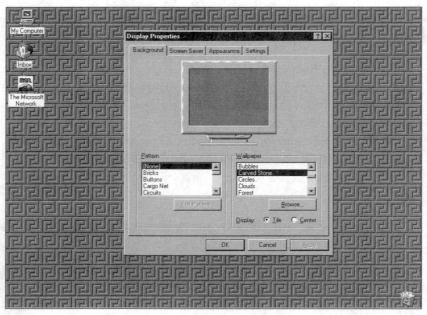

Figure 6-8: *The Windows 95 Houndstooth wallpaper.*

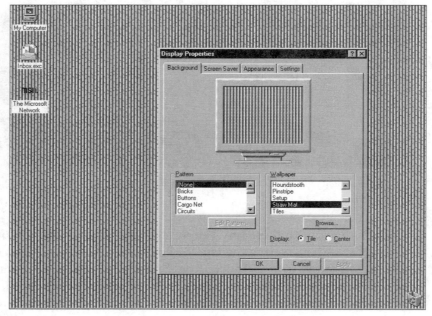

Figure 6-9: *Straw Mat.*

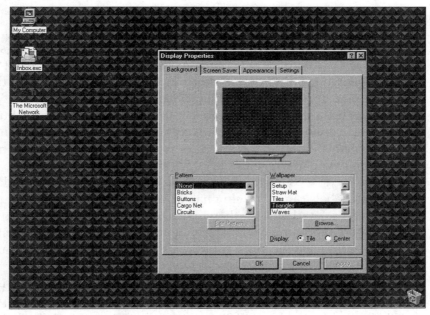

Figure 6-10: *Triangles.*

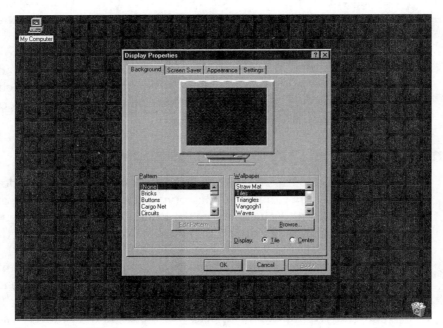

Figure 6-11: *Tiles.*

Customizing Titles

Some people like to cover their refrigerator with "sticky" notes, sports schedules, coupons. Others prefer a clean surface. Take a look at Figure 6-11. Some people will find that those white labels under the titles of the three icons in the upper left make the whole desktop look messy. The Wastebasket label has been safely hidden away at the bottom of the screen, but the My Computer, Inbox and Microsoft Network icons could be annoying. Besides, you probably know after a few days what those visual symbols mean, so you don't even need the labels.

You can do a couple of things if you want a less cluttered desktop. Unfortunately, labels cannot be eliminated. You can shorten the label under My Computer to, perhaps, "i" thereby making it less noticeable. You can also change the Inbox and MSN labels. Though at the time of this writing, changing The Microsoft Network causes a new icon and label to appear—with the original name—when you next run MSN. Now you've got two!

However, you have to be careful if you change the names of regular programs that you've copied to the desktop (by dragging, for example, their icon onto the desktop from an Explorer window). You must leave the extension alone: .BAT, .EXE, .DOC or whatever; these extensions are required. Note that you won't see the extension ordinarily. The best way to get around this is to use a shortcut to the original file. It's best not to move the actual .EXE or .BAT file to the desktop.

A second tactic to reduce the impact of objectionable titles is to change the background color to match the color of your wallpaper or, if you don't use wallpaper, the color of your desktop. To change the color, right-click on the desktop; then select Properties from the drop-down menu. Click on Appearance and change the background color.

Removing All Icons From Your Desktop

For the absolute purist, there's a way to permit nothing to intrude on the desktop. Even "My Computer" disappears (this technique is the only way to get rid of that icon). You can move the Printer, The Microsoft Network and any other icons into a folder on Explorer. (You could also dump them in the Recycle Bin.)

But My Computer is the outermost shell of the system. You can't move it to some folder. That would be like trying to move the post office into a post office box.

Making My Computer disappear—so the desktop is entirely vacant—requires that you modify the *registry*. The registry is the Windows 95 replacement for Windows 3.1's WIN.INI, SYSTEM.INI and other files that describe

Windows itself and details about software and hardware on your machine. Even something as simple as leaving the Control Panel visible when you shut down the computer is remembered by the registry. This way, the next time you start Windows running, the Control Panel can be restored to the same size and position on your desktop as you left it before.

The registry also includes all kinds of settings; it's typically 750,000 bytes (three-fourths of a megabyte) and growing. (A slight change here, running the Find utility there and, pow, it grows 15,000 bytes larger.) We'll adjust the registry's NoDesktop setting.

To make the change, click on the Start button and choose Run. Then type REGEDIT and press Enter in the Run dialog box. When the registry appears (it's in the Windows folder, if you want to locate it with Explorer), start it running by double-clicking on its name. You'll see what looks like folders labeled HKEY_CLASSES_ROOT and so on. Go down the series of locations until you get to

HKEY_USERS\Default\Software\Microsoft\Windows\CurrentVersion\Policies\Explorer

Next, double-click on HKEY_USERS; then double-click on Default, then Software, then Microsoft and so on until you've finally double-clicked on Explorer. The window shown in Figure 6-12 then appears.

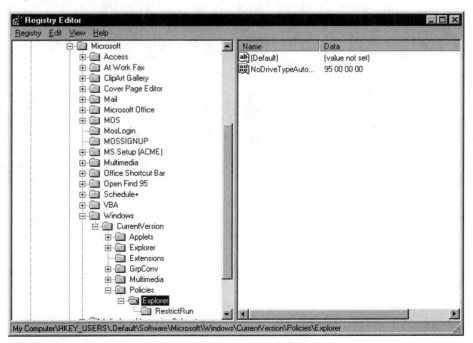

Figure 6-12: *The registry open for adjustments. Here we'll remove all icons and labels from the desktop, including My Computer.*

Now select Edit | New | DWORD Value. When you see a new entry titled New Value #1, right-click on it and then select Rename. Enter the name NoDesktop and press the Enter key. Right-click on it again, and this time select Modify. Type 1 (the digit 1) and click OK. Now shut down the Regedit program by selecting Exit from the Registry menu.

You've done it now. Click the Start button and then select Shut Down | Restart the Computer. When Windows starts up again, it will check the registry and find your change. Voila, an empty desktop. You'll notice another thing—you can no longer right-click on the desktop to change wallpaper, color schemes and so on. However, it's easy enough to click on Start, select Settings | Control Panel and then double-click the Display icon to accomplish the same thing.

If you decide that you want to go back to the way things were, if you miss My Computer, it's easy enough to reverse the process. Just start Regedit again and follow the same steps described above down to your NoDesktop entry. Right-click on it; then select Delete and close the Regedit program. **Note:** You can make this change even more easily using a program called POLEDIT (Policy Editor), which is available for Network Administrators, but you can use it for a single computer if you want to. It provides plain-English lists of options that it can adjust in the registry. If you have a CD containing Windows 95, look for POLEDIT in the ADMIN folder.

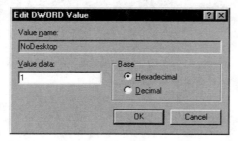

Figure 6-13: *Modifying the NoDesktop setting eliminates all icons from your desktop.*

Design Your Own Wallpaper

The little files ending in the extension .BMP that you'll find in your Windows 95 directory, like TILES.BMP and TRIANGLES.BMP, are intended to be *tiled*; that is, they are intended to be, essentially, a texture rather than a full drawing or photo. Like true wallpaper, tiled designs repeat a pattern over and over. (Recall that extensions are the last three letters of a filename, and they follow a dot: THATCH.BMP, for example. By default, extensions aren't displayed in Windows. You must request to see them; it's one of your options. To see extensions, click on the View menu in any folder. Then click on Options and select the View tab in the Options dialog box. Click on the check box for the Don't display MS-DOS file extensions for files that are properly registered option.)

It's easy enough to create your own custom wallpaper. Just start the Windows 95 Paint applet (an *applet* is a little application, also called an accessory). Here's how.

Click on Explorer or open a folder that holds the Windows 95 Paint accessory. It should be in your Windows directory. Or you can look for it by selecting Start | Programs | Accessories and looking for the one named Paint.

Now to create a small, efficient tile graphic, reduce the size of the drawing to about one or two inches. In Paint, select Image | Attributes. You'll probably see the image size described in terms of hundreds of *Pels* (pixels). Click on the Inches option and select 1 or 2 inches.

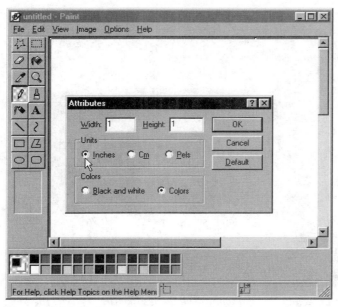

Figure 6-14: *Reduce the image to a tile-size, one or two inches.*

Then let your imagination be your guide. In the figures, we've used the Spray paint tool to create a rough texture. When you're happy with a texture or drawing, save it to the disk by selecting File | Save. Then select File | Set as Wallpaper (tiled). Now you can see how your work looks when it covers the desktop.

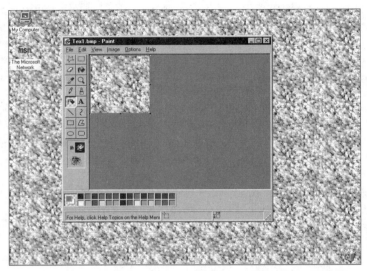

Figure 6-15: *Paint's File menu allows you to directly adjust the Windows 95 desktop wallpaper.*

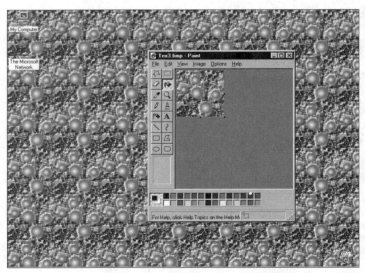

Figure 6-16: *Do whatever you want. Small tiles like this 1" x 1" tile won't slow up the redraw of your desktop or take up much space on disk or in memory.*

Here's a useful trick: If you want to really refine your art, click on the Magnifier tool in Paint; then click on your drawing. It blows up and you can make tiny adjustments with the Brush or Pencil tool, until you get the effect you're after. (To reduce it back to normal size, right-click on the picture.) See Chapter 10 for more information on the Paint accessory.

TIP You can make as many adjustments to your picture as you want, but Paint requires that you always save the picture to disk before selecting the Set as Wallpaper (tiled) option on the File menu to see the effect. Don't bother to use the 24-bit resolution option; settle for 256 color or less. You're creating a drawing without shading or gradients that would benefit from extra color depth. Besides, you don't want to slow up Windows when it's loading or repainting. Nor do you want to take up unnecessary space on your hard drive. It's more or less impossible in Paint to create a drawing that would look any better with a color range higher than 256. The only exception is if you import a high-resolution photographic .BMP file and paint onto that. In that case, go ahead and use a higher resolution to preserve the color depth of the original if you wish.

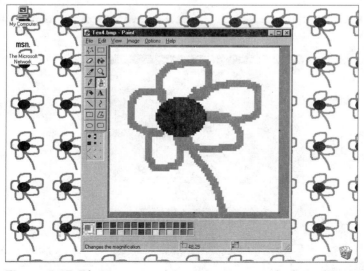

Figure 6-17: *Blow up your picture so you can make fine adjustments by clicking on the Magnifying glass tool.*

The Cleanest Screen

Some people like their desktop free of clutter. They find it less distracting. Windows 95 also runs slightly faster when it doesn't have to draw that background. And using wallpaper can cost you some memory: it takes nearly a megabyte of your RAM to use an 800x600 wallpaper image with 256 colors. But the speed difference isn't noticeable on 486 or Pentium machines, so don't let this consideration hold you back if you want a glamorous wallpaper, and have plenty of memory—more than 16mb of RAM would be generous.

If, however, you like the tidy, neat look, in the Background page of the Display Properties window, click on (None) in the Wallpaper File list box, and also click on (None) in the Pattern list box. This way, all you'll see on the Desktop background is the color that you've selected as your Desktop color under the Appearances option in Desktop Properties (we'll get to that shortly).

TIP The wallpaper and pattern options interact. You'll never see the pattern if you tile it or use wallpaper big enough to fill your desktop. The pattern option is an alternative to wallpaper—ultra high-speed redraw, almost no memory usage. You can, however, click on the Edit option to make patterns of your own if you wish.

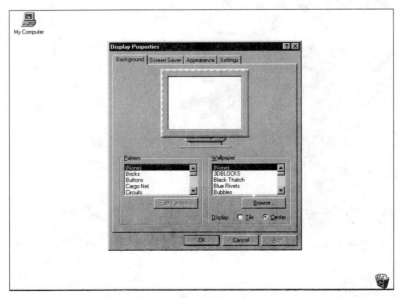

Figure 6-18: *Here's a totally clean desktop: just set both Wallpaper and Pattern to None.*

Tile Anything

Tiling isn't limited to small, texture images. If you want to use a medium-size graphic, you can still choose to tile it. Figure 6-19 shows the untiled image. Figure 6-20 shows how the same graphic looks when tiled.

Figure 6-19: *This graphic can be either Centered, as show here, or Tiled.*

Figure 6-20: *Here is the same graphic after using the Tiled option.*

Patterns

As an alternative to displaying photos or drawings to wallpaper your desktop, you can select Patterns, as shown in Figure 6-21. This option, too, is located in the Background page of the Display Properties window.

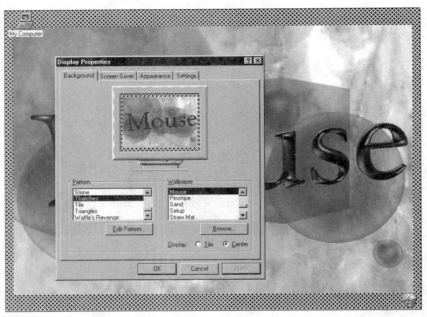

Figure 6-21: *Click on a pattern, and Windows will draw it to fill any screen space not covered by a Wallpaper graphic.*

In Figure 6-21, Windows draws your chosen pattern around any wallpaper you might have. If your wallpaper fills the screen, no pattern will be drawn. If you have no wallpaper (by setting Wallpaper to None), then the entire screen will fill with the selected pattern. (Windows 95 won't let you select a pattern unless your Wallpaper option is set to Centered or None.)

Why use a pattern? If you want a design but are using a slow computer, patterns draw faster than tiled textures (but tiled textures draw faster than large graphics that aren't repetitive or that are centered).

However, most computers these days run so fast that you probably won't notice any difference between these three approaches. Patterns, though, don't require any significant amount of memory, unlike wallpaper. If you do notice the time it takes Windows 95 to redraw your background, or if things seem sluggish when you center a graphic, see if tiling helps. If redrawing is still slow, try a pattern or just remove everything by selecting None for both the Patterns and Wallpaper options.

Patterns are the simplest wallpaper, but they are also the crudest. They usually don't look as finished or as realistic as the textures generated by tiling. Patterns are composed of black and white pixels, which limits their realism. Compare the Thatches pattern on the top in Figure 6-22 with the THATCH.BMP tiling on the bottom. Notice that the Pattern is simply a black and white, flat crosshatch. The Tiled graphic uses, by contrast, several shades of gray to achieve a smooth, 3D effect.

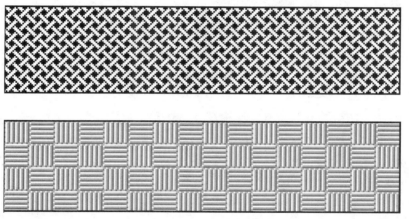

Figure 6-22: *Above, the rough black and white* pattern; *below, the smooth, more realistic* tiled *texture.*

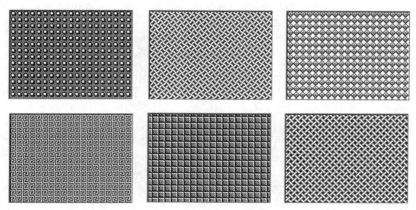

Figure 6-23: *Some of the more attractive patterns, clockwise from top left: Buttons, Cargo Net, Cobblestones, Thatches, Stone and Key.*

Screen Saver

Question: Why would you want to "save" your screen, your computer monitor? And from what? What's the danger?

Answer: Not much.

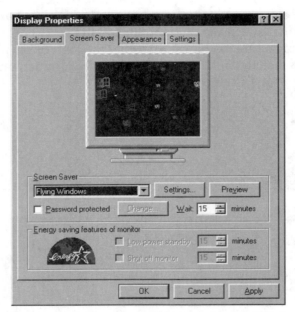

Figure 6-24: *The second tabbed panel in the Display Properties dialog box is called Screen Saver.*

In theory, if a static unchanging image is displayed on a computer monitor for hours and hours (like two days), the phosphors burn in, which is supposed to be like leaving a hot iron sitting too long on a shirt. You are supposed to get a ghostly image of the burn; whatever was on the screen is supposed to show up from then on, as a kind of faint image.

TV screens are lit from behind, by guided beams of electrons that strike against a coating of phosphorus that's painted on the inside of the glass. The phosphorus lights up. Unremitting bombardment of the beams against the exact same locations on the phosphorus is supposed to damage the phosphorus. The story goes that if you leave a word processor document sitting there overnight, you might come back the next morning and find that you can see faint outlines of the text no matter what you're really looking at.

Even after you shut down the word processor and look at your desktop wallpaper or a new fax or something, there they are, the characters of your overnight burn-in showing faintly in front of what you're supposed to see. Like rain specks on a window, you can't quite ignore them.

Fear of Burn-in

Fear of this screen burn-in phenomenon, however, is perhaps rather like the fear that if you don't cook bacon completely, you could get trichinosis. Nobody has ever known anyone to actually come down with trichinosis. Have you? What are the symptoms? Is it fatal?

Likewise, nobody has actually seen a burned-in computer screen, at least on modern color monitors (burn-in was certainly a problem with old monochrome monitors, and it can happen when displaying static graphics on an ordinary television screen). Today's color computer monitors are designed to prevent burn-in, but none of us wants to be the first to have a dreaded condition. Therefore, many people use screen savers. Besides, they can look nice.

Another reason to use screen savers is security. When you leave your desk, you may not want just anyone to be able to use your computer or examine your work in progress. Screen savers can be password-protected, so the screen saver can't be turned off without typing in a special code. Although this capability isn't bulletproof security (we'll show you how to defeat a password later in this chapter), it does provide a measure of privacy. And, of course, a truly determined intruder could turn off, then back on, the power to gain access to your secrets.

Windows 95 allows you to determine how many minutes of inactivity must pass before the screen saver kicks in. (Inactivity means you haven't pressed any keys or moved the mouse.) Next to the Wait option, you can type in (or hold down the up/down "spin" buttons by pressing the left mouse button) any delay from 1 to 60 minutes. In the Show drop-down menu (see Figure 6-25), you'll find six built-in styles of screen savers: Curves and Colors, Flying Through Space, Flying Windows, Mystify Your Mind, Scrolling Marquee and BlankScreen. For the truly brave, there's also the None option (you've been warned!).

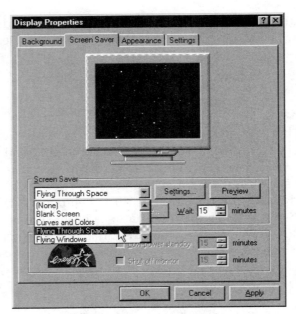

Figure 6-25: *You have six choices of screen savers, but most of them have many settings.*

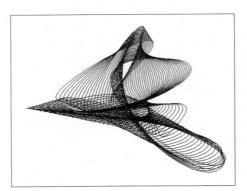

Figure 6-26: *The Curves and Colors screen saver.*

Figure 6-27: *The Flying Windows screen saver.*

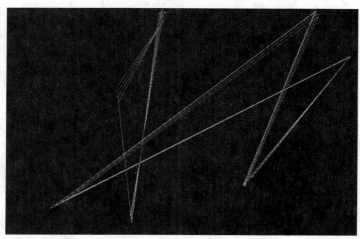

Figure 6-28: *The Scrolling Marquee screen saver.*

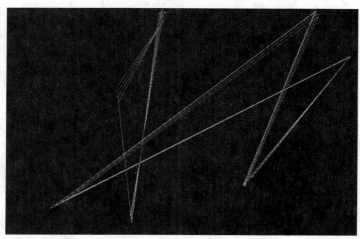

Figure 6-29: *The Mystify Your Mind screen saver.*

Figure 6-30: *The Flying Through Space screen saver.*

 TIP If you see only three screen savers listed in the Show menu when you right-click on the desktop, you probably chose the Typical option when first installing Windows 95. To load the additional screen savers, select Start | Settings | Control Panel. Double-click on Add/Remove Programs and then click on the Windows Setup tab. Click on Accessories and then click the Details button. Click on the Screen Savers option in the list; it will likely be gray, but checked, indicating that some screen savers have been installed. Click until the check box is white, but checked. Then click the OK button, and click the second OK button as well.

Variety Wallpaper

Of the various Windows 95 screen savers, the Curves and Colors screen saver and the Mystify Your Mind screen saver are quite similar—Bezier curves and polygons that range around the screen. Curves, though, erases the contents of the screen as it swirls around; Mystify works against a black background. Click on the Settings button to choose colors, number of polygons, the speed of the animation and other options. Flying Windows is similar to Flying Through Space, but instead of making you feel like you're warping through the galactic starfield, Flying Windows plunges you through a field of Windows logos. In both cases, you can select the speed as well as the number of stars/logos between 10 and 200. Try slowing down the Warp Speed, and the animation will likely seem more smooth, more realistic.

Scrolling Marquee allows you to type in a message of your choice that will scroll across the screen, centered, or at random locations. You can select the attributes of the font (its size, the typeface, the colors, italics or boldface) as well as the speed. Again, a slower speed usually looks smoother on all but the most powerful computers.

Password Protection

Each of the screen savers allows you to set a password. (It need not be the same as the logon password, if you use one, though, you could employ the same password if you wish.) If you work in a crowded office, doubtless there is a sinister co-worker or two, perhaps a lurker, a weasel or even a mountebank—someone who would like to see what you're working on. You innocently go to lunch and this person slips over to your desk. A casual bump against the desk is usually all it takes to jar the mouse and clear the screen saver.

When you select a password, you are safe from this kind of spying. Unless the lurker has guessed your password, he or she won't be able to turn off the screen saver. **Warning:** If you forget this password, you're in the same fix as the office spy. Every time the screen saver kicks in, you'll have to reboot (turn off, then back on, the power switch on your computer) to regain control.

If you've forgotten your screen saver password, here's how to delete the password. Click on Start and then select Run. Type **REGEDIT** to access the utility program that permits you to adjust Windows 95's registry, the file where most important information is kept about the state of your machine.

Once Regedit appears, select Edit | Find. Then type **Password**. Eventually Regedit will display a tree path of HKEY_CURRENT_USER, Control Panel, Desktop. Here you'll see an item called ScreenSaveUsePassword, and it will contain the following data:

0x00000001 (1)

which is a complicated computer way of saying 1, or true.

You want to change it to zero (telling Windows that you want this setting to be false).

Right-click on ScreenSaveUsePassword and select Modify. Type **0** (the digit), replacing the 1. Then click on the X button at the top right of the Regedit window to close Regedit. Things will be fine now; you have no password for your screen saver any more. (Don't show this book to any untrustworthy weasels or mountebanks in your vicinity.)

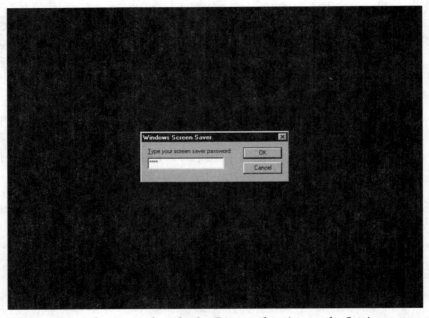

Figure 6-31: *When you select the Set Password option on the Settings page, screen savers will refuse to turn off until the correct word is typed in.*

Other Screen Savers

Files with the .SCR extension in your Windows directory are screen savers. Extensions like .SCR won't be displayed unless you specifically request them. To see extensions, click on the View menu in any folder. Then click on Options and click on the View tab. Click on the Don't display MS-DOS file extensions for files that are properly registered option. This way, you can see the full filename of all the documents.

 You can run screen savers directly from a folder just by double-clicking on their filenames.

In addition to the six savers that come with Windows 95, you can find others in the usual places—CompuServe, America Online, bulletin boards and computer stores. The most popular commercial screen saver collection, After Dark, has some gorgeous animations. Microsoft's Windows NT includes some nice ones, too, like Pipes, shown in Figure 6-32.

Figure 6-32: *You can find other sources of screen savers; this handsome one, Pipes, comes from Windows NT.*

Just as there are 16-bit (Windows 3.x) and 32-bit (Windows 95) programs, there's a distinction between old style 16-bit Windows 3.x screen savers and new 32-bit Windows 95 screen savers. What's the difference? As we discussed in Chapter 3, 16-bit programs hamper the ability of Windows 95 to preemptively multitask. Essentially, a 32-bit screen saver allows all your programs to continue running smoothly "in the background" even when obscured by a screen saver, a real boon if your computer is busy working for you—downloading a file, for example. But if you have a favorite old-style screen saver, don't let this keep you from enjoying it; just keep this limitation in mind if you wonder why your computer doesn't keep up with background tasks quite as well.

Energy saving

The final two options on the Screen Saver window are called Energy Saving Features of Monitor. Some of the newer computer monitors are capable of interacting with the computer by accepting orders to go into low power "standby" mode, or even shut themselves off completely. You can use these two option buttons to have such a monitor switch itself into lower power or shutoff, after an inactivity delay (no keyboard or mouse activity) that you specify.

If you still want to see your screen saver, stagger your timings. For example, have the screen saver appear after 4 minutes of inactivity, then allow the screen to go to standby mode after 10 minutes and then shut off after 15 minutes.

At the time of this writing, few people have monitors that can actually function this way. Your video card may support this mode, however, allowing the monitor to shut down and consume less electricity. The monitor may blank but not shut down if it's not also Energy Star compliant.

If you click on these options, however, and your monitor can't accept such orders, no harm done; nothing will happen. If these options are dimmed (grayed out), you need to enable Energy Star compliance in the Settings section, which we'll discuss later in this chapter.

Appearance

To make the Display Properties window appear on your screen, right-click anywhere on the desktop (not on an open folder or icon). Then click on the Appearance tab (see Figure 6-33). On this page, you can personalize the colors, typefaces and even some of the shapes of common items like menus, title bars, dialog boxes and background colors for the desktop and open documents.

Figure 6-33: *On the Appearance tab, you adjust color, typeface and some shapes.*

For clarity when printing screen shots and other figures in this book, we've been extremely conservative in choosing the Appearance settings—largely white backgrounds, a little gray and simple black text. But you don't have to make monochromatic choices for your daily Windows 95 look. Experiment. You might like blazing colors or muted tones. You might like large fonts; they are easier to read, but you sacrifice screen space. You can fit less on a screen when windows, menu bars or title bars are larger (to hold the larger fonts).

Decide, first of all, if you like any of the color schemes that Windows 95 provides. Click on the Schemes drop-down list, as shown in Figure 6-34.

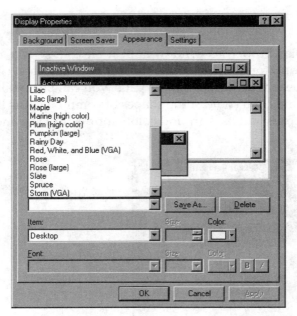

Figure 6-34: *You can choose from one of these built-in color/size desktop layouts or create your own.*

Some of the color schemes might seem garish (but they're less garish than a few that were included with Windows 3.1). In any case, you can try them out by looking at the effect after clicking on one of the schemes and seeing what happens in the sample window.

Some of the options (Rose and Lavender, for example) are designed for computers that can display 256 colors or more. Others (Marine and Plum) look best on machines capable of displaying over 65,000 colors (high color). We'll get to color and resolution issues in the following sections, where we discuss the Settings properties. However, for now, note that all these schemes are optimized for 256 colors or more, and won't look good on 16-color displays. They'll look dotty, like badly printed cartoons.

Custom Color Schemes

Look at the Default Large and Default Extra Large options in the Display Properties for Display window. They improve readability, at the expense of screen space. You might want to try different sizes and see which one is the best trade-off between readability and screen real estate.

Creating a custom scheme is easy. Here's how.

Hands-On: Creating a Custom Color Screen

1. Right-click on your desktop (anywhere on your screen you don't have any icons or folders). From the menu that appears, select Properties. In the Display Properties window are four "tabbed" pages. Click on the Appearance tab.
2. Select any layout in the Scheme drop-down list.
3. Click on any object within the sample window, and you'll see the options at the bottom of the Appearances page change to reflect the choices you can make and the current setting for those choices. For instance, click on Active Window in the sample screen. The Item text box should switch to Active Caption. This means that you can now adjust the active caption's background color, font color, font size, italics, boldface and item size (in this case, the item size is the thickness of the bar across the top of all windows). See Figure 6-35.

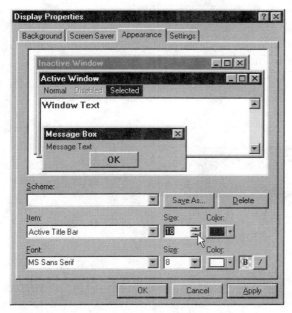

Figure 6-35: *Clicking on Active Window reveals the colors and font attributes and thickness of all your windows.*

Perhaps the most interesting option on the Appearance page is the Item Size (the Size input box next to the Item box). It can range from 15 to 100. As an experiment, try holding down your left mouse button while your mouse pointer is on the Up arrow next to the Size box. Watch as the sample seriously distorts itself as you approach 100, the maximum possible size.

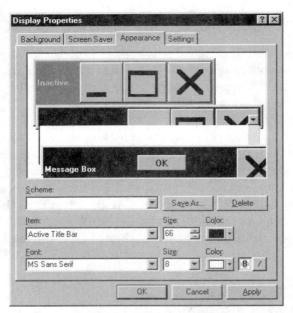

Figure 6-36: *The Size option can go as high as 100. Do that and you'll engorge the title bar on all your folders and windows (they all have title bars).*

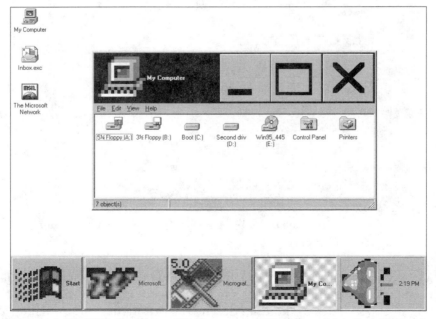

Figure 6-37: *With the Active Window set to 100, things get rather distorted, grainy and out of proportion.*

The desktop in Figure 6-37 might look good on a screen the size of a card table, but on your computer it's too much of a good thing. What's important, though, is that you can manipulate the look of Windows 95 in many ways. This freedom to go past good sense into distortion is valuable—you get to do what you think looks right, not constrained by limits placed on you at central programming headquarters (Microsoft). After all, the line where readability crosses into giantism is a different line on different screens and for different people.

Changing fonts

When it comes to changing your desktop, you know what you need and what you like. Now you can adjust things just the way you want them. Huge font sizes and giant title bars are also useful for people who have vision problems.

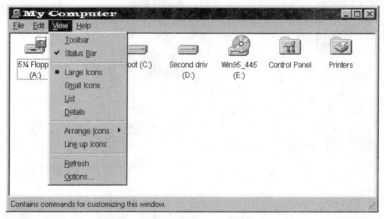

Figure 6-38: *Variety typefaces can be used freely anywhere. Here we've changed all the defaults from the ubiquitous sans serif faces to Wide Latin and Arial Narrow.*

Here's how to change the fonts on your desktop (if you're still in the sample window from the preceding "Hands-On" section):

1. Click on other elements in the sample window and change the colors, font sizes or font names.
2. When you've created a look you like, you can save it for the future. Click on the Save As button; then type in a name for your new look. From now on, it will be there on the disk whenever you feel like using it.

Creating colors

You aren't limited to the colors that Windows 95 shows as defaults. When you click on the Color (background color) or Font Color buttons, a palette of 20 colors is displayed. If you like one of them, click on it, and the change will be displayed in the sample window. You also can design your own colors if you wish. When the 20-color palette appears, click on the Other button. You'll see a new palette with 48 selected colors. Below that is space for you to create 16 of your own "custom colors."

Now click on the Define Custom Colors button, and you'll see the full color palette window shown in Figure 6-39.

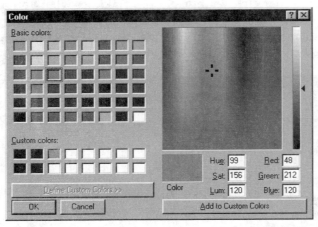

Figure 6-39: *Here you can select any of 16.8 million possible colors.*

Your video card might not be able to display as many colors as shown in this window, but it will do its best to approximate whatever you select (using a "checkboarding" method called *dithering*). You can move the crosshair pointer to find a color, or you can type in numbers. You don't need to worry about the meanings of the various color definition terms (you'll know a nice color when you see it displayed), but if you're curious:

- *Hue* is what most people think of when they think of "color." Green is one hue, blue-green is another hue, turquoise and cyan are other hues.
- *Saturation* is the intensity of a particular hue. The turquoise hue could range between a very grayish (light saturation) to an almost neon, highly intense turquoise (fully saturated) color. Another way to think of the saturation spectrum is that it represents a spread between muddy and vibrant. A turquoise ring, for instance, might be entirely of a turquoise hue but vary considerably in saturation.

■ *Luminance* is literally the amount of light. At one end, with low luminance, a hue will appear black. With full luminance, the hue will appear white. In between these two extremes is what most people think of as a range between a light pastel shade and a dark shade of a particular hue.

If you find a color you like, click on the Add to custom colors button. Then whichever custom color is selected (surrounded by a dark frame) when you click on the OK button will appear as the 21st entry in the drop-down color box on the main Appearance page. It will also be applied to whatever window element is selected in the sample window.

Video Settings

The quality of the images and text that you see in Windows 95 depends, in great part, on the video card that you have installed in your computer. To a lesser extent, the monitor also plays a part. We'll refer to this combination of card/monitor as your *video system*.

Most contemporary desktop monitors range between 14 and 21 inches, with 15 inches by far the most popular size. When you get a larger monitor, it doesn't mean that everything on your screen has to become larger—bigger folders, bigger icons and so forth. Unlike large-screen TV (which does simply make Dan Rather's face larger), computer displays are highly configurable.

When you first plug in a new, bigger monitor, you indeed will simply see larger objects. Your icons and folders will be larger. However, you'll probably want to reduce them to their previous size by switching the Desktop Area, from your previous 640x480 to 800x600, or from 800x600 to 1024x768. This way, you'll still be able to see everything as clearly, but now you'll have more desktop space to open more folders or display more windows than before.

As always, you should fiddle with the adjustments to get the best balance between readability and extra screen space. For the Desktop area, your options are 640x480, 800x600 and 1024x768. If you select a size that's beyond the capabilities of your video card, Windows will simply refuse to permit that setting. Also remember that you can adjust the size of the windows, title bars and other elements on the Appearance page of the Display Properties window, as discussed in previous sections.

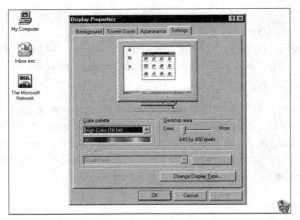

Figure 6-40: *At 640x480, the Display Properties pretty much fills the screen.*

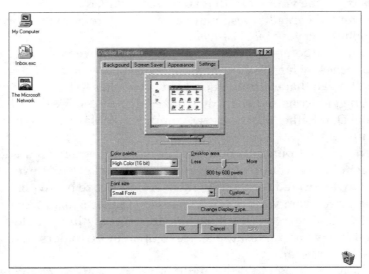

Figure 6-41: *At 800x600, you can fit more things on your new, larger desktop.*

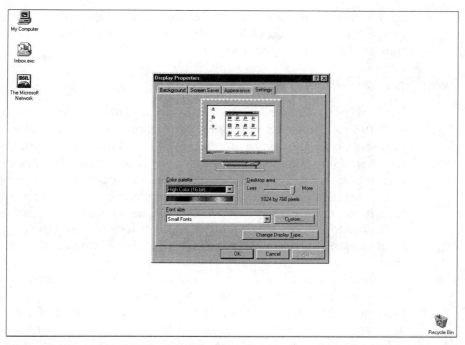

Figure 6-42: *At 1024x768, a huge amount of extra space is available for you to open notepads, additional folders or whatever you might want. Some video cards can go as high as 1280x1024.*

Color Palette Interaction

Three things interact with the Desktop area setting to determine how much space you have vs. text readability: the Color Palette setting, the size you set the fonts and the physical size of your computer monitor. If Windows 95 refuses to allow you to switch to a particular size (such as 800x600), try reducing the Color Palette setting from, say, High Color to 256 color. (Sometimes you have to choose between higher resolution, or more colors.) Quite often, a smaller color palette will permit you to enjoy a larger desktop. For example, with a megabyte of video RAM, you can either display 640x480 with over 16.8 million colors, 800x600 with 65,535 colors, 1024x768 with 256 colors or 1280x1024 with 16 colors, assuming your video card has all these capabilities in the first place. If you don't see 1280x1024 listed, your card can't handle that high a resolution.

For most work, 256 colors are plenty for a clean, clear display of text and graphics, and this setting is optimal for multimedia, games and video playback at the present time. (In the future, multimedia will gain size and resolution, but now computer video is best at 256 colors. A few video cards, though, play back video best with high color.)

Font Size

If you increase the Font size setting, you are asking Windows to enlarge such things as the captions under your icons, the titles in folder and program title bars, the text in menus and so on. Windows also makes extra room for a larger font size by automatically increasing the size of title bars, menus and so on. The result is that, when you open a folder or perform some other action, objects are larger; they take up more screen space. Therefore, if you choose a large font size (to make the text more readable on a too-high Desktop area setting), you've more or less defeated the purpose of that high Desktop area setting (which is to provide you with more desktop space).

You can make a general change to the font size on the Settings page (you can choose either large or small fonts). Notice that changing from Large Fonts to Small Fonts has roughly the same relative effect of increasing available screen space as does changing from 640x480 (VGA, for Video Graphics Adapter) up to 800x600 (SVGA, for Super Video Graphics Adapter). (However, the higher resolution of 800x600 can lend a more finely detailed appearance to text characters that some people find easier on the eyes.)

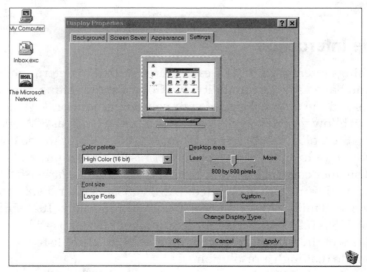

Figure 6-43: *When you select Large Fonts, your available screen space is reduced (because windows, icons and every other object grows larger to accommodate the larger type).*

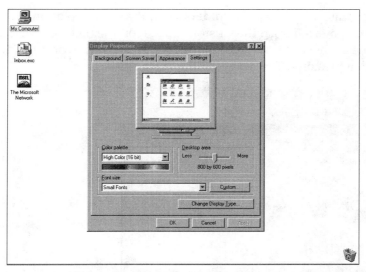

Figure 6-44: *Using Small Fonts considerably increases screen space (compare to Figure 6-43).*

You can make finer changes to font size on the Appearance page, as shown in Figure 6-45.

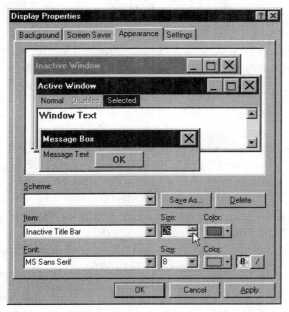

Figure 6-45: *If you want to make specific elements of your windows larger or smaller, click on the element and then change the font size.*

To change all the objects (folders, menus and so on) at once by a particular percentage, click on the Custom button on the Settings page. Here you'll find one of those subtle, smooth touches that makes working with Windows 95 such a pleasure. Try dragging the ruler.

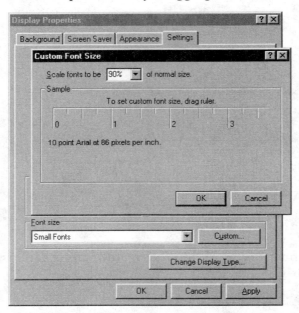

Figure 6-46: *Clicking on the Custom option on the Settings page of the Display Properties window (right-click on your Windows 95 desktop) allows you to adjust the overall size of Windows 95 objects by adjusting the font size.*

Monitor Size

The third factor that interacts with your setting for Desktop area determines how readable your screen will be at high settings. This factor is the size of your monitor. For example, if you want a comfortably readable yet spacious 1024x768 setting, a 17-inch monitor is likely to be necessary. On a 15-inch monitor, you'll have to enlarge your Font Size settings so much (in the Appearance page of the Display Properties window) that your folders and other windows will grow so large that you will have defeated the purpose of the extra space provided by going to the 1024x768 setting.

No extra burden is put on a video card at higher resolutions, any more than a TV has to work harder displaying the pyrotechnics in *Star Wars* than it does while showing the bucolic tranquillity of *Mary Poppins*. And if your monitor manages to display 1024x768 resolution without flickering (a 15" monitor is recommended), you're likely better off using this high resolution so you'll get more finely formed text characters, even if you don't opt to increase your desktop space because you chose Large Fonts. As always, try various settings—experiment. Then make up your own mind.

 If you actually take a ruler and measure a 17" monitor, the display will turn out to be around 11 x 8 inches. Following in a long tradition of TV-screen size measurement mendacity (TV screens are measured diagonally), computer monitor size descriptions are even further from the truth. A 17" monitor, even when measured diagonally, will be just over 15" in fact. The actual tube is measured, not the illuminated part that you can see and use. The argument is that the tube is rounded at the edges, so, to keep things from being distorted, the actual, usable space is less than the "full surface" of the tube. So the measurement is not limited to the usable surface. Don't expect to be able to see an 8 x 11-inch letter full size on a monitor described as measuring anything less than 21".

Color Palette

Resolution—the ability to see detail (and, therefore, a realistic picture)—depends on how many colors your monitor can display. True photographic-quality realism requires many thousands of colors. The best possible color available on most personal computer monitors permits over 16.8 million simultaneous colors. (Technically there are two factors: *actual* resolution—which can be measured using gray scales—and the *color depth* that we're dealing with here.)

Your Display

The 16-color displays have two problems. Obviously, we can see many more than 16 colors (humans are sensitive to millions of different hues). So 16-color rendering makes things look flat, unrealistic, grainy and cartoon-like. The second problem is that, paradoxically, 16-color rendition can slow down the repainting of your screen. To test the speed, try switching between 16 color and 256 color. In both modes, load a large text file into a word processor and hold down the Down arrow key to scroll down through the document. Notice that in 16-color mode you're likely to see the lines ripple and stutter as Windows 95 struggles to redraw the screen. In 256-color mode (or better), the scrolling should be smoother and more rapid.

Click on the Settings tab in the Display Properties window and look at the Color palette description. If you're using a 16-color display, click on the Color palette list box to see if any other options are available. If you can, you should increase your colors to at least 256.

Note that speed and repainting efficiency depends on the video card and the driver that you're using. You might have an odd setup and therefore find that your video is faster and smoother with 16 colors instead of 256 colors, especially when repainting large areas. If so, you need a new video card, since almost all Windows software now runs best with at least 256 colors. Again, experiment and make your decisions based on what you see.

Windows 95 is designed to display highly realistic graphics—even high-resolution photos. In fact, computer monitors can display more stable, more detailed and more colorful pictures than can a regular TV set. (Ordinary TV is capable of only about half the resolution of a computer monitor set to 1024x768. Ordinary TV is also subject to various kinds of noise and interference.)

If you're buying a monitor, consider its *dot pitch*. The smaller the dots, the more resolution your monitor will be capable of. Cheap VGA monitors have a dot pitch of .59. Average 640x480 displays expect .39. Quality SVGA uses .28 dot pitch or better. Try to get a monitor with .28 or lower. That way, when it's time to upgrade, it costs less to buy a new video card to improve your video quality than to replace your monitor, one of the most expensive components in your computer system.

Typical Resolutions

All personal computer monitors can currently display over 16.8 million colors (since they are analog monitors, they can theoretically display an infinite number of colors). This level of resolution (definition and color capability) is usually called 24-bit color or True Color and is, indeed, like looking at a glossy photograph or a magazine ad—you can see blades of grass and individual eyelashes. However, note that even though your monitor may be capable of True Color (all modern monitors are), you won't get 16.8 million colors unless your video card also supports True Color.

Somewhat less breathtaking and somewhat more common are screens capable of 65,000 or 32,000 colors (sometimes called High Color). If your monitor/graphics card combination is capable of this resolution, you should select it if you want excellent graphics. The most common resolution today is 256 color, and it does a creditable job of displaying realistic looking graphics. Here's the bottom line: If you're using 16 colors and your graphics card can go higher, choose the higher setting. (Click on the Settings tab in the Display Properties window.) And if you're using 256 colors, try selecting a higher number of colors; with quality graphics, the difference in clarity, detail and realism will be quite visible.

Dithering

What does Windows 95 do when a picture contains a color that's not possible to display on your video system? It dithers. This is the computer's attempt to improve things, but it's not too much of an improvement. The biggest problems with limited color range (16 or 256 colors) are most visible in gradually shaded regions, called *gradients*, such as the gradual changes between white and black that you might see on a bowling ball where the black of the ball gradually changes to the white of a light reflected on it. Let's see how dithering works.

With too few colors to accurately represent smooth color transitions, gradients break apart into zones that look like the marks left by ocean waves on sand. If the computer has only 16 shades, it must make abrupt transitions to represent shading, as in Figure 6-47.

Figure 6-47: *With only 16 colors, the transitions between the shades here are few and abrupt. This graphic doesn't look like a sphere—it looks like a bull's-eye.*

Figure 6-48: *This sphere is viewed at 256 colors, still too few to look like a realistic bowling ball. It still has that characteristic layered look.*

Figure 6-49: *Dithering improves the 256-color sphere, adding patterned shading to create a kind of gradient. It's not realistic, but it's closer to the original than the undithered version shown in Figure 6-48.*

The dithering shown in Figure 6-49 is a clearly a compromise. However, it's better than no dithering (see the same 256-color sphere undithered in Figure 6-48). Dithering imposes a pattern: checkers, lines, dots, brain-surface-like squiggles—there are various dithering schemes. Figure 6-49 uses darker and lighter dots to simulate the color that the computer cannot actually display. No dithering pattern really looks that good up close, but if you're far enough away or the dithered areas are small enough, dithering is certainly better than nothing.

Newspaper photographs and comic books use low-resolution images. If you really look at them closely, you can usually see the dots and patterns in the image. Imagine that you had the job of creating a particular shade of gray. You have only 16 shades, and the one you have to display isn't among them on your palette. One way to approximate it would be to paint a light background but darken it with dots, lines or some other pattern. The light background would then look darker, kind of an average of the background and how many dots or whatever you put onto it. That's dithering. Sometimes it's light patterns on a darker background; sometimes it's dark patterns on a light background—whatever compromise the computer can come up with that does the best job.

What if you don't have violet?

Also suppose you wanted to display violet but had only red and blue to work with. The solution would be to arrange a checkerboard pattern of red and blue dots; if the dots are small enough, they appear as a violet shade. Indeed, all the color you see in magazines is made up of only four shades of color. All the colors on your computer screen are formed by the electronic dithering of only three shades: red, green and blue.

A variation of dithering is called *halftoning*. Instead of varying just the density of the dot pattern, halftoning also uses various sizes of dots (tiny circles). Look closely at the smoothly shaded pictures in this book. Only black ink is used, on white paper, but halftoning creates the illusion of shades of gray.

Figure 6-50: *The solution: If you can, get a video card capable of High Color (65,000 colors) or True Color (shown here, 16.8 million colors). This graphic looks exactly like a sphere onscreen because the gradient is lifelike.*

A pure gradient, like the sphere shown in Figures 6-47 through 6-50, most quickly reveals weak resolution. But you can still see the effect of low resolution, degraded detail, in ordinary photographs and other graphic images.

Figure 6-51: *At 16-color resolution, this photo lacks contrast, looks muddy, hazy, smudged, lacking sufficient detail and contrast, smeared.*

Figure 6-52: *With 256-color resolution, you get improved contrast and clarity, but you still see visible artifacts and false textures. The sky (a gradient) is particularly badly rendered here; it looks like a skin condition.*

Figure 6-53: *Here, at full 24-bit color (16.8 million colors), areas that should be smooth are smooth. See the reflecting glass windows and the sky, see the detail in the church spire.*

When you look closely at dithering, you can see the trade-offs the computer makes when trying to create shades it cannot actually display. Magnifying the church steeple, you can see exactly how dithering works. The 16-color rendition of the sky, in Figure 6-54, displays hardly any of the transition between shades that is actually in the original (compare to Figure 6-53). In Figure 6-55, you can see a visible transition from dark to light as you look at the sky from the top to the bottom, but the transition is rough and coarse. And detail in the spire is lost in a snowstorm of blotches and spots.

Figure 6-54: *This close-up shows how dithering attempts to create a gradient in the sky, using only two shades of gray.*

Figure 6-55: *Here, in a 256-color image, the sky gradient is rendered somewhat more faithfully, but there is still considerable false texture.*

Figure 6-56: *Finally, in True Color (16.8 million potential colors), you see all the detail and no compromising dithered textures.*

Change Display Type

Another option on the Settings page of the Display Properties window is Change Display Type. (To see it, right-click on the desktop, then select Properties, click on the Settings tab in the Display Properties window and click on the Change Display Type button. The dialog box shown in Figure 6-57 then appears.)

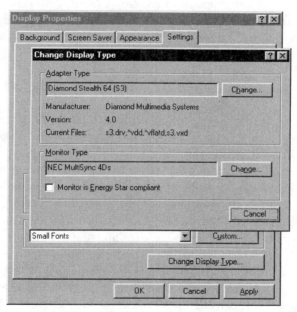

Figure 6-57: *In the Change Display Type dialog box, you tell Windows that you've changed monitors or video cards.*

If you buy a new video card to improve the speed, resolution and color capabilities of your system, or you buy a new monitor, use the Change Display Type dialog box to let Windows 95 know about your new equipment. This way, you can use drivers that are optimized for your particular card and monitor. *Drivers* are software that's been written, nearly always by the manufacturer, to provide the optimum performance for their product. But unless Windows 95 knows of these drivers, it might use a more general-purpose driver or simply not work at all with your hardware. So if you buy new video equipment for your computer, you want to tell Windows 95 about it. (Alternatively, click on Start and then select Settings | Control Panel | Add New Hardware. When asked, permit Windows to "search for your new hardware.")

When you click on one of the Change buttons in the Change Display Type dialog box shown in Figure 6-57, Windows 95 will provide a list of compatible video card drivers or video monitors that it supports. You can select from this list, or, more likely, you'll want to click on the Have Disk button.

Accelerated Cards

Windows 95 supports most types of video cards using generic drivers. For "accelerated" video cards, the most common is the S3 driver, named for the company that manufactures the chip sets for the various video card vendors. (An accelerated card does some of the video work that is normally left up to the computer's CPU. The result is swifter screen redraws, rapid response when you move or resize things and quicker drawing of circles and rectangles.)

A generic driver can't take advantage of all the special features of your video card. For that, you'll need an enhanced driver developed by the video card vendor. So, if possible use only Windows 95 video drivers. In a pinch, you can usually install a Windows 3.1 video driver, but you can't take advantage of all Windows 95 features (such as colored or animated mouse pointers). Also, many Windows 3.1 drivers are just plain too buggy, causing mysterious errors in programs. Windows 95 introduces a universal video card driver architecture, into which vendors can then plug their mini drivers to support special proprietary features of their particular cards.

All video card and most monitor manufacturers include a floppy disk that has the latest, swiftest Windows 95 video drivers for your new equipment. If you select Have Disk, you can then install these prime drivers from the floppy disk that the manufacturer supplied.

If you want to enable the energy-saving features of some of the newer monitors, be sure to enable the Monitor is Energy Star compliant check box.

The latest drivers
Manufacturers continue to work on improving the efficiency and capabilities of their drivers. You might want to check on The Microsoft Network, CompuServe, America Online or some other telecommunications service, or a BBS that the manufacturer itself runs (see your manual for the phone number). Use the service's Search (or Find) option to locate your manufacturer's forum. This way, you can upload the latest drivers.

Full Window Drag

If you have bought the Microsoft Plus! add-ons for Windows 95, and if your computer is sufficiently powerful, you can select the Full Window Drag on the Settings page of the Display Properties window. (To see it, right-click on the desktop and then select Properties | Settings.) This option shows an entire window while you're dragging that window, rather than merely showing an outline. Figure 6-58 shows how the default "outline drag" looks. As you hold down the left mouse button and move the mouse (to move the picture), the only thing that moves is the gray frame. This feature shows you the location to which the picture will jump when you release the mouse button (dropping the image onto the desktop). However, it's not that realistic.

Figure 6-58: *Windows 95 defaults to this outlined dragging style.*

For realism, you want to actually see the full window move when you drag it—the picture or filenames or whatever contents it has should seem to move. It should seem as if you are sliding a photo across your real desk in the real world; a real photo doesn't change into a mere frame while in motion. But this full-motion video is tough for the computer. It requires tremendous (by current standards) video computing power. The reason? The computer must repaint the image smoothly and continuously as you move it across the screen. Repainting at that rate is beyond the powers of most personal computers; they skip most of the job and just show a small section of the image repainted, or they flicker and jitter so much that it looks like you're rupturing, rather than sliding, the window. So if your screen flickers and looks strange when you drag things, turn off the Full Window Drag option.

Note that Full Window Drag also changes the way Windows 95 displays window resizing. If you move the mouse pointer to one of the corners or edges of a window, you'll notice the pointer change into a double-arrow symbol. Now if you drag (holding down the left mouse button and sliding the mouse), you'll change the size or shape of the window itself. With Full Window Drag turned off, you'll just see that frame until you release the mouse button; with it turned on, you'll see the computer attempt to display the continually changing interior contents of the window. Unless you are lucky enough to have one of the most powerful personal computers currently available, this effect will likely look spasmodic and ugly.

Font Smoothing

For years, Windows users have been annoyed by the jagged edges of characters in headlines or other large text. And the solutions offered (variously called *anti-aliasing* or *font smoothing*) were perhaps the most peculiar, no, let's be honest, perverse utilities in all of Windows. They blurred the edges of the characters you see onscreen when looking at text. Why would you want to blur the letters? Why sacrifice the high-contrast, sharp edges of letters in favor of smeared, washed-out gray halos around the letters in your text?

Anti-aliasing does remove the *jaggies* (a.k.a. *stairstep*) effect that you notice when you're working with huge letters. At 20 times the size of normal text (200 vs. 10 point), you can see in Figure 6-59 that the edges aren't as ragged with anti-aliasing turned on. But who works with massive letters like this most of the time? Unless you are the headline-writer for a newsletter or for some other reason must work mostly with immense letters, you probably leave anti-aliasing turned off. The effects that it has on normal-sized text are often deleterious. However, the Microsoft Plus! utilities include an intelligent, highly effective font smoothing option. For more on this feature, see Chapter 12.

Another exception: if you're fortunate enough to have a video system capable of High Color or True Color at 1024x768, the "feathering" of ordinary text characters can, to some eyes, look quite subtle and attractive, and create the illusion of much higher resolution.

Figure 6-59: *Anti-aliasing made large letters look better onscreen, but it degraded normal-sized text.*

The stairstep effect

The stairstep effect that makes some characters look ragged is technically called *aliasing*. It is a direct result of digital displays. When digitized, visual information becomes essentially a mosaic, a grid of "tiles" called *pixels* (for *picture elements*). These pixels are quite small and there are many of them on the video monitor, so you'll often be unaware of the underlying mosaic discontinuities in what you see. It's not a large mosaic like you see in restaurants and bathrooms—where you can see each tile, and the picture looks lik it was painted onto a checkerboard. Instead, computer displays have so many tiny tiles that things usually look blended and smooth.

But there is one problem with aliasing: diagonal lines. There's no difficulty displaying horizontal or vertical lines accurately, because these kinds of lines follow the pattern of the underlying pixel grid. But diagonal lines go against the grain, and the result is a rough, ripped look, like a serrated knife or, indeed, stairs.

Figure 6-60: *Horizontal and vertical lines look fine when displayed on a computer screen. But diagonal lines cause problems. The letter X and most italics are mostly drawn with diagonal lines.*

Bigger is worse

The larger the characters, the more visible and annoying the ragged diagonal lines. Usually, for most text that you'll be reading in your word processor and elsewhere, stair-stepping isn't a problem. The text is so small that your eye blends any frayed edges. Most people view text on their computer at sizes only slightly larger than the text found in books. In books, text is usually set at 9 to 11 points, and most people set their Font size option to between 11 and 13 points in their word processors. (*Points* are a traditional typesetter's way of measuring character size. There are 72 points per inch.)

In any case, it's generally only with large characters like those in headlines that you're likely to notice frazzled, shredded diagonal lines in your text (or in some small typefaces such as Script, which imitates handwriting and is slanted). Most of us usually don't even work with headlines at all; we read or write business letters and other documents at a normal text size. If you select the traditional Windows anti-aliasing features (available from various vendors and within various applications), your ordinary text can look bad. Headlines will look smoother, but regular text—the kind you read most of the time—can appear bleached out in places like a bad photocopy.

Fortunately, you can avoid this problem using the Plus! anti-aliasing method described in the following Tech Tip.

Below 8 pixels per em, Windows 95's Plus! turns on anti-aliasing but turns off hinting. The idea is that a non-gridfitted, grayscale font is actually more legible than a gridfitted one. This is especially useful for the *greeking* of text for print previews and such; you can actually read some of the extremely small sentences this way since people tend to recognize word shapes more than individual characters in a word.

Between 8 and 17 pixels per em, Plus! turns off anti-aliasing but turns on hinting. Here the idea is that when you tend to have glyphs with a single pixel that defines the stem, you wind up with diagonal strokes that tend to fade out if you turn on anti-aliasing. For example, the lowercase letters z, x, m or n in certain fonts have their vertical or horizontal strokes fully black, but their diagonals totally gray. You can get a queasy feeling as you read text this way, since the letters tend to fade in and out as you read them.

Above 17 pixels per em, Plus! always turns on both hinting and anti-aliasing. Here the strokes are generally at least two pixels wide, so none of the fuzziness that pervades the lower sizes comes through.

These cutoff points based on character size are for normal, non-bold, non-italic fonts. Italics are always anti-aliased since, by definition, every stroke is almost always a diagonal. Bold turns on anti-aliasing at much smaller sizes since bold characters are almost always at least two pixels wide in their strokes. Every TrueType font can individually control these values with the addition of a *gasp* table that Plus! will obey. Otherwise, default values that are stored in the registry are used.

Of course, all the above information is valid only for Roman text. Kanji and other Far Eastern fonts have an entirely different set of rules for dealing with this issue.

Ordinary anti-aliasing smudges the diagonals, resulting in thicker, haloed gray lines instead of the normal, thinner black lines. Figure 6-61 shows up close the smearing and lightening that font smoothing applies to normal-sized (11 point) text:

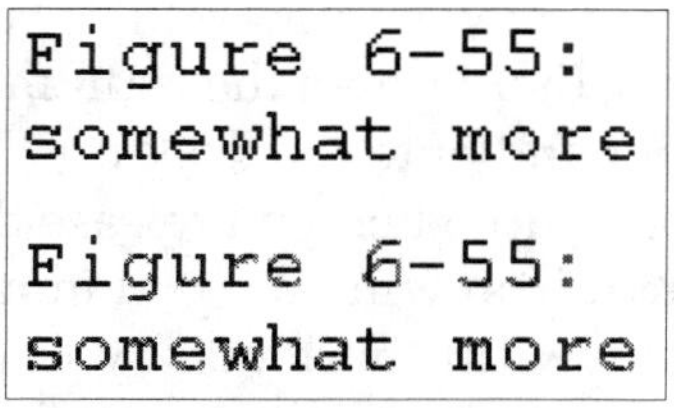

```
Figure 6-55:
somewhat more

Figure 6-55:
somewhat more
```

Figure 6-61: *A magnified view: The top two lines are normal; the bottom two lines have been smudged with Font Smoothing.*

Organizing Your Desktop

How clean or cluttered you leave your desktop is your decision—whatever you're comfortable with. Do you want dozens of icons all over the screen, so you can quickly click on one of them to start your modem, draw a picture or run your word processor? Do you want to imitate Windows 3.1's Program manager by creating a special folder for your favorite programs and have that folder the only thing visible onscreen? Do you want to actually use Program Manager? (If so, click on Start and then select Run. Type **Progman** and click on the OK button.) Or do you want nothing onscreen?

The issue is *launching*—making it as easy as possible to get a document in front of you ready to be worked with. When you launch a program or a document by double-clicking on its title or icon, you're then ready to get down to the job at hand. With programs you frequently use or documents you're currently working on, you want them to be as conveniently located as possible. You don't want to have to open the My Computer window, and then a series of subfolders just to find that document or program. Instead, you can leave these frequently needed icons directly visible on your desktop, or immediately available to you via the pop-up menu above the Start button.

Many Windows 3.x users purchased alternative desktops—more flexible systems that overlaid and hid the ordinary Windows desktop. Norton Symantec has announced that they won't release a Norton Desktop for Windows 95, and a version of the popular Hewlett-Packard Dashboard probably won't be made available either. Most everyone has acknowledged that the Windows 95 desktop is a mature and successful design. It would benefit little from outside, third-party enhancement.

The most obvious way to provide desktop icons is to create Windows 95 Shortcuts. One way to do this is to open My Computer and then other folders until you find the document or program you know you're going to want to open frequently. Then just right-drag (hold down the right mouse button while dragging the icon out of its folder and onto the desktop). Then choose Create Shortcut from the menu that pops up when you release the mouse.

Double-clicking on this new Shortcut icon will take you immediately to where you want to be. Fill your desktop with shortcuts if you want to; when you no longer need one, click on it to highlight it and then press the Del key to delete it. Remember, creating or deleting a shortcut has no effect on the file or program on your disk. Only the shortcut is deleted, not the thing it points to.

Another way to launch documents or programs is to add them to the Start button's menu. Just drag (hold down the left mouse button as you move the mouse) a shortcut onto the Start button. A copy of the icon and title of that document or program will appear in the pop-up menu above the Start button whenever you click on Start.

Moving On

In the next chapter, we'll look at the Control Panel, the place where you add new peripherals, change drivers (to make your hardware run better), adjust keyboard and mouse speed and many other things. It's like the engine room of Windows 95. You should go there if you don't like the way something is working or if you want to add a new printer or other hardware to your system.

Chapter 7

Customizing Your System

Now that you've learned how to personalize your desktop, it's time to discover the many other ways you can tailor your computer to suit your needs. Happily, Windows 95 is extremely flexible and customizable. Everyone has personal preferences, and what's more, few personal computer systems are identical. There's a wide variety of makes and models, each with unique requirements, and an even greater variety of peripherals like printers and video cards.

Windows 95 supports over 1,900 hardware items and more than 3,500 software programs. When you want to add or remove peripherals, typefaces or applications, use Control Panel. Use it also to adjust the behavior of the keyboard, mouse and the modem; modify sounds or multimedia; or change settings for faxing, printing, networks and many other properties of your peripherals and computer. In general, Control Panel is the place where you make changes to the behavior, the "settings," of your computer and its associated peripherals.

Control Panel is easy to get to. Click on the Start button and then select Settings | Control Panel (Figure 7-1). Or you can double-click on the My Computer icon on your desktop and choose Control Panel from there.

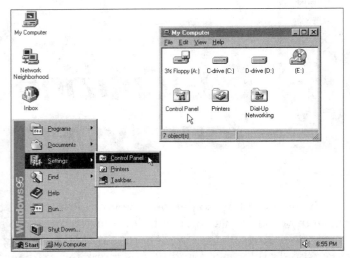

Figure 7-1: *There are two ways to run Control Panel: from the Start menu or from My Computer.*

You then see a window similar to Figure 7-2. Note that your Control Panel reflects your computer system, so it may not include all the options displayed in Figure 7-2. For example, if you haven't installed a network, you won't see an option for it. We will also skip some of the more exotic options, such as 32bit ODBC, which is installed if you use Microsoft Access or Visual Basic 4.0.

Figure 7-2: *Control Panel's wide range of customizable options are the key to configuring your computer.*

A Word to the Wise

Most things you do with a computer are benign. However, some things you could change in the Control Panel can cause problems. Not all Control Panel options are harmless. For example, with the System option, it's possible to accidentally confuse your system's list of devices, so you might end up disabling your printer port or uninstalling your CD-ROM.

We'll warn you about options that could be trouble and are therefore best approached warily. In any case, you can make a backup copy of your system files before you begin, by copying several files (SYSTEM.INI, WIN.INI, SYSTEM.DAT and USER.DAT from your Windows directory) to a floppy disk.

You may also want to copy AUTOEXEC.BAT and CONFIG.SYS from your C: drive (or other boot drive). If you do wreck your system, it may be possible to copy these files from the floppy disk back onto your hard drive and, in this way, fix the problems. Of course, this is no substitute for a complete backup of your hard drive (see Chapter 5), but it will give you a little peace of mind if you decide to boldly go where you have never gone before.

Where Do We Start?

To keep things simple, let's examine each Control Panel option in alphabetical order. We'll also preface each section with the icon representing the Control Panel option under discussion.

Windows displays several pages of property sheets when you double-click on one of the icons in the Control Panel. Each property sheet has a tabbed heading you can click on for instant access to that panel. Some settings won't take place immediately unless you click on the Apply Now button. To accept all settings from all the property sheet panels, click on OK. (Henceforth, we'll usually refer to individual property sheets as simply *panels,* as a convenient shorthand.)

 TIP Use Ctrl+Tab if you prefer to switch between the property sheets using the keyboard instead of clicking on the tab headings. Use Shift+Ctrl+Tab to go back to the previous panel.

Also note the ? symbol in the upper right of each property sheet. Click on it, and the mouse cursor changes to a *help cursor* (an arrow attached to a question mark). Use the help cursor to click on a part of the screen you'd like more information about.

To get pop-up help more quickly, right-click on a part of the screen you'd like help with, instead of using the help cursor. This makes a tiny menu open with just one entry: "What's this?" Click on the choice to pop open the Help balloon.

 ## Accessibility Options

Microsoft has taken extra care to make sure that the Windows 95 operating system takes into account the needs of those with physical challenges. Although it's still difficult to use a computer if you can't type or use a mouse, alternative input devices can make it possible. For example, a mouth stick can be used to type, and head-mounted ultrasound tracking devices can be used instead of a mouse. Research is also underway to permit mouse movement tracked by eye movements alone, using tiny muscle sensor pads placed next to each eye. This technique could in fact benefit everyone. Imagine being able to just glance about to move the cursor on the screen and deliberately blink when you want to click.

In the near future, it may even be possible to control some functions simply by thinking about the action you wish to perform, using advanced analysis of EEG information or other biofeedback techniques. This capability would leapfrog the current attempts at voice recognition, which is improving but still remains awkward.

Figure 7-3 displays the available Accessibility options for the keyboard. Many of them can also be activated via keyboard shortcuts. For example, the *StickyKeys* feature lets you press Alt or Ctrl separately from the key it modifies. In many programs and even Windows itself, special shortcut key combinations carry out some task. (Instead of *shortcut keys*, which can be confused with desktop shortcuts, we prefer the term *hotkeys*.) Hotkeys usually trigger some immediate result, so you don't have to move the mouse around or go through a menu. These special key combinations often involve holding down the Ctrl key while pressing another key, such as Ctrl+X, which in most programs deletes whatever text or item is currently selected or highlighted. With the StickyKeys feature activated, you don't have to hold down Ctrl and X at the same time to cut something into the Clipboard. You can tap Ctrl, release it and then tap X.

You can also activate StickyKeys by pressing Shift five times. This way, you can share a keyboard with someone who doesn't want these features permanently enabled via Control Panel.

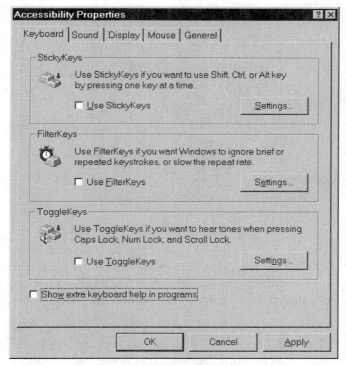

Figure 7-3: *Keyboard Accessibility features.*

The first panel in this control is for Keyboard accessibility features. We already mentioned StickyKeys, which you might like to use even if you don't have any typing handicaps. To customize it further, click on Settings to open the window shown in Figure 7-4.

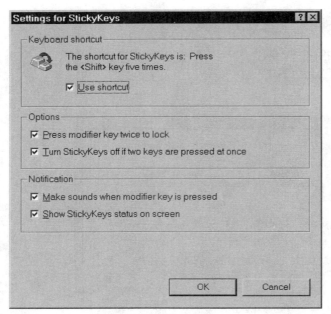

Figure 7-4: *StickyKeys settings.*

FilterKeys makes it easier if you type irregularly. It ignores repeated keys, or can delay the repeat rate, and ignores keys that are struck briefly by mistake. Its settings are shown in Figure 7-5. (To activate FilterKeys via the keyboard, hold down the Right Shift key for more than 8 seconds.)

 Years ago, those individuals with motion impairments had to purchase a plastic cover that would sit about 1" above their keyboard. It had little holes directly over each key so that you could rest your hands on the plastic cover, but to type anything you had to poke your finger through each hole and press the key. The *FilterKeys* option is a software version of this same plastic cover device. In addition to being cheaper for those people with motion impairments, it also means that they can use any machine running Windows 95 without having to bring their plastic cover along with them.

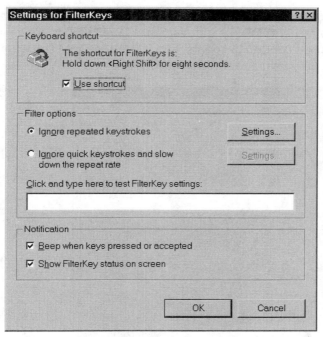

Figure 7-5: *FilterKeys settings.*

Turn on *ToggleKeys* if you want to hear tones whenever you press Scroll Lock, Caps Lock or Num Lock. (Hold down Num Lock for 5 seconds to activate it via the keyboard.) Most keyboards have small lights showing the status of these three keys. However, even if you have no trouble seeing those lights, the audible feedback may be useful to you. For most people, though, it's immediately obvious if they've pressed the Caps Lock key (all letters they type are now uppercase) or the Num Lock key (the arrow keys on the number pad now merely place numbers into the text rather than move the mouse pointer).

Returning to the Accessibility properties, click on the Sounds tab heading to open the window shown in Figure 7-6, which lets the hearing-impaired keep up with cues that would otherwise be missed. Sound Sentry substitutes visual cues for audio cues, like beeps, that accompany error messages or signal that a process is complete.

The more ambitious option called *ShowSounds* is intended to actually pop up a caption whenever a program uses digitized speech or plays a sound when you click on something. ShowSounds doesn't enable this feature all by itself. It depends on application designers to support it, just as you need a special TV to receive closed captions. Since 1994, all TVs have been required to include closed caption decoders, and it is hoped that software developers also provide universal support for ShowSounds.

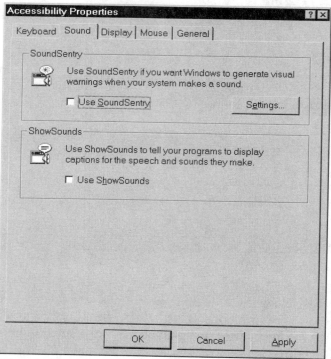

Figure 7-6: *Ways to "see" sound.*

The Display tab heading brings up a display like Figure 7-7. It lets you enable and customize the High Contrast mode. Instead of the usual black-on-gray boxes that dominate Windows's 3D look and feel, you can choose black and blue on white, or other combinations. You could also create your own custom color scheme using the Display settings in Control Panel (see Chapter 6 for an in-depth discussion of customizing), but High Contrast can be easily turned on and off when you're sharing a computer with a co-worker who's not visually impaired. (Hold down the left Shift and Alt keys while you press the Print Screen key to activate High Contrast display mode.)

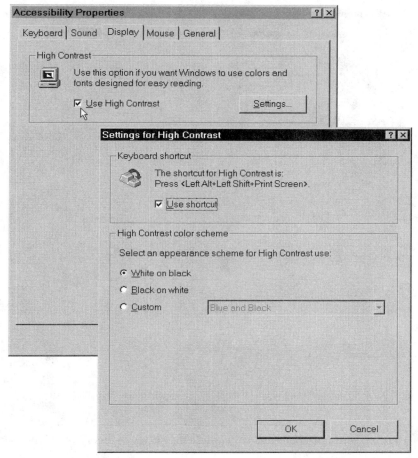

Figure 7-7: *Enable high contrast if you need to make the display more legible.*

A Nifty Mouse Substitute

MouseKeys is another feature that's useful even if you have no difficulty using a mouse. One example would be on an airplane, where there might be no room for a mouse.

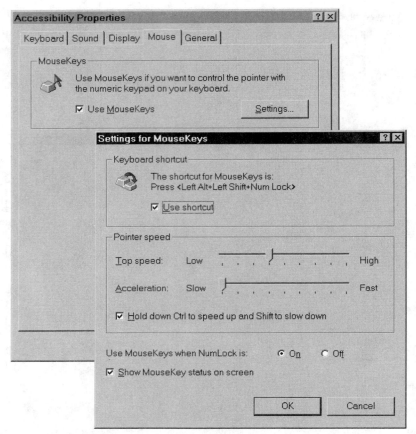

Figure 7-8: *MouseKeys lets you imitate the mouse entirely from the keyboard.*

This feature is another example of something that was originally developed for those with physical disabilities, but it turns out to be useful for everyone. This is exactly like the curb cuts on street corners that were originally put in place for people in wheelchairs, but they turned out to be extremely useful to bicyclists, rollerbladers, parents with strollers and so on.

When MouseKeys is enabled, you can move the mouse cursor simply by pressing keys on the numeric keypad (already marked with arrows, plus you can move diagonally using 1, 3, 7 and 9) while Num Lock is on.

If you want to move the text cursor using the numeric keypad, just turn off Num Lock, or use the editing cluster with its separate cursor keys if you have a 101-key keyboard. If you like to use the numeric keypad for numbers, you may want to set MouseKeys to work when Num Lock is off (see Figure 7-8). If you have an old 88-key keyboard, you'll have to disable MouseKeys if you want to use the keypad both for numeric entry and for cursor movement.

MouseKeys is also handy when you need fine control of the mouse in a graphics program. Many graphics programs don't allow you to move an object one pixel at a time. This can be improved with the MouseKeys approach. Just hold down the appropriate arrow key, and it will speed up the longer you hold it down (using the acceleration rate shown in Figure 7-8), or to really zip around, hold down the Ctrl key at the same time you hold down one of the keypad keys. If the cursor moves too fast, hold down Shift with the key to slow it down, preventing acceleration. The check box next to Show MouseKey status on screen enables a tiny icon in the Status/Clock area on the taskbar to remind you when MouseKeys is turned on.

Returning again to the Accessibility properties, click on the General tab to open the window shown in Figure 7-9.

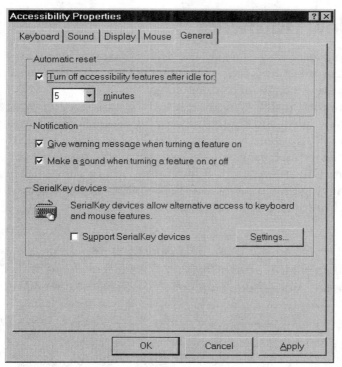

Figure 7-9: *General accessibility options.*

You can specify how to apply the Accessibility features if you are sharing the computer with someone else who doesn't use them. By choosing Apply *Changes to this Windows session only*, any features you turn on will be cleared the next time Windows starts. This option is normally not used, since the next feature, *Turn off accessibility features after idle for 5 minutes*, turns them off automatically anyway (you can change the delay in the text box next to Minutes). If you want these changes to remain part of your Windows setup until you manually disable them, you should clear this second check box.

If you use the Accessibility shortcuts a lot, you may want to turn off the *Give warning messages when turning a feature on* check box which is designed to prevent accidental activation of the features, and turn off the *Make a sound when turning a feature on or off* check box, which is also designed to alert you if you turn it on or off by mistake.

The SerialKeys feature is used with special hardware devices that substitute another device for the main keyboard. Each one is designed differently, so you'll have to refer to the documentation that comes with your special input device to see how to use it.

Add New Hardware

Windows makes it easy to install the drivers you need for your hardware. A *driver* is software engineered to provide the "hooks" Windows and Windows software needs to take advantage of the device.

When you first install Windows, it scans your computer in an attempt to automatically detect and configure your hardware, and it does a pretty good job. Ideally, all your hardware would be Plug-and-Play compatible, which makes Windows's job easy, since it can change the properties of the device via software. Other hardware often requires you to physically manipulate the card, moving tiny jumpers or flipping micro-sized switches to choose the IRQ and I/O addresses.

The IRQ (Interrupt Request) is like a flag that the hardware device waves about to get Windows's attention. It literally interrupts whatever your computer is doing (briefly) and forces it to handle the needs of the device. For example, when your modem receives a character, it interrupts everything so that your computer can read the character before it's replaced by the next one. It finds this character at a special kind of memory location called an Input/Output Address. When sending a character to the modem, it stores that character in the same I/O address. Sometimes a device can directly access your system memory using a technique called *direct memory access*, or *DMA*. Your computer has only a limited supply of available IRQ numbers and I/O addresses, so it's all too easy for the settings in your various hardware devices to conflict. Device Manager, part of the System object in Control Panel, can help you identify and sometimes resolve these conflicts. Chapter 14 goes into more detail on these issues.

We cover the mechanics of installing new hardware devices and dealing with the limited computer resources as well as explain terms like *IRQ* and *I/O address* in Chapter 15.

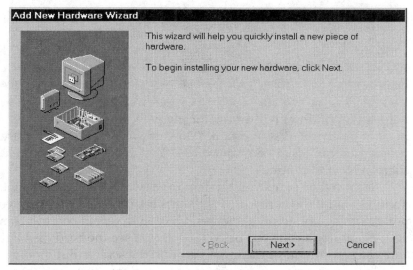

Figure 7-10: *The first screen of the Add New Hardware Wizard.*

When you run Add New Hardware, it starts the Add New Hardware Wizard, whose first screen is shown in Figure 7-10. Click Next to open the window shown in Figure 7-11, which is the actual first working screen.

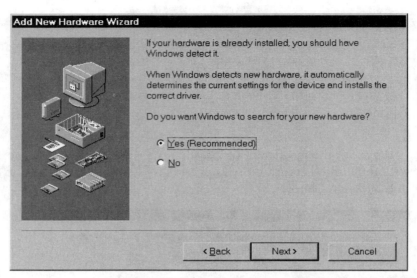

Figure 7-11: *Normally you'll allow Windows to search for your devices (hardware).*

Ideally, Windows will automatically detect a new device you've plugged in. That's why the first question, "Do you want Windows to search for your new hardware?" is already answered "Yes" by default. All you have to do is click on Next to continue.

Windows then scans your system for devices. This search can take several minutes, and if the hardware is ill-behaved, it can even lock up your computer, forcing you to press the Reset button to regain control. Don't assume your computer has locked up as long as you see the hard disk light blinking and you can still move the mouse around the screen. But if nothing happens for a long time, you may have to turn off the computer and then turn it back on to restart Windows and regain control. No harm is done, though, so don't worry about that.

On the other hand, if you know exactly what you've inserted, you can save some time by clicking on the No choice before clicking Next. Then choose the type of the device in the Hardware Types box. For example, if you just inserted a new sound card, scroll the list to Sound, video, and game controllers and double-click on it, or click on Next.

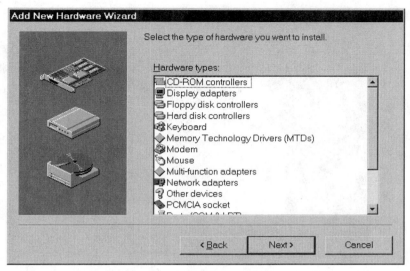

Figure 7-12: *Choose the type of device you wish to install.*

For each device detected or chosen, you get to choose a driver. Drivers are organized on the left pane by manufacturer or developer and on the right by the specific model or version. If you're installing a Sound Blaster card (or compatible), you can choose Creative Labs on the left to view the choices for the Sound Blaster or Sound Blaster Pro (Figure 7-12).

Solving Device Conflicts

Sometimes the hardware you're trying to install has a conflict with hardware already in your computer, and you get the warning shown in Figure 7-13. Conflicts occur when the two devices are vying for the same limited IRQ or I/O address resources. For example, your network card and your CD-ROM card might both be set to use I/O address 0340. In that case, you need to reconfigure one of them to use a different I/O address.

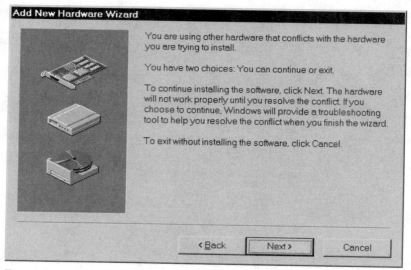

Figure 7-13: *A hardware conflict must be resolved.*

In many cases, you have to open your computer and physically reconfigure the card. Some cards, such as the Sound Blaster 16, include a setup utility that can reconfigure it using only the setup software. Plug-and-Play (PnP) hardware can be automatically reconfigured by Windows 95, so you'll rarely get this error unless you have too many non-PnP "legacy" devices that have hogged all the IRQs.

You can click on the Cancel button at this point and resolve the problem through hardware, or you may want to first identify the source of the conflict, and if possible correct the problem without having to open up your computer. If you choose Next, you get the opportunity to launch the *Conflict Troubleshooter*.

Windows 95's Conflict Troubleshooter is a part of the Help system that guides you through using the System control to see what the conflicts are. You'll want to be familiar with IRQs, I/O addresses, DMA settings (see Tech Tip above) and so forth, before you can confidently venture further. You might want to make a quick foray into Chapter 14, "Deep Inside the Machine."

For more about device settings, see the "System" section later in this chapter to find out more about Device Manager.

Add/Remove Programs

The Add/Remove Programs Control Panel option combines several separate functions into one control. The first property sheet, with a tab heading of Install/Uninstall, makes it easier to set up and remove software programs.

Application Installation Wizard

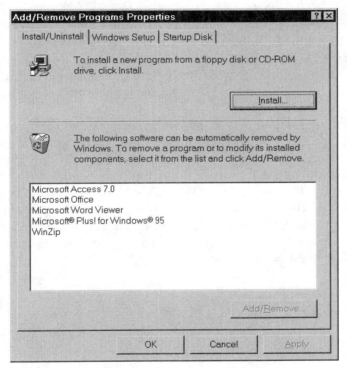

Figure 7-14: *It's easier than ever to install or uninstall programs using Windows 95.*

Click the Install button whenever you're installing a new program from disks or CD-ROM to start the Application Installation Wizard. (A Wizard is Windows's way of taking you through a task step by step, a technique borrowed from Microsoft applications such as Microsoft Word.) It's basically the same as selecting Start | Run and entering **SETUP.EXE** to run the Setup program. Windows looks for the most common types of install programs, such as SETUP.EXE or INSTALL.EXE, and launches it for you. After that, use the Setup program according to the product's own documentation.

Reverse Installation

If you realize that you're not using a program, the natural inclination is to remove it from your computer to free up hard disk space. And if you used Windows 3.1, you're probably all too familiar with the complications involved in manual uninstallation (we discussed this process in Chapter 4). The difficulty in cleanly removing old software led to a proliferation of third-party Windows "cleanup" utilities, some of which will be updated for Windows 95.

However, now Windows 95 includes a simple Uninstall feature. Keep in mind that this feature can be used only to remove new Windows 95 software. When you install Windows 95 software (with the *Designed for Windows 95* logo), the Setup program provides important uninstallation instructions that the Uninstall feature can use to cleanly remove the software, without affecting other applications.

Once you've installed new Windows 95 software, you can run Add/ Remove Programs from the Control Panel, and you'll see the name of the program in the list of installed software. Just double-click on the program name to start the removal process at any time.

Keep in mind that older, 16-bit Windows 3.1 software can't be uninstalled this way. Check the manual for your software to see if it includes an Uninstall feature. Otherwise, you'll want to use one of the Uninstall tools we mentioned earlier, but make sure you get a version that has been updated for Windows 95 for best results.

Windows Setup

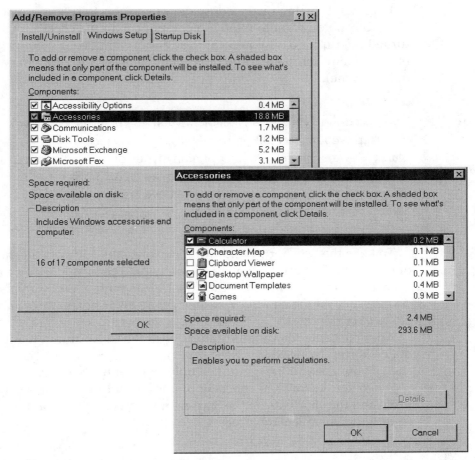

Figure 7-15: *Turn on check boxes to install; clear check boxes to uninstall.*

The second panel of Add/Remove Software lets you review and change the optional parts (components) of Windows 95. This way, you can add features that you originally skipped during Windows 95 Setup, without having to rerun the Windows 95 Setup program again. You can also use this feature to remove optional parts of Windows 95 that you aren't using, thus freeing up hard disk space.

Before you change anything, have your original Windows 95 CD-ROM or disks ready, because adding new components will require them. If you originally installed Windows from a network server, it will automatically remember which server you installed it from and will go back to that server without prompting for disks.

In principle, using the Windows Setup panel is fairly easy. Just turn off a check box if you want to remove a component, or if a check box is already turned off, turn it on if you want to add that component. You can add and remove many components before clicking on OK (you don't have to do them one at a time).

 If you used the Typical Install choice when you first ran Windows 95 Setup, you missed out on some nifty options, such as the Quick Viewers that let you look at many types of files without having to start the program that created the file. (Chapter 4 discusses Quick View.) Select Add/Remove Programs|Windows Setup to add these missing goodies.

To keep the list short, Windows Setup presents you with a general list of options first. To "drill down" to the individual choices, click on a choice such as Accessories and then click the Details button. (You can also just double-click on the choice.) You then get a new list of features and check boxes to customize.

After choosing the Details options, click the Close button to return to the main choices. Notice that a third type of check box—a gray checked box— shows you that you have installed only some of the options.

When you've finished choosing options, Windows updates your hard drive and the shortcuts on the Start menu. Usually, your computer is also restarted to complete the process.

 If you later need to reinstall Windows 95 (such as when you receive a new updated version), you might have forgotten which features you've already installed. To avoid this confusion, turn off all the check boxes to remove all the optional components. That way, you've cleaned up your hard drive prior to reinstalling Windows 95.

What's the Have Disk button for? It can be used to add Windows 95 components that weren't originally included with your version of Windows 95. Use this button only if you're instructed to do so when you receive updated software.

Instead of going through the Have Disk option, you can locate the .INF (installation information) file that comes with the software or driver, using Explorer. Right-click on the .INF file and choose Install from the pop-up menu.

Startup Disk

Your computer depends on several files to start up (boot). They include special files to start MS-DOS, which is used to load any necessary DOS drivers, before starting Windows 95. Normally, your computer finds these files and boots directly from your hard drive.

These startup files on your hard drive can get erased or corrupted, though this is an rare occurrence. (See Chapter 5, "Inside the File System." Running ScanDisk frequently can help prevent your files from being corrupted due to program errors or intermittent hardware failures.) If your boot files get corrupted, your computer won't start, and for all intents and purposes, it's an expensive paperweight.

Or is it? If you have an emergency startup disk you can still boot your computer from the floppy disk drive. If the damage is not too severe, an experienced computer user can repair the drive. If nothing else, you may be able to use MS-DOS to access files on your hard drive. That way, you can copy your most precious data files and documents to other floppy disks for safekeeping. Hopefully, you'll also have a fairly up-to-date backup of your hard drive (see Chapter 5).

 If your hard drive won't start, boot the startup disk, and use the SCANDISK command to try to repair your hard drive. If your computer still won't boot, use the SYS command from the startup disk to rewrite your MS-DOS boot files. See Chapter 22, "The Other Face: DOS 7," to see how to use DOS commands.

You were offered the chance to create a startup disk when you originally installed Windows 95. If you eschewed this choice, lost your startup disk or if your computer came with Windows 95 preinstalled, you can use Add/Remove Programs from the Control Panel to create one. Just click the StartUp Disk tab heading, insert a blank disk (or one you don't mind being overwritten) and click the Create Disk button. It's too late to create this disk if you already have hard disk problems, so you'll want to set up one soon.

Date & Time

Your computer uses the date and time to keep track of which files are more recent than others. When you save a file, it's stamped with the date and time it was created and the time it was last modified. Windows also keeps track of the time a file was last accessed (opened). Other programs need a correct date and time setting, too, such as scheduling programs that automatically run a certain program, send a fax or pop up a reminder message at a given date and time. The easiest way to open the window shown in Figure 7-16 is to just double-click on the clock on the taskbar, but you can access it from the Control Panel, too.

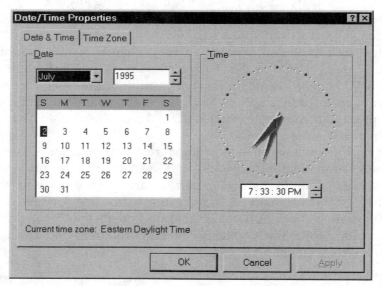

Figure 7-16: *It's important to set your date and time correctly, especially if you're connected to a worldwide network, such as The Microsoft Network.*

To set the date, just click on the day of the month in the calendar; then click the Apply button. Change the month by clicking on the month name and choosing a month from the list that drops down. You can type the year next to it or use the Up/Down spin buttons to change the year. On the right is an analog clock. You can change the time by clicking on any part of the time (hour, minute, second) and either typing a new value or using the spin buttons to increase or decrease the time. It might seem that you could just click and drag the hands on the clock to set the time, but this doesn't work. Maybe it will be supported in a future version of Windows.

The Time Zone lets you tell Windows what time zone you live in. On a network, documents are date/time stamped using Universal Coordinated Time (Greenwich Mean Time in Greenwich, Great Britain). Your time zone is used to convert your local time to UCT for international communication.

If this doesn't make sense, consider a computer attached to a worldwide network. Dates and times are always stored using UCT and then converted to your local time zone. That way, if two computers are trying to determine which of two files is more recent, the date/time stamp on the file is still relevant. Without coordinated time, a file created in Los Angeles would seem to have been created three hours earlier than a document in New York, even if both documents were actually created at the same time.

Display

With Display, you can choose your wallpaper or desktop pattern, screen saver, favorite colors, screen type and resolution, and video card driver, all in one place. Contrast this to Windows 3.1, where you had three different icons to accomplish the same purpose.

You can access the same Display options by right-clicking on any empty part of the desktop and choosing Properties from the pop-up menu.

The Display options are thoroughly covered in the preceding chapter, so we won't duplicate that discussion here, but here's a quick overview. The four following subsections correspond to the tab headings in Display Properties.

Background

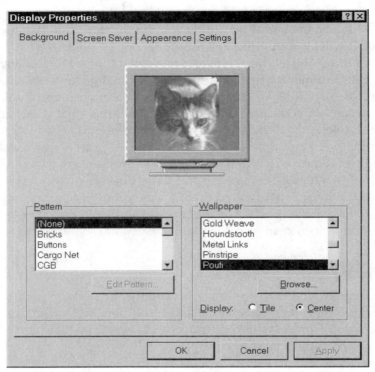

Figure 7-17: *Consider using a background pattern instead of wallpaper to save memory.*

Use the Background panel to choose a pattern to apply to your plain colored background, or choose a wallpaper design to decorate your desktop. The wallpaper or pattern appears behind any other windows or icons on the desktop. Formerly, Windows required all wallpaper designs to be stored in the \Windows home directory (folder), but you can now use the Browse button to locate any bitmap (.BMP) graphic on your hard drive.

Wallpaper graphics can be a waste of memory, so avoid them if you have a computer with less than 8mb of memory, unless you're using a very small bitmap. Small bitmaps can be tiled to fill the whole screen economically.

Screen Saver

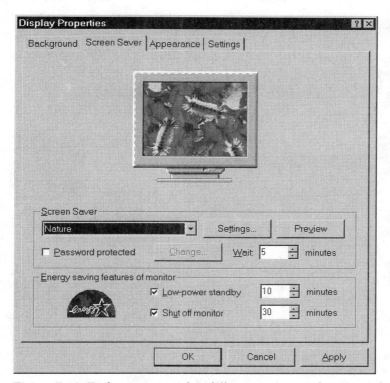

Figure 7-18: *Each screen saver has different options, so be sure to choose the Settings button to see what's available.*

We can't quite explain the popularity of screen savers, but there it is. After all, no modern color monitor is vulnerable to burn-in of a static image. Screen savers are especially ironic when you consider that they do most of their work when you're not even at your computer.

A screen saver does serve one important function: security. It's a way to preserve the confidentiality of your work and to prevent others from accessing your computer when you're away from your desk. If you're editing or writing a document or a spreadsheet that you don't want others to see, the screen saver provides a useful cover. Plus, you can set a password that prevents an unauthorized person from clearing the screen saver and using the computer.

The Energy Saving features are only enabled if you told Windows 95 that your monitor supports Energy Star power-down mode, which blanks the screen and even turns off the monitor after a while. Use the Settings panel and click on Change Display Type to enable Energy Star compliance.

Appearance

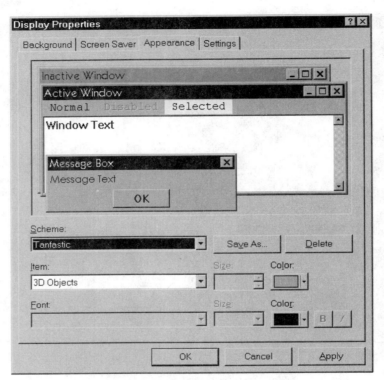

Figure 7-19: *Click the sample OK button if you want to change the plain gray color of buttons and other backgrounds to something more colorful.*

You can extensively customize the look and feel of Windows 95, such as the colors for buttons and other 3D objects, the size and font for the title bar, the font used for icons and Explorer and much, much more. The miniature Windows desktop gives you a preview of your customizations, although it doesn't reflect all the options. Be sure to save your custom Appearance scheme each time you change it. That way, you're free to try out any other scheme without risking your custom choices—just choose your custom scheme from the list to switch back to it.

Settings

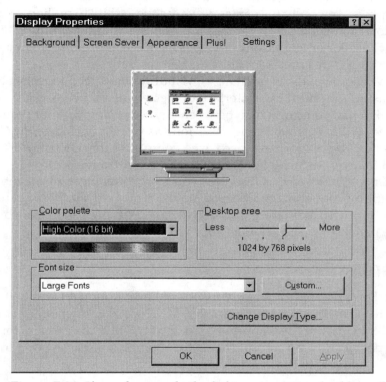

Figure 7-20: *If you change only the desktop area setting (and leave the colors and font size the same), you can switch to the new resolution without restarting Windows.*

Your video card (display adapter) probably supports many video modes, from low resolution (640x480) using rather blocky pixels (dots) to high resolution (up to 1600x1280) using very small pixels. (More pixels and higher resolution result in more desktop space and more detailed images.) To try out the higher video modes, just drag the desktop area slider to the right. (You may need to add memory to your display adapter to use its highest resolution or to get more colors.)

You may find that text is too small when you increase your resolution. In this case, try changing from small fonts to large fonts, or click the Custom button to adjust the size of the fonts to match the size of your monitor. Keep in mind that some programs (including the Windows 95 Tour) will run properly only with the Small Fonts option.

In addition to resolution, you can also choose how many colors are supported by the video mode. The 256-color option is best for high-speed graphics, especially for games, whereas the 24-bit (16 million color, or True Color) mode is superior for desktop publishing and painting. The 16-bit (65,535 color or High Color) mode is a good compromise if your video card won't support True Color at its highest resolutions.

When you make your changes, Windows may need to restart itself to adjust its graphical user interface to the new display settings. If you use small fonts, you can switch between any resolution without requiring a reboot (which is much slower), as long as you don't change the Color Palette settings. (If you normally use Large Fonts, note that choosing 640x480 forces you to revert to Small Fonts, which will require a restart.)

Once Windows 95 is installed, you won't often need to use the Change Display Type setting, unless you've just removed your video card and replaced it with a different one. In that case, Windows will take you straight to this panel so you can change your video card driver.

Fonts

The Fonts choice is not really a Control Panel option *per se*, but it is a shortcut to your Fonts folder. Originally, Microsoft had intended that the Fonts folder be part of My Computer, just as you'll find the Printers folder there. It's not clear why Microsoft made this change. The easiest way to open the Fonts folder is to first start Control Panel.

TIP   The Fonts icon in Control Panel is actually a shortcut to \Windows\Fonts. So you can browse the Fonts folder from Explorer, although it behaves a little differently than other folders, as we'll see later in this chapter.

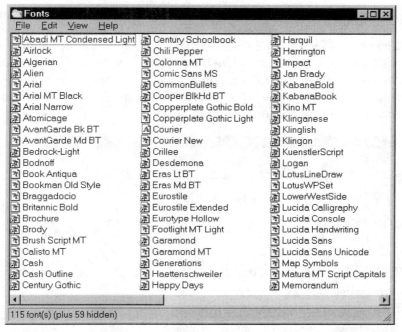

Figure 7-21: *Plentiful TrueType fonts can be an embarrassment of riches, but too many can slow down your computer.*

The Fonts folder shows you all the fonts you currently have available from Windows 95. It can show three kinds of fonts: TrueType fonts (.TTF files), screen/printer fonts (.FNT files), or a shortcut to a font file stored elsewhere on your hard drive.

Although the fonts are normally shown using large icons, you can also click on the View menu and choose either List, List Fonts By Similarity or Details to change the way you view the list. The Similarity option is especially interesting when you're searching for just the right font. Just choose a font from the *Similarity* drop-down list, and you'll see the rest of the fonts arranged in order of their similarity to the chosen font.

 Select View | Hide Variations if you want to see a shorter list of just the font *families*. For example, Arial, Arial Bold, Arial Italic and Arial Bold Italic are really just variations of the Arial font family.

Select File | Install New Font to add fonts to the list. To remove a font, click on it and then press the Del key on the keyboard, or right-click on it and choose Delete. Make sure you have a copy of a font, if you want to reinstall it later, before you delete it from the Fonts folder. Instead of deleting fonts from the Fonts folder, you can also drag and drop them into another folder. (It's okay to delete a shortcut to a font, denoted by a shortcut arrow in the lower-left corner of the icon.)

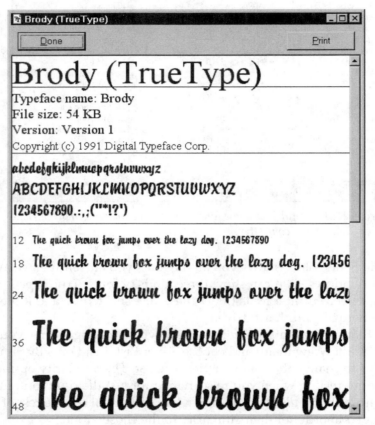

Figure 7-22: *Double-click on an installed font to view it. You can also print the summary.*

You can double-click on any font's icon to see a font summary, a kind of preview. You can also print these font samples. (Right-click on a font to more quickly print its sample.)

For more information on typefaces, refer to Chapter 12, "Personal Publishing."

Joystick

Although the mouse can be handy, most games play much better with a real joystick. You can attach a standard PC-compatible joystick to a *game port* (included on most sound cards). Windows 95 won't use a joystick itself, for example, to move the mouse cursor, but it does provide a central Control Panel tool for configuring and customizing joystick settings.

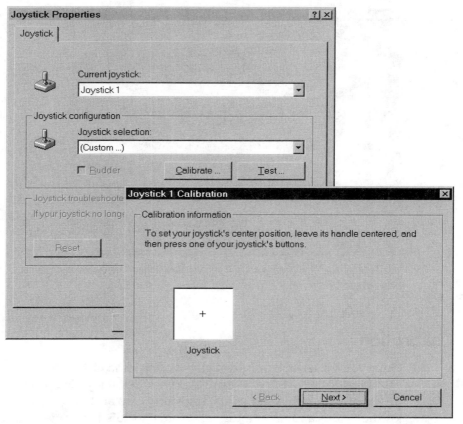

Figure 7-23: *Windows 95 games depend on Control Panel for joystick calibration.*

Of course, some joysticks aren't quite standard. You can find an amazing variety of exotic joysticks, including flight control sticks with rudder controls, racecar steering wheels, Nintendo-style joypads, even 3D controllers with multiple degrees of freedom. (A standard joystick has two degrees of freedom: left/right and up/down. A 3D joystick adds in/out. Windows 95 supports joystick devices with up to six degrees of freedom.)

The first choice in the Joystick control lets you choose which joystick you're configuring. Most of us only have one joystick, so move on to the next choice, which defines the type of joystick you have. If you have something other than a standard PC joystick, click the text below Joystick selection to open a list of joystick types, and choose your joystick from the list. If your joystick is not on the list, scroll up to the Custom type and choose it. You'll then get a dialog box like that shown in Figure 7-24.

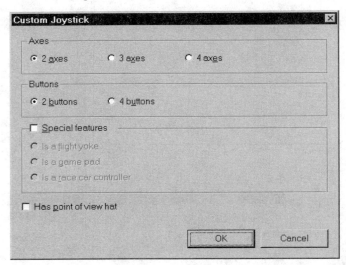

Figure 7-24: *Configure you custom joystick by turning on or off the various options on this panel.*

Calibration

Once you've set up your joystick type, click the Calibrate button. Joystick calibration is necessary because every model of joystick produces slightly different values. Instead of just registering up and down, for example, a joystick gives a range of numbers from 0 to 255. If a game is only interested in up and down, it could consider any number greater than 128 to be down and any number less than 128 to be up. The value of 128 means the stick is vertically centered. But no joystick will work within this precise range. So calibration establishes the minimum and maximum values of the joystick and the readings of the centered position.

> **TIP** You might need to adjust your calibration from week to week, as joysticks are notoriously flaky. One quick fix can be found on joysticks with adjustment sliders, which can often be used to tweak your calibration slightly without having to rerun the Calibrate option.

You can use the Test button to try out your joystick. If it's connected and calibrated, you can move the crosshair around in the box.

 ## Keyboard

When you double-click on the Keyboard icon, you open the window shown in Figure 7-25. This panel lets you customize your keyboard's characteristics.

Speed

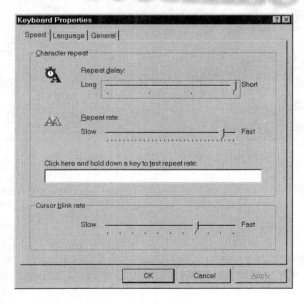

Figure 7-25: *Keyboard Speed settings.*

To adjust the Keyboard Speed settings, you move a slider left and right with the mouse to change the repeat delay, repeat rate and cursor blink rate. The repeat delay is how much time Windows waits to begin repeating once it notices you've held down a key. Set the repeat delay to short, and you'll be ttyyppinng lliiiikke ttthiiss. Once the key begins repeating, the repeat rate controls how fast the characters appear. For responsive cursor control, set the keyboard delay to short, and set the repeat rate a little higher than normal.

Language

Figure 7-26: *Keyboard Language settings.*

Click on the Language tab heading (Figure 7-26) to customize the keyboard (and your computer's symbol set) to your locale. Your locale is defined by your preferred language or country.

Normally, you'll see a choice only for your native country, the one your version of Windows has been *localized* for. You can click on the Add button to add another language. After you click on Add, choose a country setting.

This setting maps different characters onto the keyboard, matching the special designs for keyboards that are available. On a U.S. keyboard, Shift+3 gives the # (pound) symbol, but when set to British, you get the £ sign. Windows also makes it easy to type accented characters for languages that require it. Just press the accent key and then the letter of the alphabet to get a symbol like á.

When you click on Properties, you can choose your preferred keyboard layout, or variation. For example, you could switch from the standard QWERTY keyboard layout (actually designed to slow down typing, to help alleviate the jammed keys that frustrated early typewriter inventors) to the more efficient Dvorak layout.

 TIP If you frequently need to type special characters, consider using the U.S. International layout. It lets you use the trick of typing either accent (single quotation mark) symbol and then the letter of the alphabet to get symbols like á, è, ô and ñ. (You can also use the ^ and ~ symbols. To type a symbol like ö, use the " character first.) To get the symbols by themselves, just type them, followed by a space.

If you frequently change keyboard layouts or share your computer with someone using a different keyboard layout, you can enable the Enable indicator on taskbar check box. Turning on this option puts a little symbol for the current language on the taskbar's notification area (next to the clock). You can click on this symbol to change languages.

Or use the keyboard hotkey of LeftAlt+Shift to switch languages (you can also choose the Ctrl+Shift keyboard hotkey as shown previously, or disable the hotkeys altogether by choosing None).

Chapter 8 is entirely devoted to exploring the keyboard in more detail.

Mail & Fax

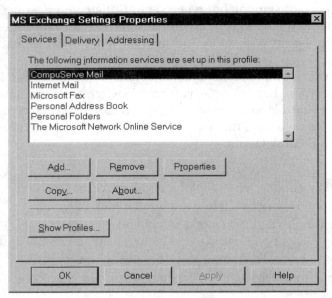

Figure 7-27: *You can customize many Exchange settings here, even if you're not currently running Exchange.*

Microsoft Exchange is Windows's new mailbox paradigm. It's intended to be the hub for all your communications: electronic mail (Microsoft Mail, Internet, Lotus Notes, CompuServe, The Microsoft Network, MCI, Sprint, America Online and so on), sending and receiving faxes, and in the future, wireless mail and more. Using the Mail & Fax icon in Control Panel, you set up your profiles, which tell Windows which services you want available for use with the Exchange Inbox. We won't go into the specifics here, since Chapter 18 explains in detail how to use Exchange on your network.

Microsoft Mail Postoffice

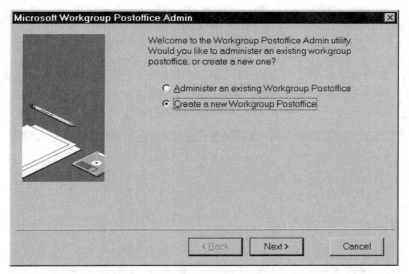

Figure 7-28: *Setting up a Workgroup Postoffice.*

The Microsoft Mail Postoffice is used with Microsoft Exchange. As shown in Figure 7-28, you can use it to either take on the administration duties of the Postoffice manager, or you can create a new Workgroup Postoffice. A Workgroup Postoffice is a special folder and nested subfolders used to hold the accounts for each user in your network workgroup. It is usually stored on a network file server, but if you're using peer-to-peer networking, and you're the Postoffice manager, it's usually stored on your computer. See Chapter 16 for more information on Microsoft Exchange.

 # Modems

Use the Modems control when you first install Windows 95 or if you buy a new modem or switch it to a different serial port (connection). Before Windows 95, every modem-related communications package had to provide its own drivers for each modem on the market. (Recall that a driver is the system software used by Windows to communicate with a device—in this case, a modem.) There was no universal modem driver, as there is for printers.

Now Windows programmers can take advantage of standard modem devices (over 800 modem types are supported) and let Windows 95 take care of the details. The Modems settings are part of the Telephony Applications

Programming Interface (TAPI), which lets Windows interface with a variety of communications systems, including central PBX exchanges and ISDN (Integrated Systems Digital Network), the successor to today's modems.

The first time you use this control, you see a window like that in Figure 7-29. The Modem Setup Wizard takes you through the setup step by step. If you permit it, Windows will attempt to automatically detect and install your modem. If you already know which modem you have and which COM port your modem uses, you can click on *Don't detect my modem* to choose it from a list of supported modem types (Figure 7-30).

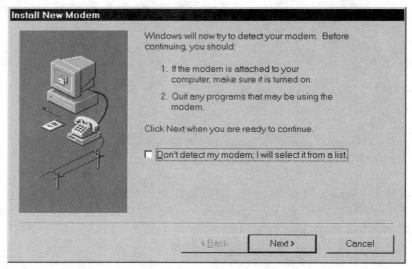

Figure 7-29: *Windows attempts to detect your modem automatically.*

 COM is short for communications. A COM port is also called a serial port, since bits are sent one at a time in sequence, serially, instead of 8 bits at a time, simultaneously, as used by the parallel printer port, LPT1. A computer can have up to four COM ports (specialized hardware permits even more), but usually you can enable only two of them at a time, since by default, COM1 and COM3 share the same IRQ (4), while COM2 and COM4 share IRQ 3. See Chapters 14 and 15 for more information on IRQ settings.

Windows then scans each COM port (skipping the port used by the mouse), and if it finds a modem, it tries to determine the make and model. If it can't determine the exact model, it may choose a generic name, such as Standard 14400 bps Modem.

If Windows 95 doesn't "see" your modem, use Device Manager (see the "System" section later in this chapter) to look for conflicts between your COM port and other devices, such as network cards. If you just recently installed the modem, and it's an internal modem, use Add New Hardware (see previous reference in this chapter) to allow Windows to detect the modem's port.

If you aren't satisfied with a Standard choice, you can open a list of all modems (shown in Figure 7-30) by clicking on Change. Using this selector, you first choose a manufacturer in the left pane and then, from the right pane, choose the specific model. Here we've selected a Hayes Optima 288 V.34+FAX.

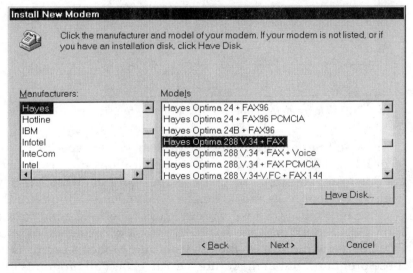

Figure 7-30: *Choosing your modem from a list.*

Figure 7-31 shows the final part of the Modems Control Panel settings. You'll see this the next time you run Modems from Control Panel. You can delete the current modem if you've changed ports, or click on Add to add a new modem or change the current modem, using the same Modem Setup Wizard we just discussed.

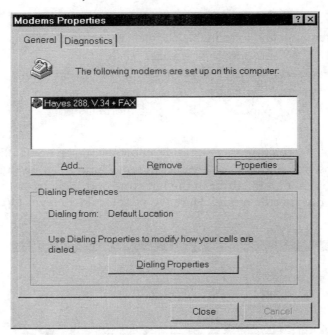

Figure 7-31: *The modem is now set up and ready to use.*

These settings are used only for software written specifically for Windows 95 or later, and by Windows itself for applications such as HyperTerminal and Microsoft At Work Fax. (See Chapter 16 for more information on these communications tools and advanced Control Panel options for the modem.)

Existing Windows 3.1 software, such as America Online, ProComm Plus, WinCIM, CommWorks and so on, have their own method of setting up the COM port and modem, so the Control Panel Modems setting is not used for those programs. But in the future, we can expect all programs to use this simple, central method of modem management.

Mouse

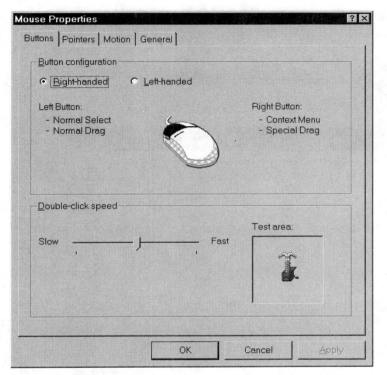

Figure 7-32: *Mouse buttons settings.*

In Figure 7-32, we've double-clicked on Mouse in the Control Panel to get the first panel of the mouse settings, which lets you customize the mouse buttons. If you're left-handed, you may want to reverse the buttons.

The other button setting controls how fast you have to repeat your clicks for it to register as a double-click. Set it too low, and Windows ignores a fast double-click. Too fast, and Windows sees most double-clicks as two separate clicks. Since two separate clicks are used when you want to rename a file, you may need to adjust this setting so Windows knows when you intend to double-click. To test the setting, double-click on Jack to make him jump out of his box.

Pointers (Animated Cursors)

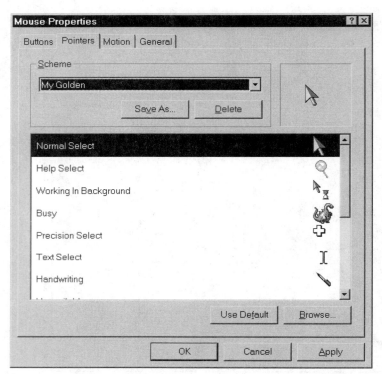

Figure 7-33: *You can customize your mouse cursor (pointer) with either plain bitmaps or animations.*

Click on the Pointers tab heading to get the panel shown in Figure 7-33. You get to customize the graphics used for the mouse cursor. Each type of mouse cursor, such as the pointing arrow and the hourglass "hold on a minute" cursor, are shown in the list, which you can scroll to reveal all the possible types of mouse cursor (some of which are only rarely used). Click on Browse to choose a new cursor file.

There are two types of cursor files. Files ending with .CUR are standard mouse cursor bitmaps. (A bitmap is a "static" picture, like a photograph.) The files with an .ANI extension are more fun: they are actual animations for the mouse cursor (like a movie instead of a photograph). For example, by choosing the file HAND.ANI (not included with Windows 95) for the Wait cursor, you get a hand with its fingers impatiently tapping on the desktop—mirroring all too well the way you feel when it appears! Figure 7-34 shows the three frames in this animation, which are looped to provide a continuous mini-movie.

If you don't get pointer animation, even if you choose an animated cursor, one of three things is preventing the animation: 1. You are using a plain VGA display driver or a Windows 3.1 display adapter. 2. You're using a Windows 95 display driver that doesn't support animated or color cursors (such as the ATI Graphics Ultra [Mach 8] driver). 3. Your hard drive is not able to enter 32-bit *protected mode*, meaning that you're using DOS *real mode* drivers (usually in CONFIG.SYS) to access your hard drive.

Figure 7-34: *Inside a cursor animation.*

When you are satisfied with your choices, click on Save As to save your custom settings. You can create more than one custom scheme, so you can rotate between them if you get tired of one, or let each user set up his or her own scheme if you share the same computer.

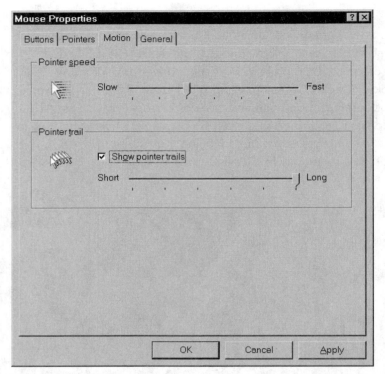

Figure 7-35: *Motion control lets you adjust the speed of the mouse.*

To change the speed of the mouse, click on the Motion tab heading to get the panel shown in Figure 7-35. You can control how fast the mouse moves by moving the slider from Slow to Fast. You have better control with Slow, but you require less desk space with Fast. Use Pointer Trails if you sometimes lose track of the mouse cursor, especially on a poorly lit or low-contrast LCD display. With Pointer Trails turned on, the mouse leaves a series of images of itself behind as it moves, like an afterimage.

For more about the mouse and these options, see Chapter 9.

Multimedia

Windows is a Master of Multimedia, and you can master its powers with Control Panel. Figure 7-36 shows the first panel, which appears when you click on the Audio tab heading.

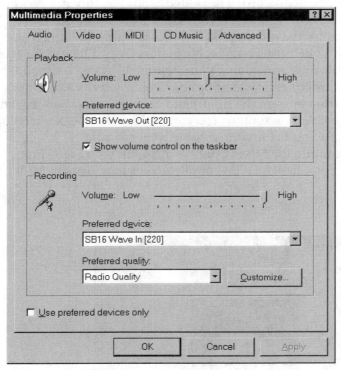

Figure 7-36: *Audio Multimedia settings.*

Audio

You should install a sound card and its drivers before you use the Audio settings. Windows Setup installs sound drivers automatically for any sound card already in your computer, but if you add one manually, you may need to use Add New Hardware to install the driver, unless it's a Plug-and-Play card. See Chapter 15 for more information on installing hardware.

It's possible (though unlikely) to have more than one sound card in your machine, so in Figure 7-36, you are choosing which driver to use for recording and playback. Normally, you don't have to change these settings; they're filled in for you. However, you may want to adjust the overall volume level for playback. For recording, the volume level controls the level of the input. If your microphone is too weak, you can "pump up the volume" to compensate.

Sound Quality Settings

The default type of sound is controlled by Preferred Quality. The greater the quality, the more disk space is needed. Radio quality is a good compromise for speech recording, and records at a rate of 11 kHz (kilohertz). Telephone quality doubles the rate to 22 kHz. Since the limit of human hearing tops out well below 22 kHz, this is as high a quality as you'll need for most purposes.

A more flexible way to mix your volume levels is to turn on the Show volume control on the taskbar option. Doing so puts a little speaker icon in the notification area on the right-hand side of the taskbar (assuming you've left your taskbar horizontal). You can click on the speaker icon on the taskbar to pop up the master volume level control.

Or you can run the Mixer Controls applet in your Start | Programs | Accessories folder. See Chapter 20 for complete information about Multimedia.

Video

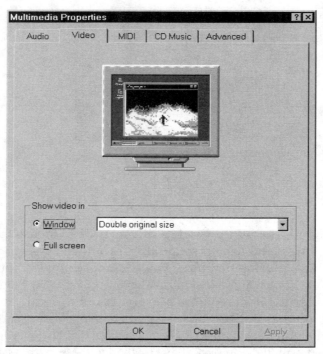

Figure 7-37: *Customize your Video playback window.*

Click on the Video tab to customize the Video for Windows playback window. (It can also be customized from within Media Player; see Chapter 17.) In Figure 7-37, you see that you can choose three sizes of playback windows: maximized (blocky, low resolution and somewhat slow unless you have a very fast computer or a special movie chip in your video card); original size (the optimal size for fast playback); or a fixed size like $\frac{1}{4}$, $\frac{1}{8}$, or $\frac{1}{16}$ screen size (which scales the video window to be the same apparent size, no matter what the resolution of your video driver). Again, if you don't have a very fast computer and a fast CD-ROM drive, you'll get best animation with the Original size option. The Full Screen choice usually behaves the same way as Maximized, but on some video cards, it can be used to play full-screen video at optimal resolution.

Musical Instrument Digital Interface (MIDI)

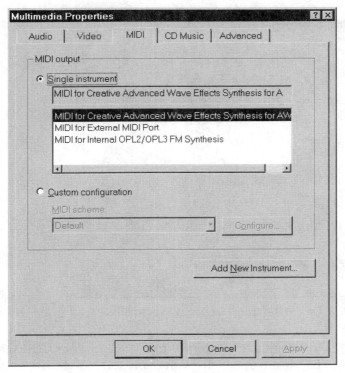

Figure 7-38: *Use MIDI to choose your instruments.*

The MIDI property sheet (Figure 7-38) looks pretty boring, and it does have a simple purpose. The Single Instrument option dedicates all MIDI output to an external synthesizer, usually attached to your sound card. The Custom Configuration lets you mix and match, sending some or all MIDI output to your sound card's synthesizer, and the rest to an external synthesizer. If you click on New, you get the MIDI Setup Wizard, which walks you through the setup of a MIDI keyboard (see Chapter 17).

When you choose Configure, you get a list of MIDI channels and the device assigned to play those channels. This is the substitute for the MIDI mapper in Windows 3.1.

CD Music

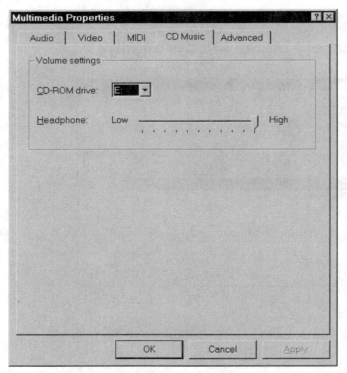

Figure 7-39: *CD Music settings let you set your volume level.*

Use the CD Music panel to set the volume level for your CD-ROM drive. You can play CD audio music discs on many CD-ROM drives, using the Windows 95 Media Player applet or a third-party tool. Here you can customize the volume level for the drive. You have to use a new Windows 95 (or later version) driver to make this work; otherwise, you use your sound card to control the volume level of your drive.

Advanced

The Advanced settings exist mainly for troubleshooting purposes. You'll rarely, if ever, need to use any of these options. For each type of multimedia device, you can click on the ⊞ symbol next to it to see what driver is used to control it. Sometimes a driver has customizable settings, so you could use Advanced to adjust it. For example, if you use the Microsoft Speaker driver for sound effects, you can double-click on the speaker driver to set the volume level and playback speed.

Network

The Control Panel Network settings are covered fully in Chapter 18, but here's a quick overview.

Configuration

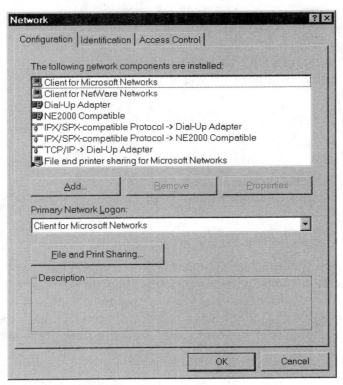

Figure 7-40: *Network Configuration.*

You use Network Configuration to choose the Network drivers. Here you see the settings for a home system that uses a modem to connect to a remote network using Remote Access Service. The Configuration box lists the currently installed networks, network protocols and network card drivers.

Identification

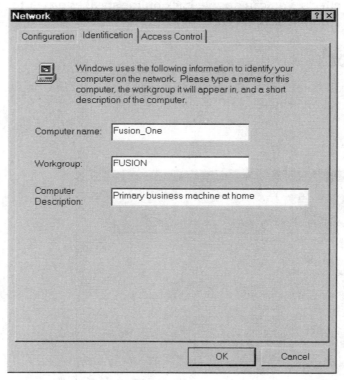

Figure 7-41: *Network Identification.*

With Network Identification, you name your computer so it will have an identity on the network, and choose a *workgroup* for peer-to-peer file and printer sharing via Microsoft Networking (not to be confused with The Microsoft Network). You can only access computers that have the same workgroup setting, so if you can't "see" the other computers on the network, this is the first thing to look for.

Access Control

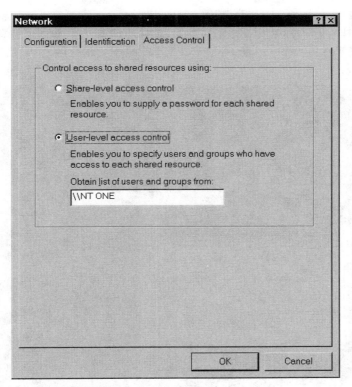

Figure 7-42: *Network Access Control.*

You use Network Access Control for peer-to-peer networking security. The default setting, Share-level, lets you create a separate password for each shared drive or printer on your computer. The other users need to know this password to be able to share your hard drive or printer. Or use User-level control if you want to set up access to your computer to specified groups of users. You define these groups using either Windows NT or Novell NetWare. Fill in the Obtain lists of users box with the name of the NT Domain or NetWare file server.

Printers

The Printers Control Panel object links you to your Printers folder, which you can also get to by clicking on Start and then selecting Settings | Printers. The printer is covered in depth in Chapter 13, so we'll just briefly mention the options here.

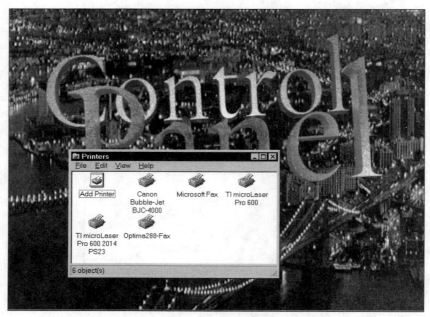

Figure 7-43: *Your Printers folder contains objects for all installed printers.*

The quickest way to control certain printer functions is to click the right mouse button on the printer icon.

 TIP   If you want to cancel your print jobs, right-click on the printer icon and choose Purge Print Jobs.

You may have many different printers installed. In some cases, you might even find something else posing as a printer. For example, in Figure 7-43, you see a strange printer labeled Microsoft Fax. It isn't really a printer at all, just a special pseudo-printer that is used to capture print jobs to be printed by Microsoft At Work Fax, the built-in fax program that comes with Windows 95. (See Chapter 16.)

Whenever you print from an application, you don't have to choose which printer to use if you set one of them as your default printer. While the printer works on your print job, you can use the Pause Printing option if you need to service your printer if it jams or runs out of paper. If you want to just start over again or change your mind about printing, use Purge Print Jobs to delete all current print jobs.

Right-click on a printer and use Create Shortcut if you want to make a copy of the printer object. That way, you can drag and drop it onto the desktop for a convenient way to control that printer without having to open the Printers folder.

TIP Be careful when using Delete, or you may lose the use of your printer until you reinstall it with Add Printer. You'll usually only delete a printer object if you replace that printer with a different one or no longer have use of a shared network printer.

If you don't like the name of a printer, feel free to rename it to something friendly. Try "My Printer" to go along with "My Computer" (or not).

To set the properties for a printer, just right-click on the printer icon, and choose Properties. Figure 7-44 shows the property sheets for the TI microLaser Pro printer.

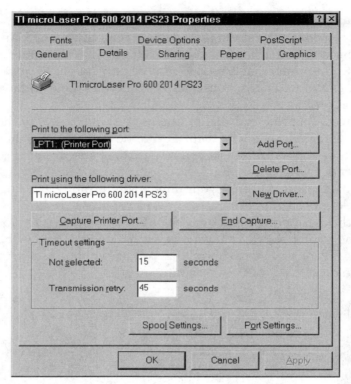

Figure 7-44: *Printer Properties lets you customize your printer.*

On this panel, you can choose the type of paper used by your printer and whether it should print top to bottom (Portrait) or sideways (Landscape). You can choose which paper tray to print from and the size of the paper tray. Some printers let you choose whether to print one page per sheet, 2-Up (two pages side by side on the same sheet), or to really save paper, use 4-Up. Specify the number of copies by either typing in the box, or click the Up/Down spin buttons.

For complete information on the Printer Properties, refer to Chapter 13.

Regional Settings

In the first screen you see after clicking on the Regional Settings icons, you can inform Windows 95 of your locale, or country. You specify your language and country in the drop-down list. Next, select Number to specify how your country displays its numbers. Normally, you won't need to change this setting if you chose the correct locale; however, these options demonstrate how far Windows goes to support international localization. Every numeric formatting option is customizable, too.

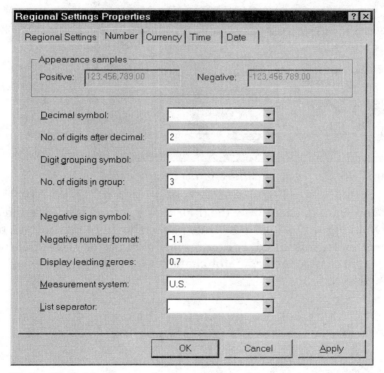

Figure 7-45: *Number settings are used for formatting numeric values.*

In Figure 7-46, you'll see the ways Windows formats currency (in the United States, "dollars and cents"). Again, you will not likely need to customize these settings unless your country is not supported by the locale chosen on the Regional Settings panel.

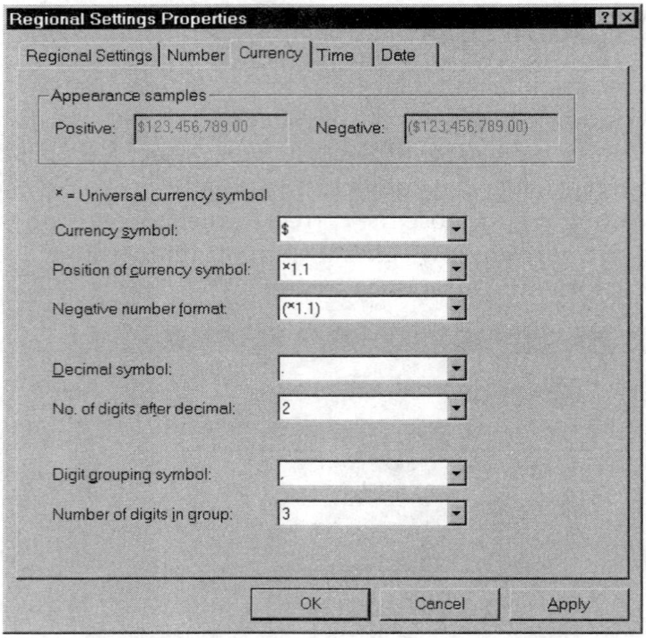

Figure 7-46: *Currency formatting for the United States.*

If you want to check how the time of day is formatted, use the Time panel, shown in Figure 7-47. Use the Date panel, shown in Figure 7-48, to modify how dates are formatted. For example, if you prefer 01-24-95 instead of 01/24/95, change the Separator character from the forward slash (/) to the hyphen (-).

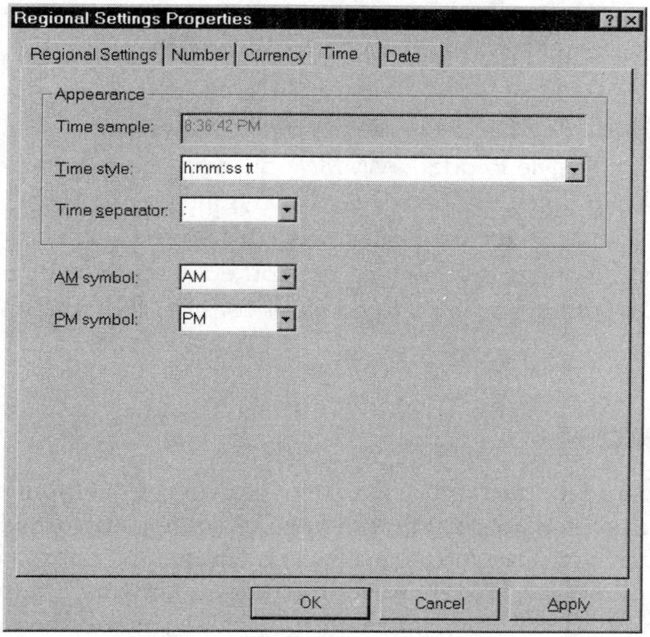

Figure 7-47: *Time formatting controls.*

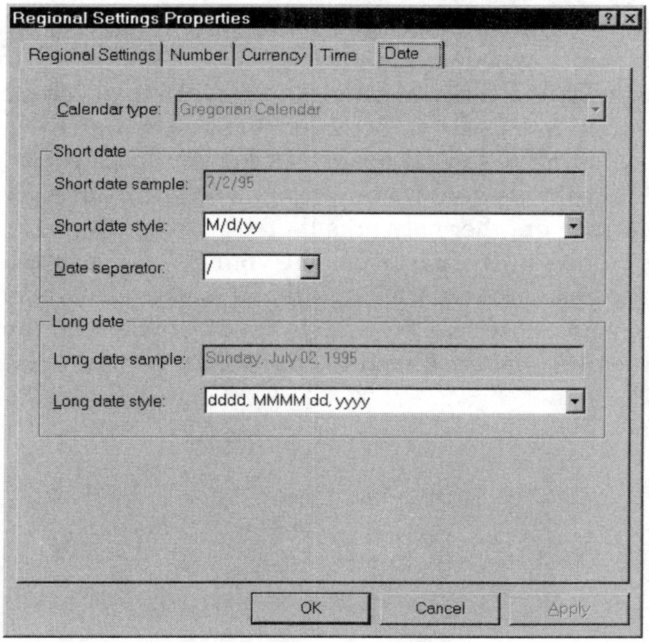

Figure 7-48: *Date formatting controls.*

TIP   Explorer uses the short date style when displaying the time/date stamp for a file in Details view. If you redefine Short date style, you change the way Explorer shows the dates. For example, change short date style to dddd, MMMM, dd, yyyy if you want it to match the long date style. This style displays the day name, month name, date and full year. (Because it also affects many other programs that can display long or short dates, such as a spreadsheet program, you want to carefully consider this option.)

 # Passwords

A password is a kind of "key" you use to lock up your computer and protect it from unauthorized access. You can have separate passwords for various purposes, such as a password to access your Exchange Inbox, a password to login to the file server, to login to your Windows network or a password to access a shared printer. For convenience, all these passwords can be accessed via a single master password. Imagine the master password as a key to a lock on a box that holds the keys to all the other locks in your house.

Using a single master password, your Windows password, is convenient because Windows will remember your other passwords for you and automatically fill them in when needed (though for the sake of security, the password is shown as a series of asterisks). You originally chose a password the first time you ran Windows 95. (If you just tapped Enter when asked for your password, Windows never again asks for your password. However, you must use a real password if you want to use Microsoft Networking, Novell Networking or other networks.)

Figure 7-49 shows how you can change your Windows (master) password. The only risk with this scheme is that if someone discovers your master password, your entire security system is vulnerable. You can also change the other passwords that are linked to your Windows password.

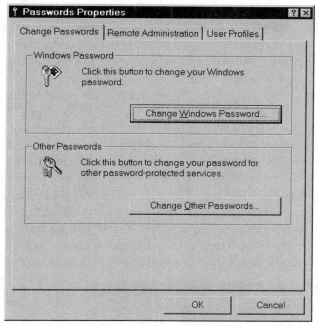

Figure 7-49: *The Windows password can control all your other passwords.*

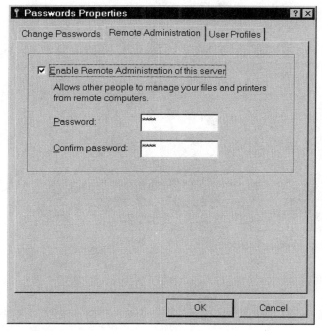

Figure 7-50: *Remote Administration settings.*

Your computer can be configured or even remotely controlled by the system administrator on the network. But to preserve your privacy, you want to make sure that not just anyone can use your computer. The Remote Administration password should only be known to you and the system administrator. Depending on your company policy, it may or may not be possible to change this password. (Some companies enable Remote Administration automatically when they set up Windows 95 on their computers.)

The User Profile Settings shown in Figure 7-51 are especially significant. By default, the Control Panel settings (and settings like the desktop colors) are always used for your computer, no matter who logs in to use it. But if you check the *User can customize their preferences* option, then a separate copy of Control Panel settings is employed for each user. You can create multiple accounts on the same computer, and when they log in, each user can have his or her own custom colors, cursors, network settings, passwords, default printers, what have you. (Actually, you can choose some settings to be shared between users if you like, but the choice is up to you.)

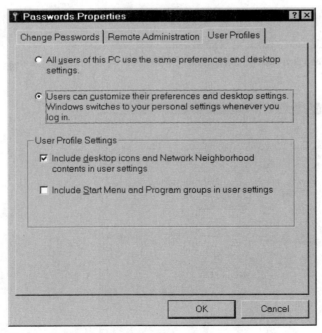

Figure 7-51: *User Profile settings.*

TIP If your network is configured properly, your user preferences will "follow" you as you move from machine to machine in an organization. Wherever you login, your personal preferences such as screen colors, desktop icons, accessibility settings, and so on will be applied to whatever computer you're using.

 # Power

You'll usually see this icon in Control Panel only if you're using a notebook (or laptop) computer that runs on battery power. Notebook computers use Advanced Power Management to save battery life by automatically powering down the hard drives and putting the central processing unit (CPU) into a low-voltage "sleep," when you haven't used your computer for a period of time.

Although power management was invented to save battery life, it can save electricity with desktop computers that feature the EPA Energy Star logo or other "green" logos. This capability allows you to keep your computer turned on all the time, if you like, sipping only enough power to keep the RAM charged, with all other components, including the video card, display monitor, hard drives, even CD-ROM drive and some printers, powered down in *standby* or *suspend* mode. If you press a key, move the mouse, if your modem starts receiving characters, or if any other event occurs, the computer springs back to life and powers up. The only disadvantage is that it can take a few seconds to power up the hard drive, which can slow you down a bit.

Power Properties

Windows 95 installs the Power icon in Control Panel if it detected support for Advanced Power Management or Intel SL Power Management (most 486-class chips support low-power SL mode) during Windows Setup. If not detected, you can still enable Advanced Power Management during Windows Setup, on the dialog box that summarizes all your setup options (the one immediately before the step where it starts copying files). Don't worry if you don't see a Power icon—you probably don't need it.

If your notebook/laptop is currently on battery power, the Power control lets you monitor your battery life remaining. (The figure shown is from a desktop computer, so it's running on AC power; in other words, it's not running on battery power.)

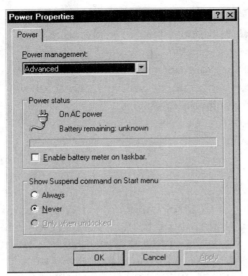

Figure 7-52: *You can enable a battery meter icon in the taskbar's notification area.*

If you want to see a visual indicator at all times of your battery strength, choose the Enable battery meter on taskbar check box to put a little warning gauge right on the notification area, next to the taskbar clock.

You can also enable the Show suspend command on Start menu, which adds Suspend Now to go along with Shut Down on the Start menu. That way, you can just select Start | Suspend when you know you're not going to use your computer for a while, to save even more power than waiting for the automatic suspend mode to kick in. You can also use Suspend before you turn off your computer if it features AutoResume. (Some notebooks power off automatically if you select Start | Shut Down instead.)

The option buttons let you choose when to show the Suspend icon on the Start menu: *Always, Never* or *Only when undocked*, that is, when your notebook computer is roaming free with you instead of inserted into a deskt⌐ docking station.

Sound Events

Sound Events are wave files that play whenever an event happens. An *event* includes actions such as starting or closing a program, minimizing or maximizing a window—you get the idea. Other applications can also create their own custom sound events, and you're free to customize them.

You can save an entire list of custom sounds as an *event scheme*, so you could define several different sets of sounds and keep them handy to use depending on your mood.

Windows 3.1 offered only a minimal library of built-in wave (.WAV) sounds, such as Chord, Tada, Ding and Chimes. These are assigned to various events. For example, click on Default Sound and then click on the Play button (shown as a right-pointing triangle in Figure 7-53) to listen to it.

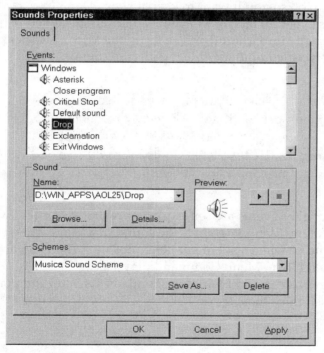

Figure 7-53: *Sound Events are fun to customize.*

 TIP   If the Play button is grayed out (disabled), you don't have a sound driver installed, or it's not working.

Windows 95 offers several coordinated sound schemes, including Musica, Jungle, Robotz and Utopia. Choose one of them from the list. If you don't see these options, refer to Add/Remove Programs, Windows Setup, and choose Details for Multimedia.

You can obtain new sounds from the huge libraries available on CD-ROM, or via CompuServe or America Online. Or "roll your own" with Sound Recorder or the sound tools that came with your sound card.

The Exclamation sound event is used whenever a message box appears with an exclamation point symbol, whereas the Question sound event appears when a dialog box asks you a question, displaying the Question symbol. Other dialog box sound events include Asterisk, Critical Stop and Program Error.

The default beep is used to get your attention or notify you of an error. You'll hear it a lot, so you'll want to keep it short. Don't choose a tiresome sound for this event. In fact, most event sounds are designed to be short, which is especially important if you're using the Microsoft Speaker driver, which freezes your computer while it plays the sound.

TIP The speaker driver, which lets you play sound effects through your computer's internal speaker, is not included with Windows 95, but you can use the widely distributed SPEAKER.DRV that was designed for Windows 3.1. (Available via *ftp.microsoft.com* and posted on most commercial online services.)

Most of the other events are self-explanatory, but you might wonder about two of them. Menu Pop Up is the sound that plays when you first click on a menu or when a submenu item pops up. When you actually choose the menu item, Menu Command plays.

Other programs can add their own sound events here, and you should feel free to customize them if you like.

System

The four following subsections correspond to the tab headings in System Properties.

General

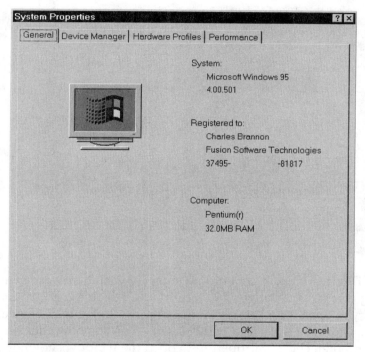

Figure 7-54: *General System properties.*

The General panel of System Properties displays a summary of your computer, shown in Figure 7-54.

Device Manager

Click on Device Manager to get to the heart of your system settings, shown in Figure 7-55.

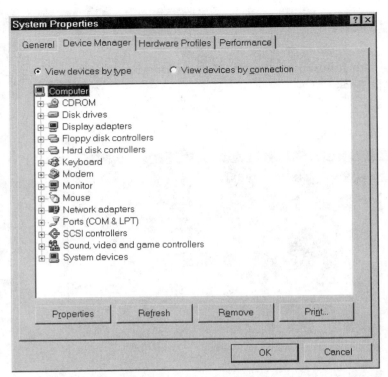

Figure 7-55: *Device Manager controls all your system resources.*

The Device Manager contains an entry for each hardware item or device in your computer, arranged by categories. Click on the ⊞ symbol next to a category to open it up and reveal its subitems. In Figure 7-55, we clicked on Ports to show the serial and parallel ports. You can now click on any of the ports and then click on Properties to open the window shown in Figure 7-56. (As a shortcut, just double-click on the item.) At any point, you can click on the Print button to print a report on your device settings.

 If you highlight the Computer item at the top of the Device Manager "tree" and choose Print, you can print out far more information about your machine than you ever thought was possible. And it's probably far more accurate than any other third-party utility of this same nature ever provided under previous versions of Windows.

Be careful with the Remove button. It removes all the entries for the driver, so if you removed the Printer Port, you wouldn't be able to print. However, you can reinstate the device using the Add New Hardware icon in the Control Panel.

The General Panel shown in Figure 7-56 lets you enable or disable the device without removing it. To disable a device, simply uncheck the box marked Original Configuration (Current). You can also choose to have a device enabled only sometimes, depending on your current hardware configuration. (See "Hardware Profiles" later in this chapter.)

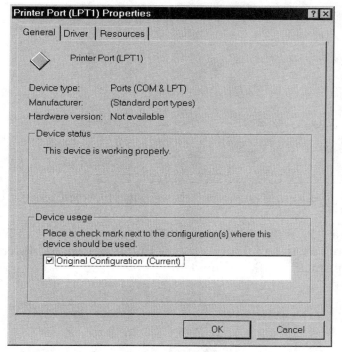

Figure 7-56: *General Printer Port settings.*

You can use the Driver panel, shown in Figure 7-57, if for some reason you want to verify the correct driver is being used. The driver is system software that permits applications and Windows itself to make use of the device. Most of the drivers you use are provided by Microsoft, but often new hardware comes with drivers provided by the manufacturer. If for some reason you need to change the software driver for the device, click on the Change Driver button.

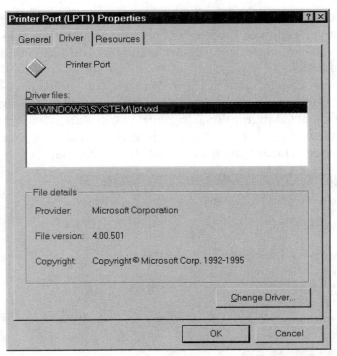

Figure 7-57: *The driver is the system software supporting the device.*

In Figure 7-58, we've "drilled down" to the deepest layer of the Device Manager to look at the resources for the COM3 port, used for serial communications, primarily with fax/modems.

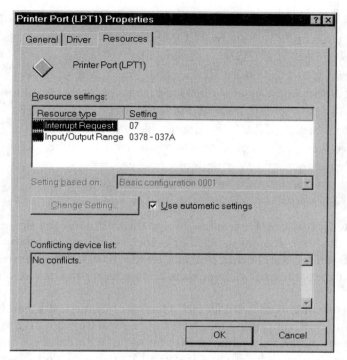

Figure 7-58: *Resource property sheet.*

What is a resource? In Windows 3.1, you may have been familiar with the infamous system resources that limited you to running only a few programs at a time. No matter how much memory you had, the old 16-bit memory model used by Windows 3.1 limited you to two 64k buffers for storing common objects such as icons and other screen graphics.

In Windows 95, Microsoft removed many of these restrictions. However, the term *resources* has a much greater significance in this discussion. Your computer has only so many hardware resources to draw upon, including IRQ settings, I/O addresses, DMA channels and memory addresses. They have to be divvied up between all the hardware requirements of your computer.

Normally, you can have only two COM ports active on a computer, since COM1 and COM3 use the same IRQ 4, whereas COM2 and COM4 use IRQ 3. The trick to getting a third active COM port is to find an otherwise unused interrupt for it. In Figure 7-58, you see the Input/Output Range is defined as 03E8-03EF, which is standard for COM3. By double-clicking on Interrupt Request, we were able to change it to IRQ5, which was not used for any other device. (IRQ5 is normally reserved for LPT2, a second optional printer port not present on this computer.)

Note the Conflicting Device List box at the bottom of the Resources property sheet. It shows the name of other devices that have overlapping resources. If you have a conflict, you can either change the resources for the device you're looking at or change the resources for the device it's conflicting with.

What else can you do with Device Manager? Using it is a good way to learn about your computer, since you can browse through all the options even without making any changes. If you remove hardware, you can remove the unnecessary hardware. If you add hardware, and it conflicts with another device, you may be able to resolve the conflict using Device Manager. Sometimes, instead of reconfiguring the new device, you can reconfigure an existing one, in which case you may need to change the Device Manager resource settings for that device.

Some aspects of Device Manager are redundant. For example, you can change the driver for your display with Device Manager, using the Driver panel and clicking on Change Driver. Or you can run the Display option from the Control Panel, choose the Settings panel and then click on Change Display Type.

Hardware Profiles

Hardware Profiles aren't very useful, except in special circumstances where your computer can be booted with different kinds of hardware— for example, a notebook computer that can be started both stand-alone or in a docking station on a network. In that case, more than one set of drivers for the different hardware may be present on the notebook as opposed to the hardware in the notebook's docking station. Once you define a profile, you can choose which devices belong in each profile. You are asked to choose one of these profiles every time you start your computer, which makes it rather inconvenient to use unless you really need it.

Performance

It seems we're never satisfied with the performance of our computer, no matter how much we expand them. How else can we explain the amazing progress of computer hardware? Whereas a 486-33 once seemed like the queen of computing, computer owners are now opting for 133 megahertz Pentiums and waiting eagerly for the Intel P6 and even P7 processors, which offer incredible speed improvements—for the right price, of course.

So we're always on the lookout for quick and cheap software adjustments, tweaks and optimizations. Although this book will help you do just that, keep in mind that Windows 95, properly configured, already runs about as fast as it ever will, barring a hardware upgrade.

The Performance panel shows you how your computer is configured. If it is indeed configured properly, you'll see a line that reads, "Your system is configured for optimal performance." You probably don't need to go any further.

But if you still insist on twisting dials, moving levers and generally fiddling with the controls, some juicy options are waiting for you behind the File System, Graphics and Virtual Memory buttons. But wait for Chapters 14 and 15 before you start exploring these options; those chapters will steer you in the right direction.

More Controls

The Control Panel is easily extensible, so over time, you'll acquire new Control Panel items, either with upgrades to Windows (such as Microsoft Plus!) or when you install new software.

 TIP If a Control Panel property sheet gets hidden by another window, you've probably noticed you can't get back to it using Alt+Tab. This is by design. Use Alt+Esc instead to switch between all open windows and dialog boxes. Alt+Tab is designed to show only the interesting windows.

Moving On

As you've seen, you can use the Control Panel to customize your Windows 95 environment. However, once you've made your Windows a comfortable place to be, it's time to get to work. In the next section, you'll see how to take advantage of your primary input devices, the keyboard and the mouse—the two most important ways you communicate your information and intentions to the computer.

Interacting With Windows

Chapter 8

The Keyboard

In this chapter, we'll introduce one of the primary tools you use to communicate with Windows—the keyboard. Chapter 9 focuses on the mouse.

Editing Essentials: Cutting, Copying, Dragging, Pasting

The mouse supplements the keyboard—both have their advantages. If you're a good typist, you can type faster than you can use a mouse to select from menus. On the other hand, using the mouse cursor to maneuver around the screen, grab objects, highlight, then visually move, resize, or delete objects is often more intuitive than trying to accomplish the same tasks via the keyboard.

In general, the mouse excels in tasks involving visuals, such as creating a drawing in a program like CorelDRAW, or manipulating Windows itself, like clicking on an icon to start a new application.

The keyboard is usually more efficient when you are working with words in a word processor or database, or with numbers in a spreadsheet. But computing increasingly involves manipulating both text and visuals at the same time—databases, word processors and spreadsheets now allow you to embed graphics. And sliding scroll bars, clicking icons, resizing windows and all the other Windows tools are designed to work with the mouse. So most people find themselves going back and forth between the keyboard and the mouse.

If you're used to typing and are good at it, you might find it annoying to take your hands off the keyboard just to, say, italicize a word. Selecting a word and then changing its font style to italics is circuitous, at best, with a mouse. You select a word by holding down the left mouse button and dragging the mouse pointer across the word to highlight it (highlighted text *reverses*—usually turns to white text on a black background, as shown in

Figure 8-1). Then you click on the italics icon in a toolbar (see Figure 8-2), or you click on a formatting menu and then click on Italics.

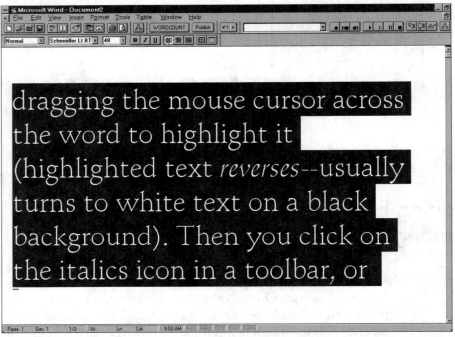

Figure 8-1: *When text is* selected, *it reverses to light letters on a dark background.*

Figure 8-2: *Toolbar icons are for the mouse's use exclusively.*

On the keyboard, you can select using the Shift+Arrow keys and then italicize that selection simply by pressing Ctrl+I. More importantly, you can go right on typing because both of your hands are still on the keyboard.

Using the mouse can be convenient enough when you're correcting or editing existing text, but reaching for the mouse can be annoying if you're actually writing—it can interrupt the flow of your thoughts.

Fortunately, Windows permits you to use either the keyboard or the mouse for virtually every task. Of course, you can't directly move the tab within a scroll bar using the keyboard (although the arrow keys and PgUp and PgDn keys accomplish the same result). Nor can you use the mouse to type in text (although it is possible to insert special characters using the mouse with the CharMap accessory).

Nonetheless, there is significant overlap between keyboard and mouse operations. To boldface text via the keyboard, you hold down the Shift key and then use the arrow keys to highlight the text you want selected. Then you press Ctrl+B (or whatever key combination your word processor uses for boldface).

The most common editing activities—for either graphics or text—are cutting, pasting, copying and moving (copying plus pasting). Here are the common techniques for both keyboard and mouse:

Action	Keyboard	Mouse
Select	Shift+Arrow keys	Drag across text
Copy	Ctrl+C or Ctrl+Ins	Click on the Edit menu, select ∣ Copy
Cut	Ctrl+X or Shift+Del	Click on the Edit menu, then select ∣ Cut
		Edit menu, select Cut
Clear	Del	Edit menu, select∣ Clear
Paste	Ctrl+V or Shift+Ins	Edit menu, select ∣ Paste
Move	Cut, then Paste	Cut and then paste

One of Windows's strong points is the general uniformity of keyboard shortcuts and mouse moves within any application written for Windows. You can expect any program to recognize that Shift+Ins means paste. However, some applications offer additional mouse techniques and keyboard shortcuts. For instance, Word for Windows 6.0 permits you to move text or graphics by dragging them. See Figure 8-3.

```
If you're a strong typist, you might find it annoying to take your hands off the keyboard just
to, say, italicize a word. Via the mouse, you select a word by holding down the left button and
dragging the mouse cursor across the word to highlight it (highlighted text reverses--usually
turns to white text on a black background). Then you click on the italics icon in a toolbar, or
click on a  Formatting  menu, then click on Italics.

Figure 5-1: When text is selected, it reverses to light letters on a dark background.
```

Figure 8-3: *Dragging selected text to move it—a non-standard technique in Word 6.0.*

When the Mouse Is Best

To move, cut or copy graphics, you almost exclusively use the mouse. For one thing, you cannot easily create an irregular section in a graphic object using the keyboard. Such a selection would be asymmetrical—not just blocks of text, but unique graphic shapes. What's worse, a graphic is usually not broken into discrete, separate entities such as letters, words, paragraphs and so on. A graphic is one object. Text is filled with characters, and each is a selectable object.

In Figure 8-4, we can see a variety of things—a dog, a hanky, a mother, a child, dresses, shoes and so on. Each of these objects, in the real world, could be selected, moved, removed and otherwise manipulated. However, inside the computer they are all welded together into a single graphic object. This presents us with problems if we decide to change parts of the image, precisely the same problems that we have when we want to edit a fax that someone sends us.

Figure 8-4: *Mom and her remarkably similar daughter—a single object in the computer, dozens of objects in the real world.*

As received, a fax is not true text. It, too, is a single object, a single graphic image. To change it into text, you must use character recognition software, which goes through the image analytically, separating white from black, and trying to determine which letter of the alphabet each graphic symbol represents. When the translation process is complete, you then have separate characters, true text. At this point, you can select individual characters, words, paragraphs and so on.

The fax software included with Windows 95 does send a fax document as a rich text message (.RTF) which is true, editable text. If this new kind of fax is received on a target computer running compatible fax software, you don't need special software to translate it before you can edit it. See Chapter 18.

A comparable translation process that can break a graphic image into its component objects is available. Some graphics programs, notably CorelDRAW, have bitmap-to-vector conversion filters, but the results are mixed at best. However, you can select an area by hand. Most graphics programs have a set of selection tools. On the simplest level, you drag a selection tool on the surface of the image, outlining the area that you want to cut, copy and so on. This process is similar to cutting a paper drawing with scissors. A more sophisticated set of graphic selection tools is shown in Figure 8-5.

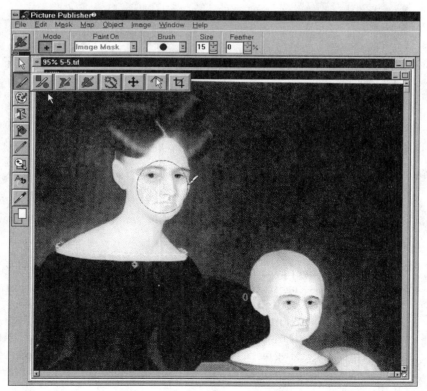

Figure 8-5: *Micrografx Picture Publisher features some of the most powerful selection facilities currently available.*

In Figure 8-5, we want to make a copy of the mother's face. A toolbar pops out providing a suite of powerful selection tools. In order, your options are Rectangular/Elliptical, Freehand, Paint On, Smart Mask (creates selections automatically, based on variations in shade) Transform, Point Editing and Crop (cut).

After choosing the Rectangular/Elliptical tool, we drag the mouse across the mother's face, selecting an oval area. Once selected, this area can be cut, moved or copied elsewhere in the image. In Figure 8-6, we have copied the new oval object.

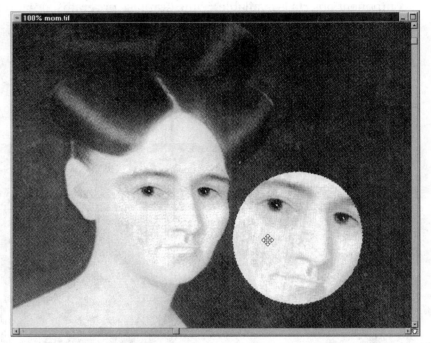

Figure 8-6: *The selection has been dragged, rotated and resized. Note the resizing cursor within the copied face.*

Each graphics application—Picture Publisher, CorelDRAW, Photoshop and all the rest—has its own way of selecting a zone within a graphic. What distinguishes the better applications is that the objects you select become *masks* or *layers*. This means that you can manipulate the new object with considerable freedom. It's as if you have created a new image that is printed onto a clear sheet of plastic. You can then superimpose the object in complex ways, even setting the amount of transparency or the kind of blending (see Figure 8-7).

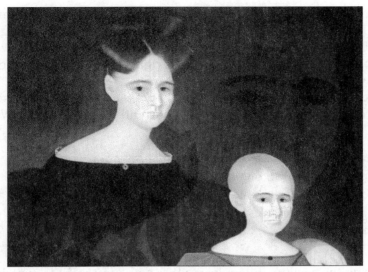

Figure 8-7: *An intricate graphic cut-and-paste job—the child's face, blown up and superimposed with high transparency.*

Keyboard Shortcuts

Windows applications, and Windows itself can be quickly manipulated from the keyboard. If you prefer, you can accomplish most anything without resorting to the mouse at all. Here is a list of the Windows's keyboard shortcut conventions, in their probable order of usefulness to you:

Instant Program Switching

◼ **Alt+Tab**   Probably the single most useful shortcut. This allows you to cycle between all the currently active programs. In Windows 3.1, this process was relatively awkward—you couldn't really see which programs you were cycling through. One of the most useful improvements in Windows 95 is the window that pops up mid-screen, and displays the icons and names of the currently running programs. (See Figure 8-8.) You can then select your choice as if you were in a cafeteria.

Figure 8-8: *With Windows 95, you get a cafeteria selection of the running programs.*

Sometimes you merely want to flip quickly between two running applications. For example, if you are writing a quarterly report, you might frequently switch between your word processor and a spreadsheet. In that case, press Alt+Tab, releasing the keys right away. The application that you were working in previously then appears.

If you hold down Alt and repeatedly press Tab without releasing Alt, you'll cycle through all the programs currently running under Windows.

 TIP   You can also cycle backward. If you have several programs running, you might tab one past the program you're after. Instead of tabbing through the whole row again, go backwards by holding down the Shift key (while also holding down Alt and pressing Tab).

During the cycling, if you decide that you don't want to switch to another application, keep holding down the Alt key, but press Esc. (Actually you can press almost any key, or even click with the mouse, to abort the program switch. But don't release Alt; otherwise, the selected application will appear and Esc will have no effect.)

 TIP   There are some "windows" that you simply can't get to with Alt+Tab. As a test, open Control Panel; then double-click on the Mouse icon. The Mouse Properties dialog box then appears. Now run another program, and try to use Alt+Tab to get back to the Mouse Properties dialog box. It's impossible. The best you can do is press Alt+Tab to go back to Control Panel and then press Enter on the keyboard to open Mouse Properties. Or you can minimize all other open windows to find the Mouse Properties dialog box on the desktop.

Why this sometimes vexing behavior? Windows 95 attempts to present only "interesting" windows to you when you cycle using Alt+Tab. Property sheets, wizards and certain other windows are not considered "interesting" for the same reason they don't appear on the taskbar at the bottom of the screen. This tactic avoids clutter. During the extensive usability testing for Windows 95, Microsoft learned that it's important for many users to avoid littering the taskbar (and Alt+Tab) with every last possible open window.

But there is a solution: use Alt+Esc. Unlike Alt+Tab, Alt+Esc will also cycle through any "hidden" dialog boxes and windows. Alt+Esc mimics the old Windows 3.0 behavior where Alt+Tab used to visit every currently open window.

As long as we're talking about *switching*, within an application that supports multiple internal child windows (also called a Multiple Document Interface—MDI—a technique that is now being discouraged by Microsoft), note that you can use Ctrl+Tab to switch between open child windows, even if they're maximized. Some applications that don't support Ctrl+Tab this way do allow you to use Ctrl+F6 instead.

Instant Exit

■ **Alt+F4**   Pressing Alt+F4 shuts down the currently active program. At that point, another application becomes the active one. (The active application is the one which, if you type something on the keyboard, will react to that typing. Sometimes it is also called the application that "has the focus.")

Pressing Alt+F4 repeatedly will shut down all running applications in turn until there are no more applications to close down. Then the final press of Alt+F4 will shut down Windows itself. Pressing Alt+F4 repeatedly works the same way as if you had clicked the Shut Down option on the Start button menu. (Yes, it's a little counterintuitive to click on the Start button in order to end your Windows session.)

Moving Within an Application

■ **Tab**   Unless you're in a text-only context like a word processor, Tab moves you through the various controls (buttons, text entry boxes and so on) within an application or dialog box.

Tabbing between controls, though, is particularly useful when there are several text boxes which must be filled in—such as a structured database entry window. Unlike with DOS applications, pressing the Enter key doesn't usually move you to the next text box; Enter is reserved for choosing the default button, such as OK. So knowing about the Tab key can be a great timesaver; you fill in one box and then hit Tab to move to the next one. To cycle in the opposite direction, press Shift+Tab.

TIP There are exceptions to the typical behavior of Enter and Tab. It's particularly useful for data entry—when you're typing in lists of information—if the Enter key performs two jobs simultaneously. One particularly good example of this kind of efficiency involves the CD Player application that comes with Windows. Pressing Enter does three things. To begin, select Start | Programs | Accessories | Multimedia | CD Player. Then click on Edit Play List in the Disk menu. Next, enter a song title in the CD play list, and press Enter. The title you just completed is entered into the list, the next title (the next track on the CD) is moved into the Edit box, and that new title is selected. Since it's there and selected, just typing in a new title will delete the selected title in the Edit box. In this way, you can just continuously type in each title, pressing Enter between each one—it's most efficient.

Because Tab is used so much for formatting purposes in writing, Tab usually doesn't cycle through controls in a word processor. Instead, it inserts a true tab (a formatting code that aligns text to the tab mark on the ruler, often about the width of five spaces) within the text.

Cancellation

■ **Esc**   Esc cancels the most recent action. If you've just opened a menu, the menu will close. If an application is displaying a message box or dialog box, the box will disappear. Many of the behaviors associated with the Esc key are particular to an application or the context within which you are currently working. However, the general effect is to stop something and return to a previous state, to escape from something you don't want. For instance, pressing Esc while CorelDRAW is redrawing the screen will cancel the redraw. If Esc doesn't seem to work, try pressing it repeatedly. Some older applications simply don't check the keyboard very often.

In an emergency, press Ctrl+Alt+Del to pop up a list of running programs. You can then use the End Task button to abort a program that's not responding. You will lose any unsaved data in that application.

TIP The Ctrl+Break sequence previously used in MS-DOS is rarely honored in Windows applications (in fact, its synonym Ctrl+C is used as a shortcut for Copy), but it can still be used to interrupt some DOS applications running from within Windows. (A few Windows applications use the Alt+<period> sequence, which is mnemonically linked with the use of the period character as a "full stop" in typesetting, to interrupt a process.)

Accessing Menus

■ **Alt+letter** This shortcut opens a menu. For example, in most applications, Alt+F opens the File menu, at which point you could press S to save your work. You don't need to hold down the Alt key during this operation (so that you are simultaneously pressing Alt and some other key). Instead, you can press Alt and then release it.

Applications differ in their behavior if you press the Alt key and then release it. You might notice that the menu button (sometimes called the Control menu) then becomes depressed (see Figure 8-9), indicating that the menus have been made active. Other applications highlight the first menu title "File." Yet other applications do nothing visible. But in all cases, you can use the arrow keys to move among the menu titles and then press Enter to open whatever menu is currently highlighted. Within the menu, press the Up or Down arrow keys to select menu entries, and make your choice by pressing Enter. (Windows trivia: The F10 key does the same thing as Alt. Press it once to move to the menu bar.)

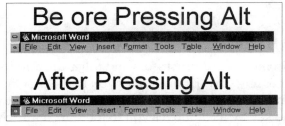

Figure 8-9: *The Menu button, unselected, then selected by pressing Alt.*

Alternatively, you can press Alt along with the character for the menu you want (Alt+E for Edit, Alt+T for Tools, or whatever menu items are available at the time). Each menu item in Windows has an underlined letter: File, Edit, Window, Help and so on. You press the underlined character to select it (see Figure 8-10).

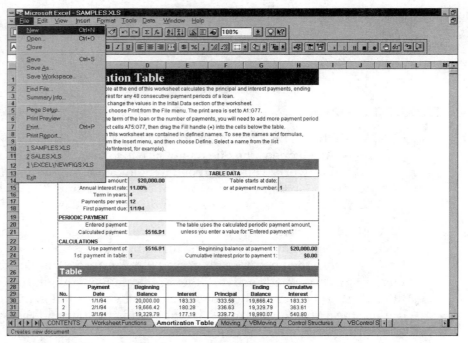

Figure 8-10: *Pressing Alt plus F opens the File menu in Excel.*

If you want to exit from a menu or simply from this Alt mode, press Alt again or Esc.

Quick Moves Within Documents

■ **Ctrl+Home**   In most word processors and other document-processing applications, pressing Ctrl+Home moves you to the first line at the top of the document. Likewise, pressing Ctrl+End moves you to the bottom. The Home key by itself moves you to the start of the current line; the End key by itself moves you to the end of the current line.

■ **Alt+<cursor left> & Alt+<cursor right>**   You can use the Right and Left arrow keys to move through the document word by word.

Toggling DOS to Full Screen

■ **Alt+Enter** This keyboard shortcut toggles a DOS screen between full screen (text mode) and windowed. (See Figure 8-11.) Using this short-cut is not the same as "maximizing," which makes a Windows-style window fill the screen. To maximize a Windows window using the keyboard, press Alt+Space+X, and use Alt+Space+N to minimize. You can minimize all open windows if you have the Microsoft Natural Keyboard (or any other 104-key keyboard) by pressing the Windows logo key, plus M (Win+M). This has the same effect as right-clicking on any empty part of the taskbar with the mouse, and choosing Minimize All. As a bonus, use Shift+Win+M to "undo minimize all."

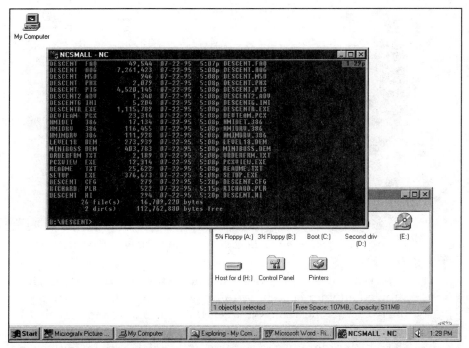

Figure 8-11: *Pressing Alt+Enter is a convenient way to enlarge or reduce a DOS window.*

Opening the Task Window

■ **Ctrl+Esc**   In Windows 95, Ctrl+Esc pops up the Start button menu, which makes it quick and easy to access your programs without reaching for the mouse (see Figure 8-12). Just press Ctrl+Esc, press the Up arrow key to choose a menu entry, and then press Enter. To move into a submenu, just press the Right arrow key.

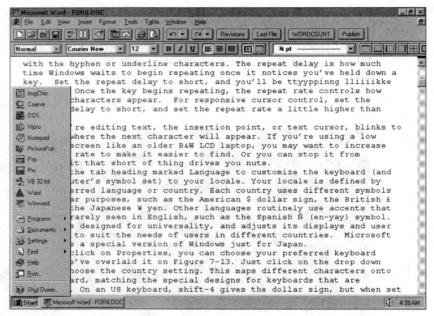

Figure 8-12: *You bring up the full Start menu by pressing Ctrl+Esc.*

In Windows 3, Ctrl+Esc brought up the useful Task Manager, which showed all your currently running tasks and let you switch between them fairly easily. The Task Manager, though, is obsolete now that Windows 95 includes the superior taskbar approach. With the taskbar, you can always see which programs are running and switch to them with a single click. (See Chapter 3.)

TIP   If you have the Microsoft Natural Keyboard (or other 104-key keyboard), you can open the Start menu by pressing the Windows key.

(In Windows 3, you also could double-click on the desktop to display the Task Manager, but now desktop left-clicking does nothing. You can, however, right-click on the desktop to find several useful shortcuts; see Chapter 4.)

 TIP Task Manager is not completely gone in Windows 95. You can still run it by clicking on the Start button, choosing Run and entering **TASKMAN** in the text box. While Task Manager is now somewhat redundant given the taskbar (and the Start button menu), you might find that you like to use it. If so, create an icon for it in your Accessories folder (or within whatever folder you prefer to locate it). You can then assign it a shortcut key to open it instantly.

To create the shortcut, right-click the Start button, choose Open and then double-click on the Programs folder. Next, double-click on the Accessories folder. From the File menu of the Accessories folder, choose New|Shortcut. When prompted, enter **TASKMAN** as the filename of the shortcut. After the shortcut is ready, right-click on its icon and choose Properties. Click the Shortcut tab, click on the Shortcut Key entry and press a keyboard sequence that you'd like to use to open the Task Manager, for example, Alt+Ctrl+~ (the tilde key directly under the Esc key). Voilà, you've restored the traditional Task Manager—for what it's worth.

Capturing the Screen

- **PrtScr** When you press the PrtScr key, you capture your entire monitor screen into the Clipboard, as if it's been photographed. (See Figure 8-13.) Once in the Clipboard, it then can be pasted into almost any application—for inclusion as a Picture Object in a word processor, for photo-retouching in a program like Photoshop, and so on.

Figure 8-13: *The PrtScr key moves an image of this entire screen into the Clipboard.*

The PrtScr key can still be used to print the screen of an MS-DOS program if it's running in full-screen text mode (press Alt+Enter to switch between windowed and full-screen text mode). If the MS-DOS program is running in a window, PrtScr will still copy the entire screen.

■ **Alt+PrtScr**   This shortcut works like PrtScr, but it copies only the currently active window (sometimes called the *client area*), not the entire screen. (See Figure 8-14.)

Figure 8-14: *Alt+PrtScr copies an image of the currently active window, not the whole screen (compare to Figure 8-13).*

Blind Program Switching

■ **Alt+Tab**   Alt+Tab brings up the round-robin cafeteria bar (the "cool switch") showing you the icons and names of currently running programs to which you can switch. Alt+Esc, however, switches visibly between all open windows. The difference here is that Alt+Tab shows you a bar with icons on it and cycles among them. Alt+Esc shows you the actual opened windows—applications and interior child windows—and cycles among them. Alt+Esc will not, however, display any applications that have been minimized and, although still "running," are now icons on the taskbar.

Child Windows

■ **Ctrl+Tab**   This shortcut usually moves among child windows. Some programs permit *interior* windows, called *child windows*. The classic example is a word processor in which each separate document that you're working on is located within a separate child window within the application's main window. You can tile child windows, cascade them, stretch and move them—in other words, treat them as if they were real windows (however, they cannot be moved outside the "parent" window of the application). (See Figure 8-15.) Similarly, Excel permits you to have more than one workbook open at any given time; each open workbook is a child window (see Figure 8-16). Technically, applications that permit child windows are said to have a multiple document interface, or MDI.

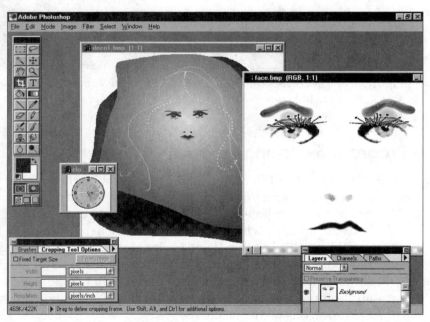

Figure 8-15: *Child windows in Photoshop—they behave much like ordinary windows but must remain within their "parent" application. Here you can see some "document" child windows (drawings) and utility child windows containing various Photoshop tools.*

Figure 8-16: *An application with the child windows feature (Excel, in this case) usually has a menu called "Window" with which you can arrange and manage the children.*

Not all Windows applications, Word included, support Ctrl+Tab. Instead, you must use the more universal, but less meaningful, Ctrl+F6 keyboard shortcut.

TIP   Windows 95 (and Microsoft Office applications) use a "tabbed" dialog box that combines several separate dialogs into one. You can click on the tab heading to switch between each "page" or "panel" of the dialog box. The keyboard shortcut is Ctrl+Tab, or Shift+Ctrl+Tab to reverse direction.

Ctrl+F4 Ctrl+F4   This closes the currently active child window, just as Alt+F4 closes the currently active main, parent or application window.

The Spacebar—Toggling

■ **Spacebar**   When a dialog box becomes visible, such as a text formatting dialog box, you can toggle (turn on or off) the currently selected
option button or check box by just pressing the Spacebar. This is an
alternative to clicking the mouse pointer on an option button. (See
Figure 8-17.) You can also "click" on a command button (such as OK or
Cancel) by pressing Tab to move to the button and then pressing the
Spacebar. (Recall that Tab will cycle you through all the options in a
dialog box, including any buttons.)

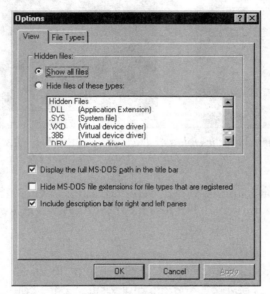

Figure 8-17: *Pressing the Spacebar toggles—turns things on and off—like this check
box in the Options for file viewing.*

Application Control Menus

■ **Alt+Spacebar**   This shortcut drops down the currently active application's Control menu, sometimes called the Document Control menu.
Although few people use it, this Control menu is available if you like it.
You can also access it by clicking the icon in the upper-left corner of
most windows. Control menus contain features that you can generally
accomplish more easily without dropping down these menus—moving
the window, minimizing or maximizing it, closing it, and so on. One of

Microsoft's and other good software providers' intelligent design decisions is to provide redundancy.

Of course, it's hammered into us at school that redundancy is to be avoided; that it's an embarrassing sign that one has lost one's way and has become merely repetitive. But often redundancy is useful. The Space Shuttle's three onboard backup computers, our two lungs, and money are obvious cases where more of the same is usually a good thing.

Redundancy in computer interface design helps the user because some people just work differently than other people. That's why, for example, Windows 95 offers the following three ways to access the mouse property sheet to change your mouse driver when you buy a new mouse:

1. Right-click on My Computer, choose Properties, Device Manager, expand the mouse tree, click on the mouse icon, choose properties and then choose Driver.
2. Select Control Panel | Mouse | General.
3. Select Help | Index | Mouse, choose Adding or changing driver, and then press the icon in the Help window to run the Device Manager.

In computing, too, redundancy is not a bad word. Keeping multiple backup files, being able to italicize using either the keyboard or the mouse, and so on. Microsoft enjoys redundancy and actively promotes it. With Windows 3, you got two word processors (Write and Notepad); Windows 95 offers Notepad and WordPad. There are two operating systems (Windows and NT), two versions of Visual Basic (regular and "professional"), two databases (Access and FoxPro), and so on down the line.

These Control menu icons in the upper-left corner of most windows are miniature versions of the program's own icon (see Figure 8-18). The things you see when you click on them—closing the application, for example—are more easily accomplished by pressing Alt+F4 or by double-clicking on that corner icon itself or the X icon in the opposite corner. But, in the true spirit of "let them do it their way," single-clicking on the Document Control icon as it's called, drops a menu down for those who prefer menu maneuvers (see Figure 8-19).

Figure 8-18: *The application window and the document window both have a Control menu, which you access by clicking on the small icons in the windows' upper-left corners.*

Figure 8-19: *When you click the upper-left corner of most windows, this Document Control menu descends.*

The Control menu for most applications is quite similar: Restore (to previous window state—minimized, maximized or normal); Move; Size; Minimize; Maximize; Close; Switch To (bring up the Task Manager window).

▓ **Alt+Hyphen**   Drops the Control menu of the currently active child window, if there is one. Interior windows (child windows) within the application often have specialized Control menus, which offer options appropriate to the purpose of the child window. For instance, in Adobe's Photoshop, the child window that governs brushes offers options to create a new brush, save a brush to disk and so on (see Figure 8-20).

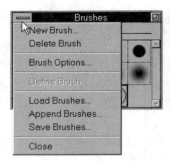

Figure 8-20: *The Control menus of a child window displays options appropriate to the purpose of the window.*

Editing

■ **Ctrl+Shift+PageUp**   You can use this shortcut to select the text from the current cursor position to the top of the page. Ctrl+Shift+PageDn selects from the current position to the bottom of the page. This behavior is supported by many word processors but isn't standard, nor is it often useful.

■ **Insert**   Pressing the Insert key toggles insert and overstrike mode. When you type in insert mode, all following text is pushed ahead as you type. It's like loading bullets into a magazine. In overstrike mode, following text is overwritten. Many writers remain in insert mode all the time. (Some programs let you use Insert by itself instead of Shift+Insert to Paste.)

■ **Alt+Backspace**   Generally, this shortcut triggers an Undo, reversing the previous action. If you just deleted a word, Alt+Backspace restores that word. Usually, several levels of Undo are available to you, so you can repeatedly press Alt+Backspace to see the effects of several of your recent actions.

■ **Ctrl+Backspace**   Use this shortcut to trigger a Redo. In other words, if you've just deleted a word and press Alt+Backspace to undo it (restoring the word), then pressing Ctrl+Backspace would once again delete that word. Repeatedly pressing Ctrl+Backspace deletes a word to the left of the cursor.

■ **Ctrl+Z**   This Undo shortcut is the same as using Alt+Backspace.

■ **Ctrl+Y**   This Redo shortcut is the same as using Ctrl+Backspace.

Shutdown or Reboot

■ **Ctrl+Alt+Del** This Shutdown or Reboot key combination (deliberately complex and spread wide apart on the keyboard so you won't hit it accidentally) was originally designed to mimic turning off the power to the computer. When you press these three keys at the same time, Windows shows you a list of currently running applications ("tasks"). You can then choose to close down any one of the tasks by clicking on the task name and then clicking on the End Task button.

This keyboard shortcut is useful if one of your applications stops responding ("hangs"). You can often selectively "un-bomb" your frozen application without having to turn off power to the computer. (Windows 3.x also permitted Ctrl+Alt+Del but was generally less successful than Windows 95 in accomplishing recovery from a bombed program. You often had to just restart the computer.)

You'll find Explorer always listed as a running task. Selecting End Task for Explorer has no effect, except to restart Explorer. Since Explorer is the Windows desktop and shell, you cannot get rid of it!

The Shut Down option, however, does close Windows. It's as if you had clicked on the Start button, selected Shut Down and then chosen the Shut Down the Computer option. (You aren't, however, given a chance to cancel this choice, nor are you shown the option of "restarting" Windows.)

Two Oddities

Keyboard real estate is expensive—you don't want any redundant or useless keys sitting there, do you? After all, your hands are only so large. They can conveniently reach only so many keys, and most of those keys are the letters of the alphabet anyway. You don't want dud keys sitting there. Given that, how do we explain the existence of the Scroll Lock key (which even has its own light on the keyboard!) and the SysRq key?

Scroll Lock was used a long time ago in a few MS-DOS file viewers and word processors. Like the utterly puzzling human appendix—that four inch long blind tube that leads nowhere and does nothing except sometimes get infected—Scroll Lock is an evolutionary remnant. Scroll Lock's existence on every computer keyboard reminds us that it must have been once useful in some way, but it's sure hard to explain now.

In theory, when you press Scroll Lock, the cursor in a few applications will be centered on the screen. When you use the Up and Down arrow keys to scroll a document, Scroll Lock keeps the cursor on the 12th line. So the cursor is "locked" during scroll.

Since, like a light switch, Scroll Lock can be toggled on and off, some applications use it for purposes that have nothing to do with scrolling. And because it actually displays a light on the keyboard, a programmer could use it as a "state" or "mode" indicator. For instance, its light could indicate that italics are on or the insert mode is in effect. However, in practice, it's rarely used for anything.

The SysRq (System Request) key is also widely ignored. It was added by IBM when they expanded the personal computer keyboard to 101 keys because there was a SysRq key on some of their commercial terminal keyboards. It means "System Request" but since applications don't use it, it's actually used to capture the screen (or current window). In other words, in its unshifted state, it nonetheless triggers a PrtScr (the shifted part of this key). To capture the entire screen, press SysRq. To capture the current window, press Alt+SysRq. (As we mentioned earlier, another relic, the Pause/Break key, doesn't have any effect in Windows 95.)

Typical Shortcuts

In addition to the Windows-wide shortcut key combinations described above, most applications have a set of shortcuts built in. In many applications, Ctrl+S will save the current document to disk. Usually, Ctrl+C will copy selected text or graphics to the Clipboard, and Ctrl+V will paste the Clipboard's contents at the current cursor position (the "insertion point"). Generally, F3 activates the search feature (but sometimes a search is triggered by Ctrl+F instead). In most word processors, Ctrl+I toggles italics, and Ctrl+B toggles boldface.

Perhaps the most common shortcut key used in any application is the Help shortcut. Even in the years when DOS was the operating system, Microsoft urged all applications to display Help when the user pressed F1. It's now become so common that even WordPerfect—long a holdout—uses the F1 key for that purpose.

But F1 is a rare example of conformity. There are hundreds of unique, application-specific shortcut key combinations. That makes life difficult. Even among Microsoft's own applications, there are variations.

Fortunately, you can usually *redefine* the default shortcut keys. In effect, you customize your keyboard. Most applications now use F3 to start a search (this feature, sometimes called Find, is located on the Edit menu of most applications). You might therefore want to change any non-conformist applications, such as the current version of Access, by redefining the purpose of the F3 key. We'll demonstrate how to make these changes shortly.

TIP In a long list box of data, you can usually type only the first
couple of letters of the item you're looking for in the list, and the
list box will jump to the location where that item is likely located.
For example, when you use the Search, Find or Index features in
Windows 95 Help, as soon as you type **pri**, you should see
listings for the printer.

Dominators

In each computer program category—word processing, graphics and so
on—one application seems to dominate. For example, in the early '80s,
WordStar was the most popular word processor. Not surprisingly, the shortcut key combinations used by WordStar, bizarre and hard to remember as
they sometimes were, became the standard. Several other word processors
borrowed some or all of the WordStar template.

As WordPerfect rose to dominance in the mid-80s, its shortcuts, in turn,
were widely imitated. Now that Microsoft's Word for Windows dominates
both the PC and Mac markets, Word's set of shortcut keys sets the standard.
This makes sense. If you are marketing a word processor, you want people
to switch from their current word processor to yours. It's easier for them to
switch if your product uses shortcuts they are already familiar with. For this
reason, and because many of Word's shortcut keys are mnemonic (easy to
remember, such as Ctrl+U for underline), even applications that don't process words, such as spreadsheets, are gradually adopting the Word keyboard template.

Even if you don't use Word for Windows, you might find the Word
keyboard standard worth considering. Many of your applications probably
use some of these key combinations. As time goes by and as more and
more applications join the bandwagon, we can expect other shortcut keys
to join F3 and F1 as universal standards. And it is predictable that many of
these universally accepted shortcuts will derive—at least in the next few
years—from Word for Windows. Windows 95's new WordPad, for example, follows most of the conventions established by Word. (After all, it
is a kind of "baby Word.")

There are anomalies, however. One common task, searching for a particu-
lar word or phrase in a document (Edit | Find or, less often, Search | Search),
is triggered by pressing Ctrl+F. Ctrl+F is used for this purpose in most
Microsoft applications and many applications from other companies. How-

ever, it doesn't work in Notepad. Notepad uses F3 to launch a search. So does Visual Basic (which also permits Ctrl+F). Word and WordPad use Ctrl+F only. You can either get used to these discontinuities, or in more sophisticated programs like Word, redefine the shortcut keys (as we'll illustrate shortly).

Function Keys

Every keyboard has a strip of keys labeled F1 through F10. Most keyboards also include F11 and F12 keys. Windows 95 itself uses these keys sparingly, but they're frequently exploited by applications. Originally, function keys were designed to be user-programmable—a way to store frequently used phrases—or to activate *macros*. We'll show you how to program your keyboard with Microsoft Word later in this chapter (similar techniques are possible with most computer applications of any substance).

Function keys are primitive and not very friendly, since the keys themselves don't have any meaning. Ideally, each key would bear on its face a tiny LCD panel, which the computer could program to display toolbar icons. As it is, you have to memorize their functions. You can also buy *templates*, pieces of cut-out plastic, which overlay the function keys. Template overlays are available for many popular programs, and you can get blank ones that you can fill in yourself.

Table 8-1 illustrates which function keys are commonly used by Windows applications. Also see Table 8-2, "Common Shortcut Key Combinations," for a list organized by the job the keys perform.

Although most programs make their own use of function keys (and there isn't much of a standard), some keys are "owned" by Windows. We also include keyboard shortcuts for common Explorer functions, which also work in any open desktop folder.

F-Key	Common Function	Other Function
F1	Help	+Shift: "What's this?" Help
F2	Varies by application	Explorer: Rename
F3	Find Next	Explorer: Find Files
F4	Varies	+Ctrl: Close MDI* window
		+Alt: Exit program
		Explorer: Drop down drive list
F5	Varies	Explorer: Refresh (redraw) file list
F6	Varies	+Ctrl: Next child window
		Explorer: Same as Tab

F-Key	Common Function	Other Function
F7	Varies	
F8	Varies	
F9	Varies	
F10	Same as pressing Alt	+Shift: Right mouse click
F11	Rarely used	
F12	Rarely unused	

Table 8-1: *Commonly used function keys.*

 TIP If you're looking for a keyboard alternative to clicking the mouse, use the Alt+*underlined letter* method mentioned previously. You can also click on a button by pressing Tab to move to the button, and press the Spacebar. Pressing Enter usually has the effect of "pressing" the default button, usually the OK button. What about the right mouse button? Windows and most applications let you use Shift+F10 to simulate a right mouse click. If you want to completely avoid using the mouse, see "A Simulated Mouse" at the end of this chapter.

Common Shortcut Key Combinations

Which keyboard shortcuts should you learn? Which ones should you program into your other applications? Table 8-2 lists some of the most useful shortcut keys in Word for Windows, the emerging standard.

Action	Shortcut
Help	F1
Search	Ctrl+F
Exit	Alt+F4
Formatting	
Change capitalization	Shift+F3
(cycles through lowercase, initial caps, all caps)	
Increase font size	Ctrl+Shift+>
Decrease font size	Ctrl+Shift+<
Toggle boldface	Ctrl+B

Action	Shortcut
Toggle italics	Ctrl+I
Center	Ctrl+E
Undo	Ctrl+Z
Editing	
Select	Shift+Arrow keys
Select	F8+Arrow keys
Select entire document	Ctrl+mouse click in left margin
Select entire document	Ctrl+A
Select vertically	Shift+Ctrl+F8 and then arrow keys
Extend a selection	F8
Cancel selection made with F8	Esc
Cancel selection made with Shift+Arrow key or mouse	Any arrow key
Select to next instance of a particular character	F8+the character
Copy	Ctrl+C
Paste	Ctrl+V
Move a selection	F2
Navigating	
Go to start of document	Ctrl+Home
Go to end of document	Ctrl+End
Go to next document window	Ctrl+F6
Go to previous document window	Ctrl+Shift+F6
The File Menu	
New Document	Ctrl+N
Open Document	Ctrl+O
Close Document	Ctrl+W
Save Document	Ctrl+S
Save As	F12
Print Document	Ctrl+P
The Edit Menu	
Repeat Last Action	Ctrl+Y or F4
GoTo	Ctrl+G

Action	Shortcut
The View Menu	
Normal	Alt+Ctrl+N
Page Layout	Alt+Ctrl+P
The Insert Menu	
Date & Time	Alt+Ctrl+D
The Format Menu	
Adjust Font	Ctrl+D
The Tools Menu	
Spelling	F7
Thesaurus	Shift+F7

Table 8-2: *Common shortcut key combinations.*

Of course, you may be interested in the key definitions for other tasks—it all depends on what you commonly use the computer for. To find which shortcut is used in you use in Word for Windows to accomplish a particular task, start Word 6.0, press Alt+H, C and then select Reference Information followed by Keyboard Guide.

What Does a Particular Key Do?

To find out what behavior Word assigns to which key combination, press Alt+T, C and then Alt+K. The Tools/Customize dialog box shown in Figure 8-21 then appears. Press Alt+N to move your cursor to the Press New Shortcut Key text box; then press the key combination that you're interested in. In Figure 8-21, we pressed the F7 key, and Word reported that this key is "Currently Assigned to ToolsSpelling." *ToolsSpelling* demonstrates the conventional Microsoft abbreviation, which includes first the menu, *Tools*, followed by the item on that menu, *Spelling*. In this book we're indicating menus and submenus in this way: Tools | Spelling.

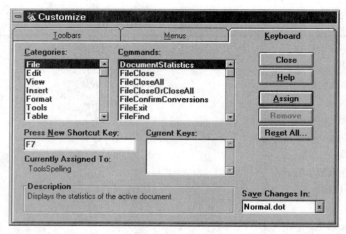

Figure 8-21: *Press a key combination in the Customize dialog box, and Word tells you what it does.*

Which Key Accomplishes Some Task?

To go the other way, to find out what shortcut key (if any) accomplishes a particular task, you can also use the Tools/Customize dialog box. Press Alt+T, C and then Alt+K; then select the menu where the task is located (in the Categories list), and select the particular task (in the Commands list). In Figure 8-22, we selected Tools under Categories and then selected Tools Thesaurus under Commands. Word informs us that this task is currently activated by pressing Ctrl+T. We are also informed that this command "Finds a synonym for the selected word." Note that some tasks will have more than a single shortcut (for example, you can toggle boldface with either Ctrl+B or Ctrl+Shift+B).

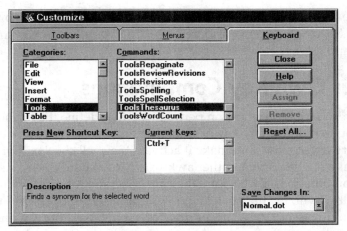

Figure 8-22: *You can also find out what shortcut Word assigns to a particular task.*

Note also that Word doesn't assign a shortcut to every task. Some tasks are so obscure that they're rarely used. And "dangerous" moves like FileClose (Alt+F4) are not only assigned to awkward key combinations unlikely to be accidentally triggered, but are also "trapped." Safety traps include the dialog box that pops up if you try to close a document that's been changed in any way from its state on the disk. If you load a document, make some changes and then press Alt+F4, Word displays a dialog box that asks if you want to save the changes to this document before closing it (and, if unsaved, losing the changes).

Microsoft does extensive "usability testing" where average users are watched while they work with an application. Perhaps it was found that people sometimes accidentally pressed a shortcut which closed the current document *without warning*. Most casual computer users would find it quite alarming if their document suddenly disappeared. It would be as unnerving as hanging a picture and poof it vanishes. Casual users generally see the computer through a real-world metaphor. When they are working in a word processor, they are perhaps thinking paper-on-my-desk or pen-and-ink.

Just because Microsoft provides no shortcut key for a particular task doesn't mean that you can't define one, however. Computer applications have become marvelously customizable. You can decide what will appear on menus and in what order; you can also decide what buttons will appear on the toolbar and what toolbars will be visible. Possibly most useful of all, you can decide what shortcut key combinations accomplish what tasks. You can reassign or delete the shortcuts that Microsoft provides by default, and you can define new shortcuts for existing tasks. You can even create entirely new tasks that Microsoft never considered (see "Macros—Power Keystrokes" later in this chapter).

Creating Your Own Key Combinations

Nearly every serious application permits you to redefine the keyboard. Most permit you to redefine any key or combination of keys. You can even redefine an ordinary letter, say *s*, and make it activate the spell checker. (Of course, this would make regular typing rather awkward.) You should resist redefining Alt+*key* combinations. By custom, they are generally reserved for opening menus. Alt+F will, in almost all Windows applications, open the File menu.

You could use the Ctrl+*keys* for your own purposes. But, again, applications generally reserve these combinations for their default shortcuts. You may as well get used to it: most applications italicize with Ctrl+I and employ other Ctrl+*key* combinations for other shortcuts. This doesn't mean that you can't assign personal definitions to these keys, but then you'd want to reassign them in every application that you use. It's much less confusing if all your applications employ the same shortcut keys for the same purposes. You don't want to have to remember different shortcuts each time you switch to a different application.

The Ctrl+Alt+key combinations are reserved for launching applications within Windows 95 itself (see "Hot Keys" later in this chapter).

So what keys should you use to customize your keyboard? You are pretty safe with combinations such as Ctrl+Shift+*key* or Alt+Shift+*key*. Word uses some of these combinations for obscure, rarely needed tasks such as Font Size Select (which you can do more quickly by pressing Ctrl+Shift+> and Ctrl+Shift+<) or merely duplicating other, simpler combinations (Ctrl+Shift+B turns on boldface, but so does the easier Ctrl+B).

But let's be realistic. There are 57 "normal" keys on most keyboards (alphabetic, digits, function keys and a few symbols). Each can be customized into a different set of shortcut keys with Ctrl+*key*, Ctrl+Alt+*key*, Ctrl+Shift+*key*, Alt+*key*, Alt+Shift+*key* or, for the dexterous, Alt+Shift+Ctrl+*key*. Therefore, you could assign 342 different shortcuts. There may be people who could keep 342 shortcuts straight, but I've never met one.

In practice, most people regularly use fewer than a dozen shortcuts—for things they want to accomplish quite often. Saving a document to disk is common, and italicizing is common, but beyond that the tasks you assign shortcuts depend on what kind of work you do. If you use many tables in your work, then you might want to create some shortcuts for Insert Table,

Delete Cells and so on. If you are a professional writer, you may want to define a shortcut for Delete Word. Anything you do regularly is a candidate for a shortcut key, but precisely how and what you define is up to you.

Macros—Power Keystrokes

Until now, we've discussed how to accomplish tasks that you could do using menus, albeit somewhat more slowly and inconveniently. However, you can do much more using keyboards. Sometimes you have to go through a series of maneuvers to accomplish something. You move through several submenus, spending time remembering which keys access the correct initial menu, reading options in the menus, pressing function keys and making selections. Macros can eliminate these repetitive series of actions—collapsing all the steps into a single "macro." And once you've created a macro, you then assign it to a shortcut key combination, just as if it were an ordinary menu item already available in Word.

Let's create a macro in Word for Windows. It's easy: you just turn on a "recorder" in Word and then carry out the series of tasks that you want "remembered." Then you can assign a keyboard shortcut to that macro, just as if your new macro were a built-in Word command.

A typical example of the value of adding macros to your applications is the job of preparing some text for publication. Whether a desktop or commercial publication, a couple of things should be adjusted. First, many people deliberately insert two spaces between sentences, or accidentally type extra spaces elsewhere; these "extras" should be removed. Double-spaces are typical of typewritten text, and they can also make text more readable on screen. But on the printed page, extra spaces look bad. Similarly, there is no key on the keyboard for the dash—so people use a double-hyphen (--). This, too, makes text look typewritten rather than professionally typeset. So our macro will search for all double spaces and double-hyphens, replacing them with single spaces and single hyphens.

Here's how to do it. Press Alt+T, M; then type in the name of this new macro—let's call it Publish. Then press Alt+O and press Enter to start the recording process. A small button bar pops up *onscreen*, as shown in Figure 8-23. When you're finished creating your macro, you can stop the macro recorder by clicking on the button with the square symbol on it.

Figure 8-23: *While you're recording a macro, this button bar appears onscreen.*

Now that Word is watching what we do, let's perform the tasks. To search and replace double spaces, press Ctrl+H. When the Replace dialog box appears, type two spaces (press the Spacebar twice) into the Find What box. Then press Alt+P and type a single space into the Replace With box. Now start the replacement process by pressing Alt+A (Replace All). When Word has finished, press Enter to remove the window that reports the number of replacements.

Now we'll do the double hyphens. Type two hyphens (--) into the Find What box; then move down to the Replace With box and press Alt+E to open the Special list. Press M to select the Em dash, as shown in Figure 8-24. Word will insert its internal code for em dash (^+). Then start the replacement process again by pressing Alt+R. Then press Enter to remove the report window and then click on Close. Now stop the macro recording process by clicking on the button with the square in it (see Figure 8-23) or, alternatively, press Alt+T, M and then Alt+O.

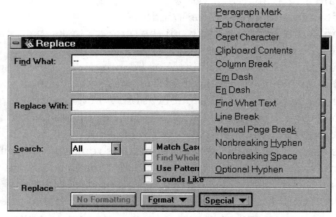

Figure 8-24: *Word offers you this convenient list of frequently needed special search items.*

Now we have a macro that will go through an entire document and make it ready for publication. Before we assign a shortcut key to this macro, let's look at the macro itself, just to see what Word constructed to describe our job. Press Alt+T, M; then type in the name of our macro, publish. Press Alt+E to edit it. Word will open a new document and display the following:

```
Sub MAIN
EditReplace .Find = "  ", .Replace = " ", .Direction = 0, .MatchCase = 0, .WholeWord
= 0, .PatternMatch = 0, .SoundsLike = 0, .ReplaceAll, .Format = 0, .Wrap = 1
EditReplace .Find = "—", .Replace = "^+", .Direction = 0, .MatchCase = 0,
```

```
.WholeWord = 0, .PatternMatch = 0, .SoundsLike = 0, .ReplaceAll, .Format = 0,
.Wrap = 1
End Sub
```

This is a computer program that Word has created. This program tells Word exactly how to behave whenever you want to run the *publish* macro. Notice that, unlike many computer languages, Word's language, called *WordBasic*, is English-like. There is absolutely no reason why computer languages should not be written in English, but only versions of the BASIC language actually strive to be as English-like as possible. (Well, perhaps job security for programmers is a reason so many computer languages resemble extraterrestrial calculus.)

Note also that Word includes all kinds of default descriptions (direction, matchcase and so on). Since these are defaults, we could remove them, and the macro would still accomplish its task.

```
Sub MAIN
EditReplace .Find = " ", .Replace = " "
EditReplace .Find = "—", .Replace = "^+"
End Sub
```

This is the essence of our macro, and, because it is in plain English, you can read what this macro tells Word to do. Also, because WordBasic is essentially just another document, you can make changes by just typing. For instance, if you decided you wanted this macro to also replace the word *hope* with the word *wish*, just type it in.

```
Sub MAIN
EditReplace .Find = "hope", .Replace = "wish"
EditReplace .Find = " ", .Replace = " "
EditReplace .Find = "—", .Replace = "^+"
End Sub
```

But let's leave the macro alone. Close the document by pressing Alt+F, C. If you have made any changes, Word will display the message shown in Figure 8-25. Just answer that you don't want any changes.

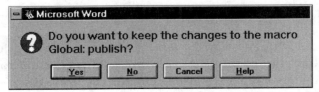

Figure 8-25: *If you've edited a macro, Word wants confirmation that you intend to make your changes permanent.*

Assigning a Shortcut Key to a Macro

We can always run our *publish* macro by accessing the Tools | Macro menu: press Alt+T, M; then type in its name (or select its name using the mouse). Press Enter (or Alt+R) to run it. But, as usual, it's more convenient to assign a shortcut key.

To assign a shortcut key to a macro, follow the same process that we discussed earlier in this chapter to assign a key to one of Word's built-in features. Press Alt+T, C and then Alt+K. Next, select Macros (in the Categories list) and select the particular macro, *publish* (in the Commands list). See Figure 8-26.

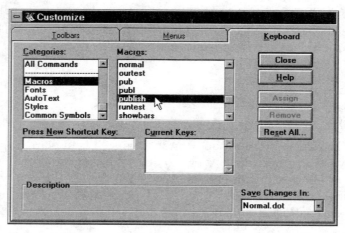

Figure 8-26: *You add shortcut keys to macros just as if macros were built-in commands.*

Now click in the Press New Shortcut Key box (or press Alt+N). Word might report that this combination is already assigned to one of its internal features. Ignore that. Let's assign Ctrl+Shift+P to our macro, so press Ctrl+Shift+P; then press Enter or click on the Assign button. That's it. Finally, click on the Close button. Now whenever you press Ctrl+Shift+P, the *publish* macro will do its job.

Which Keys to Use

Which keys should you reassign to macros? Most keys are used for typing, and you want the letter *s* to appear in a word, not trigger a macro. Many of Word's (and other programs') built-in shortcuts use the Ctrl *key*—Ctrl+P usually prints, Ctrl+O opens a file and so on. Windows itself imposes another shortcut convention involving Alt+*key* combinations—Alt+F opens the

File menu and so on. Most programs use the Function keys for additional shortcuts. What's left? Ctrl+Alt+*key* or Ctrl+Alt+Shift+*key* combinations are usually available but somewhat awkward to type. (Remember, too, that Windows permits you to launch programs using Ctrl+Alt+*key* combinations. See "Hot Keys" later in this chapter.)

Two solutions seem to work well. If you don't access menus using Alt+*key* combinations, use the Alt key as your personal macro launcher. This way, you have the whole alphabet available to you for memorable shortcuts like Alt+N for Next Window or Alt+F for Find.

Another tactic is to use the three characters that are rarely, if ever, needed in ordinary writing: the two bracket symbols [and] and the even less useful accent grave key '. Assigning these three keys to your macros eliminates the need to even press the Alt key; you just hit a bracket or accent key and your macro is triggered.

Word won't let you assign a macro to a single key like this. If you select Tools | Customize | Keyboard and press a single key such as [in the Press New Shortcut Key box, nothing happens. However, you can write a macro that assigns another macro to any key you want. Here's a macro you could type in. Name it *Assign*, if you want. Whenever you run this macro, it assigns the left bracket key to a macro named "killword." Substitute the name of the macro you want triggered in the .Name = zone here:

```
Sub MAIN
' 219 is keycode for left bracket
' 221 is keycode for right bracket
' run this macro to assign the macro
' named "killword" (delete word) to the left bracket key)
' to restore the left bracket key to normal,
' just delete the key shortcut assignment (in Tools/Customize/Keyboard).
ToolsCustomizeKeyboard .Category = 1, .Name = "killword", .KeyCode = 219,
.Add
End Sub
```

We'll have much more to say about customizing, shortcuts and macros in Chapter 21. Now let's look at Windows 95's handy shortcut key feature for launching programs.

Hotkeys

Windows, too, has a shortcut key feature, but it's limited to launching programs. A far more flexible and powerful system—Visual Basic—should be able to manipulate Windows in the next year or two. Visual Basic could control complex and sophisticated Windows behaviors, but for now we're limited to assigning a Ctrl+Alt+*key* combination to launch an application. One further limitation: You cannot directly launch the original program (such as NOTEPAD.EXE in the Windows folder). You can only create hot keys with shortcuts (such as a Notepad shortcut in the Windows\Start Menu\ Programs\Accessories folder). Right-clicking on a DOS program's icon and then selecting Properties reveals a property sheet with six pages. Choose the second page labeled Program, and you can assign a hot key there. (This automatically creates a shortcut, a DOS .PIF file, even if there wasn't one already.)

To create a hot key that launches a Windows application, right-click on the icon for the shortcut to that application in Explorer (for details about shortcuts, Explorer, folders and so on, see Chapter 4). Now select Properties from the drop-down menu. Choose the Shortcut page in the property sheet and click on Hot Key. Press whatever key you want to assign, and Windows will add the Ctrl+Alt for you (see Figure 8-27).

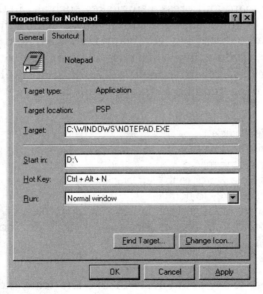

Figure 8-27: *Here's where you assign hot keys to launch your Windows applications.*

Note also that application key combination shortcuts override Windows hot keys. If you're running an application, and it has a custom Ctrl+Alt+key combination to accomplish some internal task (or you've redefined that key combination), the Windows hot key won't work while that application is the one with the focus. *Focus* means that this application is currently the one which would respond to any keystrokes—its title bar is highlighted or its icon is highlighted to show it has the focus. For example, Ctrl+Alt+N isn't used by Word for Windows, so if you've assigned that hot key to Windows Notepad, Notepad will pop up in front of Word any time you press Ctrl+Alt+N. On the other hand, if you've assigned Ctrl+Alt+E as the hot key for Explorer, pressing that combination when working in Word (or when Word has the focus) merely inserts an *endnote*, a kind of footnote that appears at the end of a book or chapter. Word has defined this key combination to trigger insert endnotes, and Word takes precedence over your hot key assignment that launches Explorer.

In this same Shortcut page of the Properties dialog box (Figure 8-27), you'll see a box labeled "Start in" where you can optionally describe a *path*, a location on your hard drive, in the Start in box. The directory or subdirectory (*folder* as Windows 95 calls them) pointed to by this path will be where the computer moves when you press the hot key.

A *path* is a list that starts with the drive letter and includes any subdirectories you might also need to specify to point the computer to a particular location. For example, C:\WINDOWS is a path and so is C:\WINDOWS\STARTUP\PROGRAMS. In any case, you might have documents or graphics or some other data used by the program that you are assigning a hot key to. You might keep all your brief notes to yourself in a folder called C:\NOTES, in which case you might want to direct the computer there if you create a hot key for WordPad. The main advantage of this shortcut is that you don't have to navigate through various directories if you want to open or save a note from WordPad's File menu; you're automatically taken to the C:\NOTES directory whenever you press this hot key.

The Run option in the Shortcut page tells Windows whether you want this hot key to launch your application as an icon (minimized), full screen (maximized), or in between (normal window).

Customizing Keyboard Behavior

If you'd like, you can customize your keyboard behavior. First, click on the My Computer icon; then select Control Panel. Or you can click on the Start button, select Settings and then Control Panel. In Control Panel, double-click on the Keyboard icon. You should see the property sheet shown in Figure 8-28. Property Sheet is the name for these things. They are different from dialog boxes.

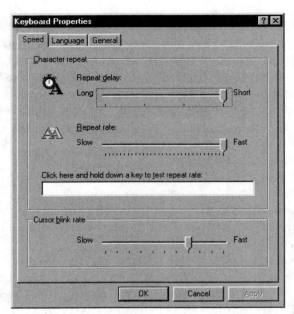

Figure 8-28: *In this property sheet you can set the speed and features of various keyboard-related options.*

The Speed page of the Keyboard Properties dialog box permits you to change how quickly the cursor begins to move once you hold down a key. Most people prefer to set the Repeat delay to Short so that you get virtually instant response when you press a key. When you hold down a key, it's handy to have it repeat automatically, especially if it's a cursor-movement key, or when you're drawing lines with the hyphen or underline characters. This repeat feature is used most often with the arrow keys, to move your cursor around a document. When you press the Up arrow key, for example, off the cursor goes, heading up the page of the document. The Repeat delay defines how long Windows waits to begin repeating once it notices you've held down a key.

Once the key begins repeating, the Repeat rate setting defines how fast the characters appear or the cursor moves when you hold down an arrow key. For responsive cursor control, set the Repeat delay to Short and the Repeat rate to Fast. This second setting, Repeat rate is a matter of personal taste. Some people prefer a slower speed so they can watch the cursor move; yet others learn to gauge how far the cursor will move in any given time. After you've adjusted the settings, you can try them out in the box labeled "Click here...."

The Cursor blink rate defines how rapidly your cursor will go on and off. While you're editing text, the insertion point, or text cursor, blinks to show you where the next character will appear. If you're using a low contrast screen like an older B&W LCD laptop, you may want to increase the blink rate to make it easier to find. Or you can almost stop it from blinking entirely, if that sort of thing drives you nuts.

The Language page of the Keyboard Properties dialog box allows you to change the default language or to define a key combination that will switch between languages.

Click on the tab marked Language to customize the keyboard (and your computer's symbol set) to your locale. Your locale is defined by your preferred language or country. Each country uses different symbols for similar purposes, such as the American dollar sign ($), the British pound sign (£) or the Japanese yen (¥). Other languages routinely use accents that are only rarely seen in English, such as the Spanish Ñ symbol. Windows is designed for universality and adjusts its character set, display and user interface to suit the needs of users in different countries. Windows 95 will be localized into 28 different languages.

Just click on the drop-down list to choose the country setting. Different characters are then mapped onto the keyboard, matching the special designs for available keyboards. On a U.S. keyboard, Shift+4 produces the dollar sign, but when set to British, you get the £ sign (keyboards sold in Britain have the pound symbol, so there's no confusion). Windows also makes it easy to type accented characters. If your language uses them, you can press the ` key and then the A key to get à. If you want to type the apostrophe key by itself, just press it twice. You can get this same functionality with the U.S. character set by choosing United States International.

The General page of the Keyboard Properties dialog box allows you to specify what kind of keyboard you're using—how many keys it has, whether the function keys are on the top or along the left side and so on. Normally, you'll leave it set to the Standard 101/102-Key or Microsoft Natural Keyboard keyboard. Alternative keyboard layouts are available, however, as we'll see shortly. (The Microsoft Natural Keyboard actually has 104 keys. Other companies also produce 104-key keyboards now, which feature two Windows logo keys and a Menu key for convenience.)

During Setup, Windows attempts to determine what kind of keyboard you use. Using the window shown in Figure 8-29, you can adjust the keyboard type. To get here, click on Change in the General page of the Keyboard Properties dialog box; then select Show all devices in the Select Device window. You can, at any time, select a different keyboard type if you, perhaps, buy a new keyboard with the function keys in a different location.

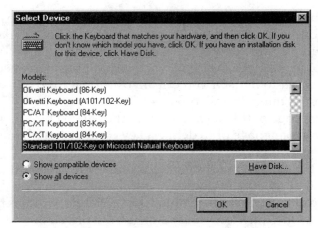

Figure 8-29: *You can change the keyboard type in the Select Device window.*

IntelliKey

If you buy a Microsoft mouse or Microsoft Natural Keyboard, you get some
software bundled with them called "IntelliPoint" for the mouse and
"IntelliType" for the keyboard. "IntelliPoint" is covered in Chapter 9, but
here we'll look at the features of the keyboard software.

Hot Win-Keys for 104-Key Keyboards	
⊞+R	Same as Start I Run
⊞+M	Same as right-click on taskbar, Minimize All
Shift+ ⊞+M	Undo Minimize All
⊞+F1	Windows Help
⊞+E	Explorer View, My Computer
⊞+F	Find files or folders
Ctrl+ ⊞+F	Find computer
⊞+Tab	Switch to next taskbar buttons
⊞+Break	Open System Properties

Table 8-3: *Hot Win-Keys for 104-Key Keyboards.*

Microsoft is now selling a new ergonomic keyboard called the Microsoft
Natural Keyboard. The keys are split and angled to make it more comfortable
for your wrists, hands and fingers when typing. After a few days, using it
becomes second nature. The keys aren't rearranged (as they are on the Dvorak

keyboard), so you can quickly be up to speed. This keyboard also has three extra keys. Either of two Windows keys opens the Start menu (or the Task Manager in Windows 3.1). Another key simulates clicking the right mouse button (opening a context-sensitive menu; no effect in Windows 3.1). (Remember that you can simulate a right-click by pressing Shift+F10 on an ordinary keyboard, but there is no equivalent for the other—often quite useful— Win+key combinations. Perhaps some enterprising shareware author will come up with a solution.)

The software that comes bundled with this new keyboard—IntelliType— also adds some new features. Figure 8-30, shows many of these features, which are also available in Windows 95 without this special software, but a few features are unique to the IntelliType software.

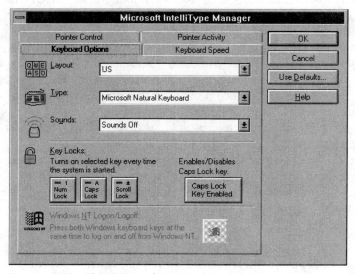

Figure 8-30: *The Microsoft Natural Keyboard provides some additional features to Windows 95.*

Under Keyboard Options, you can select various layouts specific to various languages such as Icelandic, French Canadian and so on. IntelliType also includes a Dvorak layout that isn't offered in the standard Windows keyboard property sheet.

A Better Keyboard Layout?

Another alternate keyboard layout was designed by Anton Dvorak. Curiously, the standard QWERTY layout was originally designed to be hard to use, a kind of reverse user-friendliness. Early typewriters had a problem with jamming because typists were typing too fast for the mechanism. So the typewriter was crippled with a design that's more difficult to type on than even a strictly alphabetical layout would be. Long after the jamming problems were solved though, we're still saddled with this legacy. Mr. Dvorak took the opposite tack: he studied typing and came up with a layout that was optimal. The most frequently typed characters appear near the center of the keyboard, and the weaker fingers are relegated to less commonly used keys.

If you want to try the Dvorak keyboard, remember that efficient touch typing requires that you never look at your fingers, so it's not necessary to pry off your keycaps and rearrange them, although that is not too difficult. Get a good touch typing tutor that supports Dvorak, and work with it a few weeks. You'll also need a driver for MS-DOS (available from Microsoft) if you still run DOS applications and need Dvorak support in that environment. Some typists can double their typing rate and reduce discomfort, possibly preventing the crippling possibility of repetitive stress injuries. If these changes sound extreme, consider switching to the new Microsoft Natural Keyboard, described above, which provides a more comfortable layout with which to type.

Single-handed Dvorak keyboard layouts designed for people with limited dexterity (only one hand or motion impairments) are also available. This keyboard style concentrates all the most common letters into one specific area of the keyboard to make typing go faster if you have only one hand.

In the IntelliType property sheet shown in Figure 8-30, the Type specifies various models from AT&T, Olivetti, the new Microsoft Natural Keyboard and others including Dvorak. Sounds allows you to turn on a click that will come out of your computer's speaker each time a key is pressed. If you have an outboard amplifier/speakers setup for multimedia, you can select various special sound effects like the sound of dripping water, scissors or maracas—guaranteed to drive your co-workers around the bend.

You can also specify whether that the Num Lock, Caps Lock or Scroll Lock keys should be active whenever you turn the computer on. A useful addition is the option to disable the notoriously confusing, rarely needed, but often accidentally engaged Caps Lock. Of course, different strokes for different folks—some people do use Caps Lock. Whatever suits you.

The Keyboard Speed page is redundant; these options are available in the Control Panel.

A Simulated Mouse

If you really can't stand using a mouse, you might want to try the mouse simulator. It disables the arrow keys (normally used to maneuver the keyboard cursor) and turns them into a simulated mouse. This capability is important for people with motion impairments who couldn't use a mouse otherwise. On many keyboards, all the capabilities of the NumLock-off numeric keypad are duplicated; Insert, Del, Page Down, the arrow keys and so on appear between the main keyboard and the numeric keypad. Therefore you don't lose anything by turning these keys over to mouse control (except perhaps years of practice using them to select, move, cut and otherwise edit text, if you're still a die-hard numeric-keypad-cursor-control person).

The mouse simulator is also included in the Windows 95 Accessibility Options control panel icon; see Chapter 7.

The Pointer Control page shown in Figure 8-31 allows you to decide how quickly the pointer responds to a keypress and how rapidly it reaches maximum speed. If you want warp speed, enable Fast Move. The Pointer Activity page duplicates the new Snap-to, Wrap and Sonar features described at the end of Chapter 9.

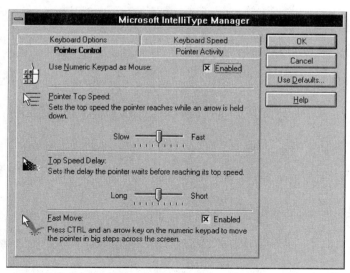

Figure 8-31: *The Pointer Control page lets you control the mouse pointer with your numeric keypad.*

Moving On

Now we'll turn our attention to the input device that's most at home in a graphical environment, the mouse. You might be surprised at all you can do with this deceptively simple tool. We were. We planned to cover the mouse at the end of this chapter on keyboards. Not exactly as an afterthought, but we thought it hardly deserved an entire chapter. However, research revealed that this little device with only two buttons and a ball is, after all, remarkably versatile.

Chapter 9

The Mouse

Until graphical interfaces like Windows became popular, text was virtually the only way people communicated with computers. The computer itself could display only plain, drab text: just letters of the alphabet, symbols like %, A, and the digits 0–9. It was a dull black-and-white world.

Sure, people made inventive attempts to create graphics out of patterns of asterisks and dashes and so on, but the results were unsatisfying at best. Even when graphical symbols were included in the character set, the resulting images still resembled crude pictographs.

And you, in turn, communicated with the computer the same way—by typing words, symbols and digits. This was the world of DOS, a monochromatic screen that more than anything resembled a blackboard in a schoolroom.

Rather unattractive. Finally things opened up, letting in color, pictures, sound and animation. Computing finally became lively.

Once you've got color and images, you need a new way of interacting with the computer. When you manipulate and interact with pictures, you need something more mobile than a keyboard. Graphics add considerable realism to computing, and in the real world you relate to objects physically—not by pushing buttons on a keyboard, but by moving things around. You need something that can quickly define (select) zones of the screen—so you can change the color, for example, of lips within a face. Likewise, you want to move things around onscreen or change their size. In short, it's inconvenient to work in the visually information-rich world of Windows with just a keyboard. It is possible but inefficient.

During the 1970s, engineers and ergonomics experts worked hard to find an alternative to the typewriter keyboard. They tried pens, fingers (touch screens), trackballs, a strange plastic pad that you put on the floor and manipulated with your feet like an organist, a microphone, an infrared headband that tracked your head movements, joysticks. They tried everything but Tinkerbell's wand.

It occurred to someone to flip a trackball on its back, like a tortoise, and the mouse was born. It quickly became the favorite pointing device. The mouse is an extension of your hand inside the computer screen, and uncannily mimics your movements. The buttons wait receptively right under your fingertips. Most people get comfortable with a mouse after their first few days using a computer, and they take their mouse for granted after that. But let's take a closer look at the little critter.

Setting Up the Mouse

Most people plug their mouse into a *serial* port (labeled COM1 or COM2 on the back of the computer). An alternative, a *bus* port, is often directly built onto the motherboard (the main circuit board) of the computer or included on a plug-in card. One type of bus mouse, the PS/2 mouse, uses a tiny round connector; it was first used on IBM's PS/2 series of computers. Both types of ports work equally well. (The advantage of a bus mouse is that it leaves both your COM ports free to use for other purposes. One COM port is used by a modem.)

When you run Windows setup, it automatically attempts to detect where your mouse is plugged into the computer and what kind of mouse it is so that it will be configured correctly. The most common arrangement is to put your mouse into the COM1 connector and leave COM2 for your modem. The most common mouse is "Microsoft mouse compatible." If you have a generic mouse, you may be able to switch it between "Microsoft compatible" and "Mouse Systems/PC compatible." Not surprisingly, Windows works best with the "Microsoft" setting. A mouse *driver*—software that controls the behavior and communications with the mouse—is also installed at this time.

If you install a new mouse, or if Windows cannot recognize your mouse during setup, you can change to a different driver using the Control Panel. When Windows runs without an active mouse, you can do virtually anything via the keyboard that you could do using the mouse. However, you'll quickly find that it's more difficult to use Windows with the keyboard alone. (Chapter 8 includes several useful keyboard shortcuts.)

Hands-On: Changing Your Mouse Driver

Here's how to change your mouse driver:

1. Click on Start.
2. Select Settings | Control Panel. The Control Panel appears (see Figure 9-1).
3. Double-click on the Mouse icon.
4. In the Mouse Properties dialog box, click on the General tab (see Figure 9-2).
5. On the General page, click on Change.
6. Click on "Show All Devices."
7. In the Select Device window, either locate a Windows-supplied driver from the lists of manufacturers shown, or, if your mouse comes with its own software on disk, click on Have Disk and load the driver from your floppy drive.

Figure 9-1: *Change the mouse driver by clicking on the Mouse icon in the Control Panel.*

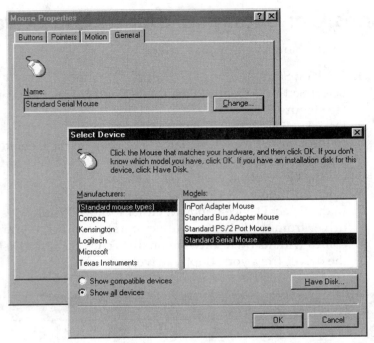

Figure 9-2: *Windows comes with a collection of drivers for the most popular mice, or you can install a driver from the manufacturer's supplied disk.*

Buttons

Macintosh users are accustomed to a one-button mouse. Some people use a three-button mouse, and the software that comes with multi-button mice permits you to assign various actions (such as pressing the Enter key) to one of the buttons. However, most Windows users have the familiar two-button mouse, although until Windows 95 the right mouse button was mostly unused.

The left button is still the primary button. It still does all the things it used to do. It allows you to drag objects (hold down the left button while moving the mouse); you also can click or double-click. (To double-click, you click the left button twice within a specified span of time. You can adjust the time span, as we will see later in this chapter.)

Generally, the left button causes *actions*—sliding or resizing windows through dragging; selecting menu items by clicking; launching a program by double-clicking on its icon.

Most of the time, a right-click opens a context-sensitive menu, which contains the most frequently used options appropriate to whatever situation you're in. If you right-click on an object like an icon, you can quickly view or change its properties. For example, if you right-click on the desktop, you'll see the options in Figure 9-3.

Figure 9-3: *Right-click on the desktop and you can manage icons; paste text or objects; create a new folder, shortcut or various kinds of documents such as text files, sound files and so on; or open the properties window of the desktop itself.*

However, if you right-click within a running program, the context menu presents options that the program's designers thought you would most likely want to see. Right-click on a document in Word for Windows, and you'll see the menu in Figure 9-4:

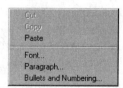

Figure 9-4: *Word for Windows responds with this menu if you right-click within a document.*

Typical Mouse Shortcuts

Remember that when you're working within a program, that the program—not Windows—governs the behavior of the mouse. There is a continuing trend toward conformity—so users don't have to remember different sets of keyboard or mouse shortcuts for each application. However, this conformity is far from complete. Table 9-1 lists mouse shortcuts you can use in Word for Windows, an application that often sets the standards for other applications. You might want to try some of these shortcuts in other applications to see if they work the same way. Few people use all the available shortcuts, but you could memorize a few of them if they provide a quick way to accomplish something you frequently want to do.

Do This With the Mouse	To Get This Result
Left-click (within text)	Move insertion cursor to the location in the text you clicked.
Left-click (in left margin)	Select line.
Left double-click (within text)	Select a word.
Left double-click (in left margin)	Select paragraph.
Left triple-click (within text)	Select paragraph.
Left triple-click (within left margin)	Select entire document.
Left double-click (within the black title bar at the top)	Toggle between full screen (maximized) and normal window.
Left double-click (in the small black bar above the vertical scroll bar)	Toggle split window (panes).
Right-click (within text)	Open a menu with cut, copy, paste, font, paragraph and bullets and numbering.
Right-click (within the black title bar at the top)	Open the standard window menu (restore, size, close, and so on) as if you'd clicked on the small icon in the upper-left corner of the window.
Shift+Left-click	Select between the previous and current insertion points, rounded off to whole words.
Shift+Right-click	Select between the previous and current insertion points, using the precise character positions.
Shift double-click (in the small black bar above the vertical scroll bar)	Open a footnotes window.
Ctrl+Left-click (in text)	Select current sentence.
Ctrl+Left-click (in left margin)	Select entire document.
Ctrl+Right-click	Move selection to location of click.
Drag	Select a section of text. If something is already selected, you can drag it (move it) to a new location in the document.

Do This With the Mouse	To Get This Result
Alt+Drag	Select a vertical block of text. Text selected in this way can then be copied rather than moved if you drag the selection after releasing the left button and then depress it again to drag the selection to a new location. To move instead of copy, select the text by dragging without pressing the Alt key. Then release and drag.
Drag in left margin	Select multiple lines of text.
Drag (in the small black bar above the vertical scroll bar)	Adjust size of window panes.

Table 9-1: *Mouse shortcuts used in Word for Windows.*

The Mouse in DOS

Although not exactly at home in the DOS environment, the mouse can be used there. First, you can use the cut-and-paste feature that allows you to move a copy of text from a DOS window into the Clipboard (and from there paste it into a Windows application). To start a DOS window, click on the MS-DOS Prompt icon on the Start button | Programs menu.

Our goal is to get to the DOS window's Document Control menu, the drop-down menu you see when you click in the upper-left corner of any window. If your DOS window is running in full-screen text mode, reduce it to a window by pressing Alt+Enter. Then press Alt+Tab to get back into Windows and thereby get a mouse pointer you can use. Click the small icon in the upper-left corner to drop down the Control menu (sometimes called the System menu). (A shortcut is to press Alt+Spacebar, which also drops down this menu.)

As soon as the menu drops, your Windows mouse appears. Move the mouse to Edit and click on Mark. Drag your mouse across some text in the DOS window. Then copy it to the Clipboard by pressing the Enter key. Now, in Windows, you can paste that text into Word or WordPad or any other text document.

You can also click on the MS-DOS toolbar to mark, copy and paste text. If these options are not shown, you can turn on the DOS toolbar by choosing Toolbar from the Control menu that appears when you click on the MS-DOS icon in the DOS window's corner (see Figure 9-5).

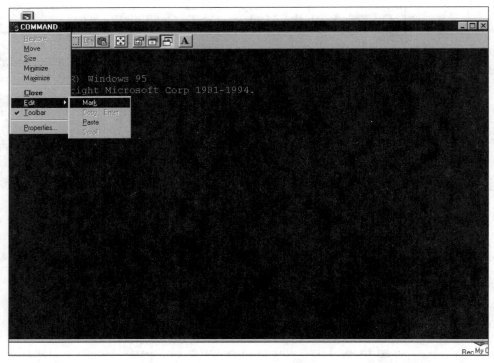

Figure 9-5: *You can make Copy and Paste a permanent part of any DOS program.*

 TIP   If you ever want to export text from Windows to DOS, just copy it to the Clipboard from WordPad or wherever; then switch to a DOS window. Press Alt+Spacebar to open the Document Control menu. Then select Edit|Paste or just click on the Paste button on the toolbar.

Recall that you can create a specialized set of properties for any DOS program. Among these properties is one that automatically permits copying and pasting—without having to go through the Control menu at all. To add this property, in Explorer choose Properties from the Control menu (or click on the Properties button on the toolbar). Then choose the Misc tab (see Figure 9-6). In the Misc page, click on the Quick Edit option. (You sometimes must turn off the Fast Paste option if a DOS application loses characters when you paste to it from the Windows Clipboard.) Note that copying and pasting works only when the DOS application is running in a window.

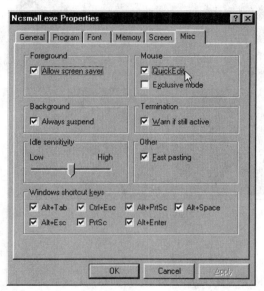

Figure 9-6: *This property sheet replaces the Windows 3.1 Pif Editor for customizing the behavior of DOS programs.*

 As shown in Figure 9-6, the Background check box button (now the default) lets an MS-DOS program continue to function, even if it loses the focus. Without it, an MS-DOS function is suspended when it loses the focus. The Exclusive mode prevents all other background applications from running so that the MS-DOS application can run full speed. This setting exists because MS-DOS applications are run with preemptive multitasking, even under Windows 3. For more information, see Chapter 22.

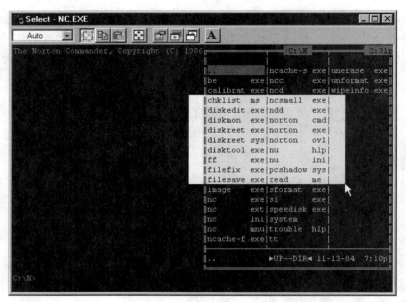

Figure 9-7: *You can use the mouse to copy text from a DOS window and paste it into any Windows application.*

If Your Application Is DOS-Aware

Of course, you don't want to use Quick Edit if your DOS application is "mouse aware," since Quick Edit lets Windows take control of the mouse away from the DOS application and fix it in Mark mode. With Quick Edit turned off (as it is normally), Windows passes through the mouse movements and clicks to the DOS application.

What's more, you no longer need to use a MOUSE driver in your CONFIG.SYS or AUTOEXEC.BAT file. In fact, you may want to remove this line if it still exists. To do so, select Start | Run. Then type **SYSEDIT** and press Enter. Now look in your CONFIG.SYS and AUTOEXEC.BAT windows, and delete any reference to MOUSE.DRV or MOUSE.SYS. Then save the modified file back to the disk.

Windows includes a 32-bit virtual mouse driver that makes mouse functions available to both DOS and Windows, without consuming any conventional memory. This driver also makes it unnecessary for you to start certain DOS applications with a batch file that pre-loads the DOS mouse driver. That kind of DOS batch file was used before Windows 95, a common technique to avoid leaving the mouse driver in memory for all applications.

Most DOS applications don't use a mouse, and Windows 3 doesn't need the DOS mouse driver either—so the batch file avoided leaving a remnant mouse driver sitting there in memory and taking up space uselessly.

Changing the Mouse

You can customize the mouse behavior and appearance—as with most everything in Windows—to suit yourself. Click on Start, then select Settings | Control Panel. Double-click on the mouse icon, and you'll see its property sheets (see Figure 9-8).

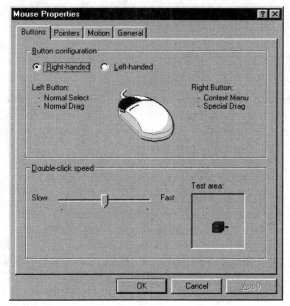

Figure 9-8: *In this properties sheet, you can switch the behavior of the mouse buttons and adjust the double-click speed.*

The Buttons Page

If you're left-handed, you might be more comfortable switching the right and left buttons. Most people favor their index finger over their middle finger, and switching permits you to use the index finger for most clicking activity.

Double-clicking is an important maneuver in Windows. Generally, it activates something—as when you launch a program by double-clicking on its icon in Explorer. Some beginners have problems with the timing of a double-click. However, if you're finding that you keep getting two single clicks instead of a double-click, try slowing down the double-click speed in the Buttons page of the Mouse Properties sheet. You also have to hold the mouse still while double-clicking. It helps to grip the mouse with your thumb and ring finger while double-clicking to minimize movement.

 TIP Since you can use two separate clicks to rename a file in Explorer (one click to select and another click to rename), you may sometimes double-click unintentionally. One way to avoid this is to set your double-click speed higher, which means you really have to hit that key quickly for it to register as a true double-click. Or just press F2 when you want to rename a file.

Fortunately, many more functions in Windows 95 no longer require double-clicking. You can launch programs from the Start menu or switch between programs on the taskbar with single clicks. If you're really against double-clicking, you can always resort to this trick: click once on an icon and then press the Enter key on the keyboard.

Programming Buttons

What good is a three-button mouse? Here's how to program the middle button of a Logitech mouse to act as a convenient substitute for double-click. Instead of double-clicking the left button, which gets tiresome, all you'll have to do is tap the middle button once. (You may be able to use the Logitech mouse driver even with a "generic" three-button mouse.)

1. Click Start | Run and enter **REGEDIT**.
2. Press F3 and look for MOUSEWARE.
3. Click the + symbol next to the MouseWare key.
4. Click the + symbol next to the CurrentVersion key.
5. Locate the key for the mouse model you use (Cordless, MouseMan and so on).
6. Click the + symbol next to the mouse model (MouseMan).
7. Click on the 000 key under that key.
8. Look for the DoubleClick value in the right-hand pane.
9. Double-click on that value (the last time you'll ever have to double-click).

10. Change the entry in ValueData from 000 to 001.

11. Close RegEdit and restart your computer.

12. Try middle-clicking on an icon to open it. Have fun!

Warning: Resist the temptation to play around with any other entries in your registry. If these changes seem too difficult, you can get updated mouse drivers from Logitech, but don't use the Windows 3.1 software that came with your Logitech mouse.

The Pointers Page

In the Pointers page of the Mouse Properties sheet, you can change the look of the various mouse pointers. The fourteen types of mouse pointers not only show where your mouse is located within text or graphics, they also provide visual clues about the mouse's current capabilities or the status of the computer itself.

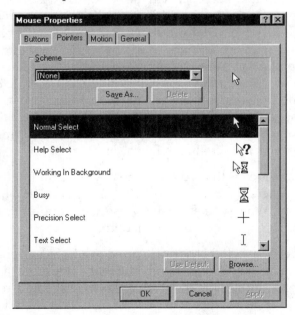

Figure 9-9: *In the Pointers page, you can select alternative mouse pointers.*

Table 9-2 illustrates the default pointers and describes their meanings.

Pointer	Description
	Normal Select is the usual pointer; all others signal temporary conditions. Normal Select changes to Text Select when your mouse is within a text document.
	Help Select appears when you enable context-sensitive help in new Windows dialog boxes that include a [?] symbol on the title bar. After you click on the [?], you can click on any part of the window to get a pop-up tip about that element. (You also can press Shift+F1 to get the same result.)
	Working in Background means that some other task is currently being carried out, but you can still type, select text, click on menus—whatever you'd normally do. This pointer means that the process in the background is sharing the computer with your current task. Such sharing is called *multitasking*. Windows shows this pointer if the background operation is busy enough to slow down your foreground application. Your foreground task might be somewhat slower than normal, or things might seem a little jerky—the effect of simultaneous tasking depends on your computer, the settings and behavior of the background application, and the task you're carrying out. Typing usually seems fairly normal, but scrolling might seem sluggish.
	Busy means that you can't do anything until the task is finished. It's taken over the computer, and you have to wait. When you exclusively use 32-bit applications, you almost never see the dreaded hourglass.
	Precision Select is normally used in graphics applications, where you're not just dragging to select text but you want to be highly specific about what you're selecting. This pointer also appears when you're selecting cells in a spreadsheet.
	Text Select is how the pointer looks when you're moving the mouse within a text document. It shows you where the text insertion point cursor will appear, so it's designed to be narrow enough to fit between two characters.

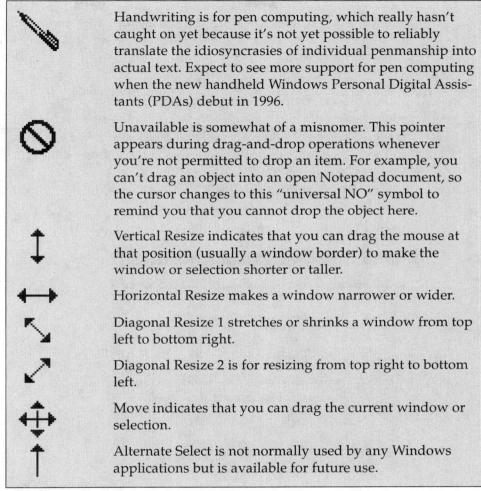

Handwriting is for pen computing, which really hasn't caught on yet because it's not yet possible to reliably translate the idiosyncrasies of individual penmanship into actual text. Expect to see more support for pen computing when the new handheld Windows Personal Digital Assistants (PDAs) debut in 1996.

Unavailable is somewhat of a misnomer. This pointer appears during drag-and-drop operations whenever you're not permitted to drop an item. For example, you can't drag an object into an open Notepad document, so the cursor changes to this "universal NO" symbol to remind you that you cannot drop the object here.

Vertical Resize indicates that you can drag the mouse at that position (usually a window border) to make the window or selection shorter or taller.

Horizontal Resize makes a window narrower or wider.

Diagonal Resize 1 stretches or shrinks a window from top left to bottom right.

Diagonal Resize 2 is for resizing from top right to bottom left.

Move indicates that you can drag the current window or selection.

Alternate Select is not normally used by any Windows applications but is available for future use.

Table 9-2: *Mouse pointers.*

Alternative pointers

As with so many other features of Windows 95, you can personalize your pointers. (We're going to use the terms *cursor* and *pointer* interchangeably here, but technically, the cursor is the horizontal bar that shows your current position within text—the place where, when you next press a key, a character will appear.) The Microsoft Plus! for Windows 95 add-on kit supplies several excellent alternatives, which are attractive and even sometimes animated. You can also download custom cursors (files ending in .CUR) or animated cursors (.ANI) from BBSes or online services such as AOL or the Microsoft Network.

 TIP   You will need to upgrade to a Windows 95 video driver to get animated or colored cursors. Some video cards simply can't support this feature, however, so you're stuck with black-and-white fixed cursors. Sample alternative cursors come with this book's Companion CD.

To see custom cursors, click on Browse in the Pointers page of the Mouse Properties sheet. You'll see the window in Figure 9-10.

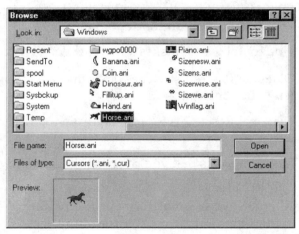

Figure 9-10: *You can replace any of the default mouse pointers with custom pointers; some are even animated.*

To change the pointer currently selected in the Pointers page, click on Browse, click on the name of the new pointer in the file list and then click Open. If you want to restore the Windows default pointer, click on Use Default.

After you've chosen a group of customized cursors, click on Save As to save the set with a unique name. That way, you can create different sets of cursors (schemes) to suite your taste and mood, which is especially useful when you're sharing a computer with someone else.

The Motion Page

On the Motion page of the Mouse Properties sheet, you can adjust the sensitivity—the relative velocity—of your mouse pointer (see Figure 9-11). Choose a speed that suits you. The difference between Slow and Fast isn't dramatic. You might want to adjust it, try it for a while, then go back and reset it if you feel the mouse is sluggish or too swift. The slower motion gives you more fine control of the mouse. You might prefer a faster speed to conserve desk space used by the mouse, but using a faster speed makes it harder to hit your target.

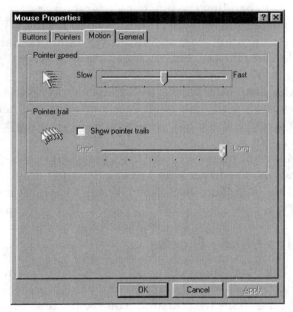

Figure 9-11: *Adjust the speed of your mouse or add a visible "trail"—a feature that is useful with portable computers.*

The Pointer Trail option adds a wake of ghost pointers that follows your pointer's movements and then fades. This feature is useful with some portable computers because the mouse pointer is often hard to see on a low-light LCD screen. The trail can make it easy to see where the mouse is and what direction it's going. It's also fun. (If Pointer Trail is ghosted or dimmed in the properties sheet, your video card driver doesn't support this feature.)

The General Page

Described earlier in this chapter, the General page is the place where you can install a new mouse driver. Since Windows detects and installs your mouse driver automatically, you probably won't need to change this setting unless you plug in a different type of mouse. You can also use the Add Hardware icon in Control Panel to change your mouse driver.

Extra Features

If you're interested in expanding the power of your mouse, various manufacturers offer specialized software and a replacement for the Windows mouse driver. Some companies even sell mice with more than three buttons. One, from Prohance Technology, comes with 40 buttons. At that point, the mouse is morphing into a keyboard.

Nevertheless, extra dexterous people with great memories can specify that individual keys on the ProMouse will launch macros or other complex behaviors. If you're using the usual two-button mouse, though, you can still expand its functionality.

If you buy the Microsoft mouse, for instance, you can choose to replace the default Windows mouse driver with Microsoft's IntelliPoint software. It gives you such additional options as Snap-to, Wrap, Line Lock and Focus. Let's take a look at what these and other IntelliPoint features can do for you.

IntelliPoint: Microsoft's Smart Mouse

Little about mouse behavior and appearance has been ignored in the eight pages of settings you can adjust in the IntelliPoint software. Does it annoy you when you're typing to see two cursors? You see the insertion point cursor for the keyboard (a bold vertical bar usually) and the I-beam mouse pointer insertion point. If you want the mouse pointer to disappear when you're pressing keys and only reappear when the mouse is moved, click on the Vanish option in the Visibility page of the IntelliPoint Properties sheet, shown in Figure 9-13. (This can be annoying when you're using keyboard controls with mouse selection, such as holding down Shift while pressing the mouse button for extended selections. It's more difficult when you can't see the pointer.)

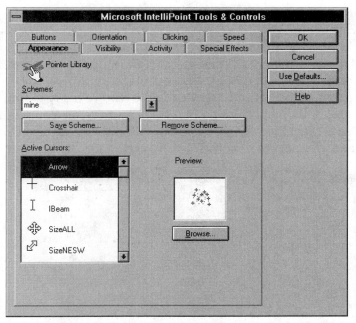

Figure 9-12: *The IntelliPoint-controlled mouse has great flexibility. On this page, you can choose from a large library of pointers and pre-written schemes (sets of pointers).*

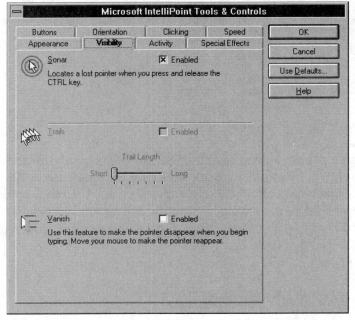

Figure 9-13: *On the Visibility page, you can make the pointer automatically disappear or choose two ways to locate a "lost" pointer on a portable's LCD screen.*

The Visibility page also provides an alternative to mouse trails as a way of seeing your mouse pointer on a portable computer (where, because of the weaker luminance, the pointer is often hard to locate). If you choose Sonar, a series of concentric circles flashes on and off, pinpointing the errant mouse whenever you tap the Ctrl key.

If you've been using a mouse for a while, you're likely to find the Activity options disconcerting, at least at first (see Figure 9-14). You might feel as if someone had switched the brake pedal with the accelerator in your car—you really have to concentrate not to have an accident.

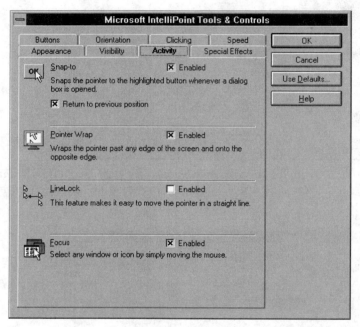

Figure 9-14: *You'll either love or hate the options on the Activity page; it's hard to remain dispassionate about them.*

For some people, however, these mouse behavior modifications doubtless make sense. For example, whenever a dialog box pops up in Windows, the button or other control most likely to be used gets the *focus*. If the Yes, No and Cancel buttons are available, and the software expects you to select Yes, that button has a black frame line around it and its shadow is darker. This button has the focus (see Figure 9-15).

Figure 9-15: *The Snap-to feature automatically moves your pointer to the button with the focus. Here, Yes has the focus.*

The button that has the *focus* is the one that will be activated if you press the Enter key on the keyboard. There is no equivalent for the mouse. When a dialog box pops up, the mouse pointer just sits wherever it was before the dialog appeared. The Snap-to option fixes this. When a dialog box pops open, your pointer whips over to the highlighted button; you can press the left button to trigger the action. (Snap-to is not compatible with some Windows applications, but you can disable it temporarily using the mouse pop-up menu.)

With Pointer Wrap turned on, when you move the pointer to the right side of the screen, it doesn't just bump there and remain pressed against the side of the screen. Instead, it reappears on the left side. Likewise, if you move the pointer off the bottom of the screen, the pointer appears at the top. This feature can either save you a lot of movement or drive you batty.

Line Lock constrains the pointer movement to straight vertical or horizontal lines. This capability would be useful, for example, in a drawing or design application that didn't provide easy access to such constraint. In general, you may find it maddening.

Focus works rather like the new menu behavior in Windows 95. In older Windows, you had to keep clicking or holding down the mouse button to activate submenus or cascading menus. Now, in Windows 95, just moving the mouse pointer automatically pops subsidiary menus open as appropriate. Focus allows you to do something similar with folders and folder icons—move the pointer onto them and, after a brief pause, they get the focus (their title bar turns black).

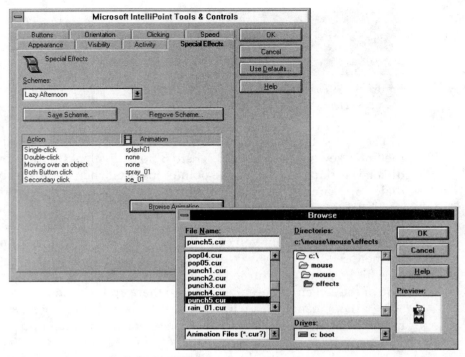

Figure 9-16: *On the Special Effects page, you can select from several* schemes, *or sets of animated pointers.*

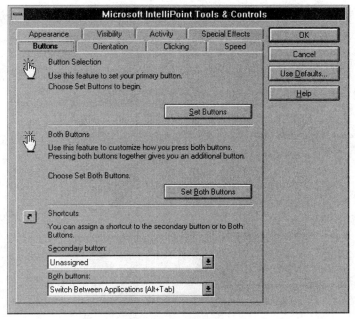

Figure 9-17: *On the Buttons page, Set Buttons lets you switch left and right. Shortcuts lets you assign a special action if you press both buttons simultaneously.*

One useful shortcut for pressing both left and right buttons is to simulate a double-click. Unfortunately, simulating pressing the Enter key—one of the most useful shortcuts—isn't offered. (Software such as the shareware Mouse manager "Whiskers" gives you a larger number of shortcut choices. Simulating pressing Enter would be useful because you often find yourself with a dialog box on which you want to press Enter (thereby triggering the highlighted option), but your hand is on the mouse at the time. You have to move your hand over to the keyboard to press Enter. (For a solution, see the discussion on Snap-to feature earlier in this section.)

Many people don't move the mouse at perfect right angles to the keyboard. Your natural arm movements may push the mouse north or northeast when moving up. By calibrating the way you move with the Orientation option (see Figure 9-18), Windows will move the mouse in a fashion that seems to you more intuitively and smoothly. You can even use it to rotate your mouse 90 percent, or upside down, and it will still work just fine, although it's hard to see how that would be useful.

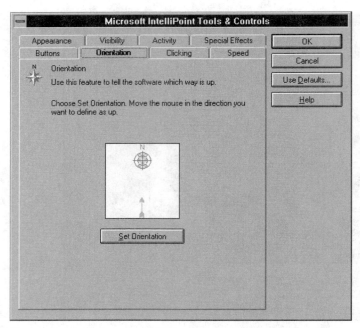

Figure 9-18: *Orientation allows you to redefine which way the mouse moves.*

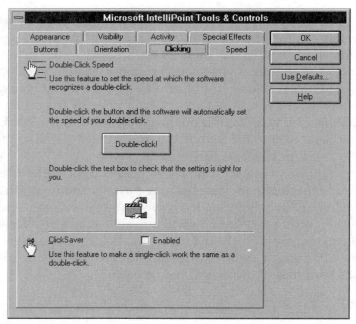

Figure 9-19: *The "Click Saver" here lets you simply move over an object to select it (without clicking it), and click on the object just once to open it (instead of double-clicking).*

In the Speed page, you can tamper with your mouse's athletics (see Figure 9-20). Some people find the second Acceleration option quite useful. Move the mouse slowly an inch on your desk. It will go about half the way across the screen. Move it rapidly 1/4 inch, and it will go across the entire screen. (These effects will vary, depending on the mouse speed you've selected.) This behavior, however, is built into Windows 95.

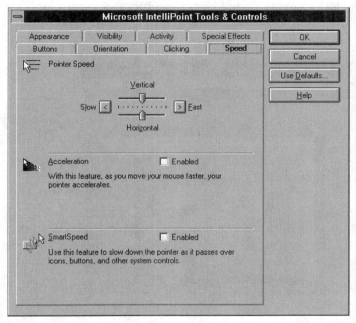

Figure 9-20: *On the Speed page, you can define different speeds for horizontal and vertical mouse movement.*

Also potentially useful is the sticky trick called SmartSpeed. Whenever you cross something you might want to stop on (icons or buttons, for example), it appears that the mouse has hit some gravel and is slowing down because of friction. If you find yourself missing your targets when you're moving your mouse, you might try this option.

The IntelliPoint Toolbar

Included with the Microsoft mouse software is the IntelliPoint toolbar, which you can use to quickly turn on and off such things as Line Lock. The toolbar can optionally be "always on top," which means that it never gets hidden behind another window. You can also reduce its size by turning off its title bar. The value of title bars in general has been questioned by some people, particularly for maximized application windows. It is perhaps hard to justify using up screen space for a bar that reminds you that you've been typing all afternoon in Word for Windows. If you've become so disoriented that you've forgotten the name of your word processor, perhaps you should stop writing at that point anyway! It might be nice to make title bars optional in all Windows applications.

Figure 9-21 illustrates the Magnify feature: the mouse pointer is over a toolbar button and the button is blown up large in the window to the left. You can set various levels of magnification with the slider at the left.

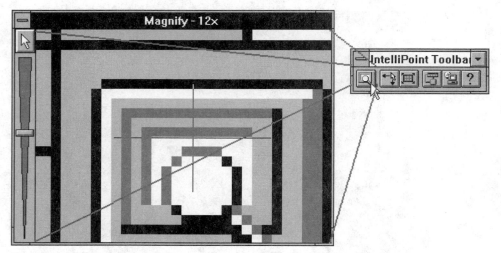

Figure 9-21: *Here is the toolbar and its Magnify option in action.*

People with vision problems could find this tool useful for the same reason that they use a magnifying glass when reading the newspaper. However, a more general solution would be to reset the properties of the desktop to a lower resolution and use the Large Fonts option. (Right-click on the desktop; then choose Settings. Make Desktop area smaller and switch to Large Fonts.) You might also use the Magnify feature to explore fine details and see how icons and toolbar buttons are drawn and shaded.

The other buttons on the toolbar are, in order: Line Lock; AutoScroll (just moving the mouse anywhere within a document that has a scroll bar will scroll the document); Customize toolbar; the IntelliPoint property sheet (shown in Figures 9-12 through 9-20); and Help.

When the Mouse Gets Dirty

Sooner or later your mouse will refuse to move smoothly. The pointer sits there when you drag the mouse, or you have to slide it two or three times before it actually does anything. You might even smack it a few times to try to knock some sense into it. But all it really needs is a mouse bath.

The mouse gets dirty like everything else. Just how often your mouse needs cleaning depends on your personal hygiene and habits. If you're a smoker with ashes falling all over your desk, if your mouse pad is stained and greasy, if your hair is held together with goop that gets on your fingers, then you might have to clean the mouse every few weeks.

If you're a very clean individual and you maintain a spotless workspace—frequently dusting, vacuuming and wiping the surfaces of your desk with toxic cleaning solutions—you might go for months without any problems. Indeed, if you cover your toaster with a quilted "cozy," cover your keyboard with a plastic overlay or put a dust cover over your computer at night, by now you've certainly bought one of those mouse hutches sold in computer stores.

But one day it happens to the best of us—the mouse will balk, and you'll have to take it apart and pick out the lint from the inside of the mechanism and clean the grease off the ball. Each manufacturer suggests different strategies for cleaning, but in most cases you twist a cover on the bottom and the ball drops out. Use foam swabs, tape or tweezers to pull out any little pills and wads of lint or whatever else has collected on the edges of the rollers inside the mouse. A blast of compressed air (cans of the stuff are available at most office and computer supply stores) can be a useful shortcut.

If the rollers themselves have mystery foreign matter on them, like smears or built up stuff that you don't know *what* it is—wipe that off too (a toothpick can be useful for this purpose). Now look at the ball. Most of them are made of a strangely heavy dense rubber (there's a steel ball inside). Some manufacturers suggest using adhesive tape to pull off "dust or lint" from the surface of the ball. However, you'll never find any dust or lint on the ball. The motions that you put the mouse through when computing guarantee that any dry matter will either rub off or be captured inside the mouse in the rollers. A rolling ball gathers no dust. Instead, the ball will over time have become slippery, coated with the natural oils from your and others' skin, as well as additional, unidentifiable contaminants. Tape won't do anything for this cleaning problem.

Some people rub the ball with an eraser, but this method really takes time. The best way to clean the ball is to take it into the kitchen and squeeze some dishwasher detergent on it and then rub it clean and rinse it off. Dry it with a paper towel, and it should be several shades lighter than when it went into the bath. Now you've restored a surface that will grip, rather than lubricate, the rollers inside the mouse.

You can also buy mouse cleaning kits. One uses a Velcro-coated mouse ball (with little plastic hooks) that you temporarily substitute for your real mouse ball. You rub the mouse around on a supplied Velcro (loop) mouse pad. This kit really cleans out the entire insides of your mouse.

Your mouse's runway surface may also need improvement. Although many kinds of mice don't need a special mouse pad, the friction available on a polished desk or table might not be ideal. It's rare to find anyone using a mouse without a mouse pad of some kind. Mouse pads, like screen savers and wallpaper, are a favorite way of personalizing your setup, even if they're not essential.

Moving On

Now that we've looked at the keyboard and mouse—the tools you use to tell the computer what to do—let's turn our attention to some things you might want done. In Chapter 10, we'll look at the generous set of accessories that Windows provides as part of the package.

We'll explore WordPad, Notepad, Calculator, Paint, the games and all the other freebie applications that Microsoft bundles with Windows 95. Some of these applications, however, are covered elsewhere in the book. Multimedia accessories (the CD and Multimedia Players, Sound Recorder) are covered in Chapter 20, and system tools (Backup, Defragmenter, DriveSpace and ScanDisk) are covered in Chapter 5.

 TIP   One accessory that you might expect to see in Windows 95 is missing. Microsoft hasn't included an anti-virus utility because as soon as they were to put it in, it would become instantly obsolete. They are leaving the anti-viral utilities to third parties. Chances are, however, that your machine running Windows 95 will not catch an older virus. That's because Windows 95 prevents any application from directly writing to the disk without "Locking the drive." (See Chapter 22.) This means, of course, that older anti-viral utilities probably won't work under Windows 95 because the very viruses that they are trying to protect you from couldn't infect your disk in the first place in Windows 95. Of course, new viruses will surely be designed to attack under Windows 95, and they will be capable of the new special disk locking technique in order to infect your disk.

Focus on Software

Chapter 10

Applets:
Windows 95
Accessories

In this chapter, we'll tour the various freebies, add-ons, applications and applets that Microsoft bundles with Windows 95. They're collected together in the Start menu under Programs | Accessories, as you can see in Figure 10-1.

Figure 10-1: *Microsoft provides a suite of programs as part of Windows itself.*

Windows 3.1 offered 13 accessories: Notepad, Write, Paint, Terminal, Cardfile, Calendar, Calculator, Clock, Character Map, Object Packager, Media Player, Recorder and Sound Recorder.

Based on the applications and applets collected in the Accessories folder within the Start menu, Windows 95 offers 29, including special sets collected within the Games, Multimedia and System Tools folders.

You might notice a file in your Windows directory called "WRITE.EXE." It isn't a copy of the Write word processor-ette included with Windows 3.1. It's merely a "stub" that always launches WordPad.

If some of the accessories described in this chapter don't appear on your Accessories menu, it means that when you first installed Windows, you didn't specifically request that they be installed. Many accessories, such as WordPad, are automatically installed if you select Complete when Setup asks how you want to install Windows 95. However, to install some of the others, such as the Phone Dialer, you must choose a Custom setup and then specifically select from the provided list of extra accessories. You can rerun Windows 95 Setup and choose Custom so that you can add these extras by hand. **Special Note:** Don't assume that because you already have a copy of WordPad you can deselect it from this Custom list of accessories during setup. Anything you deselect *will be removed from your hard drive*. To be safe, select everything listed.

An easier way to install missing Windows components is to select Add/Remove Programs from the Control Panel and then click on the Windows Setup tab. You then can scroll through the list of Windows optional components and enable (add or retain) or disable (delete and remove) each component as desired by turning on or off the check box for each one. This is also the safest way to remove undesired programs or accessories.

What's Covered in This Chapter?

Of the 29 accessories bundled with Windows 95, most of the basic ones—Notepad, WordPad, Paint, and so on—are covered in this chapter. However, other accessories seem more at home in other chapters. The Mail File Converter, Fax Cover Page Editor, Fax Viewer and Phone Dialer are covered in Chapter 16, "The Communicating Computer." The CD Player, Multimedia Player, Sound Recorder and Volume Control are described in Chapter 20, "Multimedia." The rest of the System Tools collection (Backup, Disk Defragmenter, DriveSpace, System Monitor, ScanDisk and WinBug) are explored in Chapter 5, "Inside the File System." Finally, you can find a discussion of Dial-Up Networking and Direct Cable in Chapter 19, "Getting Started With Networking." Hyperterminal connections, online registration, and Microsoft Network are located in Chapter 18, "The Microsoft Network."

What's Changed?

Some Windows 95 accessories have been greatly improved over their Windows 3.1 versions—notably the improvements in WordPad when compared to its predecessor, Write, and also the additions to PaintBrush (now called Paint).

Recorder was a way to create simple automatic behaviors, simple "macros." It was limited, though, and by most people is probably not going to be much missed. You turned it on, it watched your keyboard and/or mouse activity, and then you stopped Recorder. At this point, you could save the behaviors in a file. You could assign a shortcut key (such as Ctrl+F3) that would launch the macro and mimic the actions you had recorded.

Recorder has three main flaws. 1.) Recording mouse moves makes little sense because Recorder memorized the positions of mouse clicks and drags on the screen. Clearly, your open applications might be in different positions in the future, and the macro would fail. 2.) Recorder is too simple. Unlike the macro facilities built into Word and other applications, Recorder macros can't be edited; there is no facility for *branching* (doing different things based on current conditions), no facility for user input, and many other missing features. 3.) You have to load Recorder, then load the particular macro file and then launch the macro. There are ways around this (for example, assigning macros to icons, making Recorder load and run automatically each time Windows itself starts). However, the system is too unsophisticated and inefficient to be of much real interest. As it turns out, Recorder is also unable to cope with the sophisticated events that occur in new 32-bit applications, hammering the final nail in its coffin.

Nothing directly replaces Recorder in Windows 95, but the Windows 95 hotkey feature works well for launching programs. Also, most applications contain their own macro languages. But if you're interested in creating macros that work outside individual applications—that work in the Windows 95 operating system itself—consider purchasing Microsoft's Visual Basic. It doesn't record your actions, but it's an easy computer language to learn. (Some form of Visual Basic may yet be included in a future version of Windows.) For more information on automating Windows with hotkeys, see Chapter 8. For more information on macros and programming, see Chapter 23.

Tools at Several Levels

Microsoft has a philosophy of including similar tools at several levels of sophistication. For example, it offers Notepad for extremely simple text editing, WordPad for modest word processing tasks and Word for true, sophisticated word processing. One reason for including these tools is that you often don't need the powerhouse applications for small jobs. Notepad is often useful for a quick peek at a text file (though Windows 95 makes it somewhat less valuable now, given the Quick View feature available when you right-click on a document's icon).

The missing Windows 3.1 Cardfile—a simple database manager—was one of these lower-level tools. Far less capable than a full-blown database program like dBASE, FoxPro or Access, Cardfile was nonetheless a useful 3x5-card box simulation; it was a good place to keep notes, recipes, phone numbers or other small collections of data. You can, of course, still use the Windows 3.1 Cardfile accessory under Windows 95. So if you *have* typed a huge address book into it, just continue to use the old Cardfile. (There's nothing to replace it in Windows 95.)

If you deleted your old Windows 3.1 installation instead of upgrading it to Windows 95, some of your older accessories are now missing. The only way, then, to get back your Cardfile is to reinstall Windows 3.1 (telling it to be installed in a directory named something other than Windows—for example, OldWin). Then, after reinstalling it, go ahead and copy Cardfile and any other old accessory you want into your Windows directory. (Don't forget those .HLP files if you want Help to work.) Then delete the directory named OldWin so that you don't waste disk space.

The Windows 95 Accessory Set

Windows 3.1 Solitaire was a classic traditional version: you move cards onto one higher number, alternating red and black (see Figure 10-2). Luck plays a considerable part in your ability to win this game. The new Windows 95 FreeCell version, however, is far less dependent on luck. FreeCell is a logic puzzle disguised as Solitaire (see Figure 10-3). All cards are visible, and mathematicians claim but can't yet prove that, unlike most versions of Solitaire, you can win each game of FreeCell.

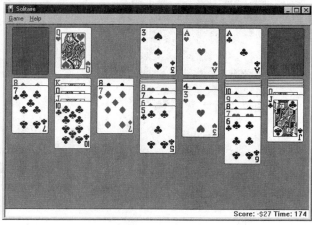

Figure 10-2: *You can still play Solitaire in Windows 95.*

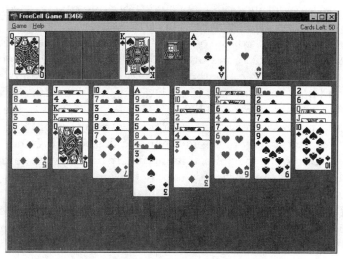

Figure 10-3: *Here's a game of FreeCell in progress.*

You also can play the Bridge-like game Hearts against the computer (your opponents are Bear, Bunny and Michele, three personalities of Windows 95) or against real people if you're on a network (see Figure 10-4). You can play Rumors only on a network.

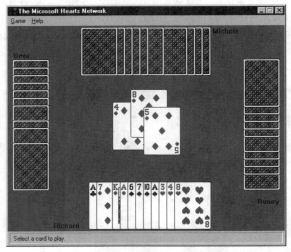

Figure 10-4: *You can play Hearts and Rumor on a network, so now you can seduce co-workers into wasting time at work.*

Multimedia & System Tools

The Multimedia folder includes CD Player, Sound Recorder, Media Player and Volume Control. These applications are described in detail in Chapter 20, but let's briefly sample a couple of interesting features of the CD Player—just to see how well integrated computers and multimedia have become.

An advanced CD Player, like those in the Sony ES series, contains a micro-processor and built-in memory—like a little version of a desktop computer. Among other tricks, you can teach the CD Player the names of the songs on your CDs and provide a rearranged order in which you want those songs played. Or you can specify that some songs be skipped altogether. Then, when you put the CD into the machine, it immediately displays the name of the record and the songs, and proceeds to play the songs the way you've told it to in your custom *play list*. How does it do this?

Each CD has an ID number burned into it, along with data about the duration of each song and other clerical information. Thus, when you put the CD into a sophisticated player, it reads the ID and checks to see if you've programmed the titles and a play list.

Similarly, when you create a CD play list, Windows saves the information you've typed (see Figure 10-5) and puts it in a file called CDPLAYER.INI in the Windows directory. Then, when you insert an audio CD, Windows gets the ID from the CD and looks through the .INI file to see if you've created a play list for that CD.

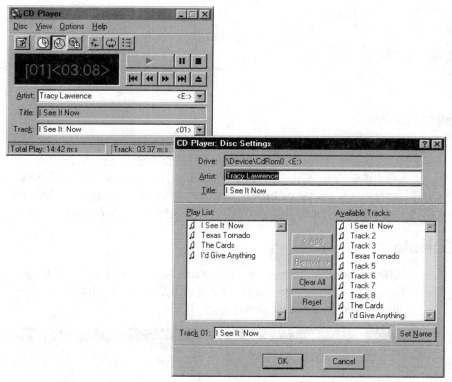

Figure 10-5: *You can create a play list and teach Windows 95 the names of the CDs, their songs and the order you want the songs played for your entire CD collection.*

In your Windows 95 directory, you'll find a file called CDPLAYER.INI, which contains any settings you've typed in to describe a CD's contents. The first number is the ID number stamped on every CD.

```
[962756]
EntryType=1
artist=Tracy Lawrence
title=I See It Now
numtracks=10
0=I See It Now
```

1=Track 2
2=Track 3
3=Texas Tornado
4=Track 5
5=Track 6
6=Track 7
7=Track 8
8=The Cards
9=I'd Give Anything
order=0 3 8 9
numplay=4

System Tools

Often called *utilities*, the collection of programs you find in Start | Programs | Accessories | System Tools are useful to keep your hard drive in top shape, get information about your hard disk, back up your hard drive to long-term storage on a tape or other backup medium, or convert a Microsoft Mail message. Most of these utilities are covered in Chapter 5.

Calculator

Although its features are largely unchanged from the Windows 3.1 Calculator accessory, few programs so vividly illustrate the visual improvements made in Windows 95 (see Figure 10-6).

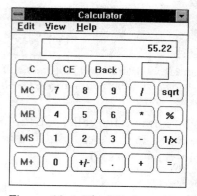 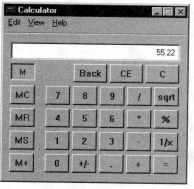

Figure 10-6: *The Windows 95 calculator on the right is more realistic looking than the Windows 3.1 version on the left.*

The buttons now look raised, and the output windows look recessed. This shading and other subtle changes lend a sculpted, 3D look to the new Calculator. To accommodate the shading, the Windows 95 Calculator is 3 pixels higher and 14 pixels wider than the Windows 3.1 version. Also changed for the better is the shape and position of the zone that shows an "M" if memory is in use. Symmetry and balance are achieved, making the older Windows 3.1 design look haphazard and clumsy by comparison.

It looks different, but are there any changes in functionality? Yes, a few. In the Standard view shown in Figure 10-6, there are no new features. But click on the View menu and switch to Scientific view, and you'll see one change. The choice between Dword, Word and Byte has been eliminated. (These three options define the size of a number, a byte being only 8-bits large and capable of manipulating or displaying numbers between 0 and 15. A Word is 2-bytes large and can handle –32,768 to 32,767. A Dword—double word—is 4-bytes large, and its range is between –2,147,483,648 and 2,147,483,647.) This feature was doubtless dropped from the Calculator because it serves little purpose to limit the range of calculations. In place of the previous range limitation, the Windows 95 version now offers three trigonometric views: degrees, radians and gradients. They affect the results you get with the trigonometric functions sin, cos and tan, which can operate in different modes, depending on what type of number they are working on.

Using the Calculator

The Windows Calculator is like a typical real-world calculator, but it's inside your computer so you can do a couple of unique things with it. You can paste results from other applications into it or copy the Calculator's results into outside applications. Use the same techniques to copy and paste. To copy the contents of the result window, press Ctrl+C; press Ctrl+Ins; or select Copy from the Edit menu. To paste into the result window, press Ctrl+V; press Shift+Ins; or select Paste from the Edit menu. You can also use this feature to copy a number from the Calculator directly into a document you're working on in a word processor or other application.

Like many real-world calculators, Windows 95's Calculator has a memory feature that is like a mini-Clipboard where you can store a single number in the midst of a calculation. (It's not the Windows Clipboard, though; you can't paste a number from memory to another program.) MC clears memory, MR recalls memory, MS stores the visible number in memory, and M+ adds the visible number to the contents of memory. When memory holds a number, the letter *M* appears in the box above the M keys. CE clears the most recent entry, and C resets the entire calculator, as if you'd just turned it on. Anything you put into the memory, however, remains. This capability is useful if you want to add several subtotals. Just add the first group of numbers, click M+, then click C and enter another group, followed by M+, and so on. When you're finished, click MR.

 TIP If you want to store various results and annotate them with text descriptions, paste the numbers into Notepad and comment them.

 TIP The % key helps you work with percentages. Most people find percentages, like fractions, a little counterintuitive. You can, however, use the % to construct a "sentence" that describes what you're after. For instance, to figure the total cost of a $200 sweater if local tax is 7%, just say it and click the buttons as you describe the problem: Two hundred plus seven percent equals (200 + 7 % =), and you get $214. To subtract a percent: Four hundred minus six percent. As you can see, pressing any of the / * – or + keys after entering a percent (like 7 %) gives you the actual number that is 7% of the first number you entered. Therefore, to get merely a percent of something, follow this same sentence structure, but don't press the equals key at the end. The hard one when working with percents is to find out what percent one real number is of another. For example, what percent of the choir is absent if 14 singers are present tonight and the whole choir numbers 18? In this case, the sentence would translate into ? % 14 18, but there's no question mark key, and you can't enter 14 18 or you'd get the meaningless value 1,418. To work these kinds of percent problems, you have to ignore the % key altogether and just divide the smaller number by the larger (14 / 18 gives you 0.7777777777778) and then multiply by 100 to translate the fraction into a percent (77.77777777778%).

The 1/X key gives you the *reciprocal* of the visible number. You can use the reciprocal to turn a divisor into a multiplicand. For example, if you want to use the result of a calculation to divide another number, you could just put the number into memory, type the other number, click the divide (/) key and then recall that number from memory. Or you can click the 1/X key and then multiply that result by the other number to get the same result. (For example, A/B = 1/B*A.)

Figuring formulae

Interestingly, the Calculator is fairly intelligent in one way. It won't let you paste a piece of text from, say, a word processor; it just ignores you if you try that. However, you can paste a simple formula, and the result is displayed. In Notepad, for example, you could write 10*5= ; then you could select it and copy it (Shift+arrow keys to select, Ctrl+Ins to copy the selected formula to the Clipboard). Then switch to the Calculator and press Shift+Ins to paste it. You would see the answer, 50. (The equals sign is required.)

 Some people learn the positions of the keys on the numeric keypad the same way they learned to type. This way, they can quickly enter numbers without having to look away from the notebook or wherever they're coping data from. To use the numeric keypad with the Calculator, just press the NumLock key.

You can access all the keys on the Calculator using the keyboard. You can, as with all Windows programs, use the keyboard instead of the mouse to manipulate the Calculator. Table 10-1 lists calculator features and the keys you must press to activate them.

Calc.	Keypress	Calc.	Keypress
%	%	hex	F5
(	(	Hyp	h
)	)	Int	;
*	*	Inv	i
+	+	ln	n
+/-	F9	log	l
-	-	Lsh	<
.	. or ,	M+	Ctrl+P
/	/	MC	Ctrl+L
0-9	0-9	Mod	%
1/x	r	MR	Ctrl+R
=	= or Enter	MS	Ctrl+M
A-F	A-F	n!	!
And	&	Not	~
Ave	Ctrl+A	Oct	F7
Bin	F8	Or	|
Byte	F4	PI	p
Back	Backspace	Rad	F3
C	Esc	s	Ctrl+D
CE	Del	sin	s
cos	o	sqrt	@
Dat	Ins	Sta	Ctrl+S
Dec	F6	Sum	Ctrl+T
Deg	F2	tan	t
dms	m	Word	F3
Dword F2	Xor	^	
Exp	x	x^2	@
F-E	v	x^3	#
Grad	F4	x^y	y

Table 10-1: *Calculator keys and their corresponding keypresses.*

Table 10-2 lists the keyboard shortcuts that work when you import numbers from the Clipboard into the Calculator.

Shortcut	Description
:c	Clears the calculator's memory.
:e	Permits you to enter numbers in scientific notation using decimal.
:m	Saves the displayed number in the calculator's memory.
:p	Adds the displayed number to the number in the calculator's memory.
:q	Clears the current calculation, moving you back to the result of the previous calculation.
:r	Displays the number stored in the calculator's memory.
\	Like clicking the Dat button. Click Sta before using this key.

Table 10-2: *Keyboard shortcuts that work with the calculator.*

The Scientific view

Click on the View Menu and select Scientific. Now you've got a plethora of statistical, scientific, computer programming, trigonometric and other features (see Figure 10-7). The uses of these various facilities is, of course, beyond the scope of this book.

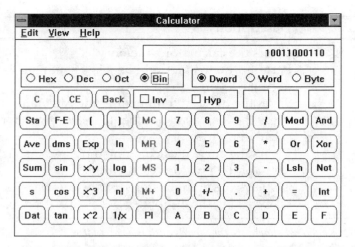

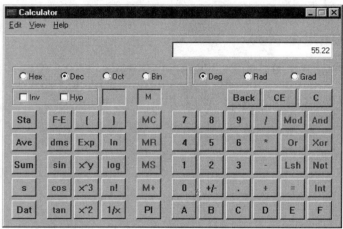

Figure 10-7: *The calculator's scientific view permits you to switch between the trigono-metric views degrees, radians and gradients, which are used with sin, cos and tan.*

What Calculator lacks

Given that Windows is most often used for business purposes, perhaps the Calculator should include a "paper roll." Having a hard copy printout would be helpful for keeping a record of all the calculations. The IRS, for example, wants you to add "on paper" all your deductions so they can see if you made an honest mistake in keying in your receipts or if something more sinister transpired. With a history of your calculation, you can also double-check for errors by proofing the "paper list" against the receipts or other data you're entering.

Of course, you aren't limited to using only the applications that come with Windows. Numerous calculator alternatives are available; some of them are inexpensive shareware or freeware. Some offer "paper tape" capability and many other valuable features, such as business calculations.

The Character Map

What do you do when you want to write the word *voilà* or *décolleté* or the famous if perplexing Greek proverb *eiz onuca,* which translates "to a finger-nail" and means "be specific"? (A more comprehensible Greek proverb— still in use today is— "You're getting up into my nostrils," which means "I'm annoyed with you.") Long a problem in DOS, the Windows Character Map accessory solves this issue neatly (see Figure 10-8). You just copy the character from the map of any font (or build whole words and then copy them). After that, you can just press Ctrl+V, or Shift+Ins, or select Paste from the Edit menu, to paste the text into your document.

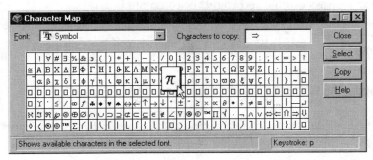

Figure 10-8: *In the Character Map, you add special characters to your documents.*

No longer do you have to search through a word processor's menus to find the "special characters" feature, look up the character you're after and then press a complicated code like Alt+0211 (to insert the copyright symbol) or some other code for an accented character. If you prefer, however, you can select a symbol and then read the Alt+*code* keystroke in the lower right of Character Map. Most word processors will recognize this combination of the Alt key and the numeric keypad numbers, inserting the desired symbol into your document, *but you must have the NumLock key on.*

Let's insert the code for the British pound symbol as an example.

1. Start Character Map and click on the pound symbol (£).
2. Look for that character's code in the lower-right corner of Character Map. It should say: "Keystroke Alt+0163."

3. Return to your word processor by clicking somewhere on its title bar or document window.

4. If the NumLock key is off, press and release it so it's now on.

5. Hold down the Alt key while typing **0163** on the numeric keypad. (Don't let go of Alt until you've typed all four digits.)

Character Map displays 224 symbols, though not all may be used. Some sets, such as the default Symbol font, include a row of blanks (shown as squares). When you first run Character Map, you'll see the set displayed in Figure 10-8. However, whichever font you last used will be shown when you restart Character Map. The default Symbol font comes with Windows and, in addition to the Greek alphabet, includes card symbols (heart, club, and so on), some mathematical symbols; arrows; copyright and trademark symbols and so on.

The Wingdings font is another popular set of symbols (see Figure 10-9). It includes a variety of *dingbats* (small icon-like characters) that you can use as bullets, designs or chained together to create borders.

Figure 10-9: *You can use Dingbats from the Wingdings font to add borders, bullets and other special effects to your documents.*

Almost every character set (also called font or typeface) registered with Windows contains at least the basic alternative symbols: various accented characters, copyright symbols (like © and ®), international symbols (such as the British pound £ and Japanese yen ¥), fractions (½, ¼), mathematical symbols (÷, ø, ±), and more. Your documents look more formal and professional when you insert these typeset-looking symbols than when, for instance, you merely type 3/4 or use a typeset "quote" instead of the tacky "inch marks." (See Figures 10-10 through 10-12.) For more about fonts and bullets, see Chapter 12.

!"#$%&'()*+,-./0123456789:;<=>?
@ABCDEFGHIJKLMNOPQRSTUVWXYZ[\]^_
`abcdefghijklmnopqrstuvwxyz{|}~□
□□,ƒ„…†‡^‰Š‹Œ□□□□''""•—―˜™š›œ□□Ÿ
¡¢£○¥¦§¨©ª«¬-®‾°±²³´µ¶·,¹º»¼½¾¿
ÀÁÂÃÄÅÆÇÈÉÊËÌÍÎÏÐÑÒÓÔÕÖ×ØÙÚÛÜÝÞß
àáâãäåæçèéêëìíîïðñòóôõö÷øùúûüýþÿ

Figure 10-10: *The Times New Roman character set.*

!"#$%&'()*+,-./0123456789:;<=>?
@ABCDEFGHIJKLMNOPQRSTUVWXYZ[\]^_
`abcdefghijklmnopqrstuvwxyz{|}~□
□□,ƒ„…†‡^‰Š‹Œ□□□□''""•—―˜™š›œ□□Ÿ
¡¢£¤¥¦§¨©ª«¬-®‾°±²³´µ¶·,¹º»¼½¾¿
ÀÁÂÃÄÅÆÇÈÉÊËÌÍÎÏÐÑÒÓÔÕÖ×ØÙÚÛÜÝÞß
àáâãäåæçèéêëìíîïðñòóôõö÷øùúûüýþÿ

Figure 10-11: *The Courier New Character set.*

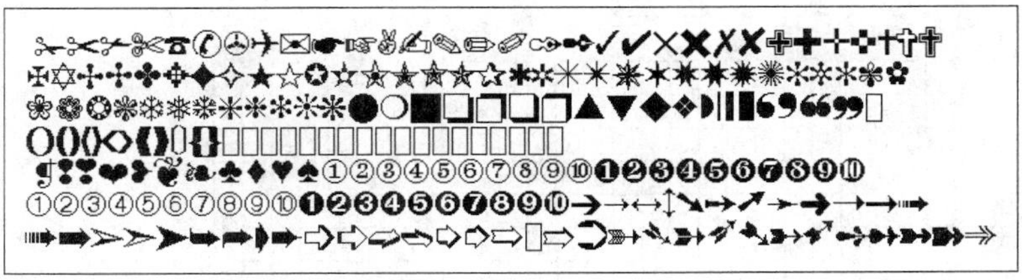

Figure 10-12: *The Zapf Dingbats set—the classic collection of bullets and borders.*

You can add new character sets to Windows quite easily. Click on Start | Settings | Control Panel and double-click on the Fonts shortcut folder. You'll see all the currently installed fonts. To add a new font, select Install New Font from the File menu.

TIP Don't overdo it. It's fun to see your documents dressed up in various typefaces. But fonts take up room on your hard drive, and they can also slow down Windows if it has to rifle through several typefaces before, for example, starting your word processor. A font file can be only 5k (approximately 5,000 bytes) or it can be as large as 200k. If you install 35 typical fonts, you'll use up more than two megabytes on your hard drive.

You can get new fonts in most computer stores for as little as $19. Hundreds of them are bundled with graphics software such as CorelDRAW. And, of course, you can download them from BBSs and online services such as CompuServe and America Online.

Alternatives

Some Windows word processors have built-in features that can accomplish the same thing as the Character Map utility. For example, in Word for Windows click on the Insert menu, then choose, Symbol, and you'll see the window in Figure 10-13. Figure 10-4 shows the Special Characters page of this window.

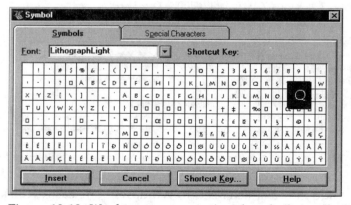

Figure 10-13: *Word processors sometimes have built-in substitutes for Character Map.*

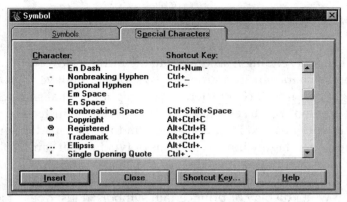

Figure 10-14: *Word for Windows Insert | Symbol feature also includes a list of frequently used symbols and predefined keyboard shortcuts for many of them.*

The Insert | Symbol feature of Word allows you to assign shortcut key combinations to any character (remember, you cannot conveniently type many special symbols using the keyboard without resorting to an awkward and unmemorable Alt+*four digit* code). Therefore, assigning a shortcut to a frequently used symbol makes sense. In fact, it's easier than calling up Character Map. For example, if you work in copyright law, you might want to assign the copyright symbol to an easily memorable shortcut such as Alt+C.

 TIP   Most word processors correctly sense the typeface that you've selected when using Character Map to insert a symbol. However, in your word processor, you might paste a character and find that it is in the same font as the rest of your document. Perhaps that's what you want. Nearly all typefaces have the same set of symbols and foreign letters; they just look slightly different in the different fonts. But let's assume that you want to insert one of the unique symbols from the Wingdings, Symbol, Dingbats or some other collection of specialized symbols. In that case, you might have to paste the symbol and then select it. Now use your word processor's Format | Font (or whatever menu it provides to allow you to change fonts) to adjust the font of that symbol so it looks as you intended.

You don't always get what you want

Most word processors will accept any character or font, displaying it properly on the screen and sending it accurately to the printer. However, if you try to import special characters into simpler, less sophisticated word processors (*text editors* might be a more accurate term), you might find that some characters won't be accepted. You'll see a black box or a rectangle instead of the symbol or character you intended to import. The Windows Notepad, useful though it is for some jobs, is highly limited in terms of typefaces. It can display only one built-in Windows font (the "system" font, such as VGASYS.FON or 8514SYS.FON)) at only one size and only one weight (bold). What's more, the system font won't display or print certain symbols; it just doesn't include them in its character set, as you can see in Figure 10-15.

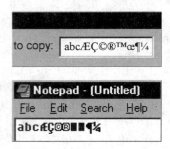

Figure 10-15: *Here we attempt to insert a string of characters from Character Map (above) into Notepad (below). Notice that the trademark symbol and the trademark character ™ can't be imported into Notepad.*

Notepad

Quite useful for taking notes or peeking into disk files, Notepad deserves its reputation as one of the most often used Windows utilities. Four changes have been made to Notepad between Windows 3.1 and Windows 95:

1. Notepad now uses the new common dialog boxes for Open, Save and Save As. This capability allows for sophisticated directory management entirely from within the dialog box.
2. It now accepts Universal Naming Conventions (UNC) names. For example, say you have a networked computer set up, and your main computer's name is FUSION_ONE. On another computer on this network, you can access the disk drives on FUSION_ONE by using Universal Naming Conventions such as \\FUSION_ONE\D-DRIVE\PROJECTS\WIN95BOOK\CHAP10.DOC.

3. It understands the new long filenames. (Windows 3.1 and previous limited you to eight characters plus a three-character extension for all filenames.)
4. It features the new Windows 95 User Interface style for the title bar caption: the document name followed by the application name. For example: MyDocument.txt. Notepad.

 TIP The *common dialog box* is the standard window that pops up in virtually all Windows 95 applications for common tasks such as Open, Save As, Print Setup and so on. Because most applications use these same user-interaction dialog boxes, Windows has achieved its longtime goal of simplifying things for users. In the old days, each application had a different dialog box for Print, Save, and so on. The options were different, and even the locations of such buttons as Exit were in different places. (Exit was sometimes called Quit or Done.) Now, thank goodness, no matter where you are in Windows 95, you engage in a *common dialog*.

Notepad is not a word processor: it lacks formatting of any significance, italics, alternative typefaces, and it can display characters in only one size and in a rough-looking boldface. It's able to display only files smaller than 64k (64,000 characters, about 6,000 words, or the size of an average chapter in an average book).

Notepad is, however, small and fast. Now that Windows 95 includes a Quick View feature, Notepad might be less frequently used than it was in Windows 3.1. Note, though, that the Quick View option doesn't permit any editing; you can look but you can't touch. And even the Quick View feature uses Notepad in certain circumstances, as we'll see.

If you try to load a file larger than 64k into Notepad, Windows explains that it's not possible and asks whether you would like to see the file in WordPad (see Figure 10-16). WordPad, like most word processors, can read a file of any size. Notepad gains some of its speed because it loads the entire file into the computer's memory. Once in memory, searches, scrolling and other activities are quite swift. However, this tactic also limits the size of files that it can view. WordPad, though, uses a different approach. It holds in memory a zone ahead and behind of whatever *part* of a document you're viewing. When you scroll, WordPad swaps the text in memory back to the disk and loads in a new zone. This process works much the same way as a microfilm viewer. Part of the film is in the viewport, and the rest is coiled on rollers waiting in "storage" if you should decide to look at it.

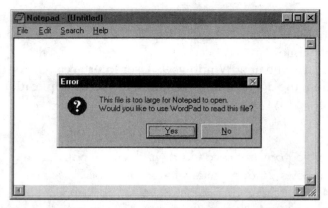

Figure 10-16: *If you try to look at a file larger than about 6,000 words, Windows suggests that you must use WordPad instead.*

You can use Notepad to jot down ideas, much like you would use a note pad on your desk. You could create a folder called Notes and store all your short files there for later review. In Explorer's File menu, select New | Folder. Another way to collect and organize ideas you jot down is to use Notepad's .LOG feature to time- and date-stamp your entries in a single Notepad file. First, type **.LOG** at the top left of a new Notepad file, as shown in Figure 10-17. Type in a note; then save the file to disk. Thereafter, any time you open this file, the time and date will be inserted automatically at the end of the text.

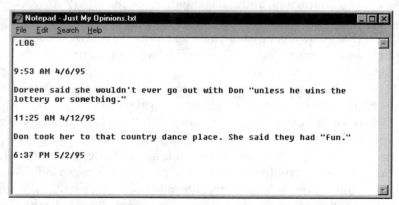

Figure 10-17: *The .LOG option inserts a time/date stamp every time you open a file.*

Notepad Menu Options

The File menu

Under Notepad's File menu, you'll find the usual document-management features. File | New allows you to start a new document. Creating a new document will destroy any existing text in Notepad, so it's like a "clear all" option. However, if it contains any edited text, Notepad will ask you first if you want to save that text to a file before clearing it. File | Open allows you to load in an existing document. In fact, unlike WordPad, you can open *any* kind of file with Notepad—not just text documents. This capability is dangerous because you could open a runnable program. If you edit and make changes to a runnable program and then save it back to disk, it's likely that you'll have damaged that application, and it won't work as it should or won't run at all.

(*Runnable*, or *executable*, files are programs that do something. These files are distinct from *documents*, the information on which a program acts. For example, Notepad is a runnable file; writing something in Notepad and then saving it creates a document file. Document files have file *extensions* such as .TXT or .DOC. Runnable programs have the extension .EXE. To request Explorer to display these DOS file extensions, select View | Options. Then deselect the Hide MS-DOS file extensions for the *File* types that are registered option. For more information, see Chapter 4.)

In any case, Notepad's File | Open feature permits you to load any file that's smaller than 64k. You'll recognize a non-text file immediately; it will look like somebody set off bombs in the file and then shook the whole thing until it contained crazy nonsense words, random blank zones, possibly mixed in with recognizable words or phrases here and there. (Word processor files can look like this, too, because of all the formatting codes they use. However, somewhere in a word processor file you'll see a zone of real text that you can understand. Open a .DOC file to see the difference.)

 If Explorer, a folder or a document icon is on your desktop, you can just drag a document onto Notepad to open the document. You can use this technique with most Windows applications. If Notepad is minimized on the taskbar, drag the item to Notepad's taskbar button and hold it there; don't let go yet. Notepad automatically restores itself to let you drop the item into Notepad's editing screen.

File | Open defaults to .TXT extensions. When you save a file from Notepad, it also adds a .TXT extension to your filename. This way, Notepad can quickly display a list of all Notepad files when you want to open one. File | Open shows just the files you're likely to want, in this case, the .TXT files. However, in the Open dialog box, you can choose All Files in the Files of type list (see Figure 10-18). You can also type in a file specification. For instance, if you type ***.EXE**, you would find only those files with an .EXE extension.

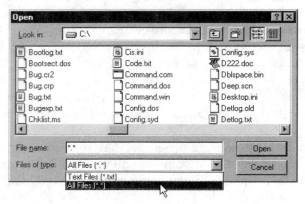

Figure 10-18: *Click here if you want to load in a file other than Notepad-style .TXT files.*

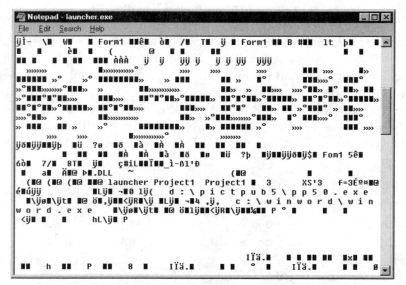

Figure 10-19: *It's dangerous to open an executable .EXE file. You might damage or destroy the application by making changes and then resaving it to disk.*

Notepad's File menu includes the familiar Save option. If you're saving a new file that's not been previously saved to disk, Notepad will prompt you for a filename. If you're saving a file that's already on the disk drive, Notepad will simply replace the older version without asking you any questions.

Following the Save option is Save As. This option is useful if you want to create another copy of the file, giving it a new name. You can also use Save As to *overwrite* an existing file (one that has a different name from the one you're working on). In other words, if you've been keeping a set of notes called BUSINESS.TXT, and you want to replace that file with the one currently in Notepad, select Save As and name your current file **BUSINESS.TXT.** Then save it to the same folder as the older version. At that point, Notepad warns you that a file with the name you're proposing to give the current file already exists. It will ask you to verify that you want to replace this existing file. Another use for Save As is if you want to save the document to a different drive or directory. You might use Save As to save the document to a floppy disk, for example, by typing **A:** at the beginning of the filename.

The next three options on Notepad's File menu control printing. The Print option sends the document to the printer to be printed. The Page Setup feature allows you to specify margins for any of the four sides, or to modify the header and footer (see Figure 10-20). By default, each printed page of a Notepad document includes the name of the file centered at the top and the word *Page*, followed by the page number, centered at the bottom.

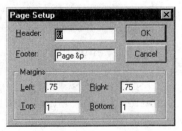

Figure 10-20: *You can make a few adjustments to the printed header and footer. The defaults, shown here, print the filename and page number.*

You can entirely remove the header or footer if you want to, but it will reappear the next time you run Notepad with a different document. Your preferences aren't persistent between sessions with Notepad. You have to make any changes you want, for each document. However, for any particular document, Notepad remembers the header and footer you've established.

You can change the default header &f to Weekly Report or whatever else you want. Add some decoration to the footer: —Page&p—. The &ff and &p

are codes to Notepad to insert *variables* (the current filename and page number). Here is a list of other variables you can insert into the header or footer text box:

&d	current date
&t	current time
&l	left-justify the following text
&r	right-justify the following text
&c	center the following text

The Print Setup option on Notepad's File menu is identical to the Print Setup found in most Windows applications. It allows you to switch the orientation to *landscape* (wider than it is tall), change the paper size or source (if your printer has various trays feeding different sizes or types of paper), change the printer (if more than one printer is available to you or if you want to send a fax) or bring up the property sheet for your printer where you can make many additional adjustments (see Chapter 13).

 TIP Many DOS text documents are formatted for an 80-column printer. Set all margins to zero to print these documents as they are intended to appear.

The Edit menu

Notepad's Edit menu is identical to most Edit menus in Windows applications. Included are the Undo, Cut, Copy, Paste and Delete features you'll find in most Windows text or graphics programs. Also, the familiar shortcut key combinations are in effect; they are faster than reaching for the mouse or pressing Alt+E to drop down this menu and then selecting one of these common editing tasks. Table 10-3 lists the editing key combinations. (Remember that to cut, copy, or delete an item, you must first *select* it. You must define the characters, words or zone within a graphic that you want the editing to apply to. In Notepad and most text editors or word processors, you can either hold down the left mouse button while you drag the mouse across some text, or you press Shift+arrow key to select. The selected text reverses to white-on-black, showing you the extent of your selection. For additional ways to select whole sentences, paragraphs or the entire document, see "Common Shortcut Key Combinations" in Chapter 8.)

	Preferred Shortcut	Windows 2.0/3.0 Compatible Shortcut
Undo	Ctrl+Z	Alt+Backspace
Cut	Ctrl+X	Shift+Delete
Copy	Ctrl+C	Ctrl+Insert
Paste	Ctrl+V	Shift+Insert
Delete	Del	Backspace

Table 10-3: *Notepad's editing key combinations.*

The Time/Date option on Notepad's Edit menu inserts a time/date stamp in your document at the current cursor location. Pressing F5 does the same thing: 5:52 PM 2/9/95, for example.

A most curious default

This a bother because most of the time you'll probably want it *on*. If you use Notepad often, you'll likely find yourself clicking on Edit and then selecting the WordWrap option frequently. There is no shortcut key for it.

Millions of perplexed Notepad users have suffered from this odd default. It's just one of those things you have to live with, like speed bumps.

It all involves the *carriage return*. In the days when typewriters were still used to create documents, they had a large lever on the right side of the machine. Every time you finished a line of text, you had to drag the lever over to the left to move the paper to the start of the next lower line. In a computer, pressing the Enter key does the same thing. It always moves you down a line and to the left. However, the Enter key also signifies a new paragraph, not just a new line. This makes sense. Why should you have to press Enter after each line you type? Why not let the computer handle this rather boring issue? When you type enough to go off the screen to the right, the computer automatically "wraps" the next word around to the right side and down one line. This way, you can just type away, pressing Return (Enter) only to separate paragraphs.

But this efficiency introduces a discontinuity with which we must all attempt to cope. We're not all using the standard 80-character-per-line typewriter anymore. Given that the width of people's screens differ and that you can select different typefaces, where the characters are of differing widths, the number of characters in a line of text can vary considerably in computer documents. Some documents you load (from alien sources like README.TXT files that come with applications and tell you things that they found out about their software too late to put in the manual) will have line lengths too wide to show up on your monitor. You'll see part of the document, but Notepad will add a horizontal scroll bar along the bottom of its window so that you can move the window horizontally to read everything. (See Figures 10-21 and 10-22.)

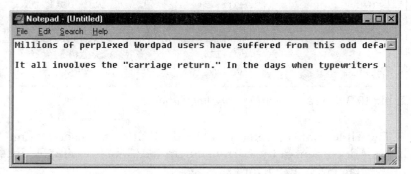

Figure 10-21: *Before: With word wrap off (the default), each paragraph is on a single line—no matter how long.*

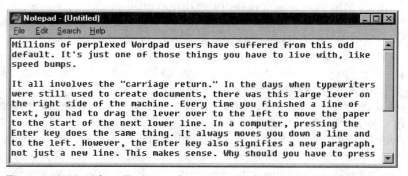

Figure 10-22: *After: Turn word wrap on, and the width of the Notepad window defines where lines break.*

The Search menu

Notepad offers an abbreviated search feature (there's no search-and-replace). However, if you want to find a particular word or phrase, press F3 and the Find window pops up, as shown in Figure 10-23.

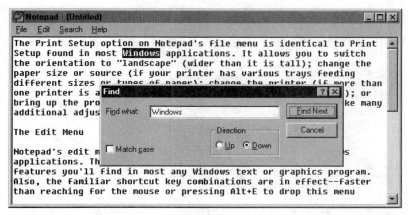

Figure 10-23: *Notepad's Find window is typical of the search feature found in most document-processing applications.*

Your options during a search are to Match case (*Spring* is a different target than *spring*) or to search up from the current cursor position rather than down. Repeatedly pressing Enter will take you to the next instance of your target down (or up) through the document until you reach the bottom (or top), and there are no more instances (see Figure 10-24).

Figure 10-24: *The search ends when Notepad can find no more instances of the text you're searching for.*

The difference between Find and Find Next is that Find Next uses the target text previously entered when you started a Find. However, it's easiest to just press F3 and type in what you're looking for.

The Help menu

Aside from giving you advice about using Notepad, the Help menu also provides some interesting statistics when you select About Notepad (see Figure 10-25). About 98 percent of Windows applications contain this About option. It might better be called About Windows since it tells you how much of your RAM is currently being used and the amount of Windows resources currently available.

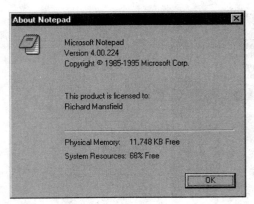

Figure 10-25: *The About window in most Windows programs tells you how much memory and resources you have left.*

Though much less a problem in Windows 95 than it was before, running low on memory or resources is still possible. If you are running, say, eight applications at the same time, you might deplete either memory or resources, and Windows might start getting sluggish or behaving erratically. The solution is to shut down a program or two, or buy and install more memory. Random-Access Memory (RAM) is the place where running programs store themselves (or part of themselves) and store the current document or graphic (or part of them). RAM is much faster to access and manipulate than reading from and writing to the hard drive. (You can learn how to install memory in Chapter 14.)

Windows uses memory in more than one way. For example, a Notepad document is held in RAM while you're working on it. That's one kind of memory usage. Another kind involves Resources, which are a special kind of storage space. Your RAM must hold not only any documents or images you're working on, it must also hold the elements of Windows itself—the frames, buttons, icons, scroll bars, fonts, palettes and so on.

In Windows 3.1, system resources often dipped precipitously as you started new applications running. It wasn't uncommon to find Windows 3.1 becoming unstable after only three or four applications were running. You'd click on Help, then select About and see loads of conventional RAM still available but perhaps only 12 percent system resources. Each application running under Windows 3.1 was given only 64k RAM (roughly 64,000 bytes) to store all the graphics elements of the windows in that application. Fortunately, this problem will be much less common now. Windows 95 has moved most resources to 32-bit memory regions that are limited only by the total amount of memory you have in your computer.

Instances

Unlike many Windows programs, you can have as many Notepads as you want open at the same time and running. Called *instances*, multiple running Notepads can be useful if you want to copy and paste visually, condense several documents into one or otherwise edit via multiple windows.

Registration (Association Types)

When you double-click on a file with a .TXT extension in Explorer or a folder, that file is automatically loaded into Notepad, and an instance of Notepad pops up onscreen. Each time you click on one of those .TXT files, another Notepad comes into existence to hold and display it (as long as the .TXT file isn't larger than 64k, in which case you're offered the opportunity to load it into WordPad). Keep on doing that and your screen will fill with Notepad clones, instances of this one program multiplied as often as you want to spawn them.

But there's more. You can *assign* (this capability was called *associate* in Windows 3.1 and is called *registering* in Windows 95) any kind of file to any application, causing that application to launch and load the file when the filename or icon is double-clicked in a folder or Explorer.

 When you want to create a new association or modify an existing one, double-click the My Computer icon (or run Explorer if you prefer). Then, from its View menu, select Options, then select the File Types tab. If you want to make a new association, choose New Type. To change an already associated file type, click on the type and then select Edit.

Another way to associate a new file type is to just double-click on the file in Explorer or a Folder view. The Open As dialog box appears, giving you a choice of programs to open the file with. If the program you want to use is not on the list, use the Browse button to locate it. You can also name the file type and choose whether to always use this program for opening that file type.

WordPad

Replacing Windows 3.1's Write accessory, WordPad's capabilities are greater than the simple text editing of Notepad, yet considerably less than a full-featured word processor like WordPerfect, Microsoft Word or Ami Pro (see Figure 10-26).

Figure 10-26: *You can put pictures, music or other objects inside a WordPad document.*

The File Menu

Let's go through WordPad's features in the order they appear on WordPad's menus. The majority of the features on the File menu are identical to those found in the File menus of 95 percent of all Windows programs (see their descriptions under Notepad above). However, the Open option includes more *filters* than Notepad's (see Figure 10-27). Notepad can read only plain .TXT text files (DOS-type ASCII files with no formatting, fonts, italics or other special qualities). You can load a Word for Windows file (or any other file, for that matter) into Notepad, but it won't make much sense. It won't be *filtered;* the codes for italics, fonts and so on will be visible as nonsense characters rather than causing the desired changes in the appearance and format of the text.

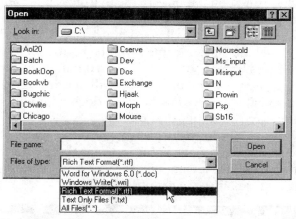

Figure 10-27: *WordPad can read and display various kinds of formatting created in other applications.*

When you select Open from WordPad's File menu, you'll notice that WordPad can translate and filter more kinds of documents than the simple .TXT file format. It can also import documents created in Word for Windows 6.0, Windows 3.1, Write (.WRI), and Rich Text Format (.RTF). Rich Text Format, similar to the format used by Word documents, stores simple formatting using its own special codes within the document, when the document is saved to a file. On the other end, when some application that can import and translate the RTF codes opens this document, the formatting is reproduced. RTF is a stop-gap measure, an attempt to preserve formatting between applications, most of which have an individual, proprietary document file format and formatting codes peculiar to them. This situation is improving somewhat, but in a rather indirect fashion; more and more applications are providing greater translation facilities than ever before. The popular word processors can now read and reproduce the format codes of most other popular word processors, with varying degrees of success. For example, Word won't open Ami Pro documents, yet Ami Pro can open Word documents.

On the other end, when you select Save from WordPad's File menu, you are offered three file formats in which to save your document: Word for Windows 6.0, Rich Text Format, or Text Only.

Print Preview

When you create a new document, it's not always easy to imagine how it's going to look when printed on paper. Are the margins right? Are some paragraphs too long? Do the font or font size contribute to the way you want the document to look? Is there an awkward line break at the end of the page? Does a major section start one line from the bottom of a page, so it would be better to press Enter above it and force it onto the next page? Rather than wasting paper by making changes, then printing, then making more changes and so on, you can view how the document will format when sent to the printer to save both time and money.

WordPad provides a Print Preview feature on its File menu (see Figure 10-28). You can see a full-page view, zoom in to see the text formatting and the font, or select a two-page view (a *spread*) to see how pages look if bound together in magazine format (see Figure 10-29).

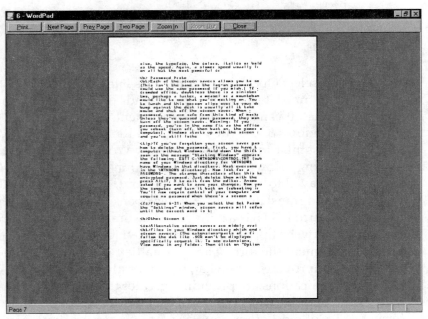

Figure 10-28: *One useful feature common to word processors but missing from simple text editors is* print preview.

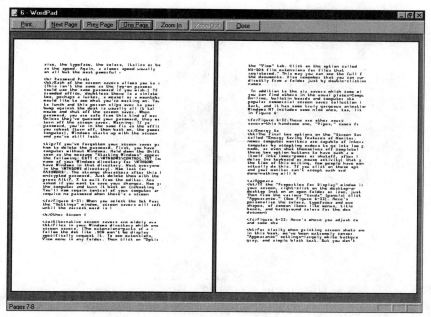

Figure 10-29: *Print Preview also features a two-page or* spread *view.*

Page Setup

WordPad permits you to select the size of paper that's being printed, adjusting the margins appropriately (see Figure 10-30). Among other choices are legal size paper and various sizes of envelopes. The Page Setup feature, in combination with the paper tray and orientation options, allows you to print envelopes with WordPad if your printer supports these features.

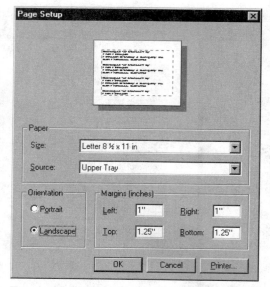

Figure 10-30: *WordPad's Page Setup includes orientation, paper size and tray features not found in Notepad (compare to Figure 10-20).*

Send

Like many applications written for Windows 95, WordPad includes built-in fax and online communication services (such as the Microsoft Network or CompuServe) capabilities (see Figure 10-31). Writing a document and then sending it as a fax or an e-mail message is as easy (if slower) than printing it to your local printer. We cover the mail options of Exchange more completely in Chapter 19, but we'll take a quick look here first.

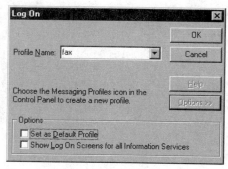

Figure 10-31: *WordPad also includes built-in telecommunications connections.*

In the Log On window, select Set as Default Profile if you usually use WordPad to send messages to a particular destination. That way, you don't have to click on the drop-down list each time to specify fax or whatever other telecommunications target you most often use.

Don't select *Show Log On Screens for all Information Services* if you want WordPad to quietly send your e-mail messages. With this option turned off, WordPad works in the background to deliver your mail, and you can keep on writing or turn to other tasks undisturbed by anything other than the sound of the phone being dialed and, perhaps, a few brief delays during screen scrolling or other activities. Of course, WordPad asks you to address your message to someone (see Figure 10-32), and you have to wait while Windows gets itself together to send the e-mail, but the online service's startup screen won't pop out and bother you while you're working. Also, see Figure 10-33.

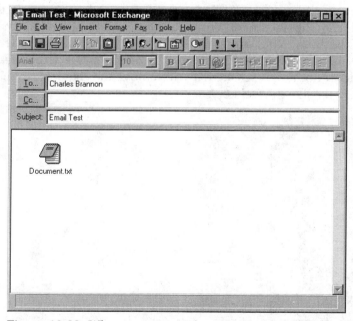

Figure 10-32: *When you request that WordPad send e-mail, it asks you to provide the addressee.*

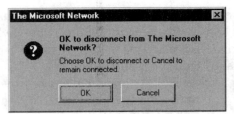

Figure 10-33: *After the mail has been sent, the Microsoft Network asks your permission to disconnect.*

The Edit Menu

Most items on WordPad's Edit menu are replicates of any other Windows application's Edit menu (see descriptions under "Notepad"); see Figure 10-34. However, WordPad uses *Clear* instead of Cut or Delete. Any selected text is removed from the document. Word for Windows has both a Clear and a Cut option. Cut removes but copies the selection to the Clipboard. Clear removes it and doesn't save it in the Clipboard. However, in Word, the Clear option is rather odd. If nothing is selected, it will remove the character to the right of the cursor (just like the Del key).

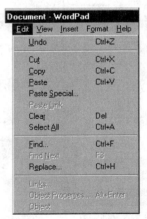

Figure 10-34: *The WordPad Edit menu offers Clear instead of Cut or Delete.*

The Clear option in WordPad doesn't behave this way; it removes only what's selected (but doesn't save it to the Clipboard the way the Cut or Copy commands do). Clear something, and it's almost gone. The Undo option doesn't use the Clipboard; it will restore something that's been cleared. In all applications, you can use the Undo option to reverse a Cut,

Clear, Delete or whatever it's called. However, you generally must perform the Undo right away, since Undo usually reverses only the last action you performed. Some applications, though, have undos six or more levels deep, and at least one, Picture Publisher by Micrografx, has an unlimited Undo feature. It remembers all the things you've done to a graphic and, on request, lets you back up as far as you want to restore the status of the graphic at any point along this trail of events.

TIP   Most Windows document-editing applications, even Notepad, use at least a few of the shortcut key combinations for the various editing options. To see the complete list of shortcut combinations (many of which work in WordPad), see Table 8-2 under "Common Shortcut Key Combinations."

Paste Special

Under the familiar Paste option on the Edit menu is a new one called *Paste Special*. Paste, as you recall, moves the contents of the Windows Clipboard to the location of your cursor in a document. In other words, if you've selected some text and then cut (or copied) that text, it went to the temporary Windows holding space called the Clipboard. Only one thing (a piece of text, a graphic) can reside in the Clipboard at any one time. Therefore, the most recently copied or cut item will be available for pasting.

Paste Special, Paste Link and the Object features lower down on the Edit menu provide access to the new Object Linking and Embedding (OLE) technology. When a document or graphic has been cut or copied into the Clipboard from another application, the Paste Special feature can insert that object into a WordPad document (see Figure 10-35). Paste Special offers several options, as shown in Figure 10-36.

Figure 10-35: *With Paste Special, you can create links to other applications and insert even graphic objects.*

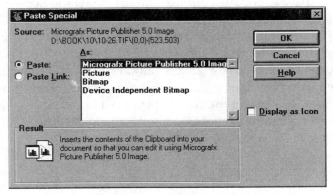

Figure 10-36: *Paste Special offers several ways to insert an object into a WordPad document.*

Selecting the "Paste" option means that when the user double-clicks on the object in your WordPad document, that object, in this case a woman's face, is loaded into Picture Publisher and can be edited. Just how the object behaves within your document is up to you. Paste Link means that this picture will be loaded into WordPad each time the document is loaded. (If you select Paste in Paste Special, the drawing is made a permanent part of the document.)

Linking vs. Embedding

The key point about the distinction between selecting Paste and Paste Link is that with Paste your document file will be much larger because it holds the picture. With Paste Link, the picture resides in a separate file on disk, so your document is fairly small. However, with Paste Link, any changes that you might make to that picture file (by editing it within a graphics program) will obviously appear within your WordPad document's version of the picture (since the picture is always loaded in from the original graphics file). Here's one problem with Paste Link: If the picture file is deleted or even moved on the disk, you'll get nothing when you load the WordPad document that contains the picture. This distinction is called *embedding* (Paste, in which the picture becomes part of the WordPad document) vs. *linking* (Paste Link, in which the picture remains separate from your WordPad document).

The Links feature of the Edit menu allows you to edit linked objects. Object Properties brings up a property sheet for the selected object. The first page, General, shows the type of object it is (its source application) and, potentially, permits you to convert the object into another format. The second page, View, allows you to switch between seeing the object itself (and possibly being able to edit it) or seeing merely an icon representing the object. The icon is generally the same as the icon of the originating application, as you can see in Figure 10-37. You can also change the icon and (if it's possible) adjust the size of the object.

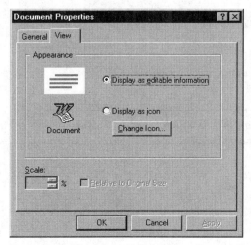

Figure 10-37: *Select Edit | Object Properties, and you can adjust various qualities of a linked or embedded object.*

We'll have much more to say about these exciting new features in Chapter 11, "Application Integration."

The View Menu

The buttons on the WordPad toolbar are, from left to right: New Document, Open a document on disk, Save current document, Print, Print Preview, Find, Cut, Copy, Paste, Undo and Insert the date/time.

Figure 10-38: *WordPad's View menu includes several typical word processor features.*

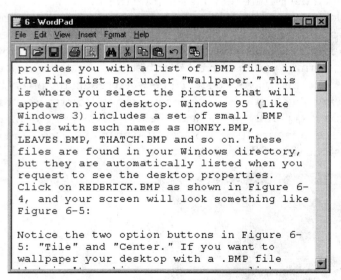

Figure 10-39: *You can click on WordPad's toolbar buttons to activate various menu items without having to open any menus.*

When you make the Format bar visible by selecting View | Format Bar (see Figure 10-40), you can quickly adjust, from left to right: Font (typeface), font size, bold, italics, underline, color, bulleted paragraphs, left-justification, centering, or right-justification. None of these items operate unless you've *selected* some text by dragging the mouse across it (or one of the several other ways to select). If you want to, say, change the typeface of the entire document, choose the Select All option from the Edit menu (or press Ctrl+A).

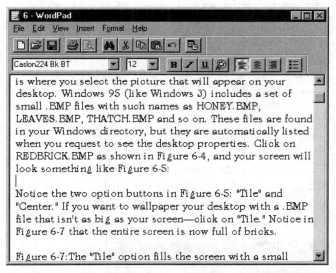

Figure 10-40: *The Format bar provides a quick way to adjust the font, font size and various other formatting qualities of selected text.*

Using the Ruler option, you can quickly drag tabs or adjust the right and left margins (see Figure 10-41). Move your mouse pointer over to the far left of your document and then hold down the Ctrl key while clicking the mouse. This way, you select the entire document, turning it to white-on-black text. Now you can slide one of the ruler pointers to reset a margin. Note that the slider on the top left of the ruler governs the position of the first line in each paragraph; the slider on the bottom left controls the indent of the rest of the text.

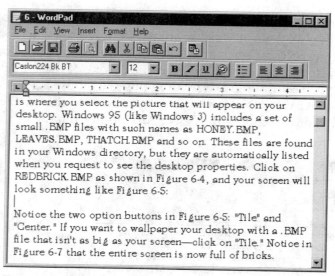

Figure 10-41: *The ruler provides a quick way to set tabs and margins.*

The WordPad status bar displays brief descriptions of menu items as you move your mouse over each option (see Figure 10-42). Those recessed areas on the right side of the status bar display the status of the Caps Lock and NumLock keys.

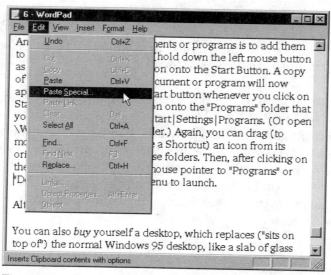

Figure 10-42: *The final option on WordPad's View menu adds the familiar Windows status bar at the bottom of the window.*

Options

The Options feature on the View menu opens the property sheet shown in Figure 10-43. The Automatic Word Selection option can make dragging your mouse across a line of text to select a group of words easier. It causes the black selection zone to jump from word to word rather than to merely move from letter to letter.

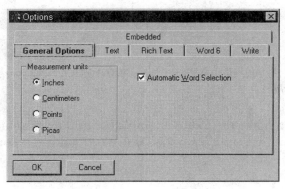

Figure 10-43: *In the General Options page of WordPad's property sheet, you can set the units of formatting measurements and toggle Automatic Word Selection.*

The rest of the pages in the Options property sheet are identical to the one shown in Figure 10-44. For each of the four file types that WordPad can work with, you can create different default conditions. Under Word wrap, you can turn off word wrap, make text wrap at the right side of the visible window, or wrap at the margins (set by the ruler). Recall that without word wrapping, each paragraph is on a single line—no matter how long. And you therefore see only part of long lines onscreen unless you scroll horizontally. With word wrap on, the lines of text are broken and displayed one on top of another, regardless of where the paragraph break (inserted whenever you press the Enter key) occurs. This way, you only have to scroll vertically.

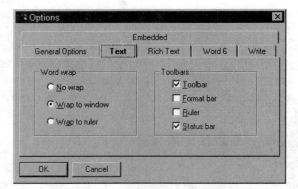

Figure 10-44: *Each of the four document file types that WordPad can work with has a page in this property sheet.*

Similarly, you can make the toolbars, status bar and ruler defaults (visible or hidden) persistent for each type of file that WordPad can accommodate.

The Insert Menu

WordPad's Insert menu offers only two choices: Date and Time, and New Object. When you select Insert I Date and Time, you're shown a list of optional formats before the actual date and time are typed into your document for you.

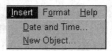

Figure 10-45: *In the Insert menu, you can insert the date and time, or an object like a picture, sound, or even a movie clip.*

When you select Insert I New Object, you'll be given several choices (see Figure 10-46). First, in the list box, choose the kind of object that you want to insert into your WordPad document. Then decide whether you want the object to be an existing file or a new object. We'll create one from an existing file. You can also decide whether or not to show it in WordPad as an icon or as its real, full-size self. In either case, you can always right-click on the object, select Properties and then reverse your decision.

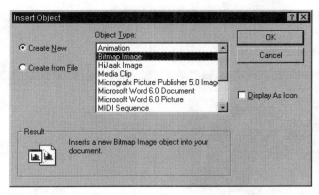

Figure 10-46: *First, select the type of object that you want to insert.*

We chose Create from File, and the result, after we specified which file by browsing the disk drive, appears in Figure 10-47.

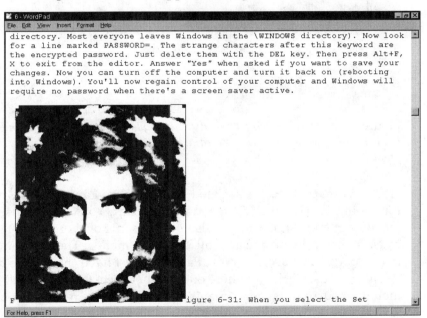

Figure 10-47: *An embedded .BMP file, a picture "object" in the middle of WordPad text.*

When the originating application appears around your object, the application isn't really, fully there. At least not visually. It's not as if you had loaded that object into the application that created it. Instead, you have *in-place editing.* WordPad combines with the other application. In our example, when we double-click on the woman's face shown in Figure 10-47, we get the result shown in Figure 10-48.

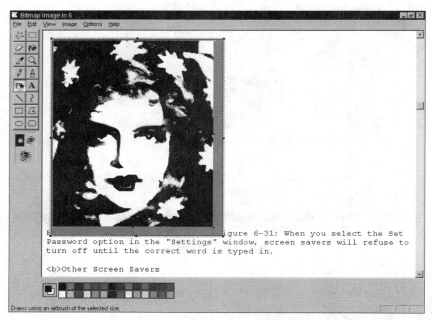

Figure 10-48: *Here, WordPad's toolbars are replaced (temporarily) with Paint's toolbars. Also, some menus are WordPad's, some are Paint's. Now we can repaint the mouth.*

This bitmap file was associated with Paint, so Paint blends with WordPad for the in-place editing when you double-click. You can then use all the facilities of Paint. But you can also invoke some of WordPad's features because some of the menus are still WordPad menus. The File and Edit menus, in this particular case, are WordPad's; the rest have changed to become Paint's menus. Click anywhere outside the object (on the WordPad document that surrounds the woman's face), and you're returned immediately to WordPad's normal editing environment. Any WordPad toolbars you had chosen to leave visible (see "The View Menu" above) and all WordPad's menus are restored. It's normal WordPad again.

This type of integration is the future of Windows applications. By combining objects, you can create your own custom applications. Add-on components will become especially useful when this kind of thing becomes more popular. Programmers are now gearing up to create these "Lego block" style programs. Most of them have to learn an entirely new approach to programming called *object-oriented programming*, or OOP. We should increasingly benefit from the fruits of these labors.

The Format Menu

As expected, WordPad has formatting features more advanced by far than Notepad's but less sophisticated than a full-featured word processor such as WordPerfect or Word. The Format menu is typical of word processors, except for the Bullet Style Option (see Figure 10-49).

Figure 10-49: *WordPad's Format menu is typical of word processors, except for the Bullet Style option.*

When you open the Font window by selecting Format | Font, you can choose typefaces from among those you've installed (see Figure 10-50). (To install a new Font, select Start | Settings | Control Panel; then run the Fonts applet and use the Install New Font option from the File menu.) You can also adjust the type size and change the style to italic or boldface, strikeout or underline. Additionally, you can change the color of the type.

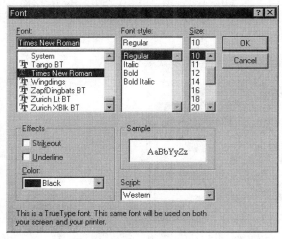

Figure 10-50: *When you select Font, you see a typical typeface-manipulation window.*

You also can turn on Bullet Style by clicking on that Format menu item. Thereafter, each paragraph (each time you press Enter) will begin with a centered black dot, and the text will be indented. Click again on Bullet Style to turn it off. If you want to toggle bullets on or off existing text, select those paragraphs (drag the mouse over them) and click on Bullet Style (see Figure 10-51).

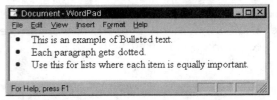

Figure 10-51: *Select Bullet Style when you want to list items of roughly equal importance.*

The Format | Paragraph item changes the indentation of your text. Changing the indent isn't the same as changing the margin, which you do with the ruler. (You can also set the indentation using the ruler.) Margin positions your text relative to the edge of the paper; indentation positions you over from the margin. The First Line margin setting (see Figure 10-52) determines whether or not the first line of each paragraph is indented differently from the rest of the lines in that paragraph. You can create a *hanging indent* or *hung* paragraph style by typing a negative number (such as –.5") in First line text box (see Figure 10-53). This way, all the lines in the paragraph, except the first line, seem to be indented. (In reality, the first line moves into the margin space and the rest of the lines are at the margin.)

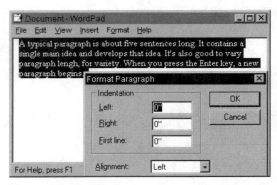

Figure 10-52: *The Format Paragraph option allows you to change indentation and justification.*

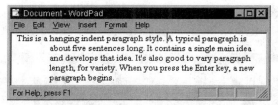

Figure 10-53: *You can create a hanging indent paragraph by setting a negative value in the First line text box.*

If you want to set the Indentation options in a different measurement unit than the default inches, select View I Options I General Options. In the property sheet, you can change the measurement to centimeters, points or picas.

The Alignment option of the Format Paragraph window determines if a paragraph is left-justified (the default), centered or right-justified.

If you need to set more tab stops than the single default 1/2 inch, select Format I Tabs. Then, in the Format Tabs window, type in any additional locations that you want the cursor to move to when you press the Tab key. This capability is useful when you're creating columns, such as the numbers in an invoice, because it will make the figures line up vertically.

Figure 10-54: *In the Format Tabs window, you can set tab stops.*

Paint

PaintBrush, as it was called in Windows 3.1 (it was derived from Zsoft PC Paintbrush, a popular Mac-like paint program for DOS), has undergone some improvements. Now called Paint, it remains limited but, like Notepad, can be useful when you want to make quick sketches or edit bitmapped (.BMP) pictures (see Figure 10-55). The .BMP graphics file format is the Windows standard. There are dozens of other graphics file formats, usually invented by a particular company and peculiar to their products. However,

.BMP, .TIF and .PCX are probably the most frequently used. For more on graphics file formats and working with graphics in general, see Chapter 12.

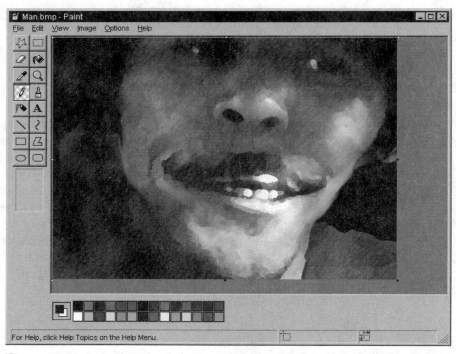

Figure 10-55: *Paint is a simple but sometimes useful drawing/retouching tool.*

There are two fundamental kinds of computer graphics applications, designed to handle the two kinds of visual art: drawings and photos. Using brushes, pens and other illustration tools on various paper and canvas textures is essentially different from adjusting the contrast or color saturation in a photograph.

Paint does simple things with both kinds of art. With Paint, you can make minor changes to existing graphics images (as long as they're in .BMP format), create or modify Windows desktop wallpaper, create simple sketches, or make copies of the screen (*screen captures*) and save them to disk files or print them.

More sophisticated graphics tasks are best left to more advanced graphics programs such as Photoshop, Picture Publisher or Corel PhotoPaint. These programs specialize in photo retouching. They include advanced facilities for *masking* (creating cutout zones and objects that can be superimposed), merging and various special effects filters such as enhancing detail, adjusting contrast and brightness, removing patterns and many other jobs. Some of these programs also let you create "paintings," and provide paper and canvas textures on which you can paint or draw with many kinds of pencils, pens and brushes. They also include styles of art ranging from impressionism through oil paint to pop art.

Within these programs, of course, is some overlap. Drawing programs usually have contrast adjustments and elementary special effects filters like sharpening. Photo retouching programs have a limited set of brushes and textures, and so on. Paint, in fact, falls pretty much between these poles, having limited features from both kinds of graphics applications.

Paint has few advanced features, and the features it does have tend to be limited, with few if any parameters you can adjust to, say, add "pressure" to a brush shape to make it look more realistic, as if a real brush had been used. For instance, if you want to imitate the look of a watercolor picture, it's possible in sophisticated drawing applications to select a brush that's "dry"; you can even see the effect of individual hairs as they apply the paint. This capability isn't possible in Paint. It has 12 brush shapes, but they are all squares, circles or diagonal lines of different sizes. Nothing with hairs.

A graphic created by Paint and its big brothers is called a *bitmap* because such images are composed of individual picture elements (*pixels*). Each pixel is represented in memory by a series of bits, so you could think of the graphic as a map made out of bits. A bitmapped picture is a more or less one-for-one translation between what you see on the screen and what is stored on disk, like a Xerox. These pictures are also called *raster graphics*, for archaic reasons having to do with the way a monitor displays graphics line by line.

The other approach to displaying and storing graphics is called Vector Graphics. Old-style vector graphics techniques, like those used in the original Asteroids coin-op game, construct images out of shapes and lines. In other words, they store a description rather than a one-to-one copy of an image. This technique is also used in drafting; Computer-Aided Design. programs such as CorelDRAW and Adobe Illustrator offer precise control over the elements in a drawing and let you create drawings from objects such as lines, rectangles, ovals and other shapes.

You can enlarge or reduce the pictures you create with these tools without introducing blockiness or blurring, as is all too common when you blow up or shrink a bitmap image. Vector Graphic drawings can also be stored more compactly in memory or on disk, and can be efficiently rendered by a printer. For these reasons, object-oriented drawings are commonly used for clip art. Whereas .BMP is Windows's native file format for bitmap graphics, the .WMF

(Windows Metafile) is used for storing object graphics. The fact is, though, that vector or described graphics always end up looking like drawings. They simply cannot define enough equations and descriptions to produce photorealistic results. For photographic quality, you must rely on the .BMP and other formats that store elements one-to-one. Visually, the difference is a cartoon versus a photograph.

For what it's designed to do, however, Paint is efficient.

Quick Sketches

Using Paint, you can draw simple diagrams, notes and reminders. Then you can save them to a disk file, print them or paste them into a word processor or other document (see Figure 10-56).

Figure 10-56: *Use Paint as you would a pen computer—draw notes or simple sketches.*

Retouching

If a picture has defects in it, like the dots in Figure 10-57, you can paint over them with the background color to clean things up. Figure 10-58 shows the new, "clean" version.

Figure 10-57: *Before: This picture contains some* noise, *some black dots.*

Figure 10-58: *After: Paint's eraser tool cleans up the noise.*

TIP If you want the Pencil or Brush tools to paint the background color (normally they paint the currently selected foreground color), right-click. In effect, you are accomplishing the same thing as using the Eraser tool (painting with the background color), but the Eraser tool has a minimum resolution of 16 pixels (4x4). The Pencil or Brush tools, by contrast, can paint individual pixels one at a time. You can use the View menu's Zoom|Large Size option to see the individual pixels, the smallest unit of visual information that can be displayed on a computer monitor. Set the Show Grid feature on as well.

Combining

You can load .BMP files into Paint. But you can also paste images. In fact, you can paste as often as you want, repositioning the new image where you want it over the earlier image. See the steps involved in making the changes to Figures 10-59 through 10-62.

Figure 10-59: *Step 1: Load in a .BMP Image by selecting File | Open.*

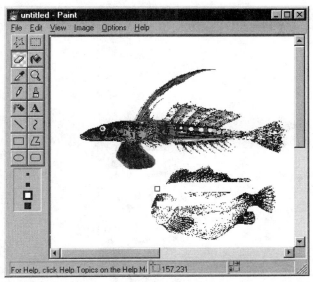

Figure 10-60: *Step 2: Use the Eraser tool to get rid of fish we don't want.*

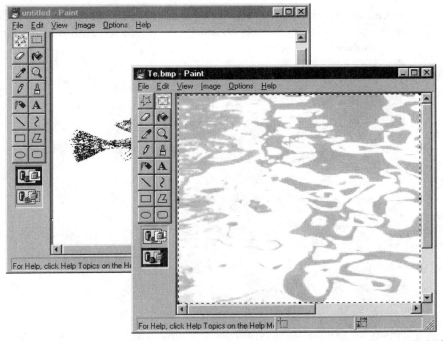

Figure 10-61: *Step 3: Reverse the direction the fish is headed (by selecting Paint's Image\Flip Rotate feature). Start another instance of Paint. Load in a picture of some water. Select it with the Rectangular select tool. Press Ctrl+C to copy it.*

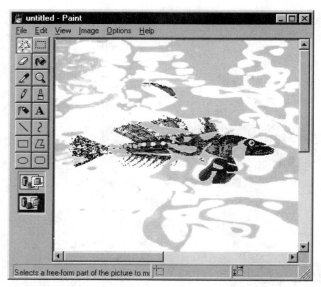

Figure 10-62: *Step 4: Click on the title bar of the original Paint window to make it active. Press Ctrl+V to paste the water onto the fish.*

Of course, more advanced photo retouching programs can accomplish more subtle effects. Figure 10-63 shows how the same constructed image looks when you can control the *level of transparency* while pasting water onto the fish.

Figure 10-63: *In some applications, you can control the transparency of a pasted image. Paint doesn't offer such subtle effects.*

Paint's Features

The File menu

On Paint's File menu, the New, Open, Save and Save As options behave as they do for most other Windows applications (see descriptions under "Notepad"). However, if you attempt to open a .BMP file that's larger than the current settings for a picture in Paint, you're asked if you want the bitmap enlarged. This way, you have the option of making the drawing surface larger inside Paint.

The File menu's Print Preview option shows you how the current picture will print on a piece of paper (see Figure 10-64).

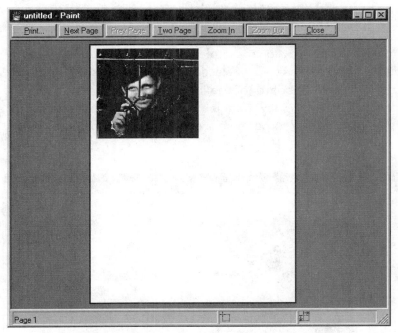

Figure 10-64: *With Print Preview, you can see how your image will look when printed.*

Page Setup works the way it does with many other applications: you can adjust the orientation of the paper, the paper source (if your printer has more than one tray feeding paper) and the margins.

The Send option allows you to mail the picture to someone via e-mail or as a fax. (WordPad and other recent Windows applications now include this nice feature. It greatly simplifies sending messages.)

The *Set as Wallpaper, Tiled or Centered* option allows you to put the current image onto your Windows desktop as a background for applications, folders and other windows. (Be sure to save your picture to a file, too, since it can be tricky to extract wallpaper back into Paint.)

The Edit menu

The only novelties in Paint's Edit menu are Copy To and Paste From. Copy To allows you to save part of your Paint picture to a disk file. This capability is the equivalent of *cropping* (removing extraneous detail from a picture). To crop, click on the Select button (top right of the button bar) and drag the mouse to select the area you want to preserve within the picture. Then from the Edit menu, choose Copy To (see Figures 10-65 and 10-66) and provide a filename.

 TIP Another, faster way to crop a picture is to click on the Select button, drag to make your selection and then press Ctrl+C to copy it to the Clipboard (or use the Copy option on the Edit menu). Then select New from the File menu to clear Paint. Finally, press Ctrl+V to paste your cropped version of the picture.

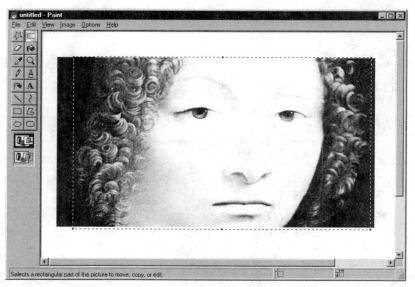

Figure 10-65: *Before: We decided to remove some of the black background from the left and right sides of this image.*

Figure 10-66: *After: Cropping with Paint is as easy as selecting, copying and pasting.*

Paste From allows you to insert a new image into a defined selection area. When an image already appears in the Clipboard (copied there from Paint or some other application), if you paste it into Paint, it will be superimposed in its entirety. After it is pasted, a *marquee* (dotted lines) surrounds it, and you can resize it by dragging the black *handles* on the marquee or move it by dragging from within the selection. However, Paste From allows you to define a marquee first into which the pasted object will fit. Paste From, however, doesn't work with the Clipboard; you must Paste From a .BMP file on the disk. (Note that you don't have to define a region first; that's just a way to paste without having to involve the Clipboard.)

Pasting With Transparency

When you click on the top two buttons of the button bar (Free-form Select or Select), two larger buttons appear below the button bar. These buttons determine whether a pasted image will cover up the underlying (original) image or whether the two images will, to an extent, blend. The upper button superimposes the new image on the old; the lower button merges them (see Figures 10-67 and 10-68).

Figure 10-67: *When the selection buttons are active, two large buttons appear below the button bar. As shown here, clicking the upper button causes a superimposed (pasted) image to cover the background image.*

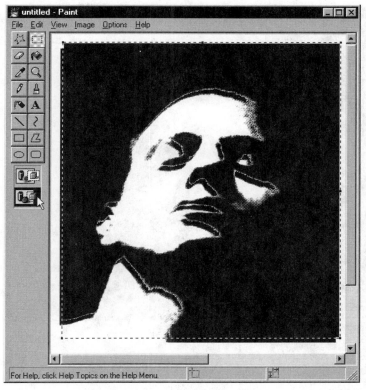

Figure 10-68: *When the lower button is clicked, a pasted image merges with the original. The new image acts like a mask, letting the old image show through in places where both images are light.*

Whatever color was the background color when the image was "picked up" controls which color is transparent. Knowing this fact is important if you want to get fancy and try some special tricks.

The View menu

Paint's View menu allows you to show or hide the tool box (the button bar where many drawing tools are only a click away), the color box at the bottom (where you select from a palette of colors or create new ones) and the status bar (the zone at the bottom which, for the most part, briefly describes whatever tool or menu item the mouse pointer is currently hovering over).

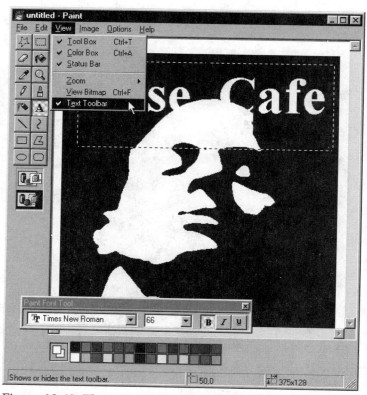

Figure 10-69: *The toolbar option activates a zone at the bottom of the Paint window that displays a brief message describing whatever the mouse pointer currently points to.*

When you select the Zoom feature, you can select Normal Size, Large Size or select a custom size from the Zoom submenu. It also features Show Grid and Show Thumbnail options (see Figure 10-70) that you can toggle on and off when in Large Size or Custom Size Zoom mode. (Also, see Figure 10-71.)

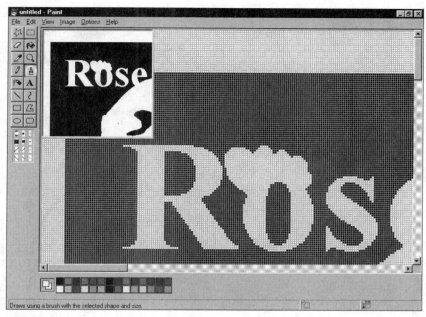

Figure 10-70: *The Grid option displays the individual pixels (the smallest units of a computer picture you can edit). The Show Thumbnail option shows you how editing in the large Zoom will look in a more realistic thumbnail picture of the original.*

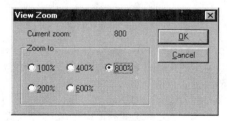

Figure 10-71: *The Custom Zoom option allows you to choose magnification up to eight times.*

The final option on the View menu is View Bitmap, which simply means display the window container. Paint takes over the entire screen and gives you a full, unobstructed view of the image (see Figure 10-72). Click anywhere or press any key to return to the normal Paint window.

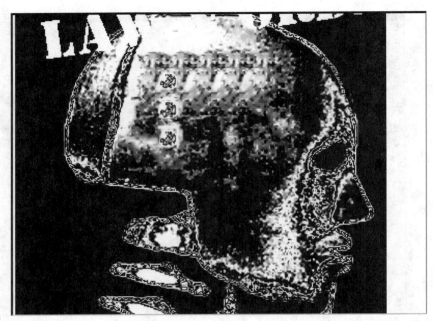

Figure 10-72: *When you click on View Bitmap, your Paint image will take over the entire screen. But if the image is large like this one, it will be temporarily cropped; there are no scroll bars in this view.*

The Image menu

Paint's Image menu contains several options that allow you to mirror, rotate and turn an image into a negative of itself. Figures 10-73 through 10-76 give you an overview of these options.

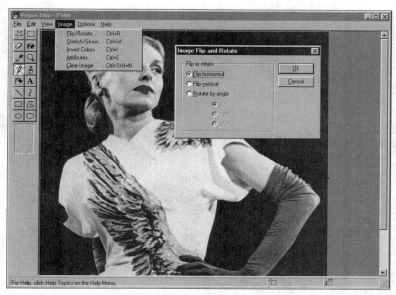

Figure 10-73: *Here you can rotate your picture by 90 degrees (to 12, 3, 6, or 9 o'clock). (Flip Horizontal makes the image look as it would held up to a mirror.) You can't mirror a picture merely by rotating it unless you also flip it vertically. The Rotate by angle option lets you choose an arbitrary angle of rotation.*

Figure 10-74: *Flip Horizontal might give you a better design. Try this option before printing your image to see if it looks better this way.*

Figure 10-75: *Skewing (here by 14%) can create a dramatic effect. Tilting the image like this gives it motion.*

 TIP   You can't enter a negative number for Skew. Paint accepts only degrees between 0 and 89. (Skewing creates an italics version of a typeface that doesn't have a special italics font. You can do this manually with Skew, too.)

Figure 10-76: *The Invert Colors filter turns a black-and-white image into its negative. If the image is in color, the results are less predictable.*

You might think that Attributes would be merely descriptive—telling you the size and style of your image. Instead, you can use this option on Paint's Image menu to crop an image (by setting different dimensions), and you can also change it from color to a severe black-and-white-only graphic (see Figures 10-77 and 10-78).

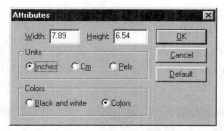

Figure 10-77: *The Image \ Attributes item tells you the size of your image (when printed) in inches, centimeters or pixels. You can also change your graphic from color to black and white here (reducing it to a monochromatic image with no grayscale—just blacks and whites).*

Figure 10-78: *When you turn a color image into black and white, you can create a dramatic effect. It removes all gradual shadings; the results are usually stark. This way, you can sometimes make a photograph look like a drawing.*

The Clear Image option on the Image Menu is a good deal faster than selecting New from the File menu. Faster yet is the shortcut key combination for Clear Image: Ctrl+Shift+N. Use it whenever you want to wipe your slate clean.

The Options menu

The first item in Paint's Options menu, Edit Colors, allows you select your foreground and background colors, and mix your own custom colors (see Figure 10-79).

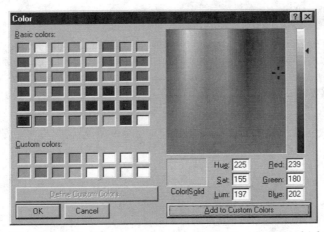

Figure 10-79: *You can create new colors or change which 28 colors appear in the color box at the bottom of Paint's Color window.*

Windows can display over 16.8 million colors simultaneously, but your video card might limit you to fewer colors. This color *resolution* is called 24-bit color, or *True Color*. Below that are resolutions called *High Color*— 65,536 or 32,768 thousand simultaneous colors. The most common resolution today is 256-color, but some machines still display only 16 colors. (You can upgrade your computer by simply buying a new video card. Modern video cards, featuring graphics acceleration, can also dramatically speed up your graphics display, making it seem like your whole computer is faster.)

Getting a card with more memory lets you display more colors, and if your monitor supports this improvement, you can increase your display resolution—how many pixels you can fit on the screen; more is better. See Chapter 6.

If you select color box in Paint's View menu (or press Ctrl+A), Paint displays a set of 28 colors below the picture (see Figure 10-80).

Figure 10-80: *Left-click on a color in the color box to make it the foreground color. Right-click for the background color.*

The Foreground color (the top color of the overlapping rectangles to the left of the color box) is the one that will appear when you use one of the drawing tools: Pencil, Brush, Airbrush, Text, Line, Curve, Rectangle, Polygon, Ellipse and Rounded Rectangle. The background color sets the page color when you select a new document; it also fills enclosed shapes. If you draw a circle and then use the Fill tool (the tilted paint bucket), the circle will be filled with the background color. The background color is also used as the background of text and will be the color that replaces the foreground when you use the Eraser tool. (Also note that the background color becomes transparent when you copy a selection and set it as transparent.)

 You can also use the Pick Color tool (the eyedropper) to get a color out of the image itself. Click on the Pick Color tool; then move the mouse pointer into the image and left-click on the color you want to become the foreground color. Right-click to get the background color.

 You can use the Fill tool to replace the white background. If there is no enclosed space, Paint Bucket simply fills the screen. Alternatively, if you want, say, a red background over your entire image, right-click on red in the color box. Then select New from the File menu or select Clear Image from the Image menu.

Adding a Color to the color box

When you first run Paint, it provides you with 8 dark and 8 lighter versions (generally of the same color) and 12 dithered colors (patterns made of two colors). In effect, you get 14 default colors and a lighter shade of those 14 colors (with a couple of exceptions). Aside from the predictable red, green and blue, various less common colors such as cyan, magenta and even something close to puce are available for your use. (Remember, with a 16-color display, only the leftmost 16 colors are "pure" colors; the other ones are made of "checkerboard" patterns of two colors. This fact is most important when you try to fill a shape. If you fill a shape with a pure color, you can change the fill easily. But if you fill a shape with a pattern, you can't fill it again with a different color, since Fill replaces only same-color pixels that are contiguous (that touch). A checkerboard pattern breaks up the colors, preventing Fill from finding all the similar colors.)

To place a different color in the color box, select Edit Colors from the Options menu. You'll then be shown the color selection window—a larger palette of 48 basic colors and below that are 16 boxes wherein you can define your own custom colors.

 TIP Instead of clicking on Edit Colors in the Options menu, just double-click on the color in the color box that you want to replace.

After the color selection window appears, just click on the color you want to move to the color box; then click on OK. To change the backcolor, double-right-click (a double-right-click is rarely used in Windows) to open the color selection window; then click on the color you're after. To create a new color, click on the Define Custom Colors button, and you'll see the color definition tools shown in Figure 10-79. Then drag within the large color window or within the vertical shade stripe to specify the particular color you're after. If you know the RGB numbers that define your color (or the hue, saturation, luminance numbers), you can type them into the appropriate boxes. Unless you have a display with more than 256 colors, most custom colors will not appear as pure color but will instead show up as patterns made of two different colors. However, if you have at least 256 colors, the custom color can be used as a solid color in your drawing.

Finally, click on Add to Custom Colors in the Color dialog box. (This is a standard common dialog box, so you'll use the same technique with other applications that let you mix colors.)

Getting Colors & Saving Colors

Your computer can display any of the 16 million plus colors available to Windows. But how many of those colors can be displayed at the same time differs considerably from video card to video card. (All monitors sold today can display the maximum; the video card determines the color resolution.)

A few video cards still in use permit only 16 colors to display at one time; many permit 256 simultaneous colors; others range between 65,536 up to 16.7 million. If your computer is a 256-color system, each application is allowed to decide which 256 colors will be displayed from among the 16.7 million available (some video cards permit a choice between only about 256,000 colors). This selection of 256 particular colors is called the *palette*. If you create a new color (see the description of the Define Custom Colors option above) that's not in this palette, the computer will approximate the color you've created by mixing a palette color with little dots or x's or other patterns made up of another palette color. This mixing process is called *dithering*, and the results are sometimes good, sometimes not so good. (Remember that if your video card handles more than 256 colors, palette is irrelevant and you can ignore the whole issue.) Dithering is also commonly used with color printers, since the ribbon or inkjet is only capable of printing a very few pure colors, but when combined in patterns, can appear to be millions of colors.

Palettes in Collision

You may have occasionally experienced a weird x-ray green or strange rose hues all over the screen or something similar. This is caused by palettes in collision in a 256-color system. When one application is running (with its particular palette) and another application's window is opened (with a different palette), you get odd neon displays that look like nothing more than bad psychedelia. (You can avoid this situation by changing to a video mode with more colors, if possible. See Chapter 6.)

When you load a .BMP file into Paint, its colors automatically define the palette (up to the number of colors in the image, or the limit of 256). Thus, loading in different .BMP files can change the current palette.

In practice, the Get Colors item on the Options menu loads in a palette (a file with the extension .PAL). The Save Colors item saves the current palette to disk. Therefore, if you define a set of new colors and want to save that particular set, use the Save Colors item to store it to disk. Later, to restore that set of custom colors, use the Load Colors option.

The final item on the Options menu is Draw Opaque, a toggle that represents the status of the two large buttons that appear beneath the tool box when either of the selector tools is clicked. The status of this item (or, alternatively, clicking on one of those two large buttons) determines whether the underlying image shows through, or is covered by, pasting into a selected area. For more on this topic, see "Pasting With Transparency" earlier in this chapter.

The Paint Tool Box

Most applications describe a collection of buttons as a button bar, but for some reason, Paint and Microsoft's Visual Basic refer to these clusters of buttons as a tool box.

Peculiarities of diction aside, a button bar by whatever name is a welcome and useful way to activate features of an application with a single click. What's more, if you forget the meaning of the symbol on one of the buttons, just hold the mouse pointer on top of it for a second, and a little description will pop out. Owing to Microsoft's thoughtful icon design, though, this is rarely necessary after you've used Paint a few times.

 TIP   A button bar provides shortcuts for menu commands (one click and you're done), whereas a tool box provides tools that you can use in the document or drawing—it actually changes the shape of the cursor, and puts you into a drawing mode. When you click on the Fill tool, you can continue to fill an object until you choose another tool. Another difference: With a button bar, you usually select something and then apply the button to it like a verb ("Text, to Bold"). With a tool box, the tool itself is the verb, and it creates its own objects ("Draw Rectangle").

Free-form Select

In the upper-left corner of the tool box is the Free-form Select tool. Using this tool, you can define an irregular selection. (The Select button next to it creates a rectangular selection.) When you click on Free-form Select, the cursor turns into a double-cross, and you can drag it over a zone in your picture to define an area that you want to cut or copy. When the area is defined, it's surrounded by a rectangular "rubber-band" of dashes, but don't worry, it's still that irregular shape you dragged. Now from the Edit menu you can select Cut (or press Shift+Del) to remove that item, or you can select Edit I Copy (or press Ctrl+Ins). After the item is placed on the Clipboard, you can paste it to move it somewhere else in the picture if you want.

Figure 10-81: *Define a free-form selection zone by dragging the mouse. Note the cursor shape is a double-cross, indicating selection.*

Figure 10-82: *After defining the cow and copying it to the Clipboard (Ctrl+C), we pasted it back into the image (Ctrl+V) and dragged it over to a new location. We wanted it small, so while the copy was still selected, we moved the cursor to a corner and dragged that corner until the cow got small.*

To remove the rubber-band dashes and cancel a selection, just click somewhere outside the rubber-band in the picture. Or click on another button in the tool box.

Select

The Select button (top right on the tool box) operates just as does the Free-form Select button. The only difference is that you can only drag a rectangle. Therefore, if you want to copy something (but leave out some details that would intrude into your copied area if you used a rectangle), just use the Free-form tool.

Eraser

The Eraser tool restores the background color; in essence, it paints the background over whatever is in the foreground. (Note that this tool doesn't work the same as Edit | Undo, which reverses your previous action.)

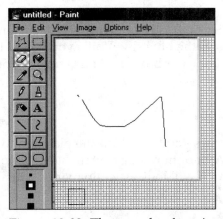

Figure 10-83: *The eraser has four sizes: 16 pixels, 36 pixels, 64 pixels or 100 pixels. Here it's set for 36 pixels.*

 If you want to erase single pixels, use the Pencil or Brush tool. Right-click to paint or draw with the background color. Set the View menu's Zoom | Large Size option to see the individual pixels. And turn on the Show Grid feature as well.

Fill

The Fill With Color tool (the tilted paint bucket) paints the foreground color into any enclosed area that you click within. If you right-click, the background color is used instead. This tool will also paint a line you click on or a character of text or any other clearly defined zone. If you click on no particular zone, it will fill to the edges of the frame of the picture and around any defined objects (lines, shapes, or whatever is a different color than the color you clicked on). One way to think of Fill is that it replaces whatever color it's clicked on, flooding across the same color until it comes to a border—a place with a different color. If things don't work out as you planned during a color flood, just click on Undo in the Edit menu (or press Ctrl+Z).

Pick Color

The Pick Color tool (the eyedropper) can come in handy when you've loaded in a .BMP file, a photo or drawing, and you don't want to try to figure out what a particular color (or shade of gray) is. Let's say that you want to extend the lips of a woman using, of course, the shade of lipstick that she's got on. Or there are some odd noise dots in a blue sky. Are you going to click on the Options menu Edit Colors feature and torture yourself trying to match the color on her lips or that sky? No. Just click on the eyedropper; then click on the lips or the blue sky. Voilà, you've got the exact color loaded into the foreground color box, and you can pencil or brush it to your heart's content.

Magnifier

The Magnifying Glass tool allows you to click on the picture and blow it up two, six or even eight times. A 1x option is also available; it restores the picture to normal size, the way it will look as wallpaper or when printed on paper.

Pencil & Brush

The Pencil tool lets you draw freehand lines, one pixel in size. The Brush does the same thing, but it allows you to select from among four brush shapes (round, square, left and right diagonal lines) and from among three sizes (which vary from 1 pixel up to 8 pixels in width, depending on the shape).

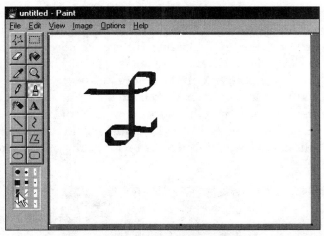

Figure 10-84: *The diagonal brushes make good curls and looks nice if you want to try some calligraphy.*

Airbrush

The Airbrush tool is rather clumsy. It fills in a circular area (you can choose three sizes) with pixel-sized dots. The longer you hold down the left mouse button while remaining in the same spot, the more the area is filled. It can add a speckled stucco-like texture, but not much else. Computers do a great job with airbrush shading and other airbrush effects, but you'll want to work with a full-featured graphics application for that, a program where you can adjust pressure, feathering and other elements of airbrush simulation. Still, with practice, you can get some interesting effects with the Airbrush tool. For example, if you want to paint some fluffy clouds, set the Airbrush to a large size using white as the foreground color, and etch out your clouds on top of the background that you previously filled with blue.

Text

You can add text of any size with any font in any color to your Paint pictures. Just click on the Text tool; then click in the picture where you want the text located. Alternatively, you can drag the mouse to describe the zone within which you want to type the text. In either case, when you release the left mouse button, a rubber-band of dashes will appear, showing where the text will go. If you want to move this text frame, drag it. To resize it, move your mouse on a corner or edge of the frame; then, when the mouse cursor changes to the double-arrow shape, drag.

If the floating Text toolbar isn't visible, click on the View menu, then click on Text toolbar. After choosing the typeface and size, type in your message. To change the color of the text, click on a different color in the color box (if its not visible, select it in the View menu as well). To change the background color behind the text, right-click on the color box.

Text almost always looks better with *no* text background. In other words, you rarely want to have the superimpose feature turned on (as in Figure 10-85), because it looks crude. Instead, click on the lower large button below the tool box to merge your text into the existing background (as in Figure 10-86).

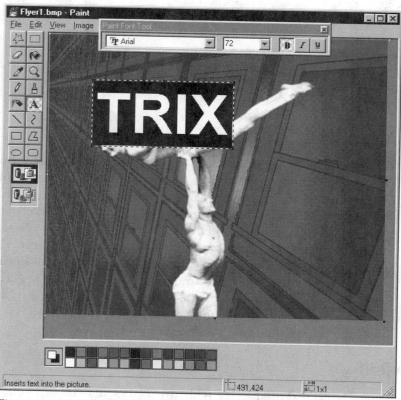

Figure 10-85: *Before: Avoid this amateurish look, caused by superimposing (onto the original image) a square background around the text.*

Figure 10-86: *After: Click on the Merge button to blend the text into the existing image.*

Line

After you select the Line tool, click within a drawing to establish the starting point of your line and keep holding down the mouse button. Then, as you drag the mouse around, you can see precisely where the line will go; it moves with the mouse (as if the line were a rubber band). When you release the left mouse button, the line is laid down. There are five thicknesses available. If you make a mistake, just press Ctrl+Z.

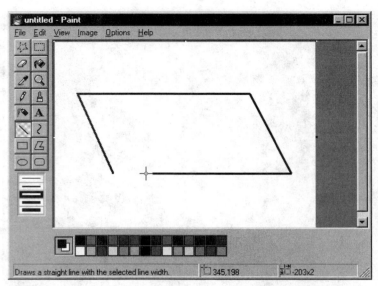

Figure 10-87: *The Line tool makes it easy to draw geometric shapes for charts, graphs and so on.*

 TIP   If you want to draw a precisely vertical, horizontal or diagonal line, press the Shift key while dragging. This way, you can constrain the line to 12, 3, 6 and 9 o'clock, as well as precisely half way between each of those angles (i.e., at 45% angles).

Curve

To create a curve, click on the Curve tool in the tool box. Then select a line width from the box below the tool box (as with straight lines, the width options are 1, 2, 3, 4 or 5 pixels). Drag the mouse to draw a straight line and then release the mouse button. Now you have *two* opportunities to deform the line, to make it curve. Click somewhere in the drawing; then drag. Release the mouse button. Now click again somewhere and drag again. Where you click and how far you drag determine the effect that your efforts have on the original line. Experiment to get a feel for what you can do.

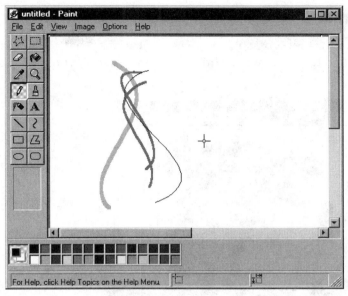

Figure 10-88: *Paint has a simple Bezier curve feature, making it easy to draw smooth arcs, semicircles and other shapes you would struggle to draw freehand.*

 TIP   All the drawing tools, including the Curve tool, can be switched from the default foreground color and made to paint in the background color. Just use the right mouse button for every action, every click and drag, instead of the usual left mouse button. Even simpler, the last action you perform with the mouse determines the color. For instance, when using the Curve tool, you drag to draw a straight line, then drag for the first arc and then drag again for the second arc. If you hold down the right button while drawing that second arc, the final color will be the background color.

Rectangle

The final four tool box tools create geometric shapes. Each of them behaves pretty much the same way. With the Rectangle tool, you can draw squares or rectangles.

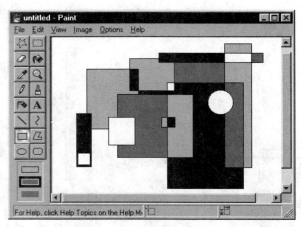

Figure 10-89: *Using the Rectangle, Fill and Ellipse tools, it's easy to build colorful, Mondrian-like wallpaper.*

Below the tool box, you'll find three styles of rectangles you can click on to select. The first one draws a frame outline only (in the forecolor). The second one draws both a frame and fills it with the backcolor. The third option draws a fill with the backcolor but no frame.

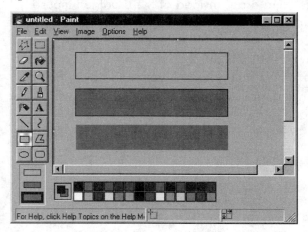

Figure 10-90: *The geometric drawing tools—Rectangle, Polygon, Ellipse and Rounded Rectangle—use three styles. In descending order, they are Outline, Outline with Fill and Fill Only.*

TIP   Line Width must be adjusted before you draw a line; you can't change the line width of an existing line or shape.

 TIP   To reverse the colors of the frame and the fill, drag your rectangle while holding down the right mouse button instead of the left mouse button.

Polygon

The Polygon tool works pretty much the same way as the Rectangle tool. The only difference is that you don't drag. Instead, you click to establish each point in the shape, then drag to see the line and maneuver it where you want it. Finish the shape with a final double-click. To constrain the polygon lines to horizontal, vertical or diagonal, hold down the Shift key while dragging the lines.

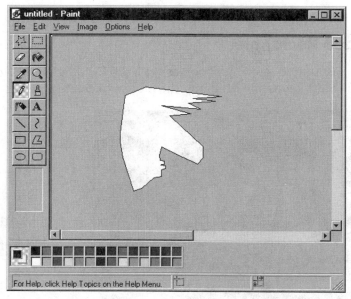

Figure 10-91: *A polygon can have as many corners as you want.*

Ellipse

You draw ellipses just as you draw a rectangle, but instead of a square shape, the Ellipse tool creates circles or ovals. To draw a perfect circle, hold down the Shift key while dragging the shape.

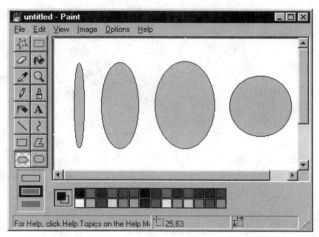

Figure 10-92: *An ellipse can be either an oval or a circle.*

Rounded Rectangle

Using the Rounded Rectangle tool, as with the Rectangle tool, you hold down the Shift key while dragging the mouse to create a perfect square.

Figure 10-93: *Nice for some kinds of labels and charts, a rounded rectangle is a square shape with softened corners.*

Clipboard Viewer

As in earlier versions of Windows, you can use the Clipboard Viewer utility to check to see what's in the Clipboard. Whenever something is cut or copied from a document (or the whole document is copied), the copy goes to the Clipboard. If something was already in the Clipboard, it gets thrown away. The Clipboard can hold only one thing at a time; it's like a scratchpad for Windows. When you request a Paste, the contents of the Clipboard are inserted into your document at the current location of the cursor. (Cut, Copy and Paste are commands found on the Edit menu of most applications. Alternatively, you can cut by pressing Ctrl+X or Shift+Del, copy by pressing Ctrl+C or Ctrl+Insert, and paste by pressing Ctrl+V or Shift+Insert.)

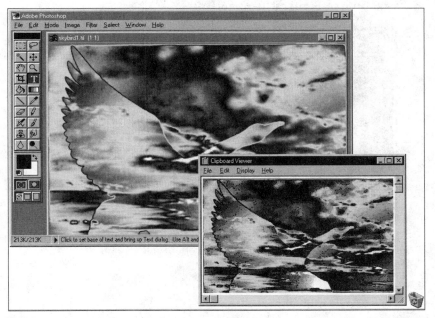

Figure 10-94: *This graphic has been copied, so a copy of it resides in the Clipboard.*

You can save the contents of the Clipboard to a file, if you wish. Click on the File menu, then select Save As. It will by default be saved as a file with a .CLP extension added to the filename. Likewise, you can open a document and load it into the Clipboard, but it must have been previously saved as a .CLP file.

The Clipboard Viewer's Edit menu has only one option, Delete, which cleans the contents of the Clipboard. You have no real reason to do this, however. Windows 95 will automatically replace the contents of the Clipboard when new data is sent into it.

The Clipboard, as a primary Windows 95 waystation, must be able to store data in all kinds of formats. This permits the transfer of data between applications (which have varying formats). The Display menu highlights the formats appropriate (or possible) for the data currently in the Clipboard. The format called Auto is active by default. This means that Clipboard picks the correct format. Graphics, however, will be displayed as best they can—fit into the current shape of the Clipboard and with reduced resolution if necessary. If you want to see what's really there, try clicking on Picture or Bitmap, as shown in Figures 10-95 and 10-96.

Figure 10-95: *Graphics can appear both squeezed and low-resolution. The information is all there, but the Clipboard Viewer might not show it.*

Figure 10-96: *To see what's really in the Clipboard, you can click on Picture or Bitmap to force an accurate display.*

In practice, you'll rarely if ever want or need to look at the Clipboard Viewer. Just let Windows 95 take care of things when you copy or paste text or graphics between applications. If you think that you might want to save something that you're going to need tomorrow, just copy it and then drag it onto the desktop. It becomes a "scrap," and you'll see it sitting there tomorrow. Open some other document and just drag it from the desktop into this document. This method is easier than trying to remember which .CLP file you saved it to, then opening the Clipboard Viewer, loading the file into the Clipboard and finally pasting it into the new document. Older Windows 3.1 applications might not permit dragging scraps out of their windows, but Windows 95 applications do.

Moving On

As we've seen, a few of the accessories in this chapter—WordPad in particular—are capable of some interesting new techniques. Object Linking and Embedding is the subject of the next chapter. We'll see how to work with compound documents—disk files that contain more than one kind of document. For example, you can embed a picture that you've created in Paint into a letter you're writing in WordPad. We'll also look at the Windows Object Packager utility, more in-place editing, the new Paste Special feature and the differences between linking and embedding.

Chapter 11

Application Integration

Windows offers an exciting technology: Object Linking and Embedding (OLE). For the user, the main benefit of OLE is *docucentricity*. OLE (pronounced olé) helps us focus on documents, not applications. It's like the way a good potter pays attention to the clay, not to the pottery wheel that spins it.

OLE helps us move away from the older, familiar style of computing where we work within a single application, like a word processor. Consider this elementary example of OLE: In Explorer, you can double-click on a text document, and your word processor automatically surrounds it. Or you can open a picture document, and Paint automatically pops up with that picture loaded. Your operating system knows the appropriate application to use with a particular kind of data file.

In other words, an application appears when you click on some data. In the old days, you started an application and then loaded data into it. With OLE, Windows "wraps" applications around data. You get to focus on the contents, not the tool you use to edit those contents.

How does Windows know which application goes with which kinds of documents? Windows looks at those three-letter extensions, such as .TXT and .BMP, that are added to many filenames. To discover which extensions Windows recognizes, open Explorer and select View|Options. Then click on the File Types tab of the Options sheet, and you'll see a list of Registered (known) file extensions and the type of data they represent.

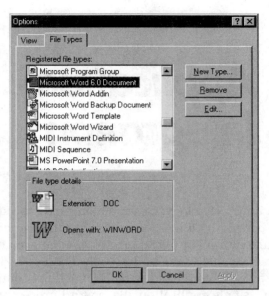

Figure 11-1: *Explorer's Options sheet allows you to view, change or delete "associa-tions" between file types and applications.*

Most of the associations shown in the Explorer Options sheet are created when you install your software. If you click on the Edit button, you can change the icon given to this particular file type. In the Edit File Type dialog box that appears, you'll see a list of commands or actions that you can per-form on this file type. The New button allows you to add additional "com-mands" (actions) that can be carried out with this file type. All the commands listed in the Actions list will appear both at the top of the Short-cut menu (the one that pops open when you right-click on an icon) and in the File menu (of Explorer itself).

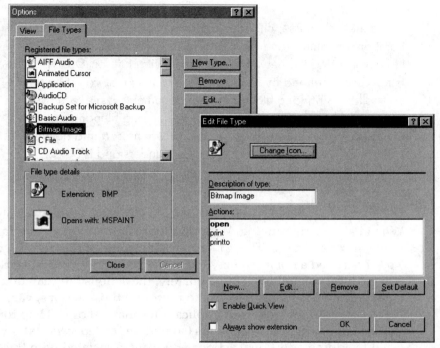

Figure 11-2: *Here's where you can modify the "actions" associated with a particular file type.*

If you click on the New button, you'll see something like this:

```
"C:\PROGRA~1\ACCESS~1\MSPAINT.EXE" /p "%1"
```

Those familiar with DOS will recognize most of this, but perhaps not the ~. The "C:\PROGRA~1\ACCESS~1\MSPAINT.EXE" part is the complete "path" showing the drive, subdirectories (folders) and filename of the application associated with this file type. The ~ (tilde) signifies that part of the subdirectory (folder) names have been removed to conform to the old DOS requirement that none of these names be longer than eight characters. Windows 95 eliminates this restriction, so the real path is

```
C:\PROGRAM FILES\ACCESSORIES\MSPAINT.EXE
```

You could, of course, change the name MSPAINT.EXE to Microsoft Paint or something, and therefore make it more Windows 95-like. However, using the new long filenames with .EXE or .DLL type files is not recommended by Microsoft. The reason that you should limit yourself to using long filenames with documents (vs. executable programs like those ending in .EXE) is that long filenames can cause various interoperability problems when used in a network. Many network remote loaders just don't understand LFNs for .EXE or .DLL files, and can't deal with them.

The /p is a symbol particular to MSPAINT (also known simply as Paint). When Paint starts running, Windows looks at this symbol and interprets it to mean "open" a file. The %1 supplies the name of that file. Together, this /p %1 is called a *command line*, and many programs, on first startup, will react to a command line. Unfortunately, the actions they can take and the command-line symbols they use to represent those actions, vary widely. However, you can look in an application's manual or its Help for information on command-line arguments (sometimes called *switches*) if you're interested in adding additional actions you want associated with this file type.

Clicking on the New button in the Edit File Type dialog box, shown in Figure 11-2, allows you to add another action and, if you wish, a different associated application. This way, you could send the document to two different applications, depending on which item you selected in the right-click pop-up menu.

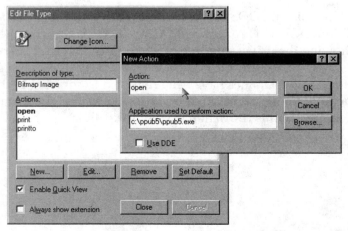

Figure 11-3: *Most OLE-capable applications recognize the simple command "open." And most of the time that's what you want to do anyway.*

The Enable Quick View option of the Edit File Type dialog box determines whether that file viewer accessory will be listed on the double-click pop-up menu (and Explorer's File menu) along with any actions you have specified for this file type. Whether Quick View is available depends on whether you installed it; it's an optional Windows 95 accessory. To install it, click on Start; then Settings then Control Panel. Double-click on Add/Remove Programs and then choose Windows Setup. In this list, click on Accessories and then click the Details button. In that new list, you'll be able to locate and select Quick View.

No more cutting & pasting

But OLE means much more than activating an application by clicking on a data file of the appropriate type. For one thing, OLE can make moving data between applications automatic. No more cutting and pasting, file filters, or any of the older, ungainly ways we used to have to move text or other information between applications. OLE greatly improves on the Clipboard.

A feature called in-place editing is also available to you. With this feature, illustrated at the end of this chapter, the menus and toolbars of the host application change to menus and toolbars (from the creator application) appropriate to editing an OLE object.

OLE also permits *mixing* various kinds of data into a single "compound" document. A document might contain pictures or music or even a video—or all of these media might be sitting in there in the document.

Clicking on the music object allows you to hear that music and also perhaps opens a music-editing application. You might want to hear the tune on a harpsichord rather than a piano.

OLE has been around for several years in a more primitive form in a few applications, in disguise. But now, with its full, robust implementation in Windows 95, OLE is finally coming of age. It's more swift now, more stable, and many more applications are capable of it. Some of this progress is hardware-dependent: an OLE event (like clicking on an embedded music object and waiting for the music player to open) can be slow on a machine with too little RAM or too slow a microprocessor. The minimum for tolerable OLE is probably a 486 computer with at least 8mb but preferably 16, megabytes.

Thanks to OLE, an important shift is taking place in the way we use computers. Several related emerging technologies from Microsoft and other companies are making computers considerably easier to use and more efficient.

These technologies, collectively referred to as *OLE*, work together to allow you to customize how applications work and how information is manipulated and stored. OLE helps you accomplish common computing tasks in novel, often much more effective, ways. In this chapter we'll explore the various elements of OLE. We'll see what you can do with it today, and what you can expect of it in the coming years.

Linking vs. Embedding

Windows is moving us toward the future of computing in ways more subtle and more powerful than simply its visual features. Object Linking and Embedding will, when fully utilized, likely change the way you work with your computer.

Embedding is quite similar to using the Clipboard. In fact, you do first select then copy the object you want to embed. Then, to actually embed it, you choose "Paste Special" from the Edit menu of the target "client" application. We'll get into some specific examples shortly, but for now let's examine the theory of embedding and linking.

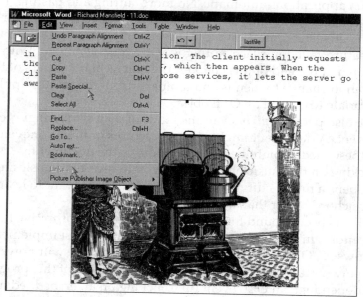

Figure 11-4: *Here is the Edit menu's Paste Special option.*

Linking or Embedding means that you can create, for example, a picture in CorelDRAW and place it into a Word for Windows document. Later, if you want to make changes to the picture while you're working in Word, you double-click on the picture, and CorelDRAW automatically appears with the picture loaded. This way, you can edit the picture in the program that created it. When you're finished, the updated picture appears where it should in your Word document. Thus, pictures and words more or less exist outside the programs that created them. Applications are available everywhere at once. The old approach of first running a program and then loading in something to work on is no longer necessary. That's one of the things that Bill Gates means by "information at your fingertips."

Embedding breaks down the barriers between *data* (like a picture) and *application* (CorelDRAW or Word). The computer will eventually seem to present you with only one big program. And you, the user, won't have to worry about loading a specific program that is optimized to create graphics or process text or recalculate a spreadsheet. You just work on the data, the graphics, numbers, data, words, music—and when you work on something, the best tool or application for the job automatically and silently appears around whatever you are working on.

Linking is quite similar to embedding, but linking performs one additional service. It can dynamically pass text or graphics between two running programs. This updating can be instantaneous and constant, or only when you request the update. (A program could also request an automatic update, even at timed intervals if desired.)

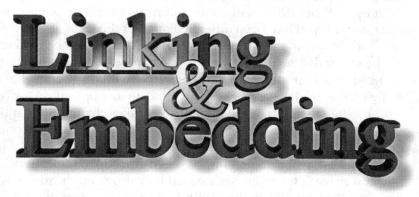

Figure 11-5: *Linking and embedding are quite similar techniques.*

Linking offers a simple way to have one application communicate with another. Most of the behaviors described as linking are indistinguishable from embedding. Say that you create a spreadsheet in Excel and save it to disk. Then you link this spreadsheet file into a Word document. You can type words and sentences in the Word document as usual. However, if you want to edit or calculate with that spreadsheet, Excel is a better tool. You can edit that spreadsheet file when you double-click on it inside Word (Excel pops up around it temporarily). When you're finished, click on the Word document outside the spreadsheet and Excel goes away, returning you to your normal Word document-editing environment. So far, this process is exactly what embedding would accomplish too.

But linking does one additional thing that embedding doesn't. Say that next time you turn on the computer you decide to spend the afternoon working with that same spreadsheet in Excel instead of Word. You add some new numbers, perform some calculations, etc.; then save the spreadsheet file back to disk. The spreadsheet has changed. What makes this a linked document is that the next time you load that document (which contains a link) into Word, the alterations you made to the spreadsheet using Excel are already there. When you double-click on the linked spreadsheet in Word, all your changes show up. You don't have to worry that the version of the spreadsheet linked in Word is an older, outdated version. In fact, it's identical to the spreadsheet that you worked on in Excel. A *linked object is a single disk file.* Therefore, any changes to it in Excel or Word (or any other application) are always current. There are no copies, no extra versions of this file floating around to confuse the issue.

Linking, then, operates on a single data file that is updatable by more than one program. Embedding inserts a copy of the original data file (or a zone, a selection of part of a data file) into another file—like stuffing an Excel spreadsheet into a Word document. Embedding creates a copy of the original spreadsheet, so now you have two different copies of this data. If you change the original document, the changes have no effect on the embedded one.

The major distinction between linking and embedding is that when a file is linked to one or more programs, it still remains as a single file on the disk. A file on the hard drive has been "linked" to an application (or two, or more). When the originating application makes changes to that file, those changes show up when another program opens a document containing a link to the original file.

By contrast, when something has been embedded, no common disk file on the hard drive is loaded when needed by various applications. After embedding, the data actually resides within the host program. It's similar to copying an Excel spreadsheet then pasting it into a Word document. Of course, the original Excel file containing the spreadsheet that got embedded still exists on the hard drive. However, this disk file is now unrelated to the embedded object. Double-clicking an embedded object doesn't result in a disk access that searches for that object. The object is part of the already-loaded document. Double-clicking a linked object causes a disk access that loads in the object from a file.

There are several implications resulting from this fundamental difference between linking and embedding. If a disk file containing the original data is renamed or moved to a new location on the disk, the embedded object is unaffected and is still usable. Recall that embedded data resides in the file saved by the host application; a copy of it has been "pasted." By contrast, linked data resides only in the original disk file, and the host application is unaware of it if that file is renamed or moved or deleted. Linked data can thus become unavailable. Embedded data is always available, sunk into the host document. The price you pay for embedding, though, is that you create a "version problem": are you working with the latest spreadsheet data? or is this embedded spreadsheet now out of date because you've since made changes to it (to the original disk file) using Excel?

(One solution to this "version" issue is to destroy (delete) the original file and maintain only the embedded copy of the data. If necessary, you can extract the embedded data later as a separate file.)

One additional penalty exacted by choosing to embed: Embedded data makes the host application's document larger. Sometimes much larger. A single embedded high-resolution graphic can boost a Word file from a few thousand bytes up into the megabyte range. Megabyte-sized files can fill up a hard drive, and of course such files also take longer to open.

Pros & Cons

If either linking or embedding were the clearly superior approach, you wouldn't have to choose between the two techniques. Each has its strong points and its weaknesses. Linking boasts smaller file sizes: only a brief description of the object, maybe an icon, and the file path is stored within the host/container application. Linking also ensures that several different applications can be working with the latest version of a particular piece of data. No matter how many applications you link it to, there is still only that one file on disk holding the text or picture.

 TIP If something is linked into a document, most applications permit you to store only the link. When you choose linking instead of embedding, an application nonetheless stores a picture of the linked item. This obviously increases the size of the document file. To change a linked picture into an icon, go to the Edit menu, then choose Links. Select the linked item you want to display as an icon and turn icon. Then turn off the *Save Picture In Document* option.

However, the weakness of linking is that this one file is vulnerable. If it's deleted, renamed or moved, the link fails. There will still be an icon or pictorial representation of the linked file in the document to which it was linked, but no updating, indeed no editing, can now take place. Double-click on it and your application will fumble around looking for the data on the hard drive, and will fail to find it.

All this was true in Windows 3.x, but Windows 95 solves this "where is it?" problem, to a degree. "Link tracking," keeping the link fresh and accurate if a linked file is moved or renamed, *does* happen automatically in Windows 95. The only proviso, the file must still remain within the same "volume" (usually this means within the same hard drive). This same kind of tracking takes place if you rename or move a program or document pointed to by a Windows 95 Shortcut. Try it: Rename the folder (directory) containing a file to which a Shortcut points. Then watch Windows 95 track it down.

In any case, you're completely safe with embedding. Embedding stuffs, you might say *grafts*, information into a "compound document." You don't have to give a co-worker a word processor file and a separate file containing a photograph that goes with the word processor file. Instead, the photo is crammed right into the text and becomes part of it. There's only one file to hand to your co-worker for further editing.

Aside from requiring rather large files and creating a problem, embedding has another drawback for people on networks. A linked object (file) can be made available to everyone on the network (by placing it in a directory on the network server). An embedded object cannot be made thus available.

Likewise, embedded objects must reside on the same computer as the container applications that edit them. A linked file, on the other hand, can be put on a network server, available freely to everyone (and always current—that file is only a copy of the data).

 ## Hands-On: Object Embedding

Here's how to embed an object within a document. As you'll see, it's pretty much like copying, then pasting, using the Clipboard.

1. Start WordPad. This will be our "client" and will contain an embedded Paint graphic. Click Start, then Programs, then Accessories, then WordPad. (WordPad is normally installed by Windows 95 Setup. If you don't see WordPad, you may need to install it. To install it, click on Start, then Settings, then Control Panel. Double-click on Add/Remove Programs, then choose "Windows Setup." In this list, click on "Accessories" then click the "Details" button. In that new list, you'll be able to locate and select "WordPad.")

2. Type in some text, such as our letter to Ms. Goez shown in Figure 11-6.

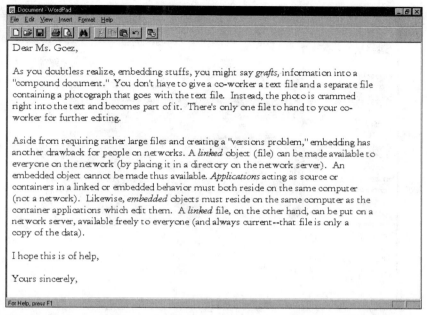

Figure 11-6: *An ordinary document, ready to get embedded with a graphic.*

3. Start Paint. (The Start button I Programs I Accessories I Paint.)
4. Draw something, or find a .BMP file on your hard drive to open.
5. In the Edit menu choose Select All so the entire image is capable of being copied. Or don't. If you want, just select a section. But *something* must be selected.
6. In the Edit menu choose Copy. Now your selection has been moved to the Clipboard.
7. Go back to WordPad. Click within your document where you want the embedded graphic to appear, to put the flashing input cursor there. From WordPad's Edit menu, choose Paste Special.

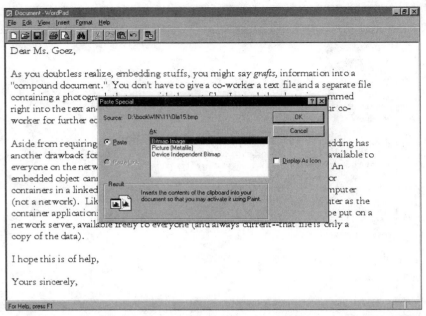

Figure 11-7: *When you request Paste Special you can choose between the full image, or reduce it to an icon.*

Notice in Figure 11-7 that Windows provides you with some alternative file types in the As list. Just ignore these types and accept Bitmap Image (.BMP), the default. You also can choose .WMF (Windows MetaFile). A MetaFile is a mathematical description of your text or image rather than a copy of each dot in the image. (For more on this distinction, see "Paint" in Chapter 10.) A .DIB (device-independent bitmap) is similar to a .BMP but has additional information that permits it to be accurately rendered on various kinds of output devices (such as a plotter).

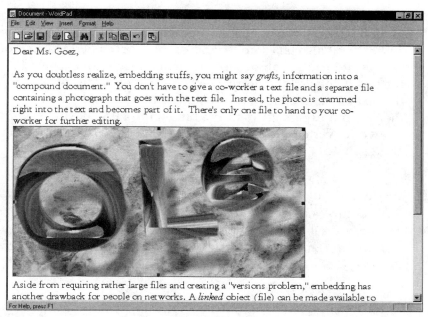

Figure 11-8: *The full image embedded into a text document.*

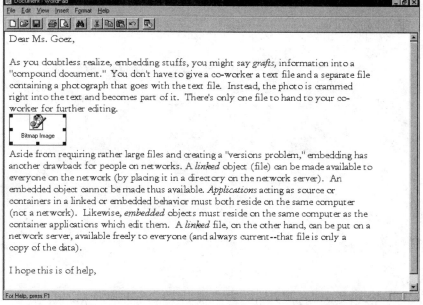

Figure 11-9: *The same image displayed as an icon only.*

If you choose to display your embedded object as an icon, you can still double-click on it (or right-click) to edit it in Paint. It takes up less screen space, but it also takes up less disk space. An embedded icon of an image can result in a file half the size of an image fully displayed. For example, the text displayed in Figure 11-6, when saved to disk, takes up 5,632 bytes; the text and embedded icon displayed in Figure 11-9 take up 187,392 bytes; the text and full image displayed in Figure 11-8 take up 355,328 bytes. (If you've converted the image into a .WMF-style graphic file, it takes up 180,224 bytes.)

 TIP The reason that an iconized object takes up less room on the disk is because Windows 95 has some built-in compression routines. It compresses the image data when it's represented by an icon and then decompresses it (which takes a few seconds) if the image is restored to real size.

What happens if you print a document with an embedded icon? The icon is printed, just as you see it onscreen. If you want to print it as a real, full graphic, right-click on it and choose Object Properties. Then click on the View tab of the Bitmap Image Properties sheet and choose *Display as editable information*. The icon will expand back to a full image.

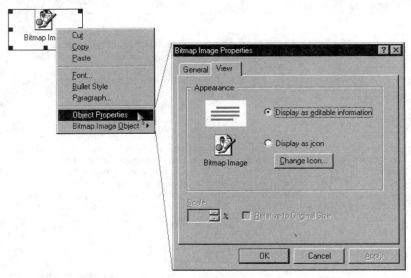

Figure 11-10: *If you want to expand an icon back to the original image, right-click on the icon and then choose Object Properties.*

There is a second way to embed or link an object into a client application using the Object option in an application's Insert menu. We'll illustrate this technique step by step later in this chapter under "Lights, Music."

 ## Hands-On: Object Linking

Linking is, at the time of this writing, more rare than embedding. That is, you aren't often allowed to link. You follow the same steps as if you were embedding, but when you click on the Edit menu in the client application and select Paste Special, the Paste Link check box is gray (unavailable for your use). This means that either the server (from which you copied the object you're trying to link) or the client application, or both, cannot link. Some applications can link and embed, others can only embed, still others cannot participate at all in Object Linking and Embedding.

However, because OLE is a fundamental technology in Windows 95 and other Microsoft operating systems, more applications are becoming OLE-capable all the time. The best way to find out if linking is possible is to try it. If the Paste Link check box won't respond, you know your only choice is to embed. (If the Paste Special menu item is missing from the Edit menu, you can neither link nor embed.)

Here's an example of linking using Hijaak—a Windows screen-capture utility—as the server and Word for Windows as the client.

1. Start Word for Windows.
2. Type in some text.
3. Start Hijaak.
4. Find a .BMP or other graphics file on your hard drive and open it in Hijack.
5. In the Edit menu choose Copy. Note that Hijaak, unlike Paint, Photoshop and some others, doesn't require that something be selected before you copy it to the Clipboard. If nothing is selected, Hijaak assumes that you want to copy the entire image.
6. Go back to Word. Click within your document where you want the linked graphic to appear. In the Word Edit menu, choose Paste Special.
7. Choose Paste Link from the Paste Special dialog box.

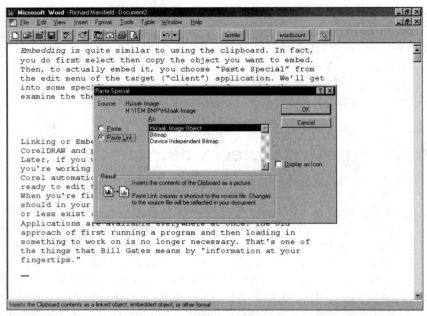

Figure 11-11: *Linking allows more than one application to share a single linked file on the hard drive.*

Note that our linked graphic object is now available to either Hijaak or Word, and it will be kept in a single file on the hard drive. The image is not stuffed into the Word document, as it would be if embedded. Instead, it resides on disk as a separate (though linked) file. If you make some changes to it in Hijaak, those changes will appear the next time you load the Word document. However, if you're impatient, you can right-click on the object and choose Update Link as shown in Figure 11-12.

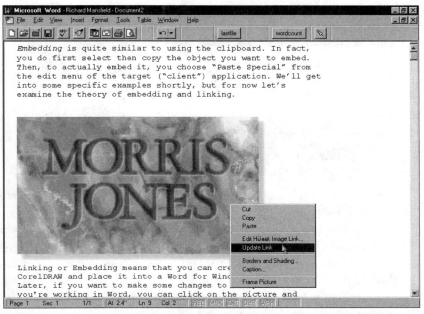

Figure 11-12: *You can manually update a linked object any time, but it also happens automatically whenever you load in the document at some future time.*

 TIP   If you want to let someone else work on a document containing a linked object, that person must have access to both the document itself as well as the server application.

Three Kinds of Update

You have considerable flexibility over how and when a linked object is updated (to bring in any changes made to the object). When a linked object is within a document in the client application, click on the Edit menu and select Links. You'll see a list of each linked object in the current document, as well as three option buttons at the bottom, as shown in Figure 11-13.

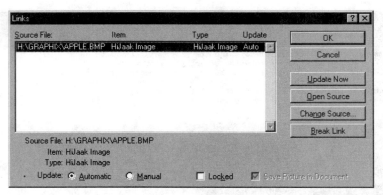

Figure 11-13: *The Links dialog box provides the various options and actions available for a linked object.*

If you click on Automatic (the default), Windows updates the linked object whenever the document is opened in the client application. In addition, if you make changes in the server application, the link can be updated automatically as well. However, this second behavior is, at this time, variable—sometimes it happens, sometimes not.

Choosing the Manual option in the Links dialog box updates the object only when you click on the Update Now button, shown in Figure 11-13, or right-click on the object, then select Update Link. The Locked option prevents any updating. The Open Source button brings up the source application with the object loaded into it, ready for editing. This is the same as right-clicking on the object, then choosing Edit Link, or simply double-clicking on the object.

The Change Source button is supposed to allow you to replace the current object with a different object of the same file type. However, at the time of this writing, this feature is not working. If you click on the Break Link button, the link to the source application (the server) will be gone. The image or other kind of object will still be in your client document, but it will not be an OLE object any longer. Instead, it's now as if you had merely copied and pasted (not pasted "special"). Any changes made to this image by the original server application will not be updated in your client document's pasted object. Likewise, double-clicking on the object won't bring up the originating server application. However, double-clicking might bring up some kind of editing facility if the client application has such a feature (as Word for Windows does for editing images).

TIP The Links dialog box has been improved over the Windows 3.x version. The earlier version didn't have a Locked option or an Open Source button. Therefore, you couldn't forbid updating (locked) or bring up the original application (open source).

OLE Adaptations

Of course, you can embed or link many kinds of objects: sound files, video clips, text and graphics. In each case, some of the options change as appropriate to the type of object involved. For example, if you copy a piece of text in a Word document, then open a new document and choose Paste Special from the Edit menu, you'll see the options listed in Figure 11-14.

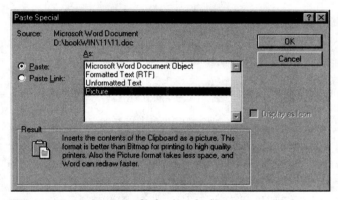

Figure 11-14: *You can link or embed text as a picture.*

The choices shown in the As list of the Paste Special dialog box (in Figure 11-14) are interesting. The first one, Microsoft Word Document Object, is what you would expect: the text originated in Word, so this choice retains all the formatting (fonts, annotations or the many other options available within Word). The .RTF option preserves italics, boldface and other formatting, but more complex or uncommon information (such as columns) is lost. This choice, the default, is sometimes the best. Most client applications will understand the formatting in an .RTF file. Unformatted text loses all boldface, italics, tabs and so on, but it will preserve paragraph breaks.

The final choice in the As list, Picture, seems at first glance, perverse. Why would you want to make some text uneditable? A picture (like most faxes that you receive) is just a "picture of text" rather than text you could go in and change in a word processor. However, if you're certain that you won't need to edit the text, this option does print quite well. Also, if you click on it to select it (or right-click on it and choose Frame picture), you can freely resize it and the text remains sharp.

The Fax feature in Windows 95 can actually send editable text via fax rather than merely a picture of text like most fax communication. The only proviso is that the receiver must also be using the Windows 95 Fax facility as well.

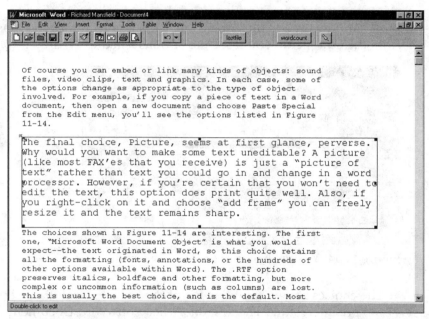

Figure 11-15: *When text is saved as a picture, changing font size is accomplished by dragging one of the tabs on the frame.*

Lights, Music

Of course, you're not limited only to text or graphics objects. You can use OLE to stuff music (.WAV or .MID files) or video (.AVI) or any other kinds of files. Here, we'll also illustrate the second way to link or embed an object into a client application.

Hands-On: Multimedia Linking & Embedding

To link either music or video, follow these steps:

1. Open WordPad (or whatever application you want to use).
2. Select Insert | Object.

Figure 11-16: *Many applications have an Insert menu that you can use as another way to link or embed.*

The Insert Object dialog box, shown in Figure 11-17, appears.

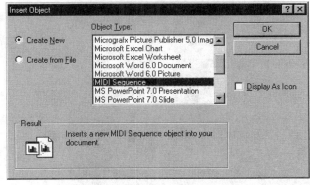

Figure 11-17: *In this dialog box, you can embed an "empty" object—one that isn't related to an existing data file.*

3. Click on Create from File. Then you can select the source file (and implicitly, the server application that's associated with it). To link this object, click on the Link check box.
4. Locate the file you want to insert as an object and then click on the OK button.

 TIP Inserted objects (whether linked or embedded) are identical in behavior to OLE objects created by using the "Paste Special" technique. The only difference is the steps you take to place them into a client document.

In-Place Editing

A feature called *in-place editing* is yet another element of OLE and further extends OLE's refusal to permit applications to dominate documents. In effect, when you request a temporary switch to a different editing mode— say from working on text in Word to retouching an image in Picture Publisher—the menus and button bars of Word will change. Precisely what happens varies from application to application, and many applications are not yet capable of in-place editing. Nonetheless, the idea is that some or all of the Word menus and buttons will be temporarily replaced by some or all of the Picture Publisher menus and buttons.

Here's how in-place editing works. Open a text document in Word. Then start Picture Publisher and open a graphic image.

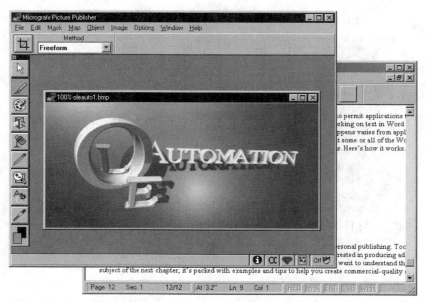

Figure 11-18: *Copy this image into Word; then click on it to temporarily change Word's menus and button bars.*

Copy the image into the Clipboard (press Ctrl+C or select Edit | Copy). Then, from Word's Edit menu, select Paste (not Paste Special), or press Ctrl+V. Your picture will appear in the Word document:

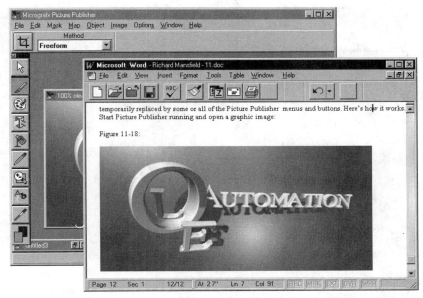

Figure 11-19: *Notice that simply pasting this picture into Word has no effect on Word's menus or buttons.*

Then right-click on the pasted image in Word and choose Edit or double-click on it. This tells Word that you want to have some (or all) of the menus and buttons available in the originating application—in this case, Picture Publisher. In Figure 11-20, you can see that although you're still working "in" Word, the text is still there and the title bar says "Microsoft Word." However, for the moment, the Word button bar has been replaced by the Picture Publisher button bar, the vertical bar on the left. Likewise, the menus have been replaced. You can now access all the retouching and image-editing features of Picture Publisher. It's not necessary that Picture Publisher even be currently running as an application in Windows 95. Clicking on the image will still bring in the appropriate buttons and menus so you can edit the graphic. Then, to restore Word's tools and menus, simply click on the text outside the image. Word's tools are restored, and you can again type, spell-check, change typefaces or do anything else applicable to working with words.

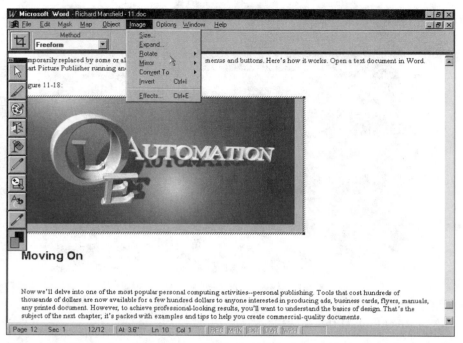

Figure 11-20: *You're still working in Word, but its features have been temporarily replaced by tools and menus useful for editing a graphic.*

How many buttons and menus or individual menu items change during in-place editing is up to the programmers who wrote applications like Word and Picture Publisher. They use OLE techniques called Menu Negotiation and Button Negotiation to define which menus and button bars appear (from either application) and the location or position of the individual menu items and buttons.

OLE in the Future

When you think of OLE, think of a frozen river breaking up during the spring thaw—things come apart into smaller objects. It is predicted that in the future we'll buy components rather than applications. Because one of OLE's goals is to make objects communicate with each other efficiently and without requiring translation, it's possible that we'll no longer buy software suites (like Microsoft Office) but instead build our own custom software from a shelf of individual objects, bound together by OLE. So you'd buy your text editor from Acme, your spell checker from IBM, your printing engine from Symantec, and so on. These components would all work together smoothly because they all speak OLE.

We're already seeing some of this capability today: componentware such as VBXs and now OCXs sold to add new features to Microsoft's Visual Basic programming language. Likewise, you can add special third-party graphics filters (that add embossing, drop shadowing and so on to images). They are called PlugIns, and all you have to do is copy them to the Photoshop directory, and they're then listed under Photoshop's Filter menu, ready to use. (The same plug-ins will also work with Picture Publisher, TrueSpace and other graphics programs.)

Note, too, that Windows 95 makes considerable use of OLE in various subtle ways. You can select a piece of text, a range of numbers or a selection from within a graphic and then just drag and drop it onto the desktop. It then becomes a *scrap*. A scrap is an independent OLE object, and the desktop is its temporary container. You can then drag the scrap into any other application. For one thing, some people will find that this feature makes moving information between applications easier. Just drag the selected range or object and drop it on the desktop. Then open the program you want to paste it into, and drag and drop the scrap into the target program. No cut and paste (OLE drag and drop invokes Paste Special automatically).

The Windows 95 shell also makes some other innovative uses of OLE, such as the Shortcut links. Shortcuts can also be dragged and dropped and used very much like OLE objects. You can drag a shortcut to a visual demo, for example, and drop it into a mail message. Then you can send it to a co-worker, and when she receives the mail, she can double-click on the Shortcut icon to run the demo, even if the demo is stored on your computer, not hers. (This trick assumes that file sharing is set up on your office's network.)

Moving On

Now we'll delve into one of the most popular personal computing activities—personal publishing. Tools that cost hundreds of thousands of dollars a few years ago are now available for a few hundred dollars to anyone interested in producing ads, business cards, flyers, manuals or any printed document. However, to achieve professional-looking results, you'll want to understand the basics of design. That's the subject of the next chapter; it's packed with examples and tips to help you create commercial-quality documents.

Chapter 12

Personal Publishing: Beyond DTP

Spreadsheets are useful tools for making financial predictions. Databases make it easy to keep track of information. But no computer application surpasses word processing in popularity or utility. With a small investment in a word processor program and a printer, the average person now has facilities for producing documents that rival professional publications. Documents that would have cost thousands of dollars to produce ten years ago are now within the reach of any computer user.

Personal publishing is advanced word processing. It means that you consider more than just what you write. You consider *design*—adding graphics, creating headlines, or otherwise manipulating and organizing the look of your pages. Because personal publishing is so popular and because the fundamentals of good page design are easy to learn, we're devoting a chapter to the topic. Above all, the graphic environment of Windows is ideal for going beyond mere typing to create handsome documents.

Because desktop publishing has become such a vital aspect of contemporary computing, this chapter offers a quick course in current styles and trends in page design. If creating professional-looking documents that impress the reader isn't important to you, go on to Chapter 13.

Windows makes it easy to create attractive, professional-looking ads, pamphlets, invitations, notices, menus, newsletters and many other kinds of documents. Windows is, above all, highly visual. You see on the screen the effect of changing the size of a headline or moving a graphic. You can drag a photo around the screen "page" as easily as you can slide a photo around on top of your desk. You can resize a graphic in seconds by just dragging one of its corners. In other words, Windows accessories and applications have all the facilities you could want when designing most kinds of documents.

Whatever you're interested in creating—a company memo, an instruction manual or just an ad to tack up on grocery store bulletin boards—you can make it look good by using Windows.

Why Bother to Design?

But of course designing a publication means more than merely typing it. So, why bother to design? What's the advantage of adding a headline, a border, a photo or other special effects to a printed page? After all, until recently most companies (and virtually all private individuals) communicated by typing their newsletters and other publications.

In the old days (before the late 1980s), things were different. If a company wanted to reach and impress a large audience, it hired an ad agency and spent thousands of dollars to have the pros create a "look" to sell a product. But for manuals, in-house instruction manuals, memos, proposals and most other communications, simple typing was good enough. The alternative—a designed page—was both time-consuming and expensive.

Personal computers have changed all that. The tools of design are available to everyone who uses Windows. But why bother?

Put simply, a well-designed page is much more attractive and more convincing. Consequently, more people will actually read what you publish. And, having read it, if it's handsomely designed, more people will believe what it says.

Whether you're printing a business advertisement for the classified ads page, a set of name badges for a convention or a church bulletin, anything you publish will look more attractive, more professional and more believable if you take a little extra time to design it. Just as you would be less convincing if you asked your boss for a raise while wearing a stained T-shirt, publications that look bad have less impact than those that look good. It almost doesn't matter what your publication says if its design is thoughtless, plain or amateurish.

Figure 12-1: *This personnel manual cover is attractive and professional.*

```
Personnel Manual
Essexe Financial
22280 Office Park Ln.
Tulsa, OK 27436

9/3/95
```

Figure 12-2: *The old-fashioned typewritten cover sheet is no longer sufficient, except perhaps for civil service or military documents.*

Figures 12-1 and 12-2 were both created in Windows Paint. But what a difference it makes when you spend an extra ten minutes to create a nice design instead of just typing your message. Both are cover sheets for a business personnel manual, but you can see a considerable difference in quality.

Getting Results From Your Publications

When you print something, you usually want to get results. You want people to be attracted to it, to read it and, finally, to act on it.

In the past decade, the tools necessary to produce publications like the one shown in Figure 12-1 have become widely available and relatively inexpensive. You already have a computer with Windows and Paint.

However, less than a decade ago, you would have had to hire a professional designer, typesetter and printer to produce this cover page. And the equipment necessary to print documents containing shadowing, proportional type, headlines and photos would have cost you hundreds of thousands of dollars. No wonder most written communication used to originate from the typewriter or the human hand.

The Extinction of the Dinosaurs

In the late '70s I went into a large Salvation Army store in Altoona, Pennsylvania. Behind the stacks of mattresses, racks of clothes and boxes of chipped china was a room containing several huge machines. I found a punch-card sorting machine the size of a pickup truck. When I turned it on, it came to life and worked fine. I didn't know it at the time, but it was utterly useless, obsolete.

The price tag on the punch-card machine claimed that it had cost a bank $250,000 and was now only $700. It seemed like a bargain. After all, those punch cards were still widely used. They always said "Do not fold, spindle or mutilate" although nobody knew exactly what *spindle* meant.

Also in this room was what looked like a table big enough for ten people to work on. But inside it was a memory for a mainframe computer—hundreds of metal tokens suspended in a matrix of piano wire for $450.

Gathering dust nearby was an accountant's immense mechanical "calculating engine." Unlike the ordinary hand-cranked adding machines of the day, this engine could multiply and divide. And, still oiled and gleaming, was a typesetting machine for $1,200. I hope nobody bought it. Within a few years, typesetters too would become as useless as the bank's card-sorter.

During the '60s and '70s, printing was already migrating to a process called *photo-typesetting*, which was a precursor to laser printing. Today, even photo-typesetting is dead; it proved to be a transitional phase between the physical typesetter and today's purely electronic technique. It lasted only a decade. Now almost all magazines and newspapers are designed on desktop systems just like the one you own.

These heavy old mechanical machines that calculated, set type, sorted cards and so on were modern in the sense that they did jobs involving information. But they were hopelessly physical and, therefore, really belonged to the dying industrial age. The information age is not physical. There is no need anymore for metal rings in a computer's memory or lead type slathered with ink to print a magazine.

The End of the Age of Heavy Metal

Just as giant reptiles gave way to tiny rodents at the end of the age of dinosaurs, heavy equipment has now given way to the personal computer. A typesetting machine was a keyboard attached to a small foundry. A typesetter would sit at the machine and type in a line of text. The lino would then pour hot metal into a form. After the letters of the text had hardened, these "slugs" were brushed with printer's ink and magazine or newspaper pages could then be pounded out. Similar techniques involving hot lead produced the illustrations and headlines too.

Now graphics and text are held in computer memory. Information stored inside a computer or on a disk is a pattern of electromagnetic fields, not that different from the way information is stored in the human brain.

No longer do text and illustrations have to be molded in metal before a page can be printed. Instead, electronic pulses travel through a cable to a printer where the information is stamped, burned or sprayed onto the paper page. And because we've now got the lead out of the process, today millions of personal computer owners can *design* their communications.

Layout & Design—Where Form Meets Content

There are many ways to make a publication attractive and inviting to the reader. The primary tools are headlines, white space, the typefaces you select for your text and various kinds of illustrations. Where on a page you place these elements (and what size you make them) has a major impact on the visual appeal of your piece. Use these elements effectively, and you're more than half way to creating a successful, good-looking publication.

The other half of the task is roughly equivalent to what editing does for writing: you polish your design. You look at your pages—preferably after putting them aside for a few days—with a cold, objective eye. And you check to see that you've got balance, contrast, variety and so on. You also check the details: crowding, hidden or floating headlines, tombstones, widows and orphans and so on. Below, in the section "A Final Checklist," we'll go through all the things you should double-check during this important second look at your work. For now, let's take a tour of the main job of first creating solid, attractive desktop publications.

One good way to start designing your publication is to pretend that you are about to paint an abstract painting in the style of Mondrian. One of the most influential twentieth-century artists, Piet Mondrian arranged squares and rectangles in attractive, balanced compositions. You've got a similar task. You have gray blocks of text, black blocks of headlines, perhaps some in-between shades of graphics, photos or charts. Finally, to glue it all together, you've got white space—the areas on the page where there's nothing but blank paper. And of all these elements, probably the most important is white space.

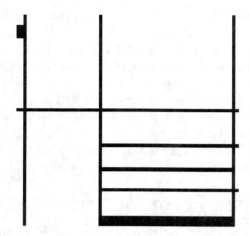

Figure 12-3: *Mondrian created balanced, attractive designs out of rectangles.*

Notice how the lines and white spaces balance in Figure 12-3. The shapes are distributed on the page so no part of the page dominates. To see how it would look out of balance, cover the little square in the top left with your finger. Do you see how the whole page is now dominated by the lower right? How it sinks down and becomes bottom-heavy.

Clearly balance isn't just a matter of comparing how much black or gray there is in the four quarters of a page. A small black square emphasized by lots of white space around it has enough power to hold this design in balance. So when you design a page, you might want to first roughly draw in the rectangles that you must include—the necessary text, any illustrations and so on. Then consider what's optional. Make a headline extra large to balance something lower on the page. Or include a photo. You can play around with the positions of various things and the margins of white around them until you get a page that looks right.

Fortunately design isn't a puzzle with only one answer. You can put together a good page in many ways. But to make your publication look its best, first consider where to put things and how large they should be.

Here's another experiment: Turn this book one-quarter turn to the right so that the black box is at the top. Does it still balance? Turn it another quarter turn, then another. It seems that Mondrian's design is balanced no matter how it's positioned, don't you think? Try this four-turns look at your own page designs—it's another good test of balance.

White Space

White space is the background—the zones on the page where no text, headlines or graphics are placed. White space wasn't used much in the past. (Designers had to worry less about balance because the pages contained less contrast.)

Until the middle of this century, white space around the sides of pages were usually thin; text took up nearly the whole page. Any blank space was filled with designs and fancy borders. For one thing, paper was expensive and the designers didn't want to waste it. While not necessarily unattractive, fully filled pages are not the current fashion.

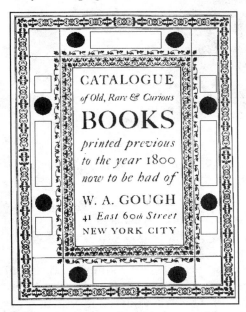

Figure 12-4: *Busy lacy borders, and jam-packed pages, have largely disappeared from contemporary publications.*

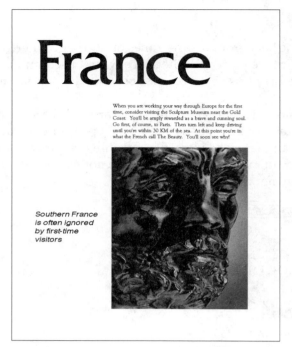

Figure 12-5: *Contemporary page design employs a lot of white space.*

Today, the reader expects smaller units of text, separated by white blank places where the eye can relax. White space also allows you to organize the text and graphics logically—to emphasize certain areas of text or to position text into subordinate areas.

A wide margin is also a good place to put a summarizing sentence or two, which tags and defines or explains the text (somewhat like handwritten notes in the margins of a book). This way, the reader can skim your publication, jumping from one summary to the next. Readers appreciate being able to scan text this way. If the reader isn't interested in the subjects on one page, it's easy to go to the next and read the summaries of that new page. By using a wide margin, your pages will have a more "open," less threatening look than the wall-to-wall gray of a page filled with text.

Headlines

Think of headlines as your darkest, heaviest design elements. They are usually the first text that will be read on a page, and are also among the first graphic elements that will attract the eye. If you put headlines in an awkward place or make them too big or too small, a page is thrown off balance.

The main headline is usually placed at the top of a page and is set in type that is considerably bigger than the text ("body text" as it's called).

Figure 12-6: *This headline is too small. It's not much larger than the callout in the margin.*

Figure 12-6, aside from being out of balance, illustrates the primary mistake made by inexperienced page designers: headlines that aren't large enough. Also, notice that headlines are generally set in a different, more plain typeface from the *serif* style usually found in body text.

> **TIP** Since they are supposed to attract and quickly inform the reader, headlines should be short. But if your headline is longer than a single line, use initial caps (capitalize only the first letter of each word) rather than all uppercase letters. And don't capitalize short prepositions, conjunctions or articles such as *in, to, a, and, an, or, the* (unless one of these short words is the first word in the headline).

Contemporary design has settled on a convention: The body text is almost always set in a serif font, and the headlines in sans serif. Serifs are the little extra jots and curlicues at the ends of a character's lines. We'll have more to say about the important distinction between serif and sans serif typefaces shortly. (For details about how Windows 95 allows you to add or remove typefaces, see Chapter 13.)

SANS-SERIF FOR HEADLINES

Serif is mostly used for body text

Figure 12-7: *As a general rule, sans serif typefaces are avoided in body text.*

The Greatest Trend

One of the most profound shifts in modern communication has been away from text and toward visuals. Clearly, movies and later television have had a major impact on the way people prefer to absorb information. In the past few years, additional shifts have occurred. These shifts are ultimately induced by television—with its expectation of a short attention span and the popular preference for seeing rather than reading.

Icons (small symbolic pictures) are relatively new to page design and derive from three separate influences: MTV, *USA Today* and graphic computer operating systems like the Macintosh and Windows.

MTV and its journalistic equivalent, *USA Today*, have had a profound impact on both print and television design styles in the past decade. MTV and *USA Today* both like to break their information into small, rapidly identifiable, easily assimilated, highly visual units. This style to reading is what dim sum, shish kabob, tappas and sushi are to eating: most cuisines have examples of meals composed solely of varied appetizers, of bite-sized portions.

When the President addresses Congress, *USA Today* will print a bulleted list of the "highlights" and maybe include some icons (such as a stack of dollars for the sound bite on the economy, a Band-Aid for health reform and so on). The *New York Times*, by contrast, will print the entire speech. The *Times* has little color, few stories, few symbols and relatively few photos. *USA Today* is filled with small, bulleted lists, graphic symbols, many short items and much color.

The emphasis on visuals continues. Nobody expects newspapers to end up with the 8-to-1 ratio of words to illustrations typical of comic books—but the trend toward graphics at the expense of words is not over yet.

Icons are frequently used in Windows to symbolize programs or actions the computer should take. You click on an icon, perhaps a small picture of a folder with a magnifying glass on top of it, and Windows's Explorer opens up—the files on a disk drive are displayed.

In page design, icons can symbolize a special section such as a summary, a caution or a helpful hint. They can also signal to the reader a regular section of a newspaper or magazine such as a lightning bolt for the weather summary.

Our local newspaper, *The Greensboro News & Record*, has taken iconization to an extreme. Every subhead—there are perhaps a dozen per page—has a little silhouette of a clock face next to it. When the paper underwent its most recent redesign and added this strange feature, it was explained that these little clocks would let readers know: here is a quick summary of this story. The clock says "save time by reading just this summary." But when they're used all over the page, it's noise. Like anything else, icons used too much become self-defeating and, let's be honest, silly.

Graphics: Diagrams, Illustrations, Clip Art & Photos

People say a picture is worth a thousand words, but of course that depends on who is writing the words. It's hard to imagine a picture that would substitute for the Bill of Rights or the Ten Commandments.

Nonetheless, contemporary page design increasingly uses as much visual information as possible. Your finished pages are not merely expected to convey information, they are expected to convey information attractively.

You want your pages to look good. And one of the best ways to avoid gray, text-heavy pages is to add illustrations. Of course, besides making your work comely, pictures can often provide more than a thousand words worth of information. If one of the goals of your publication is to tell the reader what it feels like to visit Seattle, it's much better if you can include photos of Puget Sound, the monorail and so on.

When you're selecting any graphic, consider both the goals of your publication as well as its audience:

- Would the text be enhanced or clarified by graphics?
- Do you have too much text, insufficient visual relief?
- Are you trying to demonstrate something (consider step-by-step drawings of the process)?

■ Is it an advertisement of some kind? Graphics—particularly human bodies, faces and especially eyes—force people to look. It's a prehistoric reaction: we have to look at other people, if only to decide if we need to attack, relax or flee.

■ Are you doing a company newsletter? Including photos of co-workers can greatly add to the appeal of your publication.

Illustrations

Any large graphic that's drawn (that's not a diagram or photo) is an *illustration*. It can be a drawing, an etching, a silhouette—whatever looks good or adds information to your presentation.

Figure 12-8: *Illustrations powerfully attract the eye. Did you look at anything else on this page first?*

Clip Art

You don't have to be able to draw to include illustrations in your publications. You can buy entire libraries of *clip art*, collections of professionally drawn illustrations grouped into various categories such as transportation, food, medicine, animals and so on. Some programs, such as CorelDRAW or Arts & Letters, come with collections of clip art you can paste into your documents. CorelDRAW comes with 18,000 pieces of clip art and 750 fonts.

To paste a piece of art, first run CorelDRAW or another drawing program and load the illustration you want. Select the illustration (click on it) and then press Ctrl+Ins or Ctrl+C to copy it to the Clipboard. In your word processor, move the mouse pointer to the location where you want to insert the graphic and then press Shift+Ins or Ctrl+V. At this point, most word processors surround the graphic with a "rubber band," a dashed frame surrounding the image. You can then click within the image to drag it to a new location on your page, or click on one of the sides or corners to resize it.

Some word processors, such as WordPerfect, also include a library of clip art. These libraries, though, are generally small.

Photos

Photos are often the most powerful graphic. They are highly realistic compared to icons or illustrations.

Figure 12-9: *We must look at other people. Photos of other humans are hugely attractive (attractive in the sense of magnetic).*

Computers give us complete control over photos, so retouching has become a relatively easy task. You can manipulate photographs to improve design in many ways. Several excellent photo-retouching programs are available to help you make these changes. CorelDRAW's PhotoPaint is one of these potent computerized tools. WordPerfect provides an Image Editor, which can accomplish several transformations on illustrations and photos. Windows has Paint (see Chapter 10). The most powerful photo-retouching program is Photoshop.

In Word for Windows, you can edit an embedded graphic by just double-clicking on it. First, import the graphic by selecting Edit | Paste or Insert | Picture. Then double-click on the embedded graphic, and the Microsoft drawing applet appears.

When you're using photographs, your first decision is whether or not to *crop* (trim) the picture; you can eliminate unnecessary peripheral details by cutting off one or more edges of the photo. Cropping can make a photo more dramatic, focusing the viewer on the main point. Figure 12-9 can be improved by making Gloria fill the frame. (While we're manipulating this photo, we'll also mirror the photo horizontally and remove that man's face near George's chest.) Compare Figure 12-10 to Figure 12-9.

Figure 12-10: *We've retouched this photo by cropping (trimming), mirroring and removing a distracting face from the bushes.*

One other thing to remember about photos: they are hierarchical. Sometimes you might use several photos in a given publication or even several photos on a given page. To know where to place them on a page, you can think of them in terms of their relative potency: what do people look at first? And why? What catches the eye?

The eye first goes to other eyes. That's why when you ride a subway, you avoid staring at other people. Locking eyes is, for animals and people, a challenge to combat. A direct look causes, among other things, a flood of adrenaline. Eyes are the most powerful image you can employ graphically (aside from nudity, which results in its own unique hormonal response in the viewer). Mouths and faces are second in their ability to excite the viewer.

Studies—sensors following eye movements—have revealed the following hierarchy in the excitability value of photos: 1) eyes looking at you, or body parts rarely seen by strangers; 2) eyes looking away from you or lips; 3) faces; 4) gender-specific body parts seen on beaches; 5) the whole body, nude, but facing away; 6) the whole body, clothed; 7) people in groups; 8) animals; 9) famous landmarks; 10) plants; and 11) inanimate objects such as cars, mountains and stereo sets, depending on the interests of the viewer.

Graphic Size

Your next question might be: how large should a photo be? The answer: How large is your page? Normally, your goal is to be sure that the details in the photo are clear to the viewer. The second consideration is where on the page the photo looks good as part of the page design. If you are using more than one photo, the easiest way to balance them is to make them the same size, but weigh them according to their excitability value.

Recall that when you've pasted a photo, most word processors allow you to resize the graphic. You can then click within the image to drag it to a new location on your page, or click on one of the sides or corners to resize it. If necessary, you can resize in Paint by selecting the entire image and then dragging the corners of your selection.

Photo-retouching programs have facilities for resizing photos. If one photo is to be larger than another, consider making it quite a bit larger. You want to avoid the awkward look resulting from photos of slightly different sizes on the same page. This is as clumsy looking as slightly different margins or headline typeface sizes.

Altering & Retouching

Photo-retouching programs like Adobe Photoshop, Corel PhotoPaint or Micrografx Picture Publisher offer you a generous set of tools with which to manipulate and improve your photos: detail softening or sharpening, contrast and brightness adjustments, individual color or grayscale adjustments, even sophisticated interior cutting and pasting.

When deciding if and how much retouching to do, take a hard look at the photo. Is it too dark? Adjust the brightness and contrast. Is it slightly out of focus? Try edge detect or sharpness enhance. There is much you can do within retouching programs to make marginal photos acceptable, and good photos splendid.

Shadowing

Placing a shadow behind text or graphics can add a three-dimensional look to your page, but you should use this feature sparingly. And you need not use a 100 percent black shadow. Often 50 or 20 percent black achieves a more subtle effect since shadows in the real world are only 100 percent in dungeons and at midnight in the wilderness. What's more, the most realistic shadows of all are fuzzy around the edges.

Figure 12-11: *Shadowing makes text or graphics appear to float off the page.*

Although WordPerfect, Microsoft Word and other word processors have facilities for simple shadows, to achieve the effects in Figure 12-11, you'll need to use a full-featured retouching program.

Here, though, is how you can create simple *drop shadows* in WordPerfect 6.0. In WordPerfect, you can add shadows to graphic boxes (which could include text). It includes a special Shadow menu you can use to specify position, size and color for any shadow. Press Alt+F9, 1, 1, 2 (to add the picture to the graphics box). Select 1 (Image on disk) and then 1 (Filename) to import the image into the box. Then select 6 (Edit Border/Fill), 5, 1, 5 (select lower-right for your shadow position—this is by far the most attractive and familiar shadow position). Then press Enter to get out of the menus. If you are in Graphics view, save the file (press F10), and you should see your image redrawn on screen.

Figure 12-12: *The most convincing shadows are calculated within specialized 3D graphics programs, such as TrueSpace.*

For professional-looking drop shadows, Black Box, a plug-in filter from a company called Alien Skin, works quite effectively. For the ultimate in realistic shadowing, you could use a 3D graphics program like Ray Dream Designer, Visual Reality or the excellent TrueSpace. In these programs, you can position various "lights" and set their intensity.

Silhouetting

When you remove all or most of the background from a photo, you create an interesting visual object to place into your page. *Silhouetting* means "cutting" an image out from its background. Silhouetted detail seems to thrust out of the page toward the viewer.

Figure 12-13: *Its eyes will attract the viewer, not to mention its horns. But for a stronger image, remove some background and give the beast dimension.*

Figure 12-14: *The creature now seems to be poking through your page instead of sitting flat upon it.*

Silhouetting used to be a tedious process involving scissors, squinting and lots of patience. (It's where we get the term *clip art*.) And the results would look coarse unless you were most careful. Computer photo-retouching programs such as CorelDRAW's PhotoPaint and Adobe's Photoshop, however, make this task (and others, like removing unwanted objects inside a photo) much easier. You could also paint white into a photo using Windows Paint, but it's far simpler with a retouching program's auto-selection tools.

Violate Zone Limits

Keep in mind this primary modern design rule: It's often a good idea to violate expected space. Pictures are usually square, so make one part of the picture jut out from the squareness. (In other words, silhouette it.) Objects are usually separated, so overlap some of them. Things are usually enclosed within a frame or a page, so make some of the things jut off beyond their frame or page. All of these moves make your work more dimensional, more free, and often considerably more visually exciting.

Take a look at a well-designed ad or a stylish magazine (such as *Interview, Spy, Details* or *Vanity Fair*). Notice how often things go off the page, cover each other up—or shove off beyond their frame. In fact, how many ads can you find in these magazines where everything stays within its frame or page?

When you trespass zone expectations, you are making the viewers come to grips with what they see. They have to translate your images a little, they must interpret the things they are seeing (just as they do in real 3D life). Escaping images will seem to be getting loose, perhaps dangerously leaping toward the reader.

Used with restraint, violations like this are more real. The world is not flat and packaged into neat zones. When you enter a restaurant, someone is standing in front of someone else. Someone else is partly in your peripheral vision and partly beyond it—going off the "page." In the real world, things are not contained into frames and pages.

When you employ these techniques, you are forcing your viewers to reconcile their expectations (paper is flat and has borders) with what they are, in fact, seeing—or something is on top of something else or something is going off or coming out of this page. Of course, you don't want to overdo it, or your work will look hectic and disorganized and messy and chaotic. A space violation once every few pages (or one or two within a given ad) is enough to open things up and refresh or startle the viewer.

Figure 12-15: *Modern design avoids symmetries like this, where the type and design are all neatly contained within the frame.*

Figure 12-16: *Here's a more contemporary look. The text and graphics are tilted, asymmetrical (but balanced), and they escape off the sides of the image.*

Typefaces

Now that we've covered the obvious design issues—blocks of text, photos, and so on—we'll turn our attention to a more subtle issue. The typefaces you choose, the distance between individual letters in a headline (*kerning*), the distance between the lines and paragraphs in the body text (*leading*), and other seemingly minor issues all contribute to the appearance and ultimate success of your publication.

Most readers are not conscious of these less dramatic elements of your design. But the look, for example, of the typeface you've selected can make your work look crude and amateurish or polished and professional. These "lesser" elements are like spice in cooking—they aren't the primary substance, but they contribute quite a bit to the quality of the final product.

Readers are usually unaware of typefaces. In fact, most people are only vaguely aware, if at all, that there are such things as different designs of the letters of the—alphabet. However, to the graphic artist, typeface selection is a serious issue. For one thing, a poor selection can make text less readable. For another thing, readers, although almost always unaware of the cause, can be made comfortable or uneasy depending on how well you've chosen the look of the letters to suit the purpose, tone and message of your text.

Many publications contain more text than graphics. Because your choice of typeface will have a significant impact on the reader, we are going to devote several pages to typefaces, their subtleties and their suitability for various purposes.

The most basic guideline is to use a *sans serif* typeface for headlines and a *serif* typeface for body text. Nearly all contemporary publications, ads and other professionally produced documents follow this custom.

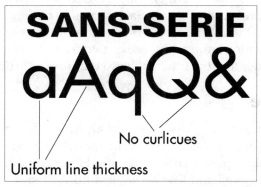

Figure 12-17: *A* sans serif *typeface, like Windows's Arial, is plain, stark—without curlicues, and has almost no variations in line thickness.*

Figure 12-18: *A* serif *is a small addition to a character, a curlicue that imitates the thinning line caused by lifting a pen from paper. See Windows's Times New Roman.*

Serif typefaces have a variety of line shapes and added strokes, bubbles and tails at the ends of the letters. These features help to differentiate the characters more than the stripped-down look of sans serif. This differentiation is the main reason that serif is often easier to read than sans serif, particularly for small text. That's why serif is almost always the choice for body text.

Sans serif typefaces are bolder, simpler, stronger looking. (Some sans serif faces have slight, almost imperceptible, variations in stroke thickness—see the lowercase *a* in Figure 12-17.) Sans serif typefaces are used when the characters are large (headlines, subheads and so on). Sans serif is also used in small doses elsewhere to indicate that the text is special such as in captions or *pullquotes*. (A pullquote is a spicy or intriguing sentence or two from the text that you blow up larger and bolder to attract the reader to the story or article.)

All Roads Lead to Rome

All serif typefaces derive from a classic, elegant alphabet designed by an unknown calligrapher, or a succession of character designers, in first century A.D. Rome. This seminal typeface consisted entirely of capital letters and was so thoughtfully designed and lovely that it continues to dominate Western printed text and probably always will.

The Roman typeface was originally chiseled into marble—on temples and statues—but it has proved equally suited to ink on paper. There have been hundreds of subtle variations on the original, but Roman or Times Roman (from the variation originally used by the newspaper, in England) is the one typeface invariably built into computer printers and included with word processors, not to mention Windows's Times New Roman.

Then, between 800–900 A.D., a second, lowercase (small letters) alphabet was developed to complement the original Roman set of capital letters. This development made life easier for the thousands of monk copyists who were hand-lettering books all over Europe. Lowercase letters can be written more quickly, and they also use up less paper (paper was then quite expensive).

Beyond that, when small letters make up most of the body text, the large letters then stand out—alerting the reader that a paragraph is beginning, that something is a headline, or that a particular word is special. Today, we generally only capitalize the first letter of proper nouns like Joyce or Tucson. However, only a century ago it was common to use "initial caps" in body text words freely, as a form of emphasis. In older books, you'll find words like Love and Fear capitalized within sentences.

Caslon's Drastic Changes

The third major change in typefaces took place in 1816. Famous alphabet designer William Caslon anticipated the simplified, spare designs that were to later dominate the artistic styles of the twentieth century: he lopped off all the extra strokes, curlicues and flourishes (the serifs) and created the first *sans serif* alphabet (however early Greek alphabets anticipated this stark simplicity).

Caslon's drastic move was at first only applied to uppercase letters, and its use was largely limited to advertising at the time. Since then, many variations on Caslon's "modern" alphabet have been designed, complete with lowercase letters. Sans serif typefaces are now used for most headlines, captions, pullquotes or any text that is positioned apart from, or larger than, the body text. The most popular sans serif typefaces are called Helvetica or Swiss. The Windows version is called Arial.

(Since the abstract design of a typeface can't be copyrighted, type foundries resort to copyrights for the name of a typeface. So we have various names, such as Arial, Helvetica, Swiss, Switzerland, Square Sans and more, all for essentially the same basic typeface. Also, sometimes you'll see strange spellings, like "Helvitica" in Figure 12-19. To the casual eye, the differences appear fundamentally indistinguishable. If you format your text as Arial and print it as Helvetica on a laser printer, the laser printer's version of Helvetica may employ thicker characters, resulting in changes in the way the page is formatted.)

AaBb&Qq	Arial
AaBb&Qq	Avant Garde
AaBb&Qq	**Futura Bold**
AaBb&Qq	Futura Condensed
AABB&QQ	**MACHINE**
AaBb&Qq	Optima
AaBb&Qq	Helvitica
AaBb&Qq	Helvitica Light
AaBb&Qq	Helvitica Narrow
AaBb&Qq	**Helvitica Black**

Figure 12-19: *Here are some variations of the sans serif style.*

Most typefaces have several "flavors" including boldface, italic and un-derlining. Boldface is most often used in headlines; it's big, black and thick. Only rarely do you see it within body text, where it jumps out at the reader and causes the bold words to be read as a group rather than within the con-text of their sentences.

Avoid the bad habit of using boldface as a way to add emphasis to certain words in the body text. Also avoid using all-capital letters or reversed, white-on-black characters, for emphasis. Likewise, stay clear of underlining words and exclamation points. This kind of thing is amateurish, an attempt to artificially add power to writing via typography instead of writing power-fully. Let the words, not the typeface or punctuation, do the talking.

You should generally remove boldface and exclamation points, and al-ways remove reversals and underlining within body text. Exclamation points should be limited to use within quotation marks, and used only when the speaker is exclaiming ("We *must* win!" the chairman said). You should remove this faux emphasis because it makes writing look hysterical, child-ish, tricky, or all three. What's more, this tactic is self-defeating since you cannot emphasize several dozen words per page and expect that the empha-sis will retain its original strength. Instead of modulating the voice, the text ends up merely shouting and screeching.

There are, however, a few kinds of newsletter articles that can benefit from boldface. In particular, a late-breaking news column or rumor column can usefully highlight the companies' or individuals' names in boldface. This is an effective way of letting the reader skim through the text, looking for names or topics of interest. It's rather like embedded subheads as a way of outlining and highlighting the various subjects in the article.

Underlined text, too, is rare in modern publications. When people wrote letters on typewriters, underlining signified italics. Only the most advanced typewriters, like the IBM Selectric designed just before typewriters became obsolete, had an italic typeface option. So underlining was used instead. Underlining is happily passing into history.

Italics are the exception. The italic version of a typeface is usually quite attractive and valuable. It's not a violently different look from normal text— just enough different to subtly convey emphasis.

The first italic alphabet was designed in 1501 by an unknown Venetian printer. The italic mode of a serif typeface endeavors to imitate the style of sixteenth-century Italian handwriting. Italics do look somewhat like script— slanted to the right, thinner, more rounded, with a connected quality, as if the hand holding the pen were not leaving the paper between letters. (When you want to emphasize something within an italic passage, revert to normal, non-italicized letters.)

Mutant, In-Between Typefaces

A few typefaces seek to combine the best qualities of both serif and sans serif styles (see Optima in Figure 12-19). They feature relatively subdued yet noticeable line width variations, and tiny, nearly invisible, serifs here and there. Such lettering is more often used in headlines than in body text, but can be used for both purposes (particularly if you don't apply it to a lot of body text; a paragraph is probably about as much as the reader would like).

Windows Typefaces

When you install Windows, you get three basic typefaces. Arial is the Windows sans serif face, though it's quite thin.

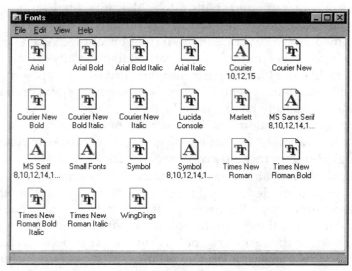

Figure 12-20: *Windows provides these fonts during Setup.*

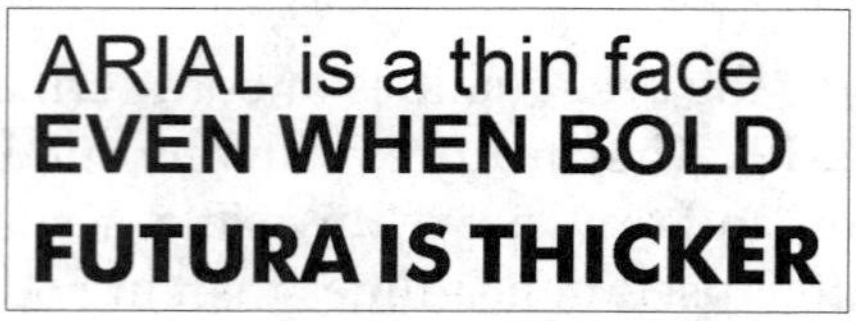

ARIAL is a thin face
EVEN WHEN BOLD
FUTURA IS THICKER

Figure 12-21: *Arial is fine for subheads, but for main heads you'll want a thicker sans serif typeface.*

The Arial typeface works okay for short sections of text or for small headlines (subheads under larger heads). But for a real headline, you'll want to use a thicker sans serif face such as Futura or Univers.

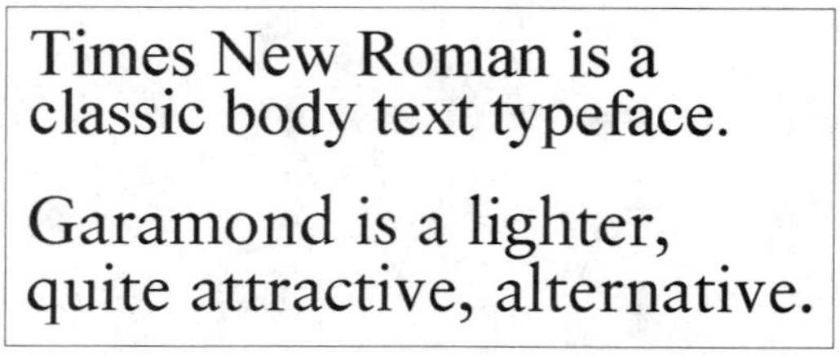

Times New Roman is a
classic body text typeface.

Garamond is a lighter,
quite attractive, alternative.

Figure 12-22: *The Windows font for body text, Times New Roman, is serviceable.*

Windows's body text font, Times New Roman, is a little darker (thicker) than you might like, but it works well enough in most publications. One way to lighten Times is to add *leading*, which is additional white space between the lines. In Word for Windows, you press Alt+O, P to get to the Indents and Spacing page of the Paragraph Format dialog box. Then you change the Line Spacing list box to Exactly and type in the point size you want in the At text box. Typically, body text is 9 to 12 points. The space between lines defaults to *single space*, which is 125 percent larger than the point size of the text itself. For example, if your body text is 12 point, the line spacing will default to 14 or 15 points. But try several different settings and see what looks good.

TIP   It's especially important to add extra white space between lines that are set in a sans serif typeface for body text. At smaller sizes, sans serif is inherently harder to read.

You can lighten Times New Roman by adding extra space between each line of text. Windows's body text font, Times New Roman, is a little darker (thicker) than you might like, but it works well enough in most publications. One way to lighten Times is to add "leading."

You can lighten Times New Roman by adding extra space between each line of text. Windows's body text font, Times New Roman, is a little darker (thicker) than you might like, but it works well enough in most publications. One way to lighten Times is to add "leading."

Figure 12-23: *If your pages look too black, add extra space between the lines.*

If you want an even lighter, more open look for your body text, consider using other popular serif fonts such as Garamond, Goudy or Caslon.

AaBb&Qq	Garamond
AaBb&Qq	Palatino
AaBb&Qq	Goudy Hundred
AaBb&Qq	Goudy Old-Style
AaBb&Qq	Caslon
AaBb&Qq	Optima

Figure 12-24: *You can use any of the several classic serif faces instead of Times New Roman for body text.*

Notice the differences in the various characters in Figure 12-24. Each of them has a "personality" and gives your body text different qualities. Optima is a special case; its design (like Zapf Humanist) endeavors to combine qualities of both sans serif and serif fonts. It falls about half way between the two major categories.

Proportional vs. Non-Proportional Typefaces

In addition to dividing fonts into the two primary categories of sans serif and serif, there is another essential division: proportional and non-proportional fonts.

Courier (Windows's Courier New) is rarely used in documents these days. Courier was the most common typewriter typeface and was used because typewriters cannot print letters of varying width. Text is easier to read on paper if the letter widths vary—the *i* takes up less room than the *m*. However, for mechanical reasons, typewriters can't vary the width of characters. So typefaces such as Courier are *non-proportional*—all characters take up the same amount of space (there's considerable white space between the letter *i* and surrounding letters). Non-proportional fonts are also called *monospaced*.

Computers, though, can produce varied spacing between letters, and your final product will look more professional if you take advantage of typefaces that vary character widths. (You can even make fine adjustments to letter spacing by hand, called *kerning*, if you wish.)

Why avoid Courier and other monospaced fonts like Prestige for body text? Studies have shown that proportional fonts (most computer typefaces are proportional) can be read 30 percent faster and use about 35 percent less paper because each character takes up only as much room as necessary. Proportional fonts are easier to read because the varying width of the characters results in greater differences in *word shapes*. And that's one more visual clue (in addition to serifs and character line-width variations).

 Courier, however, is quite readable as a screen font. Many people like to use it while writing or editing in their word processor. Then, when they print it, they choose Edit I Select All and change the entire text to Times New Roman.

Additional Typefaces

If you can manage it, acquire twenty or thirty additional typefaces beyond the ones that come with Windows. You'll have an easier time creating the appropriate look and feel in your documents if you have more than the three basic Windows fonts: sans serif (Arial), serif (Times) and typewriter (Courier).

What typefaces should you use? It depends on your goals, but here are some general guidelines. Garamond, perhaps the oldest typeface, is still extremely popular. It was created during the Renaissance, and shares with other fonts of that period (such as italics) the influence of handwriting. Garamond will probably be around as long as people use Western alphabets. It's an excellent all-around choice for body text. Another good face for body text is Palatino. The somewhat less antique-looking Times (Roman or Dutch) faces are also strong choices for body text.

You might be puzzled if you buy a set of typefaces and discover names such as *Gourmand* instead of *Garamond,* or *Palomino* for *Palatino, or Helvitica for Helvetica.* The reason for this is that laws have become so dense that even individual words can now be trademarked. Some companies that design typefaces have registered the names of the classic faces. In effect, they *own* words like Garamond. As we all know, legislators legislate but rarely repeal laws. So we are coated with new laws like a mist.

When I worked for a publishing company, one of our divisions printed books on antiques and collectibles. I was stunned to discover that the word *official* had been co-opted by a rival publishing house—the word itself was copyrighted. In essence, we could not use the word *official* in the title of any of our books, no matter how accurate that adjective might have been. If we got Erte to put together a book of his own art, we couldn't have called it the "official" book.

So, given that typefaces are sometimes called something else than their real name, how do you know what typeface you're dealing with? Often, the manufacturer will coyly include the real name by saying "Gourmond, similar to Garamond." The other way to tell is to write Adobe, the big typeface company, and ask for their official list of faces. Then look at the uppercase Q and the ampersand (&) character. These two characters are quite distinctive in each face, and if your characters match theirs, you've got it.

The Goudy and Caslon typefaces have fallen into disfavor these days because to some eyes they look fussy and out-of-date.

AaBb&Qq	Garamond
AaBb&Qq	Palatino
AaBb&Qq	Times Roman
AaBb&Qq	Goudy Hundred
AaBb&Qq	Goudy Old-Style
AaBb&Qq	Caslon
AaBb&Qq	USA Light
AaBb&Qq	**USA Black**
AaBb&Qq	Optima

Figure 12-25: *Excellent alternative typefaces you might want to add to those Windows supplies.*

Ornate Typefaces

During the dark ages, swarms of monks were spending their lives copying devotional texts, prayer books and the Bible. These monks wouldn't leave well enough alone. They drew pictures in the margins and even created elaborate decorative letters. You could still see the basic shape of the letter, but it was filled and surrounded by grapes, stars, angels in flight or whatever seemed good at the time.

Then whole new alphabets were designed featuring acrobats twisted into letter shapes, typefaces made out of flowers, and all the rest. If it bends, somebody sometime has used it to design letters. Nowadays, though, these arty typefaces are rarely used.

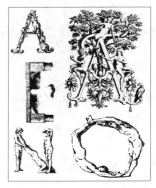

Figure 12-26: *Decorative typefaces have been out of fashion since the art-deco period in the 1930s.*

Script typefaces, like other ornate typefaces, have very few uses—namely wedding invitations and certain kinds of restaurant menus. Script unashamedly tries to look like fancy handwriting. For several centuries, but ending in Edwardian times, it was possible to hire somebody to hand-letter your calling cards and the invitations to your balls.

Hand lettering can be quite elegant. Mechanically imitated, the results are, at best, faux elegant. Besides, who has handwriting like that these days, with all those flourishes and tight curls? The script typeface has joined the lace hanky in that museum of things that are too much trouble and too ornate for our contemporary lifestyle. Forget script, unless, of course, you throw balls.

Figure 12-27: *Except for weddings and French restaurants, you won't see script typefaces.*

Type Size

Most applications and printers feature *scaleable* typefaces. This means that you can print text at virtually any size from tiny "mouse type" (4 or 6 points, used for Registered Trademark legalese) to huge headlines (72 points, for example). What are *points*? A point is a unit of measurement (1/72 of an inch) that typesetters use to specify the size of characters.

Two things to remember about type size. You'll normally want to limit yourself to perhaps three or four different sizes per publication. Too many different sizes will confuse the reader and make your pages look cluttered and disorganized. (The same problem occurs when you use too many different typefaces. In both cases, the reader ends up having less confidence in the professionalism and message of your publication. It's rather like the effect you'd have on people if you wore several unrelated garments.)

The second point to consider is that the typeface should be appropriate to the space allotted to it on the page. If you use a small typeface within a large white area, the effect is oddly disconcerting. And equally upsetting is a large typeface within too little white space.

Type Weight

You normally don't want to use more than two or three typefaces in a given publication. More than four and you start to get that kidnap note effect. However, you can add variety without creating a cluttered confused look by selecting different type *weights*. Some fonts come in several weights, meaning variations in the width of the strokes and the width of the letters. These alternatives are similar to the difference between Arial and Arial Bold. However, weight variations go beyond boldface to offer thin (condensed), very thick (black) and other styles. You'll see alternative type weights listed together in a family, for example:

Garamond Light
Garamond Condensed Light
Garamond Book
Garamond Condensed Book
Garamond Book Italic
Garamond Bold
Garamond Bold Italic
Garamond Ultra

Spacing

Leading

You can add an avant-garde look to your publication by using a sans serif typeface for body text. However, because of the lack of character differentiation, you should make the lines fairly far apart (heavy *leading*). "Leading" means widening or narrowing the white space between lines of text.

Body text can be set in sans-serif (like this Arial), but you should provide extra white space–leading–between the lines.

Figure 12-28: *Put extra white space between the lines if you use sans serif for body text.*

Interestingly, you do the opposite with headlines. Lines of text in headlines often look too loose and disconnected unless you pull them closer together by reducing the default leading. If you don't remove extra white space, readers may think that each line in the headline is a separate topic.

**HEADLINES LOOK
BEST TIGHTENED**

**HEADLINES LOOK
BEST TIGHTENED**

Figure 12-29: *Reduce white space between the lines of headlines and subheads to tighten and unify the message.*

Paragraph spacing

In addition to the distance between lines of text, you can also adjust the space between paragraphs. Adding a little white space here can open up your document and make it appear less formidable to the reader. Sure, this change is psychological and illusory (there's still just as much text to read), but many contemporary readers prefer their text in bite-size pieces. Spaced, the information appears more easily absorbed.

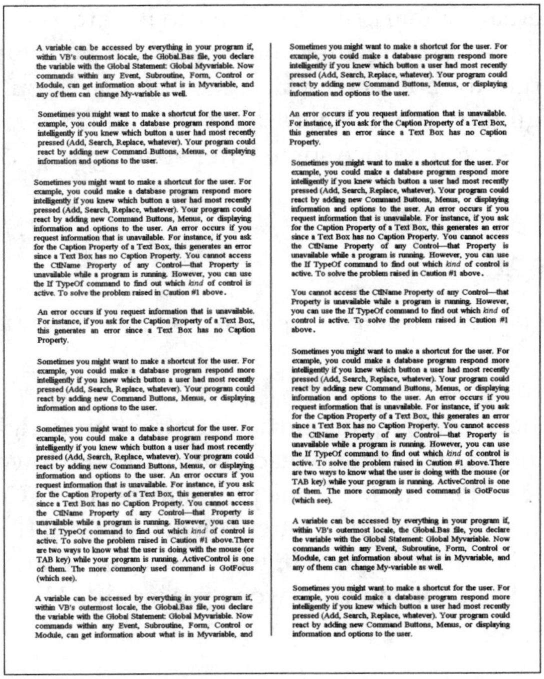

Figure 12-30: *Thanks to MTV, USA Today and other influences, readers increasingly prefer paragraphs that are separated by some extra white space because it makes the text look less demanding.*

Kerning

Most typefaces (except Courier and a few other monospaced typefaces) have variations in the spaces between the letters. *Kerning* allows you to make additional adjustments to the space between letters—specifically to bring certain letters closer together. Kerning is almost exclusively applied to headlines, where the large size of the letters and their relative positions is so visible.

If you kern your headlines, your work will look more professional and be more readable. Studies have shown that people don't read individual letters within words. Instead, most readers glance at each word and, almost instantly, recognize the shape of the entire word. If you tighten some of its interior spaces, you graphically emphasize that word's unique shape.

You don't need to kern everything, but if some characters in a headline look too loosely spaced to you, a little manual adjustment is called for. Kerning is usually applied in only two situations: where a capital letter is next to a lowercase letter or with punctuation. When an uppercase letter overhangs a lowercase letter, often an unseemly gap of white space appears between them. If you pull the lowercase letter slightly under the overhang, the results are much better. Kerning is also commonly used to tighten the space between a punctuation mark and the letter to its left.

You should adjust letter spacing after you've selected your typeface. The general rule is, the larger (or bolder) the face, the less space you'll need between letters for legibility. What's more, large or bold faces can have a checkerboard look unless you reduce some letter spacing.

This Was Not Kerned
This Was Kerned

Figure 12-31: *After kerning, the headline on the bottom is better looking and more readable.*

In Figure 12-31, notice how we paid particular attention to tightening the space between the initial capital letter of each word and the lowercase letter immediately following it: *Wa* and *Ke*. Some programs, such as CorelDRAW, make hand-kerning easy; you just drag letters on screen until the spacing looks good. It's somewhat more tedious in word processors, and each has a different approach. To kern, look in your word processor's Help | Search for Kerning or Letter Spacing.

Margins & Gutters

Besides the spacing of individual letters, lines and paragraphs, we should also consider the space around text. How much white space should you use at the top, bottom and sides of your page?

You don't want to push your text right to the edges of your pages. Unless you are designing a dictionary or other reference text, you'll want to leave a reasonable margin on all four sides of every page. People will read your publication, not look things up in it. And most readers don't want to be blasted with a mass of gray text. They want the text framed with white and often lightened further with graphics and other design elements.

Justification

People often find ragged-right columns (also called *left justification*) easier to read for several reasons. Since there is some leeway in line length, the computer doesn't have to add extra spaces in between words. These extra spaces can sometimes be quite large; sometimes only a single, long word appears on a line. This makes a page look spotty and distracts the eye while reading.

In the old days (before 1970) most text was typeset pretty much the way it had for hundreds of years—each line was built up of metal letters and metal spaces. When done by hand, justification could be achieved via subtle adjustments within the text. True justification is attractive and relatively easy to read.

In the old days (before 1970) most text was typeset pretty much the way it had for hundreds of years—each line was built up of metal letters and metal spaces. When done by hand, justification could be achieved via subtle adjustments within the text. True justification is attractive and relatively easy to read.

Figure 12-32: *Avoid justification (as in the lower paragraph here) unless you have a good reason to use it.*

Also, ragged-right decreases hyphenation and split words are always a distraction, an interruption of the thinking process. Finally, when lines are irregular in length, the eye can more easily find its place when leaving the end of one line and locating the start of the next line.

Full justification offers two primary advantages. It lends a kind of credibility to the text. Although the pages may look more stiff and more gray, fully justified type is still widely used in some kinds of business and other publications, perhaps for the same reason that suits and ties are still thought essential to convey sufficient *gravitas* if one is employed in certain professions. The second advantage of full justification is that it saves money. You can print the same amount of information on fewer pages.

Sinks

A *sink*, or *drop*, is the upper margin of a page. A fairly large upper margin can open up your design and is currently the fashion in page design. Just be sure that your sinks are the same on every page of your publication.

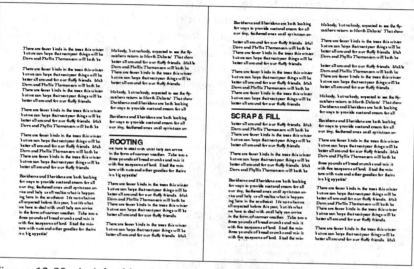

Figure 12-33: *A sink adds white space at the top and makes your pages look less threatening to the reader. But avoid uneven sinks as shown here.*

Notice that the drops in Figure 12-33 are not equal. Unless the page on the left is the start of an article and you include a headline, the different top margins break up the flow of your design. They just don't look right. Although your sinks (like all margins) should be the same from page to page, it's also a good idea to sometimes invade the sink with a photo or other graphic. Like other "space violations," this adds depth and dimension to your work.

Bleeds

A *bleed* can be text, a rule, a graphic—whatever is incompletely visible or falls partly off the page. Like other "dimensional effects," bleeds have become increasingly fashionable, particularly in advertising where you want to suggest that the product explodes beyond normal boundaries. But bleeds can also create interesting graphic effects when you use them with some restraint.

Figure 12-34: *Something that extends off the page is called a* bleed.

The easiest way to create a bleed is to crop (chop off part of a graphic or text), and position it at an extreme edge of the page. You also can use this approach to bleed characters, photos, and so on.

Common Pitfalls

Now that we've covered the main elements of design, let's look at the pitfalls, those things you should check before actually publishing. We'll start with several common problems (with uncommon names like *tombstones* and *orphans*) and then move on to more general issues such as contrast, variety and taste.

Some polishing (looking for crowding or dangling words, for example) is merely a matter of knowing what to look for, and some pitfalls are often quite simple to correct. Other things such as taste and appropriateness are more abstract; they are often harder to spot and sometimes harder to correct. Nevertheless, a good last check of your design can be what separates a clumsy amateurish publication from one that will make you proud.

A Final Checklist

Before you desktop publish a piece of work, take a break. Then print it out and look at it as if you were a reader seeing it for the first time. One approach is to check the details first: search for widows and orphans, tombstones, crowding, inappropriate typefaces, badly designed headlines and so on.

Then, when you've cleaned up the small problems, ask the big questions: Does the design make you want to read it? Is it spacious enough and inviting to the reader? Is there enough contrast and variety? Is it tasteful, yet exciting? Is the look appropriate to the topic?

Of course, you should first ask these big questions in the early stages of creating your design. For example, a design that looks respectable and solid for an official company annual report would probably be too formal for an in-house newsletter. Using this final checklist, you can make sure that you've achieved your goals. It's still not too late to make revisions. With contemporary word processors, even some major revisions can be accomplished relatively quickly, such as changing typefaces, adding space between lines, moving graphics and so on.

It's in the Details

An author will seem less credible to a reader if his or her writing contains misspellings, bad punctuation or poor grammar. These are details, but they are important details. Similarly, a publication containing widows, free-floating headlines or unreadable captions will discourage readers. The problem is one of *translation*. People don't mind puzzles when they're in the mood, but they resent it if you give them puzzles for no good reason, especially puzzles caused by mere sloppiness on your part.

When spelling or punctuation is wrong, it's briefly puzzling; it stops the reader and requires a momentary translation. A single sentence is bad enough, but keep this up across paragraphs and pages, and sooner or later you'll lose your reader. Most readers just won't take the time to translate your custom spelling into English they can understand. And if your publication contains graphic sloppiness—hard-to-read typefaces, crowded headlines, too many boxes, whatever—readers will also find your work tedious.

In the following sections, we'll look at the most common flaws in desktop publishing design. In each case, we'll state the problem—showing you what to look for—then provide suggested solutions. There are almost always several solutions to design problems, so if you solve the problem in a way we're not suggesting here, all the better. Let your imagination and common sense guide you.

Widows & Orphans

Problem: Your page will look visually rough if the page or a column within the page starts or ends with a line less than half as long as the rest of the lines in the column. A small piece of text at the start is called an *orphan*; one at the end is called a *widow*. Orphans tend to look worse than widows, but both are unpleasant, messy and usually easy to fix. Like a thread dangling off someone's pants or a piece of toilet paper stuck to a shoe, they look untidy and attract the eye for no good reason. You want to control where your readers' eyes go, not distract them with meaningless visual debris.

Solution: Editing text is the easiest way to get rid of widows and orphans. Either you or the writer should edit the text. That's the easiest fix. Adding a word somewhere in the same paragraph or taking out a word or two should solve the problem. For example, in Figure 12-35, we could get rid of the widow by changing *eliminated* to *fixed*. If you cannot edit text, adjust other elements of the page, such as paragraph spacing, to eliminate the offending extra bit of text. Thicker space between paragraphs should force a widow up to the next column or page. Thinner spacing will bring an orphan back.

> When a column
> (or page) ends with
> a short line, it's
> called a widow. This
> is considered poor
> design and should
> be eliminated by
> you.

Figure 12-35: *A* widow *is a too-short line at the end of a page or column.*

> more.
> Columns (or pages) that
> start with a short line
> are confusing. So you
> should try to get rid of
> any of these orphans
> you find in your work
> after it is formatted.

Figure 12-36: *An* orphan *is a too-short line at the start of a page or column.*

A second solution is to let your word processor eliminate widows and orphans for you. WordPerfect 6.0, for instance, has a feature called Widow and Orphan Protect. Word 6.0 prevents widows and orphans by default. If you want to make these adjustments yourself, turn off the Widow/Orphan Control option in Word's Format | Paragraph | Text Flow window.

Allowing your word processor to manage this problem, though, can result in some odd-looking spacing. For the best-looking results, you might want to edit the text yourself rather than permitting your word processor to automate the process.

Tombstones

Tombstones result from too much symmetry in your design.

Figure 12-37: *When subheads line up, the result is a set of* tombstones.

Problem: When your subheads line up and especially if the columns also match, you've got a case of bad symmetry. The result looks like a set of tombstones in a churchyard (see Figure 12-37). Readers can get confused about what goes with what: do you read the lined-up subheads horizontally across the page? Is this page organized horizontally instead of vertically (as the columns imply)?

Figure 12-38: *Stagger your subheads to get rid of tombstones.*

Solution: Add or subtract some text, change the typeface or type size, move a subhead to a new location or take some other action that will stagger the subheads. Your subheads should help organize sections of the text. To do this, they must be placed at irregular intervals—not lined up side-by-side on the page.

Crowding

Problem: Trying to fit too much on a page is false efficiency. Readers don't like gray pages with little white space. You want people to read what you publish, so don't try to save paper by cramming things together. You'll end up wasting the paper if they toss your work away unread.

intelligently if you knew which button a user had most recently pressed (Add, Search, Replace, whatever). Your program could react by adding new Command Buttons, Menus, or displaying information and options to the user.

Before you Sand

Sometimes you might want to make a shortcut for the user. For example, you could make a database program respond more intelligently if you knew which button a user had most recently pressed (Add, Search, Replace, whatever). Your program could react by adding new Command Buttons, Menus, or displaying information and options to the user.

Sometimes you might want to make a shortcut for the user. For example, you could make a database program respond more intelligently if you knew which button a user had most recently pressed (Add, Search, Replace, whatever). Your program could react by adding new Command Buttons, Menus, or displaying information and options to the user. An error occurs if you request information that is unavailable. For instance, if you ask for the Caption Property of a Text Box, this generates an error since a Text Box has no Caption Property. You cannot access the CtlName Property of any Control—that Property is unavailable while a program is running. However, you can use the If TypeOf command to find out which *kind* of control is active.

An error occurs if you request information that is unavailable. For instance, if you ask for the Caption Property of a Text Box, Sometimes you might want to make a shortcut for the user. For example, you could make a database program respond more intelligently if you knew which button a user had most recently pressed (Add, Search, Replace, whatever). Your program could react by adding new Command Buttons, Menus, or displaying information and options to the user.

Hand Finishing

Sometimes you might want to make a shortcut for the user. For example, you could make a database program respond more intelligently if you knew which button a user had most recently pressed (Add, Search, Replace, whatever). Your program could react by adding new Command Buttons, Menus, or displaying information and options to the user. An error occurs if you request information that is unavailable. For instance, if you ask for the Caption Property of a Text Box, this generates an error since a Text Box has no Caption Property. You cannot access the CtlName Property of any Control—that Property is unavailable while a program is running. However, you can use the If TypeOf command to find out which *kind* of control is active. To solve the problem raised in Caution #1 above.There are two ways to know what the user is doing with the mouse (or TAB key) while your program is running. ActiveControl is one of them. The more commonly used command is GotFocus (which see).

A variable can be accessed by everything in your program if, within VB's outermost locale, the Global.Bas file, you declare the variable with the Global Statement: Global Myvariable. Now commands within any Event, Subroutine, Form, Control or Module, can get information about what is in Myvariable, and the variable with the Global Statement: Global Myvariable. Now commands within any Event, Subroutine, Form, Control or Module, can get information about what is in Myvariable, and

An error occurs if you request information that is unavailable. For instance, if you ask for the Caption Property of a Text Box, this generates an error since a Text Box has no Caption Property.

Sometimes you might want to make a shortcut for the user. For example, you could make a database program respond more intelligently if you knew which button a user had most recently pressed (Add, Search, Replace, whatever). Your program could react by adding new Command Buttons, Menus, or displaying information and options to the user. An error occurs if you Sometimes you might want to make a shortcut for the user. For example, you could make a database program respond more intelligently if you knew which button a user had most recently pressed (Add, Search, Replace, whatever). Your program could react by adding new Command Buttons, Menus, or displaying information and options to the user. An error occurs if you

Sawdust & Grit

request information that is unavailable. For instance, if you ask for the Caption Property of a Text Box, this generates an error since a Text Box has no Caption Property. You cannot access the CtlName Property of any Control—that Property is unavailable while a program is running. However, you can use the If TypeOf command to find out which *kind* of control is active. To solve the problem raised in Caution #1 above.

You cannot access the CtlName Property of any Control—that Property is unavailable while a program is running. However, you can use the If TypeOf command to find out which *kind* of control is active. To solve the problem raised in Caution #1 Sometimes you might want to make a shortcut for the user. For example, you could make a database program respond more intelligently if you knew which button a user had most recently pressed (Add, Search, whatever). Your program could react by adding new Command Buttons, Menus, or displaying information and options to the user. An error occurs if you request information that is unavailable. For instance, if you ask for the Caption Property of a Text Box, this generates an error since a Text Box has no Caption Property. You cannot access the CtlName Property of any Control—that Property is unavailable while a program is running. However, you can use the If TypeOf command to find out which *kind* of control is active. To solve the problem raised in Caution #1 above.There are two ways to know what the user is doing with the mouse (or TAB key) while your program is running. ActiveControl is one of them. The more commonly used command is GotFocus (which see).

Against the Grain

A variable can be accessed by everything in your program if, within VB's outermost locale, the Global.Bas file, you declare the variable with the Global Statement: Global Myvariable. Now commands within any Event, Subroutine, Form, Control or Module, can get information about what is in Myvariable, and any of them can change My-variable as well.

Sometimes you might want to make a shortcut for the user. For example, you could make a database program respond more intelligently if you knew which button a user had most recently the variable with the Global Statement: Global Myvariable. Now commands within any Event, Subroutine, Form, Control or Module, can get information about what is in Myvariable, and

Figure 12-39: *This example has too little white space around the text and headlines.*

Solution: Spread the work over enough pages to allow sufficient white space so your work is easy to read and its organization is clear. Provide generous margins, white space above heads and subheads, and extra space between columns.

Typewriter Effects

```
Avoid the Courier typeface. It's the
font that's used by most typewriters
and each character is monospaced--taking
up the same amount of space as all the
others.  With Courier, your pages will
look as if they had been cranked out in
the basement of the rec hall.  Also,
remove double spaces after periods as
well as underlining.
```

Avoid the *Courier* typeface. It's the font that's used by most typewriters and each character is monospaced—taking up the same amount of space as all the others. With *Courier*, your pages will look as if they had been cranked out in the basement of the rec hall. Also, remove double spaces after periods as well as underlining.

Figure 12-40: *You should avoid the summer camp newsletter look (top). Stick with the professional typeset appearance of the second paragraph.*

Problem: If your work looks typewritten, it will look amateurish. Most people are still taught typing on a typewriter. As a result, you might be given a text file that contains typewriter effects that look unprofessional. For one thing, these people often type two spaces after each period to separate sentences. They'll also use two hyphens (--) instead of a dash (—). They'll underline instead of *italicizing* and use the monospaced Courier typeface.

Before computers, these compromises were necessary because most typewriters cannot adjust letter spacing, make dashes or create italics. But you shouldn't let these pre-desktop publishing remnants degrade the look of your work.

Most typefaces include two classic types of dashes (in addition to the hyphen): the em dash and the en dash. The em dash is longer than the en dash (just as the letter *m* is wider than the letter *n*). In whatever typeface at whatever type size, the em dash is a line the width of the letter *m;* and the en dash, of the letter *n*.

You can use either the long or short dash in your effort to eliminate double hyphens (see Figure 12-40), but some people consider the long dash unattractive and too extreme. Also, it is common practice to surround the short dash by spaces but to leave the long dash butted up against the text it separates. It's—this as opposed to - this.

Solution: First, don't use the Courier typeface. Most typewriters use this typeface, and each character takes up the same amount of space. With Courier, your pages will look as if they had been cranked out in the basement of the recreation hall at summer camp. Second, if people give you text containing two spaces between sentences, double hyphens or underlining, use your word processor's search-and-replace feature to get rid of them.

Inch Marks

Problem: Another holdover from typewriters is using inch marks (") for quotation marks (" and "). Within body text, inch marks can, in fact, be less distracting than true (non-symmetrical) double quotation marks. However, for headlines or other larger text, always take the time to insert true quotation marks. In a larger, bolder typeface, inch marks look crude. And true quotation marks look better in body text, too, if the publication is a more formal document such as catalog of elegant antiques.

Solution: Replace the inch marks by hand. You can insert special characters (such as a true dash or curved open and close quotation marks) with Windows Character Map accessory. See Chapter 10. However, some word processsors, such as Word for Windows 6.0, include an option that automatically inserts "Smart Quotes." However, you have to select this option prior to writing.

Too Much Indent

Problem: Another holdover from typewriting is the five-space indent at the start of a paragraph. The standard typewritten tab is five spaces, often too wide for a good typeset look.

> Before you desktop publish a piece of work, check for the various odd effects that might detract from the look of the document.
>
> Then, after you clean up the smaller problems, consider the big questions.
>
> Before you desktop pub-lish a piece of work, check for the various odd effects that might detract from the look of the document.
> Then, after you clean up the smaller problems, con-sider the big questions.

Figure 12-41: *With narrow columns, use narrow indentation.*

Solution: Many publications look better if you eliminate indentations at the start of paragraphs. Instead, separate your paragraphs with a blank line. This is particularly effective if your text is fully justified with a straight right margin. In that case, just don't indent at all.

If you do want to use indentation to signal the start of paragraphs, make them fairly narrow, particularly if you are using columns. The rule of thumb is that the narrower the column, the narrower the indentation should be. To remove extra indentation with the search-and-replace feature in your word processor, you need to find out whether the typist inserted tabs or five actual space characters. Move your cursor to the start of one of the indents and press the Right arrow key. If the cursor leaps to the first character, that's a tab.

"Creative" White Space

Problem: You can annoy people visually in many ways, and one of them is to use random, uneven spacing. This can be subheads unevenly spaced between sections of the text, uneven columns, using different margins on different pages, captions that are wider than the photo they describe, or strange geometric sections of text (you abandoned good taste and made a paragraph fit into the shape of a circle).

The fact that some word processors allow you to type a paragraph in the shape of a pyramid doesn't mean you should. Doing so would be like "creative" torturing of food—cooking pressed chopped ham in the shape of a fish. Serve that and most people are puzzled rather than pleased.

Solution: Look closely at all your margins, both around the edge of the page and between any columns. Adjust unequal margins. Look at captions; make sure they are the same width as the photo they describe. Are subheads equally spaced: fairly tight against the text beneath them? And you haven't poured a paragraph into some odd geometric shape, have you?

Torture Art: When Inspiration Goes Wrong

As we all know, there's a category of creativity called *torture art*. The usual examples are efforts to make a sculpture out of something inappropriate— building an Eiffel Tower out of toothpicks or hair or something. These efforts usually end up in "Believe it or not" museums, which is where they belong. One lesson to be learned from torture art: There is no necessary relationship between *effort* and *result*. If the original idea is daft, the result will be daft too, no matter how hard it was to accomplish.

Bad White

Problem: Sometimes white space can look bad. If you've surrounded a white area with text or a graphic, you've trapped, or "pooled," some white space. This white space serves no purpose and makes your page look blotchy. (See Figure 12-42.)

Before you Sand

An error occurs if you request information that is unavailable. For instance, if you ask for the Caption Property of a Text Box, this generates an error since a Text Box has no Caption Property.

Sometimes you might want to make a shortcut for the user. For example, you could make a database program respond more intelligently if you knew which button a user had most recently pressed (Add, Search, Replace, whatever). Your program could react by adding new Command Buttons, Menus, or displaying information and options to the user. An error occur if you

Hand Finishing

Sometimes you might want to make a shortcut for the user. For example, you could make a database program respond more intelligently if you knew which button a user had most recently pressed (Add, Search, Replace, whatever). Your program could react by adding new Command Buttons, Menus, or displaying information and options to the user. An error occurs if you request information that is unavailable. For instance, if you ask for the Caption Property of a Text Box, this generates an error since a Text Box has no Caption Property. You cannot access the CtlName Property of any Control—that Property is unavailable while a program is running. However, you can use the If TypeOf command to find out which *kind* of control is active. To solve the problem raised in Caution #1 above.There are two ways to know what the user is doing with the mouse (or TAB key) while your program is running. ActiveControl is one of them. The more commonly used command is GotFocus (which see).

A variable can be accessed by everything in your program if, within VB's outermost locale, the Global.Bas file, you declare the variable with the Global Statement: Global Myvariable. Now commands within any Event, Subroutine, Form, Control or Module, can get information about what is in Myvariable, and

Sawdust & Grit

request information that is unavailable. For instance, if you ask for the Caption Property of a Text Box, this generates an error since a Text Box has no Caption Property. You cannot access the CtlName Property of any Control—that Property is unavailable while a program is running. However, you can use the If TypeOf command to find out which *kind* of control is active. To solve the problem raised in Caution #1 above.

You cannot access the CtlName Property of any Control—that Property is unavailable while a program is running. However, you can use the If TypeOf command to find out which *kind* of control is active. To solve the problem raised in Caution #1 Sometimes you might want to make a shortcut for the user. For example, you could make a database program respond more intelligently if you knew which button a user had most recently pressed (Add, Search, Replace, whatever). Your program could react by adding new Command Buttons, Menus, or displaying information and options to the user. An error occurs if you

Against the Grain

A variable can be accessed by everything in your program if, within VB's outermost locale, the Global.Bas file, you declare the variable with the Global Statement: Global Myvariable. Now commands within any Event, Subroutine, Form, Control or Module, can get information about what is in Myvariable, and any of them can change My-variable as well.

Sometimes you might want to make a shortcut for the user. For example, you could make a database program respond more intelligently if you knew which button a user had most recently

Figure 12-42: *This page contains bad white space between the subhead and the picture and also in two places in the right column.*

Woodworking

An error occurs if you request information that For instance, if you ask for the Caption Property of this generates an error since a Text Box has no Caption Property.

Sometimes you might want to make a shortcut for the user. For example, you could make a database program respond more intelligently if you knew which button a user had most recently pressed (Add, Search, Replace, whatever). Your program could react by adding new Command Buttons, Menus, or displaying information and options to the user. An error occurs if you

Sometimes you might want to make a shortcut for the user. For example, you could make a database program respond more intelligently if you knew which button a user had most recently pressed (Add, Search, Replace, whatever). Your program could react by adding new Command Buttons, Menus, or displaying information and options to the user. An error occurs if you

Hand Finishing

Sometimes you might want to make a shortcut for the user. For example, you could make a database program respond more intelligently if you knew which button a user had most recently pressed (Add, Search, Replace, whatever). Your program could react by adding new Command Buttons, Menus, or displaying information and options to the user. An error occurs if you request information that is unavailable. For instance, if you ask for the Caption Property of a Text Box, this generates an error since a Text Box has no Caption Property. You cannot access the CtlName Property of any Control—that Property is unavailable while a program is running. However, you can use the If TypeOf command to find out which *kind* of control is active. To solve the problem raised in Caution #1 above.There are two ways to know what the user is doing with the mouse (or TAB key) while your program is running. ActiveControl is one of them. The more commonly used command is GotFocus (which see).

A variable can be accessed by everything in your program if, within VB's outermost locale, the Global.Bas file, you declare the variable with the Global Statement: Global Myvariable. Now

Sawdust & Grit

request information that is unavailable. For instance, if you ask for the Caption Property of a Text Box, this generates an error since a Text Box has no Caption Property. You cannot access the CtlName Property of any Control—that Property is unavailable while a program is running. However, you can use the If TypeOf command to find out which *kind* of control is active. To solve the problem raised in Caution #1 above.

You cannot access the CtlName Property of any Control—that Property is unavailable while a program is running. However, you can use the If TypeOf command to find out which *kind* of control is active. To solve the problem raised in Caution #1 example, you could make a database program respond more intelligently if you knew which button a user had most recently pressed (Add, Search, Replace, whatever). Your program could react by adding new Command Buttons, Menus, or displaying information and options to the user. An error occurs if you request information that is unavailable. For instance, if you ask for the Caption Property of a Text Box, this generates an error since a Text Box has no Caption Property. You cannot access the CtlName Property of any Control—that Property is unavailable while a program is running. However, you can use the If TypeOf command to find out which *kind* of control is active. To solve the problem raised in Caution #1 above.There are two ways to know what the user is doing with the mouse (or TAB key) while your program is running. ActiveControl is one of them. The more commonly used command is GotFocus A variable can be accessed by everything in your program if, within VB's outermost locale, the Global.Bas file, you declare the variable with the Global Statement: Global Myvariable. Now

Figure 12-43: *Move text and graphics around to eliminate pooled white space.*

Solution: Adjust your text and graphics to eliminate this unsightly, interior white space. Enlarge a graphic or a headline's typeface. Or add new text or pull some text in from the following page. You could also insert a pullquote (a brief quotation from the text, set in larger type). Any of these approaches can eliminate the trapped white space.

The 8 1/2- x 11-Inch Squeeze

Problem: If your publication is going to be on standard 8 1/2- x 11-inch letter-size paper, this width is often too narrow for a three-column layout yet too wide for one column. With a single column, the lines stretch all the way across the page and are hard to read unless you double-space or use some other tactic. Recall that it's easier to locate the start of each new line if it's not too far from the end of the previous line.

With standard 8 1/2- x 11-inch paper, the best readability is achieved with two columns, but many official publications don't look good when broken into columns. Double columns suggest newsletters rather than corporate annual reports or financial plans. What to do?

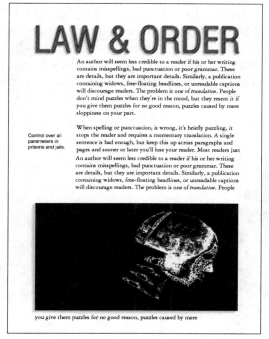

Figure 12-44: *Exterior subheads not only look good, this design is also quite readable.*

Solution: Create two columns, making the outside one narrower (perhaps one-third the width of the other column) with subheads. The wider inside column contains the text. This popular design solves the readability problem and also opens up the publication with considerable white space. Yet everything can fit well into the 8 1/2-inch limit.

Crowding & the Principle of Subtraction

Problem: At all-you-can-eat restaurants, you've seen people who don't seem to realize they can go back later. They fill their plate and then start a second layer, piling it into a mound. In fashion and design, layering rarely results in the grunge or Annie Hall look (to succeed, the layered look takes considerable care and taste). Instead, too much stuff in a page layout usually looks either gorged or accidental, as if things had crashed onto the page.

Your publication can get crowded for various reasons. Somebody might want to save paper and printing costs, and suggest that because your last page is only half full of text, why not make room for it in the earlier pages, eliminating the last page. Perhaps a writer can't cut a single precious word of his or her long article. Perhaps you're doing an ad, and your client wants you to include extensive descriptions of the product along with five customer testimonials. And he wants it all in a 6- x 4-inch space. Or maybe you've become so mesmerized with clip art, typefaces, boxes, reverses or other design elements that you're trying to put too many things into a single publication. Remember the old saying: There's no magic unless you do one trick at a time.

Figure 12-45: *Elaborate, lacy borders appealed to our great-grandparents.*

A hundred years ago, crowding wasn't a problem. It was the style. You've seen pictures of nineteenth-century parlors—crammed with horsehair-stuffed furniture dripping with doilies, figurines and vases on every level surface, walls jam packed with paintings. Publications followed this style. For the feel of a doily, designers placed complex border designs around nearly every ad. For the room full of furniture effect, ads often displayed the showroom, you saw every item the store had for sale.

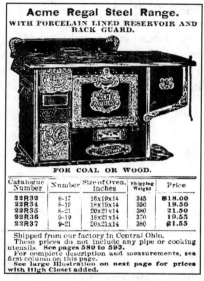

Acme Regal Steel Range.
WITH PORCELAIN LINED RESERVOIR AND BACK GUARD.

FOR COAL OR WOOD.

Catalogue Number	Number	Size of Oven, Inches	Shipping Weight	Price
22R32	8-17	16x19x14	345	$18.00
22R34	8-19	18x19x14	350	19.50
22R35	8-21	20x21x14	380	21.50
22R36	9-19	18x21x14	370	19.55
22R37	9-21	20x21x14	380	$1.55

Shipped from our factory in Central Ohio.
These prices do not include any pipe or cooking utensils. **See pages 580 to 593.**
For complete description and measurements, see first column on this page.
See large Illustration on next page for prices with High Closet added.

Figure 12-46: *One hundred years ago, advertisers didn't waste any space.*

This century we've gone in the opposite direction, stripping the decorations, gewgaws and frills so beloved by our great-grandparents. Instead, the trend—particularly in architecture and advertising-has been toward vast, clean spaces with no borders, often no pictures and few words. Gone are the gargoyles and flourishes. You need not strive for the clean, cold simplicity of the architecture of the past 50 years, but the modern eye is no longer accustomed to information and graphics packed into a page. We want at least some white space. Remember the maxim *less is more*, the essential precept of late twentieth-century style in architecture, clothing, publication design and practically everything else visual.

Solution: Subtraction. Many artists appreciate the computer simply because, aside from everything else it does, a computer allows you to easily and painlessly add and subtract words and pictures.

■ ■

The Magic of Delete & Undo

Do you recall what it was like to *type* a term paper? Before word processing, if you made a single mistake typing a page, you had to retype the whole page. Now you can rearrange text on screen with complete freedom. When it's just as you want it, print it. The same facility works with graphics.

Some designers use this trick: Put all kinds of things on the page. Then start taking things out until you've reached the degree of simplicity and cleanliness that looks pleasing and contemporary. Music composition, writing and graphic design have all been profoundly affected by computerization. Computers free the artist by giving him or her two powerful new tools: the commands *Delete* and *Undo*. And some programs, like Picture Publisher, offer *unlimited* Undo. Click on their Undo and you see a list of each change you've made to the original document. This way you can go back and undo any change.

■ ■

Variety & Balance

A perfectly symmetrical thing is, of course, always in balance; its components are equally distant from the four sides of the page and equidistant from each other. Although they are in perfect balance, they are also usually boring. In cooking, the only truly safe ingredient is water; it has no flavor, so it merely dilutes whatever you add it to. Similarly, too much symmetry can reduce your page design to blandness. You want to learn the tricks of placing things so they result in a good compromise between variety and balance.

How can you check for balance? Print a copy of your page, tape it to the wall and squint. Squinting blends the text elements into masses of gray so you can weigh them against the graphic elements as shapes. Your goal is to arrange these elements on the page so they don't tilt the page in any one direction. Turn your page upside down and then sideways. Does it hold together?

Figure 12-47: *Relentlessly symmetrical, this design is perfectly balanced but could be more lively.*

Figure 12-48: *After resizing and repositioning the elements, the page is now more compelling.*

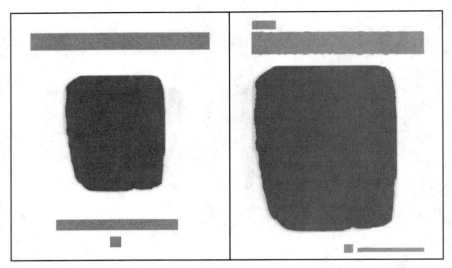

Figure 12-49: *Check balance by looking at your designs as if they were blocks of grays.*

Anti-Aliasing

Feathering, stroking, font smoothing—anti-aliasing goes by many names, but the idea is to get rid of the notorious "stairstep effect." Straight vertical or horizontal lines always look great. But diagonal lines get ragged in the digital domain.

Diagonal text (or graphic lines) looks rough when displayed onscreen or printed because a computer monitor or printer creates text out of individual pixels or dots. You can easily visualize the problem if you dump a few hundred postage stamps on a table and then try to put them together to display your initials. If your name is Iris Thomas, no problem. *IT* can be constructed so all the lines of the letters line up clean and straight. But if your name is Nick Carson, part of the *N* and most of the *C* will be impossible to make smooth without resorting to scissors. No matter how many stamps you use (the more stamps, the higher the resolution), you'll always get what looks like a stairstep along diagonal lines.

Figure 12-50: *The horizontal lines in the Z are clean, but curved or diagonal lines are "stairstepped."*

A remedy is available, but it's not a cure-all. Anti-aliasing is an option offered in many word processing programs. When you select anti-aliasing, diagonal lines are smoothed in two or more ways. If possible, smaller squares are used to reduce the sawtooth effect. Also, some of the squares are lightened so the diagonal line seems to blend less abruptly into the background.

Figure 12-51: *Compare this anti-aliased* C *to the more ragged one in Figure 12-50.*

Figure 12-52: *A close-up of the top of the letter* C. *The smaller squares and gray-shading show up in the anti-aliased character on the right.*

One drawback to anti-aliasing is that it blurs the text, making your work look somewhat out of focus. It's a trade-off. In general, today's monitors and printers have high enough resolution that they automatically use very small pixels or dots when creating diagonal lines. They already look good enough; the stairstep effect isn't bothersome. The only thing anti-aliasing can contribute to most contemporary high resolution monitors and printers is to add a haze of gray to diagonal lines. The bottom line: you might want to leave anti-aliasing off. When you print out your work to see how it's going to look when published, see if you notice any bad stairstepping. If you do, try it again with anti-aliasing turned on. See if the blurring is worse than the stairstepping. It's your choice whether you want anti-aliasing on for normal viewing on your monitor during your ordinary work.

How do you turn on anti-aliasing? Different graphics applications call it by different names. Try looking in Help I Index under Font to see if there's an entry for "Smoothing." Or try to find "feathering" or "stroking" or "font smoothing."

Plus! The Best Solution

In addition to the anti-aliasing in many Windows 95 applications, Microsoft Plus for Windows 95 also offers it via an option called *font smoothing*. This feature works well because it applies smoothing only when the typeface is of particular sizes. It doesn't just smooth everything, thereby smearing ordinary body text sizes.

Plus! is an optional set of tools, desktop designs, pointer styles, sounds and other useful, well-designed features. To change Font smoothing if you have installed the Plus!, right-click on the desktop. Select Properties and click on the Plus! tab.

Recall that anti-aliasing of normal body text sizes (12 point and smaller) can make the text appear out of focus. That's one of the reasons the font smoothing option in Plus! selectively applies anti-aliasing. For larger-sized text (usually, above 18 pixels per em, or *ppem*), it can really help. Try loading a PowerPoint slide show on a projection monitor using font smoothing and see how good the text looks. (To see it, you'll need a color card that supports at least 16 bits per pixel color depth. Or just turn it on and see if it helps in almost every Windows 95 application. You get the best of both worlds: anti-aliasing when it's needed, plain text when that's sharpest.)

Anti-aliasing also is handy for extremely small text on the screen (*Greeking*). At sizes less than 6 pixels per em, turning off hinting but turning on anti-aliasing actually makes the text appear legible. Remember that people tend to read by recognizing word shapes rather than individual letters. So if you turn on font smoothing in Plus!, you'll find three major cutoff points for the font smoothing option:

0 to 6 ppem:	Turn on anti-aliasing, turn off hinting.
7 ppem to 18 ppem:	Turn off anti-aliasing, turn on hinting.
18 ppem on up:	Turn on anti-aliasing, turn on hinting.

Of course, these specifications are for normal roman text. Italics and boldface have different cutoffs, as do non-Western glyphs such as Kanji. In any case, you can further refine the selectivity of font smoothing if you want to. You can override the system's default behavior by whacking some values in the Registry.

Moving On

Appropriately enough, our next subject is the printer. We'll cover what's new in Windows 95, how to install a printer, set it up, adjust its properties, control print jobs and, in general, get the most out of this most useful computer peripheral.

Focus on Hardware

Chapter 13

The Printer

What you'll likely notice first about printing under Windows 95 is that it's smooth—it doesn't tie the computer up very much. Printing now mostly works in the background. After a brief pause, you can get back to typing or drawing or whatever you were doing. Underneath, essentially unnoticed, the text or graphic that you sent is being fed automatically to the printer. And, in its own good time, the printer will eject the results.

In earlier versions of Windows and DOS, sending something to the printer would "freeze" the computer—you couldn't use the keyboard or mouse. You were locked out until the job was well along, or even finished.

Some people, particularly those printing images and drawings (which take so long to print), bought *spoolers*, which were like a small, computerized memory bank that you plugged in between your computer and the printer. When you printed something, it would flow into the spooler. This gave you back your computer so you could use it while the printing job was completed. The spooler sent the information to the printer as fast as possible.

To be fair to printers, they have a tough job. It takes much longer to physically make marks on paper in the material world than it takes to bounce electrons off your monitor screen in the "virtual" world of the computer. Printers must "organize" and interpret what they print. They can accept only so much data at one time. Another delay is caused by the great number of different printers people can attach to their computers. A color-capable Epson printer expects a different "code" than a Hewlett-Packard LaserJet II to alert it to make the next letters italic rather than normal. This delay is caused by the fact that Windows 95 supports over 800 different printer models (Windows 3.1 supported only 300). But, in any case, your text or graphics must flow through a filter that explains to your particular printer (via a code) that italics is now expected. Windows uses *drivers* to flow data from the computer into the printer. This process also takes time.

A *driver* is software, a kind of specialized computer program that governs a video card, a printer or other peripheral. Some drivers are supplied by the manufacturer and are copied into Windows's system folder when you install a new peripheral. (This is why you sometimes see Have Disk as an option on some property sheets.) Other drivers are built into Windows 95 itself.

Windows uses an Enhanced Metafile language to describe how to build a printed page. A *metafile* contains a description of your text or image rather than a literal picture like a dot-for-dot copy of the original. A description might say: draw a 2- x 3-inch rectangle 5 inches down from the top and 3.45 inches over from the left; then fill it with blue dots.

The printer driver is responsible for converting the metafile to the codes used by a particular printer. With no buffering, this conversion takes up all the computer's time, resulting in a seemingly "frozen" computer while the printing churns out.

In Windows 3.x, the Print Manager applet could make printing appear to occur "in the background," allowing you to continue using your computer while it prints. Instead of feeding the printer codes directly to the printer, they are stored on the hard drive, and Print Manager *spools* a little bit of this data to the printer every so often (during moments when you're not typing or editing). By cooperating with other running programs, Print Manager created the illusion of background print spooling, even though this method does increase the overall time it takes for the document to print.

Windows 95 improves on the old Print Manager spooler in several ways. First of all, it's written using 32-bit programming and is fully integrated into the printing system. As a result, it *multitasks* much better (allows you to do other things with the computer at the same time it's working). It also doesn't require running a separate "print manager" program. Thanks to the new printing system, you don't notice as much halting or jerkiness if you are scrolling through a document, for example, while printing.

Second, instead of waiting for the printer driver to convert the entire metafile to a spool file, it can spool the Enhanced Metafile first. That way, the printer driver can do its work in the background. (Some printers can even accept Enhanced Metafiles directly.) You can also set up a printer to start printing as soon as the first page is spooled, so you don't have to wait as long for printing to begin. It can simultaneously print and add new data to the spool file. All of these changes make printing with Windows 95 smoother and more efficient than it was with Windows 3.1.

You can also set up a printer to avoid Enhanced Metafile (EMF) spooling, in case this process causes problems with a particular program. After all, it's a new technology. With *raw* spooling, printing works similarly to Windows 3.1; the entire metafile is first converted to printer codes, which are then spooled to the hard drive for background printing. PostScript printers already use a special type of metafile—a PostScript program file—to describe a page's layout to the printer. That's why PostScript printers don't have a separate EMF spooling method; they always use raw spooling.

Setting Up a Printer

When you first install Windows on your computer, Windows tries to determine what peripherals you have attached to your machine. It looks for a video card, a modem and so on. However, until the new Plug and Play technology is further along, Windows can't always determine which printer you use. Increasingly, printers also report themselves for Plug and Play duty, via a bi-directional printer port that permits two-way communication between the computer and printer, so your printer can sometimes be installed automatically by Windows. If not, Windows presents you with a list of the over 800 printers it can "talk to." From this list, you are asked to specify which brand and model you use.

However, you might install a new printer months after setting up Windows 95. (Some people have two printers attached to their computers—one for high-quality business letters and graphics, one for quick rough drafts, or one for color.) Indeed, any time you want to install a new peripheral such as a sound card or printer, you don't have to run the entire Windows 95 Setup program again. Instead, you can click the Control Panel icon labeled Add New Hardware. (For information on installing modems or other peripherals, see the chapter devoted to the particular device you're installing, or Chapter 15 for general information on adding hardware to a computer.)

Unlike earlier versions of Windows, the Windows 95 Control Panel doesn't contain a generic Windows Setup option. You could, however, use your original Windows 95 CD or disk to run Setup again. In this case, running Windows 95 Setup from within Windows 95 itself works just like it does from DOS. But instead of going to this trouble when you want to make fundamental changes to the peripherals attached to your computer under Windows 95, you should merely look for the Add/Remove Programs and Add New Hardware icons in Control Panel (click on Start and then select Settings | Control Panel). Various parts of Windows require separate setup routines, but no umbrella setup program is available. To install a new printer, you can follow an even more simple tactic: click on the Start button and then select Settings | Printers.

 Sometimes you'll want to follow the process of "installing a new printer," but you're not really adding any hardware. Printer manufacturers sometimes offer an updated "device driver," which makes their printer run faster or adds new features. This is just a program on a floppy disk that will replace the older device driver you previously installed in Windows 95. To make this replacement, follow the steps below for installing a new printer, but in step 5, click on the Have Disk button.

 ## Hands-On: How to Install a Printer

Here are the steps to install a new printer:

1. Click on the Start button and select Settings | Control Panel. Alternatively, you can click on the My Computer folder. In either case, you'll see the Printers icon.
2. Double-click on the Printers icon. Then, in the Printers window, double-click on the Add Printer icon.

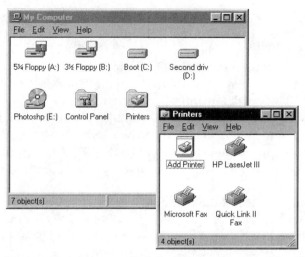

Figure 13-1: *You can find the Printers icon in either the Control Panel or the My Computer folder as shown here (or select Start | Settings | Printers).*

3. When the Add Printer Wizard appears, click on the Next button.

Figure 13-2: *The many Windows Wizards help you accomplish various goals. The Add Printer Wizard helps you add a printer to your computer.*

4. If your computer is connected to a network (even if you only have the Dial-Up Networking adapter installed), the next page of the Wizard prompts you to choose if you're installing a local printer (connected directly to your computer) or if you want to install a driver for a network printer. If you are installing support for a

network printer, you are asked to locate the printer on the network (see Chapter 19). For example, the primary printer on a Novell network might be found via \\SERVER\PRINTQ_0. If you want to print to the printer from MS-DOS applications, click the Yes option button under the heading "Do you print from MS-DOS based programs?" Then pick a printer port (other than LPT1:) that will be used to capture the output from the MS-DOS program. For example, if you choose LPT2:, when MS-DOS prints to LPT2:, the output is captured and redirected to the Windows printer spooler. If you don't have a local printer at all, you can use LPT1: for the network printer.

5. Click on the name of the manufacturer of your printer in the left-hand list box. If your manufacturer isn't listed, look in your printer's manual to see whether a printer in the Wizard's list is compatible with yours. As a worst case, select the one called "Generic," and expect your printer to produce only severely limited (typewriter text-only) results. If you are just installing a new or updated printer driver (see the Tip above), click on the Have Disk button instead.

6. After you select the manufacturer, double-click on your particular printer model in the right-hand list box. (Or just click once on the printer model and then click Next, if you prefer.)

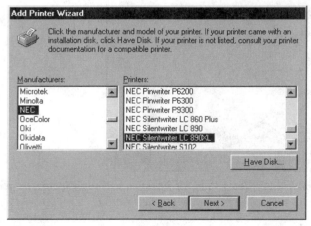

Figure 13-3: *Click on the manufacturer of your printer; then click on the specific model.*

7. In the next Wizard window, you are asked to select the *port* (the plug where your printer is attached, usually in the back of the computer). The correct answer here is almost always LPT1: (Printer Port), as shown in Figure 13-4. Click on the Next button.

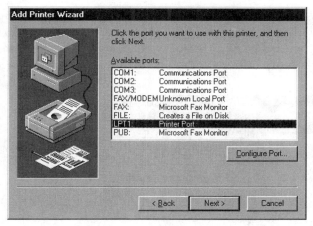

Figure 13-4: *Almost all printers are attached to the Printer Port called LPT1.*

8. In this Wizard window, you can type in a personalized name for your printer, which will be the title under the new icon for your printer.

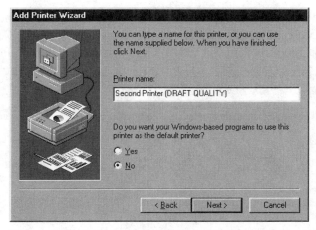

Figure 13-5: *Here you can type in a custom name for your printer, or just use the default name supplied by Windows. We changed Windows's suggestion to Second Printer (DRAFT QUALITY).*

9. If you're adding a second printer, you'll probably want to leave your primary printer as the default. If so, click on Yes.

(*Default* here means that when you click on a Print icon in a word processor toolbar, the document will automatically go to that printer. If you want to send your text to the secondary printer, you'll have to specifically tell the word processor to do that. Different programs have different ways of switching, but most use a Printer Setup option on the File menu, as shown in Figure 13-6.)

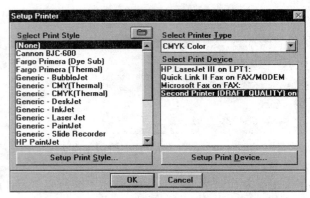

Figure 13-6: *In this typical Setup Printer window, you tell a word processor where to print the current document.*

10. In the same Wizard window, click the Next button. In the next window, you see the Test Page option, shown in Figure 13-7. Because it's a good idea to request a test, click on Yes, then click on Finish.

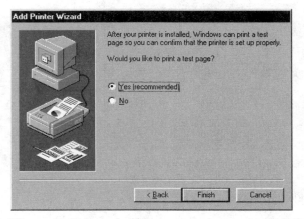

Figure 13-7: *You should try a sample page to see if the printer is hooked up right and if the driver is working as it should.*

11. At this point, Windows 95 will try to load the driver software for your particular printer so the computer can make itself understood when requesting that document be printed. It's possible that Windows 95 will respond that a driver for your new printer is already on your hard drive. In this case, accept Windows's suggestion that you not replace the existing driver unless you are attempting to install an updated driver.

Most likely, though, Windows 95 will request a particular disk from the set of disks (or a CD) you used when originally installing Windows 95 (see Figure 13-8). Don't worry if you installed Windows 95 via CD (or the manufacturer of your computer did). Just get out the CD and put it in the CD drive. Windows 95 is smart enough to remember where to look on the CD to find the driver.

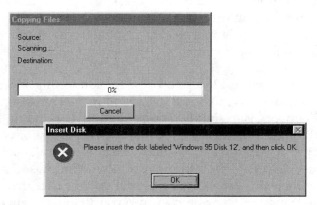

Figure 13-8: *Don't be alarmed at this message if your Windows 95 installation disk is really a CD. Just pop the CD into the drive.*

12. After the driver software is installed, Windows will attempt to print the test page. Be sure your printer is turned on. If all goes well, the printer will eventually eject a page with the Windows 95 logo, the title "Windows 95 Printer Test Page" and a brief list of your printer's technical specifications beginning with the message "Congratulations!" and ending with the message "This is the end of the printer test page."

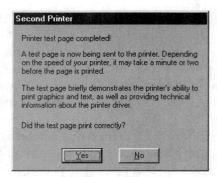

Figure 13-9: *If all goes well, you should see this message. Click on the Yes button.*

If something goes awry in your test printing, though, Windows will assist you in locating the problem. You'll first experience a brief delay while Windows sets up some Help information. If you follow the steps suggested by the Printer Troubleshooter, you'll be able to solve the most common printing problems. In the following sections, we'll review some of the steps you might take to fix things.

Note that the proceeding 12 steps are fine for connecting a local printer, but there are far easier ways to do all this if you're on a network. The easiest approach on a network is to simply browse the network and find a printer that is already shared from a Windows 95 server. Then just drag the printer icon into your printers folder and Windows 95 automatically copies the necessary printer drivers for you from the remote Windows 95 server. Most corporations will use this capability because it's a lot easier than even walking through the Windows 95 printer setup Wizard. In fact, you can even *mail* a printer configuration to someone else using Exchange. Can you imagine a corporate helpdesk person solving someone's problem by simply mailing the end-user a "printer" and telling them: "Here, just drag this into your printers folder and you're good to go."?

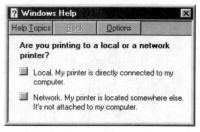

Figure 13-10: *Here is the first help message you'll see if something goes wrong during the printer test.*

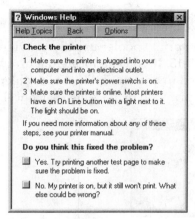

Figure 13-11: *If you tell Help that you've just got a local printer (no network), it will make these suggestions.*

Removing a Printer

Nothing is easier than getting rid of a printer from Windows 95: just double-click the Printers icon in Control Panel or the My Computer folder. Then choose the printer you want to remove by right-clicking on its icon. Then select Delete from the pop-up menu, as shown in Figure 13-12.

Figure 13-12: *Removing a printer couldn't be simpler. Just right-click on its icon.*

Troubleshooting: If You Have Printer Problems

If you have a printing problem, the print spooler usually provides a helpful error report, as shown in Figure 13-13. If you can locate the problem (needs paper, isn't turned on, isn't plugged in and so on), fix the problem and click on Retry. Otherwise, call off your print job by clicking on Cancel.

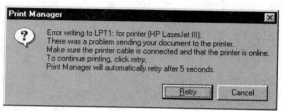

Figure 13-13: *This problem report from the print spooler offers helpful suggestions when things go wrong.*

Here, in order of likelihood, are the various problems that might be preventing your printer from printing:

■ One: By far the most common problem when a printer doesn't work after it's first installed is that the printer isn't turned on. Make sure that it's plugged into the wall and that a light is on somewhere (most printers have a power-on light).

■ Two: The second most common problem is that the printer isn't plugged into the computer properly. Most printers have a wide plug (more than twice as wide as any other plug that goes into the computer). The receptacle on the computer is called a *parallel printer port*, and you'll usually find only one of these receptacles. So it's hard to make a mistake plugging in a printer. Nonetheless, check that the cable is plugged securely, both into the back of the computer and into the printer itself.

Futurism update: Soon we can forget about cables. In a not-too-distant "tune up pack release" (as Microsoft is calling their, what will be ongoing, upgrades to Windows 95) they will be shipping native Win95 support for "IRDA infrared drivers" for most new laptops and printers (IBM Thinkpads, Gateway Liberty, HP Omnibooks, HP LaserJet 5 series, etc). If you have one of these new machines, you'll merely need to make sure your computer is pointed in the general direction of the printer. No physical cable connection will be required.

■ Three: Is the printer "Ready"? Some printers have separate Power, OnLine or Ready buttons. When you first turn on the printer, it will likely take a moment to warm up and, perhaps, run some tests on itself to make sure it's in good working order. If you try to print before the printer has gotten itself together, you'll get an error message (a window will pop up on your screen) and nothing will be printed. Likewise, if you've pressed the Pause, OffLine or other button that momentarily disables the printer, you'll get the same message. So check to be sure that the Ready or OnLine button (if available) is pressed or lit up. In other words, the printer must be engaged and ready to receive text or graphics from your computer.

■ Four: Mechanical problems can prevent printing. Paper might be jammed inside the printer, or the paper feeder tray might be empty. Other possibilities include the following: the ribbon might need to be replaced, a cartridge is empty, something mechanical is jammed, the top of the printer isn't securely shut, or some other foul up. Some printers display an error code in a small window, describing the problem. Others merely jam and wait for you to figure out what's wrong. Check your printer's manual.

■ Five: Relatively rare computer problems can also prevent printing. You need at least 2 megabytes of free space on your hard drive (for the spooler to store information before sending it on to the printer). To check your available space, double-click on the My Computer icon. Then right-click on your hard drive icon, and from the drop-down menu, select Properties, as shown in Figure 13-14.

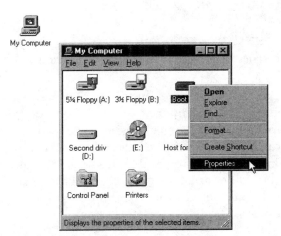

Figure 13-14: *To find out if you have enough disk space to run your printer, look at the Properties of your hard drive.*

If your hard drive is almost filled with files, programs and so on, you'll need to delete some of them (or copy them to floppy disks) until you free at least 2mb. In practice, though, it's a good idea to always leave 20 megabytes or more free on a hard drive; Windows itself uses the hard drive, too, and it will run faster and better if some vacant storage room is free on the drive.

In Figure 13-15, you see the hard drive's properties sheet that Windows displays. Notice that Windows is reporting that drive C: has 404 total megabytes, with 337 in use by programs and files. Therefore, 67.1 megabytes are free—more than enough for the print spooler and other Windows activities.

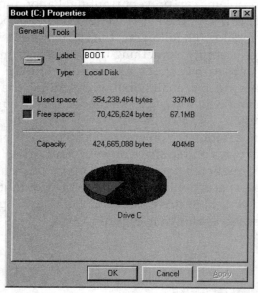

Figure 13-15: *This properties sheet is a typical report on the status of a disk drive.*

■ Six: The least likely problem when installing a printer is that Windows incorrectly identified your printer or selected the wrong device driver for it (or perhaps you erred when choosing the brand and model). In any case, you can check to see if the currently used printer driver is correct. Click on the Start button and then select Settings | Printers. When the Printers folder appears, right-click on the icon of the printer you just installed. Then select Properties, and a window like the one in Figure 13-16 appears.

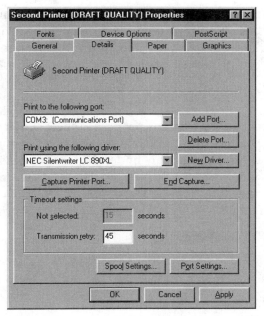

Figure 13-16: *A printer's properties sheet tells you what printer Windows thinks it's dealing with. Here, it's the NEC Silentwriter.*

After you've opened your printer's properties sheet, click on the Details tab to see what Windows says is your printer's name. If the name is wrong (or the port is wrong), go back to step 1 of the previous section and reinstall the printer. (You might as well also delete the icon in the Printers folder for the printer that was incorrectly installed. Right-click on the icon; then select Delete. When asked whether you're sure you want to delete it, click on Yes.)

Adjusting Your Printer's Properties

By far the most common adjustment you'll want to make to a printer is adding new fonts (typefaces) to it, to give your documents character and variety. (See Chapter 12.)

However, you might want to change the title that appears beneath the printer's icon or the orientation of the paper, and so on. You can make these changes in two ways: from within an application or from the Windows desktop. But applications usually offer a limited subset of the printer's properties, so usually you'll want to access the Properties window via Start | Settings | Printers.

Click on the Start button and select Settings | Printers. When the Printers folder appears, right-click on your printer's icon and choose Properties. Then you'll see the tabbed window shown in Figure 13-16. Here you can access a full range of your printer's features.

General Options

The General Options page of the printer's properties sheet shown in Figure 13-17 simply shows the name of your printer (you can type in any name here you wish; it's merely the title that appears under the icon). Especially useful is the Comment field. As you can see, we noted the date when we last changed the printer's toner cartridge (the "ink" of a laser printer). You can also write notes to yourself describing the location (on a network) of this printer.

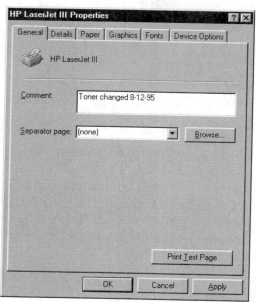

Figure 13-17: *Here you can change the icon's title, insert a separator page or print a test page.*

A separator page, if you want one, is inserted between each document printed. This page helps you keep different documents apart when a printer is busy turning out multiple copies or documents from various people on a network. You could also use it as a simple title page. Windows 95 offers two styles. To access them, click on the drop-down arrow on the Separator page box.

The Full option prints a bold Windows logo and, using a large bold type-face, the title "Windows 95 Separator Page." Below it prints the name of the document, who it was printed by, and the date and time of printing. The Simple option prints the same information, but without the logo and in the small regular typeface of the document's text. The Simple option isn't nearly as easy to spot when you're flipping through a stack of pages, so it doesn't serve the main purpose of a separator page.

If you want something really distinctive, click on the Browse button of the General Options page to locate a Windows Metafile (.WMF) graphic. You could use a drawing, your company's logo or whatever. The separator, however, must be a Windows Metafile-style graphic. Unfortunately, per-haps, the Windows Metafile graphic storage technique hasn't really caught on. Few graphics programs allow you to save pictures in that format; even Windows Paint doesn't. (CorelDRAW, though, does a good job if you want to edit a .WMF file.) Also, many applications (including Microsoft Office) provide .WMF files. (To see if you've got some on your hard drive, click on the Start button and then select Find. In the Named text box, type **.WMF**.)

The Print Test Page option is the same as the option offered during printer setup when you add a new printer. See step 11 under "Hands On: How to Install a Printer," earlier in this chapter.

Details

When you click on the Details tab of the printer's properties sheet, you'll see the options shown in Figure 13-18. The Details options govern how your documents are sent to the printer (which printer, how fast, what delay and so on). In the first drop-down list box, you can select which printer you want to send your documents to—if more than a single printer is available. Some networks and even individuals have one printer for swift, crude draft copies and a second, slower final printer for the finished product. In Figure 13-18, note that you must specify which port the desired printer is attached to. The primary printer will almost always be on LPT1.

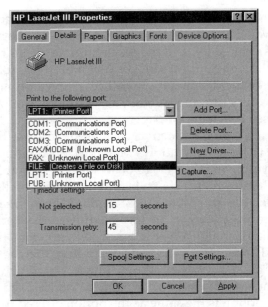

Figure 13-18: *Switch printers by selecting a different printer port from this list.*

You can also select different drivers, though at this time it's rare to find more than one driver for a single device. This list, however, will display a separate driver for all printers available to your computer. This way, you divert the document from your printer to a fax machine, for example.

The Capture Printer Port button allows you to "map" a printer to a network drive. This is necessary for MS-DOS applications and some older Windows applications. Most Windows applications are designed to print to a specific printer, not a specific printer port (like LPT2:). DOS, however, can print only to a port.

A network printer is not physically present, so the Capture button fools MS-DOS into believing that your LPT2: port (which most computers don't really have anyway) is a local printer. In fact, the printer data sent to LPT2: is rerouted to a network printer. If you don't have a printer attached to your local computer, you can capture LPT1: and redirect it to a network printer. If you do have a local printer, you'll probably want to redirect LPT2: or LPT3: instead. Chapter 19, "Getting Started With Networking," provides more detail on network printing.

Timeout settings determine Windows 95's behavior when you send a document to the printer. The *Not selected* setting determines whether the printer is detected to be physically available, and the *Transmission retry* setting determines whether the printer has actually begun printing the document. The Not selected option governs how many seconds Windows should wait for a printer to come online (for example, if the printer's power is turned off, how much time should pass before you're notified of that fact). The Transmission retry option is similar, but the delay determines how many seconds Windows will wait before reporting that the printer isn't responding or isn't yet ready to print. Printers need time to "digest" and understand documents before they actually start ejecting pages. You should increase this setting if you get timeout error messages when printing large or complex documents.

Spool Settings

To choose when, if or how the spooler intervenes in the printing process, click the Spool Settings button at the bottom of the Details page of the printer's properties sheet.

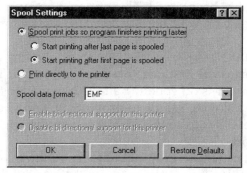

Figure 13-19: *In the Spool Settings window, you can customize this useful utility.*

Most people will want to leave spooling on because it more quickly returns the computer to your use (unfreezes it) when a document is sent to the printer. The computer briefly freezes when you first print a document because Windows wants to focus all its attention on formatting the document. If spooling is turned on, the resulting formatted document is saved to a temporary file on your hard drive. Then the computer will respond again to your typing and mouse moves. In the background, without affecting your interaction with the computer, the contents of that file will then be fed to the printer. Likewise, you'll also want to select the EMF rather than RAW (unchanged) format for most printers. EMF (Enhanced Metafile format) simply prints faster than raw, unmodified data because it results in smaller spool files.

Without EMF, the entire burden of translating codes (like italics) falls on the printer. You could also choose the *Print directly to the printer* option, thus avoiding spooling entirely. However, why would you want to do this? The spooler only uses a few megabytes on your hard drive; after the printing is finished, the hard drive is cleaned and the spooler is removed. The only reason for changing any of these default spooling settings is if you're having problems printing or if your printer's manual instructs you to.

There *are* some applications which get confused by the new EMF spooling and in some cases Windows 95 will automatically notice the problem and turn EMF spooling off for you. One example of this is if you have older versions of Adobe Type Manager installed. In that case, Windows 95 is forced to turn off EMF spooling (however, Adobe is currently in beta of a new version of this, so this "problem" will go away over time).

The *Start printing after last page is spooled* option unfreezes the computer faster than ordinary spooling. All formatting is calculated by the computer, and then the printer file is saved to the disk. Nothing is sent to the printer until the entire document has been saved. This option, however, can require a large temporary (spool) file on your hard drive, particularly for big or complex documents.

The *Start printing after last page is spooled* option starts sending the document to the printer as soon as the first page has been formatted. The *Print directly to the printer* option turns off spooling altogether. On most computers this should be avoided: it's slow to return control to you, and you can't pause print jobs in progress. Resort to this only if you are having problems getting your printer to work.

The Bi-directional options will be gray and not respond to mouse clicks unless your printer is capable of two-way communication with the computer. If your printer can send messages, these reports can be useful if problems occur; therefore, you should leave this option turned on.

Port Settings

You also can set the correct printer port by clicking the Port Settings button in the lower-right corner of the Details page of the printer's properties sheet. The Port Settings option allows you to specify whether printing from MS-DOS windows should also be spooled. (Turning off this option can sometimes speed up DOS print jobs but can cause conflicts if you try to print from Windows while the DOS program is printing.)

Paper

Ordinarily, you'll use your word processor to make any adjustments to margins, envelopes, feeder, page size and page shape. Because word processors have access to the Windows Setup information, however, you can adjust these options in the Paper page of the printer's properties sheet.

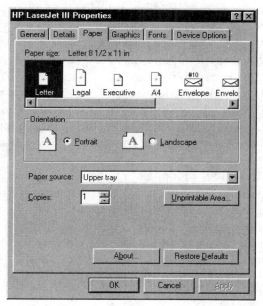

Figure 13-20: *In the Paper page, you can adjust the virtual margins of the document.*

You can put various sizes of paper into most printers—from a business card to a 1-foot-by-infinite roll of computer paper. What's more, the printer will print on these various sizes without your changing any settings. The purpose of setting a paper size, orientation and margin is to have your word processor format the text (or graphics) so they stay within the physical boundaries of the paper and so some white margin frames the text.

If you see an icon labeled Custom in the Paper size panel at the top of the Paper page, you can click on it and define a unique paper size. PostScript printers, for example, permit various custom paper sizes, including huge formats that are used with *imagesetters* (typesetting machines).

In the Orientation section shown in the middle of Figure 13-20, you can set how your text is printed on the page. You can choose from Portrait or Landscape. Click on Portrait if you want to print the long way on the paper—the orientation that most artists use to create human portraits. Click on Landscape if you want to print so the page is wider than it is high—the way landscape scenes are painted. Portrait is by far the most common because people have a harder time locating the next line when the lines of text are extremely wide. Landscape, however, can be superior for printing graphics or if you are designing a newsletter with two side-by-side pages. Just fold a 14- x 11-inch page in half, and you have a four-page 7- x 11-inch newsletter format.

Some printers have various trays holding different sizes of paper or envelopes. You can specify which tray should be the source of the paper for a particular print job by choosing from the Paper source drop-down list. Which options are listed here will depend on your printer model. Here you can also request that multiple copies be printed.

The Unprintable Area option specifies the margins. The word processor is forced to keep the text or graphics within this frame of white space. In other words, you can specify how far over from the left side of the paper the document should be printed and how far down from the top, over from the right and up from the bottom of the paper. Most laser printers have a quarter-inch unprintable area on all four sides of a page because the grippers and rollers need some space to move the page or because the image area of the printer's drum is slightly smaller than a page. You'll find that photocopiers also have a narrow unprintable region, and some even automatically reduce a page to fit. Inkjet printers typically have a more sizable unprintable region of about one-half inch on the top and bottom.

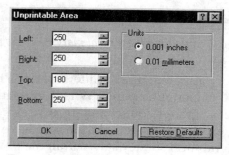

Figure 13-21: *Here's where you can adjust the margins.*

As you can see in Figure 13-21, the margins are adjustable for the Hewlett-Packard LaserJet in increments of 1/100th of an inch and default to one-quarter inch on all sides except the top, which is a bit less than one-fifth inch. On many printers, you cannot reduce the margins to the very edge of the paper. One-quarter inch is about the narrowest possible margin permitted; this thin zone is truly "unprintable" unless you fool the printer by claiming to be using a larger page size than you really are.

Graphics

In the Graphics page of the printer's properties sheet, you can tell Windows what kinds of compromises it should make if an image must be printed at a low resolution. Note that this discussion assumes you are not using a PostScript printer. A PostScript printer bypasses the universal printer driver and uses a different set of dialog boxes.

Dithering

The Dithering option of the Graphics page conveys to the printer what it should do if you send it a picture that's more complicated than it can cleanly reproduce. Complicated here means that some printers can only print, for instance, 64 shades of gray (or that many different shades of color). However, you might want to print an image with 256 shades. Dithering is a compromise—a way to display in-between shades by adding patterns (crosses, scattered dots and other patterns) to simulate areas that, in the original graphic, are really a shade of gray that the printer cannot reproduce. You also can use dithering to improve the quality of color printing.

A printer can't really print shades of gray. It can only impress black or white dots (pixels) on the paper. By arranging clusters of black and white dots, or checkerboard patterns of black and white dots, it can fool the eye into seeing shaded regions. The size of the printed dots affects how smoothly and how finely the shaded patterns can be produced, so a typical 300 dpi (dots per inch) laser printer can only display 64 shades or fewer. By quadrupling the resolution, a 600 dpi printer can display about 256 shades of gray. Color printers also use these techniques to create a range of pseudo-colors using only three primary colored inks.

Dithering is also sometimes seen on the computer screen if you're displaying, for instance, a True Color image on a 256-color display card or a 256-color image on a computer that can display only 16-color graphics. However, the Dithering setting on the Graphics page will affect only the printer, not the screen. Your choices are None, Coarse, Fine, Line art and Error diffusion. See Figures 13-22 through 13-26 for examples of these options.

Figure 13-22: *This is the original, undithered image. Something close to this will be printed if you select the "Fine" setting. Better yet, if the image is of high quality and your printer is capable of very high resolution (above 600 dpi), choose None.*

Figure 13-23: *If you choose None on a low-resolution printer, the printer will make its own decisions if it has to compromise on shading. Here's one possible result.*

Figure 13-24: *This image is printed at the Coarse dithering setting. Coarse can actually yield more shades of gray, but the whole picture looks fuzzier.*

Figure 13-25: *If you set dithering to Line art, you'll see no grayscale shading at all— just black and white.*

Figure 13-26: *Error diffusion creates noodle patterns, irregular blobs, something like rough paper. This setting is often a good compromise if your printer must dither. Error diffusion is similar to the* halftoning *effect you see in newspapers. PostScript printers can perform true halftoning.*

The various dithering options are unfortunate, but better than nothing. Each attempts to soften the blow when reducing resolution (detail) to accommodate a printer with fewer dots per inch than the original image enjoys. Something's got to give if you try to write a letter with a brick dipped in ink. Of all the options, Error Diffusion is often the best, but you should really experiment. Send various images to your printer, using these various dither options, to see what produces the best results with different kinds of graphics.

Resolution, or DPI

Also on the Graphics page, you can adjust how cleanly images will be reproduced. "Rough" printing goes faster and can be used if you just want to see a draft of a drawing. For the final product, though, you'll want to use the maximum *resolution* of which your printer is capable—the highest dpi (dots per inch) setting.

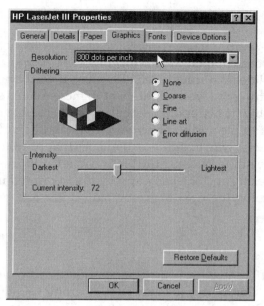

Figure 13-27: *How many dots per inch you can choose here will depend on your printer's capabilities.*

Resolution means how much detail you can see. The lowest resolution, usually 75 dpi, produces a cruder, rougher graphic than higher settings. Some printers can achieve a density of 600 dpi or even 1200 dpi with special interpolation. The fewer dots per inch that are printed, the looser, more blurred and less detailed the result. You can see the difference in Figure 13-28.

Figure 13-28: *300, 150 and 75 dots per inch—decreasingly sharp, smooth and detailed results at different dpi settings.*

Intensity

The final setting on the Graphics page, Intensity, is similar to those found on copier machines—you can compensate for printing that's coming out too light or too dark. This slider is normally left alone, but if your printer ink cartridge or toner is getting old, you might want to increase this setting. However, you'd probably be better off just replacing the ink in your printer and restoring the slider to the midpoint between dark and light. But adjusting Intensity can be a great way to lighten up images that print too muddy or dark, as an alternative to retouching the picture in a Paint program. Keep in mind that both Dithering and Intensity apply only to printed images that use shades of gray or color; these settings won't affect line art, text or solid black objects.

Fonts

Of the thousands of different fonts, some offer elegant traditional letter shapes ("Garamond," "Goudy"), which are subtle variations on the classic Times Roman design. Others are highly specialized, like "Shotgun," which features thick black letters with holes—as if the characters had been blasted with buckshot. You can use Garamond in almost any document, but Shotgun is pretty much limited to Tex-Mex restaurant menus and playbills for the musical *Annie Get Your Gun*. Nonetheless, it's nice to have a variety of fonts available beyond the few supplied by Windows (Arial, Courier and Times New Roman) and the few built into your printer (Courier, Times, Line Printer and Univers in a LaserJet).

 TIP Where do you get alternative typefaces? They're widely available on CompuServe, AOL and bulletin boards. Some commercial applications give them to you—hundreds of high-quality fonts are included with CorelDRAW, for instance.

In Chapter 12, we go into detail on which typefaces are appropriate for various kinds of documents. Here we'll limit the discussion to cartridges and installing new printer fonts. Note that this Fonts page in the Printer property sheet is printer-specific. The options here will differ from printer to printer: what cartridges, if any, the printer can accept and what printer-specific fonts, if any, are available. You can easily ignore this Fonts page entirely because it represents an older technology: cartridges. Printer-specific fonts are written in *font languages*, which are largely dying out and being replaced by Windows's TrueType language.

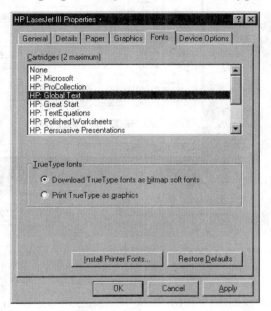

Figure 13-29: *In the Fonts page, you can manage cartridge typefaces.*

One way to add new typefaces is to buy cartridges to plug into your printer. Cartridges are expensive and generally contain only a few fonts. If your printer can utilize cartridges, check the list box in Figure 13-29 to see which ones will plug in and how many you can use at the same time. If you already have cartridges installed, you can identify them in this list box. Thereafter, they will appear in your word processor and other applications as a font that you can select. Remember that the options on the Fonts page are printer dependent. For Hewlett-Packard's LaserJet III, you can select up to two different cartridges, each adding one or more new fonts (typefaces).

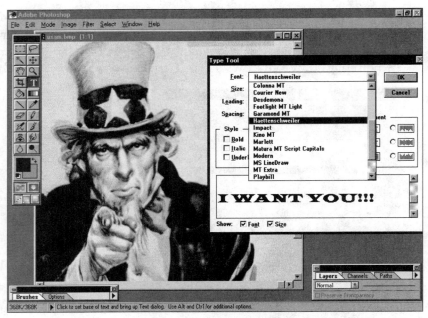

Figure 13-30: *You can select a new typeface (font) from within Adobe's Photoshop, for example.*

TrueType fonts are typefaces conforming to a standard established by Microsoft. These fonts are *scalable* (you can freely resize them from tiny "8 point" to huge "120 point"). They are also going to look essentially the same when displayed on the screen as they will when printed. (They are the same shape but can be a little ragged around the edges if printed or displayed in low resolution. For example, if you select 75 dpi in the Graphics page of the printer's properties sheet, curves and diagonals within the characters will stairstep and look rough. Similarly, some screen resolutions can produce ragged characters. See Figure 13-31.)

Figure 13-31: *The character on the left illustrates font smoothing (anti-aliasing). The character on the right is ragged.*

TIP If you install Microsoft Plus! For Windows 95, you can turn on font smoothing, which produces smoother lines and curves, especially with large typefaces, on your computer screen. It doesn't suffer from the usual problems induced by anti-aliasing—blurry characters at body text sizes like 10 or 12 point.

Soft Fonts or Graphics?

The next option in the Fonts page of the printer's properties sheet determines how Windows will send characters from the computer's hard drive to the printer (downloading them). Normally, you should leave the default setting *Download TrueType fonts as bitmap soft fonts* selected because your documents will print faster.

For example, if you select a TrueType font from within a word processor and then start printing a document, the font will be loaded into your printer. Windows will read the font off the disk drive and send it as a description of how that font should be geometrically reproduced. Many printers are capable of accepting such a description and then reproducing the look of the characters.

This description is like telling someone how to print a black square by saying: "Start with a black dot 5 inches over from the left of the paper and 4 inches down from the top. Then draw a line 2 inches to the right, 2 inches down, 2 inches left and 2 inches up. Now fill with black." Such a description can be transmitted to the printer rapidly.

The alternative, printing TrueType fonts as graphics, is essentially like taking a snapshot of each page of your document and sending a dot-by-dot message to the printer. (This "snapshot" approach is almost always the way that a drawing or other graphics are sent to the printer. Many printers are not equipped to reconstruct a drawing from a description. They require a copy.)

The computer sends a stream of information, dots that will be reproduced by the printer. If you've chosen 300 dpi resolution (in the Graphics page of the printer's properties sheet), a 2-inch black square will be reconstructed by the computer saying, in effect, "Start at this position on the paper. Now: black dot, black dot, black dot..." 600 times for the first line across the top. Stop. Start at this new position: black dot, black dot... then repeating this 600 more times to go down 2 inches. A total of 360,000 messages to the printer are required to print those black dots. This approach is obviously slower when communicating between the computer and the printer because there's much more information to pass along.

So, it generally makes sense to leave the *Download TrueType as bitmap soft fonts* option selected. However, if you are printing documents with many graphics but very little text, you might speed up the printing if you select the alternative *Print TrueType as graphics* option. The increase in speed, however, isn't much in most cases. Also, you can achieve some special effects (graphics partially covering characters) using this option, but you have more control over such effects using a drawing/retouching program such as CorelDRAW or Photoshop.

Installing Printer Fonts

You make *printer-specific* fonts available to your printer by installing them in a special folder recommended by the printer manufacturer. This means you can copy fonts from a CD or a bulletin board into a folder named PCLFONTS, for example, depending on your printer's brand.

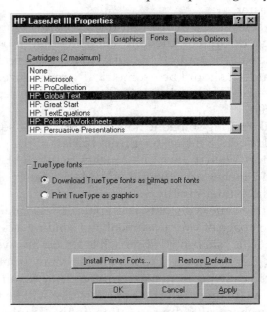

Figure 13-32: *You tell Windows 95 the location of printer-specific fonts you want to install on the Fonts page.*

Although it's a rather outdated idea now, a few years ago one of the best ways to use fonts was to collect some that were compatible with your printer. Some printers can accept fonts that you download into the printer's memory when you turn on the computer. Alternatively, these fonts can be downloaded selectively if you choose them within your word processor. This tactic isn't used much any more because it's easier and more convenient to let Windows 95 manage things for you.

However, you can still use this download technique if you wish. You must put a new font into the folder in which the printer expects to find it. In the case of the Hewlett-Packard LaserJet, the folder is called PCLFONTS. To start, click on the Install Printer Fonts button on the Fonts page. When the Font Installer appears, as shown in Figure 13-33, click on Add and enter the folder name (PCLFONTS, here) in the Add Fonts window. Then click on OK.

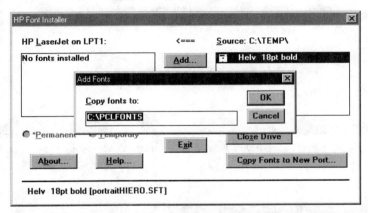

Figure 13-33: *When you select a printer-specific font and click Add, you can specify the folder where your printer looks for downloadable fonts.*

Windows Fonts

A more practical and efficient approach to adding fonts is to install fonts into Windows 95 itself and let Windows's Print Manager convert the fonts to codes that your particular printer understands. To add Windows fonts, click on the Start button and then select Settings | Control Panel. When the Control Panel appears, click on the Fonts icon. Then a window will open showing all the fonts you currently have installed. Select File | Install New Font. After you select your fonts from the Add Fonts window, click on OK. The fonts then are sent to your Fonts folder.

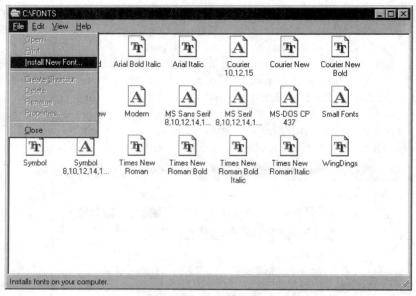

Figure 13-34: *Here's where you should add fonts; Windows 95 True Type has become the standard format.*

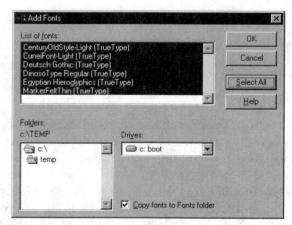

Figure 13-35: *Locate the fonts on your hard drive; then click on OK. They'll be sent to your Fonts folder if you leave the default Copy fonts to Fonts folder option selected.*

Windows's native TrueType font files end in .TTF. Printer-specific fonts end in .FON or .FNT or a bevy of other filename extensions.

Device Options

The final page of the printer's properties sheet, Device Options, allows you to select additional options for your particular printer. What appears on this sheet depends on the memory—how much RAM—your printer contains. The printer's RAM is just like the RAM in your computer. (Remember that most printers have microprocessors and RAM; they are "computers," too. They are just dedicated to the process of producing documents rather than being general-purpose machines like your main computer.)

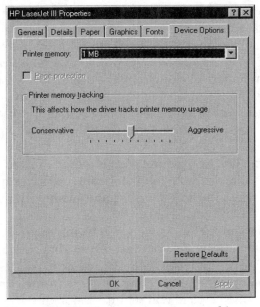

Figure 13-36: *The options you see on this page will depend on your particular printer.*

All printers have some memory, but some printers, like computers, allow you to add additional memory. Why would you want to? Ordinary text is generally no problem at all, but graphics can create huge files, requiring several megabytes to hold a single page. Some printers can be expanded to contain as much as 4 or 5 megabytes to hold such complex graphics, but even they can struggle to print the most difficult graphics. If the work you do frequently results in an "Out of memory" message from your printer, consider investing in additional RAM for the printer.

To make your printer capable of printing documents with more complex graphics (or, in some cases, print faster), you can add RAM. Some printers let you add RAM via a cartridge; others require that you open up the printer and push in a memory board.

The list box at the top of the Device Options page will display the amount of memory that was included with your particular printer when you bought it (the default amount). In the case of the LaserJet III, it's 1 megabyte. If you add more memory, you must let Windows know by clicking on this list box and selecting the correct total of RAM from the drop-down list. Note that some printers communicate with Windows 95. If you have this kind of printer, this memory-adjusting option will be unchangeable (by clicking), and Windows will already display the correct RAM.

You might have wondered: if complex documents require so much memory, why not divide them in pieces and feed the pieces one at a time, like a bucket brigade? The next option on the device options, Page protection, permits you to zone off some of the printer's memory (into a "page"). If you get an "Out of memory" message from your printer when you try to print a complicated graphic, try clicking on Page protection. In some cases, selecting this option will make it possible to print the tough document. Normally, leave it off. (If your printer doesn't have enough RAM, the Page protection feature isn't possible, and this check box will remain gray (disabled), so you can't click it.)

The final option on the Device Options page is a fudge factor. The Printer memory tracking slider allows you to tell your printer's driver how conservative to be when estimating the amount of printer memory required to print each page sent to the printer.

If you get an "Out of memory" message when trying to print a complex page, this memory tracking option is your last resort, short of adding RAM to the printer. Try moving the slider to the right, toward "Aggressive."

Here's what's happening. Among its other duties, a printer driver predicts how much printer RAM a page will require, before it releases that page to the printer to be printed. If the driver calculates that a page will exceed the RAM available in your printer, it will refuse to waste your time by sending the page on and having the printer grind away and then fail to print. Instead, the driver will immediately notify you that there's insufficient printer memory to print this page. However, the driver can't always predict accurately. It might be too conservative, and some borderline-sized pages might actually print, even though the driver doesn't think so.

If you set this slider too far toward Conservative, you won't have to wait until the slower printer fails to print a complex page. The drawback is that some pages that could have printed will be reported as too complex by the driver before the printer ever gets a chance to even try. Set the slider too far toward Aggressive, and you'll cause the driver to send pages that it estimates are going to overflow the printer's memory. The drawback here is that the printer will waste your time while it tries, and sometimes fails, to absorb these dubious pages.

Printing Documents

Ordinarily when you want to print a document or a graphic image, you can just press Ctrl+P. Most applications use this key combination as a shortcut to printing the current document.

Alternatively, you can press Alt+F and then P. This shortcut drops down the File menu and then selects the Print option; it works in nearly all Windows applications.

In Windows 95, you can drag a file out of a folder window or the Explorer and drop it onto the printer icon on the desktop. This presupposes that you've left the printer icon on your desktop, of course. Many people prefer to remove it (to dump it in the trash can) because printing from within an application is so easy.

Although standards are being developed, each Windows application still has its own particular window that pops up when you choose Print. And each has its own way of displaying messages concerning the printer's status.

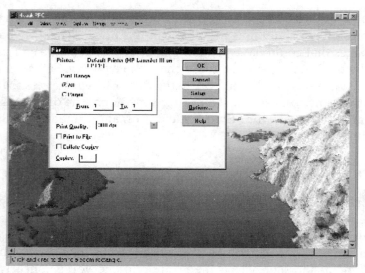

Figure 13-37: *Hijaak, an excellent screen capture and image conversion program, displays this dialog box when you request printing. Sadly, though, Hijaak has some known incompatibilities with Windows 95. See the PROGRAMS.TXT file that's installed by Windows 95 in your Windows directory for more info on this. When you're in that file, though, search for* Yijaak. *Somebody misspelled it.*

As you can see in Figure 13-37, most applications have provisions to allow you to select the number of copies and to define a range of pages. Typically, graphics programs provide additional options relating to resolution (dpi), positioning and other graphic-related issues. When you click on the Options button shown in Figure 13-37, you see the Print Options window shown in Figure 13-38.

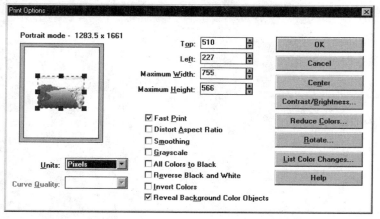

Figure 13-38: *Many graphics-related options are available when you select Options from the Print window in Hijaak.*

A word processor, by contrast, provides options related to text instead of graphics: collation, reverse print order, annotations, summary information and so on. Each application offers different options and different levels of control over the printed document.

When you click on Print, you'll almost always see one button, Setup, no matter which application you're in. By clicking on this button, you can switch printers, switch from printer to fax, change page orientation and select a different paper tray in the Setup window. These options, and others, are also available when you right-click on your printer icon and then select Properties.

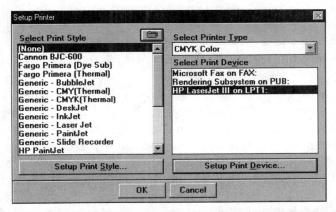

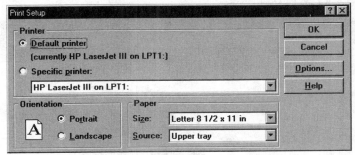

Figure 13-39: *Picture Publisher (above) and Hijaak (below) display different printer setup windows, but the options are essentially the same.*

TIP While a document is printing, the printer icon appears next to the clock on the right side of the taskbar. Double-click on it if you want to pause, purge or just watch the progress of the current print job.

Controlling a Print Job

Once you've sent a document off to the printer, you still have some control over the situation. Your choices are pause or purge. If you double-click on your printer's icon, it will open the window shown in Figure 13-40.

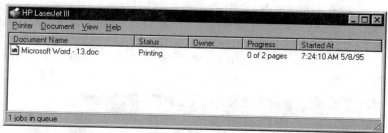

Figure 13-40: *Here's where you can pause or cancel a print job.*

After you begin printing, things happen pretty fast. Windows 95's Print Manager composes pages according to the rules described in your printer's driver. This action is swift, and unless there's a problem, the printer should start ejecting pages within a few seconds after you click Print. But if you have a large document and want to pause it, select Printer | Pause. The printer might eject a few more pages (based on how much memory it has and how many pages have already been composed and dumped). But shortly the job will be halted.

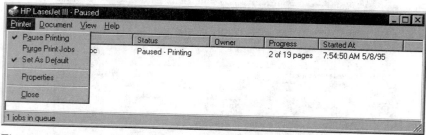

Figure 13-41: *To pause the printer, select Printer | Pause Printing.*

Likewise, if you for some reason want to purge (cancel) all pending print jobs, click on "Purge Print Jobs" under the Printer menu.

 TIP If you are printing several documents, they'll all be listed in order in the printer window. To reorder them, just drag them above or below each other.

TIP If you're a notebook or laptop user, you can set your printer to work offline. That way, you can travel without a printer yet still print your jobs as if you had one. When offline, the printer driver stores the printed jobs. When you get back to the office, just hook up the printer and turn the printer back online; then watch all the print jobs start printing automatically. Right-click on a printer icon to choose the Offline feature.

Help

If something goes wrong during printing, help is only a few mouse-clicks away. Windows 95 has a little quiz you can take that should lead to the solution of your problem. Click on Start, then Help. Double-click on Troubleshooting, then "If you have trouble printing."

Figure 13-42: *In the Help window, you can likely track down any printer problems.*

Deferred Printing

Here's a nice feature if you use a laptop, a docking station, a shared network printer—or otherwise sometimes don't have a printer available when you want to print something. If a printer is currently unavailable because one isn't connected or available to your computer—print a document anyway. Windows 95 knows that there's no physical printer, so it invents a virtual printer and makes a note to itself to print this thing later when a real printer is available. When Windows does detect a printer—the files are then spooled over to the printer automatically. If you want to adjust this feature (say you're on a network and have other reasons for deferring print jobs), take a look at the Printers Folder (in My Computer). Double-click on the Printers folder, then click on the icon of the printer that you want to target for printing. Open its File mehu and select Print Offline. (This option won't be available unless you're working on a portable or on a network. If you don't see Print Offline on this menu, you can select the Pause Printing command instead. Note also that if you've turned off the "spooling" option in your printer's property sheets, offline printing isn't available.)

Moving On

Now we'll turn our attention to the computer itself and go "Deep Inside the Machine." We'll explain everything you ever wanted to know about how your computer works: buses, microprocessors, RISCs and the rest. You might find this discussion a solid background for optimizing your computer or adding new equipment, which is covered in later chapters.

Chapter 14

Deep Inside the Machine

You probably take your computer for granted. Once it's set up and plugged in, your focus shifts from nuts and bolts to bits and bytes.

Software is where the action is. Windows itself is software, and so are all the applications you use each day. Unless you've had to open your case and install new hardware, you probably haven't had much cause to ponder how the magic of software is enabled by the incredible technology underneath it—your computer hardware.

Some people think that a computer should work like a mere appliance, a "black box" that absorbs disks and CD-ROMs, fueling the engine that draws your graphics, calculates your spreadsheets, sorts your databases and processes your words. It's power on tap, so you should only have to turn it on, right?

Figure 14-1: *It seems your computer is always hungry for the newest version of the latest software.*

Yet no one would expect an automobile to drive itself or operate with the push-button simplicity of a blender. A computer is more like a car than it is like a washing machine. It's amazing that with all the knowledge, skill and experience we put into driving that we really can take it for granted, yet we do because transportation is so important to us. More and more, computing is becoming just as important to us, and as we drive our machines onto the "information superhighway," it pays to learn a little bit about what goes on under the hood. That's the topic of this chapter.

Anatomy of a Computer

Your computer is composed of a few obvious parts. There's the TV-like monitor (sometimes called the CRT, an acronym for the cathode ray tube that forms the picture—unless you're using an LCD screen on a laptop, of course). You have your system unit (variously called the case, or the console, or chassis). And of course, you have your peripherals all wired into the system unit: a printer, modem, perhaps a scanner, touch tablet, microphone. And finally, you have the primary input devices: your mouse and keyboard.

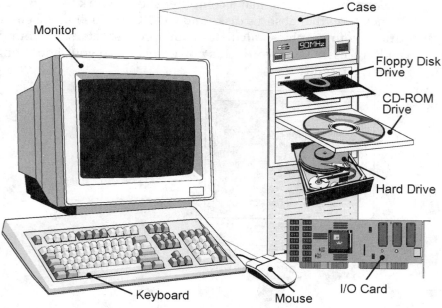

Figure 14-2: *Parts of a computer.*

In the next few chapters, we'll explain what you need to know about these items in order to get the most out of Windows. The mouse and keyboard are covered in Chapters 8 and 9.

Some people think that the system unit is just a storage box and simply call it "the hard drive." Of course, the hard drive or drives in your computer are indeed installed in the system unit, along with your floppy drives and CD-ROM drive. These memory devices are controlled by flat electronic modules called *cards,* or sometimes, *boards.*

These boards work like the specialized regions of the human brain. They are plugged into the central nervous system of your computer, the *motherboard* (which makes the cards themselves *daughterboards* by convention). Other daughterboards, like your video card or sound card, would be analogous to the vision or speech centers of your brain. Extending the analogy, your hard drive is akin to your brain's long-term memory, whereas solid-state RAM is somewhat like short-term or working memory.

All this activity converges at the *system bus,* which is like a roadway divided into multiple lanes. Just as nerves convey messages to your brain, the system bus routes and coordinates signals within your computer. Each "lane" of the system highway conducts a stream of individual on/off signals, or *bits* of information.

And just as a six-lane superhighway can move more traffic at higher speeds than a simple two-lane expressway, a 32-bit system bus can move twice as much data as a 16-bit bus, which is to say it can transfer the same amount of data twice as fast.

The system bus is like your spinal cord: It connects your computer's sensory and motor organs (input/output devices like the mouse or monitor) to the central processing unit (CPU, sometimes called MPU for microprocessor unit). So the CPU is like the cerebral cortex of the brain, where all the computing actually occurs.

The Computer Inside Your Computer

Intel's 80X86 chips, along with MS-DOS and now Windows, are what define a computer as a "PC." You probably know that the 80386 or 80486 "chip" is the CPU of your computer. We usually leave off the '80' and just call them 386 or 486. The successor to the 486 isn't a 586, but rather the Pentium. Other chip makers have offered their own alternative "586" chips, such as the Cyrix M1 or the NexGen NX-586.

When you subtract the hardware that merely supports your computing needs—memory, hard drives, video card, case, power supply, wiring and circuit boards—you're left with a single square chip. Even the chip is really just a ceramic package for an even tinier silicon wafer. This wafer may be less than 1/4" wide, and contains millions of microscopic transistors. It's the computer inside your computer, and does all the real work. The heart of your computer would comfortably fit inside your ear.

Figure 14-3 is an actual microphotograph of a Pentium microprocessor. It uncannily resembles a satellite picture of a major metropolis. Its roadways are the pathways for electrons, flowing like quicksilver through the webs of transistors that flip on and off to create custom circuits: In effect, your computer is continuously rewiring itself, dynamically, in each instant inventing a new design to solve the latest calculation.

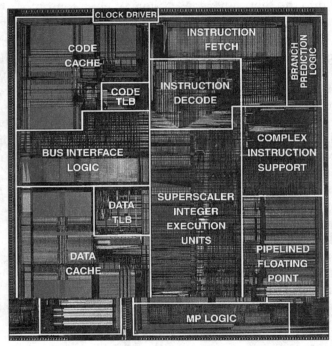

Figure 14-3: *The Pentium microprocessor is composed of multiple independent subprocessors.*

The CPU acts upon (*executes*) individual commands stored in memory and relayed via the system bus. These commands are very simple, such as a command to move a number into a storage area, add or subtract, compare two values, jump to a new memory location and so on. (Although some software is written directly using these assembly language codes, most software today is created with high-level human-meaningful languages such as C, Pascal or BASIC. BASIC is the all-time most popular computer language, and Microsoft's Visual Basic is the lingua franca of Windows. It's an easy way to automate your applications, and you can even learn to build your own custom programs. In fact, you'll learn some of these techniques in Chapter 23, "Automation & Programming.")

The System Bus & the Data Bus

The system bus transfers data to and from memory. Your computer has millions of memory locations, like the cells of a honeycomb, and each one is assigned a unique number, called an *address* (just as your house is numbered with its own address).

The system bus has two levels. Think of them as a freeway raised on pillars above another freeway underneath. The CPU uses the address bus to select a memory address it's interested in and finds the value of that memory location on the data bus. If the CPU wants to change a value in memory, it sends the number representing the location of a memory cell over the address bus while simultaneously sending via the data bus the new value to be stored.

When executing programs, the address bus points to a region in memory containing the command instructions for the CPU. The data bus pipes the instructions directly into the CPU, and the CPU executes each command and then points to the next memory location to get the next command and so forth.

Ticking away like an ultra-high-speed metronome, a quartz crystal called an *oscillator* generates regular pulses, so all this traffic moves in discrete coordinated spurts. Each tick or tock is a *clock cycle*, and one packet of information can be processed (read from or written to memory, or one command acted upon) in each clock cycle. Actually, most computer instructions require more than one clock cycle to complete, although the Pentium is optimized to perform many instructions in just a single clock cycle.

This heartbeat is unimaginably, frantically, rapid. In fact, the heart of your computer beats millions of times per second. That's what the speed rating of your CPU means. A 386-33 CPU is ticking away at over 33,000,000 cycles per second. One cycle per second is known as a *hertz*, so 33 megahertz (MHz) is 33 million clock ticks per second. Radio waves are also measured in hertz, and computer transistors flip on and off so fast they emit a furious crackling whine on the radio frequency spectrum. In principle, this RF interference can wreak havoc with FM, cordless phone and television reception, so most computers are certified as Class B Business machines. If you use an FCC Class B-certified computer at home, you are responsible for correcting any problems your RF interference causes for anyone else. (FCC Class C machines are designed by the manufacturer for home use.) Fortunately, most computers are sufficiently shielded, and the RF interference rarely extends more than a few feet away from the computer.

Apples & Oranges

Even if all CPUs run at the same clock speed, they won't necessarily compute at the same speed. First of all, consider the 386SX versus the 386DX chip. While both run at 33 MHz, the DX chip would outpace the SX chip because the 386SX has a 16-bit data bus and the 386DX has a 32-bit data bus, so the DX can in principle transfer data twice as fast, even at the same clock speed. When not accessing memory, the SX runs just as quickly, though, so the 386DX is not quite twice as fast. In fact, it's about 75 percent faster than a 386SX.

The 486 chip runs faster than a 386 chip with the same speed rating, merely because it can do more during each clock cycle. Many of the commands (for example, a command to multiply two numbers together) run more efficiently on the 486, so a multiply operation takes fewer clock cycles to complete. Since each command has been streamlined, a 486 can process more commands than the 386 in the same amount of time. The 486 also includes a small amount of onboard memory (8k) so that it can continue to feed itself instructions and data even while it's busy working on others. (This memory buffer, called a *cache*, is accessed extremely quickly since it's part of the chip and doesn't need to be accessed via the system bus.)

In addition, the 486DX has a built-in, specialized numerical processor (or FPU, for floating point unit), so it can perform sophisticated math operations at hardware speeds. Owners of 386 systems can install a low-cost 80387 chip to add an FPU to their motherboard, but the 486DX includes an improved FPU directly on the chip. Sometimes the FPU is called a *math coprocessor*.

Do You Need a Math Coprocessor?

The typical 486 computer system actually uses a 486SX chip, which is a 486DX with the numeric processor disabled. Without a functional FPU (floating point unit), the 486SX costs much less, and that translates into less expensive computers, which is why the majority of low-cost 486 systems use the 486SX. (Intel actually only manufactures the 486DX chip, but if the FPU on a 486DX chip fails any quality checks, the FPU is excised—intentionally burned out—and as long as the rest of the chip passes the tests, it is then sold as a 486SX. Ironically, the demand for the low-cost 486SX occasionally required Intel to cripple working 486DX chips to meet its quotas.)

The 486DX chip is also used as an add-on FPU for 486SX motherboards, and it plugs into a spare socket. Once installed, the 80487 chip simply disables the original 486SX CPU and takes over as a full-fledged 486DX.

But it's a waste to use your spare socket for an 80487. The introduction of the clock-doubled 486DX/2 and the clock-tripled DX4 chip allows easy upgrades to faster speed without risking incompatibilities. You can install these "Overdrive" chips directly in your spare CPU socket. While the quartz "heartbeat" of your computer's motherboard may continue to run at 25 MHz, a clock-doubled CPU sneakily runs at 50 MHz internally. That means that memory access to the system bus is still served up at the normal rate, but an *internal* command like a multiply can complete twice as fast, due to the revved-up internal clock speed.

The Intel DX2/66 chip is for 33 MHz motherboards. The fastest 486-class chip is the 100 MHz DX4, which plugs into a 33MHz motherboard yet provides nearly the same performance as a Pentium. Another reason the DX4 is so fast: it doubles the 8k internal memory cache to 16k. (However, the DX4 is not four times as fast as a normal 486 chip, as the name seems to imply. It actually is a clock-tripled chip; it internally runs at three times the rate of the system bus. The "4" in DX4 simply refers to its 486 compatibility.)

The Pentium chip, on the other hand, flies along at a minimum clock speed of 60 or 66 MHz, and there are now 90, 100, 120, and soon to be 133 and 150 MHz versions. The special Pentium Overdrive CPU can be installed in your spare 486 socket, too, although the full 64-bit capabilities of the Pentium are somewhat limited by the 32-bit data bus on a 486 motherboard.

Inside the Pentium

To get its speed, Pentium does more than just burn cycles faster. The Pentium splits the incoming stream of instructions into two parallel command streams and attempts to execute more than one command at the same time. Moreover, the Pentium is so efficient, it can handle most of the basic commands it encounters in only one clock cycle. It also sports a souped-up FPU. The Pentium has separate cache RAM for instructions and data, with a total of 16k of on-chip cache.

The Pentium has also gathered a reputation for running so hot that it requires its own mini cooling fan, since the faster a chip's heart beats, the higher its "blood pressure," just as a faster-revving auto engine runs hotter at higher RPMs. The new Pentiums operate at lower voltage, so they run cooler and more reliably, even without supplemental cooling (although they do sport a large honeycombed "heat sink" to radiate heat, and a fan is still a good idea).

Of course, Intel is not the only player in the PC-compatible CPU market. Chips from AMD, NexGen and Cyrix offer 486 features at competitive prices and with attractive performance while retaining full compatibility, and new "586" chips from these companies provide a less expensive alternative to the Intel Pentium.

Yet with all the variations in chip design, it's not easy to compare apples with apples when shopping for a computer. For example, a 40 MHz 386 runs a little faster than a 25 MHz 486. Did you think a 486 always ran faster than any 386? Even though a 386 is not as efficient, if it runs at a high enough clock speed, it can still outpace a 486 running at half the 386's clock speed.

Even though a 486DX chip has a speed-boosting numerical processor, a 486SX computer usually runs most applications just as fast. Why is that? Because only a few programs, notably certain spreadsheet functions and 3D software, actually bother to use the FPU, especially since software publishers want their software to run well on the more popular, less expensive 486SX systems. The most efficient computer calculations are carried out on *integers* (whole numbers without fractions), and you don't need an FPU for that.

But for some graphics packages, there is no substitute for an FPU. For example, Pixar's Typestry creates stunningly realistic three-dimensional type, and we use it in this book for several illustrations. For a typical complex 3D image, Typestry completes the picture in about 40 minutes on a 486SX-25 but takes less than 15 minutes with the 486DX-25. (A 386DX/25 with no FPU requires nearly an hour and a half.)

TIP You've read about the Pentium floating point error that can result in slight (some say trivial) inaccuracies when dividing certain numbers. If this overly concerns you (and it shouldn't), run System from the Control Panel, and click the Device Manager tab heading. Look for the System Devices item, and click the filename striplu.tif symbol to show its subitems. Double-click on the entry for Numeric Data Processor, and choose the Settings tab heading. Finally, turn on the check box for "Use only if the processor passes all diagnostics." However, this effectively disables your Pentium's FPU. If you use your machine for 3D rendering, this will drastically slow it down, and for no good reason—the division inaccuracies are vanishingly small, and have no real-world impact.

Putting It to the Test

Since commands run twice as fast, but system bus access is unchanged, a clock-doubled 486DX/2-66 runs about 70 percent faster than a 486DX-33. The DX4-100 is over twice as fast as a 486DX/2-66. The average 60 MHz Pentium is about two and a half to three times as fast.

There is a rather more scientific way to compare CPUs, using a benchmark test. A *benchmark* is a standard program written specifically to compare computer systems or components. It can measure the speed of a CPU, its video display or hard drive. For example, to test the speed of a computer, a benchmark could sort a list of 1,000 numbers or compute all the prime numbers to some arbitrary limit.

Intel has developed the *iCOMP* benchmark to compare the speeds of microprocessors running typical software. Table 14-1, courtesy of Intel, compares the effective speed ratings of all the microprocessors in the Intel family. Other benchmarks are usually published by computer magazines, such as *Windows Magazine*'s WinBench, often quoted to compare video card speed. (Note: A CPU's MHz rating doesn't really tell you how fast it runs. The iCOMP index, based on eight typical operations, is much more useful when comparing CPUs. The higher the iCOMP number, the faster the microprocessor.)

Microprocessor	MHz	iCOMP
Pentium™	100	815
Pentium	90	735
Pentium	66	567
Pentium	60	510
IntelDX4™	100	435
IntelDX4	75	319
IntelDX2™	66	297
IntelDX	50	231
IntelDX	40	182
IntelSX2™	50	180
i486DX™	50	249
with OverDrive™	(100)	231
i486DX	33	166
with OverDrive™	(66)	297
i486DX	25	122
i486SL™	33	166
i486SL	25	122
i486SX™	33	136
with OverDrive™	(66)	182
i486SX	25	100
with OverDrive™	(50)	231
i486SX	20	78
with OverDrive™	(40)	182
i386DX	33	68
i386DX	25	49
i386SL	25	41
i386SX	33	56
i386SX	25	39
i386SX	20	32

Table 14-1: *iCOMP CPU Speed Ratings*.

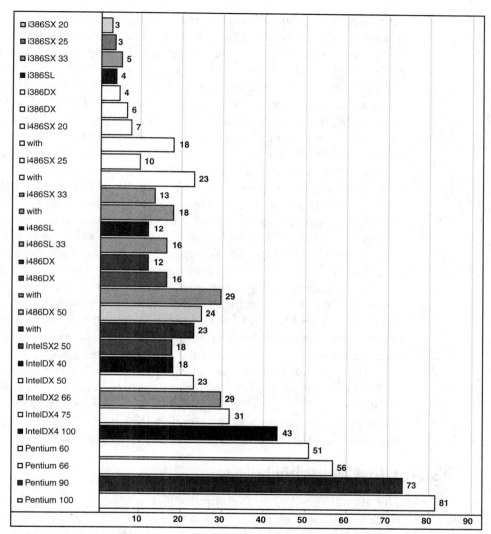

Source: iCOMP: A Simplified Measure of Relative Intel Microprocessor Performance, *Intel Corporation, 1993.*

RISCy Business?

In the future, Windows will no longer be an Intel-only club. Windows 95 will only run on Intel-compatible CPUs (and there are no plans to change this). Windows NT, an advanced workstation-class operating system, runs most Windows 3.1 (16-bit) and new 32-bit Windows software, and it includes powerful networking capabilities that makes it one of the best file servers on the market. Windows NT runs on advanced RISC microprocessors such as the DEC Alpha AXP, the MIPS RS6000 and now the Motorola PowerPC, as well as the familiar Intel chips.

RISC processors achieve their power by oversimplifying their instructions so that they always complete in a single clock cycle. The Pentium has many RISC features, but true RISC processors are simpler in design, so they can often cost much less to produce and don't overheat as they are made increasingly faster. The PowerPC runs so fast that it can pretend to be a 486 chip and run standard Windows at about the same speed as a slow 486SX-25 (some people say it's more like a 386, really). With Windows NT for the PowerPC, however, Windows programs will run at amazing speeds. New chips from Intel will give the PowerPC a run for its money, including 133 MHz Pentiums and the new P6 design that is designed especially for multitasking, and can be easily paired up with other P6 chips for economical multiprocessing.

While Windows NT will run on a wide variety of microprocessors, Windows 95 will only run on Intel CPUs because it contains embedded, highly optimized assembly language code that Microsoft is loath to reengineer (the original programmers don't even work for Microsoft anymore!). Tinkering with such low-level, undocumented code risks "breaking" Windows features that are essential for compatibility with existing Windows 3.1 software.

Also, the advanced user interface features of Windows 95 will probably not be a part of Windows NT until 1996, however, and Intel still has a few tricks up its sleeve (such as the Hewlett-Packard/Intel P7), so the 80X86 legacy of PC machines will be with us for some time to come.

It's Not Just Megahertz

The overall speed of your computer is determined by more than just the clock speed, or even how efficient the CPU is. In fact, with Windows, the transfer rate of your hard drive and how much RAM you have make more difference in terms of how fast your computer feels. If you had to choose between upgrading your computer from 4 to 8mb of RAM versus upgrading the CPU from a 386 to a 486, the memory upgrade would probably give you more bang for the buck. (That's because with only 4mb of RAM, Windows has to borrow spare memory from a swap file on your hard drive—and your hard drive is much slower than your RAM.)

Windows 95 doesn't care if you have a 386, a 486 or a Pentium—as long as you don't have a 286. The very first version of Windows 1.0 could actually run on a lowly 8086, although in this first version, Windows was little more than a graphical shell for running DOS programs. Windows 2.0 required the 286 chip, and Windows 3.0 would still run on a 286 machine, but poorly. Windows 3.1 led to the rapid embrace of the speedier 386 machines, and Windows has driven the sale of ever more powerful hardware. Yes, Windows has had a reputation for sluggishness, but one reason is that it has been chained to the lowly abilities of a 286 computer. Until Windows 95 debuted, very few programs took advantage of the special 32-bit features of the 386 processor.

Sadly, even now we are limited by older CPUs. The 386 is now fast becoming obsolete, yet there are special software features in the 486 CPU and powerful new commands available for the Pentium, which will probably languish for years just because too many people still need to run Windows on older hardware.

Of course, for many people, Windows 95 still runs acceptably on a 386DX-16 with 4 megabytes RAM—that is, unless you've ever been spoiled by running it on a DX4 or Pentium—then there's no going back!

TIP On the other hand, a 386SX chip, no matter how fast it is, is not suitable for use with Windows 95. The 386SX chip uses a 16-bit data path, so the 32-bit code in Windows 95 truly suffers when forced to run in such a tight space, leading to significantly poorer performance. Fortunately, it's very inexpensive and easy to upgrade a 386SX chip to a 386DX. While you're at it, consider using one of the popular "386 to 486" upgrade kits.

From Punchcards to Pixels

Windows seems so slow on older 386 computers because it's graphics-intensive. In DOS, applications are character-based, meaning that the screen displays are "drawn" from alphabetic and numeric characters, plus a few graphic symbols. In fact, the video display evolved from the line printer. On old time-sharing computers (this was just after the age of punch cards that forbade you to fold, staple or mutilate), computer users basically pecked away at electric typewriters (teletypewriters, or TTYs) to communicate with the computer. The amazing invention of video terminals allowed you to type on a "video printer," or glass TTY, instead.

A generation later, we are finally leaving this era behind. We still communicate using a keyboard most of the time—we've even preserved the archaic QWERTY layout (designed to make typing so difficult that fast typists wouldn't jam the mechanism!). But now that personal computers have crossed over from teletype to television, primitive text-only displays have been updated with graphics, animation and sound.

We won't belabor here the obvious advantages of a graphical user interface: the old arguments put forth by die-hard DOS fans against the Macintosh now seem rather quaint to all but the most reactionary—now that Windows has brought us all to graphical, intuitive computing. Indeed, Windows 95 combines the best features of Windows 3.1, Apple's Macintosh and IBM's OS/2 to create a new operating system of unparalleled power and elegance. Defending the bleak monochromatic world of DOS computing is as useless as defending black-and-white TV or gaslight.

Figure 14-4 shows a sample user interface for a DOS menu. Instead of entering a number from 1 to 7 from a list of choices, we can simply click on attractive 3D buttons (Figure 14-5).

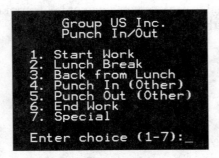

Figure 14-4: *Many DOS applications use only alphanumeric characters and require keyboard input.*

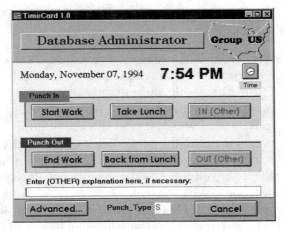

Figure 14-5: *A Windows design can make use of colorful 3D buttons that you can click on with the mouse.*

Instead of typing Y for Yes or N for No, we just click on a button labeled OK or Cancel. Rather than type a cryptic command like XCOPY C:\RAINBOW C:\GRAPHICS\ /S /E, we can simply drag and drop one folder onto another.

Character-based DOS applications need only write a single number to memory to display the letter *A* on the screen. Windows draws the shape of the *A* dot by dot, looking up the patterns of the letter in an image library called a *font*. By displaying text using graphics patterns, it's easy to mix graphics and text on the same screen and render the text exactly as it will appear when printed. Multiple sizes of type, in many fonts, in boldface or italics, can all be drawn on the screen together, making WYSIWYG (pronounced *wiz-zi-wig* and means "what you see is what you get") publishing a dream come true. By contrast, a DOS text-only screen displays all characters the same size and from the same font. The only variation is color.

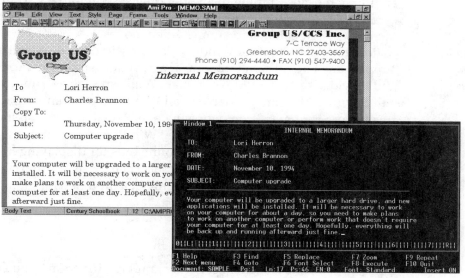

Figure 14-6: *Unlike the dull character-based DOS word processor (inset), Windows permits you to work with the actual typeset document on the screen.*

Even DOS applications that do use graphics are often limited to some least common denominator, since there are few standards for graphics in DOS. Early computer users basked in the cyan and magenta glow of CGA graphics and then graduated to the 16-color capabilities of EGA enhanced graphics before finally succumbing to the exotic 256-color VGA video modes. Windows made VGA graphics the new standard and thankfully laid to rest the bad graphics that PC users were saddled with. We now enjoy graphics resolution as high as 1280x1024, with over 16 million colors per pixel.

And even when DOS games and graphics packages use VGA graphics, they are usually limited to 320x200, 256-color displays, since the Super VGA 800x600 modes are implemented in a different way on every make and model of video card. The lack of standards for DOS video proved to be an intractable mess.

Not only are there few standards for video, but most other peripherals are eccentric too. Every printer manufacturer has its own version of a printer control language, with different commands to display boldface type, for example. A DOS word processor has to be programmed to work with every printer on the market and has be updated to support each new model that came out. The same DOS word processor had to be tested with each brand of video card, too. Every publisher had to spend time and money developing and testing their products for these variations.

In fact, before Windows, there were few useful software standards for anything: the closest thing to an operating system for PCs, MS-DOS, concerned itself only with your disk drives and included a few routines for memory management and simple video modes.

Perhaps the best gift of Windows is that Microsoft designed it to invisibly support any and all standards—as if all printers spoke the same language and all video cards would work alike. While specialized, unique drivers are still required, they are available to all Windows programs alike, and they free the programmers from worrying about such low-level issues. And instead of having to reinvent the wheel, Windows programmers can draw upon standard Windows graphics commands for displaying lines, circles, boxes and images. Another boon is that when a driver is improved for speed, all Windows programs suddenly benefit too, without having to be individually redesigned or enhanced.

Busting the Bottleneck

Since even the most efficient software graphics drivers are limited by the speed of the CPU, many new graphics cards now feature *coprocessors*. In effect, an extra computer is built into the video card itself, designed expressly for fast graphics. Rather than bogging down the main CPU with redrawing the gridlines, symbols, button bars and pie charts needed by a spreadsheet, accelerated graphics hardware does the hard work and frees up the CPU to run programs and make other kinds of calculations. A fast video card includes a "bit blit" engine for pumping graphics onto the screen, so animation, video playback and scrolling are smooth and speedy. The coprocessor can draw lines and rectangles as fast as Windows by itself can draw a single dot. Instead of having to draw and erase the mouse cursor, the hardware can float the cursor like a pixie "on top" of the rest of the graphics. These fast graphics cards sport optimized memory chips for fast redraws, transferring data up to 64 bits at a time.

If it weren't for Windows graphics standards, these hardware advances would have been adopted slowly and remained expensive toys, but these new graphics accelerators can simply substitute their hardware features in place of the old graphics software and transparently speed up graphics displays. Nobody has to rewrite software to support the new cards.

Since so much of Windows's sluggishness can be cured with an accelerated graphics card, two computers with the same CPU will seem to run Windows at different speeds just because one computer has a faster graphics card. A 386 with a fast graphics card and fast drivers can outperform the fastest 486 if it's stuck with an old-style VGA card.

Catch the Local Bus

Another recent innovation is the use of local bus graphics cards. In addition to the fast system bus, your computer employs a much slower input/output bus. The I/O bus sends data from your hard drive to the CPU or from the CPU to the video card. Your computer may run at 25 or 33 MHz, but the typical ISA bus pokes along at a paltry 8 MHz. (ISA means Industry Standard Architecture, the first PC standard for expansion card designs.) ISA bus transfers originally were limited to 8 bits at a time, but when the 286 CPU arrived, it brought a new ISA design that widened the I/O highway to 16 lanes (16 bits).

Even with 16 bits, the 8 MHz speed limit prevents sophisticated high-speed graphics. Squeezing data through such a slow, narrow channel creates a bottleneck that hampers throughput (the rate that data can flow). Fortunately, a way was found to hot-wire the graphics card directly into the data bus of the CPU, and local bus graphics were born. Within a year, the proprietary local bus standards were replaced by a uniform VESA local bus standard, and a booming market for VLB graphics cards soon developed. VLB features proved inexpensive to add to a motherboard design, and now all new computers feature local bus slots (although they don't all yet come with VLB graphics cards).

Figure 14-7: *Local bus lets graphic data punch through at maximum speed over a wider path, while the traditional ISA bus is like a bottleneck, throttling performance.*

At the same time the VESA committee (VESA stands for Video Electronics Standards Association) ratified the VESA local bus (VLB), Intel became concerned about the limitations of the VESA local bus. Since the VLB interfaced directly with the processor, it was limited to the 33 MHz top speed of the motherboards available at the time, which made it inappropriate for use with 60 and 66 MHz Pentium motherboards. Additional VLB cards could actually slow down the computer, since the VLB cards steal cycles from the CPU, inducing *wait states* that temporarily prevent it from accessing its own memory.

Intel's PCI standard is an alternative to local bus. (PCI stands for Peripheral Connection Interface.) PCI is usually called a local bus, but it really adds a new high-speed data bus that is independent of the CPU's speed, so PCI can transfer hundreds of megabytes per second. Whereas the VESA local bus was limited to a 32-bit-wide path, the PCI standard has no trouble grabbing 64 bits of data at a time.

VESA countered PCI with an improved local bus design, but PCI is perceived to be technologically superior, and Intel made the PCI chips available at a low enough cost that the PCI standard is quickly overtaking the popularity of the VESA local bus. PCI is also catching on with non-Intel manufacturers, including new models of the Apple Macintosh and IBM's PowerPC machines. It's theoretically possible to design a video card that will work with any of these machines, further assuring the future of PCI.

Once local bus technology caught on, other controllers, especially hard disk drive controllers, benefited from the new, fast access as well. For the consumer, VESA local bus will continue to be popular for a while, since so many new computers were sold with VLB slots. As a bonus, an unused VLB slot can still be used as a standard ISA slot, whereas PCI slots can only be used for PCI cards. PCI is used extensively on Pentium and high-end 486 computers, and will replace VLB in a year or so.

Local bus accelerated graphics cards are dozens, if not hundreds, of times faster than plain-Jane VGA graphics cards, and although they once cost thousands, you can now buy a quality local bus fast graphics card for about $150.

After ISA and before VLB was a fast design called EISA (extended ISA), which doubled the peripheral bus width from 16 to 32 bits and increased its speed. Unfortunately, EISA motherboards were considerably more expensive to produce than ISA boards, and 99 percent of available add-on cards were still ISA-based, so EISA remained a high-end bus standard reserved for the upper echelons of wealthy power users or for corporate file servers and mainframe substitutes.

IBM's own MCA (Micro Channel Architecture) has floundered for years, ever since IBM introduced it to try to take back the reins of PC system design. But MCA came too late. The standard ISA bus had become too firmly entrenched, there were never many cards designed to the MCA spec, and, even when IBM opened up the specifications to the MCA bus, it was also too expensive and ahead of its time. However, the MCA bus offers the kind of automatic configuration features that we are only now seeing in the new Plug-and-Play specification, an improvement over the standard ISA and local bus designs.

Getting Ready for Plug & Play

Plug and Play is the solution to a quagmire of technical incompatibilities that plague computer users when they try to plug in their own expansion cards. Competing for limited computer resources, expansion cards trample on each other in their quest for supremacy. With patience and organization, it's possible to make it work, and we'll discuss how in the next chapter. In the near future, Plug and Play will make expanding your PC as easy as loading bread in a toaster—well, almost as easy.

Plug and Play also promises new intelligence in the way Windows treats your hardware. It allows a notebook to be unplugged from its base station, automatically copying needed files from the desktop hard drive, and updating them when plugged back in. Plug-and-Play features allow your computer to transparently attach to a network. In fact, with a wireless interface, your notebook will log on to the network and attach to shared printers as soon as you enter the building.

Most computers sold in the latter half of 1994 fully support Plug and Play, and manufacturers are introducing new Plug-and-Play peripherals, some with *Microsoft At Work* technology. Now a scanner or a label printer can share a serial port with a modem. A fax/modem can send editable documents instead of just graphical images of pages—without the complication of modem software. You'll soon be able to print on your copy machine like a laser printer, with a full array of sorting, collating, duplexing, stapling and paper selection choices.

Moving On

Now that you have some background, we'll continue with a discussion of Plug and Play and hardware expansion issues in the next chapter, where we show you how to upgrade your computer: adding more memory, a larger hard drive, a new sound card or a better video card. Windows makes it easy by reconfiguring itself almost automatically.

Chapter 15

Upgrading Your Computer

In this chapter, we'll get mechanical. Just as any driver should know at least a few things about cars (how to open the hood, change a tire, locate the fuses), it's worth knowing a little about the inside of your computer. Not only can a few simple tricks save you expensive repair shop bills, doing some simple things yourself is also a lot quicker.

In this chapter, we'll cover how to upgrade various cards, speed things up with a new microprocessor, add memory, add an extra hard drive, resolve conflicts and provide various other hardware tips and tricks that most any computer user should find worth knowing. We'll also tell you when you need to call the repair shop.

Even the most modern 486 or Pentium Windows 95 system inherits many of the design strategies (or limitations) of the original 8088 or 80286 computers running DOS. Although PCs have always had a generous expansion capability (a feature inspired by the Apple II computer, yet conspicuously absent on Apple Macintoshes for many years), PC makers assumed that you would have a computer dealer or repair shop install any necessary expansion cards. That assumption turned out to be quite wrong.

In the early '80s, you could void your warranty by opening the computer and installing cards. This restriction was dropped when it became obvious that users were indeed installing their own video cards, sound cards, game cards, memory cards, even hard drives on cards. Now, you're expected to know how to do these things—or pay a high price to get someone else to do it.

Although the great majority of today's computer owners aren't the tinkering hobbyists of the 1980s, and most just don't have time to learn the intricacies of PC hardware, neither do they want to surrender all control over their computers or pay someone to do everything for them. Particularly when most of this stuff is simple and easy to learn.

If you have even a slight do-it-yourself bent, or if you're interested in saving time and money, it could be worth your while to read this chapter and explore some of the fundamentals of PC hardware expansion. We'll also see how to deal with some of the frustrations that can arise when trying to get multiple cards from different manufacturers to cooperate within your computer.

Hardware Configuration

While most of us would never dream of disassembling our VCR or opening the back of our microwave oven, it's actually quite commonplace for people to crack the case of their computer, to add expansion devices such as multimedia cards (sound, video), drives (hard disks, CD-ROMs, tape drives), additional RAM or even a microprocessor upgrade.

Although the manuals for these upgrades provide your best instruction on how to specifically install them, in this chapter we'll cover some general techniques that help when you're working inside a computer, including important safety precautions. Before you actually get started, though, it's important to read the manuals, and the rest of this chapter, so that you'll have an understanding of configuration issues.

Another reason to read the manual and this chapter is that you may be called upon to configure your card manually, setting the dreaded IRQ, DMA and I/O addresses (explained later in this chapter).

Cracking the Case

To begin working on your computer, you'll need to remove the cover, or case. Ideally, you'll prepare a well-lit work area, protecting the desk or table you use with some newspapers or a desk blotter to prevent scratches. It can be handy to have a bright desk lamp or flashlight that you can shine into the crevices of the case, especially when you drop a screw. (If you do drop a screw into the case, make sure you retrieve it, since a lost screw can create disastrous connections—otherwise known as short circuits.)

You won't need many tools: a cordless power screwdriver with a Phillips-head bit comes in handy. You may also want to use a non-magnetic (nylon) screwdriver when installing a floppy or hard disk drive, although they're usually well shielded. For everything else, a magnetized screwdriver makes it much easier to position a screw exactly before you drive it into place. Sometimes you'll have to configure a card by repositioning jumper caps on the card. Needle-nosed pliers or a set of sturdy tweezers make it easy to pull off the tiny jumpers. If the manual tells you to remove a jumper, you may actually want to place the jumper so it covers only one of the pins (it won't make a connection), but you'll have the jumper handy if you ever decide to configure the card a different way.

You'll also want to have a cup of some kind to hold the screws you remove (an empty egg carton makes it easy to sort the screws if you like).

Don't Get Fried

Your computer's worst enemy is static electricity. The tiniest spark, even one you can't see or feel, can carry 10,000 volts. The only reason it doesn't kill you is that despite the major voltage, the amperage is tiny. But if you were shrunk to the size of the circuitry in your computer chips, you'd get the shock of your life. RAM chips and SIMMs are especially sensitive. Their finer-than-hair connections can melt, or the tiny transistors can fuse, in a microscopic wisp of smoke.

Some engineers insist on using a grounded wrist strap, available at most electronics supply stores and computer stores, but this may be overkill for the average person. However, spending a few dollars on a disposable wrist strap (now included with many upgrade kits) can be effective insurance. You should try to avoid handling the metal (conductive) parts of a card. Instead, hold it by the insulated fiberglass board or the metal bracket. Always ground yourself by touching some large metal part of your computer, such as the chassis, before picking up a sensitive part.

Obviously, you want to unplug and turn off the power to your computer before you work on it, right? Actually, many professionals recommend that you keep the computer plugged in, but turned off, of course. That way, the metal case of the computer remains grounded via the grounding terminal in your wall socket and can rapidly drain away static. After all, the only dangerous voltage is inside your power supply unit (the metal box with the fan in it, shown in Figure 15-2). You must never open the power supply box, even if the computer is unplugged, since dangerous high voltage can be stored in the power supply capacitors for hours after it's shut off.

Better Safe than Sorry

Throughout the rest of the your computer, however, the voltage is only about three to five volts DC. If leaving it plugged in still makes you nervous, you can always attach the wrist strap to something that is grounded if you want to be more well-protected from static. But you still want to make certain that the power is shut off, since inserting or removing a part with the power on can lead to damaging power surges, and you could ruin the component. (For the same reason, you may want to avoid plugging or unplugging cable connectors from the back of your computer while it's on, although we've done it for years without any problem.)

Another way to damage a component is to plug it in backward. Many parts, such as memory SIMMs, are keyed to prevent you from inserting them incorrectly, and cards can only plug in the right way.

If you insert a replacement chip, like a BIOS or processor upgrade, be sure to follow the directions on how to align the chip so that pin 1 (usually marked with a notch or a white dot) lines up with pin 1 on the socket (also marked with a notch, a dot, or a tiny "1" on the motherboard). If you still can't tell which way to put in the chip, look at how the other chips are oriented. Most of them are going to be "pointed" the same way.

Now you're ready to begin working on your computer. Remove the screws that secure the case (don't remove the screws surrounding the power supply). You usually want to leave the back panel of the computer facing you while you work on it. If you have a tower case, you'll have to orient it tower-wise while removing the case, but you'll want to lay it on its side while working inside it.

The case will either slide away from you or lift straight up (or sometimes slide forward a bit and then up). Be patient until you've figured out how to remove it, and don't force anything. If it still won't budge, make sure you've removed all the necessary screws. (Sometimes there are screws under the computer, along the sides, too.)

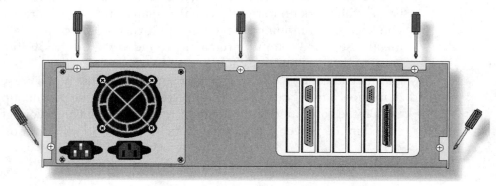

Figure 15-1: *Remove the screws marked here, but leave the others alone.*

With the case off, take a look around to get oriented. Assuming the rear panel of the case is still facing you, you'll see the various cards plugged in the back of the computer, and the power supply will usually be on the left. The power supply has wires leading to the motherboard and wires (red, yellow, black, white) leading to the hard disk and floppy drives. Figure 15-2 shows the inside of a typical (ISA/VL-BUS) computer case.

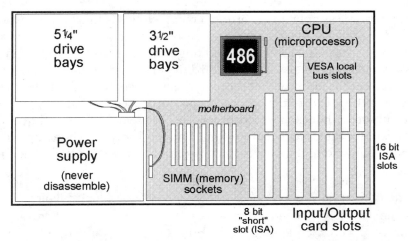

Figure 15-2: *It's a good idea to get familiar with the innards before you poke around.*

Shuffling Cards

To remove a card, follow the rear of the card bracket forward to locate the actual card, and trace this back to where it's held in place by a screw at the rear of the computer. (The screw is usually about half an inch to the left of the actual card, unless it's a PCI card, in which case the bracket screw is on the right.) Remove the screw, and get a good grip on the front and end of the card, avoiding the conductive components. Also try not to press too hard into the back of the card where all the little leads are sticking up—they can be sharp and break your skin.

Easy Does It

The best way to pull out the card is to rock it gently but firmly back and forth while pulling up. Don't try to yank it straight out. Just use your fingers—any tools may damage the card. If it's still stubborn, you can press against the bracket that shows through the back of the computer while pushing up to loosen it.

Removing the card is the easy part. Inserting one is a little more tricky. You have to align both the card's edge with the slot socket and the metal "tongue" of the bracket against the back of the computer (the tongue must fit into a slot found along the plane of the bottom of the case). Gently rock the card into place to align it; then press it firmly straight down at the front and back of the card. Use a bright light and inspect the card to make sure it is completely and correctly inserted front to back. The most common failure when installing a new card is simply not inserting it completely. As long as it's seated evenly and the bracket fits flush with the case, don't be concerned if you can still see the top part of the leads (the gold fingers) above the slot socket. Typically, only the lower one-third of the card fingers actually fit into the slot.

If a card is not installed properly, there's usually no harm to it when you power it up, except that your computer may beep plaintively and refuse to continue with its usual startup process. To save the time and trouble of having to remove the cover a second time, you might want to hook up the monitor and keyboard and give it a quick bootup before you reattach the case.

 TIP   The gold or tin "fingers" on a card can oxidize, reducing their conductivity. When you remove a card, lightly rub a pencil eraser across the contacts to polish them brightly before you reinsert the card. (Don't overdo it; you don't want to rub off all the metal.)

This trick can sometimes fix an old card that's been giving you grief. You can also polish the leads on a RAM chip. Also, with RAM chips, you should match the type of metal on the leads with the type of metal in the SIMM socket; Intel recommends that you avoid mixing metals (such as gold on tin) to avoid corrosion and prevent spurious crashes. So before you purchase new memory SIMMs, check to see what kind of metal is used in the socket, since you can buy SIMMs with either gold or tin leads.

Figure 15-3: *This detail shows you exactly how a card fits into the backplane of the computer case.*

Don't worry if the bracket doesn't align perfectly with the back of the computer. It's common to have to "shoehorn" the top of the bracket into place before you can drive the screw to hold it in place. (Don't shoehorn the card, just the flexible metal bracket, if necessary.)

Some computers have a mixture of different slots (the paired plastic bars—sockets—on the motherboard in the computer into which you fit expansion cards). The short 8-bit slots can be used only with a corresponding "short slot" card, most commonly internal modem or serial port cards. The 16-bit ISA card slots have two sockets, separated by a gap. The VESA local bus is a third type of slot. (You can read more about the various types of slots—ISA, VESA, PCI and others—in Chapter 14.)

Sometimes a card will fit into a smaller slot than it's designed for, but, even so, it won't work. On the other hand, it's okay to plug a "short" 8-bit card into a 16-bit slot, and you can also plug a standard 16-bit card into a VESA local bus socket, which is actually a 16-bit socket with an extra connector. PCI slots are completely unlike ISA slots, though, and you can only plug a PCI card into them.

Sometimes a motherboard will have a dual-purpose ISA/PCI slot, which share the same bracket position. The only way you can put both cards into that slot is to remove the bracket from the ISA card, which isn't a good idea (unless you're desperate for another ISA slot), because then there's no way to securely lock down the card.

DIP Switches

Sometimes you'll be asked to set some *DIP switches* on a card, which are tiny on/off switches made of plastic. (DIP stands for Dual Inline Package, in case you wonder, although it's a pretty meaningless acronym.) DIP switches are fairly easy to work with; you can use the tip of a ballpoint pen to flip them. The easiest way to customize a card, though, is via software so on some cards you don't have to set any DIPs. After you get the card in, you run some setup software from a manufacturer-supplied disk. (Later in this chapter, we'll also discuss the new Plug-and-Play cards, which can be interrogated and reconfigured on the fly when your computer starts up.)

 Before you fiddle with a card, you might want to sketch the default configuration of any switches.

Sometimes it will be difficult to determine how to set these switches and jumpers. The worst case scenario is if you've lost the manual to a card. For example, you might need to disable the external COM port (communications) on your hard drive (IDE) card because you're adding an internal modem. In this case, you might try changing only one jumper or DIP switch at a time, turning on the computer to see if it worked and then switching it back if it didn't and trying the next one (this is usually harmless, but we can't be responsible for wanton acts of desperation on your part).

Out With the Old

Once you've got your computer case off, you can install one of the easiest upgrades. You can actually remove the computer's CPU (central processing unit) and replace it with a faster one. In many cases, this task only involves popping out one chip and sticking in a new one, and you get anywhere from a 70 percent to 150 percent boost in speed.

A variety of CPU upgrade kits are available, including ones that replace a 286 with a 386 or pseudo-486 chip. You can also replace a 386 with a special kind of 486 chip package, although you won't get the same performance as a whole new 486 motherboard. If you have a 386SX, you can add a 387 math coprocessor to your spare slot (see Chapter 14, "Deep Inside the Machine") to boost some operations such as spreadsheet calculations, 3D programs and graphics programs like photo-retouching—things that depend on heavy-duty math.

In With the New

If you have a 486SX, you can nearly double your speed by adding an Intel OverDrive 486DX2 chip to your spare "487" socket. If you don't have a spare socket, you can usually just remove your old chip using the chip puller included in the OverDrive kit and push the new chip into place. Some motherboards include the coveted Zero Insertion Force (ZIF) socket that includes a little lever to release the chip. That makes it easy to replace the chip without any special tools.

Make sure you get an OverDrive kit that matches the speed of your old processor. 486SX-25 users need a ODP25/50 chip, whereas 486SX-33 users should get the ODP33/66 chip. As we mentioned in Chapter 14, the OverDrive chips runs internally twice as fast, slowing down when accessing memory at normal speed. On average, a DX2 OverDrive chip runs about 70 percent faster. If you're replacing an SX chip, which lacks a floating point processor, your speed will increase even more dramatically with some types of software.

The Intel DX4 chip gives you an even bigger boost, since it runs internally at three times the clock speed of your bus. A 100 mHz DX4 chip makes your computer run nearly as fast as a 60 mHz Pentium. That's a good thing, because the promised Intel Pentium OverDrive chip is not compatible with some older motherboards.

If you're interested in the Pentium OverDrive upgrade, make sure your motherboard supports the P24T (the technical name for the chip), and includes a jumper setting to enable *write-back cache*. Without this support, you won't get Pentium-class performance. You may also need to upgrade the BIOS chip in your computer—it's often cheaper to just replace the motherboard with a modern one.

On some computers, the 486SX chip is hard to get to. You may need to partially remove the motherboard. To do this, first remove all the cards (you don't have to remove the cables from the hard disk card; just lay it out of the way on top of the hard drive). Examine the motherboard for a few screws that you can remove. Be gentle with the motherboard—too much flexing can lead to cracks in circuit traces. You can usually move the motherboard enough to get at hard-to-reach areas without unplugging anything. If you do need to remove the power supply connectors on the motherboard and forget how to plug them back in, keep in mind that the black wires on the two connectors meet in the center.

Once you can figure out how to remove the motherboard, though, you may get better performance by replacing the entire motherboard instead of swapping the CPU. Keep in mind that if you substitute a new Pentium motherboard with PCI slots, you may not be able to use your existing VESA local bus cards (see Chapter 14 for more about VESA local bus), and you'll need a new type of SIMM memory (more about this in a moment.) The only real complication with changing the motherboard is keeping track of all the connectors for the speaker, LEDs (status lights), turbo, reset and keylock controls on the panel. It's a good idea to make notes before you disconnect the wires. For example, you'll note that the connector with red and black wires is for the speaker; the one with orange, black and brown wires goes to the turbo switch and so on. If you lose track, follow the wires to see where they go—usually to an LED or switch on the case.

TIP When you're plugging the connectors (especially LED connectors) into the motherboard, make sure that the "hot" wire is
plugged in so that it matches up with the + or 1 symbol on the
motherboard. Typically, wires marked black or brown are
ground, and red, white or yellow wires are positive ("hot") wires.

Memory Expansion

If your computer has spare SIMM sockets, you can add more RAM simply
by plugging in new SIMMs. A SIMM (Single Inline Memory Module) is like
a tiny version of the full-size cards we've already discussed. A SIMM is
usually inserted at an angle and then pushed upward and sideways to rotate
and lock it into place (see Figure 15-4). It's usually easiest to put all the
SIMMs before locking each one. The SIMM can be inserted only one way—
orient new ones the same way as the existing SIMMs. Examine the installed
SIMMs closely under a bright light to make sure they are fully seated and
firmly locked into place. (They click when correctly seated.)

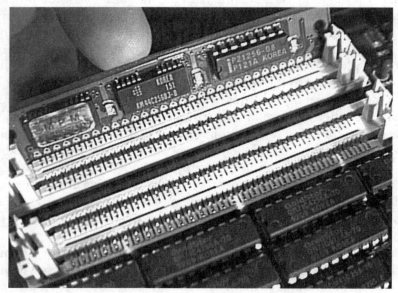

Figure 15-4: *How to insert a SIMM memory module.*

Typically, a 4mb computer uses four 1mb SIMMs, with four SIMM sockets left empty. You can add four more 1mb SIMMs to go to a total of 8mb RAM. If you already have 8mb RAM, your only choice is to remove all the 1mb SIMMs (you might be able to sell them) and buy some 4mb SIMMs. With eight SIMM sockets and eight 4mb SIMMs, you can insert up to 32mb. SIMM memory costs about $40 per megabyte, though, so it's usually not affordable to install more than 16mb, and Windows won't run much faster with more than 16mb RAM, unless you run intensive CAD or DTP work. Some motherboards can accept 8mb and 16mb SIMMs and theoretically allow as much as 64 or 128mb RAM (or more).

One way to reuse your old 1mb SIMMs is to put four 4mb SIMMs in the first four SIMM sockets (Bank 0) and put four 1mb SIMMs in Bank 1 to get a total of 20mb RAM.

Many newer, inexpensive motherboards have only four SIMM sockets, so you have to switch to 4mb SIMMs right away if you want more RAM. If you're lucky, the motherboard will already use a 4mb SIMM, so you won't have to get rid of the old 1mb SIMMs.

Pentium and newer 486 motherboards use a 72-pin "double-sided" SIMM and won't accept the standard 36-pin SIMMs. Since Pentium motherboards have only four SIMM sockets, it's best to buy one with a single 16mb SIMM instead of starting with an 8mb SIMM and adding another 8mb SIMM later, since this preserves your option of populating all four with 16mb SIMMs. (You can even buy 64mb SIMMs and configure a system with a whopping 256mb of RAM.)

Standard memory chips use eight bits per byte for data storage, plus an extra *parity* bit for error checking (the parity bit is the sum of all the bits in a byte, although only the rightmost bit is stored). The memory chips can detect when the parity doesn't match up, and halt the system. This may seem severe, but consider what happens when a memory failure goes unnoticed. If it's RAM used for your hard drive cache (the cache is explained in Chapter 5, "Inside the File System"), it can corrupt the hard drive. If it's RAM used by a program, it could cause an error that leads to incorrect calculations, scrambled spreadsheets or gobbledygook documents, and you might not discover it in time to protect yourself.

Some computer manufacturers are starting to use memory chips without parity checking, since memory prices are still running high, and the parity bits in an 8mb computer add up to 1mb extra RAM. The rationale here is that the system can run a memory test on powerup (Windows also tests memory on startup). But sometimes a memory error can occur spontaneously (and temporarily), often due to a cosmic ray from beyond the earth or a gamma ray emitted from the ceramic packaging surrounding the chip itself (all ceramics are feebly radioactive, as is driveway gravel and the bricks in your house).

So you may want to pay that little bit extra for more protection parity bits provide. If you start to get a lot of parity errors, you may need to replace one of your RAM chips. Tracking down which one went bad can be tough, though; for that you may have to take your computer to be serviced.

In any case you should find out whether your computer uses parity RAM chips or not. Parity chips are marked 1x36x9 for 1mb chips, whereas the less expensive (Macintosh-compatible) 1x36x8 chips are required for computers without parity. (A new kind of SIMM computes parity on the entire SIMM, rather than on each byte, and creates a "simulated" parity bit that fools the computer into accepting the SIMM as a parity SIMM, without using extra RAM chips. These SIMMs are less expensive, but you do give up a little bit of protection.)

You should also match the speed of the SIMMs with those already on your motherboard. For most computers, a 70ns (nanosecond) SIMM will work just fine. While it's okay to use faster SIMMs (smaller numbers are faster), there's no point adding faster SIMMs than you already have, since the computer accesses all memory at the rate of the slowest chips.

Installing a Hard Drive

The two most common hard drive designs are IDE (Integrated Drive Electronics), also called AT or ATAPI drives, and SCSI (Small Computer System Interface), popularized by the Macintosh. SCSI is highly favored by power users. However, the new EIDE (Enhanced IDE) specification, improves on IDE and is comparable to SCSI in terms of speed.

Ideally, you'll be installing the same kind of drive that's already in your computer, so you won't have to remove your interface card and configure a new one (as you'd have to do when moving from IDE to SCSI). On this note, you usually can't add a second IDE card to a system that already has one. If you need more than two IDE hard drives, you can buy specialized IDE adapters that allow this.

You might want to change your adapter anyway. For example, you might be upgrading to one of the new high performance IDE drives that can be controlled with an Enhanced IDE (EIDE) controller. They allow 32-bit data transfer over the local bus and can be used with large capacity drives (540mb, 730mb, 1gb or more). Look for IDE cards that include built-in 16550 (*not 16450*) serial ports, a game port and a printer port (the newer ones support super-fast Enhanced Parallel Port [EPP] or Enhanced Capability Port [ECP] printer ports). If you have trouble with the joystick/game port on the IDE card, it may conflict with the one on your sound card. Disable one of them.

 TIP Not all "enhanced IDE controllers" truly support all features of enhanced IDE. One hallmark of enhanced IDE is the ability to read several blocks from the hard drive at once (multiple block transfer) and transfer them 32 bits at a time over the local bus. But another important feature is Logical Block Addressing (LBA). Without LBA support in your computer's BIOS or on the substitute BIOS of the EIDE card, you won't be able to successfully use the new large IDE hard drives with 540mb, 730mb, even gigabyte capacities.

Doctor & Igor?

When adding a new IDE hard drive to an existing system, you have to configure one of them as a *Master* and the other one as a *Slave*. (Not too politically correct. Why not just Primary and Secondary, or Skipper and Gilligan?) You really need the manuals for the drives to figure out this configuration, and it may only work with two drives made by the same manufacturer. (You may be able to get this info faxed to you by the manufacturer if you call their technical support line.)

Examine how your existing hard drive is attached to the computer chassis, either directly screwed into a 3.5-inch drive bay or with a 5.25-inch mounting kit (two brass brackets) in the larger bay. The drive may also have rails screwed into the side to slide it into place in the drive bay, and it may be attached either with more screws along the side or two screws at the front. You may have to remove the plastic front panel of your computer to slide the drive in, especially when installing a drive with a front bezel, such as a CD-ROM drive.

Perfect Alignment

The Master (or the only drive on a single-drive system) should be plugged into either connector at the end of the IDE ribbon cable, with the red stripe on the ribbon corresponding to Pin 1 on the drive. (Pin 1 on the drive is usually marked with a tiny number on the circuit board behind the connector. But check the manual to be sure.)

In addition to the data cable, you need to plug in one of your spare power plugs from the power supply. They have white trapezoidal plugs on the end, so you can't insert them upside down. If you don't have enough spare plugs, you can buy a Y-splitter from a computer/electronics supplier.

The second, Slave hard drive usually plugs into the middle connector, and the far end of the cable plugs into the pins on the IDE interface card. (The usual term *interface card* is somewhat of a misnomer. IDE drives *integrate* the interface intelligence on the drive itself, so IDE cards can be manufactured cheaply. Hence the term IDE—Integrated Drive Electronics. SCSI cards, on the other hand, may contain an embedded microcomputer to provide the intelligence needed to coordinate up to seven attached devices.)

The red stripe on the ribbon cable should also align with pin 1 on the card's IDE connector. (If the connector doesn't have enough pins, you may be trying to connect it to the floppy drive pins.) Pin 1 is almost always toward the rear of the card (assuming the rear panel of the computer faces you), and it is usually marked with a tiny 1 on the circuit board.

You'll also typically attach the floppy cable to the same card, and a two-wire connector from the hard drive status light LED (attached to your front panel). This light usually has red and white wires and is often marked HD LED on the little black connector. Plug the LED connector so that the red wire aligns with the "1" or a "+" symbol on the card. (If it's reversed, it won't hurt anything, but the LED won't flicker during drive access.)

Mind Your P's & Q's

If you're installing a SCSI (Small Computer System Interface) drive, make sure that it is properly *terminated*. A terminating resistor keeps the SCSI signal from rebounding from the end of the cable like a confusing echo. The last internal drive on the SCSI chain must be terminated (with little plug-in terminating resistors, a resistor pack, a jumper or switch setting). If there are no external devices (or if you have external ones only), the card itself must be terminated. If you have external devices, the last SCSI device must have an external SCSI termination block. Remember, both ends of the SCSI chain (with the host adapter in the middle) must be terminated for proper results. Also, the total length of the internal SCSI cable should be no longer than one foot, and the total length of the external cables should not exceed three feet.

A single SCSI host adapter card is a jack-of-all-trades, controlling up to seven attached SCSI devices. SCSI can also be much faster than IDE cards, supporting up to 10 megabytes per second data transfer on a local bus. (Fast Wide SCSI can boost this transfer to 40 mbps.) The new Enhanced IDE is catching up, though, with up to 11 mbps, and it can control more than two devices, including a new breed of IDE (ATAPI) CD-ROM drives.

Each device on the SCSI bus must have a unique identifier, or SCSI address. The SCSI hard drive must be set to unit 0 in order to boot (to be the drive that the computer looks for when power is turned on in order to bring up DOS or Windows). Typically, SCSI address 1 is reserved for a second hard drive, and address 7 is for the SCSI host adapter itself. You can use any number from 2 to 6 for other devices, such as a SCSI CD-ROM or scanner, as long as it is a unique address number and doesn't conflict with the address of another SCSI device on the same bus.

If you mix both IDE and SCSI drives in the same computer (yes, it's possible), keep in mind that the IDE drive will always be configured as drive C:. You may also need to load SCSI drivers in your CONFIG.SYS file to access the SCSI drives if they are not configured as unit 0 and unit 1, or if you have more than two SCSI drives. Check with the manufacturer of your SCSI hard disk controller to see if they have updated Windows 95 drivers available.

When you've installed the hard drive, you need to configure your computer's CMOS settings to recognize the drive. To enter the BIOS/CMOS setup, press the F1, F2, Esc or Del key while you power up. (Check your manual if pressing a key doesn't do the trick. Some older computers require booting a Setup Disk, and some clones have their own unique method. Often, when you first turn on power, you'll see a memory check and a message about which key to press to enter Setup. Some computers use the Ctrl+Alt+Ins sequence to enter the BIOS Setup.)

BIOS Basics

The system BIOS (Basic Input/Output Subsystem, pronounced *bye-oss*), which contains the core code required to boot your computer and support simple input/output for DOS, is not actually used by Windows, except when Windows can't directly control your hardware. Future PCs may not even contain a BIOS, relying on Windows 95 to take charge immediately. The BIOS settings you enter (or those set by the factory) are stored in a special kind of memory chip that is kept "alive" by a tiny battery, since all RAM chips lose their settings, their data, when not powered.

The Complementary Metal Oxide (or CMOS, pronounced *see-moss*) technology used in fashioning these chips accounts for the acronym and for their low power consumption. (CMOS technology is used extensively in notebook computers for this reason, even though it costs a little more.) The built-in battery is usually trickle-charged while your computer runs, but if you leave the computer turned off a long time, your computer forgets its BIOS/CMOS settings.

Sometimes the BIOS settings get wiped out when you insert or remove cards. You also may need to replace a battery after about five years (assuming your computer isn't completely obsolete five years from now!).

Rarely, a computer crash can get so out of hand that it scrambles the BIOS settings, and your computer won't boot and won't even let you enter BIOS Setup to correct the problem. To manually wipe out the CMOS, you can remove the battery and let the CMOS "drain" for a few hours. You usually just remove a jumper to disable the internal battery. The pins for the external battery can be shorted to quickly drain the CMOS. This wipes out your now-insane CMOS settings, restoring them to the factory defaults, and you can start anew. Since the "permanent" BIOS settings are actually subject to these problems, it's important to write down your settings, especially if your BIOS doesn't include a hard drive autodetect option, since you can't boot your computer without the proper settings.

The newer BIOS designs include an option to automatically detect the configuration of attached IDE hard drives, but with other types, if you lose your BIOS settings, you will have to type into Setup the number of heads, cylinders (tracks) and number of sectors per track into a drive-type table. The BIOS includes a list of standard drive types (that are in fact usually outdated), so look for a custom drive type (usually type 46 or 47) that lets you enter the actual description, the settings listed in your hard drive manual. If you get it right, the BIOS should display the correct size of the hard drive (200mb, 420mb or whatever it is).

Truth in Advertising?

Don't be dismayed if Setup reports a drive size that doesn't match the "real" size of your hard drive. Most hard drive manufacturers pretend that a megabyte is one million bytes. In their opinion, a megabyte is 1,000 kilobytes, and a kilobyte is 1,000 bytes. Everyone else knows that a kilobyte (k) is 1,024 bytes, and a megabyte (mb) is 1,024 times 1,024 bytes, or 1,048,576 bytes. So a 540mb hard drive, according to the manufacturer, has 540,000,000 bytes. But divide 540,000,000 by 1,048,576 and you get the true size: 515mb. You can check this calculation by multiplying the cylinder count times the number of heads times the sectors per track times the number of bytes per sector (512). The result is the exact number of bytes actually available on your hard drive. (This drive size inflation is similar to the notorious "measurements" given by television and computer monitor manufacturers. For a dismal surprise, measure your monitor screen diagonally. You may have thought you had a 15" monitor—check again! The specifications are based on the size of the tube, not the visible area inside the monitor's bezel.)

As we mentioned before, some BIOS designs won't let you enter a custom drive type with more than 1,024 cylinders. As a result, you may be forced to configure your 540mb drive as a 512mb drive. That's one reason to buy an enhanced IDE controller if you get one of these big drives—they usually support the larger drive types.

Drive controllers can contain their own settings for drive types. SCSI host adapters always query the drive to determine its settings, so here too you don't enter a drive type in the BIOS Setup. Instead, use setting Type 1 or Not Installed.

After All That, It Doesn't Work

Assuming you have the correct BIOS/CMOS settings, and the hard drive still won't boot, either the cable is plugged in upside down (usually no harm done, just reverse it), or the drive's not getting power (check the power supply connector), or the IDE card/SCSI adapter card is not seated firmly or configured properly.

Another reason a drive won't boot is that it was never formatted. In this case, you'll have to use a DOS boot floppy to start your system, and run the FDISK and FORMAT commands to prepare the computer for installing Windows 95. (See Chapter 22, "The Other Face: DOS 7" for a quick reference to DOS commands like FDISK.) Windows offers to create just such an Emergency Boot Disk when you run Windows Setup. (You can also make one by running Add/Remove Programs—via the Control Panel—and clicking on the Startup Disk heading.)

If you purchased Windows 95 as the "full" version, rather than as an upgrade, the Setup program can automatically partition and format a new (empty) hard drive as part of Windows 95 setup. Just boot your computer from Windows Setup Disk 1.

With other types of devices, even if you've installed them correctly, they may yet fail to function properly (or at all). In most cases, this failure is the result of the new card conflicting with another device in your computer. That's our next topic.

Software Configuration

Cards naturally need to communicate with your computer's CPU (central processing unit). They can interrupt the CPU to request immediate service, using one of the IRQ (interrupt request) lines, or they can be passively scanned by the CPU. The communication between the CPU and the hardware is supported by special software drivers. You'll have to configure Windows 95 (which is software) to support your add-on peripherals (the hardware).

EyeRocks, DeeMays & EyeOhs

The three methods used for this communication with the CPU are IRQs, DMAs and I/O addresses. You might find it easier to deal with acronyms if you pronounce them as words, hence "EyeRock," "DeeMay" and "EyeOh." (Of course, using acronyms can lead to silly pronunciations such as "Miz Dose" for MS-DOS.)

One way to pass data back and forth is by sharing a section of memory (either computer memory or memory on the card itself) with the CPU. The CPU is said to have Direct Memory Access (DMA) to the shared block of memory, and it can give commands or send data to the card by writing to the memory block, and look for replies or read data directly from the memory on the card.

A Big Chunk, All at Once

Many hard drive controllers use DMA to speed up disk access. Instead of making the CPU read one byte at a time and store each byte in memory, the hard drive controller fetches an entire block of data from the hard drive directly into a memory buffer, bypassing the computer's own CPU. This frees up the CPU to continue its work and makes everything run more smoothly.

When Windows plays a .WAV audio file, it copies a fragment of the .WAV file directly to the DMA buffer, and the sound card plays the digital data as analog sound. Your computer doesn't wait for this snippet of sound to finish but continues running your other software. The instant the chunk of sound concludes, the sound card fires off an IRQ alarm so that Windows will drop what it's doing and transfer the next part of the .WAV sound. Any delay will introduce choppiness into the otherwise smooth playback of the sound.

Or Just One Byte at a Time

Another, simpler method than DMA is to assign several *input/output ports* to the card. They are accessed something like memory but are controlled via an entirely different bus (see the preceding chapter for more about the system bus), and relatively few of them are available, so they are best for simple actions like sending commands and receiving replies. When your sound card plays MIDI music, Windows has to send only the pitch, voice and velocity of each note, so it takes only a few bytes (characters), communicated through a few I/O ports.

Similarly, there are I/O ports for your modem or mouse COM (communications) port and the LPT1 or LPT2 printer port (LPT stands for line printer). A single I/O port is used to send one character at a time to the device, and the I/O port can be queried to see if the device is ready for the next character.

Typically, cards use these resources in conjunction. When you're connected to an online service via modem, each incoming character appears at the COM port's I/O address. It's quickly displaced by the next character, so the COM port fires off an IRQ "Attention!" signal to the CPU, which drops whatever it's doing, reads the character, copies it to a memory buffer and then returns to what it was doing before. At high connection speeds, these interrupts can occur so frequently that Windows may not always be able to catch every interrupt in time, and the result is dropped characters, resulting in either errors or slowed access due to the need to resend characters.

Windows 95 now includes high-priority serial port drivers, making dropped characters much less of a problem, but the best solution is to use an enhanced COM port. Whereas the old-fashioned 8250/16450 COM port chip can hold only one character at a time, the enhanced 16550 chip can buffer up to 16 characters before sending an interrupt signal. Therefore, the CPU is interrupted less frequently, which makes for smoother coordination between the COM port and the computer. We'll go into more detail on how this works in Chapter 16.

There's Only So Much to Go Around

If you've ever lived in one of those charming older homes—say one built in the '40s—you know that whatever their good qualities, electricity was still viewed as a novel luxury. One outlet per room was quite enough before TV, stereos, VCRs, humidifiers and all the other plug-in items that now populate our houses.

Likewise, early personal computer designers cramped the style of a generation of computer users by grossly underestimating the memory, speed and connection needs of today's computers. A decade ago, less than one-tenth of a megabyte of memory (64k or 128k) was considered lavish. This gives you some perspective when puzzling over the limitations of PC system design, which, constrained by the need for compatibility with old hardware, hasn't really changed very much in the last 15 years. Of course, computers are faster now, and have more "goodies" like large hard drives and fancy multimedia equipment. But the foundation was laid in the early 1980s.

Adding a card (to run a new peripheral like a sound card) often requires finding an IRQ and DMA that's not being used. Your computer needs Interrupt Requests (IRQs) and Direct Memory Access (DMA) channels for its own purposes too, so it doesn't take much, even in a modest computer system, to run out of unique IRQs. And since the IRQ number tells the CPU which device needs attention, each device that uses IRQs must have exclusive use of it. The original IBM PC could use up to eight IRQ lines ranging from 0 to 7, so many cards are still limited to using 3, 4, 5 or 7. To make it worse, COM1 (serial port #1) needs IRQ4, COM2 (serial port #2) needs IRQ3, and LPT1 (parallel printer port) is assigned IRQ7. Often the only free IRQ is IRQ5.

Since IRQ5 is reserved for the second parallel printer port (LPT2), which few people actually have, it's a prime target for new card installation. Although IRQ7 is traditionally reserved for LPT1 (where most people put their printer), neither Windows 95 nor DOS actually uses interrupts when printing, so IRQ7 can usually be reassigned to another purpose. It's frequently co-opted by sound cards, for example.

If you want to add many cards, it may mean sacrificing one of your COM ports to get the extra IRQ, and this means giving up your modem, since Windows needs one COM port just for the mouse. Worse, you have to find out how to disable the COM port on your serial or IDE card so that it won't conflict with the IRQ you've chosen for the new card.

Fortunately, many cards now allow you to choose among the higher IRQs between 8 and 15. These new IRQs were made possible by turning IRQ2 into a "cascade interrupt," which fools the computer into thinking it has more than the standard eight interrupts. This means that IRQ2 by itself can't normally be used.

It's also possible to suffer conflicts between I/O addresses (each I/O port is assigned an *address*, usually given in hexadecimal notation, such as 02E8H or 0340H). Although most cards are smart enough to stay out of the way of the I/O addresses used by the printer and communications ports, there are few industry standards for most I/O addresses. Many sound cards, following the lead of Creative Labs's SoundBlaster, use addresses starting at 220H, but so, alas, do some CD-ROM interfaces and network cards.

Find Some Fresh Settings

When you install a new card, you may be required to choose an unused IRQ as well as an unused I/O address and sometimes a unique DMA address as well. To keep track of these addresses, it's a good idea to write down all the information on your computer and its installed components on a written chart, as shown in Table 15-1.

To dig out all this information, you may have to turn to the manuals that came with all your peripherals and your computer, and look for the specifications or interface requirements. You may also want to photocopy the pages that show what the jumper settings mean, for quick access during the hair-pulling sessions that are almost inevitable. You can find this information more easily by using new Windows 95 facilities that we'll get to shortly (for example, the Device Manager).

When installing a new card, just check your table, and you'll have no problem avoiding IRQ or I/O conflicts, assuming the card lets you pick settings that aren't in use. If not, you may have to change the settings on other cards in order to free them up for the new card. Each card stakes out its turf to prevent I/O rumbles. Of course, make sure you revise your table when you change anything—it's like balancing your checkbook.

While you're making your table, it's also a good idea to write down your computer's CMOS settings, since as we mentioned previously, you may not be able to make your hard drive boot if your CMOS battery dies!

Device	I/O Ports	IRQ	DMA	Notes
System Timer		0		RESERVED BY SYSTEM
Keyboard interrupt	0060	1		RESERVED BY SYSTEM
Cascade interrupt		2		RESERVED BY SYSTEM (allows IRQs 8 through 15)
COM1: (Serial port #1)	03F8-03FF	3		Used for mouse on this computer
COM2: (Serial port #2)	02F8-02FF	4		Used for modem on this computer
COM3: (Serial port #3)	03E8-03EF	3		NOT INSTALLED Can't be used together with COM1 except with a unique, nonstandard IRQ
COM4: (Serial port #4)	02E8-03EF	4		NOT INSTALLED Can't be used together with COM2 except with a unique, nonstandard IRQ
LPT2: (Parallel printer #2)	0278-027A	5		NOT INSTALLED IRQ5 not used in this computer for LPT2
Disk drive	03F2-03F5	6	2	RESERVED FOR FLOPPY DRIVE
LPT1: (Parallel printer #1)	0378-037A	7		IRQ7 not used by LPT1 But is used by SoundBlaster
SoundBlaster Pro/CD ROM drive	0201, 0220-0237, 0240-0257, 0388-0389	7	1	(DMA 1 is default, 8 bit DMA) Joystick port uses 0200-207H, so I disabled game port on IDE card
Real time clock		8		RESERVED BY SYSTEM
IDE interface	03F6-03F7, 01F0-01F7	14		CMOS Settings (C: 1024 heads, 15 tracks, 32 sec/trk; D: 1001 heads, 15 tracks, 17 sec/trk)

Table 15-1: *A typical PC-AT-Type computer system.*

There Is a Better Way

Up to now, we've been discussing techniques for managing your computer's configuration with DOS and Windows 3.1. Windows 95 includes many enhancements that will make your life much easier when you're upgrading or installing new equipment.

For one thing, Windows 95 does a pretty good job of detecting all the hardware on your computer and figuring out what IRQs, DMAs and I/O addresses are being used by each peripheral. Microsoft has programmed Windows 95 to recognize many common types of hardware devices, and it will attempt to discover the settings of hardware it hasn't been told about.

The first step in this detection process occurs when you first install (or reinstall) Windows 95. Redetection can also occur automatically when Windows discovers that you've altered your computer or added a new device, such as a PCMCIA (notebook card) device or a new modem. Or you can force Windows to redetect all hardware or certain types of hardware when you run Add New Hardware from the Control Panel.

This detection process is well designed, but it's not magic. Sometimes the detection process will seize up your computer, when one of Windows's tests runs afoul of some hardware it's trying to examine. If this happens while you're installing Windows 95, you can simply run Windows 95 Setup again and choose the Smart Recovery option. This makes Setup skip over the hardware detection that failed the first time, which may require you to manually configure the device (more on that a little later).

During Setup, a text file called SETUPLOG.TXT is created in the root directory of your C: drive. If Setup fails, you can run failsafe boot (pressing F5 while Windows starts) and read this file using Notepad, or if Windows won't run, press Shift+F5 at boot time to jump to DOS 7 and read the file with the DOS EDIT command. SETUPLOG.TXT shows the status of each step in the Setup process, and you'll be able to see the last thing it tried to accomplish (before failing), at the end of the file. On the other hand, this file might not make any sense to you, since it's rather cryptic.

Another informative file called IOS.LOG is created if there is any problem starting the file system, such as having to resort to real-mode drivers. It won't exist if all goes well, but if you have problems, you can find it in your \WINDOWS directory.

Windows does its best to detect conflicts and even disables devices that conflict, when necessary, to prevent your computer from locking up. It can offer you suggestions on how to overcome these problems, but it usually can't fix the problem for you. That requires a Plug-and-Play BIOS.

What Is Plug and Play?

The idea of Plug and Play is that you should be able to insert any card or hook up any device without having to worry about conflicts with other devices. If you have a computer with a Plug-and-Play BIOS and use only Plug-and-Play devices, this ideal can be achieved.

Plug and Play is not only a philosophy, but also a technical specification developed by industry leaders including Microsoft, Intel and Compaq Computer. Although well supported by Windows 95, it is not specific only to Windows: it's supposed to work with any operating system, including future versions of "alternate" operating systems like OS/2 (which at this time has only limited PCMCIA Plug-and-Play functionality). But Windows 95 is where Plug and Play truly lives up to its potential.

At bootup, all the Plug-and-Play cards are temporarily disabled and then asked to report on their configuration. If any conflicts are found, the Plug-and-Play BIOS can change the I/O, IRQ and DMA settings on the cards automatically until all the cards are in harmony. Then they are reenabled and Windows starts. Windows then takes into account any changes in the setup and offers to install the necessary software drivers.

Hot Stuff

Plug and Play also allows *hot docking* of devices such as PCMCIA modems and hard drives. If you have a document open on a removable hard drive, Windows 95 can warn the application that you've requested to eject the hard drive, and the application will prompt you to save your file before the hard drive disappears.

Instead of unplugging a card, you might unplug the entire computer, if it's a laptop or notebook computer, removing it from the docking station. The docking station might have its own hard drive, a different video card, maybe a CD-ROM. Ideally, you can yank the notebook out of the docking station without even powering off and rebooting. Plug and Play puts Windows into a video mode compatible with the notebook's LCD display and silently detaches from the network.

While on the road with the notebook, you might enter another building with a wireless network. Plug and Play can automatically connect to the network server and allow you to login. When you return to your desk, the video switches back to the monitor, the mouse on the desktop docking station takes the place of the trackball mouse on the notebook, and you can synchronize the files on the notebook's hard disk with those on the docking station's hard drive or on the network (read about the Briefcase in Chapter 19, "Getting Started With Networking"). If you printed any documents on the road, they can begin printing automatically when you return to the docking station. In fact, if you merely walk into a room containing an infrared-linked printer, a printer connection can be instantly established and printing begins.

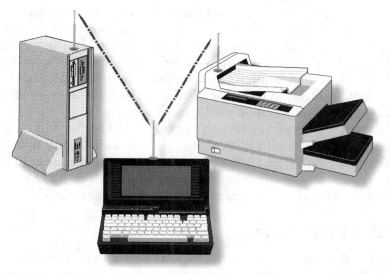

Figure 15-5: *As soon as you enter a building, your future notebook can establish wireless links with other devices "automagically."*

Plug and Play is especially useful with PCMCIA devices. A typical notebook computer has only one or two PCMCIA slots, so a user might want to yank out the modem to insert a flash memory card (used like a removable hard drive). When the modem is reinserted, Windows is ready to communicate again. None of this requires rebooting the computer.

Stranger than Fiction

This functionality may sound like science fiction, but it's already in testing with major hardware and software developers and will be a part of your life in the next year or so.

The first PCMCIA cards contained flash EPROM or battery-powered RAM disks for storing files, but the standard has been advanced to cover all kinds of miniaturized components, including modems, network interfaces, multimedia cards, SCSI adapters, even incredible tiny 2" hard drives. You can even get a PCMCIA reader for your desktop computer and install it in one of your floppy drive bays, so you can share your cards between your desktop and notebook.

Truly, PCMCIA is a killer acronym—*Personal Computer Memory Card Interface Adapter*. (Or is it "People Can't Memorize Computer Industry Acronyms?") It's amazing that it took so long for a more user-friendly term to be invented for these handy credit card-sized devices that plug into most new notebooks and PDAs. The PCMCIA industry finally recognized what a mouthful PCMCIA was and rechristened them as *PC Cards*. Somewhat of an improvement, although it leads to some confusion with standard ISA cards for PCs. So in this chapter, we'll continue to call them PCMCIA.

PCMCIA is due to be replaced by new CardBus devices that run faster, a kind of local bus for credit card-sized devices.

Even if your computer doesn't have a Plug-and-Play BIOS, Windows can configure most Plug-and-Play cards automatically. (Most new computers have a Plug-and-Play BIOS now, and many computers sold in the last year have a Flash BIOS, which can be upgraded from a disk to have a new Plug-and-Play BIOS. Contact your vendor for more information.)

Old Cards Can Play, Too

Devices developed prior to the Plug-and-Play specification are coyly referred to as *legacy devices*. Millions of them are in use, so Windows works hard to accommodate them. Once Windows identifies the resources used by these devices (or you inform Windows about them), it can reroute any new Plug-and-Play hardware you install to tiptoe carefully around the legacy devices.

Your master control panel to device configuration and Plug and Play is called the Device Manager. It's available when you choose the System icon in Control Panel. You can also right-click on My Computer on the desktop and choose Properties to get the System Properties (see Figure 15-6).

 Tip: With the Microsoft Natural Keyboard or other 104-key compatible keyboard, use the ⊞+Break key sequence to quickly get to Device Manager.

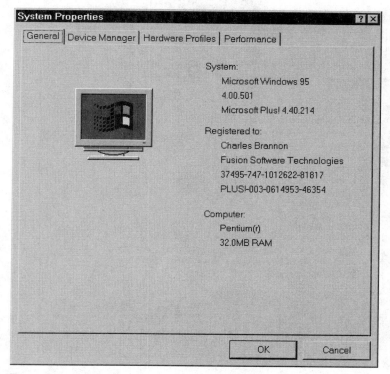

Figure 15-6: *System Properties initially displays some general facts.*

We covered some of these options briefly in Chapter 7, "Customizing Your System," and discussed the performance settings in Chapter 5, "Inside the File System." Now we'll take a detailed look at Device Manager, and see how you can use it to diagnose or repair a faulty setup.

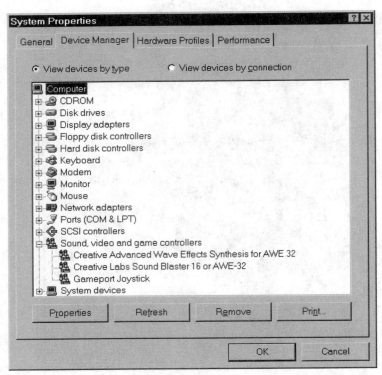

Figure 15-7: *You can view devices by type to help you find a specific kind of device.*

Figure 15-7 shows the first view of the Device Manager, a list of all devices on your system, grouped by type. Each major category of devices is listed. Most of them will have a ⊞ symbol next to them. This means that you can click on the ⊞ symbol to find out more about one of the device types. In Figure 15-7, the Sound, video, and game controllers category has been expanded to show the hardware devices for the SoundBlaster 16 that's been installed in this computer.

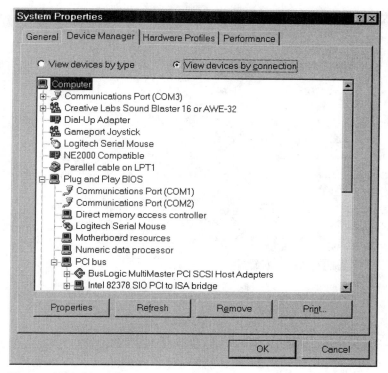

Figure 15-8: *You also can group devices by the device they are connected to.*

Two Ways to Organize Your Views

You can click on View Devices by Connection in the Systems Properties to get another point of view. You can now more clearly see that the SoundBlaster EMU (the wavetable music option of the SoundBlaster 32 AWE) is a subset of the SoundBlaster 16, as shown in Figure 15-8.

Each view has its own advantages. If you don't know how to find something, try both views. Viewing by types is logical when you know what type of device you're looking for. Viewing by connection makes sense when you know what something is attached to or a part of.

When you've found a device to explore, double-click on it, or click on it and choose the Properties button. (You have to click on the Properties button if you're viewing by connection, and the device is also a connection type. For example, the SoundBlaster 16 is both a device and a connection type.)

You get a properties sheet for the device, which for the SoundBlaster 16 looks like Figure 15-9. The first page, General, has only a few items (Device Type, Manufacturer, Status) and a check box next to the configuration(s) where this device should be used.

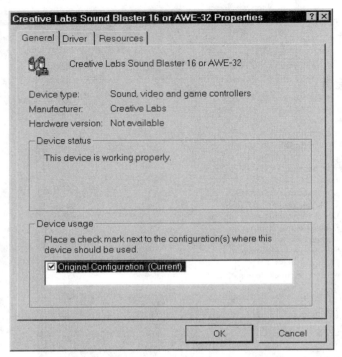

Figure 15-9: *The General page of the properties sheet is minimally informative.*

To disable a device, simply uncheck the Original configuration (current) box. You can also choose to have a device enabled only sometimes, depending on your current hardware configuration.

Hardware Profiles aren't very useful, except in special circumstances where your computer can be booted with different kinds of hardware—for example, a notebook computer that can be started either stand-alone or in a docking station on a network. In that case, there may be more than one set of drivers for the different hardware present on the notebook as opposed to the hardware in the notebook's docking station. Once you define a profile, you can choose which devices belong in each profile. You are asked to choose one of these profiles every time you start your computer, which makes it rather inconvenient to use unless you really need it.

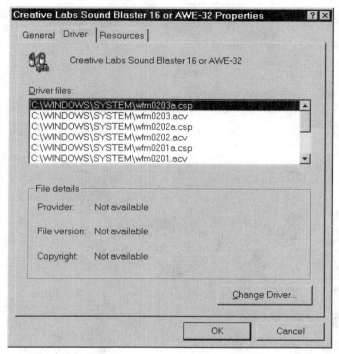

Figure 15-10: *The Driver page of the properties sheet lets you confirm that you're using the right software.*

The Driver page of the properties sheet (Figure 15-10) is more informative than anything else. It shows you which software drivers are installed to support the device. You can click Change Driver and choose a different software driver for the device, but there is usually a better way to do this. For example, when viewing the properties for your display card, you could use Change Driver to change the driver, but the preferred method is to use the Display icon from Control Panel.

The Real Goodies

The meat of Device Manager is in the Resources page of the properties sheet (see Figure 15-11). Here you can directly view the settings for a device, including the all-important IRQs, DMAs and I/O ports. If you're having a problem with a device, such as an I/O conflict, you can first check here to see that the settings are correct for the card.

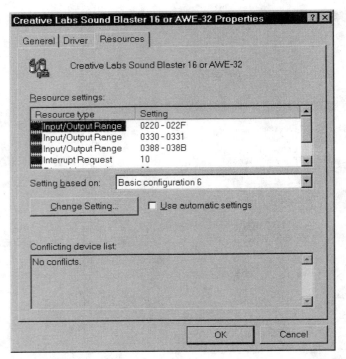

Figure 15-11: *The Resource page of the properties sheet gives you direct access to the device's configuration.*

For example, if Windows didn't detect the card properly, the settings may be incorrect. When the SoundBlaster card was first installed, Windows set the IRQ to 5. While this setting didn't conflict with anything, the actual IRQ on the card is 7, so the sound card didn't play sounds properly. One alternative would be to reprogram the sound card to use IRQ5. On some cards, this requires opening the case, removing the card, and repositioning a jumper or flipping a tiny switch.

Although it's easy to reconfigure the SoundBlaster 16 using a DOS utility, using IRQ7 is a good idea since that leaves IRQ5 available for future upgrades. However, by default, IRQ7 conflicts with the settings for the Printer Port (LPT1). By convention, IRQ7 is reserved for LPT1, even though Windows doesn't even use IRQ7 for printing.

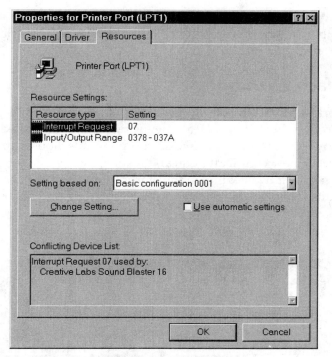

Figure 15-12: *Solving an IRQ conflict is sometimes easy.*

Figure 15-12 shows the Resource page for the Printer Port. In the Conflicting Device List, it clearly shows a problem with the SoundBlaster 16. We can cure this problem by clicking on the Settings Based On drop-down list box and choosing a different Basic Configuration. Choosing Basic Configuration 0 allows the use of the same I/O port (0378, required for LPT1), but without any IRQ setting.

Sometimes you can directly modify these settings. You can click on a setting, such as Interrupt Request, and then click on Change Setting (or just double-click on Interrupt Request). This pops up another little window that lets you type in a new value, or use the Up/Down spin buttons to change the value.

Shut Down, Boot Up

After making a change, you may need to let Windows 95 reboot your computer. That way, it can adjust any other drivers (such as the SoundBlaster 16) more safely, since during bootup, the devices aren't enabled until the drivers are loaded and initialized. Yet ideally, Windows should be able to "rewire" itself automatically, since this is a requirement of Plug and Play. This is not always possible, but as Microsoft refines Windows, it will be able to adjust itself ever more automatically.

Your Personal Tech Wizard

If all this work seems a little daunting or confusing, Windows has a way to walk you through these steps one a time, using a Help tool called the *Conflict Troubleshooter*. Windows may offer to start the Troubleshooter automatically when it detects a new conflict that it can't resolve by itself.

Or you can start it by clicking on the Start button and then choosing Help | Contents. Then double-click on Troubleshooting and choose *If you have a hardware conflict*. Or you could alternatively locate Conflict Trouble-shooting in the Help Index (see Figure 15-13).

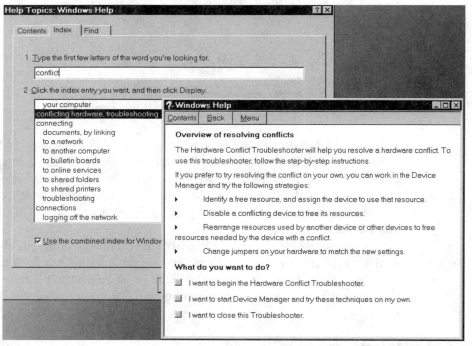

Figure 15-13: *Use Help from the Start button to locate the Conflict Troubleshooter.*

While you're using the Conflict Troubleshooter, a Help window pops up for each step and stays on top of all other windows until you're through with it. The help panel includes tiny buttons you can click on, shown in Figure 15-14. Click on the "jump" arrow to open System Properties, and follow along as it tells you to choose the Device Manager tab. We won't illustrate all the possible screens you might see (there are too many!), but some of the possibilities include checking to see if a device is listed twice, checking to see how many resource conflicts exist, narrowing down which devices conflict with each other, deciding when to disable a device, and more. The Conflict Troubleshooter is a valuable tool. Indeed, it's a kind of "Intelligent Assistant," based on Microsoft's own in-house techniques for troubleshooting and problem solving, distilled into a simple expert system.

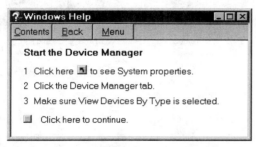

Figure 15-14: *Click on the little "jump" arrow to open System Properties.*

You might also want to try the PCMCIA Troubleshooter, Modem Troubleshooter, Printer Troubleshooter, the MS-DOS Troubleshooter and the Memory Troubleshooter, all available from the Help Index under the Troubleshooting index entry. (These features are also mentioned in the appropriate chapters of this book.)

Another Approach

Sometimes the easiest way to fix a hardware problem is to just reinstall the driver. Click on the device in Device Manager and choose the Remove button. You may need to restart your computer, depending on the device. Now we can run the Add New Hardware icon from the Control Panel.

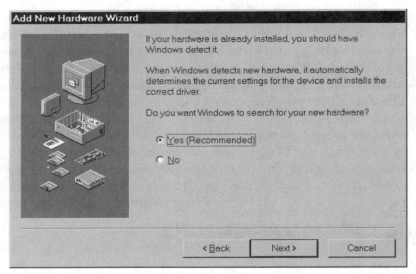

Figure 15-15: *Choose Yes and then click on Next to let Windows analyze your hardware automatically.*

We first looked at this Wizard in Chapter 7. Figure 15-15 shows the second page of the Hardware Installation Wizard. (The first page is just an intro that confirms that you want to start the Wizard.) It's convenient to let Windows 95 automatically detect new hardware. As we said, it can often do this automatically at startup and even instantly when you insert a new device like a PCMCIA card, but if you install some new hardware and it isn't recognized, you can use the Hardware Installation Wizard to scan for it.

Ideally, Windows will automatically detect a new device you've plugged in. That's why the first question, "Do you want Windows to search for your new hardware?" is already answered "Yes" by default. All you have to do is click on Next to continue.

Windows then scans your system for devices. This search can take several minutes, and if the hardware is ill-behaved, it can even lock up your computer, forcing you to press the Reset button to regain control. Don't assume your computer has locked up as long as you see the hard disk light blinking, and you can still move the mouse around the screen. But if nothing happens for a long time, you may have to turn off the computer and then turn it back on to restart Windows and regain control. No harm is done, though, so don't worry about that.

On the other hand, if you know exactly what you've inserted, you can ̄e some time by clicking on the No choice before clicking Next. Then ̄e the type of the device in the Hardware Types box. For example, if you just inserted a new sound card, scroll the list to Sound, video, and game controllers and double-click on it, or click on Next.

For example, let's say we haven't yet installed a SoundBlaster 16. We first select *Sound, video, and game controllers* and then choose the manufacturer—in this case, Creative Labs. We then click on the model of the sound card, the SoundBlaster 16.

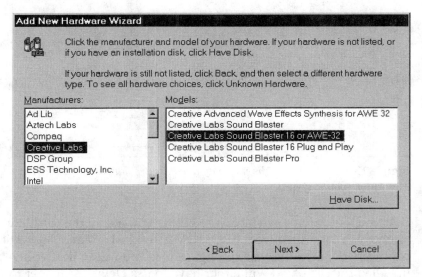

Figure 15-16: *To manually install a hardware device, choose the manufacturer or vendor on the left and the specific model on the right. For best results, make these selections before you actually install the hardware.*

(If you don't find the name of the device you're looking for, but the hardware came with a driver disk, you can choose Have Disk to install the driver from the disk. You'll also use this button when you are installing an updated driver that is newer than the drivers included on the Windows 95 Setup disks or CD-ROM. On the other hand, try the Windows 95 drivers before you resort to using old Windows 3.1 drivers.)

Now You're Cooking With Gas!

Now that we've installed the drivers, the Add New Hardware Wizard tells us how to set up the card (see Figure 15-17). You may have to configure the card physically by moving jumpers, or install it and run the configuration program for the card. (You may need to configure some cards using DOS 7 before you restart Windows. Press Shift+F5 while booting to jump straight to DOS.)

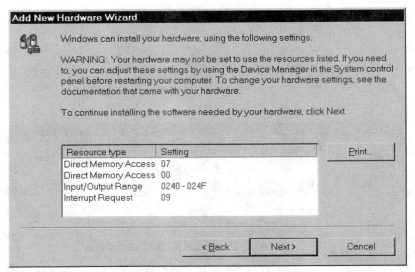

Figure 15-17: *Windows tells you how to configure your new hardware, even before you install it.*

If you use Add New Hardware before you install the card, it can identify a set of available resources (IRQs, DMAs and so on) and suggest that you configure the card to those settings before you install it. If you've already installed the card, you will either have to use Device Manager to set these resources to match your card, or pull your card out and reconfigure it to match the suggested settings.

This method can also be a handy way to cure a configuration conflict. Rather than try to figure out the conflicts, remove a problem device (an improperly installed device is "crossed out" with a red X or a red circle with a band through it) and use Add New to reinstall it, and follow the recommendations on how to configure the card.

In this case, the recommended configuration is not the one we wanted to use. As we discussed above, we wanted to let the SoundBlaster 16 use IRQ7, since it would otherwise go to waste. We could manually reconfigure the device using Device Manager, but the simple solution here turns out to be to remove the device driver (using the Remove button on the Device Manager panel) and use the Hardware Installation Wizard option to automatically scan the system. In this case, the Wizard detected the resources already in use by the SoundBlaster 16 (IRQ7) and automatically installed it using those settings.

Other Features of System Properties

Returning to the main System Properties sheet, consider the Hardware Profiles page, shown in Figure 15-18. You can use this page to set up different sets of system configurations, but you'll rarely want to do this.

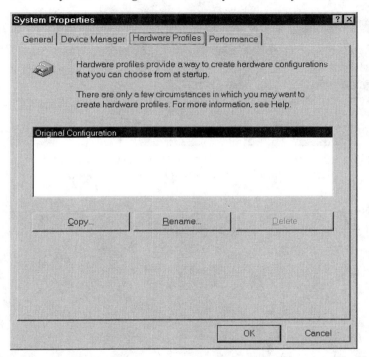

Figure 15-18: *You'll want to avoid creating a hardware profile, since you then have to choose one every time you start your computer.*

If you create more than one hardware profile, you'll have to choose which one to use whenever you boot your computer and start Windows. Having several profiles could be useful if your computer has to accommodate unusual configurations, such as running with different network cards or video cards at various times. (This might be the case in a testing lab, for example. Another case would be a laptop computer that docks at different stations with different hardware, such as home vs. office.) But Plug and Play should resolve most situations where your hardware configuration varies, so you'll want to probably avoid the hassle of using multiple hardware profiles.

The Print button is also available from the main Device Manager page (Figure 15-7). When you click on Print, you get three choices: System Summary, Selected Class or Device, and All Devices and System Summary (the longest, most complete report). Refer to Figure 15-19. You can only choose Selected Class or Device if you've clicked on a specific device. Table 15-2 shows an excerpt of the settings for the SoundBlaster 16.

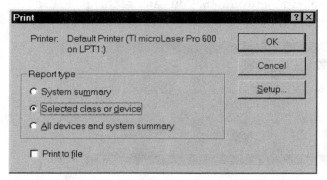

Figure 15-19: *You can choose how detailed to make your system report. It's a good idea to file a copy of these settings for reference when troubleshooting.*

Class: Sound, video and game controllers
    Device: Creative Labs SoundBlaster 16 or AWE-32
    Resources:
    IRQ: 10
    I/O: 0220h-022Fh
    I/O: 0330h-0331h
    I/O: 0388h-038Bh
    DMA: 03
    DMA: 06
    Device drivers:

C:\WINDOWS\SYSTEM\cspman.dll
    File size: 0 bytes.
    Manufacturer: Creative Technology Ltd.
    File version: 4.00
    Copyright: Copyright © Creative Technology Ltd. 1994-1995

C:\WINDOWS\SYSTEM\sb16.vxd
    File size: 54363 bytes.
    Manufacturer: Creative Technology Ltd.
    File version: 4.00.493
    Copyright: Copyright © Creative Technology Ltd. 1994-1995

C:\WINDOWS\SYSTEM\sbfm.drv
    File size: 4128 bytes.
    Manufacturer: Creative Technology Ltd.

File version: 4.00
Copyright: Copyright © Creative Technology Ltd. 1994-1995

C:\WINDOWS\SYSTEM\sb16snd.drv
File size: 46000 bytes.
Manufacturer: Creative Technology Ltd.
File version: 4.00
Copyright: Copyright © Creative Technology Ltd. 1994-1995

C:\WINDOWS\SYSTEM\wfm0200.acv
File size: 13456 bytes.
Manufacturer: Creative Technology Ltd.
File version: 4.00
Copyright: Copyright © Creative Technology Ltd.

C:\WINDOWS\SYSTEM\wfm0200a.csp
File size: 2238 bytes.
No version information.

C:\WINDOWS\SYSTEM\wfm0201.acv
File size: 5184 bytes.
Manufacturer: Creative Technology Ltd.
File version: 4.00
Copyright: Copyright © Creative Technology Ltd.

C:\WINDOWS\SYSTEM\wfm0201a.csp
File size: 6776 bytes.
No version information.

C:\WINDOWS\SYSTEM\wfm0202.acv
File size: 9056 bytes.
Manufacturer: Creative Technology Ltd.
File version: 4.00
Copyright: Copyright © Creative Technology Ltd.

C:\WINDOWS\SYSTEM\wfm0202a.csp
File size: 9004 bytes.
No version information.

C:\WINDOWS\SYSTEM\wfm0203.acv
File size: 9056 bytes.
Manufacturer: Creative Technology Ltd.
File version: 4.00
Copyright: Copyright © Creative Technology Ltd.

C:\WINDOWS\SYSTEM\wfm0203a.csp
File size: 9004 bytes.
No version information.

Table 15-2: *SoundBlaster 16 settings.*

Moving On

This chapter dealt with a lot of technical issues, but you should now have a solid understanding of computer installation, configuration and trouble-shooting. In the next chapter, we'll dive into communications issues, including setting up a modem and telephone, accessing a BBS with HyperTerminal and using Microsoft Exchange, your "Universal Inbox," for sending and receiving faxes and electronic mail.

Getting
Connected

Chapter 16

The Communicating Computer

You're talking long-distance with a friend. Where is the conversation taking place? Somewhere "out there," in *cyberspace*—your communication is flashed across the country as thin lines of electron patterns. "Jacking into cyberspace" means taking part in a booming online community, through local BBSes (bulletin board systems), commercial online services like CompuServe, Prodigy and America Online, and to a greater extent than ever before, via the Internet (the Net), the predecessor of tomorrow's "information superhighway." And the pioneering Microsoft Network, included with Windows 95, promises to extend and redefine how we interact with a commercial online service.

Sure, "cyberspace" is becoming a cliché, and you're probably weary of all the "information superhighway" metaphors, but it does help communicate the idea. If Bill Gates is right, one day we'll all truly have "information at our fingertips."

The online experience can be overwhelming, partly because there's a lot to learn, but mostly because of the staggering *amount* of information that awaits you on the other end of the modem line. The Internet alone transfers several terabytes (billions of bytes) of information every day. (One terabyte is sufficient to contain every publication in the United States Library of Congress.)

In this chapter, we'll help you with the first part, learning how to use a modem to get online. We'll also pass along some guidelines for finding cool and useful online resources. Then we'll see how to exploit Windows 95's other communications features, such as desktop faxing. We'll save a discussion of the other kind of computer connectivity, networking, for the next chapter.

What Is a Modem?

You use a hardware device called a *modem* to connect to other computers over a phone line. Since the telephone is designed to carry sound, not digital information, you need a device that can *modulate* (convert) the computer's binary language of ones and zeros into various music-like tones that can be streamed at high speed over ordinary phone lines (often called POTS for "plain old telephone system"). On the other end of the line, another modem *demodulates* (translates) the audio tones back into computer data. The word "modem" comes from combination of the terms MOdulation/DEModulation.

Some modems are external boxes that attach via a cable to a *serial port* on the back of your computer. Your mouse usually plugs into your first serial port, a small trapezoidal socket. Since the computer port has pins sticking out, it's called a male connector. The plug on the mouse cord or modem cable, then, has to be a female connector. (In terms of gender, it's the pins that define the male connector, even though the female serial cable actually plugs into the male connector.) In addition to the small DB9 (9-pin) serial port, your computer may have either a second DB9 port or a DB25 (25-pin) serial port.

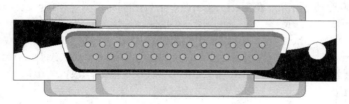

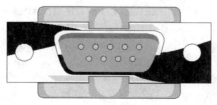

Figure 16-1: *Types of serial ports: 25-pin (top) and 9-pin (bottom).*

The serial port is attached to an RS-232 serial interface inside your computer. (RS-232 is just an industry designation for the most common type of serial port.) In the PC world, these are also commonly called COM ports (COM for communications).

A typical PC has two COM ports, and your mouse is usually attached to the first one, COM1, which on almost all computers is a small DB9 connector. The second COM port, COM2, is usually a DB25 connector. If both COM ports are the small DB9 connectors, your mouse can be plugged into either one, or you can use a DB9-DB25 adapter to plug a mouse (which almost always has DB9 female plugs) into the wider DB25 COM port.

Another type of modem takes the form of a plug-in interface card. Like a VGA display card, hard disk interface, sound card or CD-ROM interface, it plugs into an empty socket inside your computer. Although internal modems are less expensive than the external modems in a box, they are more trouble to install and configure. Two advantages to an external modem: 1. you can easily move it from one computer to another, and 2. you can reset it by flipping it off and on, whereas an internal modem can't be reset without turning the whole computer off and on. (Sometimes a modem won't hang up the phone if it "locks up," requiring a power off/on reset.)

Tech Talk: Internal Modems

Some configuration pitfalls may await you if you install an internal modem, and the topic is a little complex. Some of the concepts, such as I/O and interrupt conflicts, are better understood once you've read Chapters 14 and 15. (If you're avoiding these problems by using an external modem, you can skip ahead to The Telephone Connection below.)

Your modem card has to communicate with your computer using a *COM port*. (A port is an external junction point used to connect equipment to your computer.) But since your computer already has two COM ports, you'll have to disable one of the them so it won't conflict with the COM port used for the modem card. Some modem cards can be configured to use COM3 or COM4. Those COM ports are supported by Windows 95, although they share the same interrupt (IRQ) as COM ports 1 and 2. (The interrupt is a unique channel used to signal the computer that data is ready from the modem. See Chapter 14 for a complete discussion of interrupts and I/O ports.)

So you can't use both COM1 and COM3 or both COM2 and COM4 in the same computer, since there would be interrupt conflicts. However, setting a modem card to use COM3 or COM4 will keep you from having to disable (turn off) the COM1 or COM2 ports, since this avoids the more serious I/O address conflict (each COM port has a unique I/O address, but not a unique IRQ).

If you do have to disable one of the computer's COM ports, the jumper settings to do that are usually on the card that's attached to your hard disk drive, unless the COM port is integrated into your computer's motherboard.

In that case, turning off one of the ports will be documented in your computer's technical manual.

For the more adventurous, it's possible to configure more than two COM ports, if the hardware allows you to choose unique IRQ settings for each COM port. For example, if you set COM 3 to IRQ 5 and COM 4 to IRQ 10, you can use them at the same time as COM 1 (IRQ 4) and COM 2 (IRQ 3).

 Video cards using the S3 graphics chip conflict with COM4. You won't be able to set up a COM4 port if you have an S3-based graphics card.

Your computer may have a combination of short, 8-bit slots and double-connector 16-bit slots. Most cards these days require 16-bit slots, but most modem cards can fit into either an 8-bit or a 16-bit slot. If you have an open 8-bit short slot, use it for the internal modem to keep your other slots free for other add-ons.

To learn how to open your computer's case and install add-on cards, check Chapter 15, "Upgrading Your Computer." Of course, the easiest way to use an internal modem is to buy a computer with one pre-installed.

Or, if you have a portable computer, buy a Plug and Play PCMCIA (PC Card) modem. These credit-card style adapters simply plug into the side of the notebook computer. Windows 95 lets you plug and unplug PCMCIA cards even while the computer is turned on. This convenience is hard to ignore, which is why vendors are adding PC card slots to even desktop computers, so you can share PCMCIA cards between your notebook and desktop computers.

The Telephone Connection

There are two RJ11 telephone jacks on the back of a modem or modem card, one labeled LINE or WALL, and one labeled TEL or PHONE. (They might also be labeled IN and OUT.) Plug one end of a telephone cord into the wall socket and the other end into the jack marked LINE/WALL/IN. You may have to unplug the cord from your telephone. In that case, you can plug a second (shorter) telephone cord into the modem jack labeled TEL/PHONE/OUT and the other end into the telephone, restoring your telephone's capability. (If you don't use a telephone in the room with the computer, you don't need to plug anything into the TEL/PHONE/OUT cord.)

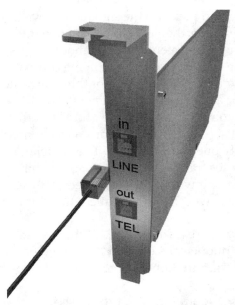

Figure 16-2: *Making the telephone connection.*

If you have trouble dialing with the modem, make sure the phone connections are properly seated and in the right jack. (Some older homes or those in rural areas may lack RJ11 wall connectors, but they can be installed by an electrician or by following the instructions on an adapter available at stores like Radio Shack.) Likewise, some hotels don't use standard RJ11 jacks; check with the front desk before you plug in, or you may damage the modem or the hotel's phone system.

The same may be true where you work: A standard RJ11 looking jack may actually be an electronic phone interface, part of a "key system" that is incompatible with analog phones or modems. If so, you may be able to get an analog jack installed or bring in a separate phone line for the modem. (If you have to dial 9 or another number to make an outside call at work, you'll have to add the same sequence to the beginning of any numbers you dial with your modem. Later, we'll see how to configure Windows to add this automatically.)

Since fax machines work like modems, you may be able to share a phone line with a fax machine, especially if you use a phone/fax/modem switchbox device, which can determine how to route an incoming call to the correct device. Some of these devices work by answering the phone and "listening" for detect a fax tone or a modem carrier tone. If they find one, then the switchbox re-rings the attached line to fool the fax or modem into thinking that the phone is still ringing and picks up the signal. However, many modem calls don't make a sound until after they're connected, so many of these switchers can't truly distinguish between voice and modem calls.

The easiest to use of these switchers rely on a phone company service called *distinctive ringing*, (available for a small monthly fee) which gives you different phone numbers for a single telephone line. Each phone number causes the same phone line to ring in an unusual and easily distinguished fashion, so you can give out separate numbers for your fax, modem and voice phone, yet pay for only one incoming line. The switcher electronically recognizes the rings and routes the call accordingly. Some new modems also feature distinctive ringing (along with other advanced features such as digital Caller ID), so they don't answer the phone unless they know the call is for the modem.

Of course, you can't truly share a single line. While you're on the modem line, you can't receive phone calls or send or receive faxes. That's why many people, especially in a family home, have a second phone line set up for the modem.

If you do use only one line, you might want to subscribe to your phone company's voice mail (Memory Call) service, so that callers who reach a busy signal can at least leave you a message, something impossible with an ordinary answering machine.

 TIP Almost all modems sold today include fax capability, but using a computer fax requires the computer to be turned on and the fax software to be active. To activate fax answering in Windows 95, start Microsoft Exchange.

Another problem can occur if someone picks up the phone in another room during your modem session. That usually disrupts the signal enough to hang up the modem and abort your link to the other computer. Attaching your phone to the modem prevents you from picking up the phone and disrupting a modem session, but it doesn't prevent someone in another room (on the same phone line) from interfering.

You can avoid this by attaching "privacy" or "modem protector" boxes to the other phone extensions (but not on the modem extension). Such devices also prevent anyone from picking up and listening in on an extension during ordinary telephone conversations.

More vexing is the problem caused by another popular telephone company service, Call Waiting. It causes a momentary lapse in the phone connection (heard as a click) when someone calls you while you're busy with another caller. As you know, you then briefly "hookflash" the phone to take the other call. This doesn't work with a modem, and the click is usually interpreted as the other computer's hanging up the phone, canceling your modem session.

To avoid this, ask your phone company what buttons you can press to disable Call Waiting (usually *70 or 1170). Those codes disable Call Waiting only for the current phone call, and you can add the *70 (or whatever) sequence to the start of the phone number of the computer you're calling. (After you hang up, Call Waiting is restored for subsequent use.) You can also add this sequence to the Dial Setup of your modem/fax software. Later, we'll see how to set up the Windows TAPI (Telephony Applications Programming Interface) to support the disabling of Call Waiting. Future Windows 95 applications that support TAPI (explained later) can automatically benefit from Windows 95's ability to configure dialing features.

Setting Up The Modem

Assuming that your modem is plugged into the computer and to the telephone line, you're ready to install the Windows TAPI support for the modem. If your modem was hooked up to your computer when you installed Windows 95, your modem may be ready to use right now. But let's look at how to do it, in any case.

First, click the Start button, then click Settings and choose Control Panel from the Settings submenu. You can also find the Control Panel by double-clicking the icon for My Computer (assuming you haven't renamed that icon to something like "JimBo's Computer").

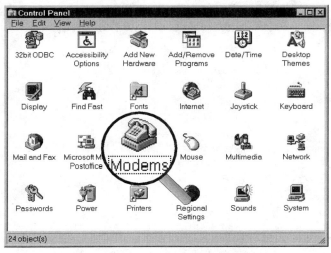

Figure 16-3: *Use Modems in the Control Panel to set up your modem for Windows 95.*

Once you're in Control Panel, double-click the Modems icon. The Modem Setup Wizard starts up to help you install support for your modem, as shown in Figure 16-4.

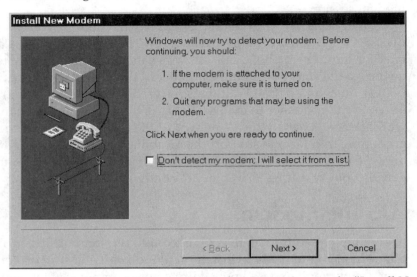

Figure 16-4: *The first time you use Modem Properties, use the "Install New Modem" Wizard to install a modem.*

Most of the time, you'll let Windows 95 detect what kind of modem you have and let it determine which COM port it's using. Rarely, this detection won't work properly or won't recognize your modem, so you have the option of choosing it from a list.

For now, don't click the box marked *Don't detect my modem.* Instead, just press the button marked Next to continue with the Wizard.

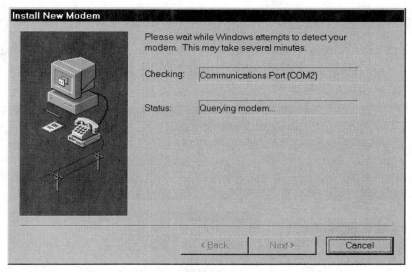

Figure 16-5: *Windows is searching for a modem.*

Now Windows 95 starts looking for your modem. It tests each COM port on your machine (except the one the mouse is using—it knows that can't be a modem), and when it finds something that responds, Windows 95 asks the device whether it's a modem and what kind of modem it is. Usually this information is sufficient to let Windows figure out what kind of modem you have, and then you'll see the Wizard page shown in Figure 16-6.

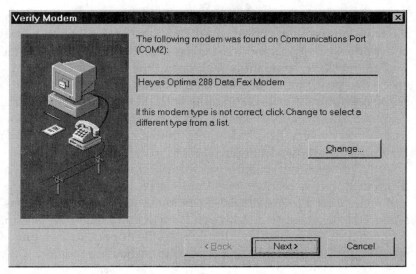

Figure 16-6: *Windows 95 can identify most modems automatically.*

If the modem make and model shown doesn't match the kind of modem you have, or if it shows something like "Standard modem," you might want to click Change to search the list of modems. You can also choose this option in the first page of the Modem Setup Wizard by clicking the box marked *Don't detect my modem*.

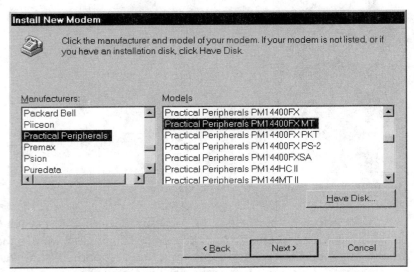

Figure 16-7: *First choose the modem's manufacturer on the left, and the modem model on the right.*

If you still don't see your specific make and model, don't despair. First, the Standard modem choice works fine most of the time. You only have to choose the speed your modem supports in the list on the right. Second, your modem might be compatible with one of the known modems. If Windows chose the wrong modem when it auto-detected your modem, it's probably because your modem is compatible with the one it selected. Finally, modems designed after Windows 95 shipped may come with a setup disk with new or updated drivers for Windows 95. In that case, click the button marked Have Disk (as shown in Figure 16-7) to install the new drivers.

After you've completed the wizard, Windows 95 support for your modem is installed, you're ready to use Windows 95 applications like HyperTerminal, and you're ready to install Dial-Up Networking for Internet access (covered later in the next chapter.) However, keep in mind that most existing Windows 3.1 programs are naïve about the new TAPI support, so each one will have to be configured separately to support your particular modem.

Why So Many Modems?

Why does Windows 95 have to know what kind of modem you have? If all modem manufacturers adhered to a single modem standard, this wouldn't be necessary. In fact, most modems do use some form of a modem standard established *de facto* by Hayes Microcomputer Products, Inc. (which was the leading manufacturer of modems many years ago). Those modems are configured by sending them commands preceded with the "attention" code AT. For example, the code ATDT555-1212 tells the modem, "Attention: Dial (Touch Tone) the telephone number 555-1212." The standard code ATH0 hangs up the modem, ending the call. Therefore, the standard became known as the Hayes AT standard.

Figure 16-8: *The computer sends the code AT to get the modem's attention.*

Although there is a core set of compatible modem codes (which is what the Standard modem type uses), your modem probably has special features, such as data compression, that might not use the same command code as another manufacturer's brand. The Modem Setup program keeps a list of all the common types of modems, along with all the command codes they use, so that Windows communications applications can control even the more advanced features of modems. Windows supports thousands of types of modems, right out of the box.

Toward a better standard

As you might expect, Microsoft has been pushing for a better, more compatible modem standard. New modems that support the new modem protocol also feature an exciting feature that lets you switch easily between your modem and the telephone, without breaking the current connection. Imagine playing an interactive computer game via modem and being able to talk to your friend during the game. When you make your move, the telephone makes a beep, during which the conversation is briefly muted to allow the modems to exchange information, then you can resume your conversation.

This VoiceView feature will also make modems more practical for business applications like teleconferencing, where employees at different sites can share a document and mark it up with colored pens or annotation, all the while conversing by telephone—on the same phone line.

In the near future, Digital Simultaneous Voice and Data, or DSVD, will make it possible to talk on the telephone while the modems exchange data on the same line, with no need to pause the data transfer during your conversation.

Just How Fast is Fast?

A serial communications port on a PC can transfer data as slow as 300 bps or as fast as 115,200 bps (bits per second). It's called a *serial* connection because data is sent one *bit* at a time. Each character is represented by a number. For instance, the letter A is represented by the number 65, which is 01000001 in the computer's binary language. The serial port transfers each bit in order, 0-1-0-0-0-0-0-1, and the other end of the connection collects these bits and reassembles each group of eight bits into a *byte*. (Your parallel port, used to connect to your printer and some kinds of external devices, sends all eight bits at the same time, in parallel.)

Just a few years ago, 2400 bps (bits per second) modems were "state of the art," and many people still used 1200 bps modems (even 300 bps modems were common just ten years ago). Now, 9600 bps is the minimum you need for adequate online interactivity. You can buy 14,400 bps modems for under $100 now, and today's state-of-the-art 28,800 bps modems are available between $200 and $300.

Most modems *negotiate* the speed when the call is first attempted. You'll hear awful squalling sounds when the modems are *handshaking*, testing each other to see how fast they can connect.

Figure 16-9: *Modems negotiate the highest speed that's supported by both devices, using a technique known as handshaking.*

Of course, the actual connection depends on the highest speed supported by *both* modems. If your 28,800 bps modem calls a friend's 2400 bps modem, you'll have to connect at the 2400 bps rate.

Many online services let you dial in via networks such as SprintNet or Tymnet, and your speed is determined by the type of modems installed at your local switching center. Most online services are limited by this arrangement to 9600 bps, so if all you do is call CompuServe, you might save some money by buying a 9600 bps modem. However, these networks are constantly being upgraded, and many cities have local access to 14,400 bps dial-up networks, with 28,800 support just around the corner. As we'll see, 28,800 bps is the fastest speed that ordinary telephone lines can possibly support, so a purchase of a 28.8Kbps (Kbps=kilobits—thousands of bits—per second) modem can be a wise choice that won't be outmoded too quickly.

Not a baud

You may have heard the term "baud" used interchangeably with bps (bits per second), as in a 2400-baud modem. Originally, a baud was a transition between frequencies that represented approximately one bit of information. However, now a single baud can encode multiple bits of information, so it's incorrect to use term *baud* for speeds faster than 2400 bps.

If you're more comfortable thinking in terms of characters per second (or bytes per second), just divide the bits-per-second rate by eight. So a 2400 bps modem really transfers 300 characters per second, and even a 28,800 bps modem can send or receive data at only 3,600 characters per second.

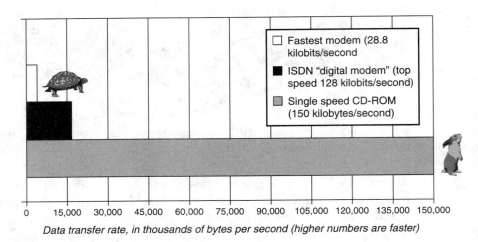

Data transfer rate, in thousands of bytes per second (higher numbers are faster)

Figure 16-10: *The tortoise vs. the hare. The fastest modem is much, much, slower than the slowest CD-ROM drive.*

By contrast, even a slow (single-speed) CD-ROM transfers data at 150,000 characters per second. Your hard disk can be a hundred times faster still. Today's business networks can communicate at ten megabits per second, or 1.25 megabytes per second, and some businesses enjoy ten times that speed. Clearly, even the fastest modems are ill-equipped to keep up with the kind of data transfer we're accustomed to with our other peripherals. See the sidebar, The Next Generation of Modems, for a possible solution.

The Next Generation of Modems

In the next few years, ISDN—Integrated Services Digital Network—will become an increasingly attractive alternative to modems. Using special telephone company switching equipment, ISDN creates a pure digital link between your computer and other computers with ISDN support. An ISDN connection gives you at least 57,600 bps, and up to 128,000 bps (depending on how your connection is implemented), fast enough for real-time videophones, color faxing, and lightning-quick file transfers. In some areas, ISDN access is available for as little as $18/month, and in a few years it won't cost any more than a normal phone line.

An ISDN adapter is not a modem—it doesn't have to translate back and forth from digital to analog—ISDN is a pure digital format. ISDN cards and external interfaces are beginning to appear at less than $400.

Even the 128,000 bps top speed of ISDN is slow compared to hard disks or even CD-ROMs (the popular quad-speed CD-ROMs can send data at a rate equivalent to nearly five million bits per second.)

Another promising technology uses your cable television wiring as a high-speed one-way connection. So graphics and so forth appear on your screen quickly, although you still need a modem connection so your keystrokes can be sent back to the online service. Future two-way cable connections will further enhance this technology, leading to interactive television and video on demand, with the side benefit of very high-speed data links.

With the increased use of fiber optic "wiring" in the telephone system, extending eventually into every home, we can hope that one day computer communications will catch up with the expectations delivered by hard disks and CD-ROMs. When that day comes, we may find that hard disks and CD-ROMs are obsolete.

■ ■

A Modern-Day Tower of Babel

In addition to a standard for sending command codes to the modem, modems also support various international standards (or protocols) to varying degrees. These protocols are designed to allow modems from different manufacturers to communicate with each other, taking advantage of advanced features such as *data compression* and *error correction*. The modems on both ends of the connection have to support compatible protocols for all this to work.

Make no mistake about it

Error correction allows modems to automatically ensure that the data is sent without mistakes. Without hardware error correction in your modem, it's up to the software in the computer to ensure that the data is sent properly. When you're reading a news article on the screen, you wouldn't mind a few mistakes here and there, but if you're transferring digital documents and program files, a single mistaken character can ruin the entire file. Most online services and communications packages feature built-in software error correction, but hardware error correction is faster.

How does error correction work? Let's say I wanted to send you three numbers and make sure that you got them correctly. If I sent you 5, 2 and 9, I'd ask you to repeat the numbers to me, and if I heard 5, 3 and 9, I could resend the 2.

But having to send the entire data stream in both directions can really slow down the data transfer. Instead, perhaps I could also send you the three numbers: 5, 2, 9, then the sum, 16. That way, when you add up your three numbers 5, 3, 9 and get a total of 17, you know you need to have the data resent. This adds only one extra number to the data you're sending.

Instead of sending three characters at a time, it's more effective to send a *block* of 128, 256, 1024 or more characters at a time. With good-quality connections, you want more characters to be sent at one time, to avoid wasting time with error correction. On the other hand, if a poor-quality phone line makes many corrections necessary, a smaller block size makes more sense, since less time is wasted retransmitting the smaller blocks.

Modern error correction is even more advanced. By sending along some redundant ECC (error correcting code) information, the receiving modem is actually able to reconstruct lost data most of the time, without requiring a time-wasting retransmission.

The error-correction technique also monitors the number of corrections. If they are excessive, the modems can agree to switch to a lower speed. High-speed communication requires high-quality phone lines with no noise or interference, but by switching to a lower speed, the modems can continue the data transfer even if the phone line conditions deteriorate. Some modems can even attempt to upgrade the speed if line conditions improve.

The big crunch

With today's information explosion, you've been hearing a lot about *data compression*—making thousands of bytes fit into a few hundred bytes' worth of space.

Data compression can seem like a black art. It seems nonsensical that you can fit a big file into a little space, as you'd squeeze water out of a sponge. Compression works because ordinary data contains redundancies that can be identified and coded more efficiently, then reconstructed later (decompressed). Abbreviations and acronyms are a form of data compression in language, such as lb. for pound, Mr. for Mister, FBI for Federal Bureau of Investigation, etc. (et cetera). Professional stenographers and secretaries using shorthand also employ data compression in their techniques for abbreviating the written word.

With modems, smaller files mean faster transfers, so in effect, data compression accelerates the modem connection. A compression rate of 2:1 (read as "two to one") doubles the modem speed. Some modems can compress up to 4:1 with some types of files.

On average, 2:1 is the most that data compression can achieve, but some files, such as text files (like the words in this book) are extremely compressible, since there is so much redundancy in language. For example, if all you did was replace every occurrence of "and" with "&" (and converted back again when read), you'd save two bytes for every use of the word "and." That can add up in a large document.

Many graphics files are also very compressible, such as images with large areas of a single color, which can be encoded as a single pixel of that color, paired with a number that specifies how many pixels to repeat. (So-called "lossy compressors" can compact images even more dramatically, but degradation of the original image resulting from approximations made during compression is inevitable. Modems can't use lossy compression, since their job is to ensure accurate data transmission.)

If you have a 14,400 bps connection with 4:1 compression, you might have a *throughput* rate of 57,600 bps, assuming that the data compresses at the maximum ratio of 4:1. The data travels between the two modems in compressed form at 14,400 bps, but it's decompressed "on the fly" fast enough to feed into your computer at 57,600 bps. That means there are really two connections involved here: the connection between the modems (which sends compressed data at the line speed of 14,400 bps) and the connection between the modem and your computer (the modem uncompresses the data and sends it to the computer at 57,600 bps).

Some files are always stored in compressed form. These include graphics formats such as .GIF (CompuServe Graphics Interchange Format), most .TIF (Tagged Image File Format) files, and PC Paintbrush .PCX graphics. Those files can't be compressed any further. And some file types, such as program files, consist of complex, code-like patterns that don't compress very well.

Before modem compression standards became common, people were already accustomed to compacting their data before sending it. On the PC, the popular PKZIP program can combine many separate files into a single, compressed *archive* file. This one file is a lot easier to send over the phone line than a bunch of separate files—and with better than 2:1 compression, it's a lot faster, too. The recipient then runs PKUNZIP to unpack the archive into a directory of individual files on his hard disk.

PKZIP is not the only game in town; similar programs include LHA, ARC, LHARC, and ARJ. (Macintosh users typically use a program called *Stuffit* for the same purpose.) Files on the Internet may be archived using other formats like .z, gzip or tar.

To help you compress and decompress these files, we've included on our CD-ROM the 32-bit shareware version of WinZip, which is designed for Windows 95. It can compress in several formats including PKZIP, and it can decompress many other formats. It's such a great accessory for your online forays that you'll immediately appreciate the benefit of sending in your shareware registration fee.

Since files vary greatly in their compressibility, and since many files are already compressed, take modem compression with a grain of salt. If you buy a 14.4Kbps modem, count on getting 14,400 bits per second. Consider anything you get with data compression a bonus.

A Few Standards

We've summarized below some of the most popular modem standards, or versions (hence the "v" in the name of the standards).

- **MNP Levels 1-4:** These are various levels of error correction. Some 2400 bps modems were misleadingly marketed as 9600 bps modems, assuming best-case data compression. (MNP stands for Microcom Networking Protocol, after the company that invented it.)
- **MNP Level 5:** This was one of the first data compression standards, and it's required for true *v.42bis* support.
- **v.32:** The first 9600 baud modem standard, with a simple form of optional error reduction.
- **v.42:** Combines LAP-M data compression with error correction. Does not have to support MNP 5 or *v.32*.
- **v.42bis:** Supports MNP 1-5, LAP-M, and *v.32*. Supports the most types of connections.
- **v.terbo:** A proprietary method used for 19,200 bps speeds. Not compatible with *v.34* or *v.fast*. Fortunately, some *v.terbo* modems can be upgraded to *v.34*.
- **v.fast, V.FC:** An pre-release version of *v.34*, "V Fast Class," was implemented by most 28,800 bps modems before *v.34* was ratified. All *v.fast* and *v.34* modems also support *v.42bis*, to permit throughput as high as 115,200 bps (assuming the data is highly compressible).
- **v.34:** Supports 28,800 bps and adapts better than *v.fast* to problems with phone-line quality. Compatible with *v.fast* in most cases. Most v.fast

modems can be upgraded to v.34 with a software "patch" transmitted to the modem, but many v.fast modems require you to return them to the factory and pay for the upgrade.

Although 28,800 bps is the highest theoretical rate possible with phone lines (like Einstein's "speed of light" limit in physics), the updated *v.34bis* standard will further improve support for marginal phone connections and increase data compression.

In a nutshell, you should look for a modem with *v.42bis* support, and if it's a 28,800 bps modem, you'll want to get *v.34* support in preference to *v.fast*.

The reason we can't expect today's phone lines ever to exceed the 28,800 bps limit is because phone lines were designed to send low frequency (voice) transmissions. They just can't send dit-dit-dot-dit information that vibrates faster than the vocal cords of a screaming woman with a high voice. And even a scream is attenuated. You wouldn't listen to opera over the phone.

Getting Online

Enough about modem standards, let's get online! After setting up your modem with Control Panel, you're ready to fire up HyperTerminal (the modem software included with Windows 95) and make some calls.

First, you have to find someone to call.

Although you can use HyperTerminal to call CompuServe, the CompuServe Information Manager (WinCIM) is a much better way to get online, featuring icons and enhanced menus, and it's included if you purchase a CompuServe Membership Kit. Other services, such as America Online and Prodigy, have their own dedicated software and can't be accessed via a program like HyperTerminal. Support for *The Microsoft Network* is included with Windows 95, and it works with Explorer and the Microsoft Exchange E-mail (electronic mail) software. If you're not interested in HyperTerminal, skip ahead to Commercial Online Services.

BBSes: Online, On the Cheap

The first stop is finding a local BBS, or bulletin board system. BBSes are computers set up by people in your community who are dedicated to providing free or low-cost online services.

A BBS provides a way to communicate. You can send electronic mail to others in your area and take part in discussion groups on a variety of fascinating topics. Via Fidonet or Internet links, your messages can be passed along to other BBSes in your state or even around the world. BBSes are a great way to make friends, and they're a growing alternative to the singles scene for meeting and dating.

Some BBSes are dedicated to particular groups, such as a computer users' group. You can find Christian BBSes, anarchist BBSes, alternate lifestyle BBSes, programmers' BBSes and the notorious adult BBSes, where any topic is fair game.

You can also play computer games on a BBS, via a feature called Doors. If the BBS supports multiple phone lines, you can play interactive computer games with other members and engage in online conversations known as chats. Your typing appears on the other person's screen and vice-versa. (Online services extend the concept of the chat to host online conferences and Q&A sessions with celebrities and computer experts.)

Many BBSes also feature a fine collection of files for your perusal, including lots of shareware, utilities and demos. You'll also find plenty of graphics and pictures (especially popular on adult BBSes). Receiving a file is called *downloading*. Many BBSes also encourage, even depend on file contributions from members, or *uploading*. (We'll see how to upload and download with HyperTerminal, below.)

Increasingly, many bulletin board systems feature online CD-ROMs stuffed to the gills with files, many of which are quite recent. You can save a lot of money by checking out your local BBS before you pay to download the same file from an online service. Many BBSes are free (actually, they depend on voluntary contributions), and many fine BBSes are available for a very low annual subscription fee.

Some local BBSes have become so successful that people call them from all over the world. We've collected some of the biggest of these in Table 16-1. Keep in mind that some of these numbers may be out of date by the time you read this. Try calling during the day to avoid waking up someone who has been reassigned the telephone number of a disconnected BBS.

Bulletin Board	Phone Number
Advanced Systems	503 657-3359
Albuquerque ROS	505 296-3000
Blue Lake	503 656-9790
BorderTown	410 876-5101
Bytes'n Bits	201 437-4355
Bytestream	314 657-1318

Cajun Clickers	504 756-9658
Charlie's	314 442-6023
Chrysalis	214 690-9295
Dark Shadows	609 627-8369
Digital Concepts	602 292-0065
Download America	203 676-1708
EXEC-PC	414 789-4210
GearBox	201 692-1110
Glass Menagerie	215 376-1819
Hal 9000	313 663-4173
HAWG WILD!	402 493-2737
Heart of Tennessee	615 890-8715
Hollywood News	301 373-5965
HyperLinc East	215 356-1630
Infinite Space	407 856-0021
Laser Connection	201 472-7785
Log On America	401 739-4100
Microfone Infoservice	908 494-8666
Mission Fun House	203 374-0101
Nashville Exchange	615 383-0727
NMC TBBS	406 265-4184
Northern Lights	207 761-4782
Other World	615 577-9342
PC-Ohio	216 381-3320
Perfect Visions	513 233-7993
Prime Time	404 667-0885
Public Access	209 277-3008
RunWay	215 623-6203
Shareware South	404 370-0736
Sleepy Hollow	310 859-9334
Software Creations	508 365-2359
St. Louis Online	314 973-4073
Starship 2	201 935-1485
Starship Enterprise	201 283-1806
Synergy Online	201 331-1797
The Batboard	314 446-0475
The Castle	213 953-0040
Twilight Clone	301 946-8677
Windows Online	510 736-8343
WorldNet	301 654-2554

Table 16-1: *Select National Bulletin Board Systems.*

To find numbers for your local BBSes, try asking around at local computer stores or regional computer newspapers. Joining a computer user group in your area makes it easy to find out who's online.

If you have a lot of time on your hands, a spare computer, and an extra phone line, you can even set up your own BBS, and it can be a rewarding (though taxing) hobby. We'd recommend that you talk to several established *sysops* (the term for BBS system operators) before you take the plunge and purchase a BBS package. You might not realize just how much time and effort this hobby can require.

Many computer companies also offer free technical support and updates with an online BBS. It's a good way to post your support questions and look for new versions of drivers and utilities. Other companies provide similar levels of support on CompuServe, America Online, Prodigy, and increasingly, on The Microsoft Network.

About HyperTerminal

HyperTerminal is an example of a type of modem communications software called a "terminal program." On early mainframe computers, the console you used to type and view computer output was called a terminal. A terminal is not a computer, although it superficially resembles one. Its keyboard simply relays the keystrokes to the mainframe, and its screen displays characters being sent to it by the mainframe. But a "dumb terminal" doesn't do any computer processing on its own. (Terminals are still in use today on networks, but some of them do have computer processors to handle the display of Windows-style graphical user interfaces.)

Some of these terminals could be connected to the mainframe over the telephone line via modem. So when personal computers became popular, programs were written to take the place of a dumb terminal. These programs were called *terminal emulators* or simply, terminal programs.

Some types of common terminal emulation: VT-52, VT-100 (and other VT series), 3270, TVI series, Data General, ADDS, and WYSE, to name a few. There's also the TTY (teletypewriter—the first terminals that replaced a printer terminal with a CRT were called glass TTYs). A TTY terminal is also called an ASCII terminal, since it uses the American Standard Code for Information Interchange, the same code used by personal computers to represent text numerically. (For example, the ASCII value of the letter A is 65.)

Unless you're connecting to a mainframe, you probably won't be using terminal emulation per se. The ASCII or TTY emulation is sufficient for most cases. But there's another popular standard that's commonly used with BBSes called ANSI-BBS. It's based on a variation of ASCII and includes codes to display text in various colors and attributes, such as blinking or highlighted text. It gives the plain-text world of the BBS a much-needed facelift.

(Some bulletin boards have begun exclusively using a new method called *RIP graphics* (Raster Image Processing) that gives the BBS a Windows-style graphical user interface. You don't need Windows to view these graphics, though. All you need is a terminal program that is compatible with RIPTerm. Note that HyperTerminal does not include support for RIP.)

We'll see below (in "Advanced HyperTerminal") how to set up terminal emulation, if you need it.

HyperTerminal lets you connect to these BBSes by configuring a connection that tells it what phone number to dial. Each connection you set up creates a new icon in the HyperTerminal Connections folder.

Getting Started With HyperTerminal

With a telephone number for a local BBS in hand, open the HyperTerminal Connections folder from the Start | Programs | Accessories menu (Figure 16-11).

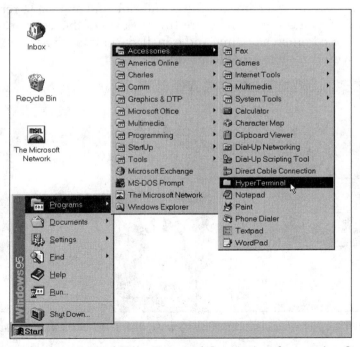

Figure 16-11: *Find HyperTerminal Connections by pressing Start and clicking Programs, then Accessories.*

Since you don't have any existing Connections, double-click HyperTerminal to create one.

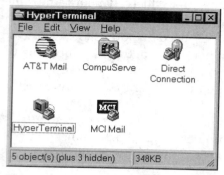

Figure 16-12: *Double-click the HyperTerminal icon to create a new connection. The other icons shown here are HyperTerminal Connections that we've already set up.*

When you start the HyperTerminal program (instead of a connection icon), it assumes that you want to create a new connection, and pops up a box to let you choose a name for the connection and an icon to remind you what kind of connection it is (Figure 16-13). Some of the icons are obviously designed for commercial online and e-mail systems, such as AT&T and MCI Mail. But you can choose any icon you like.

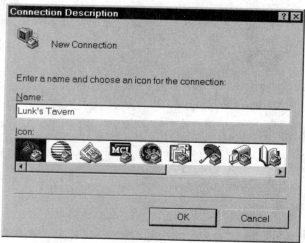

Figure 16-13: *To create a new connection, make up a name for it and choose an icon.*

The next step is to fill in the phone number for the BBS, as shown in Figure 16-14. The modem you've already installed is shown automatically. (If you have more than one modem or other communications device, you can choose between them. If you haven't yet configured a modem, you'll be walked through modem setup first, which we covered above.)

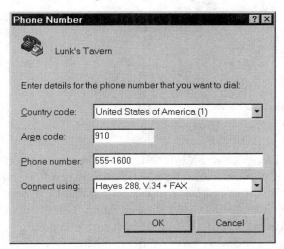

Figure 16-14: *Enter the phone number for the BBS and the device (modem) you want to use to make the call.*

You're now ready to dial the number and make your connection. (If you're just setting up a connection for later use, you can press Cancel to avoid dialing right now. Be sure to use File I Save to write your Connection settings to disk.)

When you're ready to connect, press the Dial button. If you're calling a popular BBS, you may get a busy signal, reported as Busy in the status box of the Connect dialog box. Just press Dial Now when you want to retry the call.

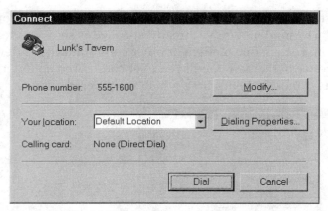

Figure 16-15: *Making the call is as easy as pressing a button.*

(If you think you have the wrong number, press Cancel. Then use Properties from the File menu to examine the phone number and change it if necessary. Make sure the box marked *Use country code and area code* is checked only if you're dialing a long distance number. Then use Connect from the Call menu to try your call again. Note that you can also change the number directly from the Connect dialog box by clicking Modify.)

When the other computer answers the call, you'll hear the usual modem noise while the two modems check each other out. You may also need to press Enter or Esc to declare your presence as an actual modem call instead of a wrong number (which wastes time for the BBS).

After the greeting and title screen for the BBS, you're asked to enter your name. If this is the first time you've signed on, enter your name anyway. Assuming someone else doesn't already have an account by that name, you'll probably be asked if you typed the name in correctly (sure you did), and if so, do you want to create a new user account. Then, just follow the prompts and answer all questions accurately to set up your online account.

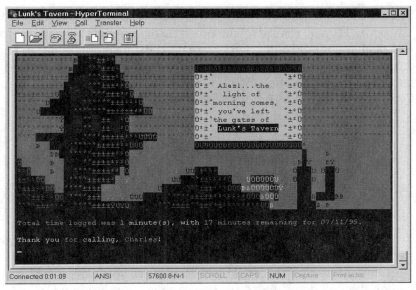

Figure 16-16: *Online graphics don't draw correctly using a normal Windows font.*

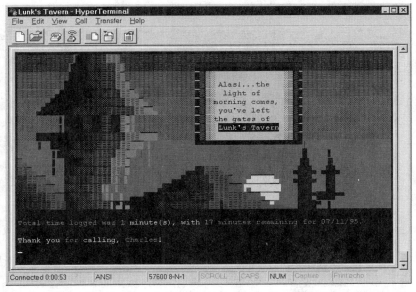

Figure 16-17: *Here's how they're supposed to look, using the Windows Terminal font.*

Once online, the first thing you'll probably want to change is the font used by HyperTerminal. For some reason, the default font doesn't display IBM character graphics, which are used extensively by BBSes running on or for IBM-compatible PCs. Choose Font from the View menu, and try another font, such as Terminal. (MS LineDraw, if you have it, is also a good choice, since it's a resizable TrueType font.)

 For quick access to menu commands, turn on HyperTerminal's toolbar using View|Toolbar (shown in the above figures just below the menu bar). From left to right, the toolbar commands are New, Open, Connect, Disconnect, Send, Receive and Properties.

Once you're signed on, you'll be whisked through a fairly standard procedure. Notices will be displayed, your account will check for waiting mail (giving you a chance to read it if you want), you'll be given an option to view the BBS newsletter, and you can view any updated online bulletins. Then you arrive at the BBS's main menu, which may look something like Figure 16-18 (many BBSes use a common foundation like WildCat!, but even those that do often customize their menus extensively).

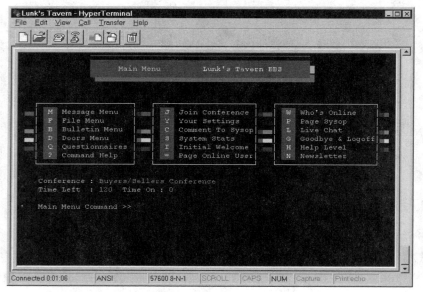

Figure 16-18: *A typical BBS main menu.*

The choices on the main menu are broadly divided into these categories: bulletin-board maintenance (such as changing your user setup, reading bulletins and so on), engaging in electronic mail with other users, playing online diversions (Doors), and uploading or downloading files. Everyone has a favorite BBS activity, and some boards favor one type of activity over another (messaging vs. files, for instance).

Since so many BBSes are in operation, we can't tell you how to use each one, but here are some general guidelines:

Messaging

1. When you first create your account, you're often given the choice between a line editor and a full-screen editor. If you're using a 9600 bps modem or faster, you'll prefer to use the full screen editor, which lets you move the cursor around, just as you can with NotePad.

2. When you reply to a message, it helps the recipient if you quote a small part of the original message that you're commenting on. Some BBSes have features to help you with quoting. Or, you can use the clipboard: highlight the text in the original message and choose Edit | Copy (Ctrl+C), then compose your reply and use Edit | Paste (Ctrl+V) to insert the original text. To set the quoted text apart from the original, you can add > to the beginning of each line of the original quote, enclose it in quote marks, separate it from your reply by a series of dashes, or just write something like "In reply to So and So's message, where he said: " Try to avoid quoting the entire message; that wastes valuable network resources.

3. Messages in a BBS are organized into topical sections or conferences. In the messaging menu, you can choose a message base to browse through or post messages on.

4. Some BBSes require you to use your real name, others let you use a "handle," at least when messaging. But don't assume your handle will provide you with perfect anonymity.

5. We won't go into all the details of online "Netiquette," but here are a few tips that will help you relate better to other online users. This advice has been culled from a number of online guides:

   a. Try to avoid posting an inflammatory or personally critical attack. This is known as flaming and it generates a lot of heat, but very little light. Remember that the recipient is a real person. Don't write anything that you wouldn't say in person. Politeness is as important online as it is in daily life.

b. If you're writing about something that affects you strongly, consider waiting to post it until the next day, then reevaluate it when you've cooled off.

c. In most cases, especially in Internet news groups, never post a commercial message. There are separate, clearly identified areas where online business is conducted. On a BBS, look for a Classifieds or Buy and Sell message section.

d. Target your mail correctly. One of the worst mistakes is to send a message indiscriminately to thousands of users (aka Spamming) or to the wrong newsgroup or message section.

e. Respect the conventions of a BBS or news group. Don't criticize someone's religion on a Christian BBS or complain about obscenity in an uncensored adult area. Also avoid posting messages off the subject of the section or newsgroup.

f. Before posting any questions, look for a FAQ (Frequently Asked Questions) file. The FAQ may already have the answer you're looking for, and you avoid wasting the time (and network *bandwidth*, or capacity) of everyone else with common questions. You'll also probably hear the admonition RTFM (Read the *Friggin'* Manual).

One more Netiquette tip: Use the BBS's main menu option to log out (usually G for Goodbye), rather than simply hanging up your modem. This is referred to as "dropping carrier," and is considered rude, because it can take a BBS several minutes to detect the hangup and reset itself for the next caller. If you drop carrier routinely, you may find that your BBS account has been deleted.

Downloading Files

The text connection

The simplest way to transfer data is to simply capture it off the screen as it appears. This is useful only for plain text, since you can't simply capture computer files and programs. Use Transfer | Capture Text from the HyperTerminal menu to begin capture. Anything sent to you from the BBS, and any keystrokes you type, are stored in the capture file until you end the connection. Or you can repeat Transfer | Capture Text. If you're currently capturing text, the menu changes to a submenu with the choices Stop, Pause and Resume. You can use Pause and Resume to temporarily prevent the capturing of text, perhaps while you navigate the BBS menus.

Transfer | Send Text File can be handy when you compose e-mail. You can use it to send any text file you create with Notepad or save as text only from a word processor.

Figure 16-19: *Turn on capture by choosing a file to store the text, then click Start.*

Instead of capturing text to a file, you may simply want a printed log of your session. In that case, use Transfer | Capture to Printer. When you want to stop printing, use Transfer | Capture to Printer again, which also turns off the check mark next to the option on the menu.

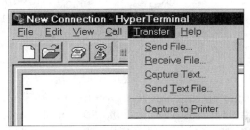

Figure 16-20: *Use the Transfer menu to send and receive files, capture text to a file, or send it to the printer.*

Protocols

To download binary files (most files other than text), you need to use a download *protocol*.

A protocol is an agreed-upon way of doing something, kind of like a diplomatic treaty. Protocols are essential for standardized communication.

When you first create your BBS account, you may be asked to choose a download protocol, or you might be asked at the time of downloading. Transfer protocols include Xmodem, Kermit, BiModem, Ymodem and Zmodem. They are designed to transmit data accurately and in binary form to preserve program data exactly. Zmodem is the best all-around protocol for speed and accuracy, and it's supported by HyperTerminal.

Protocols like Zmodem were developed before error correction became standard issue with modems. They send a block of data with a checksum code, which lets the recipient verify the integrity of the block and request a retransmittal of that data if necessary. This is especially important with program files, where even a single misplaced number can be disastrous.

If you're sure you have an error-free connection between two modems, you can use the Ymodem-G protocol, which simply streams the data continuously without error checking. Because there is no pause to exchange checksum information, Ymodem-G is faster than Zmodem, but not much. Another advantage of Zmodem is that if your connection is lost, you can continue the download where it left off when you call back.

The file catalog

The files on a BBS are organized in categories. There is usually a List command to let you choose a category and display all the files in it. From the list, you can mark the files you're interested in retrieving and download them all at once as a *batch* (for batch downloading, use the Zmodem or Ymodem-G download protocol). Some ASCII files can be viewed online.

Better Safe Than Sorry

We suggest you perform a virus scan on any files retrieved from a BBS or online service, even though almost all BBSes have instituted automatic virus scanning or only use certified virus-free CD-ROMs. Viruses are especially notorious on the Internet, so protect yourself.

A computer virus is a small program that is designed to make copies of itself [reproduce] by attaching itself to other programs or infesting the boot sector of a floppy disk or hard drive. (The boot sector contains a tiny program used to start DOS or Windows on your computer and it's ideal for infection. When you insert a new floppy, the virus copies itself to it, to better pass along to another computer.)

Viruses are programmed by malicious computer thugs trying to prove their "hacking" abilities. A virus may simply be annoying, displaying a message or playing a silly tune, or it may be destructive, wiping out files or even the entire hard drive. The actual risk of a virus infection is considerably exaggerated in the press, but it pays to be careful. Nevertheless, we have never encountered a virus from BBSes in over 15 years of downloading files. And our experience is typical. Do you know anyone who's been attacked by a computer virus? It's rather like the fears that people have about undercooked pork. Nobody has ever heard of anyone getting trichinosis; or even knows what the symptoms are.

The file catalog is usually divided into sections by content, and you can browse through the files in any section. When you're viewing a list of files, you can use the description of it to decide whether you're interested, then mark the file by typing its number (or just write down the filename on a piece of paper).

The files you've marked will be displayed in a list, and you'll be asked whether you want to start the download or add other files to the list. If you haven't marked any files, you can type in the filenames you wrote down. Remember, so far, none of this depends on any features of Windows or HyperTerminal—your interaction is through the text menus of the BBS.

Downloading can be confusing. Do you start the download with HyperTerminal or does the BBS take the initiative?

The answer: Once you've selected all the files you like, use the BBS Download feature to start a download first. After choosing to start the download, you may be asked again to choose a Download protocol. Again, Zmodem is your best choice. You then press a key, perhaps D, to start the download. The BBS then waits for you to tell *your* computer to start its download procedure. At this point, use Receive File from HyperTerminal's Transfer menu to start the download.

 TIP Turn on HyperTerminal's toolbar using View I Toolbar. You can then start a download by clicking on the toolbar icon resembling a file folder.

When you use Transfer I Receive File, HyperTerminal pops open a dialog box to let you choose where to put the file. It also lets you pick the download protocol to use (Zmodem, the default, is shown, and is the best choice if the online service supports it).

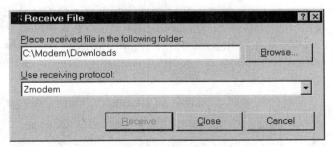

Figure 16-21: *When you download a file, it is normally stored in the HyperTerminal folder, which can get cluttered. Consider creating a Modem folder on your hard drive, and create a subfolder for Uploads and Downloads within this folder. That way you can organize all your online activities.*

The BBS will usually wait about 30 seconds before timing out, so use Transfer | Receive file immediately after you tell the BBS to start the download. If for some reason you need to cancel the download, most BBSes let you press Ctrl+X several times to interrupt. Otherwise you'll see streams of nonsense characters spilling onto your screen, the binary data that the BBS is still trying to send you.

When the file download has completed, use the BBS's Exit or Goodbye command to end your session (unless you have more files to download). You can then open your Downloads folder and examine the goodies you've retrieved.

If the file ends with an extension of .ZIP, you need to use a program like PKZIP (widely available for download) or WinZIP (included on this book's Companion CD-ROM), to unzip (decompress) the files to a new folder. You can run the program's Install or Setup (WinZip can also do this for you), or simply copy the files to a folder on your hard disk where you keep your program files. After you've extracted the files, you can delete the original .ZIP file to save disk space.

Some downloaded files appear to be a runnable program, ending with an extension of .EXE. In fact, many of these are actually self-extracting archives. Like a .ZIP file, they contain numerous individual files in compressed form. Unlike .ZIP, you don't need a separate program to decompress .EXE files. Copy the .EXE file to the folder where you want to store the files, and double-click on it to run the self-extractor. When the files are extracted, you can delete the .EXE file to save space.

Contribute something

Some free BBSes expect user participation and set a limit on the number of files you can download unless you do your part and upload files that you've gathered elsewhere. But uploads of old or existing software aren't appreciated. This policy is actually becoming outmoded, as CD-ROM libraries have begun to replace the individual file collections of many BBSes. But there still may be a limit, expressed in terms of credits or number of minutes allowed per day. Even if you have lots of credits, avoid hogging the BBS, especially if there's only one line.

 TIP Turn on HyperTerminal's toolbar using View | Toolbar. You can then start a download by clicking the toolbar icon that looks like a flying page of paper.

To upload a file, first use the bulletin board system's menus to tell it you want to upload a file. The BBS will prompt you for a description of the file and a file area that best matches the type of file you're contributing. When it tells you to start the upload, use the Transfer I Send File menu choice to begin.

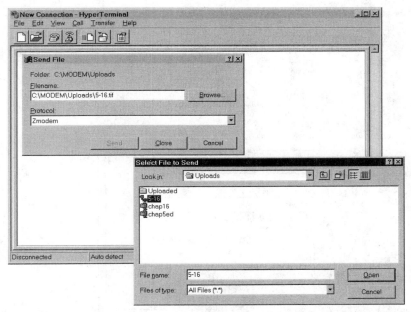

Figure 16-22: *You can use the Send File dialog box to choose the location of the file you're sending and the protocol to use (Zmodem is recommended).*

One on One

Another good use of HyperTerminal is to exchange files with another computer. In this case, decide which computer will be used to accept the call. Since HyperTerminal doesn't have a way to answer a phone call, you'll have to use a special trick.

 There are other ways to exchange files. You can use Microsoft Fax to send editable documents to another computer running Microsoft Exchange. Or you can use Dial-Up Networking or Direct Cable Connection to attach your computer to another computer and exchange files using Microsoft Networking. We'll cover these options later in this chapter and in Chapter 19.

First, open the HyperTerminal folder, and when asked to create a connection, create one called Direct Connection. Instead of filling in a phone number, click the *Connect Using* box and select Direct to COM x (where x is the port your modem is on).

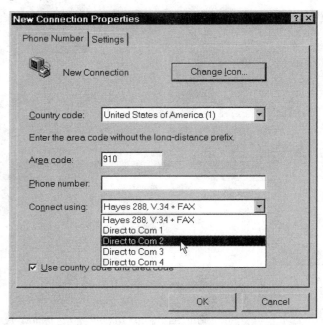

Figure 16-23: *Use Direct to COM to create a direct connection to your modem.*

Once you've chosen a direct connection, you'll be asked to set up the communications port's characteristics, such as speed, data bits, stop bits, and so on. Normally, you'll only change the speed. The default speed is 2400 bits per second, which is incredibly slow; use your modem's fastest speed (14,400 bps or 28,800 bps).

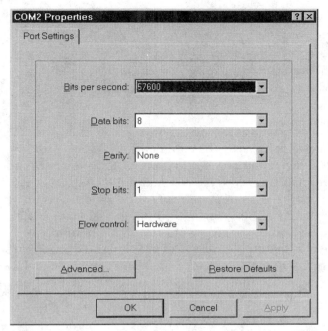

Figure 16-24: *All you have to change on the Port Settings property sheet is the speed of the connection.*

A direct connection opens up a line of communication between HyperTerminal and the modem. It can also be used to connect a special cable, called a null modem cable, between two computers' serial ports. You can then act as if the two computers were connected by modem, transferring files and so on.

If the serial port is attached to a modem, the direct connection lets you type modem commands. As we mentioned earlier in this chapter, a modem command is a sequence starting with the letters AT. For example, the sequence ATH0 means "hang up the phone." When you send a command, the modem will respond OK. If you don't get a response, or if your typing is not echoed to the screen, your direct connection isn't working: Check to see that you're using the correct COM port.

Now that you have a direct connection, you're ready for one-on-one communication. The computer on the other end of the phone line (the remote computer) uses a normal HyperTerminal connection to call you, using your modem's phone number. You'll use the direct connection, because you have to make your computer answer the phone.

TIP You can use the modem command ATZ to reset your modem's settings, in case you have difficulty with a call. Some modems use the command AT&F to completely reset the modem to factory defaults, similar to turning the modem off and on.

When the remote computer calls you, you'll see the word RING appear on the screen. At this point, type the command ATO. This puts your modem online, and it answers the call. If you'd prefer to have your modem answer the phone automatically, type the command ATS0=1 before the other person calls you. This puts the modem into *auto-answer* mode. You'll probably want to use the command ATS0=0 when the online session is over, to turn off answer mode, so you can answer your telephone normally.

When you and the remote computer are connected, both parties can use the Transfer menu to send or receive files. You can also chat back and forth simply by typing. Use Transfer | Capture Text or Transfer | Capture to Printer if you want a record of your online session.

Advanced HyperTerminal

One problem you might encounter when you connect two computers directly: one or both of you might not be able to see what you're typing. When you browse the HyperTerminal menus, you won't find an option for "local echo." Instead, choose File | Properties (or right-click the connection icon in the HyperTerminal folder and choose Properties). The first panel of the property sheet shows you the Phone Number settings, which we've already discussed.

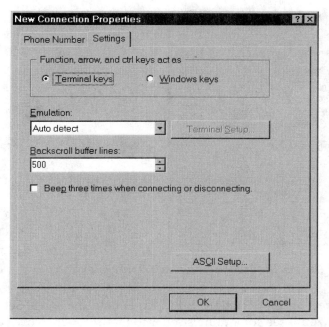

Figure 16-25: *New Connection Properties let you control some useful HyperTerminal options.*

Instead, click on the tab heading for Settings. Here, you can customize how the HyperTerminal terminal operates. Under the Emulation box, you can choose the terminal type that the remote computer expects. Normally, you'll use Auto Detect, but you can also choose from ANSI, Minitel (the French standard), TTY, ViewData, VT100, and VT52.

The backscroll buffer is used to store lines that have "scrolled off" the top of the screen. You can use the scroll bar on the right side of the Hyper-Terminal screen to review the session, but the buffer size is not unlimited. Here, you can increase the default size of the backscroll buffer from 500 lines, if your computer has enough memory.

The choices for *Terminal keys* and *Windows keys* let you decide whether to transmit these keys to the other computer or whether the keys have their normal use with Windows. If you set it to *Windows keys*, then keys like F1, which opens Help, operate as usual. Otherwise, the F1 key is simply trans-mitted to the remote computer.

You'll also see a check box for *Beep three times when connecting and discon-necting*. Turn it on if you want an audible alarm after the dialing succeeds or if the connection is terminated.

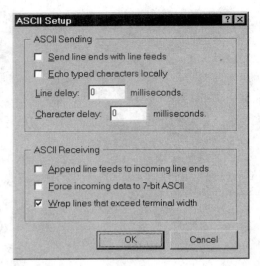

Figure 16-26: *Use ASCII Setup to set up features like local echo.*

Another nest of useful options is hidden behind the ASCII Setup button. Press it, and you'll see something similar to Figure 16-26. Now you can finally turn on the local echo that's necessary to see your own keystrokes when you're directly connected to another computer. Just turn on *Echo typed characters locally.*

You can turn on local echo, but you may have another problem: All your typing stays on the same line. You need a way to send a line feed along with each "carriage return" (the end of line character). Just use the checkbox for *Send line ends with line feeds.* The options for line delay and character delay are not needed except when communicating with old, slow and cranky telecommunications devices.

If the incoming characters all end up on the same line, use the *Append line feeds to incoming line ends* check box. Also, if you're seeing lots of "garbage" characters on the screen, you might need to use *Force incoming data to 7-bit ASCII.*

Normally, you'll leave the box checked to *Wrap lines that exceed terminal width.* Otherwise, long lines will simply be chopped off to fit the screen.

Other Modem Goodies

As we mentioned, Windows provides a standard interface to the telephone using the Telephony Applications Interface, or TAPI. HyperTerminal is one example of a TAPI application. Another mini-application (applet) that uses TAPI is Phone Dialer.

Phone Dialer is part of an attempt by TAPI to unify all your phone numbers. Right now, each Windows communications program, fax utility, and personal information manager (PIM) keeps its own separate, and usually incompatible, list of phone numbers. With TAPI, you can compile just one master phone book, and all TAPI-aware applications can use it for dialing.

That's the idea, anyway. Actually, it appears that many programs will still create their own phone books.

The Phone Dialer lets you start or maintain a phone book. You can dial any number to initiate a voice conversation. How can your computer dial the phone? Right now, the best way to do this is to plug your telephone in the TEL or PHONE jack on the back on your modem, instead of using a Y connector or putting your phone on another extension. This way, the computer can send a command to the modem to dial the phone, just like when the computer dials another modem, but instead of going online, it tells the modem to go into voice mode, which lets you have a normal conversation.

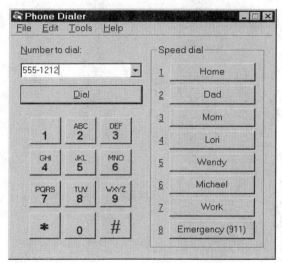

Figure 16-27: *Phone Dialer is handy, but it's not much smarter than the average memory telephone.*

Phone Dialer (Figure 16-27) looks like a telephone touch-pad, and you can even dial by pressing the buttons. Or you can type the phone number in the *Number to dial* box. Notice the down-arrow next to the box. Click it, and you'll be able to retrieve the most recent phone numbers you've dialed. Click the Dial button to make your call, or just press Enter after you type in the phone number.

When you dial a number, the dialer pops up a box that tells you to click the Talk button to pick up the telephone handset. When you click Talk, the modem hangs up, so make sure you've already lifted the handset off its cradle (or pressed your speakerphone button) before you do so. Just give the modem a chance to dial first.

 TIP Use the international format for long distance calls. It's +1 followed by the country code, then the city/region code and the phone number. Conveniently, the country code for the United States is 1. To dial national directory assistance for North Carolina, you'd use +1 (910) 555-1212.

You can also assign your favorite phone numbers to the memory dial button on the right. Just click the memory dial button, then enter the name and telephone number to assign to it. You can use the Edit | Speed Dial menu command (Figure 16-28) to reassign the phone numbers.

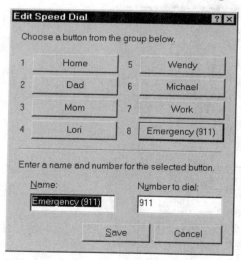

Figure 16-28: *Edit your speed-dial numbers the easy way by choosing Speed Dial from the Edit menu.*

 TIP If your phone system needs a pause between digits, like when you have to dial 9 to get an outside line, use a comma. However, if you have set up your dialing options correctly, you don't need to specify the 9 each time you dial. (Use Tools | Dialing Properties.)

More About TAPI

Before you can get the most out of TAPI-aware applications, you have to configure your dialing properties. If you installed Microsoft Exchange with the Microsoft Fax feature when you set up Windows, you've already seen the Dialing Properties. From Phone Dialer, use Tools | Dialing Properties to access it. Or run the Modem icon from Control Panel (covered in Chapter 7).

When you click on Dialing Properties, you get a dialog box similar to that shown in Figure 16-29:

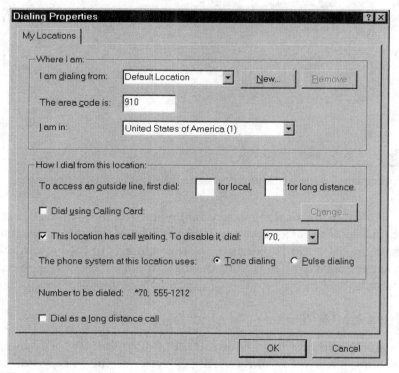

Figure 16-29: *Dialing Properties tell TAPI where you're calling from, among other things.*

If you're using a notebook computer and you travel a lot, you'll want to click on the New button to set up a separate dialing-properties location for each city you travel to. That way, modem programs know when they need to dial 1 for long distance, based on your *current* area code.

The dialing properties are fairly self-explanatory. Make sure you fill in the area code box and the country, at least. If you know your telephone system doesn't support TouchTone dialing, use the *Pulse Dialing* option at the bottom of the property sheet.

In the *How I dial from this location* section, fill in the boxes with the special digits you need to place an outside call (some phone systems use a different sequence for local versus long distance calls). Otherwise leave them blank. If your phone has Call Waiting, fill in the code that turns it off for the current call (usually 1170 or *70) in the box next to *This location has call waiting.* (You can click the arrow next to the box to display a list of common choices for call waiting disable.) Otherwise you can turn off the check box.

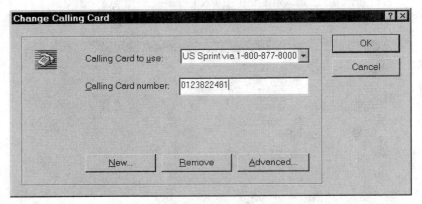

Figure 16-30: *Using a calling card can save you money when traveling.*

To dial using a calling card (ideal when you're traveling), turn on the check box for *Dial using calling card,* and choose your type of calling card from the list of cards that appears, then enter your calling card number. If you ever need to change your calling card, use the Change button from the main dialog box.

The Future of TAPI

In the near future, TAPI will reach out to PBX (private branch exchange) systems, key systems and hybrid key systems—in other words, telephones in offices. You'll be able to dial your business phone from your computer and even answer the phone if you have a handset attached the computer. In the slightly more distant future (but only slightly!), you'll further integrate your computer with your phone system for applications like voice mail and fax retrieval, blurring the distinction between telephones and computers. Soon they'll be the same thing.

Microsoft At Work

A related TAPI technology, Microsoft At Work, extends the Windows technology used in desktop PCs into other office equipment, such as copiers, fax machines, printers and who knows what else. With your fax machine on the network, you can send Windows faxes directly to it or receive a fax from the fax machine. Yes, you can do this already with a fax modem, and in fact, it's Microsoft At Work technology that supports fax modems in Windows for Workgroups and Windows 95. But the marriage between PCs and office equipment is even more intimate: copiers and fax machines (some now entering the market) sport touch-sensitive LCD screens with Windows-style graphics and icons. You can also set up a copy job from your desk, selecting options like duplexing, sorting and collating, and paper type. Your original will go to the copier as if it were a laser printer—and in fact, there soon won't be any difference between copiers and laser printers.

You can already buy devices that combine computer scanning, standalone and computer faxing, copying, and printing, all in the same box for much less than buying the equipment separately. Microsoft At Work technology ties the elements together cohesively and provides the link to the Windows PC.

Microsoft At Work Fax (MAW Fax) makes desktop faxing convenient, and it has some unique advantages over other fax add-ons (although many of them will fall in line as enhancements to the core functionality of MAW Fax).

 TIP If you want to solicit a fax from a service like SprintFAX, use Start | Programs | Accessories | Fax | Request a Fax. This will fast become a popular alternative to using your telephone to contact a company's fax-back system. A fax service can also accept faxes for you, ideal for when you're traveling. If you subscribe to a fax service, use Request a Fax to retrieve your waiting fax messages. You can even rely on this feature for exchanging files, as long as they're sent as editable documents (which requires Windows 95 or a Microsoft At Work fax machine).

The power (and some of the complexity) of MAW Fax comes from its reliance on Microsoft Exchange, a powerful new electronic mail system that also forms the backbone of another communications tool we'll cover in Chapter 18, "The Microsoft Network."

You might not now exchange electronic mail, but in a way, fax was the earliest form of electronic mail, even if it's sent and received on paper (and even that's changing; now that we can send and receive faxes from our computers). Since you need an address book/phone book for faxing and a way to type fax memos and affix attachments, using an electronic mail package for faxing makes a lot of sense.

Here's another way faxing is like electronic mail: with MAW Fax, you can elect to send a computer document as an electronic file. It arrives as a copy of the original word processing file (or other type of document, like a spreadsheet), and the document is ready to open for viewing or editing with the same or a compatible application.

This is in sharp contrast to a traditional electronic fax, which arrives as a simplistic drawing of the original, like a black-and-white photograph. The only changes you can make to a picture are graphical, similar to writing on a paper fax with a pencil.

The Bigness of Exchange

Since faxing depends on Exchange, let's look at Exchange first. Even if you only use it to send faxes now, you'll probably use it for electronic mail in the future.

Microsoft Exchange is your universal Inbox, with links to online services (like CompuServe), your Internet account, The Microsoft Network, company LANs (local area networks) running Microsoft Mail or Microsoft Exchange Server, and in the future, you'll also be able to attach to Lotus Notes servers and other mail systems such as MCI Mail and AT&T Easylink. Exchange is crucial to Bill Gates's vision of "information at your fingertips."

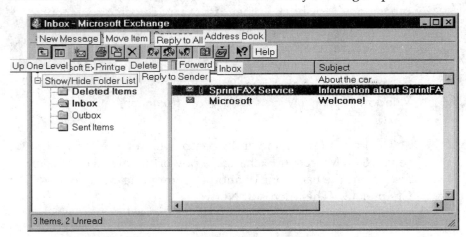

Figure 16-31: *Exchange works something like a filing cabinet, as does Windows Explorer. (Tooltips for all toolbar icons are shown here for quick reference.)*

Cosmetically, Exchange resembles something we've already learned a lot about: Explorer. Exchange, too, has a two-pane window, with the names of folders on the left-hand side and a view of documents (mail or fax messages) on the right-hand side. A handy toolbar keeps the most useful commands at your fingertips.

 TIP Use Tools I Customize Toolbar to change which menu commands appear as icons on the toolbar.

Normally, only the contents of the Inbox are shown. If you want to display both panes, click the *second* toolbar button (Show/Hide Folder List). Now you can see that, in addition to your Inbox, you have several other folders, including Outbox and Sent Mail. (The difference: Outbox holds messages that are in the process of being sent. Once delivered, the mail moves to the Sent Mail folder. Deleted messages are saved in the Deleted Items folder.)

Unlike earlier e-mail systems such as Microsoft Mail, Exchange messages and faxes can be sent with all their fonts, formatting, colors and embedded objects (including pictures, sound files, and more) intact, ushering in a new way of communicating creatively. Exchange also can send plain text to systems that don't support all this graphical tomfoolery—the goodies are in a separate part of the e-mail file, so that the receiving system can use whatever it's capable of deciphering.

Setting Up Exchange

If you rushed to sign up for The Microsoft Network (MSN) when you first installed Windows 95, Exchange is already set up on your computer. If you haven't done so yet and intend to, you might want to check out Chapter 18 first.

If you choose to install Exchange when you set up Windows 95 (it happens automatically if you install Microsoft Fax), then there's already an Inbox icon on your desktop. In fact, you might have been walked through the setup for Exchange by the Windows Setup program.

Getting an Inbox

If you don't have an Inbox icon, it's easy to remedy. First, open Control Panel (Start I Settings I Control Panel). Then double-click the Add/Remove Programs icon.

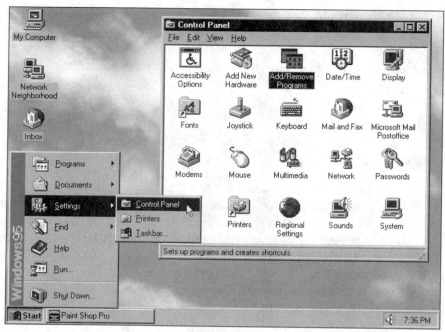

Figure 16-32: *Use Control Panel's Add/Remove Programs to add Microsoft Exchange.*

When Add/Remove Programs opens, click the tab heading for Windows Setup, which will look similar to Figure 16-32. Here you'll see an X in the checkbox for each part (or component) of Windows that you originally installed. Some of the items are actually categories of components, such as Accessories. If you have installed only some components in a group, that group will be marked with a gray square. If it's clear, then nothing in that group has been installed. To add or remove items within a group, double-click the group or click the Details button.

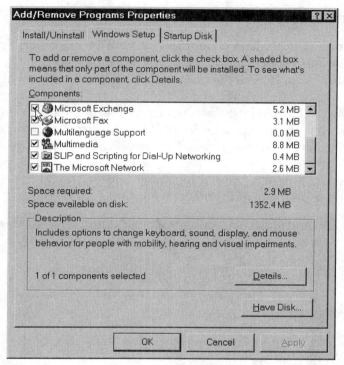

Figure 16-33: *Turn on the checkbox for* Exchange *and* Fax *to install an Inbox on your desktop.*

If you want to remove some components, just click the check box to clear it. (The associated files are actually deleted from your hard drive to free space.) Or to add a component, click the empty check box to mark it (this will add files to your hard drive).

To add Exchange, just click the empty box next to Exchange. If you add Fax, you also have to add Exchange, so it'll be turned on for you automatically. (If the boxes are already marked, Exchange is installed. If you still can't run Exchange, try first unmarking it, then click Apply to remove it, then mark it again and click Apply to add it back.)

When you're done, click the Apply or Close button. Now Windows Setup makes the changes necessary to reconcile your choices. If you cleared a box, that component will be removed. If you checked a new box, Windows adds that component. Nothing happens to components you didn't change. To make the changes, Windows usually requires you to insert some of the original Windows 95 installation diskettes or insert your Windows 95 CD-ROM. Some changes also require you to restart the computer.

Initializing Exchange

To get started with Exchange, double-click your Inbox to start the Exchange Setup Wizard. If you still don't see an icon for Inbox, you can start the Exchange Setup Wizard from the Control Panel. Open Control Panel with Start | Settings | Control Panel, and double-click the icon labeled Mail and Fax (*not* Microsoft Mail Postoffice, which we'll explain next).

The first step of the Exchange Setup Wizard instructs you in setting up an Exchange Profile. Your profile tells Exchange which services you'll use. While it's common to put all your services in the same profile, you may prefer to set up alternate profiles for some services, so you can choose whether to log on to outside systems when you start Exchange.

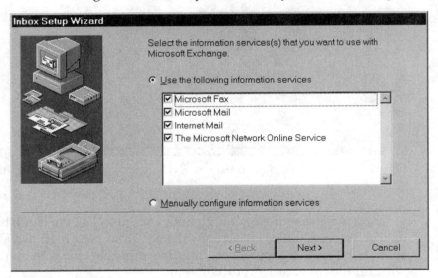

Figure 16-34: *Choose the services and providers you want available from your Exchange profile.*

As shown in Figure 16-34, mark the check boxes for each service (or provider) you want to use with Exchange. In the following discussion, we'll assume you checked all the boxes so that we can review the additional steps you follow to complete the setup.

If you installed Microsoft Mail, you'll be asked for the path to the Workgroup Postoffice (ask your network administrator if you didn't create it yourself). After that, you'll be asked to enter your user name (account name) and your password. See Chapter 19 to learn how to set up a WGPO.

If you chose to use Microsoft Fax, you'll be walked through modem setup (discussed earlier in this chapter), if you haven't already installed your modem.

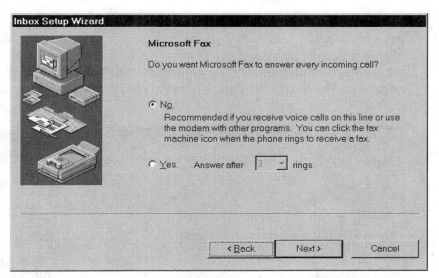

Figure 16-35: *If you receive phone calls on your modem line, or if you want to use other modem programs while your Inbox is open, make sure Microsoft Fax is not set to answer the phone.*

The next Microsoft Fax step is to enter some information for sending and receiving faxes. Some of this information will appear on the fax cover page. If more than one person uses your computer to send faxes, you'll want to set up a separate *profile* for each person, so the information will be unique. Use the Mail and Fax icon in Control Panel to manage your profiles.

You'll also have to decide whether you want Microsoft Fax to answer the phone line attached to the modem. If you do, Microsoft Fax will pick up the line, answer the call, receive the fax and put it in your Inbox—all automatically. But if the call isn't a fax, Fax will intercept every phone call. That's why using a modem/telephone autoswitcher, available from office supply and computer stores, can be very useful. Otherwise, you'll want to tell Microsoft Fax not to answer all calls. (There's also a manual option that alerts you when the phone is ringing and automatically pops open a box that lets you choose to answer the call.)

 If you use your computer with other modem software, make sure you set up Microsoft Fax so that it does not answer the phone. When MS Fax monitors the phone line, no other modem program can access the modem unless they've been updated with TAPI support.

If you want to use Exchange with the Internet, you have your work cut out for you. First, you must have already set up your Internet account with Network Setup and set up a connection with Dial-Up Networking (unless you access the Internet via your company's TCP/IP LAN.) Since we don't cover Dial-Up Networking until the next chapter, you might want to set it up later.

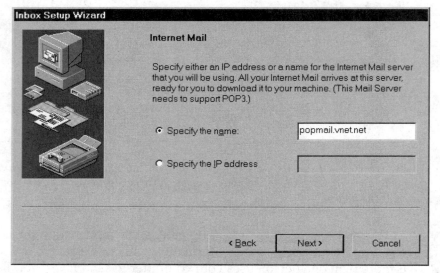

Figure 16-36: *Setting up Internet mail can be daunting the first time you try it.*

All you need for Internet mail is a few facts and figures, such as your mail address and the name of your provider's mail server. This information should be obtained from your Internet provider—you probably already know this information if you previously used a Winsock-compatible mail program with Windows 3.1. (Turn to Chapter 17 if you're eager to get started with Internet mail.)

Now that Exchange is ready, let's get back to faxing. We'll look into using Exchange for electronic mail in Chapter 19.

Sending a Fax

When you first start Exchange, it can be a little intimidating, because it has a lot of features. Right now, we'll focus on sending a fax. Choose New Fax from the Compose menu.

The first time you send a fax, you'll be asked to choose your current location, which is really useful only if you're traveling with a notebook or laptop computer. Choose the check box labeled *I'm not using a portable computer* to prevent this box from appearing again.

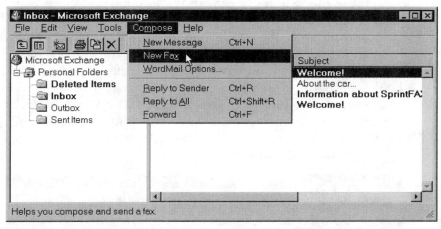

Figure 16-37: *Send a fax by choosing Compose | New Fax.*

The first step in sending a fax is to choose the recipient. If you've already sent this person a fax, the name will be in your personal address book (PAB), otherwise you can add an entry to the PAB.

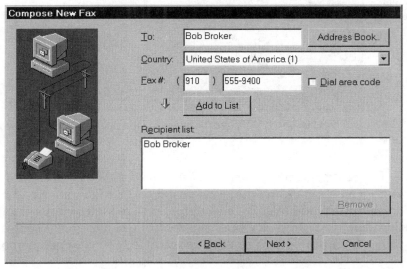

Figure 16-38: *To send a fax, first enter the person's name and phone number.*

As shown in Figure 16-38, you type the recipient's name in the *To* box. Choose the country for the recipient in the *Country* box, if necessary. Then enter the fax number in the *Fax #* boxes. (If it's a long-distance call, turn on the check box for *Dial Area Code*. While you can leave off the area code for local faxes, filling it in makes your phone book portable if you travel with your computer.)

When you finish the phone number, click the *Add to List* button to add the number to your fax list.

If you send faxes routinely to the same group of people, use the Address book (see below) to create entries in your personal address book. Unlike the Microsoft Mail version of Fax that shipped with Windows for Workgroups, Exchange does not automatically add new phone numbers and addresses to the Personal Address Book. Use Tools | Address Book to manage your e-mail addresses and fax numbers.

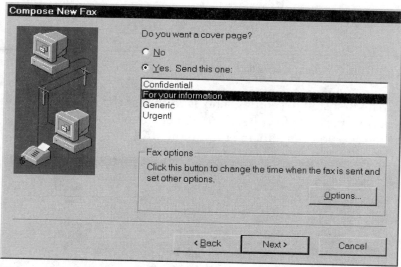

Figure 16-39: *Choose a cover page to send, or choose No to send only the memo you type.*

The next page of the *Compose New Fax Wizard* lets you choose a cover page. You can pick any of the Microsoft cover pages or a cover page you've created with the Cover Page Designer (covered later in this chapter). Also on this page, you can click Options to control when the fax is sent, among other things (Figure 16-40). When you're ready to type your fax memo, click Next.

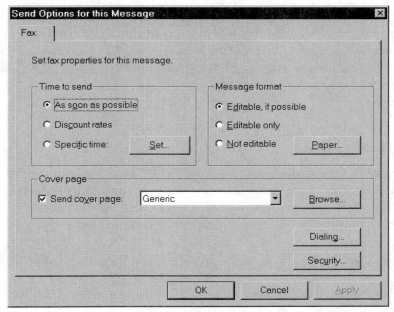

Figure 16-40: *Send Options let you control when the fax is sent and whether to send a file as an editable document.*

Now you can type your fax memo. Enter a subject line, then press Tab to switch to typing the memo. (Normally, you'll leave the check box marked for *Start memo on cover page*. If the memo is short enough, it will all fit on the cover page. Otherwise, it will be continued on a blank page.)

When you're done typing, click Next. The next-to-last page of the wizard lets you attach files to your fax. Normally those files are simply printed along with your fax on the destination fax machine, but if you used the Options button to send your fax as an editable document, the attachments will show up as icons in the message when opened from the recipient's Inbox.

If you have no files to attach, just click Next. The final page of the wizard simply asks you to click Next to begin the transmission. This is your last chance to cancel the fax if you change your mind. Click Finish to send the fax.

The Microsoft Fax Status program pops up and shows you its progress as it dials and sends the fax.

You don't have to wait around while the fax transmits. Thanks to *multitasking*, the fax is sent in the background. You can continue to use your computer for other things while the fax is transmitted.

An Alternate Route

Instead of using the Compose New Fax Wizard, you can simply create a new Exchange message by clicking the New message icon on the toolbar or choosing Compose | New Message. Or choose Start | Programs | Accessories | Fax | Compose New Fax.

 The keyboard hotkey for New Message is Ctrl+N.

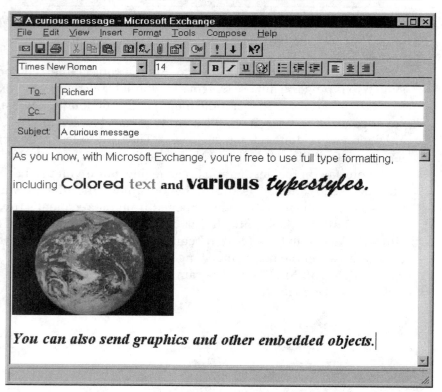

Figure 16-41: *Use Compose | New Message to open the New Message window (shown).*

This pops up the full-featured message editor, shown in Figure 16-41. Most of the time, you'll just fill in the subject and body text of the message. You can click on To: to open the address book and choose an address for sending the message, or just type the name of a person that you know is in your address book. (Use the Check Names icon on the toolbar to confirm that your recipient is in the phone book.)

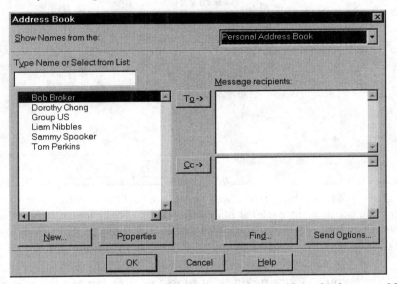

Figure 16-42: *You can choose a name from your address book, or use New to create a new entry.*

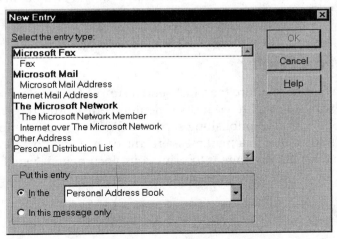

Figure 16-43: *After choosing New, choose the type of address you're creating, such as Fax.*

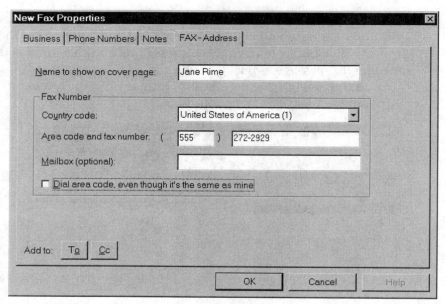

Figure 16-44: *Use the Fax Address panel to set up the recipient's name and fax number. You can also store related information such as telephone numbers, business/ mailing address, even a page of notes, about each recipient, by clicking the appropriate tab headings.*

While you're working on your message, you can use the editing toolbar to choose the typeface, type size, style (bold, italics underline, color) and other options like bulleting and indenting. In this way, New Message works a lot like WordPad, the little brother of Microsoft Word. (For more about Word-Pad, consult Chapter 10.)

The Microsoft Fax Printer

Often you want to do more than just send a simple fax memo. For example, you might want to prepare your document in your word processor or with a spreadsheet or desktop publishing software. While you can simply attach the original document to a mail message, the easiest way to get the document into a fax-mail message is to print your document as usual, using the Microsoft Fax printer driver instead of your regular printer driver.

Figure 16-45: *The Microsoft Fax Printer lives in the Printers folder, which you can open by using Start | Settings | Printers or by opening My Computer.*

Most programs have a Printer Setup option on their File menu that lets you choose a printer. Or, the setup option may be in the dialog box that appears when you choose File | Print. An alternative is to use the Send or Send As Mail option, if your word processor supports it.

Just remember to change your default printer back to your regular printer driver when you've finished faxing, or the next time you print, you'll really be faxing. (Unless that's what you want—it's possible to use a fax machine as a kind of slow remote printer. Indeed, that's exactly how it works: when you print your file, it appears on your recipient's fax machine, just as if that fax machine were a printer.)

When printing is completed, Exchange pops up to ask you the phone number (fax address) to use for the document, and you can also choose your cover page options. The document you just printed appears as an icon in an otherwise empty e-mail message.

 TIP   E-mail attachments are created when you print to the fax printer and appear as icons in the message. You can also create an attachment by copying something into the clipboard and pasting it in the mail message. (Some items, like pictures, appear within the document literally as a picture, instead of an icon. If you want an icon, use Paste Special from the Edit menu).

Since you can use the clipboard to create attachments, this should suggest to you that you can use almost any drag and drop operation to put objects (attachments) into the mail message. If the receiving fax machine is also a

Microsoft At Work fax machine or fax modem, you can choose to have the objects retain their identities as computer files. Instead of being rendered (printed) as a fax, the objects will be sent intact. If the object was a waveform (.WAV) file, the recipient can click the speaker icon to play the sound or voice mail message. If it's a document, the recipient can double-click it to view it in a word processor.

To make sure these objects are sent as objects instead of pictures, make sure both fax modems are being used with Microsoft At Work Fax. Use Tools | Microsoft Fax Tools | Options to set the way the fax is sent. Send it as Editable, If Possible, instead of Not Editable.

 TIP When you send a fax or a mail message, the message is temporarily moved to the Outbox folder until it's sent. If you change your mind about sending a message or a fax, you can remove it from the Outbox if you act quickly.

If you aren't sending the fax as an editable document (when the recipient has an ordinary fax machine), then when you send the fax, Exchange opens up the appropriate program to print the attached objects (of course, some objects, such as .WAV audio files can't be faxed to an ordinary fax machine—they'll just appear as icons).

 TIP Sent faxes are copied to your hard drive and they aren't deleted automatically when sent. Look in your Sent Mail folder from time to time and delete old mail messages and faxes. (If you need to resend a fax, look for it in your Sent Mail folder.) You may also need to empty your Deleted Mail folder, unless you've set it to delete mail automatically when you exit Exchange or Shut Down.) To do this, choose Tools | Options and check the box for *Empty the 'Deleted Items' folder upon exiting.*

Viewing a Fax

Nothing could be easier than looking at a fax in the Exchange. Just double-click the name of the fax in your Exchange Inbox, as shown in Figure 16-46. Or, if the name is highlighted, you can just press Enter.

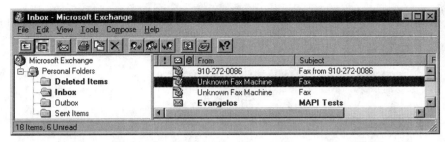

Figure 16-46: *Opening a fax for viewing is as easy as pressing the Enter key.*

You'll see the Exchange Fax Viewer open up with your fax inside it, ready for zooming, rotating or whatever's necessary to see the picture. And do remember, faxes are pictures (unless sent as editable documents from within Windows 95 to another Windows 95 recipient). Because they are graphics, they can be upside down and the Fax Viewer is ready to rotate them if required.

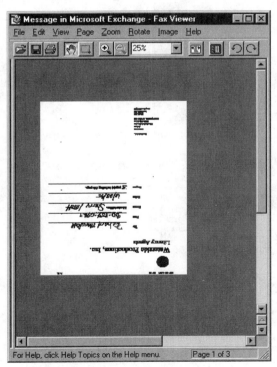

Figure 16-47: *The Fax Viewer, ready to rotate and zoom.*

As you can see in Figure 16-47, faxes can come in skewed. To fix this one for viewing, we'll click the Rotate menu and select Flip Over, then click on the Zoom menu and choose 50% to get the readable results shown in Figure 16-48:

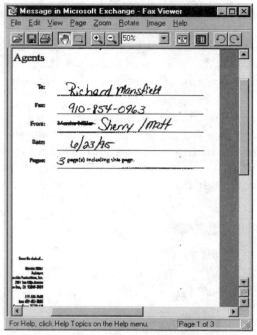

Figure 16-48: *That's better. Now we can read the main information.*

To see more detail, zoom further, as shown in Figure 16-49.

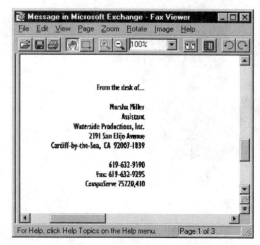

Figure 16-49: *At 100%, you're as close as you can get. If it's unreadable at this magnification, ask them to resend it.*

TIP The easiest way to slide the page around when it's zoomed is to click on the hand symbol on the toolbar, or choose Drag from the Edit menu. As you can see in Figure 16-50, your mouse pointer is replaced by a tiny hand icon. Now hold down your left mouse button while moving the mouse around. The images slides quite easily. Another tip: to scroll the image in any direction, drag the Drag pointer over against the frame of the Fax Viewer and hold it there. The image will then slide continuously.

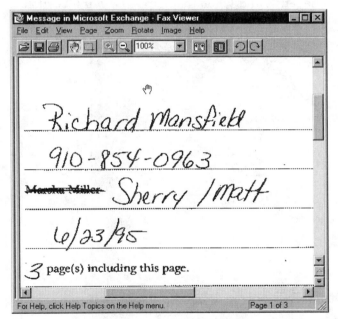

Figure 16-50: *The Drag mode (Edit | Drag) is effective when looking at a document close up.*

Many of the menu items on the Fax Viewer are found on most any Windows 95 window—Print, Save As and so on. However, a few, like Drag described above, are unique to the Fax Viewer. Let's look at some other special features you can use to more easily view and manipulate your faxes.

If you choose Select from the Edit menu, or click the Select Button (next to the hand), you can then drag a zone within the page. This selected area can now be copied (Ctrl+C or Edit | Copy) and pasted into Paint or another graphics program.

On the Zoom menu are the options Fit Width, Fit Height and Fit Both. Fit Width makes sure you see the entire width of the fax page, within whatever size you've currently got the Fax Viewer window. Fit Both shows the entire page. There's also a Fit Both icon on the Toolbar to the right of the Zoom drop-down list.

A useful *Show Thumbnails* feature (Figure 16-51) splits the Fax Viewer window and lines up all the pages on the left side. Clicking on any of these thumbnail sketches brings up that page on the right pane, in larger magnification. The Thumbnails option is in the View menu and also on the Toolbar, third icon from the right. Finally, the Image menu has only one feature— Invert. It turns black to white and white to black. Sometimes a Fax comes in looking like a negative and when that happens, you'll be glad the Viewer includes inversion among its tools.

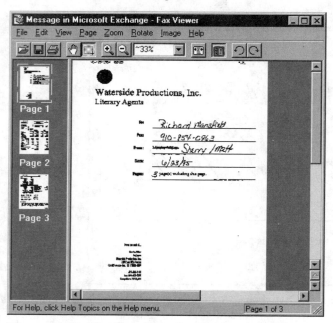

Figure 16-51: *The Show Thumbnails view displays all the pages of the fax in the pane on the left. Click on the page you want to see in the larger right pane.*

Creating a Cover Page

If you want to design a snazzy cover for your faxes, Microsoft Exchange includes a full-featured design tool. In Exchange, click the Compose menu, then select New Fax. The Fax Wizard will appear and ask for the address. Then, when you click Next, you'll see the Wizard window shown in Figure 16-52:

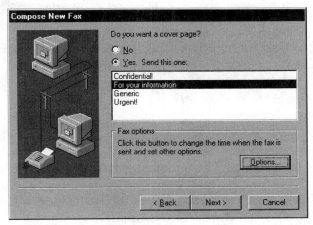

Figure 16-52: *Choose from one of the predesigned cover sheets from this list if you wish.*

If you have a collection of cover sheets, you can locate them by clicking the Options button shown in Figure 16-52. Fax cover pages have a file extension of .CPE.

However, if you want to design a new cover page, click the Start button, then Programs | Accessories | Fax | Cover Page Editor. If you haven't used this feature before, you'll also see the Tips window shown in Figure 16-53.

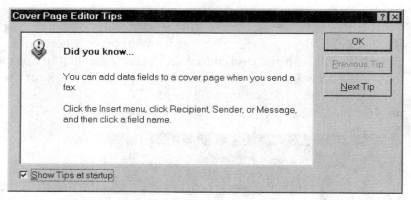

Figure 16-53: *The Fax Cover Editor displays tips when first started (or every time, if you leave* Show Tips at Startup *selected).*

The easiest way to compose your own cover sheet is to just modify one of the sample cover sheets that Windows 95 supplies. Click on the File menu in the Cover Sheet Editor, select Open, then move to your Windows folder where you'll find the four prebuilt samples: Confidential, For Your Information, Generic and Urgent. Load one of them and work with it. Generic, as you might guess, is a good choice for a template.

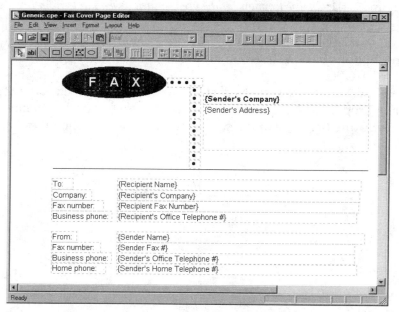

Figure 16-54: *Open the Generic predesigned cover sheet and use it as a template to create your own.*

The Cover Sheet Editor works with *fields*. These are zones, surrounded by faint gray dashes that include a "trigger" enclosed in braces. Take a look at Figure 16-54. See where it says {Sender's Company}? That's a field. You don't want to have to type in your name, company, address, fax number and all the rest each time you send a fax. Items on the fax cover page enclosed within brackets {} will be replaced by information already known about you, like your phone number and company name. Likewise, information about the recipient of your fax will also be filled in from your address book or from whatever you type into the second page of the Compose New Fax Wizard in the Exchange.

Let's take the Generic cover sheet and make some modifications, a little customizing, to see how the Editor works. Click the black oval. Let's make it fatter. When you click on it, you'll see the "handles" that you can drag to reshape it. Drag the lower-middle handle downward. You'll see the results shown in Figure 16-55.

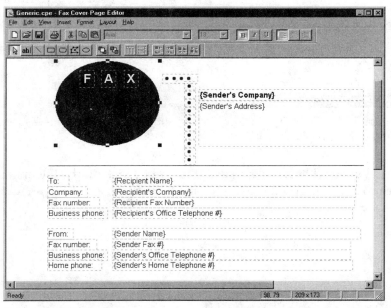

Figure 16-55: *You can reshape geometric objects easily by dragging. Compare to Figure 16-54.*

To deselect (to get rid of the frame and handles), click outside the selected zone. Now we want to change the font of the letters F A X from bold to normal. To select all three letters (which are separate objects, each with its dashed-line frame) drag the mouse around the outside of them. When they're selected, just click on the *B* icon on the toolbar to turn off boldface.

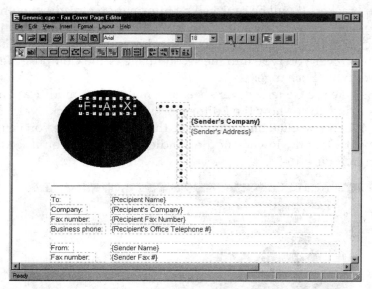

Figure 16-56: *Select a group of objects by dragging around them—as we did here around the letters* F A X.

Let's see what it looks like at this point. Click on the File menu and choose Print Preview. You'll see the finished product, as shown in Figure 16-57.

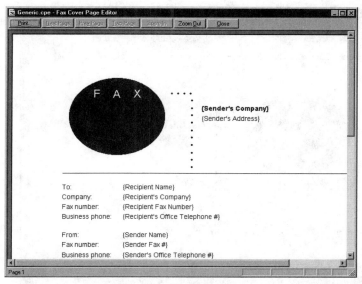

Figure 16-57: *Print Preview displays the page pretty much as it will look when sent, but the fields will be filled in later.*

Click the Close button to get back to the Editor. Now we want to put a .BMP graphic into this page. No problem. Load the graphic into Paint or some other graphics application. Select it and Copy it (from the Edit menu). Reposition it by dragging, and resize as described above. You can also import graphics as objects (Insert menu, Object), but at the time of this writing a graphics object will pixelate— appear in very low resolution. It's best to bring in a graphic from the clipboard by having copied it from a graphics application.

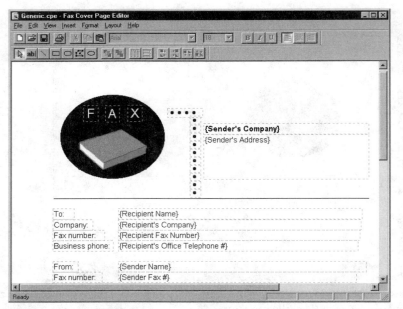

Figure 16-58: *We sell books, so we wanted this, our book logo, on the cover page.*

Or go wild, and get really creative. Transform your logo into a texture in a graphics program, then blend it into the background. To get the look in Figure 16-59, we used Micrografx's Picture Publisher and took the book icon, lightened it (Map menu, Contrast/Brightness), then saved it as a texture (Edit menu, then Copy To | Texture). Then we filled a new image with this texture (File | New), copied it to the Clipboard (Edit | Copy) and placed it behind the other Fax cover elements by pasting it into the Fax Cover Page Editor. The Send to Back button on the toolbar moved it to its correct position behind everything else on the page.

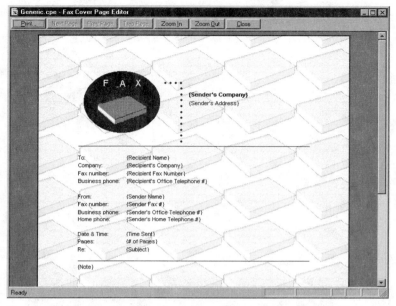

Figure 16-59: *We flung our book logo all over the background here. Why not create your own great fax cover page? Windows 95 gives you the tools.*

Of course there's much more you can do within the Fax Cover Page Editor. There are tools to create shapes; to align layers on the Z axis (bring layered objects to the front or push them behind other objects); to space or align a selected group of objects; insert all kinds of fields (the Insert menu); draw borders (Format menu, Line, Fill & Color); and the usual font options to format and adjust text found in most Windows 95 applications. These options are largely self-explanatory, and we don't have space to illustrate each feature in this book. Play with the Cover Page Editor; it's easy to use. Now let's turn our attention to the outside world—the Internet and the new online service that everyone's talking about, The Microsoft Network.

Moving On

We cover some additional Exchange options in Chapter 19, where we discuss using Exchange for electronic mail on a network. In the meantime, get ready for some fun as we explore the Internet and The Microsoft Network in the next two chapters.

Chapter 17

The Internet Connection

You can't ignore it. The Internet is growing larger and stronger every day. Although constantly under construction, the information superhighway is fast becoming an essential part of our lives. Most of this is probably due to the success of the World Wide Web, a friendly and colorful way to present text, graphics and multimedia with a Windows-style look and feel.

The Internet is growing all the time and is changing the world, and Microsoft recognized this by building Internet connectivity right into Windows 95. While there's no Web browser yet, we'll show you how you can easily acquire Microsoft's Internet Explorer and use other browsers such as the popular Netscape Navigator, as well as other Internet tools like FTP file transfer.

Of course, there's a limit to how detailed we can get; we won't attempt to compete with the hundreds of Internet books out there. In fact, if you want a full-fledged Internet guide, check out *Internet Guide for Windows 95* (Ventana Press). So instead of a tutorial on how to use the Internet, or a compilation of exciting sites to visit, in this chapter we'll focus on the Windows 95 Internet connection.

Figure 17-1: *Microsoft's Internet Explorer is an example of a Web browser, a program that lets you "surf the Net." Here we are using it to view Ventana Online's home page.*

Obtaining an Internet Account

We'll assume you already have an Internet access account through an Internet provider. Local dial-up access to the Internet is now available across the country, from both local vendors and large, national providers. Microsoft is also selling Internet access through The Microsoft Network. A "provider" is a company that offers, for a fee, a local toll-free number you can call to get onto the Internet.

Make sure you have what's called a PPP (Point-to-Point Protocol) connection with your provider. The older SLIP protocol can be made to work, but we won't get into that here, since it's not installed for Windows 95 by default. If your provider only gives you a shell or SLIP account, get a PPP account instead, or choose another provider. (While you're shopping, also ask whether the provider supports CHAP or PAP authentication—don't worry about what this means yet—for easier online access with Windows 95. Also inquire about support for 28,800 bps modems—you'll be upgrading within a year to get the top modem speed that's necessary for smooth Internet browsing.)

 TIP   If SLIP is your only choice, read the \ADMIN\APPTOOLS\SLIP\ SLIP.TXT on the Windows 95 CD-ROM for information on using and configuring SLIP. Or purchase Microsoft Plus! for Windows 95, which can automatically configure your setup for SLIP. But SLIP is slower and less efficient, so insist on PPP for best results.

Connection Checklist

You'll need to find out the following information from your network provider before you can install Windows 95 Internet support. We've provided a checklist on the next page. We've also provided a sample of the data you need so you can see how the necessary information is formatted. You could even copy this page, fill out the form, and use it as a quick reference. Yes, a lot of information is required. In the near future, the process of setting up Internet access will become largely automatic. But in the meantime, you'll need the information shown below. Some entries are optional. For example, many providers automatically assign you an IP address instead of a fixed IP address. (We'll explain what that means later.)

Property	Example	Your value	Also called	Note
Local access number	555-5555	_____	phone number	1
Host	cbrannon	_____	username	2
Domain	vmedia.com	_____	server	2
DNS Server IP Address	199.72.13.1	_____	Host IP address	3
Backup DNS Server	199.72.1.1	_____		3
Gateway IP Address	199.72.13.250	_____	gateway	3
News Server	kells.vmedia.com	_____		4
POP3 Mail Server	popmail.vmedia.com	_____	mail server	5
Mail account	cbrannon@vmedia.com	_____	user account	6
Mail password	yeah_right	_____		6
Password	you_wish	_____	PPP password	7
Your IP Address	199.72.13.137	_____		7
Subnet mask	255.255.255.0	_____		7
Supports CHAP/PAP?	no	☐ Yes ☐ No	authentication	8

Table 17-1: *Before you can set up Internet access, get the following information from your provider.*

Connection Properties

In Table 17-1, fill in the blanks under *Your value*, using the Example column as a guide to the format and syntax of each item. Let's review each item in Table 17-1 to get the terminology out of the way. The Note entry in the table refers to one of the following notes:

1. Local Access Number: This is the modem phone number of your local Internet provider, not the voice line used for technical support or customer support.
2. Host and Domain: It doesn't make sense, but *your* username is the host, and the domain is the name of the provider's server. These are combined in the format host@domain to form your user account and mail account name. (However, it's possible to use a mail account separate from your user account.)
3. DNS and Gateway IP: An *IP address* is a set of four numbers (separated by periods) that uniquely identify an Internet resource. (The Net is fast running out of numbers, which will likely lead to a fifth number in the address). Instead of using a fixed DNS address, some providers are moving toward creating a unique DNS address on the spot. In this case, you won't need the DNS address at all, but check to make sure. Many providers don't use a gateway or let you use the default gateway. So this entry might also be blank.

4. News Server: While you won't need this to configure Windows 95, you'll want to know your news server when configuring your newsreader software or Web browser. You might also want to find out the name of your *time server* if you want to be able to set your computer's time, correct to the millisecond.

5. POP3 Mail Server: Microsoft Exchange Internet Mail requires a mail server that supports the POP3 protocol. Some older providers limit you to sending standard text-only mail, and you won't be able to use that type of mail account with Windows 95 (although you can still dial up using Telnet or another mail program to read your mail the old-fashioned way). If your provider offers both types of mail systems, ask for the name of the POP3 server. (You may need to use the Mail Server's IP address instead if no name is available.)

6. Mail account and Mail password: Your mail account is usually the same as host@domain (mine is cbrannon@vmedia.com). However, if you require a separate PPP account, use that for the host and domain. The mail password is also not necessarily the same as your PPP password.

7. Password, IP Address, Subnet mask: Each user on the Internet also needs to have a unique IP address. This leads to a proliferation of addresses, however, and what happens if you move to a different network location? The solution is to let the provider assign you a unique (but different) IP address every time you sign on to the network. In that case, leave this entry blank. Otherwise, fill in *your* IP address (not the DNS address). The subnet mask is almost always 255.255.255.0, unless you're part of a subnetwork. (Leave this blank if your IP address is assigned automatically.) You also need a password that goes with your account or IP address. This is sometimes called a PPP password, if it's not the same as your mail password.

8. Supports PAP/CHAP: If your provider has support for an Authentication Protocol, Windows 95 can fill in your username and password automatically. If this doesn't work, you'll have to set up a *script* to complete your connection or enable a *terminal window* so that you can type them in. We'll discuss these issues below.

Alternatives to Microsoft

In this chapter, we'll teach you the standard method for connecting to the Internet from Windows 95. If you buy an Internet kit from another company, it may use an entirely different approach. The Windows 95 method, although it can be a little tricky to set up, will give you the best results.

You can use Internet kits designed for Windows 3.1, but you'll want to get the new Windows 95 versions as soon as they're available. The CD-ROM that accompanies this book also contains Internet *shareware* that gives you almost everything the expensive Internet kits offer. (However, shareware is *not* free. You are obligated to pay a registration fee to the software author if you continue to use the software after its trial period expires. If software is clearly labeled as *freeware*, you don't need to pay for it. Check the license. Some shareware allows free use to educational customers, a flat registration fee for personal use, and a larger sum for business and site licenses.)

Hands-On: Getting Ready for Networking

If you don't see an icon for Network Neighborhood on your desktop, networking support hasn't been installed. See Chapter 19 for full documentation on setting up a network. If you're on a network, you can contact your network administrator for help if you access the Internet via a company gateway or firewall. Here, we'll cover just the steps required to install the TCP/IP protocol and the Dial-Up Networking adapter.

Support for Dial-Up Networking may not be installed on your computer, depending how you originally installed Windows 95. To make sure you have it, run Add/Remove Programs from Control Panel, then click the Windows Setup tab heading. Choose the Communications option and click Details. Turn on the check box for Dial-Up Networking. See Figure 17-2.

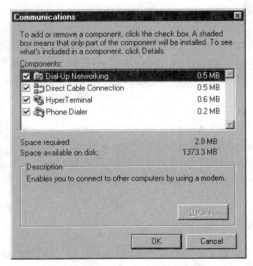

Figure 17-2: *Use Control Panel's Add/Remove Programs to make sure you have the Dial-Up Networking support installed.*

1. Click Start | Settings | Control Panel and double-click the Network icon to open Network Properties. If you already have a Network Neighborhood icon, right-click it and choose Properties.

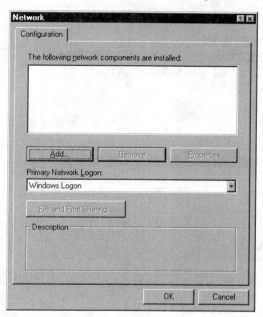

Figure 17-3: *The first time you set up the network, the list of network components is empty.*

2. If you already see entries for Microsoft Networking, TCP/IP and Dial-Up Adapter, the support is already installed. See Chapter 19 to learn how to configure your existing setup. Or just click everything and use the Remove button to start from scratch.
3. Click the Add button, and then choose Protocol (Figure 17-4).

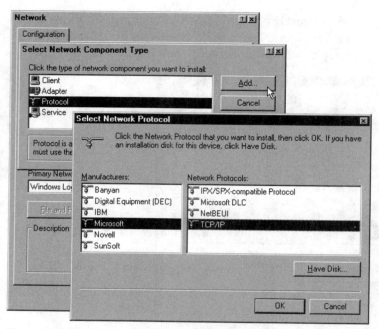

Figure 17-4: *To install TCP/IP, choose Protocol, and install the Microsoft TCP/IP protocol.*

4. Using the leftmost pane, scroll down to the Microsoft entry and click it. Then click TCP/IP on the right.
5. Network Properties will now resemble Figure 17-5. The Dial-Up Adapter is automatically installed. If you don't see it, click Add, then Adapter, and choose Microsoft Dial-Up Adapter.

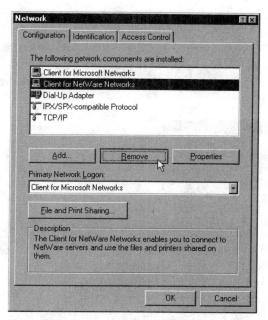

Figure 17-5: *After TCP/IP is installed, remove the NetWare and IPX/SPX entries, unless you are also on a Novell network. If you are, refer to Chapter 19.*

6. If you only want to use the Internet, click the entry for NetWare and click Remove, then click on IPX/SPX and remove it, too.
7. Proceed to Configuring TCP/IP below.

Configuring TCP/IP

The Internet and Windows 95 use TCP/IP to communicate. TCP/IP stands for Transmission Control Protocol/Internet Protocol. TCP slices up your network communication into *packets*, which are routed individually (and automatically) to the IP address of the destination computer, where they're reassembled.

Most of the settings above are used only to set up TCP/IP. Once this is out of the way, using the Internet is much easier.

If you still have your Network Neighborhood open, just double-click the TCP/IP entry. Otherwise, use Networks from the Control Panel or right-click the Network Neighborhood icon and choose Properties.

Now let's look at each TCP/IP property sheet. The headings below correspond to the tab headings for the property sheets. (Click on any tab heading to switch to it, or use Ctrl+Tab.)

IP Address

As shown in Figure 17-6, fill in your IP address and subnet mask from Table 17-1. The figure shows the example data. If you don't know your IP address, or if your provider fills it in automatically, click the option button for *Obtain an IP address automatically*.

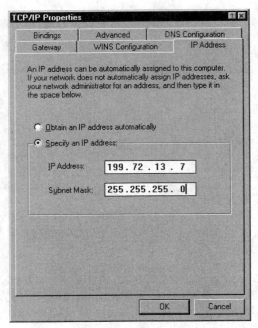

Figure 17-6: *Use* Specify an IP address *if you your provider has assigned you a fixed IP address.*

DNS Configuration

First, you'll need to enable DNS (Domain Name Server) support almost every time. (Some archaic providers haven't upgraded to DNS yet, but you'll need it for best results.) Click the *Enable DNS* option button. Fill in the host and domain from Table 17-1. (Our figure shows the example data, *not* your personal information that you need to obtain from the provider.)

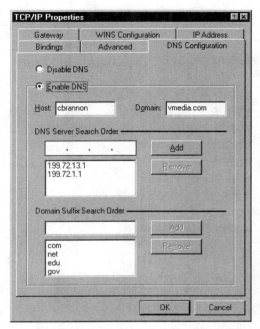

Figure 17-7: *Enter the DNS IP address (not your IP address) and click Add.*

Enter the DNS Server's IP address in the box after DNS Server Search Order. (You can type a space between numbers to skip quickly to the next box.) Then be sure to click Add (otherwise it has no effect). If your provider doesn't use a specific DNS address, fill in the host and domain, but leave the DNS entry blank. You can enter additional DNS addresses to use as a backup when the primary DNS is unavailable.

You don't need to fill in the DNS Suffix Search order, but if you want to, add the entries *com, net, edu* and *gov.*

Gateway

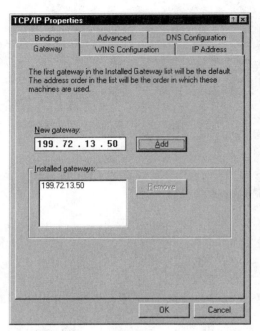

Figure 17-8: *If your service requires a specific gateway, enter the gateway IP address here.*

Many providers don't require a gateway. If your gateway is 0.0.0.0, leave the gateway entry blank. Otherwise, fill in the provider's gateway IP address, and be sure to click Add to put it on the list. You can add more gateways to be used when the primary gateway is clogged.

Ignore the others

You don't need to configure the property sheets for WINS Configuration, Bindings or Advanced. They are used only to connect to a Windows NT server or to use TCP/IP as a protocol with networks other than the Dial-Up Adapter. Believe it or not, you're finished setting up TCP/IP! Just click OK at the bottom of the property sheets to return to the Network Properties, and then close that box, too. Let Windows restart your computer to install the necessary network software. (You'll also be prompted to insert some of your Windows 95 Setup disks or the CD-ROM, unless you installed Windows 95 from a network server.)

Dial-Up Networking

Now that you've configured TCP/IP, you're ready to establish a Dial-Up Networking connection to your Internet provider. Choose Start | Programs | Accessories and choose Dial-Up Networking (Figure 17-9).

Figure 17-9: *The Dial-Up Networking folder holds all your connections to other computers.*

Double-click the *Make New Connection* icon to start the Make New Connection Wizard. Click Next to proceed to the window shown in Figure 17-10.

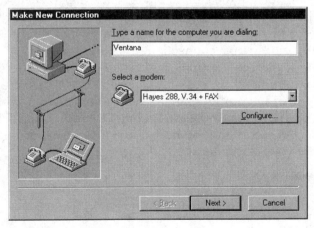

Figure 17-10: *Connection settings.*

Make up a descriptive name for this connection (such as the name of your Internet provider) and enter it in the first box. Use the *Select a modem* box to choose the modem you want to use for the connection. Most of us have only one modem, so just click Next to continue. If you haven't installed a modem yet, see Chapter 7, "The Control Panel," or Chapter 16, "The Communicating Computer."

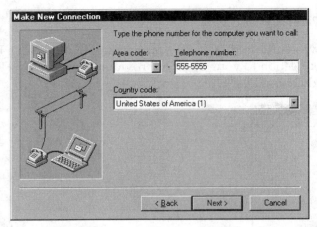

Figure 17-11: *Use the next page of the Wizard to enter the access number of your Internet provider.*

You then tell Windows 95 the phone number of your Internet provider. This is the data or modem number, not the telephone number you call for customer or technical support. Fill in the area code, even if it's a local call. If you're calling from outside the United States, click the box beneath *Country code* to choose the correct international dialing code. Click Next to continue. You're rewarded with the last page of the Wizard, which tells you that you've completed setting up a connection. Click Finish.

You can create several connections, if you like. Some providers let you dial a long-distance number to access high-speed (28,800 bps) modems, if they aren't supported in your local area. Create another connection for this phone number, with a name like "Faster, Long Distance" and fill it out identically otherwise. Or you might use more than one Internet provider, especially if you share your computer with another person.

Figure 17-12: *Your new connection is now shown in Dial-Up Networking.*

New versions of The Microsoft Network support using MSN as your dial-up Internet provider. (MSN updates are transferred to your computer automatically if you use MSN.) The MSN setup will automatically create a Dial-Up Networking connection for you, and we anticipate that many other providers will also allow easy "plug-and-play" connection installation. They'll even configure TCP/IP for you.

 You can also use Dial-Up Networking to access files and folders on another computer via a modem or with direct cable connection. The computer you're accessing needs to be running the Dial-Up Server, which is not included with Windows 95, but is available in the Microsoft Plus! add-on. Once you connect, you can log on to the network just like any other network citizen—albeit a somewhat disgruntled one because of the slow speed of a modem connection.

Getting Connected

You must connect before you can run any other Internet-related software. Some programs, such as Microsoft Internet Explorer, can automatically dial your chosen connection. Once you've created a new connection, double-click the icon you've created to start a connection to your provider.

Actually, you're not ready yet. When you first double-click your connection, you see a window similar to Figure 17-13. Here, you'll enter your username and your password (from the table you filled out above). By default, your Windows login name will be shown, which will almost certainly be incorrect. Use the username and password given to you by your Internet provider. If you have a separate mail account, you need to use your PPP username and PPP password in this box. Click the *Save password* check box, and you won't have to enter them again. You also get a chance to change the phone number. Click Dial Properties to change your local area code or to tell Windows 95 to disable Call Waiting. See Chapter 16 to learn more about Dial Properties.

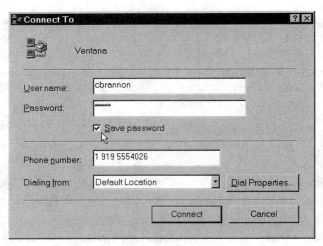

Figure 17-13: *Enter your login name and password (which displays only asterisks as you type for security).*

Now click the Connect button to go online. Windows 95 pops up a box while it's dialing (Figure 17-14). You'll also hear the modem squealing and screeching as it handshakes with the other modem. (You can use the Modem icon in Control Panel to turn off your modem speaker or adjust its volume. External modems usually have a volume control dial.)

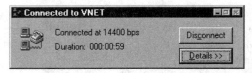

Figure 17-14: *Windows informs you of the progress of your dial-up connection.*

If all goes well, the status box will change to Connected after about half a minute. You can now run any Internet utility program or other Internet software, as long as the software is *Winsock-compliant*. You can even access other online services like America Online and CompuServe via Winsock, which can be advantageous if your only high-speed local number is for your Internet provider.

Troubleshooting Connections

Alas, many readers will discover that the steps above don't work for them. You may need to take additional steps to configure your connection correctly. This is necessary if your provider doesn't automatically assign an IP address, or if you manually log in to the server.

Figure 17-15: *Choose Properties for a connection to configure it further.*

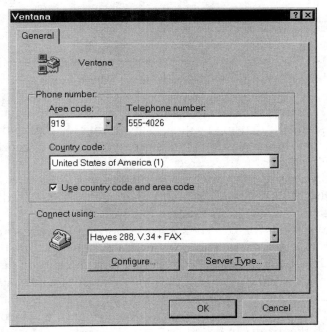

Figure 17-16: *The Connection property sheet lets you configure the modem and the server type.*

Right-click your connection's icon and choose Properties from the pop-up menu to edit the connection properties, as shown in Figure 17-15. You can also change the phone number from this panel. Enable *Use country code and area code* only if the call is long-distance. Or, you can change the modem you use (more about that in a moment). But this panel doesn't show any of the *meat* of the connection properties. For that, click Server Types, which is shown in Figure 17-17.

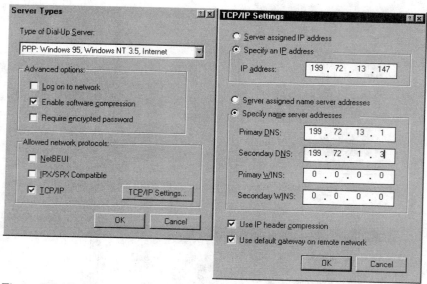

Figure 17-17: *Click the TCP/IP Settings button to troubleshoot your Internet connection.*

Figure 17-17 shows you how to configure the Server Types panel for Internet access. If you're using Dial-Up Networking to access a different kind of computer, like a Windows NT server, you'll need to check with the network administrator for the correct settings.

Under *Allowed network protocols*, turn off all the check boxes except TCP/IP and click the *TCP/IP Settings* button to change the TCP/IP settings used by this connection (which is also shown in Figure 17-17).

The normal settings for TCP/IP are *Server assigned IP address* and *Server assigned name server addresses*. That's wrong if your provider gave you a fixed IP address. Choose the *Specify an IP address* option and type in the same IP address you used when configuring TCP/IP. Choose *Specify name server addresses*, and fill in the IP address of the DNS server. If you filled out a copy of Table 17-1, you'll have those numbers at your fingertips. The other two check boxes on this page can be left on.

Manual Log-in

After the last few steps, you may be able to connect to your provider. Or not. Windows 95 can log in to a wide variety of providers automatically, by taking advantage of standard methods called authentication protocols. Most providers support either CHAP or PAP, or are planning to add support for them soon. In the meantime, you'll have to log in manually.

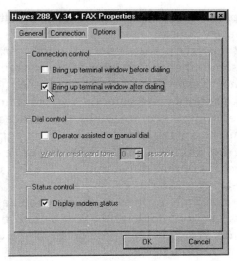

Figure 17-18: *Click Configure from the panel shown in Figure 17-16 to access the modem properties.*

Right-click your connection icon and choose Properties, as shown in Figure 17-15. Next, click the Configure button to set up your modem. Figure 17-18 shows the first panel of the Modem properties sheets. We discussed these settings in both Chapter 7 and in Chapter 16, so let's go straight to the Options property sheet (Figure 17-19). Turn on the check box for *Bring up terminal window after dialing* and Close the modem properties.

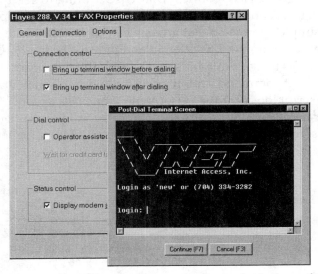

Figure 17-19: *Turn on* Bring up terminal window after dialing *if you need to manually log in to your service provider.*

Double-click the service provider connection icon. This time, after the dialing is complete, another window pops up, as shown in Figure 17-20. This is a *terminal window*, a plain-text interface to the service provider's computer. You may have to press Enter or some other character to announce your presence to the server. The server will then display a prompt for you to enter your username and password. (Sometimes you'll enter the password first.)

Pay close attention to the prompts sent to you by the service provider. For example, your server might use the text Username? or Login name: or Account. Write down the exact phrase. It might ask for your Password or Enter your password. Write this phrase down, too. We'll use it to automate this process using the Dial-Up Scripting tool.

When your manual login is complete, press the F7 function key to exit the terminal window. Windows 95 now completes the connection, and you're ready to run Internet software. We'll get into more detail on the things you can do with your Internet connection, below.

Dial-Up Scripting

It's inconvenient to have to go through this rigmarole every time you connect. Fortunately, Microsoft provides a special Wizard to help you automate the login process. Before we go any further, use the steps we describe above to reverse the change you made: Turn off *Bring up terminal window* from the Options panel of Modem Properties. It's not necessary when you use the scripting tool.

Click Start | Programs | Accessories | Dial-Up Scripting to set up a *login script*. The login script automates login. A script is a type of computer program, but it's simple enough so that anyone can create one. Each line of the script is a computer command, written in an English-like language. The computer interprets these commands and acts on them in order. It won't move on to the next command until it's finished with the current command.

Typically, a script looks for the "Username?" and "Password?" prompts and feeds your name and password automatically. All you have to do is customize the script to reflect the actual prompts used by your service.

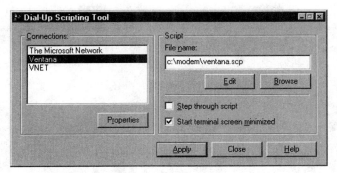

Figure 17-20: *Choose the connection on the left and a script File name in the box on the right. Use Browse to open some sample Dial-Up scripts.*

As shown in Figure 17-20, just choose one of your connections on the left. This is the connection that will be linked to the script. (Some connections don't require scripting, such as The Microsoft Network.) On the right-hand side, type in a filename for the script file you want to use. The script file is a plain-text document that you can create with Notepad. Or click Browse to choose one of the sample scripts that Microsoft provides. For example, the CIS script links you to a CompuServe node for PPP access. Use PPPMENU.SCP as a starting point for creating your own PPP script. (The SLIP entries are commonly used for SLIP connections, which we don't discuss in this chapter.)

You can also turn on the check box for *Step through script* if you want to watch the script one line at a time while it connects. That lets you see more easily what line is causing problems if the script doesn't work. Once you have the script working properly, you'll probably want to enable *Start terminal screen minimized* so that you don't have to look at the terminal window.

Figure 17-21 shows the contents of the PPPMENU.SCP file. We've simplified it to remove some lines that you probably don't need.

```
proc main
; Delay for 3 seconds first to allow host time
; to send initial characters.
delay 3
transmit "^M"
; Wait for the login prompt before entering
; the user ID
waitfor "username:"
transmit $USERID
transmit "^M"
; Enter the password
waitfor "password:"
transmit $PASSWORD
transmit "^M"
endproc
```

Figure 17-21: *Customize this example script to automate your dial-up connection.*

Note that any line beginning with a semicolon is a *comment* and is not really used for scripting activity, but rather as a way to leave notes to yourself. The entire script starts with *proc main* and ends with *endproc*. Most of the time, you'll use only three commands in your script. Use *delay* to force the script to pause for a number of seconds. It's used in Figure 17-21 to give the server a chance to get its act together before beginning the login sequence.

Use *transmit* to send information (text) to the remote server. The characters ^M signify the act of pressing the Enter key. (The ^ symbol is equivalent to the Ctrl key. In terminal mode, Ctrl+M is the same as Enter. ^I is the tab key, ^G is the "ring bell" key and so on.) Enclose your text in quotation marks.

Usually you want to pause the script until it detects a key word or phrase from the server. The key phrase is the cue that's needed to send a response. Follow *waitfor* with the name of this key phrase, enclosed in quotes. In Figure 17-21, we wait for the phrase "username," which could be part of a longer phrase like "Enter your username." As soon as "username" is detected, we use transmit to send the username. $USERID is a special word (a variable) that holds the text you entered in the Connect dialog as your username. Similarly, $PASSWORD holds the password you typed. Notice that no quotation marks are used in this command, otherwise we'd send the actual characters $ U S E R I D. After sending either text sequence, the script uses *transmit* again to send the Enter key.

When the script encounters *Endproc*, it stops processing and Windows 95 completes the connection. Your service provider may also require you to choose a menu option before Windows 95 can complete the connection. You would have discovered that when using the Manual Login feature we discussed above. If that happens, add more *waitfor* and *transmit* commands, as necessary, to your custom script. The PPPMENU.SCP sample script shows you how.

Once you get the hang of it, you may be tempted to automate other processes, especially if you want to control your service provider's computer via shell mode, where you can get mail and so forth using text menus. There's no tool to let you interactively record your session automatically. However, you can enable the option for *Bring up terminal mode after dialing* (discussed earlier), take notes of the prompts you're given and the text you enter to accomplish a task, and then write a script that fills in the blanks automatically. That makes you a power user, and you'll want to refer to Figure 17-22, excerpted from the Dial-Up Scripting help file, for quick reference.

---

proc *<name>*
Begins the script procedure. All scripts must have a main procedure (proc main). The script begins running at the main procedure and stops at the end of the main procedure.

endproc
Ends the script procedure. When this command is reached in the main procedure, Dial-Up Networking will start PPP or SLIP.

delay *<n seconds>*
Pauses for *n* seconds before executing the next command. For example, delay 2 will pause for two seconds.

waitfor "*<string>*"
Waits until the specified characters are sent by the computer you are connecting to before executing the next command. The value you specify for <string> is case-sensitive. For example, waitfor "USERNAME" waits until "USERNAME" (in all capital letters) is received from the computer you are connecting to.

transmit "*<string>*" I *$USERID* I *$PASSWORD*
Sends the specified characters or your username or password to the computer you are connecting to. The username and password variables are automatically set to the username and password for the Dial-Up Networking connection that you assign to the script.

set port databits <integer>
Changes the number of bits in the bytes that are transmitted during the session. You can specify a value between 5 and 8 bits. If this command is not used, then the settings specified in the Properties for the Dial-Up Networking connection that you assign to the script will be used.

set port stopbits <integer>
Changes the number of stop bits for the port during the session. You can specify 1 or 2. If this command is not used, the settings in the Properties for the Dial-Up Networking connection that you assign to the script are used.

set port parity none I odd I even I mark I space
Changes the parity scheme for the port during the session. If this command is not used, the settings in the Properties for the Dial-Up Networking connection that you assign to the script are used.

set ipaddr
Sets the IP address for the session.

set screen keyboard on I off
Enables or disables keyboard input to the terminal window.

getip <optional index>
Reads an IP address and uses it as the workstation address. <optional index> specifies which IP address to use as the workstation address if the remote computer sends more than one IP address. For example, set ipaddr getip 2 uses the second IP address sent by the remote computer.

halt
Causes Dial-Up Networking to stop running the script. The terminal window will stay on your screen so you can enter information manually. To establish the connection, you must click Continue.

; comment
Indicates a comment. All text preceded by a semicolon is ignored.

strings
You can use any character as part of a string, including the following:

^char If char is a value between @ and _, then the character sequence is translated to a single-byte value between 0 and 31. For example, ^M is converted to a carriage return. If char is a value between a and z, then the character sequence is translated to a single-byte value between 1 and 26. If char is any other value, then the character sequence is not treated specially.

\<cr\>	Sends or receives a carriage return.
\<lf\>	Sends or receives a line feed.
\"	Includes a double quote as part of the string.
\^	Includes a caret as part of the string.
\<	Includes a < as part of the string.
\\	Includes a back-slash as part of the string.

For example, transmit "Joe^M" sends Joe, followed by a carriage return, to the remote computer; waitfor "Joe\<cr\>\<lf\>" waits to receive Joe, followed by a carriage return and a linefeed, from the remote computer before executing the next command in the script.

Figure 17-22: *Dial-Up scripting command reference.*

Online With the Internet

From this point on, we'll assume you've connected to your Internet provider. You usually maintain your connection as long as you want to use your Web browser to view World Wide Web pages, or while you're using FTP for file transfer. It's important to realize that you can do all these things at the same time. You can download a file (with FTP) while simultaneously viewing Web sites (with Internet Explorer or some other browser application). Of course, the more Internet tools you run at the same time, the slower things go, since your connection can only transmit data at the top speed of your modem (and the provider's modem). You disconnect only when you're ready to end your online session. If you don't connect manually, your online charges could grow larger and larger, which can be disastrous if you forget to disconnect.

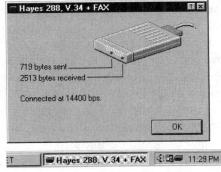

Figure 17-23: *Use the little modem icon to view your online statistics.*

While you're online, you'll notice a modem icon in the taskbar notification area (the special region containing the clock). Double-click this icon to pop up the modem status box, as shown in Figure 17-23. You can tell how many characters have been sent, how many have been received, and how long you've been connected. This is handy for estimating your bill. (Some providers charge by the minute or hour, others charge a flat rate for a certain number of hours every month.) To disconnect and hang up the phone, click the taskbar button for the connection status box and choose Disconnect.

Browse the Web

By far the most popular online activity is Web browsing. Browsing requires a special program called a Web browser to connect to Internet computers. These servers host special files called *HTML documents* that are similar to word-processing documents. The documents can contain text formatting, embedded pictures, even forms, buttons and other special controls. The best feature of HTML is that it lets the author of an Internet document embed a *link* to other Web pages, which gives you the power to navigate your way around the globe in seconds. (Many Web sites are located in other countries. You don't pay any more to access them, but communication tends to slow.)

You can also design your own Web pages. Many Internet providers are now offering space on their servers for a low monthly cost that you can use to host a Web page of your own. Composing HTML (HyperText Markup Language) documents from scratch can be tedious, but we've included a few shareware tools on this book's CD-ROM, that make it easy to create your own pages.

Microsoft has developed the Word Internet Assistant, which gives Microsoft Word the power not only to view Web pages, but also lets you create your own using Word's convenient features. Word Internet Assistant is available free from Microsoft at the Internet address: *http://www.microsoft.com.*

An Internet location can take several forms, but the Uniform Resource Location format (URL) makes it easy to go to any Internet resource, regardless of its type. With a good browser you can access Web pages and FTP files, use Gopher to look up the addresses of sites of interest to you, or take part in discussions in newsgroups. A URL is preceded by the characters http:// and is usually followed by www for a Web site, ftp for file transfer, or the name of a USENET newsgroup. The name of the location on the Internet follows (often the name of a company followed by *.com*) and can include additional / characters to specify a particular folder (directory) on the Internet computer.

Because MS-DOS computers use '\' instead of '/' (the UNIX standard) to form network addresses, you can usually use either symbol with the Internet, especially if you're using Internet Explorer or Netscape Navigator for Windows 95, which are designed to take advantage of Windows 95.

Microsoft's Internet Explorer takes URLs and turns them into Windows 95 shortcuts. You can drag any underlined text (which signifies a hotlink to a URL) and drop it onto your desktop as a shortcut icon. To return to that Web site, just double-click the shortcut. The Internet Explorer automatically dials your connection and links you to that Internet location.

As we went to press, the latest 1.2 beta version of Netscape Navigator was released, which also features Windows 95-specific user interface techniques such as drag-and-drop URL shortcuts and an easy-to-use FTP interface. Look for the latest version of Netscape at *http://www.netscape.com*.

 Internet Explorer also lets you open a URL by choosing Start | Run from the Start menu. Then just enter any properly formatted URL, such as *http://www.msn.net*.

Although we haven't included any Web browsers on our companion CD-ROM, they're easy to obtain from other online services. You can also buy a Web browser (just like any other software) at a computer store, including kits that sell for less than $10. Many book/disk combos also include the original or enhanced versions of the Mosaic Web browser.

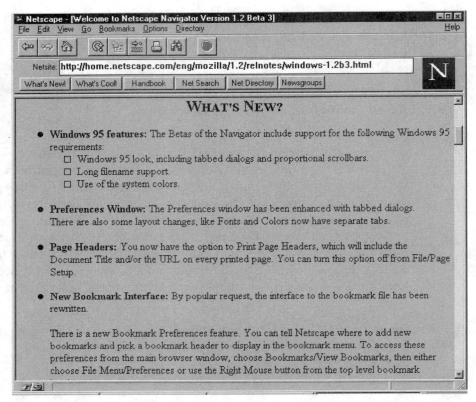

Figure 17-24: *Netscape Navigator is the industry standard for WWW software.*

Netscape's *Navigator* is widely considered the leader in Web software, and it has helped to introduce innovations in Web page design, including textured backgrounds and secure transmission of confidential information, like credit card numbers for online shopping. You can usually get the latest Netscape version via FTP (discussed below) using the address *ftp.netscape.com*.

The Microsoft Internet Explorer is included with *Microsoft Plus! Companion for Windows 95*, but Microsoft intends to make it available for free download from The Microsoft Network. You can also probably find it on Microsoft's Web server (a kind of Catch-22 if you don't have a browser yet) or via *ftp.microsoft.com*.

Download Files

The Internet is the world's largest repository of non-commercial software. (There's plenty of the other kind out there, too, but it's almost always illegally distributed copyrighted software.) The File Transfer Protocol is your key to these riches.

An FTP *site* is a location on a computer on the Internet that hosts files available for download. When you download a file, it travels from "up high" (the remote computer) *down* to your computer. You can also *upload* files to the remote computer to contribute to a collection. Some businesses also FTP to exchange documents.

The easiest way to connect to an FTP computer is with an FTP client program. Windows 95 includes an MS-DOS *command-line utility* to duplicate the FTP commands used by UNIX servers, but that's ancient history. Instead, just link to an FTP site via your Web browser or run a graphical FTP program.

We've included the excellent shareware program WS_FTP32 on this book's Companion CD-ROM. (WS_FTP32 is actually free for personal and educational use, but it requires a license when used in a business setting.)

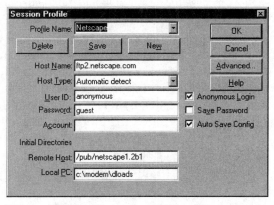

Figure 17-25: *Choose the FTP host you want to access, filling in your account name and password if necessary (otherwise use anonymous login).*

To download a file, start your connection from Dial-Up Networking and run a program like WS_FTP32, shown in Figure 17-25. When you first run WS_FTP32, you must configure a host (or choose one from the drop-down list). See Figure 17-25.

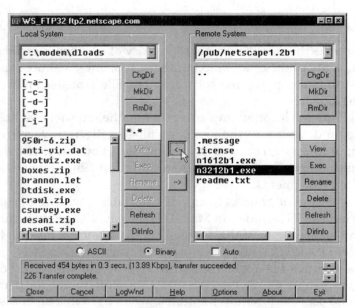

Figure 17-26: *With WS_FTP32, choose the destination folder on your computer on the left, and pick the folder or file you want to access on the right.*

Once connected, WS_FTP32 is easy to use. Choose a folder on the left-hand side to receive downloaded files. On the right, you can choose a folder on the FTP server by double-clicking it. To receive a file, click on it, or to grab a bunch of files, use Ctrl+Click to select them from the list. Click the <- button to transfer the files to your computer. You can also reverse the flow by choosing a file from your computer and clicking -> to send them to the current FTP directory.

Use WS_FTP32's Help menu to learn more about this full-featured utility.

Read Newsgroups

Recall that you can access most Web resources using a browser like Netscape Navigator or Microsoft Internet Explorer, including messages in newsgroups. A newsgroup is like a CompuServe forum or a BBS on The Microsoft Network. A newsgroup hosts related files on particular subjects. Many newsgroups are accessed using the prefix *alt*. For example, *alt.paranet.ufo* contains messages and replies to messages concerning UFOs and similar close encounters. From your Web browser, use the format *http://alt.paranet.ufo* to browse the messages, which are displayed without any special formatting.

You can put your own two cents in, too. Newsgroups encourage participation, so you can reply to a message that interests (or inflames) you. We won't get into all the details of Netiquette here (although we included a few pointers in Chapter 16), but perhaps the best rule is to treat others online as politely as you would if you met them on the street.

To access a newsgroup, you have to "subscribe" to it. That doesn't imply a long-term commitment, it just means that you want the news server to hook you up to the newsgroup. If you lose interest in a newsgroup, unsubscribe to it to free resources.

We've also included on the Companion CD-ROM the program WinVN. WinVN offers a convenient way to read newsgroup messages, although it does take a little work to configure WinVN. You'll need to know the name of your provider's news server (although you can use any news server that you have permission to use), and the name of your mail server. Read the WinVN help file for more information.

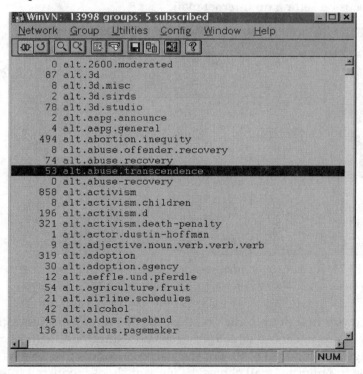

Figure 17-27: *WinVN lets you browse newsgroups easily.*

You can also use WinVN to read files that have been encoded as text files. WinVN includes a built-in decoder for the most popular file formats. You can download photographs and pictures from areas like *alt.binaries.pictures*, or get the latest version of Id Software's Doom from *alt.binaries.doom*. So in a way, a newsgroup can also take the place of an FTP site—you can download files, not just view text. Also, some people find newsgroups easier to use than FTP sites. However, newsgroup file transfer is slower than FTP because the files have to be converted to text symbols, not actual computer files (*binary files*).

Internet Mail

Electronic mail is second in popularity only to the World Wide Web. Windows 95 provides a peerless Internet mail application via Microsoft Exchange. Refer to Chapter 19 for complete documentation of Exchange e-mail. Here, we'll focus on setting up Internet mail.

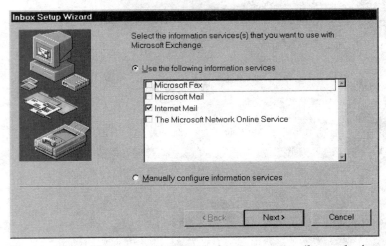

Figure 17-28: *If you're only interested in Internet mail, you don't need to choose the other services. See Chapter 16 for more about faxing.*

When you first double-click on the Inbox icon on your desktop, you're usually asked to choose which services you want to use with Microsoft Exchange (see Figure 17-28). For the purposes of this discussion, we'll only examine the Internet mail choice. When you choose to install Internet mail, you're walked through a series of pages that let you configure Exchange for your Internet mail account.

If you don't have an Inbox icon, double-click on the Mail and Fax icon in Control Panel. You might also need to add Microsoft Exchange using Control Panel's Add/Remove Programs option, under the heading Windows Setup (which we discussed in Chapter 16).

The next step (Figure 17-29) simply has you choose between using a modem to connect, or your company's network. We only discuss the modem option in this chapter, since configuring TCP/IP support for a network is a job best left to experienced network administrators.

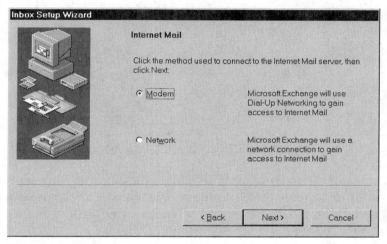

Figure 17-29: *Choose* Modem *unless you access the Internet via your company's network.*

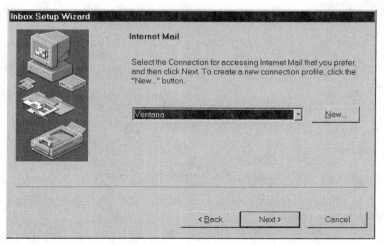

Figure 17-30: *Choose one of your Dial-Up Networking connections.*

You then choose one of your Dial-Up Networking connections to use to retrieve Internet mail. Use the connection we set up earlier in this chapter.

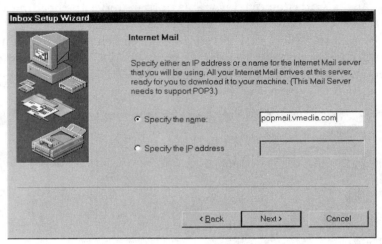

Figure 17-31: *Now fill in the name of your POP3 mail server.*

On the next page (Figure 17-31), fill in the name of your mail server. (This server must support POP3, an Internet mail protocol that allows formatted text and graphics attachments.) You probably wrote this down already in your copy of Table 17-1 at the start of this chapter.

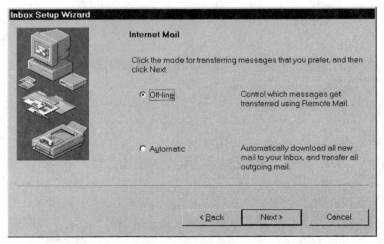

Figure 17-32: *Choose Automatic for easiest mail delivery; off-line if you want to manually download your mail.*

The next page of the Inbox Setup Wizard lets you choose how your Internet mail is delivered. Choose Automatic if you want Exchange to automatically dial your Internet provider and download all mail. Exchange will also automatically dial up and send your mail. However, this can be inconvenient if you're also using Exchange for other services. If you open your Inbox just to send a fax, you may not want to wait for the Internet mail to be processed. One solution is to put the Internet Mail service in a different profile. We discuss profiles in Chapter 19. Otherwise, use Off-line if you want to manually download your mail. (See "Remote Mail" in Chapter 19.)

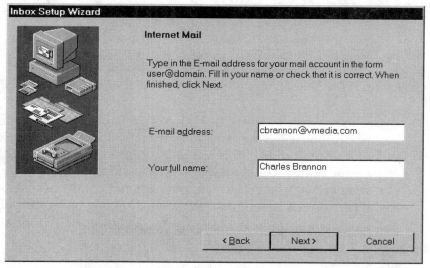

Figure 17-33: *Fill in your e-mail address and your full name.*

In Figure 17-33, enter your Internet mailbox address, and underneath, your full (real) name. This is the same as your user name, the @ symbol, and the domain of your Internet provider. You probably filled this out in your copy of Table 17-1 just for this occasion.

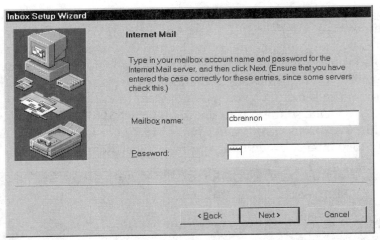

Figure 17-34: *Your Mailbox name is the account used to access your mail.*

The above screen (Figure 17-34) looks similar to the one we just filled out. But the mailbox is not the same as your mail address. It's often just the first part of your mail address (e.g. cbrannon without the @vmedia.com suffix). If you use the same account for mail as you do for PPP access, you'll use the PPP account name here. Use your mail account password here, which might not be the same password that you use for logging into your PPP account.

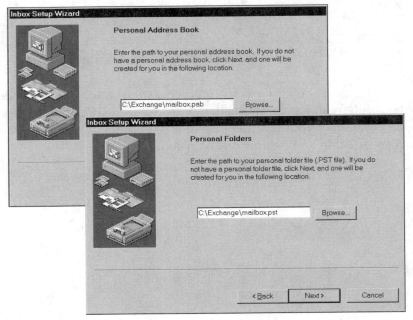

Figure 17-35: *Just click Next to bypass the next two screens.*

You're then asked to specify the location and name of your personal store file and your Personal Address Book. Just click Next to accept the names shown, unless you want to create a separate set of folders for your Internet mail than you use for other Exchange mail (not recommended). The last page of the Wizard (not shown), simply asks you if you'd like the Inbox icon added to your Start menu. It's a matter of preference, but you already have an Inbox icon on your desktop, so it's not necessary.

You're now ready to use Internet mail. For more details on using Exchange for electronic mail, see Chapter 19.

Hunt With Gopher

Many Internet sites are moving all their information onto the World Wide Web, but the Web's predecessor was Gopher, a way to read text messages on remote computers. Using Gopher is different from newsreading, which lets you view messages organized by topic. You also can't reply to Gopher messages, so it's more like a library. Gopher searches for topics you specify and provides the addresses of Internet sites where files or information on those topics can be found. Most people will prefer to use their Web browser for Gopher searches, too, using the format http:\\gopher.

Gopher is all too passeé, but it's still necessary for many purposes. However, there are now much better search tools. Check out these URLs to help you find what you're looking for:

Yahoo Internet Catalog
     http://www.yahoo.com
World Wide Web Virtual Library
     http://www.w3.org
Carnegie-Mellon Lycos Catalog of the Internet
     http://www.lycos.com
Savvy Search
     http://132.239.54.5:2000/cgi-bin/savvysearch
WebCrawler Search Engine
     http://webcrawler.com

Windows 95 Web Sites

As we close this chapter, we present a small list of Windows 95-related Web pages. This list will grow tremendously as time goes by. For reference, we also include the link to Ventana's site, and the Web page for this very book, where you can obtain the latest versions of the shareware included on the book's Companion CD-ROM. We'll keep the site fresh with new shareware submissions, hints and tips and additional tutorials, not to mention links to the best and latest Windows 95-related sites.

The Windows 95 Book
http://www.vmedia.com/win95.html
Ventana Communications
http://www.vmedia.com
The Windows 95 Page
http://biology.queensu.ca/~jonesp/
Barry's Windows 95 page
http://sashimi.www.com:80/~barry/home.html
Barry's Windows 95 SLIP How-to
http://sashimi.www.com:80/~barry/html/Win95slip.html
Craig's Windows 95 Page
http://www.bucknell.edu/~cbonsig/win95.html
Windows 95 Info Page
http://www2.pcix.com/~snipe/win95home.html
The (Unofficial) Windows 95 Home Page
http://www.southwind.net/~leeb/win95.html
Net Ex Unofficial Windows 95 Software Archive
http://WWW.NetEx.NET:80/w95/
Stroud's Consummate Winsock Apps List
http://www.netppl.fi/consumate/win95.html
The Computer Paper
http://www.tcp.ca/
The Windows95 TCP/IP Setup FAQ
http://www.aa.net/~pcd/slp95faq.html
Windows 95 Dial-Up Networking White Paper
http://www.wwa.com/~barry/wn95slip.html
InterNet Direct Win95 HelpDesk
http://www.idirect.com/win95/index.html
Techweb
http://techweb.cmp.com/techweb

Moving On

Now that you've used your modem to connect to the worldwide network, let's look at Microsoft's own corner of the online universe. In Chapter 18, we'll examine MSN, Microsoft's easy-to-use, yet powerful online service. If you find the Internet as a whole to be just too big (and connecting to it somewhat intimidating), the carefully planned contents and superior organization of The Microsoft Network is a pleasant alternative. It's the best way to get Windows 95 support too.

Chapter 18

The Microsoft Network

How and whether the new The Microsoft Network will be available is, at the time of this writing, up in the air. Microsoft's announcement that it intended to embed its new online service into Windows 95 caused an uproar. Unfair, said competitors, so the Justice Department is looking into it. A subpeona has been served. Stay tuned.

The argument against Microsoft asserts that plugging its own service right into the operating system used by 90 percent of personal computer users amounts to unfair competition. It's the equivalent of the water company's going into every kitchen and putting in a second faucet that dispenses its new line of soft drinks.

Microsoft's argument is that the gateway to The Microsoft Network (MSN) is merely an icon on the Windows 95 desktop. Anyone can place a CompuServe or America Online icon on the Windows 95 desktop, too. And removing MSN from the desktop is simply a matter of right-clicking its icon and choosing Delete. How built-in is that?

Figure 18-1: *The Microsoft Network icon on the Windows 95 desktop.*

Whatever compromise is reached, there's no denying that when Microsoft enters the world of online services, things are unlikely ever to be the same again. For one thing, it's widely predicted that the online charges for MSN will be lower than the competition, perhaps considerably lower, given the economies of scale.

What's more, MSN *is* "built in" to Windows 95 in a more profound sense than just that little icon on the desktop. MSN is integrated into Windows 95 because MSN looks like and works like the shell, the Explorer, and the other elements of Windows 95. Once you understand how to use features like Find in Windows 95, you know how to use them in MSN.

This chapter is somewhat different from the others in that we're not going to attempt to cover *every* feature and show every little corner of The Microsoft Network. MSN is, at the current time, a boiling pot—everything is moving around, and new things are being added all the time. Instead, we'll take a survey of highlights and emphasize how you navigate this virtual world. In other words, we'll concentrate on describing the tools you should master to get the most out of MSN. We'll leave it up to you to explore on your own the content, zones, destinations and topics of personal interest to you.

Signing On the First Time

When you first install Windows 95 and click on the MSN icon to access The Microsoft Network, you'll see the Connection Settings box shown in Figure 18-2.

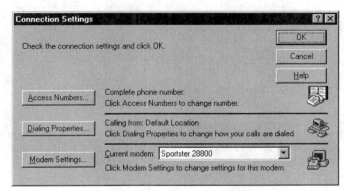

Figure 18-2: *You have to answer some questions the first time you log on to The Microsoft Network*

Each town of any size has a free "access number" or two that your computer can dial to connect to The Microsoft Network. But first you have to tell Windows 95 where you live. Click the Access Numbers button, and you're presented with the two text boxes shown in Figure 18-3.

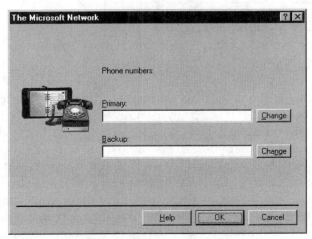

Figure 18-3: *If you already know the access numbers, type them here.*

If you don't know the access numbers, click Change and you can look them up for your geographic location, as shown in Figure 18-4.

 TIP These access numbers are normally filled in for you when you first sign up for The Microsoft Network. The list of phone numbers is also updated automatically from time to time. Microsoft is also working on expanding its network of 28,800 bps dial-up sites (also called POPs—for Point of Presence). These let you connect to the Internet via MSN.

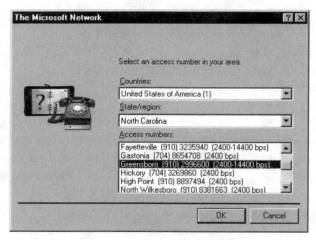

Figure 18-4: *Once you tell Windows 95 your location, you probably won't have to change these numbers again.*

If you see more than one local access number listed for your location, you can enter a secondary one. If the primary number is busy, MSN will dial the secondary (backup) number.

Notice in Figure 18-2 that you can also adjust the Dialing Properties. Change the properties if you work in an office, for example, that requires you to dial 9 for an outside line. Dialing Properties also lets you switch from tone to pulse dialing or select an alternative location (if you often call from a hotel in LA, you can have MSN remember the necessary settings and access numbers). You can also disable Call Waiting or use a calling card.

Finally, if you have to adjust the Modem Settings, click that button to see the property sheets for your modem. Here you can select a different port, change transmission speed, and otherwise modify the way Windows 95 deals with your modem. In general, you can leave these settings the way that Windows 95 set them up for you. However, for a complete discussion of these settings, see Chapter 7.

Into the Network

After telling Windows 95 the access phone numbers you want MSN to use, you're ready to travel out into the world of this young and promising online service. You'll next be asked to provide a member ID, as shown in Figure 18-5.

Figure 18-5: *Enter your member ID and password here.*

As with most online services, you can identify yourself by your real name or, if you prefer, by a nickname. The member ID is the name. Prudence suggests that you not give your real name to *everyone*—MSN, like life, has a few loose cannons sliding around. Also type a password. To avoid having to type the password each time you log on to MSN, click on the Remember my password check box.

Now, click Connect.

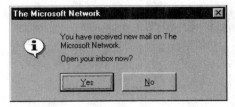

Figure 18-6: *If any e-mail has come in since your last session, you'll see this message. You can read your mail immediately or leave it in your Inbox in the Microsoft Exchange. See Chapter 16 for a complete description of how to use the Exchange.*

Figure 18-7: *This window greets you at the entrance to MSN.*

Figure 18-8: *Then the window improves the resolution of the images.*

If there's no new mail, two windows open: the main MSN window and another called MSN Today. Whatever's going on—special chats, appearances by celebrities, new forums—will appear in the MSN Today window. Notice that some of the icons here can hardly be called icons. Instead, you'll see some rich, colorful, almost photographic images. Click any of these pictures to go to the location described.

You'll see the images' resolution improve as the detail seems to pour into them. This clarification takes place over about 10 seconds or so, unless your modem is very fast and your local access number connection can support high speed.

The Main Window

Alternatively, you can switch to the main MSN window, which looks and behaves remarkably like any other opened folder in Windows 95.

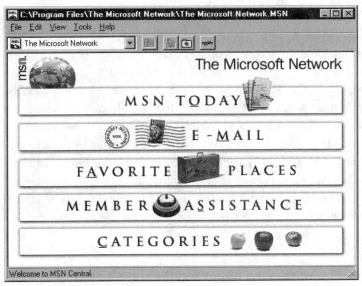

Figure 18-9: *The Main MSN window resembles Windows 95's Explorer and folders.*

As you can see in Figure 18-9, there's not much new to learn about navigating around within MSN. If you've grasped the essentials of Windows 95 itself, you'll feel quite at home in the online environment as well. Look, for example, at the File, Edit, View, Tools, Help menu listings. Seem familiar?

Likewise, you can decide—as in Windows 95 folders—whether or not you want a toolbar or status bar displayed (click on the View menu, then select Toolbars or Status Bar).

Of course, the contents of the MSN menus differ from those in the Explorer or an opened folder. They contain options appropriate to MSN. The File menu includes "Up one level" and "sign out." Up one level won't work at first—it will be gray on the screen, as shown in Figure 18-9, because that's the top level. But if you're in a forum or several layers down inside MSN, this option returns you to your previous, higher, location.

Sign out disconnects you. You can also disconnect by clicking the small icon at the right side of your taskbar on the bottom of the screen. Another way to log off is to close the Main MSN window or click the sign-out button at the far right of the toolbar.

The Edit menu has three options within the Goto selection. You can always get back to the top menu (MSN Central) or go to Favorite Places—a list of locations on MSN that you define by clicking on File | *Add to Favorite Places* within any location in MSN. So, if you find a forum or other locale that you want to revisit, drop down the File menu and click Favorite Places to add it to your personal list.

TIP We interrupt this message...you shouldn't have to suffer unnecessary charges simply because you got called away from the computer and forgot to sign out of MSN. Every so often, an inactivity warning message box will appear in the middle of your screen. It says: "Disconnecting in 25 seconds. Click Cancel to remain connected. The Microsoft Network is disconnecting because there has been no activity recently. To increase the length of time before disconnecting, go to MSN Central, click View, then click Options." (See Figure 18-11.) The default inactivity time is 10 minutes, but you can increase it to as much as 59 minutes if you want.

The final option on the Edit | Goto list in the MSN Central window is Other Location. Here you can enter the name of a particular location if you know it.

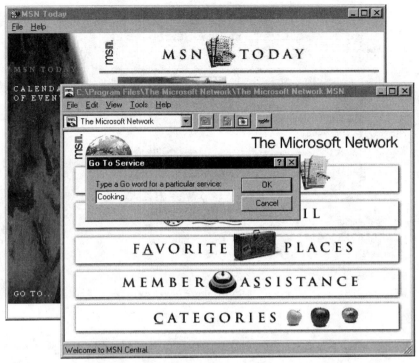

Figure 18-10: *If you know where you want to go, type the location here.*

You'll notice, though, that the Edit menu is context-sensitive, like all menus in Windows 95. If you're in a different location, Edit might offer cut, and paste, find, and other options appropriate to the zone displayed by the window.

The View menu of MSN Central lets you to display or hide the toolbar on the top and the status bar on the bottom of the window. It also includes a refresh option that redraws the window. At the bottom is an Options item that displays the properties sheet shown in Figure 18-11.

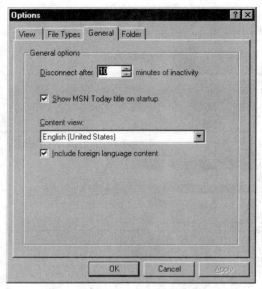

Figure 18-11: *Customize MSN to your heart's content.*

The Property Sheet

It's unusual, but by default you're shown the *third* instead of the first page in the property sheets for MSN's options shown in Figure 18-11. The options available on that page are the most online-specific, the ones you'd likely change. The Inactivity setting determines how long MSN will wait after you've stopped using the mouse or keyboard to interact with the online service. It doesn't want to charge you for three days' connect time if you had to rush to the airport to go to Florida to accept your $10,000,000 prize in the great sweepstakes. If that happened, of course you couldn't care less. But most of the time, the reasons for abandoning an active online session are more mundane—you checked on the baby and got fascinated; you answered the door and got fascinated or whatever.

The *Show MSN Today title on startup* option decides whether you always see that "what's happening" screen when you log onto MSN, the screen shown in Figures 18-7 and 18-8. If you consider it a waste of time, deselect the check box and you'll then only see MSN Central, the window shown in Figure 18-9.

The Content view option lets you avoid seeing messages or other things in languages you don't understand. The View and File Types pages shown in Figure 18-11 let you decide what files you're shown and whether to display the DOS-style "extensions" (like .DOC). Both pages of options are identical to those described for the View | Options menus found on the My Computer window or Explorer. See Chapter 4 for more details. The Folder option gives you a choice between opening a new window for each folder you open, or limiting your display to a single window showing the currently opened folder.

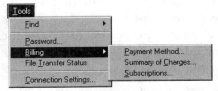

Figure 18-12: *The Tools menu on The Microsoft Exchange's MSN Central window.*

In the Tools menu you'll see the same Find (files, folders or MSN location) utility that appears under Tools in the Windows 95 Explorer. The Password option allows you to change your password. This offers security because you first must type in the existing password—thus you must know it— before you can change it to something else.

The Billing selection allows you to change how you pay for MSN, as shown in Figure 18-13.

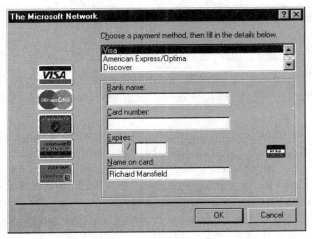

Figure 18-13: *The way you pay for MSN online time can be changed here.*

Next on the Tools Menu under Billing, you'll find a summary of your current charges and a list of your current subscriptions to various services. You can set a monthly ceiling—the amount you're willing to spend each month. You can choose to be notified when you're about to exceed that limit. At that point, you can decide whether to continue and spend the extra money.

Following the Billing options is the option that opens a File Transfer Status window—showing files awaiting download and files that have been downloaded. (Downloading means copying a file from a remote computer, like MSN, to your hard drive over the phone. Uploading means copying from your computer to the outside machine.) By clicking the File Transfer Status window's Tools | Options menu, you can tell MSN whether you want files downloaded as soon as you add them to your "download queue" or retrieved when you specifically request them.

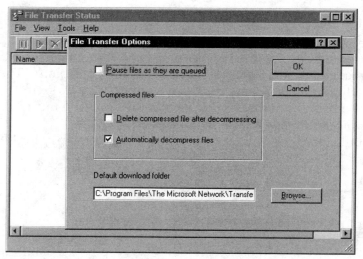

Figure 18-14: *Decide how files are to be copied from MSN to your computer.*

Many computer files you'll find online are compressed. This saves space on the online service's disk drives and also speeds transfer when you download. Most files are compressed using the popular PKZIP utility, and such compressed files end in the extension .ZIP. MSN will automatically unzip (decompress) these files upon download to your machine, and even delete the then redundant .ZIP file from your hard drive. You can bypass these automations, though, if you prefer. Likewise, you can specify the folder on your hard drive where downloaded files are to be stored.

The Connection Settings option on the MSN Central Tools I Options menu brings up the same window shown in Figure 18-2 and discussed above.

The Help menu includes a troubleshooting wizard and a list of customer support numbers, as shown in Figure 18-15. If you want to try getting answers from the wizard before making a call, click on Help I Member Support Numbers, then select *Troubleshooting, Signup & Access Problems*.

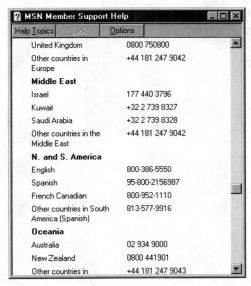

Figure 18-15: *You can get customer support from anywhere in the world.*

Into the World

Online services are justly popular, and many people spend more time and money on them than they do on TV. MSN, like America Online and CompuServe, to name two, opens a world to the computer user. Whatever subject interests you—games, history, mechanics, cooking, you name it— you'll find useful information about it, experts willing to answer questions, and other enthusiasts ready to talk live in "chat" sessions. It was no accident that Microsoft chose a picture of the world as the MSN logo.

When you connect to MSN, you can take several pathways to explore the world out there. Just click any of the pictures or icons you'll see on the MSN Today window and in Figure 18-16.

Figure 18-16: *Click on any of these images to go immediately to that location on MSN.*

Alternatively, you can click on the words "GO TO…" in the bottom left of the MSN Today window to see the general, top level of MSN categories. (You can also get here by clicking Categories in the MSN Central window.)

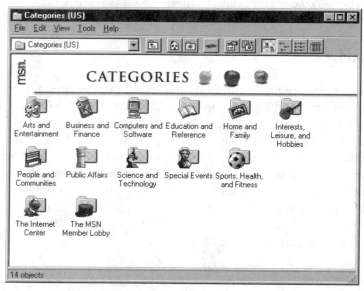

Figure 18-17: *MSN's general categories are grouped here. Click Go To in the MSN Today window, or Categories in the MSN Central window.*

If you're interested in astronomy, click the Science and Technology icon in the Categories window shown in Figure 18-17.

Notice the toolbar in Figure 18-17. Much of MSN resembles the Windows 95 Explorer or an opened folder, and MSN can be manipulated and navigated in ways similar or identical to the rest of Windows 95. For example, the icon on the far left of the toolbar in Figure 18-17 moves back up to the previous folder in MSN. The next button, with the picture of a house, returns you to the MSN central window. The folder with the asterisk sends you to your Favorite Places folder, which contains the categories and places you like to visit frequently on MSN. The next icon disconnects you from MSN. The hand holding a paper displays the properties of this folder, and the icon with the + adds the current folder to Favorite Places. The final four icons behave just as they do in Windows 95 Explorer or folders—allowing you to select large or small icons or a list or details view of the current window.

The drop-down list box on the left in Figure 18-17 includes Member Assistance, Favorite Places and Categories. Here you can choose between US and Worldwide versions of these folders.

Tunneling Down

Let's burrow down a way to see where it gets us. Let's go to Categories, and say we're interested in astronomy. Click the Science and Technology icon, and you'll see something like the folder shown in Figure 18-18. (We say *something like* because MSN is in a continual state of adjustment and refinement—and it always may be. The particular folders and categories you'll see will depend on when you look.)

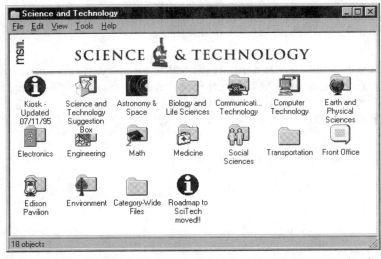

Figure 18-18: *Going down from Categories into Science & Technology.*

At the level we've moved into in Figure 18-18, you'll find a list of *forums* or gathering places for people of like interests. Technically, this Science & Technology group is also a forum, but doesn't have some of the features—messages and files, for example—of a forum at the lowest level.

Notice on the left of Figure 18-18 the Kiosk. This is like a bulletin board for the entire forum, and it contains details about new additions to the forum, special rules and the name of the forum manager (or SYSOP, for SYStem OPerator). The Kiosk also describes the general contents and purpose of the forum.

Science and Technology Category Kiosk   (07/11/95)

Come Chat with us In Chemistry!!!!

What and Who: Come to the opening of Chemistry Chat! This live event is designed for members to meet and get acquainted. There is no defined topic so anything goes -- -- from a possible chemical explanation of the Bermuda Triangle mystery to a discussion on how nature's chemicals can improve health. Interested non-chemists are encouraged to attend. You are guaranteed to learn how chemistry can impact on your life so swing on by!

Date: Wednesday, July 12 at 6-7 p.m. PDT.

Where: Chemistry Chat (Navigate to Science & Technology/Earth & Physical Sciences/Chemistry Forum or use the go word "Chemistry".

Recently updated forums:

Robotics has expanded their forums

The Nursing Network has added Health Care Professionals

Amateur Radio has added the Satellite BBS

Figure 18-19: *Click Kiosk to see general information about a forum. There's more information than we can display in this figure.*

Next to the Kiosk is a Suggestion Box where you can send comments to the forum manager. At the bottom is an exclamation point icon with information the manager wants you to see immediately, something too urgent to put into the Kiosk. Double-click the exclamation point for further details.

TIP For an example of the deep integration of MSN into Windows 95, and something truly impressive, try clicking a Kiosk icon. You'll see MSN download (copy to your machine over the phone) an RTF file (rich text format, that preserves font sizes, color, italics and so on). This information will then appear within the word processor you've assigned to display .RTF files on your computer, such as Windows 95's WordPad. (See Chapter 4 for more details on associating file extensions with a particular application.)

In any case, you'll sometimes see *shortcuts* embedded within the word processor document. Double-click one of them and you're back in MSN at the location pointed to by the shortcut! The walls between Windows 95 applications and the MSN online service are fairly permeable.

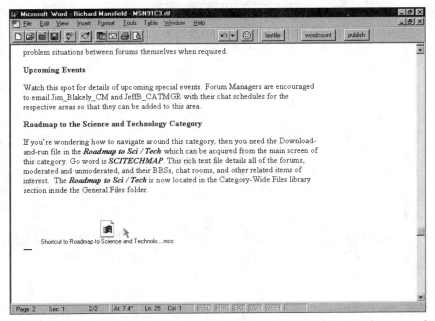

Figure 18-20: *This word processor document includes a shortcut that can take you to a location within MSN.*

There are other specialized icons within the Science & Technology Forum window (refer to Figure 18-18). The "Edison Pavilion" is an *auditorium* for this forum, a place where meetings are held, during which you and other MSN users can talk to somebody famous for an hour or so.

 TIP You can also create your own MSN shortcuts by dragging and dropping any MSN icon to your desktop (or any folder, really). To return to that area on MSN, you can just double-click the shortcut icon. If necessary, Windows automatically dials up and connects to MSN, and takes you directly to that location. You can even send your favorite MSN shortcuts to others by embedding (pasting) them into your e-mail.

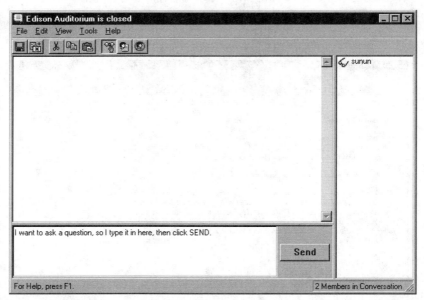

Figure 18-21: *Go to a pavilion to interact with visiting celebrities and special guests. This virtual auditorium is empty right now.*

Select the Category-Wide Files icon to download recent or older files or upload files of your own. Notice that this is a collection of general files relating to science and technology. If you want to find files specific to a sub-category like math or electronics, click those icons in the Science & Technology forum.

Into a Bulletin Board

Click the Astronomy icon to go down to that more specific forum within the general science forum.

Figure 18-22: *Now we're near the bottom level—a special-interest forum.*

The Chat icon takes you to a "room" where you can interact with other astronomy aficionados who happen to be connected to MSN now and are talking to each other (by typing notes). Chat screens look just like the pavilion screen shown in Figure 18-21.

The BBS (Bulletin Board System) icon takes you down to the messaging center for this forum. It's not e-mail—you're not sending a private letter to a particular person. Nor it is a chat room where you're talking with others in real time. A BBS is in between: faster than e-mail, slower than chat. In a BBS, you post a message in response to someone else's message or start a new topic. Think of a BBS as a slow chat room. You connect to MSN, then click on Favorite Places where, presumably, the BBSes of interest to you have been gathered. (Remember that from virtually anywhere within MSN, you can click the Add-to-Favorite-Places icon on a toolbar or select that option from the File menu in most MSN windows. The *Add to Favorite Places* icon is the one with the +. And if the toolbar isn't visible in an MSN folder, but you do want to see it, click the View menu, then click Toolbar.)

As you might expect, a MSN BBS window is highly customizable and extremely flexible. Similarly to Explorer, you can list messages by subject, author, size or date. Just click those titles at the top of the list to rearrange them. There are three View styles: Conversation, List and Attached Files. (Choose among them from the View menu.) The Conversation view is shown in Figure 18-23. An arrow indicates messages you haven't read, and messages with a + symbol have been responded to, but the responses aren't visible. Click the + to reveal the subset. Some of *those* messages might also have a + indicating responses to *them*.

Subject	Author	Size	Date
New BBS Section for Astro...	Lenny Abbey	520 bytes	4/18/95 1:51 AM
Astro Magazine Library	Lenny Abbey	860 bytes	4/18/95 2:51 AM
Astro Library	Lenny Abbey	555 bytes	4/19/95 1:21 AM
RE: New Services	Maurizio Incani	674 bytes	4/29/95 7:34 AM
RE: New Services	Lenny Abbey	670 bytes	4/30/95 2:21 AM
Micro-Keck ?	Allan Symonds	1.14KB	5/2/95 12:36 AM
Astronomy Lab, Astronomy ...	Eric Bergman-Ter...	518 bytes	5/2/95 10:37 AM
Buying a new telescope.	Vincent Denich	687 bytes	5/2/95 3:21 PM
Saturn's Ring Plane Crossing	Lenny Abbey	1.82KB	5/4/95 1:24 AM
Where is everybody?	Avishay Greenberg	340 bytes	5/5/95 4:46 PM
RE: Earth Centered Universe	Boyd Swartz	735 bytes	5/6/95 11:53 PM
RE: Earth Centered Universe	David Beach	795 bytes	5/7/95 5:00 PM
RE: Earth Centered Universe	Anthony Kent	694 bytes	5/10/95 7:00 AM
Radio Astronomy	Eric Ford	638 bytes	5/11/95 5:57 PM
The "Place" of the Astro BBS	Allan Symonds	594 bytes	5/12/95 2:33 AM
CLEA	Eric Ford	503 bytes	5/17/95 8:12 PM
Ready to Go!!!	Lenny Abbey	942 bytes	5/18/95 2:08 AM
RE: Earth Centered Universe	Steven Hunter	600 bytes	5/24/95 7:52 PM
Newtonian Telescopes	Vincent Denich	583 bytes	5/25/95 7:34 PM
New Saturn Images	Lenny Abbey	561 bytes	5/27/95 3:39 AM

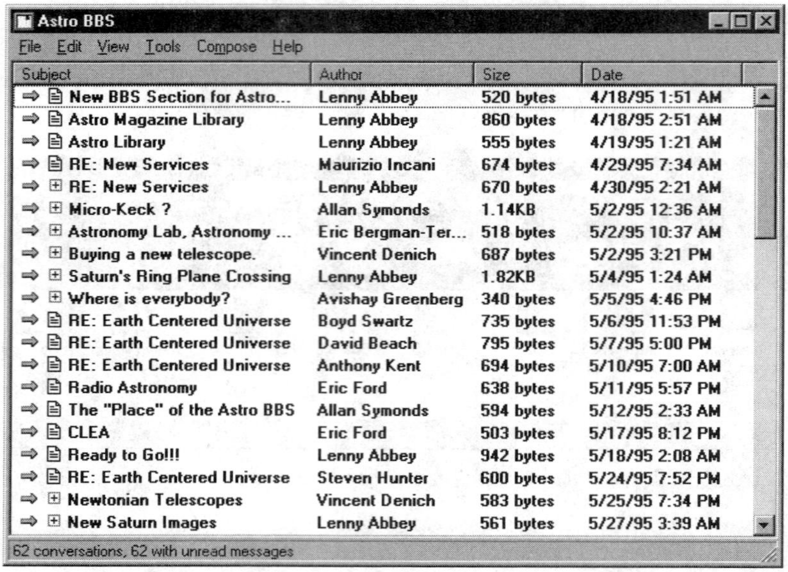

Figure 18-23: *The Conversation View style of a BBS window.*

TIP To see every message on a BBS, click on the View menu, then choose Expand All Messages. You'll see an outline-style, indented, subordinated view of the original messages, and sets of replies to them.

The second View style, "List," displays every message, and it can be relisted by Subject or Author (alphabetically) or by size or date (click on the bar above the message window). The third View style displays only files to be downloaded rather than text messages to be read. (In the List view, you'll see a paper-clip symbol next to any files.)

Notice that many messages are a few hundred bytes (text characters), the typical size of an ordinary BBS message. You'll see some huge messages, though—1 megabyte or more. Those messages contain an embedded picture, sound or even video file. In MSN, you can paste (from the Edit menu) things that you've selected, then copied from a graphics, music or multimedia program's Edit menu. Sure, it will take a while to download a huge embedded item—but no other online service lets you do this. Only in MSN can you send multimedia embedded in a message.

The BBS Window Menus

Many items on the BBS Window menus will be familiar to you from other Windows 95 applications, the Explorer in particular. However, some items here are unique to MSN. On the File menu, you can click "Create Short-cut," which puts an icon on your Windows desktop. This way, the next time you want to go to that location, you can double-click its icon, and you're off and running.

The Edit menu has a GoTo selection, with shortcuts to MSN Central, Favorite Places or, if you know the name of the location you want to jump to, Other Location. You'll see the dialog box in Figure 18-24.

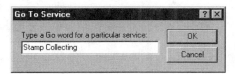

Figure 18-24: *Type the name of your target location here. MSN calls these "Go Words."*

On the View menu you'll see "Expand All Conversations" or "Collapse All Conversations." This switches you between a display of *every* message or a collapsed display of only the messages that started a topic. Expanding and collapsing only has an effect if you're using the Conversation View described above. The Options item on the View menu provides the same properties sheet described above and shown in Figure 18-11.

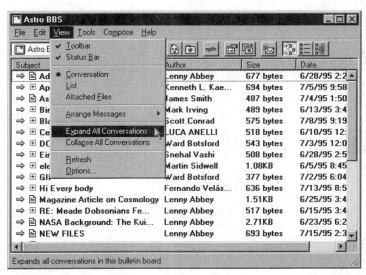

Figure 18-25: *The View menu determines how messages are displayed.*

The Tools Menu lets you manage the marking of messages. You'll remember that in Conversation view, there are arrows next to unread messages. The messages aren't necessarily to *you;* the arrows just mean that you haven't read them. In the menu shown in Figure 18-26, you can choose to mark or unmark the currently highlighted message or conversation. (A conversation is the first message on a new topic, plus the chain of messages responding to the topic.) You can also mark all messages as Read, which is a useful way of allowing MSN to highlight (place arrows only by) messages that have arrived since your last session. You could, of course, just click the Date bar at the top right of the message window, then simply look for any messages posted after your last session.

Figure 18-26: *Select how to tag messages you haven't read in the Tools menu.*

 To view all messages in a single conversation, press Shift and click the + symbol. To show a single message and all the replies to that message, click the + symbol. To collapse a particular conversation, click the − symbol.

MSN Central

If you've been trying things out on MSN while reading this chapter, you're in the BBS (bulletin board system). Click the Bulletin Board's Edit menu and choose GoTo MSN Central. This deceptively simple window is, as you might guess, the heart of MSN. You can get *anywhere* from here. And if you click enough "Up One Level" buttons on the various toolbars in other "lower" MSN windows—you'll end up back here. The Up One Level icon is a file folder with an up-arrow symbol, and you can also find it as an item on the File menu of most windows. The MSN Central window is shown in Figure 18-9.

MSN Central has five wide buttons: MSN Today, E-mail, Favorite Places, Member Assistance and Categories. We've already looked at all the locations except E-mail, so let's conclude with a brief look at MSN's approach to this increasingly popular method of communication. MSN uses the Microsoft Exchange that comes with Windows 95. For an overview of the Exchange, see Chapter 16. For an in-depth discussion of all of the Exchange's features and menus, see Chapter 19.

Electronic Mail

If you don't like talking on the phone, or if the US Postal Service isn't fast enough for your purposes—e-mail is the answer. Sure, there's always fax, but conventional fax machines are probably a transitory technology like cassette tapes or mimeograph machines. Faxes can be messy, hard to read, relatively slow to transmit and print. And above all, faxes are *read only*. You can't just put a fax in your word processor and edit it.

If someone sends you a fax that you want to edit or reformat or copy into a word processor document, you've got problems. You have to use a translator program that scans through the graphic image and attempts to change the character symbols into a true text file. This process is usually less than perfect.

However, if you send a fax using the Fax accessory that comes with Windows 95 to someone who also has Windows 95—no problem. The fax will be sent in an editable format that the recipient can drop into Word for Windows, WritePad or another word processor. This technology—we might call it true data faxing—is another nail in the coffin of fax as we've known it.

Sending e-mail in Windows 95 is easy. You don't have to be connected to MSN to write someone an electronic letter or read something that's been sent to you. Just click the Exchange icon on your desktop.

Figure 18-27: *Click the Inbox desktop icon to activate Exchange and see your mail.*

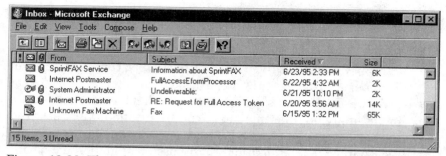

Figure 18-28: *The Inbox of the Microsoft Exchange. Here's where you'll find any messages that have arrived.*

The Microsoft Exchange is an all-purpose mailing service. It can send and receive faxes, e-mail messages and messages sent over an office network. Any time you start Exchange, you'll see any mail in your Inbox. The mail stays there until you delete it or move it. You can also look in three other folders within the Exchange: Outbox, Deleted Items and Sent Items. Of course, there's a full search feature: Click the Tools menu and choose Find.

 ## Hands-On: Sending E-mail

Sending a new electronic message is easy.

1. Click the Microsoft Exchange icon on your desktop. (If you don't see it, click Start, then Settings, then Control Panel. Click the Add/ Remove Programs icon. Then click the Windows Setup tab and locate the Microsoft Exchange. Click, and follow directions to install the Exchange.)
2. In the Compose Menu, click New Message. (Or, if you've chosen to have the toolbar visible, click the third icon from the left—the spar-kling-letter symbol shown in Figure 18-29.)

Figure 18-29: *Click this symbol to create a new message.*

3. After you choose New Message, you'll see the entry form, the text box shown in Figure 18-30.

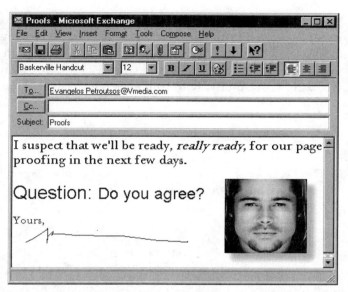

Figure 18-30: *This full-featured mini-word processor allows you to check spelling, adjust formatting, attach a disk file and generally control the content and style of an outgoing message.*

4. If you know your recipient's address, just type it in. Otherwise, click on the To button. You'll see the address book shown in Figure 18-31.

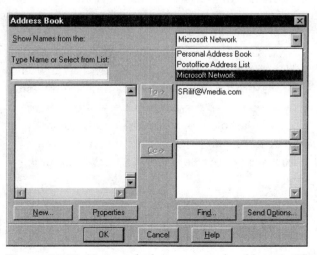

Figure 18-31: *You can look up someone's address in The Microsoft Network, in your Personal Address Book, or in a Network ("post office") list.*

5. Once you've typed the address, formatted and spell-checked the message (press F7), attached a disk file or otherwise composed your missive, just click on the flying-letter symbol at the far left of the toolbar or click the File menu and choose Send. (Pressing Ctrl+Enter is another way to trigger Send.)

Figure 18-32: *This flying-letter symbol sends your message out of your computer and into the world—on its journey to the recipient.*

TIP   Any message that you *receive* will contain the address of the sender. So you can reply easily by merely clicking the Reply to Sender icon on the toolbar (a face with an arrow pointing toward the nose). You can do the same thing by clicking the Compose menu and selecting Reply to Sender. (Shortcut: pressing Ctrl+R is another way to reply to sender.) For the most part, people's e-mail addresses are in the Internet format. Such addresses normally end with a dot, followed by a three-letter abbreviation such as .com, .edu, .net and so on. Also, somewhere within an Internet address you'll also find the @ symbol, separating the name or ID of the recipient from his or her address. For example, to write to your friend Jason, whose name on AOL (America Online) is JASONX, type the address: **jasonx@aol.com**. Likewise, if his userID on CompuServe is *77777,333*, you would type: **77777.333@compuserve.com**. Addresses on MSN (when sending e-mail from some online service *outside* MSN) are: jasonx@msn.net. Some Internet-style addresses can be quite lengthy: jasonrtasko@cs.unc.edu for example. It's best to put frequently used addresses in your Personal Address Book in the Microsoft Exchange.

6. Unless you're actively connected to MSN or some other online service, your message will be put into your Outbox folder. The next time you activate MSN or some other e-mail-capable application, the mail might be sent automatically. However, applications vary in their awareness of outgoing mail in the Exchange. To send the message manually, click the Tools menu and choose Deliver Now. (To get to the Outbox, click on the Microsoft Exchange's Up One Level icon on the toolbar until you see the Outbox folder displayed. Or, click the View menu and choose Folders.)

Find

We've tunneled down from MSN Central at the top to Bulletin Board Systems and e-mail messaging at the bottom, but don't take this to mean that the geometry of MSN is vertical, like a deep well. Rather, MSN resembles a pyramid—spreading out from the top in all directions and extending horizontally as you move more deeply down into it.

This enormous and continually metamorphosing bundle of information would be daunting if there weren't a way to find your way around efficiently. Fortunately, there is: the Find utility. And here again, competing online services have some catching up to do (not to mention libraries, the Internet, and other data masses). Put simply, Windows 95 Find is the among best general-purpose search engines we've ever seen.

We covered Find several places within this book, but it's slightly different when you use it with MSN so we'll take a brief look at it here. Find appears on the Tools menu of folders and Explorer, and on any window within MSN itself. You'll see the input window in Figure 18-33.

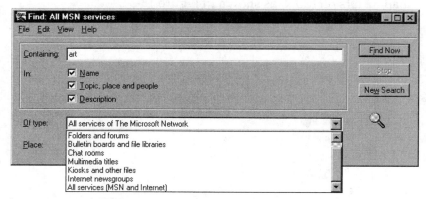

Figure 18-33: *Here's where you can start your search for anything within MSN.*

Type in any word or phrase that you're searching for, then click on any or all of the In: check boxes. Note that you can further limit the number of hits by specifying a particular location in the drop-down list shown in Figure 18-33. We've chosen the second most broad search by selecting "All services of The Microsoft Network." For the broadest possible search, click on the selection at the bottom of this list, "All services (MSN and Internet)." (The *Place* text entry box can also be used to narrow the search: type in a geographic location, such as Los Angeles.)

And or Or

You can further refine your search criteria by using the words *and* or *or*. For instance, if you want to see any location involving *both* art and music, type: **art and music** in the *Containing:* text box. To see all locations related to *either* art or music, type: **art or music**. Using the word *and* will of course result in fewer hits than will the word *or*. As a shortcut, you can just punctuate these two kinds of searching. For an *or* search, you can use a comma: art, music. For an *and*-style search, leave out the comma: art music. Likewise, you can use the DOS-style "wild card" characters. For example, *per would find any word or phrase ending in per (supper, reaper, etc.). per* would trigger anything starting with per (perfect, perhaps). *per* triggers anything with per inside it (papers). The ? wild card ignores a particular letter: d?t would trigger dot, dat and so on. If you want to search for an *exact match* to a phrase, use quotes: "art and music" would hit only on locations with that entire phrase in them. Searches ignore upper- and lowercase letters: *publish* will result in the same hits as *Publish*.

When you're ready, click on the Find Now button. Searching for "art," we had 52 hits on MSN, as shown in Figure 18-34.

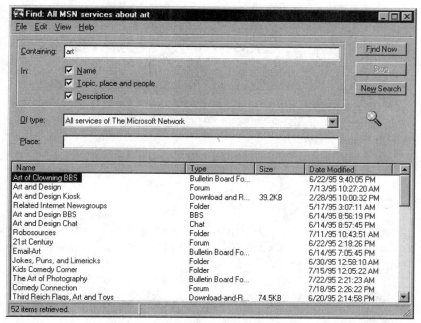

Figure 18-34: *There were 52 locations within MSN having something to do with* art.

To got to any of the locations listed after Find has finished compiling its list, just double-click on the desired location. Notice in Figure 18-32 that the various zones within MSN are listed under the heading "Type." Forums, BBS Forums, BBSes, Chat Rooms, Folders and, at the bottom, one called "Download-and-R..." (As always, if a word is cut off, you can drag one of the headings to make more room. In this case, if you drag "Size" over to the right, you'll see "Download-and-Run" as the type of this item.

 TIP   If you double-click on a "Download-and-Run" object in MSN, the file will be sent to your computer and will be displayed in whatever application is registered (associated) with the file type. At the time of this writing all Download-and Run files we've tried have been .DOC files, so they trigger Word for Windows or WordPad in our computers.

The similar "Download and Open" feature is available when you download files yourself from MSN, as we'll see shortly.

There are several things you can do with the list that Find provides you. Sort it by clicking on any of the column headings such as Size, Type, and so on. If you want to create a shortcut to a particular location, or put it into your MSN Favorite Places folder—just right-click on its name and make your choice. To put the entire search itself on your desktop, click on the File menu and choose *Save Search*.

Downloading & Uploading

A frequent pleasure when using online services is downloading shareware, graphics or other goodies. MSN makes it easy, blending the files right in with the messages on the BBSes.

To try downloading, go to a BBS. Files you can download are indicated by a paper clip symbol. In the View menu, click *Attached Files* to see only the downloadable files listed (as opposed to mere messages which can be read online rather than downloaded). You don't have to switch to the *Attached Files* view—you can scroll through all the messages in *Conversation* or *List* view, looking for paper clip symbols.

If you want to see if there's any charge to download the file, you can right-click on the message name and choose Properties, as shown in Figure 18-35. (You'll always be warned prior to a download if there's an extra cost.)

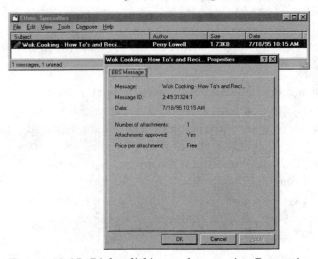

Figure 18-35: *Right-clicking and requesting Properties provides additional information about a file.*

Once you've found a file you want to download, you can double-click on the filename to see the message and the icon for the attached file.

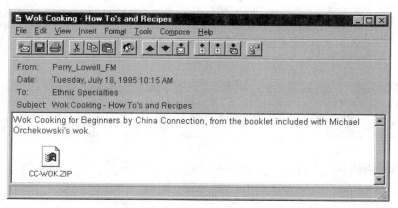

Figure 18-36: *A downloadable file looks like this: an icon within a message.*

Right-click on the file icon and you'll be offered several options, as shown in Figure 18-37. The Open option is similar to the *Download-and-Run* feature described earlier—the file will be downloaded, then opened within whatever application you have registered as "associated" with its file type. A .TXT file will be displayed in Notepad, etc. The Download option transfers the file from MSN to your hard drive, but doesn't automatically display it within an application. Properties shows you a fairly complete description of the file, including how many people have downloaded it and so on.

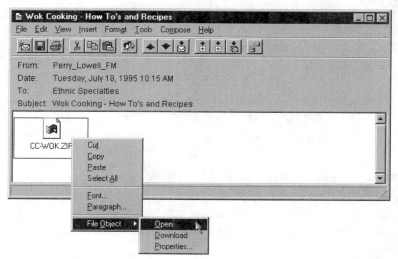

Figure 18-37: *Right-click on a file's icon to download it.*

Click Open or Download as shown in Figure 18-37 to transfer the file from MSN to your hard drive. By default, the file will be stored in a folder of its own. For example, the path on your hard drive where you could find the file "WOK.ZIP," shown in Figure 18-37, after downloading would be: C:\PROGRAM FILES\THE MICROSOFT NETWORK\TRANSFERRED FILES\CC-WOK.000.

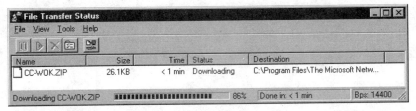

Figure 18-38: *During downloading, you see this status window.*

An Alternative Download Strategy

If you want to specify the directory in which the downloaded file will be stored, don't right-click on the file's icon. Instead, click on the icon to select it, then choose Save from the File menu (or press Ctrl+S). Click on the file's name, to select it within the list box shown in Figure 18-39, then use the *Folders* and *Drives* boxes to specify the target folder.

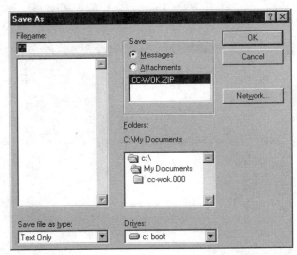

Figure 18-39: *You can specify where on your hard drive a downloaded file will be stored.*

Recall that MSN offers an option of automatically decompressing compressed (.ZIP) files. See Figure 18-14 and the surrounding text for more about downloading options.

Uploading

If you have some shareware that you've enjoyed, or a great picture you've drawn, or any other file you'd like to share with others on a MSN BBS, reverse the process of downloading. Uploading means sending a file from your hard drive to MSN.

First, create a new message on the BBS (Compose | New Message). Click within the message to move the cursor to the location within the message where you want to insert the file you're uploading. From the Insert menu on the BBS window, choose File. Browse your hard drive and click on the name of the file you want to send, then click the OK button (or just double-click on the filename of the file you're sending). Note that you can insert more than one file into a message.

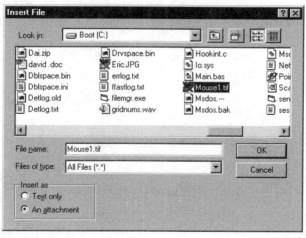

Figure 18-40: *We've selected the file MOUSE1.TIF for uploading.*

To complete the process of uploading, click on Post Message in the File menu, or, if you've got the toolbar visible, click on the leftmost icon, the picture of a flying envelope. Your uploaded file and any message that you wrote will appear in the BBS as soon as the forum manager (sysop) has checked it for viruses, legality and so on.

Moving On

Now we'll turn our attention to one of the most complex issues in contemporary computing—networking, tying more than one computer together in an office. Fortunately, Windows 95 contains sophisticated and extensive networking support. Networking is, of course, easily a book-length topic. However, in Chapter 19 we'll provide the basics, showing you the steps to take to make computers talk to each other under the supervision of Windows 95.

Chapter 19

Getting Started With Networking

Networking connects your computer with other computers. The other computers can be in the same room, the same building, across town or anywhere in the world. Networking lets you share files and printers with co-workers and colleagues.

There are many kinds of networks. The global telephone and telecommunications network was the first and is still the biggest network. Television also comes to mind, although the four major "networks" (CBS, NBC, ABC, FOX) are really networks of affiliates, not a network in the technical sense, just as television "programming" has nothing to do with computer software.

As far as true computer networks go, the Internet takes the top prize for being the biggest and most pervasive network, encompassing thousands of machines across the world. But when we talk about networking, we usually mean the more ordinary type: computers in a business hooked together via cables for file and printer sharing. This distinction blurs slightly when you take into account Dial-Up Networking: using a modem to connect an off-site computer to a company network. Indeed, The Microsoft Network, in effect, puts your computer onto Microsoft's global wide area network. (Don't worry about terminology yet; we'll get to that a little later.)

Home offices and individuals are also discovering networking, as many families realize that just one computer isn't enough. A home-based network lets you pool your resources.

Complete coverage of Windows 95 networking topics would fill an entire book. While we'll cover a wide variety of topics in this chapter, we'll focus on personal networking and on using Windows 95 with a company network. We'll also get into more detail on using Microsoft Exchange for electronic mail.

What Good Is a Network?

Before the age of personal computers, only mainframes and terminals were in use. The mainframe performed all the computing. Individual users interacted with the mainframe using a dumb terminal. The terminal's only job was to display text sent from the mainframe and relay keystrokes to the mainframe. The network was simply the wiring needed to communicate between the mainframe and the terminals.

The advent of personal computers changed all that. Each desktop has its own complete computer system with its own operating system and software. Every user creates files on his or her own hard drive and prints on his or her own printer.

SneakerNet

Without a network, you cannot directly share files. Employees rarely work alone; instead, they collaborate. One employee generates a document or spreadsheet, which is reviewed by another. Yet another person may incorporate the document in a report. It may need to go back to the original author or other co-workers for revision.

Figure 19-1: SneakerNet *is a poor substitute for networking.*

For years, many companies relied on floppy disks to do the trick, and far too many small businesses continue to depend on *SneakerNet*. Let's say Joe needs some financial data for a report. He calls up Barbara, who copies a spreadsheet to a floppy disk and walks over to Joe's desk with it. Joe takes the floppy, copies it to his hard drive and tosses the floppy in an ever-growing stack of "scratch" floppies to be reused eventually. If he discovers a mistake in the spreadsheet, he can correct it, but now he needs to copy the file to a floppy and give it back to Barbara again. But Barbara has already updated the spreadsheet, so she now has to carefully compare her version with Joe's.

This situation gets even more complicated if Barbara and Joe work on different floors of the same building, or worse, if Joe works in Cincinnati and Barbara operates out of Cleveland. Then the files have to be transmitted via modem, mailed or shipped overnight.

File Sharing

With a network, only one copy of the spreadsheet resides in a central location (it doesn't matter where for this discussion). If Joe needs a copy of the spreadsheet, he just looks for it on the network hard drive. He can modify the spreadsheet if he has the necessary permissions (set up by the network manager), and when Barbara loads the spreadsheet, she'll see Joe's changes have been incorporated. The network also can prevent more than one person from making conflicting changes to a document at the same time. It also helps prevent "versionitis," which happens if everyone works on his or her own copy of the file without being able to reconcile the differences between versions of the file.

While today's personal computers typically have large hard drives, many companies prefer to use a huge, shared hard drive, called a *file server*. That way, individual PCs don't need big hard drives, and centralized storage makes it much easier to manage files and folders company-wide. For example, all the information on the file server can be backed up to tape from a single location. Without a network, every employee is responsible for keeping backup copies of all his or her important files, and that's something you simply can't rely on.

Networks also provide another important advantage: security. With a centralized hard drive, the network manager can decide who gets access to which files. Individual files or directories (folders) are marked so that only authorized users or groups of users can access the files. Files can be set as read-only to prevent changes except by authorized users, and files, folders, even entire file servers, can be hidden. For example, the accounting system must be shielded from an employee who's curious to find out the salary of a rival co-worker.

While most networks are confined to a single building, larger companies can link their branch offices together, so collaboration is possible even across long distances.

Networks also avoid redundancy. Software can be installed to the file server just once, and with appropriate licensing, employees can run the software from the central location. If software needs to be updated, only the primary copy needs to be changed, instead of having to reinstall it on every computer individually.

Printer Sharing

Instead of each employee using his or her own printer, companies can leverage their investment by sharing equipment. So rather than buy a cheap desktop printer for each employee, the company can purchase a few high-volume sophisticated laser printers and use the network to connect the printers to every computer in the building. Joe doesn't have to change the way he works; he prints his documents as usual and then walks over to the laser printer to pick up his printouts. Employees can also continue to use their personal printers, yet they can use the network to share them with co-workers who lack a printer of their own.

Companies can also share other peripherals, such as modems, scanners and CD-ROM drives. While you can buy devices, like switch boxes, to share printers and modems, inexpensive networks are a much better alternative.

Workgroup Computing

As we mentioned earlier, networks foster group and team computing. Special sub-networks can be set up to allow teams to focus on the documents they work with. Even without a central file server, it's possible to link together individual PCs into a network. The files on each employee's hard drive can be read by an employee using a different computer. And the sharing is not indiscriminate. Employees or workgroup managers can decide which files or folders are shared on which computers, and which are private.

Collaborative computing also relies on software designed to take advantage of networks. For example, if everyone uses the same (or compatible) scheduling software, you can look at another employee's schedule to see if he's available for a meeting or when he'll return from vacation. Workgroup word processing allows you to route a document to a distribution list. Each employee makes changes or notes, which are shown using electronic "sticky notes" or revision marking (underlines for insertions, strikethrough for deletions). The document is automatically sent to the next person in the team.

Electronic mail, or *e-mail*, is a boon for company communication, making it much easier to send memos and correspondence. It provides a straightforward mechanism for routing documents. E-mail also provides a link to outside network services and desktop faxing.

Even more exciting, users on a network can use desktop conferencing to communicate face to face using video cameras, and they can work on the same document at the same time, dynamically. You actually see the other person moving the cursor, highlighting or deleting text, right on your screen, and when it's your turn, the other person can watch as you work. It's as if you both were working on the same computer using dual keyboards and mice.

Windows 95 Networking

Windows 95 is an excellent tool for taking advantage of a computer network. It includes the network features of Windows for Workgroups, it interacts with Windows NT, and it fully supports third-party networks such as Novell NetWare.

Windows for Workgroups was a pretty good solution for using Windows on a network, but Windows 95 does so much more. Windows 95 is easier to use on a network. No complicated steps are required to log in, attach or browse a file server—just open up the Network Neighborhood icon, and you'll see a list of all the computers you can explore.

Networking is fully integrated into the desktop, so you can view files on file servers just by opening a window. You can even use long filenames with most networks, once they're set up properly. Performance is also enhanced with full 32-bit protected mode drivers (as opposed to the older real-mode MS-DOS drivers that gobble up conventional memory) and file system features such as *caching* that speeds network file access (see Chapters 5 and 21 for more about caching). Robustness is also improved: No longer will your computer lock up if the file server connection is dropped or if someone accidentally disconnects a cable.

Windows 95 also enhances networking with techniques such as *shortcuts*, which let you refer to files on other computers or servers as if they were stored locally on your computer. You can even e-mail shortcuts, so you don't have to tell Joe where to find a file on a network—just send him a shortcut to the file, and when he double-clicks on the shortcut, he is automatically connected to the network resource, and the file is opened on his computer.

Introducing Network Neighborhood

If your computer is already set up to run on a network (as it would be if your PCs are managed for you by the company), you'll see an icon called Network Neighborhood right on your desktop. Double-click on the Network Neighborhood icon to see a list of all the computers that you can browse for files.

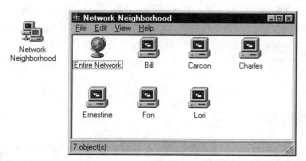

Figure 19-2: *Double-click on Network Neighborhood to browse your network.*

Network Basics

Ideally, a network should be as unobtrusive as possible. At its simplest, a network is simply a big hard drive out there somewhere (in the file server closet or on another employee's desktop computer). The goal of a network is to make it seem that these hard drives are no different than the real hard drive inside your computer.

Drive redirection

You're familiar with "C:", the drive letter of your computer's hard drive. If you have more than one hard drive or a CD-ROM, you may also have a D: drive or an E: drive. If you're connected to a network, you might also have a drive letter corresponding to a file server or a folder on another computer. Your F: drive would look and act like a normal hard drive, but it's actually not part of your computer. The only requirement to use this drive is that you have to attach to the network.

This trick of relocating the server hard drive to your computer is known as *redirection*. You simply "map" a network drive to whichever drive letter you like. (This may have already been done for you by your network supervisor.) The main server drive (or volume) is mapped to a drive letter like F:

on your computer. A server can also map folders (directories) to a drive letter, so that when you open G:, you're actually opening something like F:\WORDPROC\DOCUMENTS. But you only see the files because G: is the "root" of F:\DOCUMENTS.

Windows 95 also makes it easy to browse network drives without using drive letters, which is especially important when you realize that you have only 26 drive letters total. Since you need some drive letters for your own computer, that gives you fewer than two dozen possible network drives or folders.

So instead of using the G: to get your documents, you double-click on Network Neighborhood, then on the file server's icon, then on the Word-Processor folder and then double-click on the Documents folder. Or you can open a file directly using the Universal Naming Convention (UNC), something like \\Publications\Word Processing\Documents. But it's up to you (and your network supervisor) which method you use. If you prefer drive letters, you can keep right on using them.

Cabling

The information on a network is usually transmitted over actual wiring, or cabling. The cabling may resemble the type used for cable television (*coaxial*) or telephone-style wiring (*twisted pair*). The network wiring may have been installed when your office building was constructed, along with the electrical wiring, or added later by a network installer. We'll also show you how to set up your own cabling for a small business or home office.

In a way, the cabling is what makes a network a network. It's not the file server, since you can share printers and files without one. It's not really even the network software. The network cabling is the foundation that makes the network possible.

For a price, you can also set up a wireless network that communicates via radio waves or infrared signals. Wireless networks are also useful for connecting separate buildings using microwave signals. We're also seeing the adoption of wireless communication between notebook computers, networks and printers. On the road, a wireless network carrier can relay information between your laptop and your company's network, using cellular telephone or pager technology.

Another alternative uses modems or telephone lines to link computers into a network. The Dial-Up Networking built into Windows 95 makes it easy to tap into off-site computers, the Internet or The Microsoft Network.

Packets

A busy network has to send and receive thousands of files all at the same time. Data is flowing between the server and every computer on the network, and also between computers on the network. If you're opening a large document, do all the other users have to wait until you're finished before they can take their turn?

No, because all the files are atomized into *packets*. So your 100k spreadsheet file would be split into dozens of smaller sub-files. These packets can be more efficiently routed. If your computer is too busy to retrieve a packet, the file server can resend it. If the packet suffered some noise or errors during transmission, the network can send just that packet again, instead of the entire file. And everyone can access the network at the same time because your packets are *interleaved* (mixed in sequence) with everyone else's packets.

The network interface card in your computer samples all the packets that travel through the network, but it picks out only packets that are stamped with your address. Your address is a number that identifies your computer (or *node*) on the network.

Routing

Sometimes packets have to be shipped outside your local network to outside networks. This process is called *routing*. Special hardware devices called bridges and routers do the work of routing—it's not something you have to be concerned with.

LAN vs. WAN

You'll often hear networks referred to as LANs, or local area networks. This means that the entire network is contained within a single building or campus. If your LAN is hooked into another LAN via a bridge or router, then the combined entity is called a WAN, or wide area network. In effect, the Internet is one huge WAN.

Server vs. Peer-to-Peer

Typically, a computer network ties individual PCs into a central hard drive, stored on a special computer called a file server, so named because it "serves up" files, just as a waiter serves a meal at a restaurant. But a file server isn't limited to this role. It can also run programs for the users of the network. Instead of processing a database file on your local PC, you can just tell the file server which records you're looking for, and it can perform the necessary queries and sorting automatically. This is much more efficient because the server has direct access to the data on its own hard drive. This technique is known as *client-server* computing. Often, such a file server is actually called an *application server*.

The file server in such a network is dedicated solely to the task of serving up files and running applications for users. You typically don't have an employee using the file server as a desktop computer. So it's called a *dedicated file server*. An example of a dedicated file server is a computer running Novell NetWare.

While a Windows NT server doesn't have to be dedicated solely to serving files, typically it's not used as a desktop computer. (Some desktop users use Windows NT Workstation, which is very similar, but not dedicated to serving files, although it can also be used as an application server or a secondary file server.)

The other side of the coin

A popular alternative to server-based computing, *peer-to-peer* networking simply makes the files on each individual computer available to the users of every other computer. So if I had a file on my hard drive to share with you, you'd look on your H: drive, which points to the C: drive on my computer. But it appears that my hard drive has been mysteriously transplanted into your computer and assigned the drive letter H:.

Peer-to-peer networking also makes it easy to share printers. Even if you don't have a printer, you can print your documents, and they'll emerge from my printer (or vice versa, if you're the one lucky enough to have your own printer).

The disadvantage of peer-to-peer computing is that there is no centralization. It can also be inconvenient because I can't access the files on your computer if you have it turned off.

For these reasons, many peer-to-peer networks rely on at least one computer that is turned on all the time, and acts in effect like a file server. But it's not a *dedicated* file server; you're free to use it as a desktop computer, too. (For best results on a peer-to-peer network, select the fastest computer with the most storage as the main server. That way, the local user won't notice the demands of file sharing too much. Ideally, a non-dedicated file server will have another, smaller hard drive set aside just for the local user.)

NetWare vs. Windows NT

The two most popular network operating systems for IBM-compatible computers are Novell NetWare and Windows NT. (Versions of UNIX are also available for PCs, but we can safely ignore it for this discussion.) Windows 95 provides excellent client support for both. A *client* is an individual PC that's connected to a network. (If you've implemented a peer-to-peer network, your computer can be both a client and a server, but usually the client is the *user* of a network.)

Novell NetWare does not use MS-DOS, but its own unique disk operating system that makes it easy to secure the files on the file server. Even if you boot the file server from a DOS disk, you can't access the files on it. You must attach to the operating system from a client machine to actually use the network, although there are some management tools that run from the file server console (the monitor and keyboard attached to the file server computer).

Windows NT is the "big brother" of Windows 3.1 and Windows 95. Before Windows 95, it was the only Microsoft operating system that could run 32-bit Windows applications. Windows NT is fast gaining ground, displacing NetWare and other network operating systems. Because Windows NT has a friendly Windows-style user interface (and can now run the Windows 95 user interface), it is much easier to set up and maintain. Windows NT is also more powerful with full multithreaded multitasking and the ability to exploit multiple CPUs (symmetric multitasking—see Chapter 3 for more about multitasking).

Both Windows NT and Novell NetWare are sophisticated network operating systems that simply can't be covered in a single chapter. Fortunately, hundreds of books are available for those of you who are responsible for running a network. In this chapter, we'll show you how to set up your own peer-to-peer network and focus on the client side of network computing.

Workgroups

What if you don't have (or can't afford) the hardware and software resources required for Windows NT or NetWare? You can set up a peer-to-peer network using Windows 95. (You can also use Windows for Workgroups 3.11, but it's an older technology that is completely supplanted by Windows 95.)

With Windows 95 peer-to-peer networking, you have almost all the advantages of a dedicated network. You can even dedicate a computer to act like a file server and use it as a desktop computer when needed.

Windows 95 networking (also called Microsoft Networking) revolves around the concept of a *workgroup*, which is often a subset of a larger network. You can mix Windows 95 networking on the same network with Windows NT and NetWare, or you can use it to connect just a few computers together.

Usually, only computers within the same workgroup can communicate using Microsoft Networking. The idea is that the accounting department will have its own workgroup network, marketing will have another, product development yet another workgroup. This setup may seem to be a serious limitation, but it's by design. Workgroup networking is easier to manage and maintain by employees who aren't full-time network supervisors. If you prefer to have all the computers in your company work together, all you have to do is use a single workgroup for all of them, instead of individual workgroups for each team or department.

Even if your company uses more than one workgroup, you aren't necessarily prevented from using shared resources on a different workgroup. Using the Entire Network icon in Network Neighborhood, you can view a list of all workgroups.

You define your workgroup in Network Neighborhood's Identification property sheet, which we'll discuss in the "Configuring Network Neighborhood" section later in this chapter.

Network Components

Before we get started building your network, let's get some terminology out of the way.

Clients

A *client* is a user of a network. More specifically, a client is the network software, or driver, that Windows 95 uses to communicate with a network operating system. The two primary clients with Windows 95 are NetWare Networks and Microsoft Networks. (Don't confuse Microsoft Networking with The Microsoft Network, although we understand why you might!)

Only one client can be your *primary* client, but you can be logged into both types of networks at the same time. If you use Microsoft Networking as your primary client, it can automatically log you into a NetWare network at the same time.

Windows 95 supports several other network clients, including Banyan Vines and SunSoft NFS, but we won't discuss them in this chapter, since they aren't very common.

Protocols

A *protocol* is the language used to communicate over the network cabling. Traditionally, Microsoft Networking has used the NetBEUI protocol, while NetWare uses IPX/SPX. With Windows 95, Microsoft recognized the popularity of IPX/SPX by making it the primary network protocol (although NetBEUI is also installed by default). The protocol used by the client has to match one of the protocols supported by the file server or by other clients on a peer-to-peer network.

TCP/IP (Transmission Control Protocol/Internet Protocol) is fast becoming the world's most popular networking language. Its use as the universal protocol of the Internet helps explain its ascendance. TCP/IP is also the only protocol that supports some of Windows NT's advanced system management features.

Which protocol should you use when setting up a new network? For small networks, NetBEUI provides the best performance, but IPX/SPX is also a good choice. IPX/SPX can be routed between different file servers (see "Routing" earlier in this chapter), unlike NetBEUI. You'll need IPX/SPX if you intend to link your workgroup network with a Novell network, even if you only use Dial-Up Networking.

TCP/IP is ideal for slower network connections, so it's preferred for transport between networks on a wide area network. For a complete technical discussion of the merits of various protocols, consult the *Microsoft Windows 95 Resource Kit*, available from Microsoft Press.

You can use more than one protocol on the same network and even on the same computer, although multiple protocols can result in somewhat slower network operation. For our discussion, we'll use IPX/SPX as the best all-round small network protocol.

Adapter

An *adapter* is a device that physically connects you to a network. Usually, this means a Network Interface Card (NIC), a plug-in circuit board (similar to the video card, modem card, and so on that you insert inside your computer). Like most plug-in cards, the NIC requires an unused I/O address and usually a unique IRQ setting. See Chapter 15 to learn about configuring hardware.

Your NIC has to be compatible with the cabling used by the network, although it is possible to mix both cabling and different network cards. For our purposes, the type of NIC you buy will either use twisted-pair (telephone-style wiring with modular jacks) or BNC (coaxial cable). Many NICS support both types of connections.

You can also buy PCMCIA credit-card type network cards for notebook/ laptop computers, and network interface modules that plug into the parallel port of a PC or laptop. They are easier to configure but are more costly and sometimes not as fast as a true network card. Before buying, check the list of adapters in Network Neighborhood (we'll show you how below) to make sure the adapter is supported by a Windows 95 driver. If it's not on the list, check with the manufacturer to see if they have a Windows 95 driver for the device.

Dial-Up Networking is another type of adapter. It's a software adapter that converts your modem into a network interface device. The Dial-Up Networking adapter takes care of all the details required for placing a call and connecting with the remote computer. It otherwise works identically to a network card, except that it's much slower than a typical network card. (The remote computer at the other end of the connection also has to use the Dial-Up Networking adapter or run a program that can communicate with it, such as the Remote Access Server, or RAS, in Windows for Workgroups and Windows NT.)

Service

A *service* is special software that provides utility to a network client. One kind of service is an *agent* that's used by the network to control some aspect of your computer. For example, the Arcada Backup Agent is a service that can be used by the Arcada Backup software for NetWare or Windows NT to access the files on your computer to back them up to tape.

More typically, the service refers to either File and Printer Sharing for Microsoft Networks or File and Printer Sharing for Novell Networks. You must install one of them to allow peer-to-peer networking. If you aren't on a Novell network, use the Microsoft Networks file sharing service. It allows each user to set permissions for access to his or her files and folders using passwords. Any user who knows the right password can access your files. This is called Share-Level Access Control.

If your network is part of a Windows NT network, you can also assign permissions to authorized Windows NT users or groups of users. Windows 95 verifies the user's request using the Windows NT server. This is called User-Level Access Control.

With File and Printer Sharing for NetWare Networks, you can choose to set permissions based on NetWare *groups* and *users*. This too is User-Level Access Control.

Wiring Your LAN

In this section, we're going to show you how to install a typical small network. We can't cover every possible way to install network wiring, or all ramifications. We'll just focus on one type of economical network cabling: thin Ethernet. (While stringing telephone-style twisted-pair cabling is easier, it requires a more expensive network *concentrator* to route all the telephone lines. It's even possible to use the unused pair of wires in your normal household telephone wiring as network wiring.)

The Office LAN

Most readers will be using a company network that's already wired, so you may want to skip ahead to "Installing Network Neighborhood." However, you can apply the techniques we discuss in the following sections to most small businesses and get good results. Check your locality for laws and regulations regarding wiring installation; your best bet may be to hire an electrician with network experience to install your cabling.

About Dial-Up Networking

You can use Dial-Up Networking (DUN) to connect a computer at your home or branch office to a computer attached to a local area network. It's also possible to use devices such as the Shiva Netmodem to connect to a network without requiring a computer to answer the phone. When connected via Dial-Up Networking, you have all the resources of "being there," including the ability to share files and print to remote printers. But Dial-Up Networking is slow. Plan on running all your applications from your local hard drive, and use DUN only to access documents and data files over the link. Printing to a network printer is also possible but may not be practical if you're printing large files or documents with graphics. We recommend nothing less than a 28,800 bps v.34 modem for Dial-Up Networking.

Perhaps a better alternative to Dial-Up Networking is something loosely known as "remote control." Using software packages such as Carbon Copy (Microcom), ReachOut (Stac) or PC-Anywhere (Symantec), you can dial up a computer at another location.

When you're connected, the remote control program puts you in complete control of the other computer. Instead of your normal Windows desktop, your monitor displays the same image as the monitor on the remote computer. Your keyboard "types" keystrokes on the other computer. And moving the mouse moves the pointer on the other computer. Although still sluggish, the perceived performance can be still quite adequate over even a 14,400 bps modem.

These packages also feature file transfer capabilities, since you are actually using the other computer to do all the work—your computer is transformed into a "dumb terminal" in effect. If you need to work on any files using your own computer's software, you'll need to copy the files to your computer first. Windows 95 does not include any built-in remote control software. Existing Windows 3.1 remote control software won't work with Windows 95 either. The makers of remote control software have developed Windows 95 versions, so contact your vendor for an update.

About Direct Cable Connection

Using Direct Cable Connection (DCC), you hook a cable between two computers to network them. It's very similar to Dial-Up Networking, but instead of using modems and the telephone system to make the connection, you have a direct connection between the two computers via a cable attached between the two serial ports. You can also use a parallel cable for higher speeds. Indeed, new computers feature Enhanced Parallel Ports (or Enhanced Capability Ports) that permit much faster data transfer, approaching the speeds of a true network. It's a near-ideal way to connect two computers together. DCC is mainly useful in the home (or very small business), since you don't need to buy network cards or run any wiring. But you can only use it between two computers; so far there's no way to "daisy-chain" a cable to a third computer. For that you'll need a regular network card and cabling.

Direct Cable Connection is ideal for transferring data between a notebook and a desktop computer. Like Dial-Up Networking, the connection extends to the entire network. Your notebook computer can access files not only on the desktop computer, but can also log into the network attached to the desktop computer, giving you access to all files and printers on the network (as long as you have the necessary passwords and permissions).

Do It Yourself

To get started with wiring your own network, you'll need at least two computers, two network cards and a length of network cabling. For this discussion, the network cards should be thin-Ethernet (CheaperNet) cards with BNC connectors. See Figure 19-3.

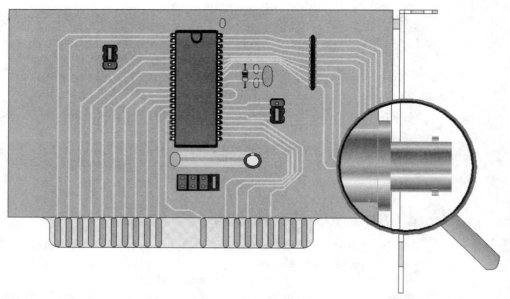

Figure 19-3: *The most common type of Ethernet card uses BNC connectors, similar to (but not compatible with) those used for VCRs and cable TV.*

The cabling should be RG58/U-type cable, which you can purchase from Radio Shack or another electronics or computer store. It should have a solid center core and braided copper shielding, although you can also use cabling with aluminum tape shielding. For unobtrusive installation, you'll need to drill a hole through the floor and run the cable under the house, or run the cable up the wall through the false ceiling of an office. Make sure you measure the distances and buy the correct length of cable, and get a little extra too.

You'll need to attach BNC connectors to each end of the cable, as shown in Figure 19-4. Or purchase pre-built thin-Ethernet cables with the connectors already attached.

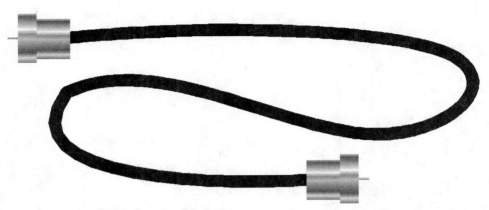

Figure 19-4: *The Ethernet cables will have male twist-on connectors on either end.*

You'll next plug a BNC T-Connector into the jack on the back of each network card (these tees usually come with the network card).

You'll also need two network terminators. They typically don't come with network cards, so ask for BNC-type terminators when you shop at the computer or electronics parts store. A network terminator uses the same type of connector that you attached to the cabling, but is really just a "stub" that prevents the radio frequency signals from bouncing off the ends of the cables and causing confusing echoes. (Yes, Ethernet uses radio signals transmitted over wires, just like cable television.)

We'll cable the network like a string of Christmas tree lights, with the bulbs replaced by computers. The first computer in the chain has a terminator attached to one side of the tee (which one doesn't matter). The first length of cable is attached to the other side of the tee, and is attached to either side of the tee on the second computer in the chain. If the network has only two computers, you'll put the terminator on the other side of the second computer's tee. Otherwise, you'll run another segment of cabling from the second computer's tee to the third computer, and so on. The last computer in the chain (like the first one) needs to have a terminator installed on the dangling end of the tee.

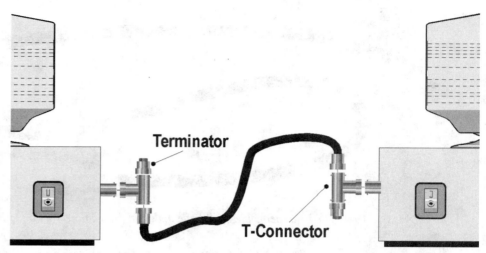

Figure 19-5: *The network cable runs from one computer to the next, with each end terminated.*

When running the wiring, you may be tempted to put the tees in the ceiling or under the floor and run a single cable from each tee to the connector on the back of each network interface card. We tried this arrangement years ago, and it doesn't work. The extra length of cable interferes with the RF signals, and you have a network that doesn't function reliably.

Safety issues

Since network cabling communicates using low-voltage radio frequency signals, you don't have to worry about an electric shock. You should be concerned about static electricity, though, so ground yourself by touching the metal case of your computer before plugging or unplugging cables. It's also a good idea to ground both terminators. Attach a wire to the end of a terminator (or wrap it around the terminator if it lacks a loop or grounding strap) and run it to the center screw of any properly grounded electrical outlet. This will help drain power surges that can get transferred to the network cabling during lightning storms or when large electrical motors (such as A/C or refrigerator compressors) turn on and off. (Using a surge suppressor with a computer is important, but when it shunts surges to ground, some of this is sent through the ground of the network cabling. Grounding the terminators allows the discharge to be harmlessly transferred to earth, instead of running through the network card and damaging the card or the computer.)

If you are installing the cabling adjacent to ventilation or heating/cooling ducts, you will have to use *plenum* cabling, a more expensive type that uses

Teflon-coated cables. This prevents toxic fumes from being released into your air conditioning system in the case of an electrical fire.

Installing Network Neighborhood

Once you're wired, the next step is to install the Windows 95 drivers for the network. If you already have a Network Neighborhood icon on your desktop, skip ahead to "Configuring Network Neighborhood."

Networking support is automatically configured once you've added a network adapter. Even if you don't have a physical network, you may want to install the Dial-Up Adapter, which lets you access the Internet and other dial-up servers. For now, we'll assume you've installed a network interface card (NIC) or a PCMCIA network card.

If you add a network card designed for Plug and Play, Windows 95 will detect it and install the drivers for it automatically. Otherwise, use Add New Hardware from the Control Panel (see Chapter 15) to get Windows to recognize your NIC. Windows 95 searches for your NIC card, but if it can't detect it, use the manual install feature of Add New Hardware, or use the Windows 95 drivers that came with the card. Note that the default hardware settings that Windows 95 uses for your NIC will likely be incorrect. Use Device Manager or configure your network adapter with Network Neighborhood (see below).

After the card is installed, Windows reboots your computer, and you'll see an icon for Network Neighborhood.

Configuring Network Neighborhood

Before you can configure your network, you'll need to access the property sheets for Network Neighborhood by right-clicking on the icon and choosing Properties from the pop-up menu (see Figure 19-6).

Figure 19-6: *Right-click on the Network Neighborhood desktop icon and choose Properties to view the settings for your network.*

TIP If your desktop is cluttered, you can also right-click on the Network Neighborhood icon that's shown in the Explorer folders list (the left-hand pane).

Configuration

The first property sheet, Configuration, is shown in Figure 19-7. The main window shows all the network components that are currently installed (which won't necessarily match up with what's shown in the figure). A network component can be a client, adapter, protocol or a service. You must have at least one client, one adapter and one protocol to use Windows 95 networking. Before we get into specifics, let's finish describing some other items on the Configuration property sheet.

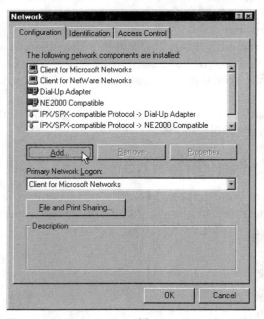

Figure 19-7: *You can add, remove and set the properties for any network component from the Configuration page of the Network Neighborhood property sheets.*

Use the box labeled Primary Network Logon to choose between the clients you've installed. This will be the client that actually logs you into the network. If you use both the Microsoft Networking and NetWare Networking client, choose Microsoft Networking, which will automatically log you into the NetWare network.

 TIP   If you travel with a portable computer, you may want to choose Windows Logon as the Primary Network Logon so that you're not asked for a name and password when you're not connected to the network.

Enabling file & printer sharing

Use File and Printer Sharing if you want to set up peer-to-peer networking and share your hard drive and/or printer with other users. File and Printer Sharing uses the Primary Network Login setting to install either File and Printer Sharing for Microsoft Networks or File and Printer Sharing for NetWare Networks. (Use the Microsoft version if you have any computers running only Windows for Workgroups-type networking. If all computers in the workgroup are using the Microsoft client for NetWare, use the NetWare version of file and printer sharing. You can install either type by choosing the Add button, regardless of the Primary Network Logon setting.) We'll explain more about File and Printer Sharing later in this chapter.

Adding components

Before you can configure a network component, you may need to add it to the list. Just click on the Add button to install components, as shown in Figure 19-8.

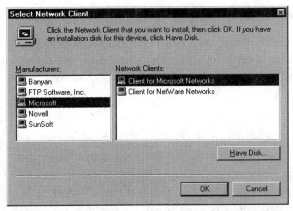

Figure 19-8: *Choose the manufacturer/vendor on the left and the name of the component on the right. (Use Microsoft for most components.)*

Client for Microsoft networks

Figure 19-9 shows the properties for the Client for Microsoft Networks. If your computer is part of a Windows NT network, turn on the Log on to Windows NT domain check box and fill in the name of your Windows NT server (the domain). You can also choose between Quick logon or Logon and restore connections. You may prefer the latter if you want to make sure your network connections (mapped drives) are available before you start working.

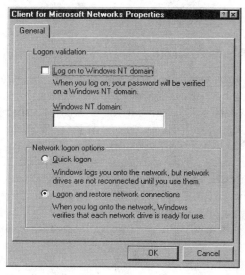

Figure 19-9: *You don't need to fill in a domain if you're only using Windows 95 for peer-to-peer networking.*

Client for NetWare Networks

Windows 95 may install the Client for NetWare Networks, even if you don't attach to a Novell file server. In this case, you can click on the icon for NetWare and then click on the Remove button. Removing this option frees up memory.

TIP   A few programs use network copy protection to make sure you're running only licensed copies of software. If you have the NetWare client installed, but you're not logged into the network, these programs, which include Aldus (Adobe) PageMaker 5.0, will refuse to run. The solution is to remove the NetWare client.

If you are on a NetWare network, double-click on the icon for Client for NetWare Networks to see something similar to Figure 19-10. On the General panel, type in the name of your NetWare file server. If your location uses multiple servers, you can choose one from a list by clicking the arrow next to the text box. Use the other drop-down box to choose which drive letter will be assigned to the first NetWare volume (normally F:).

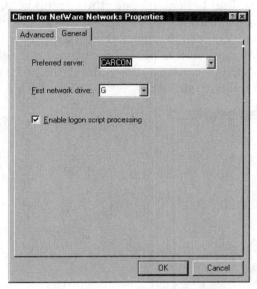

Figure 19-10: *The General panel for NetWare lets you specify your favorite file server and which drive to use as the first network drive.*

Part of logging into a Novell file server is executing the *login script*, a special batch file that NetWare administrators use to set up default printer assignments and so forth. You can prevent this script from running by turning off the Enable script processing check box. You might need to turn off this option if the login script attempts to start any TSR programs, which is verboten in Windows 95.

Instead of using the Microsoft Client for NetWare networks, you may for some reason need to use the standard DOS drivers (IPX, ODI or VLM drivers). You will not get the full benefit of Windows 95 networking (such as File and Printer Sharing) with these drivers. Delete the Microsoft Client and choose the Add button to install either the NetWare Shell 3.X or 4.X driver.

Adapter

The next thing you'll want to do is verify the settings for your network adapter (shown in Figure 19-7 as *NE2000 Compatible*). Click on the adapter and choose Properties. You can also double-click on any component to access its properties. (But you can't right-click to get the properties as you can with other Windows icons. Right-clicking opens the pop-up help, which you can also get by clicking on the ? in the upper-right corner of the property sheet to get the help cursor. You can then click the help cursor upon any item to get more information about that part of the property sheet.)

The properties for the NE2000 card are shown in Figure 19-11. (The properties for the Dial-Up Adapter are similar.)

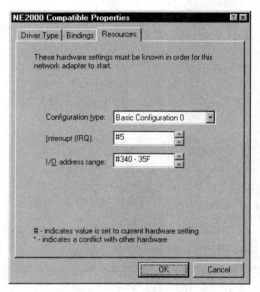

Figure 19-11: *Choose the Resources page to configure your network card.*

The Driver Type page lets you decide what type of driver to use. We recommend sticking with the 32-bit drivers, unless you're forced to use older Windows 3.1 drivers or DOS drivers.

The Bindings panel tells Windows which protocol the adapter uses. Normally, the protocol will be set automatically. A network adapter must be *bound* to (associated with) at least one network protocol.

On the Resources panel, use the Up/Down arrows or type in the correct values to configure your card to match its hardware settings (unless it's a Plug-and-Play card, which is configured automatically).

The Dial-Up Adapter uses an Advanced panel instead of Resources, since it has no resources to configure. Since you won't need to change any of its settings, we'll move on to the properties for your protocol.

Protocol

Earlier in this chapter, we discussed why you need a network protocol. The protocol you use must match the protocols used by the computers you want to link with. If the protocol isn't shown on the list, use the Add button to create it. For example, add the Microsoft TCP/IP protocol to get Internet connectivity. (We cover TCP/IP setup in Chapter 17.) Use IPX/SPX to connect to NetWare and later versions of Windows NT. Use NetBEUI to connect to earlier Windows NT servers and Windows for Workgroups.

You'll see one protocol entry for each adapter that protocol is bound to. Double-click on a protocol to get its properties, as shown in Figure 19-12.

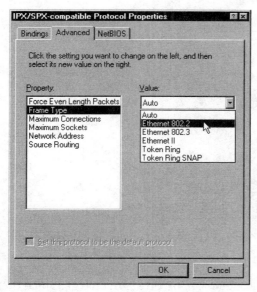

Figure 19-12: *IPX/SPX properties let you bind the protocol, enable NetBIOS and fiddle with advanced settings.*

The Bindings panel is the place where you link the protocol to an adapter. (You can also bind from the adapter's property sheet.) Use the NetBIOS page if you want to turn on NetBIOS support, which isn't used very much these days but is required for some network applications. (Exchange also uses NetBIOS, if enabled, to flag urgent messages.) We won't cover the Advanced settings here because you'll rarely have to change them. (However, if Windows 95 doesn't detect the IPX frame type correctly, you may have to choose it manually.)

File & printer sharing for Microsoft Networks

If you've chosen to use File and Printer Sharing (discussed earlier), you can double-click on it in a list of components to get its properties, as shown in Figure 19-13. The only one item shown that you may want to fool with is Browse Master.

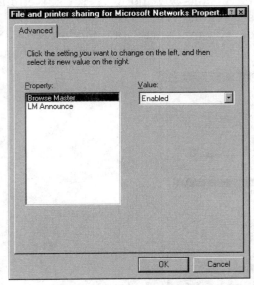

Figure 19-13: *Set Browse Master to Enabled on at least one computer for best results with peer-to-peer sharing.*

On a pure peer-to-peer network, no one is in charge. Since there's no server, though, where is the "master list" of all computers kept up-to-date? Normally, this is handled cooperatively. One of the computers in the network is elected a *browse master*. The process of choosing a browse master is complicated, but it's usually the machine that's turned on first or has been left turned on the longest. One or more computers are elected as a backup browse master, which update the list periodically from the browse master. If a browse master computer is turned off or logged off from the network, one of the backup browse masters takes over the job of primary browse master.

All this can take up to 15 minutes to be updated. This explains why you sometimes can't see every computer on the network, even if everything is set up properly. Wait 15 minutes before deciding that you need to troubleshoot.

To save time and trouble, you can tell Windows 95 to always use a specific machine as the browse master. For best results, choose the fastest computer, one that is rarely turned off or logged off. From the File and Printer Sharing property sheet, click on the entry for Browse Master and use the box on the right to set its value to Enabled.

On the other hand, a slow computer might suffer from serving as a browse master, so you can set the Browse Master property to Disabled. Otherwise, the value is set to Automatic. With Automatic, Windows is free to elect a browse master. It's like being chosen for jury duty.

File & printer sharing for NetWare Networks

Normally, with File and Printer Sharing for NetWare Networks, shared resources are organized by workgroup. Shared drives will be listed along with the other computers in the workgroup. This option is called *Workgroup Advertising*. Alternatively, you can use *SAP Advertising*. With SAP Advertising, your computer appears to be a Novell file server. When SAP Advertising is enabled, other computers using the Novell client software NETX can attach to your computer, even if they're not running Windows 95. It's a great way to make a device like a CD-ROM available to all users on a mixed network. (If all computers are running Windows 95, you're better off using Workgroup Advertising, which is more convenient for the users.)

You might think this is a way to get a Novell-type network without paying for a NetWare license and going through all the work of setting up a Novell network. Unfortunately, it's not that easy. While your computer can act like a Novell file server, the lists of users and groups have to be obtained from an actual NetWare file server. So your computer can act like a secondary NetWare file server, but it can't replace the real one. But this feature is still very handy. Shared printers appear as NetWare print queues, and you can use the standard Novell network management commands (SLIST, PSERVER, FCONSOLE and so on) to manage the settings for a Windows 95 computer.

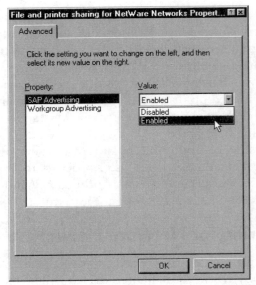

Figure 19-14: *Enable SAP Advertising if you want to masquerade as a Novell file server.*

Figure 19-14 shows the options for File and Printer Sharing for NetWare Networks. If you're using Workgroup advertising, set its value to Enabled: Can Be Master. This is equivalent to the Automatic choice we mentioned above—your computer can be elected as the browse master. Use Enabled: Preferred Master if you want to set your computer to be the browse master, or Enabled: Will Not Be Master if your computer is too slow to serve as a browse master.

For SAP Advertising, all you have to do is choose Enabled or Disabled.

Identification

Returning to the main Network Neighborhood property sheet, click on the Identification tab heading (see Figure 19-15).

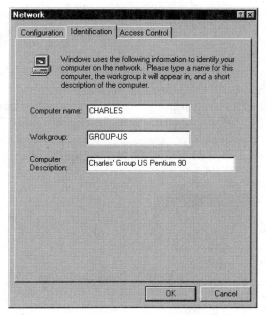

Figure 19-15: *Set your computer's name and workgroup using the Identification page of Network Neighborhood.*

Here you name your computer and specify which workgroup it belongs to. Remember that, by default, you can only "see" computers that use the exact same workgroup name, which helps you limit the scope of a network. However, the Entire Network icon in Network Neighborhood can let you view other workgroups, too, unless this feature has been disabled by the network administrator.

 TIP When setting up a small office network, use any name you like, such as the name of your company, but keep it simple so there's no ambiguity in spelling. Otherwise, you might not realize that two computers are actually using different workgroup names.

Every computer within the same workgroup must use a unique machine name. If every user has his or her own machine, you'll probably want to name the machine after the primary user. If many employees share the same machine, make up a name that meaningfully identifies that computer. You can use up to 15 characters for the machine name; use the Description box to fill in a more complete name, which is also shown when users are browsing the network.

Access Control

When you're finished with the Identification panel, click on the Access Control tab heading (see Figure 19-16). Here you're choosing a security method used to validate peer-to-peer sharing. If your computer is not part of a NetWare or Windows NT network, you'll have to choose Share-Level. With Share-Level security, you can set up a password for each drive or printer that you're sharing. Any user with the same workgroup can access a drive you're sharing, if he or she knows the password.

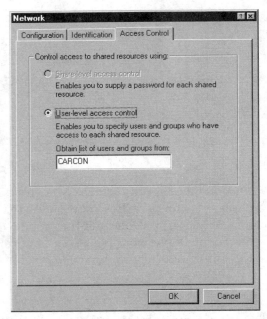

Figure 19-16: *Use Access Control to choose between password protection (Share-level) or server-based authentication (User-level).*

For enhanced security, consider using User-level access control. This gets a list of authorized users from a NetWare or Windows NT file server. When you share your local drives and printers, you can choose by name which users (or groups of users) are allowed access.

Using Network Neighborhood

After you've configured your network and restarted your computer, you're ready to get started with networking. Once again, Network Neighborhood is the key.

Browsing for Computers

Double-click on the Network Neighborhood icon to open a folder-style view of all the computers on the network, as shown in Figure 19-17. Or you can right-click on the icon and choose Explore to get an Explorer view. (From within Explorer, you can just click on the Network Neighborhood icon.)

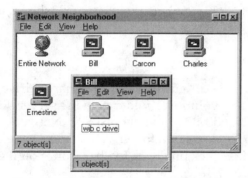

Figure 19-17: *The Network Neighborhood folder shows all the computers in your current workgroup. Double-click on an icon to view the shared drives and folders on that computer.*

The Network Neighborhood folder normally shows your preferred server (if you're on a Novell or Windows NT network) and any computers within your workgroup. Your own computer's name is also on the list, although you'll usually use My Computer or Explorer to access your own computer.

Also shown is an icon for Entire Network. This expands your view to show all the file servers that are part of your companies' local area network, including off-site servers that are part of a wide area network. When you double-click on a server, you may be asked again for a login name and password, unless it's the same as that used by your normal server. The Entire Network icon also shows the names of other workgroups, including your current workgroup. Double-click on any workgroup to see the computers contained within it.

Double-click on a machine name to "drill down" into the hierarchy and view the drives and folders shared on that machine. They are also called shared resources, or simply *shares*. (The user of that computer must also be using File and Printer Sharing, and have previously set up sharing for the drives and printers on his or her computer.) Or double-click on a file server's icon to view the volumes available on that file server. (Your network administrator can control which volumes you have access to.)

When you see the drive (or folder) that you want to examine, double-click on it. If User-level access control is set for that share, you need to type a password (asterisks will be shown as you type) to open it. (You don't need a password if the user didn't choose one or if the share is set for User-level access. However, if you're not one of the users authorized for that share, you won't be able to open it.) The next time you start your computer, you'll have to enter the password again. However, when password caching is enabled (which it normally is unless your system administrator forbids it using Policy Editor), your computer remembers the password (shown as ****), and all you have to do is click on OK.

Mapping Drives

You may find it convenient to *map* a drive letter to a shared drive or folder. You can also map a drive to a volume or folder on a file server. Right-click on the Network Neighborhood folder and choose Map Network Drive. You can also map a drive from Explorer or a folder view, if you have the toolbar enabled (View | Toolbar). Just click on the 🖳 toolbar icon. You'll get the dialog box shown in Figure 19-18.

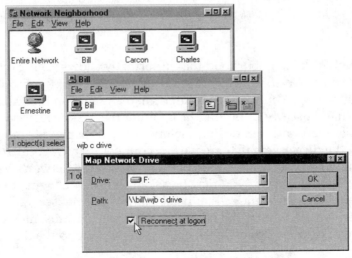

Figure 19-18: *Choose a drive and a network path, and you'll be able to access that drive or folder more conveniently.*

Click on the box next to Drive to choose a drive letter to assign to the shared drive or folder. In the Path box, you can type in the name of the network resource you want to use or choose it from a list of shares you've used recently by clicking the Down arrow next to the box. This box is blank the first time you use it, so you'll have to type in a path to the resource. Finally, turn on the *Reconnect at logon* check box. This will ensure your mapped drive will be preserved from session to session. Otherwise, the mapping will disappear when you shut down Windows.

Universal Naming Convention

Note that there is no Browse button—you have to know how to specify the name of a shared folder. To do this, use the Universal Naming Convention. For example, if your network file server's name is PRIME, and you want to assign a drive letter to the APPS folder on the WIN volume, you'd use the UNC of \\PRIME\WIN\APPS. For a Windows NT server, the first part of the UNC (\\PRIME) would be the name of a domain on that server. You can also refer to a shared drive on another computer (using peer-to-peer networking) by using something like \\CHUCK\C-DRIVE or \\CHUCK\CD-ROM\WIN95. The second part (after \\CHUCK) is the name of the shared drive, or it can be the name of a shared folder.

Actually, there is an easier way to map drives. Just open the Network Neighborhood folder, navigate to the folder you want to use and choose Map Network Drive from the File menu (you can also click on the toolbar icon). This automatically fills in the path to that resource.

You might need to map a drive when running DOS or Windows 3.1 applications, since they probably won't understand UNC names. But drive mapping will eventually be obsolete, since Network Neighborhood makes it so easy to browse for folders. You can also navigate to a shared folder within the Common Dialog Open and Save boxes, which we discussed in Chapter 5.

UNC names have another advantage. Sometimes you aren't able to browse the network if your computer is running low on memory or if the browse master is temporarily unavailable. But you can always open a folder by referring to its UNC name.

 Select Start|Run and enter a UNC name to jump directly to that folder, opened on your desktop.

Finding a Computer

On large networks, select Start | Find | Computer to more quickly locate a shared drive or server. This can be a lifesaver if you're trying to access a computer that's linked via a slow connection, such as Dial-Up Networking, since browsing can be very slow over a phone line. For the same reason, you'll want to rely on UNC names rather than the Browse button when you're opening or saving files from an application.

Sharing Your Drives

Sharing is a two-way street. It's one thing to be able to access files and folders on somebody else's computer, but others may need to use your computer's files, too. First, don't be worried that you're opening a Pandora's box: you have full control over which folders are shared, and you can use a secret password so that only authorized users can "get in." (Or you can limit access to only certain users.)

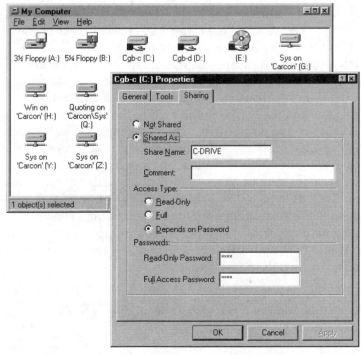

Figure 19-19: *Use passwords to protect a shared drive.*

The easiest way to share a drive is to first open My Computer. Next, right-click on a drive you want to share, and choose Sharing from the pop-up menu. You then get the Sharing page shown in Figure 19-19. (You can also open this page by choosing Properties for a drive and clicking on the Sharing tab heading.)

Sharing a folder works identically. Just right-click on the folder you want to share and choose Sharing, or click on the Share Drive button on the toolbar. The difference is that when you share a folder, the user sees that folder as if it was a hard drive. Only the files on that folder (and any subfolders it contains) are visible.

To share a drive or folder, first click on the Shared As option button. By default, the share name is simply the drive letter of the hard drive. You can use any name you like, but it makes sense to be consistent with these names network-wide. For example, if everyone shared his or her drive as C-DRIVE, you wouldn't have to guess when composing a UNC to someone's computer. You'd know to use \\BILL\C-DRIVE when referring to drive C: on Bill's machine.

 TIP It's possible to share a drive or folder yet make the drive invisible to casual users browsing Network Neighborhood. Just add a $ symbol after the share name. If you shared your C: drive as C-DRIVE$, it would not be shown when users browse the network. A user would have to know the hidden name and use a UNC name like \\LORI\C-DRIVE$\DOCS to access a folder. This convention adds an additional layer of security, but you'll probably want to use User-level or Share-level access control, too.

Use the Comment box to provide a more meaningful description of the drive if you like. This is shown when someone uses Network Neighborhood to browse your computer.

Share-level Access

Next, choose the type of access you want to allow. For a CD-ROM, you'd naturally use Read-Only. Use Full to allow someone unlimited read and write access to your drive. Or click on Depends on Password if you want to allow some users to have read-only access and others to have full read/write access, depending on which password you give them.

You don't have to use passwords. Indeed, if your company is "one big happy family," sharing is a lot more convenient without passwords.

User-level Access

If you configured your computer for User-level access (see "Configuring Network Neighborhood"), the Share dialog box looks like Figure 19-20. Here, you can pick the names of the users you'd like to give access to your files.

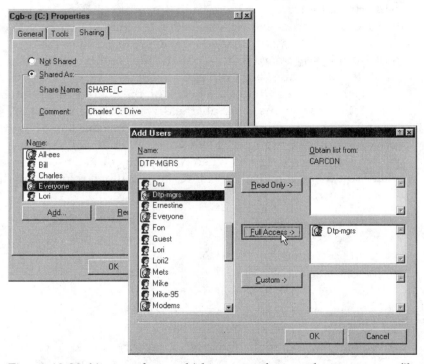

Figure 19-20: *You can choose which users can have read access to your files and which can have read/write access.*

Sharing Your Printer

You can also share your printer, which allows others on the network to send their files to your computer to be printed. Select Start | Settings | Printers to open your Printers folder. Right-click on the printer you want to share and choose Sharing to get the Sharing property sheet, as shown in Figure 19-21. (Note that there is no toolbar button to share a printer, nor is it available from the File menu. But you can also get to the Sharing panel of the printer by choosing the Properties toolbar button 🖼 or choosing Properties from the File menu or right-clicking to open a pop-up menu.)

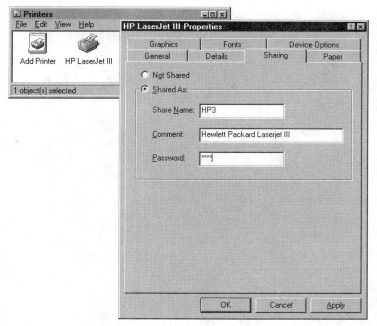

Figure 19-21: *The share name of the printer is visible when a user chooses Install Network Printer.*

Installing a Network Printer

To print to someone else's shared printer, select Start | Settings | Printers to open your Printers folder. Double-click on the Add Printer icon, and from the Add Printer Wizard, choose Network Printer. Then click on Next. When you do this, you'll be asked to enter a network path or the name of a file server printer queue (see Figure 19-22).

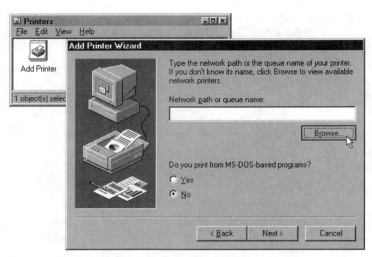

Figure 19-22: *Click on Browse to quickly find a network printer.*

 TIP   Answer Yes to "Do you print from DOS" only if you are using MS-DOS applications with that printer. Windows applications print to a printer driver, not to a printer port. But MS-DOS can only print to a port like LPT1: or LPT2: If you choose Yes, you then have to choose which LPT: port to assign to the network printer. If you assign LPT1:, you won't be able to access your local printer (assuming you have one).

For example, the primary printer on a NetWare file server might be \\PRIME\PRINTQ_0. A printer shared as HP3 would be accessed via \\CHARLES\HP3. More conveniently, click on the Browse button. As shown in Figure 19-23, you can navigate easily to the desired computer. Click on the ⊞ symbol, if necessary, to show the printers shared by that computer. You can even drag and drop a printer from the network server into your Printers folder to easily install it.

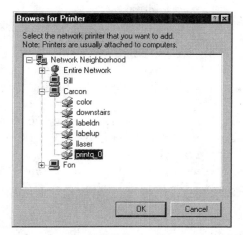

Figure 19-23: *Find the computer that hosts the printer you want to use.*

Ideally, Windows 95's *Point and Print* feature will automatically install the drivers for the printer. After all, the computer that's sharing the printer already has the drivers it needs, so they're passed along to your computer. On a Windows NT or NetWare file server, however, the network administrator has to set up Point and Print. Otherwise, you'll have to choose a printer vendor and printer model from the list of printers (see Figure 19-24).

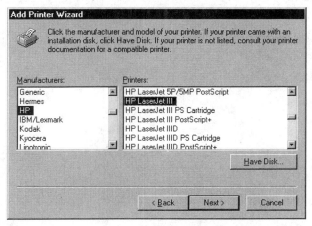

Figure 19-24: *Choose the printer's manufacturer on the left and the specific model on the right.*

Dial-Up Networking

In principle, Dial-Up Networking works exactly like a real network connection, but it's a little slower. Dial-Up Networking also relies on a host machine at the main network location, which serves as a bridge between you and the main network.

Since Dial-Up Networking is crucial to Internet access, we've already discussed it in Chapter 17. You can also use Dial-Up Networking to access files and printers on your computer at work while traveling with a portable computer (that's not the only scenario, but it's a common one). Unfortunately, the Dial-Up Server is not included with Windows 95. You'll have to get Microsoft Plus! for that.

Direct Cable Connection

We'll set up a direct cable connection between a desktop computer and a portable notebook computer. It can also be used to link two computers together into a mini-network. To get started, choose Start | Programs | Accessories | Direct Cable Connection. In Figure 19-25, choose which computer will be the host, the one that shares its files, and which computer will be the guest, which is allowed to access those files. Usually the desktop computer is the host and the portable computer is the guest, but this can be reversed at any time.

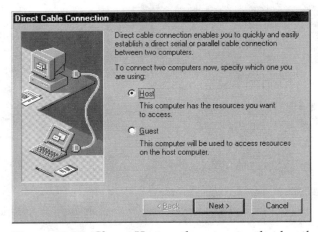

Figure 19-25: *Choose Host on the computer that has the files you want to access. Configure the other machine as Guest.*

TIP   Both computers need fast 16550 serial ports, or you'll be limited to 19,200 bps when sending files over a serial cable. With a 16550, you can use speeds as high as 115,200 bps.

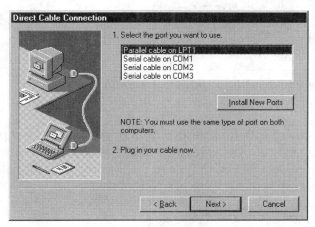

Figure 19-26: *Choose a cabling method next.*

To set up the host, you next need to choose how you're connecting the two computers, via either a parallel "LapLink" style cable, or a serial *null-modem* cable. The parallel cable (which plugs into the printer ports on both machines) is fastest, but it has a length limitation of about 10 feet. You can string serial cables much farther without data loss. In Figure 19-26, we've chosen the parallel cable option. At this point, you should go ahead and plug the cable between the two computers if you haven't already.

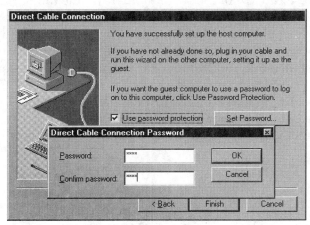

Figure 19-27: *Click Set Password if you want to have a more secure connection.*

In Figure 19-27, you'll see that we've set a password by clicking the Set Password button. Realistically, it's doubtful that you need a password, since the connection only exists as long as you have the two computers cabled up. Once you've completed this step, the desktop computer perks up and starts listening for the guest computer.

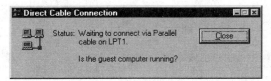

Figure 19-28: *The host computer might get impatient if you wait too long to start the Guest connection.*

When you connect with the guest computer, you might see the warning message shown in Figure 19-29. If you want to view the shared folders on the host computer, you'll need to type in the *machine name* of that computer (which you configured using Network Neighborhood).

Figure 19-29: *If Direct Cable Connection can't figure out the name of the host computer, you'll have to type it in.*

Finally, you'll see a view of the shared folders on the remote computer. At this point, treat Direct Cable Connection exactly like any other form of Windows 95 networking. Just as with a direct networking connection or Dial-Up Networking, you won't be able to see anything on the host computer unless that user has installed File and Printer Sharing and has shared some drives or folders.

You can't actually print to a shared printer via Direct Cable Connection if you're using the parallel printer port for the connection. You can either use the serial cable method to connect, or add a second parallel port to the host machine.

Your Briefcase

The *Briefcase* is an anomaly: most people don't even know they need it. If you have a portable computer, you're already familiar with the process of transferring files between your desktop computer and your portable machine. When you're finished with files on the portable computer, you have to remember to transfer the file back to the desktop machine. This can get tedious if you like to transfer large numbers of documents between machines.

The Briefcase automates the process. Select File | New | Briefcase to create a Briefcase folder on your portable computer. Connect your portable computer to your desktop computer via a network or Direct Cable Connection. Then drag and drop the files from the desktop computer into the Briefcase folder on the portable computer. (To make this process easier, you can create the Briefcase first on the desktop computer, copy all the files to it and then move the entire Briefcase to the notebook computer.)

 You can also host a Briefcase on a floppy disk for ultimate portability, but doing so limits how many files you can use. But a removable hard drive, such as the Iomega Zip drive or a Syquest cartridge, makes an ideal place to keep a large Briefcase.

You edit the files within the Briefcase on the portable computer (don't move the files out of the Briefcase). When you're ready to update the documents on the desktop, connect the portable computer to the desktop machine. Use the desktop computer to double-click on the Briefcase on the notebook computer to open it.

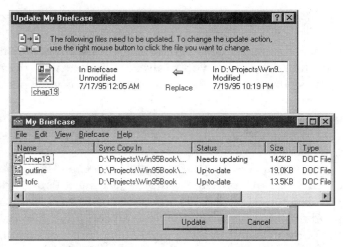

Figure 19-30: *Open the Briefcase to update the original files.*

If you're using Details view (View | Details), you can see which items need to be updated.

Use Briefcase | Update All to copy the modified documents from the Briefcase to their original locations on the desktop computer. Or you can select only certain files and use Briefcase | Update Selected.

Use Briefcase | Split From Original to break the link between a file in a Briefcase and the original. You can then move that file out of the Briefcase and keep it anywhere you like on the portable computer. Even if you make changes to the file, it will no longer be updated on the original (desktop) computer.

The Briefcase has another powerful potential: files can not only be transferred between computers, but they can be synchronized, too. What happens if you changed the document on the original (desktop) computer and on the notebook computer in the Briefcase? If you reconnect, you have a problem: you can't just replace the original file, or it would lose its changes, being replaced by the Briefcase version.

Although there is no easy fix for this, Windows 95 allows programs to set up special synchronization for files that they create. For example, Microsoft Access for Windows 95 can compare the tables between the two machines. Any records added on the desktop computer are merged with the database in the Briefcase on the portable computer and vice versa. Both copies are complete and up-to-date. We look forward to more applications that support this feature, especially when applied to contact managers and scheduling software.

We've used the Briefcase to synchronize files between a desktop computer and a notebook computer. This description covers only the most typical use of the Briefcase. You can also use it to synchronize files between a notebook and a hard drive in the notebook's docking station, or use the Briefcase along with Dial-Up Networking to more conveniently transfer files. With some experience and a little trial and error, you'll probably figure out some innovative ways to put the Briefcase to good use.

Shared vs. Local Windows Installation

For the best network performance, you'll want to install Windows 95 on your local hard drive. Some network administrators prefer to keep a centralized Windows 95 directory on a network drive. They believe that this setup makes Windows 95 easier to maintain. But we don't recommend this option; Windows needs all the speed it can get, and even a sluggish local hard drive is much faster than a network connection. Running Windows from a file server also significantly increases network traffic. If your computers are diskless workstations, you may have no choice but to run Windows 95 from a file server directory, but the network traffic will get horrendous, since the Windows swap file will also have to be located on the server.

However, even if you don't implement a common Windows folder on the network, it's still useful and necessary to create a Windows 95 installation directory. This way, users can upgrade or reinstall Windows 95 without needing the original disks or CD-ROM. (Of course, your company must still arrange with Microsoft to obtain the necessary number of software licenses for Windows 95.)

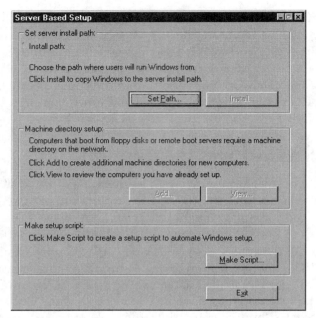

Figure 19-31: *NetSetup is ideal for automating network installation.*

The easiest way to create a network install directory is to copy the \WIN95 folder from the Windows 95 CD-ROM to the network. Users can run the SETUP program from the network from either DOS or Windows 3.1. Or you could set up a share to a CD-ROM drive that hosts Windows 95.

Expert network administrators will prefer a more optimal method, however. You'll need the Windows 95 CD-ROM. Look in the \ADMIN\NETTOOLS folder, and run the program called NetSetup. This way, you can create a custom Windows 95 folder on your network drive and an automated batch script for installing Windows 95. It's possible to create a setup script that completely automates Windows 95 setup, which is a lifesaver for administrators of large companies. The Windows 95 files are also decompressed for faster searching and lookup on the LAN.

We can't get into all the complex details of using NetSetup here. For more information, open the Windows Resource Kit help file located in the \ADMIN\RESKIT\HELPFILE folder of the Windows 95 CD-ROM and search for NETSETUP. You'll also find sample setup scripts and polices in the \ADMIN\RESKIT\SAMPLES folder.

The Policy Editor

Thanks to Policy Editor, configuring Windows 95 on local workstations is easier than ever. You can even access a computer's registry from your own machine. With Policy Editor, you can set certain default registry settings which are enforced on each users' computer. Policy Editor also lets you improve security. For example, you can prevent a computer from running MS-DOS programs, or in fact, prevent access to any programs except those on the Start menu, and you can lock the Start menu to prevent modification.

Policy Editor can also hide all of the desktop, although this also prevents the use of desktop shortcuts and scraps, which we covered in Chapter 4. You can also prevent access to certain Control Panel items or property sheets.

Run POLEDIT from the \ADMIN\APPTOOLS\POLEDIT folder of the Windows 95 CD-ROM. Use File | Open Registry to modify the policies of your local computer. Then click on the ⊞ symbol to expand the list of settings. Turn on a check box for the policies you want to implement. Figure 19-32 shows some of the shell restrictions you set up.

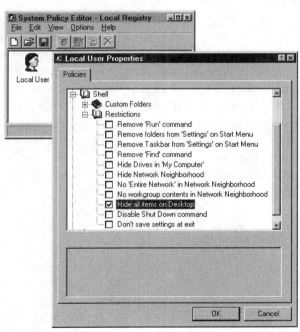

Figure 19-32: *Use POLEDIT (Policy Editor) to control access to Windows 95 features.*

You can then save the policy template to a folder that's accessible to all computers, such as the SYS\PUBLIC directory of a NetWare file server. If you're running only peer-to-peer, you'll have to copy the POLICY.DAT file to the local hard drive of each computer.

This is just an overview of Policy Editor. For more complete documentation, search for POLEDIT in the Windows 95 Resource Kit help file (as we discussed above).

Microsoft Exchange E-Mail

We first discussed Exchange in Chapter 16, where we used Exchange to send faxes. In Chapter 18, we used Exchange to send electronic mail via The Microsoft Network. In that chapter, you found out more about the ways you can creatively format your messages using the message composer. In this chapter, we'll present a quick reference to Explorer, a kind of quick tour.

What's *Not* Covered Here

- **Exchange Server**   Larger networks will benefit from implementing Microsoft Exchange Server, which runs on Windows NT and provides a complete electronic mail and forms database. Exchange Server takes over all the responsibilities of managing electronic mail and boosts the responsiveness and improves the reliability of Microsoft Mail and Exchange. Exchange Server can also link you to other mail services, such as Lotus Notes and MCI Mail.
- **Fax**   Turn to Chapter 16 to learn how to get started with Microsoft Fax and how to compose faxes.
- **Internet**   Consult Chapter 17 to see how to set up Exchange for Internet mail.

The Workgroup Postoffice

The Workgroup Postoffice (WGPO) is a special set of folders used to store and route electronic mail across a network. The network could be anything from a two- or three-computer Microsoft Windows network to a thousand-computer corporate LAN. You only need a WGPO to route Microsoft Mail using Exchange; a WGPO is not necessary for other Exchange services like fax, Internet or The Microsoft Network.

Setting Up a WGPO

If you are setting up Windows 95 for networking for the first time, you'll need to first create a Workgroup Postoffice. Otherwise, if you used Microsoft Mail with Windows for Workgroups (or used the stand-alone Microsoft Mail), then your network already has a Workgroup Postoffice, and you should not create a new one. A given workgroup should have only one WGPO—duplicate postoffices will prevent mail from being routed properly.

You create a WGPO by running the Microsoft Mail Postoffice icon from Control Panel. Windows first asks you if you are going to set up a new postoffice or administer (manage) an existing postoffice. You can do the latter only if you are an authorized administrator, in which case you'll know the user name and password of the WGPO administrator. If you create the WGPO, then you are the administrator.

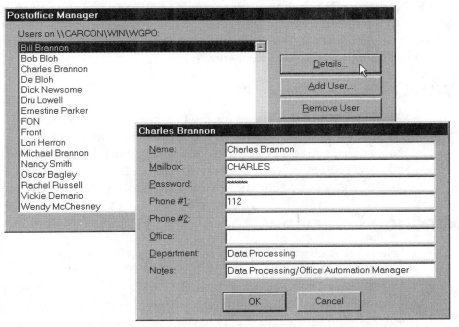

Figure 19-33: *The Workgroup Postoffice manages all the Microsoft Mail users on your network.*

Once you've either created the WGPO or logged in as the administrator, you get to add, modify or remove mail accounts. For each account, you can set the user's full name, account name, password and some other entries to help you keep track of the mail user. (See Figure 19-33.)

Before anyone can log into your postoffice, make sure you are sharing the WGPO folder (for example, create a share called MAIL that shares the C:\WGPO0000 folder on your hard drive). (We discussed sharing earlier in this chapter.) Another alternative is to store the WPGO in a folder on a network drive that's accessible to all employees.

Exchange Mail users will need to know the share name or network directory that contains the WGPO when they run Exchange Setup (discussed in Chapter 16).

On a big LAN, it can be tedious to set up hundreds of individual accounts. If new users attempt to run mail for the first time, they'll just need to know where to find the WPGO. Then they'll be asked if they already have an account on the postoffice and, if not, if they want to create a new account.

This is the same situation you're in if you are setting up Exchange to work with a postoffice managed by someone else. The Exchange Setup Wizard walks you through the steps needed to attach yourself to the mail system. All you need to know is the *path* (drive and directory) of the WGPO and whether you need to create a new account for yourself—ask the WGPO administrator if you aren't sure.

WGPO Address Book

The list of users you create for the Workgroup Postoffice is used as the master address book for Microsoft Mail. Every user in your workgroup can choose this address book when composing mail. Mail users can also create address groups, so you could send mail to all managers, for example. Refer to the reference section later in this chapter for more information.

Exchange Overview

Microsoft Exchange is the key to Windows 95 electronic mail. Out of the box, Exchange only includes services for Microsoft Mail, Microsoft Fax, the Internet and The Microsoft Network. We'll also show you how to add CompuServe to Exchange for easy access to your CompuServe Mail messages. In the future, we expect to see additional Exchange clients for other online services.

Exchange & Microsoft Mail

Exchange sends e-mail using Microsoft Mail. This means you can send and receive mail with users running Microsoft Mail with Windows for Workgroups, even DOS machines running Microsoft Mail. However, unless the recipient is running Windows 95, you can send and receive plain text messages only. Any custom colors, embedded objects, fonts and formatting will be stripped off the message when it's sent.

Profiles

When you set up your Inbox (see Chapter 16), you chose which services (Exchange clients) to include in your default profile. A *profile* determines which services Exchange will use to communicate. Sometimes it may be useful to set up more than one profile. For example, if you use Internet mail infrequently, you can create a separate profile for it. When you use more than one profile, Exchange lets you choose which profile to use when you first open your Inbox. (You have to log off from Exchange if you want to switch between profiles.)

Run the Mail and Fax applet from Control Panel to inspect or manage your profiles. You can also get to the same place by right-clicking on the Inbox icon on your desktop and choosing Properties. If Exchange is already open, you can choose Tools | Services.

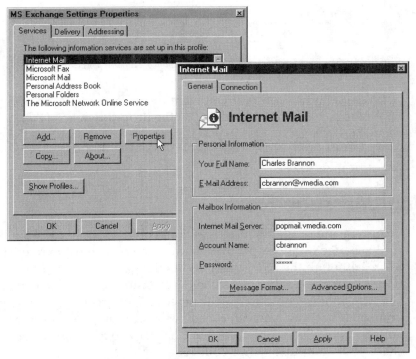

Figure 19-34: *Use Properties to edit the settings for a service.*

The Add and Remove buttons let you change which services are set up with your profile. Use Copy if you want to transfer one of your services, already customized, to another profile. (To move the service, just delete the original after you've copied it.) The Properties button lets you customize all the details for a service. Use the About button to get some general information, such as the version number, about the selected service.

Figure 19-35: *The Profiles view lets you set up custom Exchange sessions.*

Click on Show Profiles if you want to add or remove a custom profile. If you have more than one profile, use the drop-down box (*When starting Microsoft Exchange, use this profile*) to choose which profile is the default profile. When you open your Inbox, Exchange shows this profile first on the list of profiles to use.

Personal Message Store

Incoming and outgoing messages are kept in a special file, stored as C:\Exchange\Mailbox.pst by default. The PST extension refers to a *Personal STore*, although the PST is simply called your "Personal Folders" most of the time. (Your personal address book is also stored in C:\Exchange.)

If you share a computer with someone else, create a separate profile for yourself. That way, you can each have your own personal store and personal address book. See "Passwords" in Chapter 7 to learn more about how to share your computer with a colleague.

Personal Folder Structure

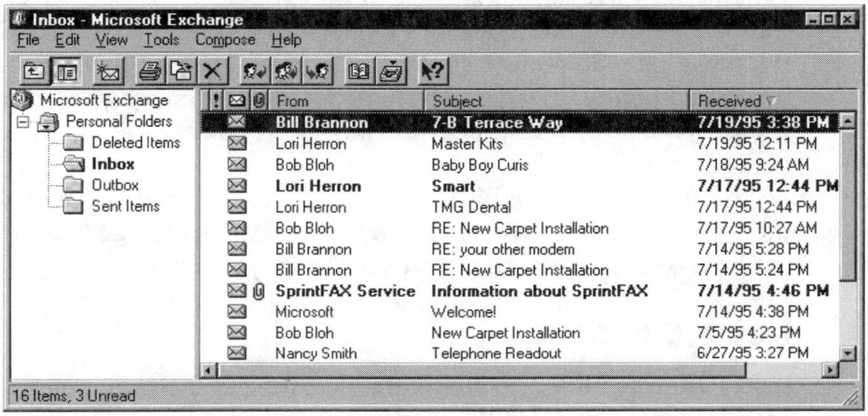

Figure 19-36: *With the folder pane open, you can easily view the structure of your personal store.*

When you first open your Inbox, you only see one folder, your Inbox. Click on the 🔲 toolbar button (or choose View | Folders). That gives you quick access to any of your other folders.

Inbox

When you receive mail, it appears in your Inbox. (A message waiting icon also appears on the taskbar notification area, next to the clock.) You can also save unsent messages in your Inbox. When you're composing a message, simply close the Message Editor. You'll be asked if you want to keep the message. If you do, it will be in your Inbox, ready to send again later.

Outbox

When you click on the Send button, your message is temporarily moved to your Outbox folder. With some services, like Microsoft Mail, your mail is automatically sent rather quickly. If you're online with a service like The Microsoft Network, your mail is also dispatched within a short time. So if you wrote something rash, you had better open your Outbox quickly if you want to cancel the send. Delete messages in the Outbox to prevent them from being sent.

If you're not currently online with a service like Internet Mail, you have to use the Tools | Deliver Now menu choice to force the items in Outbox to be sent. You can also flush your Outbox using Remote Mail (see below).

Sent mail

When a message is sent, a copy of the message is kept in your Sent Mail folder for future reference. It's a good way to review your mail and verify if a message was sent. (Use Receipt Requested with the Message Editor, discussed below, to get concrete proof of your message's reception. However, this only proves that your message was received, not that it has been actually read.)

You'll want to periodically browse your Sent Mail folder and delete old messages to prevent wasting disk space. See "Exchange Options" below to see how to prevent Exchange from keeping Sent Mail.

Deleted mail

Just as there's a Recycle Bin on the desktop, Exchange gives you a Deleted Mail folder in case you change your mind. So when you delete a message, it is simply moved to the Deleted Mail folder. However, normally the Delete Mail folder is emptied when you exit Exchange or shut down Windows. We'll see how to change this if you want to keep your deleted mail until you manually delete it. Naturally, if you delete mail items from Deleted Mail, the mail is permanently removed.

Custom folders

You can create your own custom folders, too, which lets you use Mail as a simple message database. Use File | New Folder to create whatever organization structure you like. You can move messages from your Inbox or Sent Mail folders to your custom folders.

Shared folders

Microsoft Mail also supports the use of shared folders, which are stored in the Workgroup Postoffice. This lets you set up a filing system for the office. For example, you could keep memos relating to corporate policies in a custom shared folder called Office Procedures. The creator of a shared folder can choose which users can access the folder and whether others are allowed to add items or delete items from the folder.

The current version of Exchange does not support shared folders, but this feature is expected to be added to Windows 95 in an upcoming maintenance release.

> **TIP**   Exchange opens separate windows when you compose a message, view a message, open the address book and so on. Use the taskbar buttons to help you bring any window to the top of all other windows if you have trouble finding it.

Browsing Messages

The right-hand pane of Exchange (or the only pane if you've turned off the folders pane) shows you the messages (entries) in the current folder. (The current folder is Inbox unless you choose a different folder from the folders pane.) Each entry is shown in the order that it's received. Notice the headings marked To, Subject, Sent and Size (you may need to resize the Exchange window to see all these headings). These headings are "hot": you can sort the list by any heading just by clicking on it. (Unlike Explorer, you can't click on it a second time to reverse the order of the sort.)

You can also resize the columns by placing the mouse pointer exactly between any two headings. Click and drag without releasing the mouse button toward the left or right to move the boundary between columns, which resizes it. Exchange remembers your custom view the next time you use it.

To open a message for viewing or editing, just double-click on it. Or to compose a new message, choose an option from the Compose menu.

For more information about the main Exchange window, refer to the section "Exchange Menu Reference."

Address Books

When you're sending mail, it's very convenient to keep your most common contacts in a personal address book. You can also use the Postoffice address book (see "Workgroup Postoffice" earlier) to address your mail, and other services like The Microsoft Network and CompuServe Mail also let you keep addresses or access the master address book for the entire service. While Internet mail doesn't have a master list (it would be unimaginably large), the Internet Mail client can verify that the address you use actually exists.

The only address book you can edit yourself is your personal address book. If you share a computer with another person, he or she can create his or her own Exchange profile using a separate address book.

When you're running Exchange, select Tools | Address Book or click on the address book icon 📖 on the Exchange toolbar.

TIP Notice that when you use menus, keyboard hotkeys are shown for popular commands. You can use Ctrl+Shift+B to open the address book.

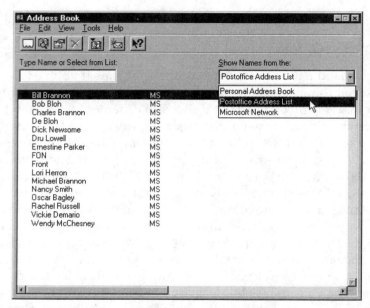

Figure 19-37: *Choose the address book you want to use from the Show Names box.*

Figure 19-37 shows the first panel of the address book. By default, it shows you the Postoffice address book if you're using Microsoft Mail. Click on the box beneath Show Names to choose a different address book, such as your personal address book.

When the address book becomes very large, you'll find it easier to type in part or all of a person's name in the Type Name box to quickly jump to the first address that matches what you've typed. You also can select File I Find or click on the 📇 toolbar icon.

To add an address, choose File I New Entry or click on the 📖 icon on the toolbar. (If the toolbar isn't shown, choose View I Toolbar.)

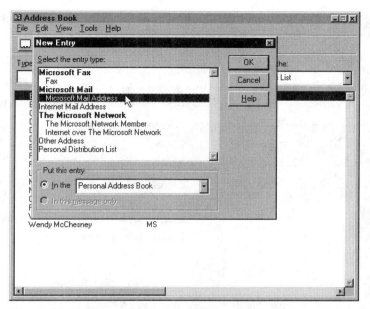

Figure 19-38: *Choose the type of address you want to create.*

As shown in Figure 19-38, the next step is to pick the type of address you want to add. We showed you how to add a fax address in Chapter 16. If you choose Microsoft Mail address, you'll see the dialog box shown in Figure 19-39.

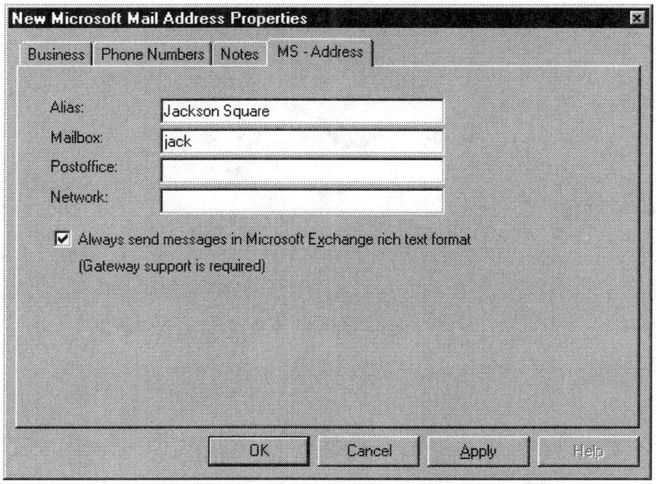

Figure 19-39: *Customize an address by filling in the boxes shown on this panel.*

The rightmost tab heading is shown by default. For Microsoft Mail (MS-Address), fill in the person's real name (Alias), mailbox name, Postoffice (workgroup) and which network hosts the postoffice. Since the Postoffice address book is available for most mail users, you'll rarely need to create it from scratch. You get the same dialog box if you click on an entry in the address book and choose File | Properties or click on the ⌾ icon on the toolbar.

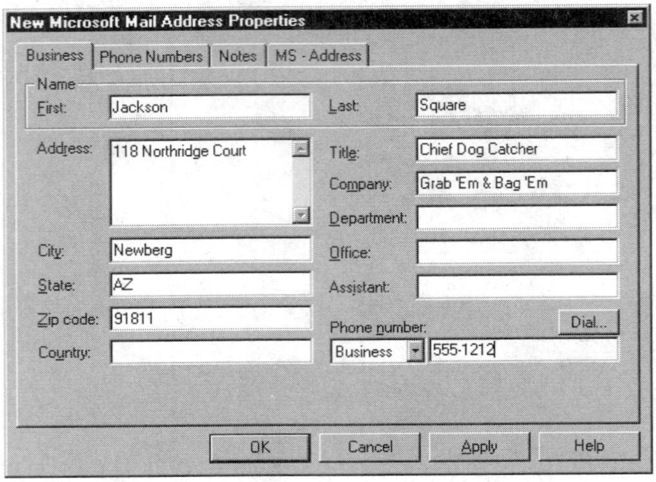

Figure 19-40: *The Business page of Address Properties lets you keep the "snail mail" address for a contact, which can be shown on a fax cover page.*

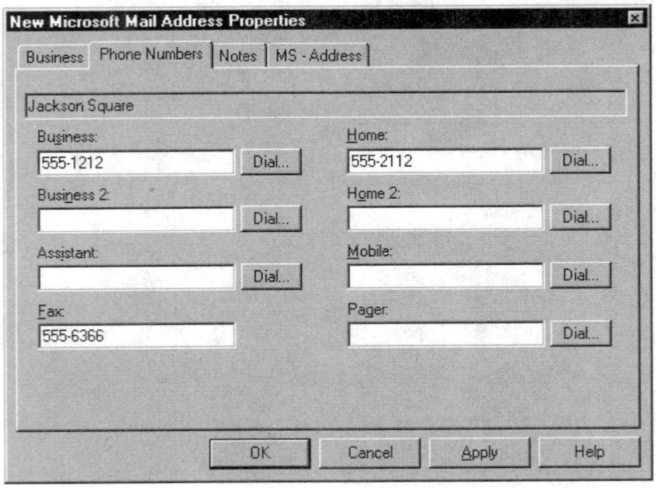

Figure 19-41: *Use the Phone Numbers page of Address Properties to keep track of phone numbers and other contact information. The Notes page lets you write a free-form reminder to yourself about the contact.*

The other tab headings let you use your address book as a simplistic contact manager. Use Business to fill in the complete name, address, title, mailing address and more. The Phone page stores all the related telephone numbers. You can even click on the Dial button to pop up Phone Dialer (see Chapter 16) to connect you automatically with the person, using your modem as a dialing device. (If your company links your telephone system to Windows 95 via TAPI, you can dial without even using a modem. See Chapter 16 for more about TAPI.)

For convenience, you can click on an address and then choose File | New Message or click on the ▣ icon the toolbar to send a message directly to that recipient. If you want to send the message to more than one person, just hold down Ctrl while clicking on names in the address book. Or to select a range of names, click on the first name and then Shift+Click on the last name in the range.

Address Groups

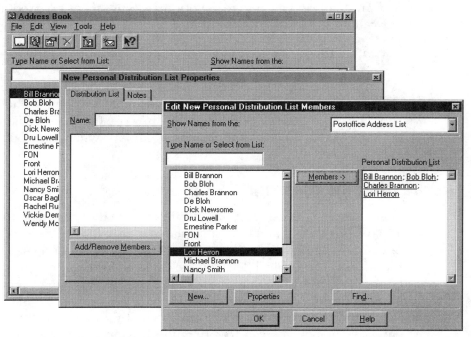

Figure 19-42: *Click on Add/Remove Members to pop up your address book and use it to add the entries you want to include in your list.*

If you frequently send messages to more than one person at the same time, it's more efficient to create an *address group*, also called a *distribution list*. This list can be especially handy for broadcasting a fax to a list of phone numbers, hands-free. First use New Entry to open the list shown in Figure 19-37 and then double-click on Personal Distribution List. As shown in Figure 19-42, type the name of the address list (for example, All Employees) in the Name box. Use Add/Remove Members to pop up one of your address books, also shown in Figure 19-42. Choose the entries you want to add to your distribution list on the left and click on the Members-> button to add them to your list on the right. To delete a member, use the mouse pointer to select the person's name and press the Del key to delete it. (Editing the distribution list box works like editing any other text message. Make sure each entry is separated from the next by only one semicolon.)

Message Editor

The message editor has many talents. It's used to create new mail, reply or forward mail, and even to read your mail. Since it has no fixed name, we'll just call it the Message Editor.

Composing a New Message

When you want to send a message, just click on the ▨ icon on the toolbar (or choose Compose | New Message) from the main Exchange window. The shortcut key is Ctrl+N. While you'll mainly use the Message Editor to compose messages, you also use the Message Editor when you double-click on a message to view it.

Addressing the Message

When sending a message, you can simply type the name of a person in the To box. To verify that the person's name is an actual address, press Ctrl+K or click on the ▨ toolbar button. Or click on the To button itself to pop open the address book, which lets you pick a name from one of your address books. You can also create a new address entry. This works very much like creating an address book entry, which we discussed earlier in this chapter.

Use the CC: (carbon copy) box to specify the name of a secondary recipient or recipients. You can specify multiple recipients in the To box by separating their names with semicolons (or just click on To or CC: to fill in addresses from an address book). But CC: lets the recipient choose to reply either to just the original sender or to all the other recipients shown in the

CC: box. Below, we'll show you how to enable a BCC: (blind carbon copy) box that you can use to send a copy of a message without revealing this fact to any other recipients.

To help the recipient manage his or her mail, try to invent a meaningful Subject line that succinctly summarizes your message. You'll appreciate this helpful tip all the more when you receive mysterious messages titled "Note" or "For your information." Since the same subject line is used when you reply or forward a message, consider whether the subject title is still appropriate if the topic of your conversation shifts. A message about "Crustaceans" may end up talking about "Copapods" after it's replied to over and over again.

Replying to a Message

Another way to send a message is to reply to someone else's message. When you reply, the original message is pasted (quoted) below your message, and your typing is shown in a different color (normally blue). (We'll show you how to choose options for Replying, such as changing the color and font of the reply text.) Normally, you'll use Reply to send a message back to the original composer of the message, so the To: box is filled in automatically. Use Reply All to send a reply to the original author, and send a copy of the reply to the CC: recipients shown in the original message. On the other hand, your CC: box is used to send a copy of the reply to another recipient.

Forwarding a Message

When you receive a message intended for someone else, or if you just want to pass a message along, use Forward. The original message is pasted into your new message, along with the original addressing information. You can type an explanation of why you are forwarding the message, or a message of your own, above the quoted message. The characters "FW:" are added to the subject line. Use the To and CC: boxes to choose who will receive the forwarded message.

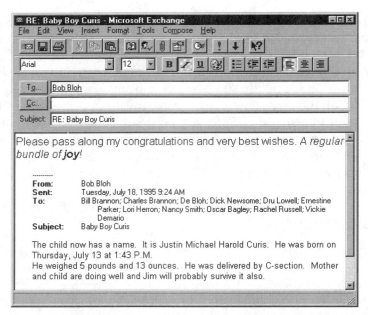

Figure 19-43: *The Message Editor works like a full-featured mini word processor.*

Formatting a Message

We discussed message formatting in Chapters 16 and 18, so we won't belabor the point here. But feel free to use the formatting toolbar or Format menu (see quick reference later in this chapter) to create messages using whatever fonts, colors, type sizes and type styles you prefer.

You might want to limit yourself to the Windows default fonts (Arial, Courier New and Times New Roman) if you want to make sure the recipient can see your message as you sent it. If you use a font that the recipient doesn't have installed, the fonts will be replaced with one of the default fonts that matches your font most closely. For example, if you used Century Schoolbook, a serif typeface, the recipient will see the message formatted with Times New Roman, the default Windows serif typeface.

Inserting Objects

You can even mix graphics with your message. The easiest way is to open the program you used to create the graphic, copy it to the Clipboard and select Edit | Paste in the Message Editor to add it to your message. This method actually works with just about anything you can copy into the Clipboard (use the application's Edit | Copy menu choice).

You can also use the Insert menu to add text to your message from existing files on your hard drive or insert any other kind of object, such as a complete word processing, spreadsheet or presentation document. These objects appear as icons in the message, and a copy of the object is sent to the recipient. The recipient just double-clicks on the object icon to edit it, assuming he or she has a copy of the same program you used to create it. If both parties use Microsoft Fax, you can even send these objects as a fax, and the document arrives not as a traditional fax image, but as the original editable file, just like receiving any other mail message.

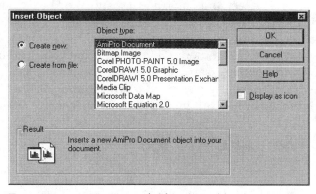

Figure 19-44: *Use Insert | Object to add a document, spreadsheet, graphic or other OLE object to the current message.*

If you select Edit | Paste Special, you can choose the file format appropriate to the object. Just click OK to accept the default association that's active in your computer for the object's file type.

Drag and Drop Mail

You can also insert objects with the mouse by selecting some text or part of a document or graphic image. Drag and drop the selection from the original application to the mail message. If you drag and drop a shortcut to a document or program, the original file is not sent along with the message. Instead, when the recipient double-clicks on the message, he or she opens the original file that's on your hard drive.

To make installing software less tedious, some network administrators will embed a shortcut to the Setup or Install program within a message and mail it to all the users. When you get such a message, just double-click on the program shortcut to start the setup program, which is usually configured to automatically install the program "hands-free"; that is, you don't have to make any choices or decisions. It's theoretically possible to even distribute Windows 95 this way to upgrade Windows for Workgroups users to Windows 95.

See Chapter 11 for more information about using Object Linking and Embedding to mix various objects in your messages.

Sending From Applications

Another way to create a mail message is from the File I Send menu of many applications. For example, when you use File I Send from Microsoft Word, the Word document is "bundled up" into an icon within a mail message, just as if you used Insert I Object and chosen Microsoft Word Document as the object to insert. This can also be a convenient way to send a message as a fax. When sent as a fax, the inserted objects are opened by the program that created them, in order to print them. This printed file is captured and sent as a fax. However, with mail messages or when sending a fax as an editable document (the default when two computers run Microsoft Fax), the objects are not rendered for printing, but just sent intact as icons.

Message Editor Menu Reference

Toolbar

Figure 19-45 shows you all the options available from the Message Editor toolbar and the formatting toolbar. Each toolbar button corresponds to one of the menu choices discussed in the following sections.

Figure 19-45: *Let the mouse pointer rest briefly over any toolbar button to pop up a ToolTip that describes that button.*

File Menu

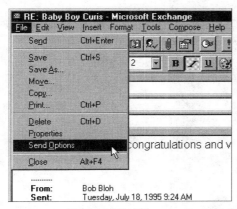

Figure 19-46: *Use the File menu to manage your current message.*

Here are the Message Editor's File menu options:

- **Send**   Transmits the current message by moving it to the Outbox.
- **Save**   Stores the message as a separate file on your hard drive. You can open the message using WordPad.
- **Save As**   Lets you change the name of a message you've already saved.
- **Move**   Transfers the current message (unsent) to a different folder. Just choose the folder you want to use from the list that pops up next.
- **Copy**   Puts a copy of the current message in a different folder. Keeps the message open for editing.
- **Print**   Sends the message to your printer, with all formatting intact.
- **Delete**   Sends the current message to the Deleted Mail folder.
- **Properties**   Pops up an informative box. (See Figure 19-47.)

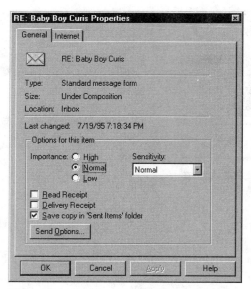

Figure 19-47: *Message Properties lets you see when a message was sent or received, and it lets you change the message's importance (priority).*

■ **Send Options**   Lets you change the Fax send options for a message. See Chapter 16.

■ **Close**   Equivalent to clicking the Close box for the message. Allows you to keep the message in your Inbox in case you want to complete it later.

Edit Menu

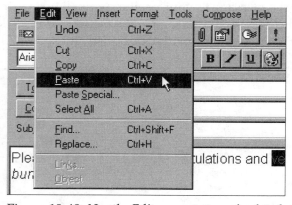

Figure 19-48: *Use the Edit menu to transfer data between applications or between messages.*

Here are the Edit menu options:

- **Undo**   Reverses the last action you performed.
- **Cut**   Deletes the selection and copies it to the Clipboard.
- **Copy**   Copies the current message to the Clipboard.
- **Paste**   Inserts the contents of the Clipboard into the current message.
- **Paste Special**   Lets you choose what type of object to use when inserting the contents of the Clipboard into the current message.
- **Select All**   Highlights the entire message. Use this option prior to copying or cutting the selection to the Clipboard.
- **Find**   Searches within the current message for a word or phrase.
- **Replace**   Same as Find, but also lets you replace each phrase found with a different word or phrase.
- **Links**   Choose this option if you used Paste Link from the Paste Special dialog box to insert a link to an object. You can then update or break the link. (See Chapter 11.)
- **Object**   Choose this option if you used Paste Special to insert an object. You can then edit the object or change its object type.

View Menu

Figure 19-49: *Use the View menu to customize the Send Message user interface.*

Here are the View menu options:

- **Toolbar**   Displays (when checked) or hides (when unchecked) the toolbar.
- **Formatting Toolbar**   Displays (when checked) or hides (when unchecked) the Formatting toolbar. If you're sending messages to a recipient who can't see your formatting, you might turn off the Formatting toolbar to free up some screen space and remind you not to bother with fancy formatting.
- **Status Bar**   Displays (when checked) or hides (when unchecked) the status bar at the bottom of the window.

■ **BCC Box**   Enables (when checked) or disables (when unchecked) the display of the BCC Box, which you can use to specify a blind carbon copy for a recipient. Other recipients will not know that you send that person a copy of the message, hence *blind*.

■ **Previous**   Skips ahead to the next message in the current folder.

■ **Next**   Backs up to the previous message in the current folder.

Insert Menu

Figure 19-50: *Use the Insert menu to add special contents to your message.*

Here are the Insert menu options:

■ **File**   Inserts the contents of a text file or other document, such as a Word or WordPad document, as message text.

■ **Message**   Inserts the contents of a different mail message into the current message.

■ **Object**   Inserts an entire file or document into the current message. The object is usually shown as an icon. When you insert an object, you can also choose to create a new object, such as a Paint picture, on the spot rather than insert one from a file.

Format Menu

Figure 19-51: *The Format menu is highly redundant—just use the formatting toolbar.*

Here are the Format menu options:

■ **Font**   Pops up the Font formatting dialog box. You'll find it's more convenient just to use the Formatting toolbar.

■ **Paragraph**   Left-justifies, right-justifies or centers the current paragraph or paragraphs you've highlighted with the mouse. It's more convenient to click on the corresponding buttons on the toolbar.

Tools Menu

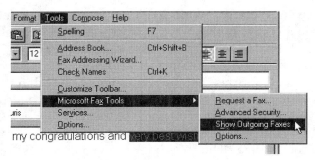

Figure 19-52: *The Tools menu is a busy place. Use it to run Exchange utilities or set special options.*

Here are the Tools menu options:

■ **Spelling**   Runs a spelling check on the current document. Or checks only the current word or phrase if you've selected something with the mouse.

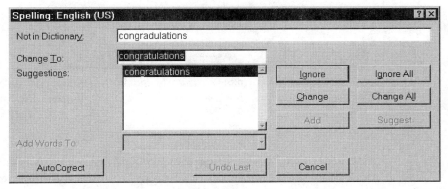

Figure 19-53: *The spelling checker suggests replacements for incorrect spellings. If it doesn't recognize a word that you know is spelled correctly, use Add to add the word to your custom dictionary.*

■ **Address Book**   Opens the address book, which we discussed earlier in this chapter.

■ **Fax Addressing Wizard**   Works like Compose New Fax. Instead of walking you all the way through the process, the Wizard returns you to the Message Editor to actually compose your fax. This way, you have far more control over how you format your fax.

■ **Check Names**   Confirms that the names you've typed in the To: and CC: boxes match names in one of your address books. It also replaces the name you typed with the full name of the recipient. For example, if you typed *Bill*, it would be replaced by *Bill Brannon*. This feature works best if you set the default address book to the one you use most frequently.

■ **Customize Toolbar**   Lets you turn on or off toolbar buttons.

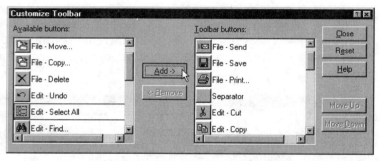

Figure 19-54: *Choose the buttons you want to add on the left and click on the Add-> button, or use the <-Remove button to "put back" a toolbar button. Click on Reset to restore the normal toolbar.*

■ **Microsoft Fax Tools**   Choose either Request a Fax, Advanced Security, Show Outgoing Faxes or Options from the flyout submenu. See Chapter 16.

■ **Services**   Opens the dialog box discussed in the "Profiles" section. See Figure 19-33.

■ **Options**   Lets you customize all Exchange options. See "Exchange Options" later in this chapter.

Compose Menu

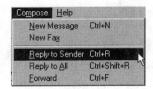

Figure 19-55: *Use the Compose menu to create messages. These menu entries also exist as toolbar icons.*

Here are the Compose menu options:

- **New Message** Opens a new Message Editor window to compose a message.
- **New Fax** Starts the Compose Fax Wizard to walk you through creating a fax memo.
- **Reply to Sender** Normally disabled when you're editing a new message. But when you're viewing an existing message, you can choose to reply to it.
- **Reply to All** Same as above, but sends the message to the author and recipients shown in the original message's To: and CC: boxes.
- **Forward** Instead of composing a reply or a new message, you can simply forward the current message you're looking at.

Message Editor as Message Viewer

The appearance of the message editor changes when you are merely reading a message from one of your folders. At first glance (see Figure 19-56), the message viewer looks quite similar. But note that it lacks the formatting toolbar. You also can't change the addressing information. The toolbar gains convenient previous/next message arrows. If you want to edit a message you're reading, use Forward to open the message using the editor mode.

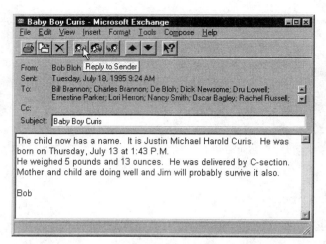

Figure 19-56: *You can't edit a message while reading it, but you can Reply or Forward it.*

Exchange Menu Reference

Although the main Exchange window (often called Inbox) appears to offer most of the same options as the Message Editor, many of the menu choices actually work a little bit differently.

Toolbar

Figure 19-57 points out the toolbar icons that are unique to the Inbox window. Refer to Figure 19-45 for the other buttons. These buttons correspond to the menu choices in the following sections. Some menu options let you work on more than one message at a time. Ctrl+Click to select more than one message, or click on the first message and Shift+Click on the last message to select a group of entries. (Unlike Explorer, you can't drag a selection "lasso" around items to select them.)

Figure 19-57: *The Inbox (Exchange) window sports a convenient toolbar for quick reference to menu commands.*

File Menu

Figure 19-58: *The main Exchange File menu lets you manage message entries.*

Here are Exchange's File menu options:

- ▓ **Open**   Lets you retrieve a message you saved from the Message Editor as a separate file on your hard drive.
- ▓ **Save As**   Converts the current or selected messages.
- ▓ **Move, Copy, Print**   Transfers the current or selected messages between folders or prints them.
- ▓ **New Folder**   Creates another folder. Turn on the folder view with Tools | Folders if you want to view all your folders instead of just the contents of the Inbox folder.
- ▓ **Delete**   Removes the highlighted item from the current folder by moving it to the Deleted Items folder. (Deleting from the Deleted Items folder is permanent, however.)
- ▓ **Rename**   Changes the name of a folder.
- ▓ **Properties**   See Figure 19-47. You can also view the properties for a folder.
- ▓ **Import**   Lets you open another document as a mail message. It's similar to using Import File from the Message Editor.
- ▓ **Exit**   Closes Exchange, freeing up memory and unloading any Exchange services, such as Microsoft Fax. Make sure you send any outgoing mail before you exit.
- ▓ **Exit and Log Off**   Not only exits Exchange, but also logs you off from Microsoft Mail. This option is useful if another person wants to log onto his or her mail account on your machine using a different profile. If you're running any other mail-enabled programs, such as Microsoft Schedule+, those programs also shut down.

Edit Menu

Figure 19-59: *The main Edit menu lets you change the status of messages or choose them all for subsequent File menu operations.*

Here are the Edit menu options:

■ **Select All**   Highlights all the entries in the current folder. You can then copy, move, print or delete all messages at once.

■ **Mark as Read**   When you first receive a message, it's marked in bold-face type to show that it's new, that you haven't read it yet. Use Mark as Read if you plan to ignore a message without ever even reading it, yet you don't want to delete it outright.

■ **Mark as Unread**   Once you read a message, it's no longer boldfaced to remind you that it's a new message. Use Mark as Unread if you want to tell yourself to review the message again later.

View Menu

Figure 19-60: *Use the View menu to change the way the Exchange window appears.*

Here are the View menu options:

■ **Folders**   Turns on (when checked) or turns off (when unchecked) the left folders pane.

■ **Toolbar**   Enables or disables the toolbar.

■ **Status Bar**   Enables or disables the status bar.

■ **New Window**   Opens another main Exchange window for the current folder.

■ **Columns**   Normally, the right-hand pane of Exchange (or the only view if you don't have the folders panel enabled) shows only these columns: To, Subject, Sent and Size. You may need to resize the Exchange window to see all these columns. Use View I Columns if you want to choose from a wide array of additional message properties. This way, you can create a custom view and easily sort by any property.

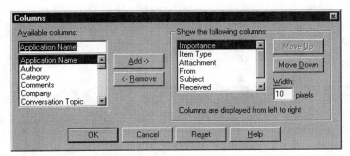

Figure 19-61: *Use View I Columns to design a custom view of your Inbox or other folders.*

■ **Sort**   While you can simply click on any column heading to sort by that column, you can also use View I Sort to display the list by any other message category, even if that column isn't currently shown.

Tools Menu

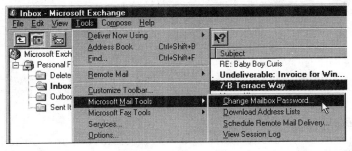

Figure 19-62: *The Tools menu offers utilities and options for Exchange.*

Here are the Tools menu options:

- **Deliver Now Using** *(Service)*   Lets you send and receive mail from any of the services in your profile. May cause Exchange to connect to a service using your modem or other network connection. Use All Services to completely update all your mail.
- **Address Book**   Opens your address book, which we covered earlier in this chapter.
- **Find**   If your Inbox or other folder gets crazy with too many messages, use Find to attempt to locate a message. For convenience, most of the features of the main Exchange menus are also available. Use the Advanced option to narrow your search to specifics such as the date it was sent or to search by the size of the message, among other things.

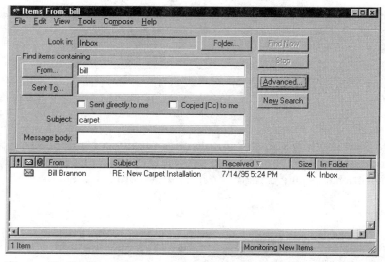

Figure 19-63: *Choose From to search by author or choose Sent To if you want to search by recipient. Click on Folder to search from another folder. Use the Subject line to search for any phrase within a message or use Message body to search the message text. The new messages appear in the box below. Click on a heading to sort the list by that category.*

- **Remote Mail**   See the "Remote Mail" section.
- **Customize Toolbar**   Lets you add or remove items to the Exchange toolbar.

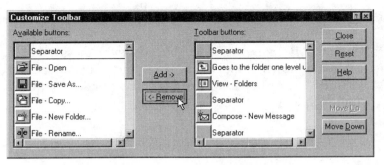

Figure 19-64: *Choose the buttons you want to add on the left and click on the Add-> button, or use the <-Remove button to "put back" a toolbar button. Click on Reset to restore the normal toolbar.*

- **Microsoft Mail Tools**   Choose Change Mailbox Password, Download Address Lists, Schedule Remote Mail Delivery or View Session Log from the flyout submenu.
- **Microsoft Fax Tools**   Choose either Request a Fax, Advanced Security, Show Outgoing Faxes or Options from the flyout submenu. See Chapter 16.
- **Services**   Opens the dialog box discussed in the "Profiles" section. See Figure 19-33.
- **Options**   Lets you customize all Exchange options. See "Exchange Options" later in this chapter.

Compose Menu

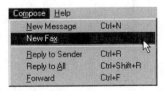

Figure 19-65: *Use the Compose menu to create messages. These menu entries also exist as toolbar icons.*

Here are the Compose menu options:

- **New Message**   Opens a new Message Editor window to compose a message.
- **New Fax**   Starts the Compose Fax Wizard to walk you through creating a fax memo.

- **Reply to Sender**   Opens the Message Editor to reply to only the author of the current or selected messages.
- **Reply to All**   Same as above, but sends the message to the author and recipients shown in the original message's To: and CC: boxes.
- **Forward**   Transfers a copy of the current or selected messages to another recipient.

Help

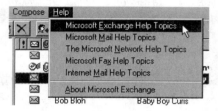

Figure 19-66: *The Help menu displays separate choices for each Exchange service.*

Use the Help menu to find out more about Exchange. You'll find specific help available for whatever task you're currently working on, or you can browse through the entire Exchange online manual. Remember that Help also lets you search by index entries, or even search for a key word or phrase. You can also print help topics for convenient reference.

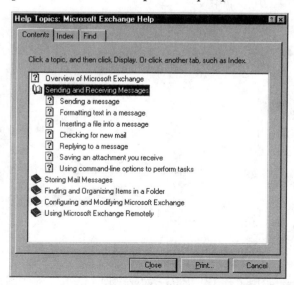

Figure 19-67: *Turn to Help whenever you get stuck.*

Remote Mail Menu Reference

Some services require a modem connection to transfer mail. Since this process can be sluggish, especially with a modem slower than 14,400 bps, you may prefer to use the Remote Mail version of Exchange. Remote Mail is only available for Internet Mail, The Microsoft Network and optional services like CompuServe Mail.

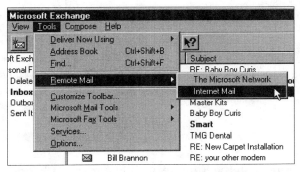

Figure 19-68: *Choose Tools | Remote Mail from the main Exchange menu, and choose the service you want to use from the flyout menu.*

You can use Remote Mail only if you configured your service for "Download remote headers." (See "Exchange Options" later in this chapter.) The idea of Remote Mail is that you want to call up the remote service, download just the headers (subject lines) of your messages and then hang up the phone.

You can then mark the messages that you want to actually retrieve or mark messages to be deleted from the remote service. Then you reconnect with the service to actually retrieve or delete the messages and finally you disconnect.

You can read and reply to your messages *offline*, that is, without relying on a continuous and often expensive telephone connection. When you're ready to send your replies and get any new message headers, you reconnect again. So your interaction with the remote services takes place in fits and starts, bursts of frenetic activity punctuated by leisurely reading and replying.

If you have a fast modem connection to the service, you might prefer to use the Tools | Deliver Now Using option from the main Exchange windows. This is ideal if you like to keep a running telephone or network connection, which is common if you're also using Dial-Up Networking to access files and printers on the remote network.

Toolbar

Figure 19-69: *Let the mouse pointer rest briefly on any toolbar icon to pop up a helpful ToolTip description.*

File Menu

Usually, the only option on the Remote Mail File menu is Properties, which we discussed earlier in this chapter.

Edit Menu

The Edit menu is disabled if you haven't yet transferred remote headers. Following are the available menu options.

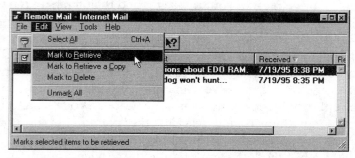

Figure 19-70: *Use Remote Mail's Edit menu to manage your message headers.*

■ **Select All**   Highlights all message headers for a subsequent Edit action. You can use Ctrl+Click to selectively choose messages, or you can click on the first message and Shift+Click on the last message to select a group of messages.

■ **Mark to Retrieve**   Flags the message to be retrieved the next time you connect. When the message is retrieved, the original is deleted from the remote service so it doesn't keep coming back to haunt you.

■ **Mark to Retrieve a Copy**   Same as above, but leaves the original mail in your remote service's mailbox.

■ **Mark to Delete**   Flags the message to be deleted the next time you connect.

■ **Unmark All**   Turns off all Marking flags.

View Menu

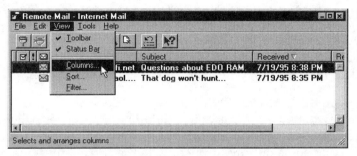

Figure 19-71: *Use View to enable the toolbar or sort the entries.*

Remote Mail's View menu options are the same as those discussed for the main Exchange window. However, instead of Find, use Filter to transfer only the message headers that match the search specifications you choose.

Tools Menu

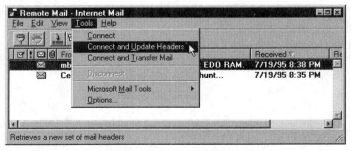

Figure 19-72: *Use Remote Mail's Tools menu to connect to the remote service and update your mailbox.*

Here are Remote Mail's Tools menu options:

- ■ **Connect**   Dials up the remote service and keeps you online. You still have the advantage of selective message retrieval, but you don't have to make a series of modem telephone calls.
- ■ **Connect and Update Headers**   Dials up the remote service, updates the list of message headers (which show only the Subject of each message) and disconnects (hangs up the modem).
- ■ **Connect and Transfer Mail**   Dials up the remote service, sends any outgoing mail, retrieves any messages you've marked and then disconnects.
- ■ **Disconnect**   Forces a disconnection from the remote service.
- ■ **Microsoft Mail Tools**   See "Exchange Menu Reference."
- ■ **Options**   See "Exchange Menu Reference."

Exchange Options

You can open the Exchange Options from the Tools menu of any Exchange window. Now let's take a look at its plethora of Properties panels. Most of the options here are self-explanatory; we provide the figures for your reference. Note that some options apply only to the current message or selected messages. If you don't have anything selected, the Options set the default properties for Exchange. The Services panel is covered earlier in this chapter.

TIP   While you have the Exchange Options open, you can't click on or use any other Exchange window until you close it. That may explain the mysterious beeps you get and the occasional inability to actually use Exchange: You have the Exchange Options dialog box (or other dialog box) open, and it's probably hidden by other windows. Repeatedly press Alt+Esc to switch to the dialog box and then close it.

General

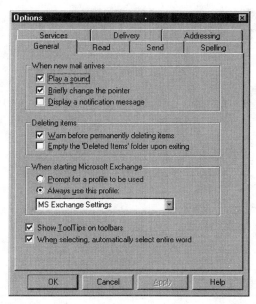

Figure 19-73: *When you receive new mail, you can choose how you're notified, to play a "mail beep," flash the mail icon in place of your arrow pointer or even pop up a message box on the General panel. Under the When Starting Microsoft Exchange section, choose the Prompt for a profile to be used option if you're using more than one profile (see "Profiles").*

Read

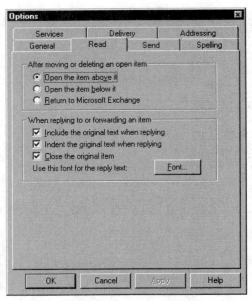

Figure 19-74: _Read options let you customize the way you open and reply to messages. Click on Font to choose the typeface and color used when you're replying to a message._

Send

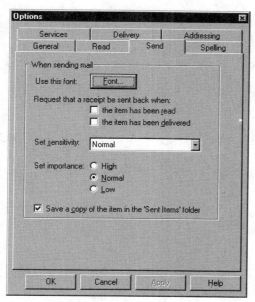

Figure 19-75: *On the Send panel, click on Font to choose the default typeface and color for composing messages. Use the Request receipt option if you want a message notifying you that your message has been either read or delivered. Use the Sensitivity option to choose between Personal, Private or Confidential, which causes a special icon to appear next to the message in the recipient's mailbox. Importance affects the urgency of the message: High causes an immediate notification to be sent to the user. Turn off the Save a copy of the item option if you don't want to clutter up your Sent Items folder.*

Spelling

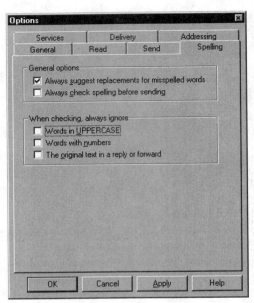

Figure 19-76: *By default, all the check boxes are turned off on the Spelling panel. If you want only misspelled words to be flagged, turn on the Always suggest option. Or use the Always check option to perform an automatic spell check. You can ignore certain types of misspellings using the When checking section.*

Delivery

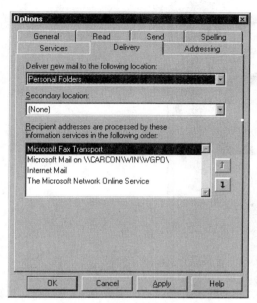

Figure 19-77: *Normally, you'll receive mail in your Personal Folders message storage location. On the Delivery panel, you can choose a different personal store to receive your messages, perhaps when you're on vacation. The Secondary location option is used in case mail can't be received at your normal location. The last part of the box specifies the order in which destination addresses are processed. For example, if you move The Microsoft Network above Internet Mail, then any mail sent to an Internet address will be sent via MSN, not via your Internet connection.*

Addressing

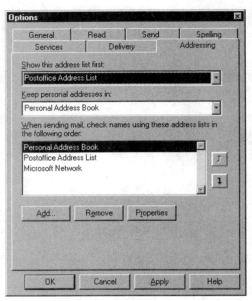

Figure 19-78: *Use the first box of the Addressing panel to control your default address list and the second to choose where you create new addresses (normally you have only the Personal Address Book choice). When you use Tools \ Check Names, the list at the bottom of this page determines which address books take precedence. For example,* Mike Young *might be a name in your personal address book, and* Mike Brannon *might be listed in the Postoffice address list. By default, if you type* **Mike** *in the To: box, it will be converted to* Mike Young. *Reverse the order in the list if you prefer one address book to another.*

Moving On

Now that you're an expert on networks, don't be surprised if colleagues begin to rely on you for help. You might even end up as an ad-hoc network administrator if you aren't careful!

Now let's have some fun. In our next chapter, we'll take a dazzling tour of Windows 95 multimedia features and learn how to get the best game, graphics and sound performance out of your PC.

Expert Windows

Chapter 20

Multimedia

Multimedia is a fancy term for what used to be called A-V, audio-visual, in high school. Remember? There was a room or large closet stuffed with carts holding record players, audio tape machines, film projectors and so on. In recent years, CD players and VCRs have joined the older technologies. Multimedia exploits what was called *son et lumière* in the nineteenth-century—sound and light. Multimedia is both audio and video, capabilities relatively new to computers.

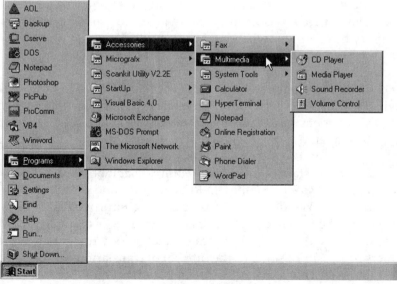

Figure 20-1: *Click on Start, then Programs, Accessories and finally, Multimedia.*

Until recently, computers displayed black-and-white text but were silent, except for the odd, primitive squawk coming through the computer's tiny built-in speaker. Now, computing can include movies and high-quality sound. Those features can greatly enrich the computing environment. You can now insert a spoken message into a letter to a friend or add a short video of your family to your e-mail Christmas cards. You can compose and even edit music or video with your computer. And of course, games and educational software become much more compelling when they include realistic video and CD-quality stereo sound.

What's New In Windows 95

Windows 95 comes with several built-in multimedia programs—software accessories that communicate with and govern the behavior of your CD-ROM, sound card and video peripherals. We'll explore each of these accessories, but first, here's some background on new multimedia features in Windows 95.

One improvement in multimedia capability in Windows 95 is Plug and Play. Sound cards, and to a lesser extent CD-ROM units, were notoriously touchy in Windows 3.1. They often required setting complicated switches, and sometimes they interfered with other hardware or software. Plug and Play (see Chapter 15) is designed to eliminate those problems and turn the burden over to the computer when you want to add a new multimedia peripheral.

Windows 95 also includes an auto-start feature that triggers the CD and makes it do something simply by putting a CD into the CD drive. If the CD includes a startup file (named AUTORUN.INF), Windows 95 will follow whatever instructions it finds in this file—opening a menu, starting a game. All this happens automatically, as soon as you slide the CD drawer back into the CD player. (Nothing will happen, though, if your CD-ROM unit isn't compliant and recognized as a unit supported by Windows 95. You can still use it, but this startup triggering requires that it be on Windows 95's list of known types. Contact your CD-ROM vendor and get a Windows 95 driver.)

Other new Windows 95 features include improved audio and video compression (the files take up less space with no loss of quality). MIDI music has been improved via a "polymessage" technology that, in effect, relieves your microprocessor of some of the burden of translating complicated, dense MIDI music. This reduces the likelihood that you'll hear any "hiccups" or interruptions during playback of complex MIDI music. No longer must you have a separate program (Video for Windows) to play video—video support is built into Windows 95. If your CD-ROM unit permits it, you can listen to audio CDs while you work at the computer. This is possible because of Windows 95's multitasking facilities (more than one thing can be happening at the same time), and also because Windows 95 now includes a CD player with many features for playing audio CDs.

CD-ROM games and other programs benefit from improved performance—faster response and near-hard drive speed of access—thanks to Windows 95's new 32-bit CD file management system (CDFS), caching (holding frequently accessed data in RAM—random access memory), and higher speed CD-ROM units (2X, 3X, 4X and even 6X speeds). The CD is rapidly becoming an essential computer peripheral.

Some of Windows 95's multimedia features, though, aren't very practical, at least for now. There's support for Pioneer LaserDisc players—by adding a special video card you can view movies on your computer screen and control the player (pause, skip, etc.). Beyond that, you can add special cards to control a videotape player (VISCA), record digital video, display regular television (in a window or full screen) on your computer monitor, play FM radio and so on.

However, for many people, playing LaserDiscs, recording or playing videotapes or watching TV are best accomplished with a normal TV or a normal video camera. After all, the viewing area of your computer screen is valuable real estate. Why use it to watch regular TV? If you want to watch TV while you work at your computer, you might be better off—and you'll certainly save money—if you just buy a $200 TV and put in on your computer desk next to the monitor. Likewise, even a few seconds of digitally recorded video can take up many megabytes of disk space. If you want to make video recordings, ordinary videotape is far more efficient. You can store hours of video on a $4 tape. These few multimedia applications seem dubious—at least until RAM becomes far cheaper and computer monitors become wall-sized. However, much other multimedia is not only useful now, it's a major advance in the utility and pleasure of computing itself. Let's consider what's ahead in the next few years.

The Game Plan

Microsoft and other companies understand the importance of multimedia. For one thing, computers compete with television. There's no inherent reason why computers shouldn't be as entertaining as TV and, indeed, far more flexible. The idea of combining computers and television into one super-appliance isn't new, but this goal has never been closer to realization. Multimedia is the wave of the future. It changes the emphasis—moving computers from a business-oriented machine to an entertainment center. That shifts the focus from text-based computing—tasks you're required to do—to "programs" that you want to watch and interact with. In other words, Microsoft is moving from its traditional role as a language and operating system purveyor (MS-DOS, Windows, etc.) to an entertainment empire.

It's intriguing to note that the Microsoft "Home" line of products (games, the Encarta encyclopedia, Cinemania, Art Gallery, Mozart, Baseball and all their other multimedia titles) is expected to become Microsoft's biggest division in the next few years. Bill Gates has predicted that Microsoft will be "coming out with a new title every week" in a few years.

Also, CD isn't the only medium for delivering high-quality video and audio to the computer. Introductory versions of Encarta and Microsoft Bookshelf are available on the Microsoft Network (see Chapter 18). This means you can get multimedia over the telephone. Sure, the first time you use it you have to wait 10-15 minutes while Bookshelf's engine (the search program) is downloaded from the Network onto your hard disk. But after that, you can search nearly as fast as you could if the CD were in your local machine. And telephone communication speeds will vastly improve in the coming decade. Eventually, your computer should be able to interact with the Microsoft Network as swiftly as your TV receives the nightly news.

Interactivity transforms television from passive, voyeuristic viewing into engaging, personalized learning and recreation.

The famous difference between TV and computers is *interactivity*. With traditional TV, you listen to the news that Dan Rather wants to describe, in the order he wants to present it. With interactive television, you'll be able to filter the news based on your preferences and interests. What's more, you'll be able to vote or send other messages *back* to the broadcast. How these new capabilities will eventually change our lives is under debate; that they *will* change our lives, though, is certain. Let's take a look at some of the multimedia technologies you can use today in Windows 95.

Multimedia Terminology

Before we start playing movies and music, let's define some terms: digitization, sampling, .WAV files, MIDI, MPC and codec.

Digitization

Computers work with numbers, *digits*. There are of course, only ten digits: 0-9, but combinations of digits can describe all kinds of numbers—negative, fractional, huge. (Internally, computers use *binary* symbols, different from our familiar decimal digits. But this doesn't matter—the number 5 is still 5 no matter what symbols you use to describe it. It's always that number of fingers on a hand in any language.)

When you gang sets of numbers together, these series of numbers can describe (and store) all kinds of things: pictures, symphonies, whatever can be seen or heard. But reality—a sunset, a rose, the sound of a piano—is not digital. Reality, as we see or hear it, is in a state of flux, continuous, seamless. For example, when you listen to a piano, your eardrum is responding to sound waves coming through the air. You can't see them, but they're disturbances in the air just like waves on the ocean are disturbances in water.

Perhaps the easiest way to grasp the meaning of *digital* information is to compare the old fashioned vinyl record with today's CD. A record is an *analog* recording; it's like an analogy to the music it stores. A soft master disk spins on a turntable while the music plays. The sound waves bump against a membrane in a microphone, which in turn causes a needle to cut wavy patterns—grooves—in the disk. In short, the air waves are mimicked in the soft vinyl. It's an analogy of the wave patterns in the air, and when played back, a needle again moves through the grooves, riding the waves and sending this continuous pattern to the speakers so they can pump in and out, causing waves in the air.

A CD is *digital*. It starts out the same as a vinyl record. The band plays, and the air vibrations are detected by a microphone. But instead of moving a needle, the waves are translated very rapidly into numbers—individual, discontinuous symbols. These numbers (or "samples") describe how high the waves are (the "amplitude" or loudness of each sound wave) and how often the waves occur (the "frequency" or pitch). A laser burns patterns of microscopic pits in the CD that represent the series of numbers. After this laser burn we now have purely *mathematical* descriptions of waveforms—a CD is like a thick book with page after page containing lists of numbers. This is quite different from the sculpture in vinyl, a long, winding bas relief that looks like the original air-wave patterns. Analog *imitates* the original; digital *describes* it.

If you could get very tiny and walk along a groove in a vinyl record, it would look as though you were walking through a deep canyon. You'd see warps, ripples along both canyon walls. A few huge, deep bends along the walls would represent a drum hit; a piccolo would appear as many shallow ruffles. You'd be seeing a frozen image of the original music—warps and waves that look just like the air would look, if you could watch it vibrate while listening to this music.

By contrast, if a tiny you walked across the surface of a CD, the landscape would be perfectly flat, metallic, with faint, shimmering rainbow reflections. In the metal film sandwiched between plastic layers, you'd see many millions of tiny pits, pinpricks where the metal had vaporized as the master recorder laser set down lists of numbers. These seemingly random patterns of pits don't look like waves at all. They are instead a code, symbols like the bumps on elevator buttons that represent numbers to the blind. On the futuristic surface of a CD, there is no visible *analogy* to anything in the real world. The relentless sameness you see in all directions appears unnatural, and it *is* unnatural. It's pure information.

Digitized sounds or images have several distinct advantages over analog storage methods. Digital information takes less room. You can describe a deep wave (a low frequency) with a single large number rather than by carving out a big chunk of vinyl. What's more, you can *compress* numbers. If there's twenty seconds of silence, you can compress it into a description like this: (20) 0 rather than 00000000000000000000. If you try to compress analog silence, you just get fewer seconds of silence, so it's impractical.

Also, because numbers can be easily manipulated by the computer, you can effortlessly achieve all kinds of special effects—equalization (emphasizing certain tonal ranges), delay, echo, reverb, etc. Attempting these same effects in the analog realm is much less direct, and the results are less precise. But best of all, digitization avoids distortion, or noise. Once you've made your pitted number codes in a CD, it's essentially impossible for the information to be degraded—numbers are stable. The number 15 isn't going to turn into the number 439 no matter how roughly you handle the CD or how long it sits on the shelf. Analog records are subject to everything from heat to dust to the violence of a needle scratch. From day one, a vinyl record is slowly dying, sinking into noise from contamination. When enough time passes, you can hardly bear to listen to the music through a haze of hissing, popping noise.

All the advantages of CD's over vinyl records (or cassette tapes, for that matter) apply equally to digitization of visual images. Morphing, *Forrest Gump*, and hundreds of other kinds of special effects are impossible without the digital intervention of the computer. Likewise, extreme clarity can be achieved with digital images. In the next few years we should see television cross the digital border to high-definition TV (HDTV). When that happy day arrives, we'll no longer suffer from the ghosting, snow, smearing, dot crawl, sparklies, false color and all the other visual noise that's been with us since the advent of commercial TV in the early '50s.

Sampling

How is something digitized, turned from a continuous natural wave into discrete numbers? Assume that we're going to sample a flying bird. We first decide how often to take a snapshot of the bird. (This frequency of the samples is called the *sampling rate*. CDs sample music at 44.1kHz, roughly 44 thousand samples per second! Thus, a 60-minute CD would contain over 180 million numbers (samples). A lower sample rate results in a rougher, less accurate sound.

But back to the bird. You can sample a flying bird at 24 times per second and when you play the "frames" back, the eye will think it's seeing a continuous movement as the wings wave up and down and the bird moves smoothly across the sky. Our *movie* camera, then, takes 24 *still* photos per second. If you look at a film strip you'll see the individual still shots, each slightly different from the one before. Yet fluid motion results when the frames are run continuously past a projector lamp. If you sample at too low a rate, the wings will seem jerky and the bird will seem to lurch across the sky. What you would then be seeing is the true discontinuity that underlies sampling.

Of course, a traditional celluloid movie isn't actually *digitized*—the samples remain analog photos. To digitize images, you have to sample enormous amounts of information: 921,600 samples *per second* for a 640 x 480 video on your computer screen. That's why even a short digital video clip (an .AVI file) is so huge. For an example, click on Start, then Programs | Accessories | Multimedia. Click on Media Player. In the Device menu, select Video for Windows. Now, find SKIING.AVI, the sample video clip that comes with Windows 95. It will be in your Windows\Media directory. Open it.

The *skiing.avi* file is only installed if you choose "Sample sounds and video" from the Multimedia options during Windows 95 setup. (It's also only available on the CD-ROM version of WIndows 95.) You can use Add/Remove Programs, Windows Setup from Control Panel if you want to put it on your hard drive. Or just open one of the videos in the \funstuff folder of the WIndows 95 CD-ROM.

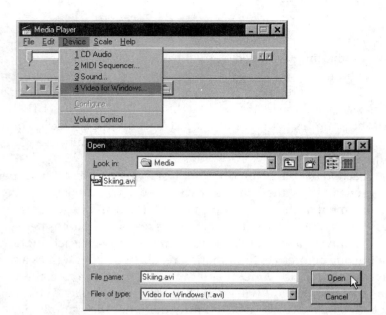

Figure 20-2: *This sample video clip, SKIING.AVI, is located in the Media folder in your Windows directory (assuming you installed it. See Tip).*

Figure 20-3: *The skiing clip has 154 frames and lasts 10 seconds.*

Note that SKIING.AVI is far from full-motion, high-definition video. It has just a little over 15 frames per second, so the motion is somewhat rough—not continuous. It's also only 1/4 screen size. You can make it larger on your screen by selecting Configure from the Device menu. However, if you make the clip full screen, you'll see further degradations, the vivid results of a sampling rate that's too low. At this magnification, the image displays the classic telltale low-sampling-rate "mosaic" pattern—squares and rectangles. A high enough sampling rate would reduce these blocks to invisibility. Your eye couldn't detect the individual samples, and the image would appear accurate, clean and highly detailed. High-resolution video is, in a word, *realistic*. The obvious blocks of sampling in Figure 20-4 would disappear, and the clip would look like a movie instead of a lurching mosaic slide show. Enlarging also makes the 15-frames-per-second rate more annoying: the skier seems to wobble rapidly down the slope, and some frames are simply skipped—the computer can't redraw the screen fast enough to display them all. There's nothing fluid or graceful about it.

 The best way to improve the fluidity of video is to invest in an accelerated video card. Many new video cards feature hardware support for *interpolation, color conversion and scaling*. These relieve your CPU of the burden of translating and enhancing the size and resolution of a video. Otherwise, you'll need a fast Pentium machine and at least local-bus video to get best results when playing video. Use *Original Size* for fastest playback.

Figure 20-4: *Enlarged, the video reveals its individual samples—rectangles and squares.*

Yet even though SKIING.AVI is far from true high-definition digital TV, its mere ten seconds requires 1.5 million bytes on disk! You can imagine the storage requirements of a high-definition digitized two-hour movie. Nonetheless, there have been several recent breakthroughs in compression techniques and increased densities of optical media like CDs. As a result, a consortium led by Toshiba will introduce a consumer video technology in 1996 that will contain a complete movie on a single CD. The new movie-on-CD format is a step in the direction of true digital HDTV. These "super density" discs, (SD), can hold 18 *gigabytes* of data, vs. the 650 megabytes of current CDs. This is an increase of more than 10 times the amount of information on current CDs. You can imagine what this storage space will do for computer games and for general computer applications, and how quickly this medium will become the must-have computer peripheral.

TIP Normally, whenyou double-click on an AVI file, that movie plays and then the playback window closes.Double-click on the movie while it's playing if you want to open Media Player,which lets you play it again, pause or rewind it. You can also right-click on an AVI file and choose Open Properties from the right click popup menu to get the video specs (frames per second, etc.) and copyright information (author, etc.) You can even play the video from its property sheet.

.WAV Sound

.WAV files contain a digitized sound. Like .BMP files, which contain a bit-by-bit copy of a graphic, .WAV files contain a bit-by-bit copy of a sound. In other words, a .WAV file is a digital recording. A .WAV can be voice, sound effects, music, whatever. But regardless of what it is, *it will be brief.* Though less demanding than digital images, digitized sound nonetheless eats up enormous amounts of disk space or RAM. A "radio quality" (FM stereo) recording gobbles 43k per second. A "CD quality" recording uses 172k per second. In other words, you'll use up a megabyte of hard drive space for every six seconds of music you record at CD quality.

However, if you're just recording some spoken words or a simple sound effect, you can safely reduce the sampling rate and consequently the resulting sample size, and switch from stereo to mono. As you can see in Figure 20-5, the crudest digital recording you can make via PCM is a sampling rate of 8kHz, mono, storing each sample in 8 bits. Recording at this rate uses up only 7k per second.

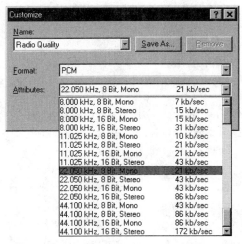

Figure 20-5: *The sampling rate and, to a lesser extent, the sample size determine the quality of your digital sound recording.*

To see or change your recording options as shown in Figure 20-5, click on Start, then Programs | Accessories | Multimedia. Select the Sound Recorder accessory, and from its Edit menu, select Audio Properties. Finally, in the section labeled Recording, click on Customize.

Notice in Figure 20-5 that Windows's Sound Recorder accessory allows you to choose three factors that will determine the quality of your recording:

the rate (kHz), sample size (bits) and mode (stereo or mono). Your goal is to choose the settings appropriate to what you're recording, bearing in mind that a higher-quality requires more space on your hard drive.

Sound formats

As you can see in Figure 20-5, you can select various formats. PCM (Pulse Code Modulation), however, is a standard that has been used in telecommunications for years. One alternative, ADPCM, is somewhat more efficient, because the sounds are compressed when saved to disk. However, PCM is the default and the standard.

What settings should you use?

 When recording voice, you can use the sampling rate used by the telephone company: 11kHz. The human voice generally falls below this upper limit, unless someone breaks into song. For singing, you might want to bump it up to radio quality, around 22kHz. This is equivalent to FM radio. For the best recording of singing accompanied by instruments, go up to CD quality at 44kHz—and watch the resulting file grow huge on your hard drive. Most sound cards default to 11kHz (telephone quality), but Windows 95's default is radio quality. For general purposes when recording music, you can leave it at radio quality and get fine results. The only practical situation where you might want to briefly go up to CD quality is to capture the full impact of extremely high-frequency sound, like breaking glass. Remember, too, that there's no point in recording at frequencies (rates) greater than your attached amplifier and speakers can reproduce. The best rule of thumb is to try a couple of settings by making some test recordings, then go with the setting that sounds good enough.

Although the *rate* at which you sample audio or video is the more important factor, the *size* of each sample also contributes to the quality of the result. Using a movie analogy, think of the sampling rate as the number of frames per second and the sample size as the quality of each frame (how well the film displays detail or color). When digitally recording music, the *sample rate* is expressed in kHz (kilohertz), 1000 per second. (Therefore, 8kHz means 8000 samples per second will be taken during the recording.) The *sample size* describes how many bits will be used to store each sample. The more bits used, the greater the silence between the sounds. The bits-per-sample factor is usually called the *quantization* level. This factor is difficult to describe, but recording at low quantization produces a result similar to tape hiss. The purity of the silence, or absence of hiss, brings out the high frequencies of the cymbals, for example, because they're contrasted with silence, rather than blended into a background hiss. Try plugging a microphone into your sound card or playing a CD, and recording (with the Windows Sound Recorder accessory) a sound, such as your voice. Adjust the bits per sample (BPS) from 4 bits per sample to 16 and play back the recordings to hear the difference. (You can get down to 4 bits per sample by changing the Format option from PCM to Microsoft ADPCM.)

For generally good recordings, the minimum setting for the Sound Recorder should be 22.050kHz at a 16-bit quantization level. If you record at 8-bit, you'll hear the background noise even through a moderately good amplifier and speakers.

Figures 20-6 through 20-9 illustrate the concepts of sample rate and sample size. A sample rate that's too small results in a blocky texture—in effect, you're seeing each sample. A good sampling rate results in samples too small to see—and the picture then looks realistic.

Figure 20-6: *When the sampling rate is too small, detail disappears into the mosaic of visible samples. You can see this effect in Figure 20-4, as well. In this case, we're using 4 dots per inch (dpi).*

Figure 20-7: *With the sample size too small, the possible variations in grays are reduced. Here we're using 4 bits per sample, and the result is only four possible shades.*

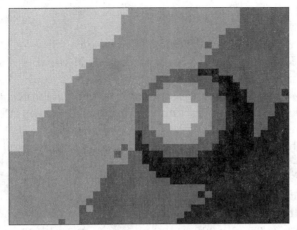

Figure 20-8: *The worst possible result. We used a 4 dpi rate and a 4 bps sample size. Now we've got few shades, causing the mosaic tiles to form larger, cruder rectangles.*

Figure 20-9: *A good, clean picture. Here the dpi rate is 100 and the bps size is 256.*

Increasing either the rate or the size wouldn't improve the picture in Figure 20-9 because of limitations imposed by the paper and printing methods used in this book. And, for an image without color, 256 is about the resolution limit humans can detect. Magazines, however, sometimes go up as high as 1200 dpi on shiny paper stock for color images.

MIDI

Given that digital recordings, .WAV files, use up so much space, there must be an alternative. There is. If your sound card is MIDI-capable, you can have the card re-create music on the fly. In other words, the sounds are stored in a MIDI file (.MID)—a kind of sheet music description of the notes, the instruments that should play those notes, and the timing. This takes up much less space than a digital recording.

The quality of the result, though, greatly depends on how well your sound card can re-create musical instrument sounds. There is a great range—from the boring, unvarying honks and beeps of a toy organ to the accurate timbres of actual instrument recordings on ROM chips.

MIDI, Musical Instrument Digital Interface, is a standard music description language that was established in the mid-'80s. In addition to the pitch, a MIDI file describes the tone (timbre, the difference between a trumpet playing middle C and a French horn playing the same note); duration (and any fading of the volume); vibrato (changes in pitch); tremolo (changes in loudness); sustain; and dozens of other aspects of music.

A computer can store and manipulate sound in two ways: symbolically (coded, like the MIDI descriptions of a sound) and imitative (sampled, like a .WAV recording of an actual sound). You can see this same distinction in the visual domain. .WMF (Windows metafile) images are mathematical descriptions of a picture—shapes, textures, colors—and they are re-created on the fly when the file is brought into the computer from disk to be displayed. .BMP files, by contrast, are sampled copies of an image, and they're merely displayed line for line across the TV monitor. There's no *drawing* or calculating necessary—each dot on the screen is already saved in the .BMP file. This distinction parallels the difference between analog (imitative) and digital (descriptive) recording, as discussed earlier in this chapter. However, both .WAV and MIDI, are *stored* digitially. True analog is stored on a vinyl record or as patterns on an audio tape more or less like a *carving*, like a sculpture.

Human languages also evidence this same division between symbolic and imitative techniques. English is symbolic. It uses 26 symbols to represent everything. English represents a stork with symbols like this: STORK. Japanese or ancient Egyptian, by contrast, *imitate* the object they're describing, like this:

The goal of an imitative approach is to accurately reproduce the sound or image. The goal of a descriptive approach is to create a recognizable *symbol* of the sound or image. For example, a photograph is imitative, whereas a caricature is symbolic. Imitative (.BMP or .WAV) files more or less reproduce the original; symbolic files (.WMF or .MID) more or less *suggest* or *re-create* the original. That's why a photo of Jesse Helms looks like him and a caricature exaggerates his unusual features—pinched mouth, big glasses, unusual head shape, etc.

The primary benefit of symbolic data storage is its efficiency; it just takes a lot less space to store the symbols for "ten seconds of middle C" than to store that 10 seconds as an actual sample. You can imagine how huge the Bible would be if it were written in hieroglyphics instead of an alphabet. And you'll never see a Chinese typewriter—it would require many thousands of keys. Think of this distinction between symbol and copy as the difference between sending your friend the recipe for your fantastic Christmas cookies vs. driving over to his house with a tin of the cookies themselves.

 TIP When choosing a sound card, insist on Level 2 MPC compliance, but if you're interested in or sensitive to music, also listen to MIDI played through several different cards to find the one that pleases you the most. Just getting Level 2 MPC doesn't guarantee that you'll like the MIDI you hear. The cards differ considerably in their approach to reproducing music.

MIDI orchestras

The idea behind MIDI is that a disk file (.MID) will say "snare drum & piano G# at this moment in the music." It will say this with a few symbols like 12/22#4, taking up only a few bytes. Your sound card will then play its drum and piano sounds. The accuracy of the sounds stored on the card makes all the difference.

SoundBlaster cards use "FM synthesis," which uses complex mathematics to imitate natural instruments. However, in the past few years, synthesizers used by professional musicians have moved away from this "synthesis" in favor of sampled (or "wavetable") instruments. This technique involves making a CD-quality digital recording of real instruments, and storing it on the sound card. A drum sample might require only a few seconds. It dies away fast. But a piano sample taken with the sustain pedal held down can decay over many seconds before silence. And, too, for the best quality, you have to take a sample of each key on the piano—you can't just adjust the pitch of a single sample, because the low notes have a quite different timbre from the high notes. In any case, you put all the sounds in RAM chips on the card, then when the MIDI asks for Piano/G#/10 seconds, that sample is played through the speakers. For instruments like the flute, which don't have problems with overtone dynamics (changes in the timbre while a note is sustained), you can take a relatively short sample and *loop* it (repeat it over and over with no seam of silence between, so it sounds like a continuous, pure tone). More complex instruments like the cello, whose sound changes character over time, require long samples that aren't looped.

In any event, high-quality sampled sounds produce the most realistic MIDI music: a virtual band in a box. You've got the best of both worlds. You're not filling your hard drive with an actual digital recording of the original music, but you *are* reproducing the music with digitally recorded, sampled, real instruments.

Recommended sound cards

Some sound cards boast sampled instrument sounds; no old-style FM synthesis at all. Others rely on synthesis, but offer add-on "daughterboards" that cancel the synthesized sounds and replace them with the superior sampled sounds.

- **Roland** SCC-1 (Sound Canvas), RAP10 (Roland Audio Producer) and the SCD-10 daughtercard. Roland is a respected name in the music world, producing high-quality synthesizers. Their wavetables—originally recorded for their professional synthesizers—are quite good. The wavetable daughtercard can be plugged into any 16-bit version of the SoundBlaster card to change the SoundBlaster from synthesis to true digital samples.

▨ **SoundBlaster** by Creative Labs, is a wildly popular board. The SoundBlaster 16 has a plug (the WaveBlaster connector) to which you can add Creative Labs's daughtercard of sampled sounds. (You can also add daughtercards of other manufacturers to the WaveBlaster socket—it's the de facto standard socket.) Be sure you get a 16-bit SoundBlaster if you're at all serious about the quality of your multimedia sound. SoundBlaster's AWE 32 card features the E-mu Proteus samples—widely considered among the finest digitized samples of real instruments. Many musicians feel that the E-mu sampled sounds are best for classical music, while the Korg sampled sounds (see Media Vision below) generally work best for rock music.

▨ **Monterey** by Turtle Beach uses their "WaveFront" sounds, and features complete MPC Level 2 compliance. Turtle Beach also makes a WaveBlaster compatible daughtercard.

▨ **Media Vision's** wavetable daughtercard is also WaveBlaster compatible, and thus can be used to upgrade a SoundBlaster 16 from synthesis to sampled sounds. The Media Vision set of samples comes from the Korg line of professional synthesizers. The appeal of these samples is a matter of some debate. Some musicians feel they are too "bright" or "hard." Others find them just the ticket for punchy, gutsy rock music.

The bottom line: if you're buying a sound card for the first time, try to get one that's MPC Level 2 compliant, 16-bit, is SoundBlaster compatible, and includes a WaveBlaster-compatible connector so you can add one of the daughterboard sample sets described above. If you already have a sound card, the single greatest improvement you can make is to add a daughterboard. This immediately replaces the synthesized sounds with the sounds of real musical instruments. And the process is relatively painless—you just plug the daughtercard into the sound card, and that's it. There's no rewiring or software to worry about.

MPC—The Industry Standard

Before 1990, CD-ROM drives and sound cards each had their own, manufacturer-supplied, custom formats for saving and reading sounds, video and music. Microsoft and other vendors got together and created a multimedia standard, MPC (Multimedia PC). The goal of this standard is to permit various multimedia devices to read and manipulate each other's songs and movies, as well as work harmoniously together (the sound card, for example, can play *Für Elise* while the CD-ROM unit displays a picture of Beethoven).

Level 1: 1990

MPC defined two levels of multimedia standardization. In 1990, the Level 1 specification described the minimal hardware requirements as: 386SX computer; 2mb RAM; 30mb hard drive; color monitor with 16 colors at 640 x 480; Windows 3.0 with Multimedia Extensions; a CD-ROM with a 150k/second or faster data transfer rate and an average access time of 400 milliseconds or less. (The *transfer* rate is the speed at which information can flow from the CD into your computer. The *access* time is the speed at which the laser can be repositioned to any zone on the CD, no matter how far from its current location.) The sound card had to meet these minimal requirements: an 8-bit digital-to-analog converter that could record at 11.025kHz and play back at 11.025kHz or 22.05kHz sampling rates (we'll define this shortly); and a four- or nine-voice, multitimbral synthesizer (that is, it can play different sounds simultaneously), that could produce at least two drum sounds at the same time.

As you might guess, multimedia effects on a Level 1 system are crude, at best. The most you could expect would be a little fake organ music to accompany text or a tiny, postage-stamp-size animated cartoon.

Level 2: 1993

The Level 2 specification was defined in 1993. It expands on Level 1 and is more typical of today's computers: 25Mhz 486SX computer; 4mb of RAM; 160mb hard drive; color monitor with 65,536 colors at 640 x 480; and a joystick. The CD-ROM unit must feature a 300k/second or faster data transfer rate and an average access time of 100 milliseconds or less. The sound card must meet these minimal requirements: a 16-bit analog-to-digital converter that can record at sampling rates of 44.1, 22.05, or 11.025kHz; a six-voice multitimbral synthesizer; can mix various audio inputs into a single stereo output (two RCA jacks on the back of the card that feed into an ordinary stereo amplifier or receiver); a MIDI (Musical Instrument Digital Interface) port featuring MIDI Out, MIDI In, and MIDI Thru; a volume control; PCM (Pulse Code Modulation) sampling for realistic recordings; and microphone input.

Most CD-ROM units and most sound cards sold today are MPC Level 2-compliant, at least to a degree. There are different "levels" of compliance, all the way up to "full." If you're buying a CD-ROM, check to see whether it can meet the essential MPC CD speed specification. The most important specification is the *speed* of the CD-ROM unit. You'll hear the CD-ROM speed described as 1X, 2X, 3X and so on. 1X means the Level 1 minimal speed (150k/second with 100 milliseconds seek time). 2X is twice that fast, and so on. Buy the fastest one you can afford, at least a 2X unit. Nothing else will have a greater impact on the quality of your multimedia.

To be MPC compliant at the lowest level, a sound card need only be able to play back prerecorded (.WAV type) files (like older Ad-Lib, SoundBlaster, and other cards). It need not be capable of more sophisticated music or voice synthesis, nor need it feature MIDI. However, "fully" Level 2 MPC-compliant sound cards do feature FM synthesis and MIDI (like more recent SoundBlaster, Roland and other cards). Fortunately, Windows 95 is *extensible*: if you buy a fancy new multimedia device that can do things not anticipated by MPC or Windows 95 itself, the device will come equipped with software that can manage the new capabilities. Finally, buy a Plug gand Play sound card to take advantage of Windows 95's auto configuration abilities (see Chapter 15).

CODEC

You can more or less ignore codecs. Windows 95 will select the right technique when you play a compressed file. Codec stands for *co*mpressor/*dec*ompressor, a technique that permits sampled sounds and images to be stored more efficiently as compressed data. Then, when played back, the data is decompressed and restored to its original state. Compression not only saves storage space (on a tape, in computer memory, or on an optical disc), it also saves space during *transmission* from the storage medium to the final display. For one example, current TV channels are allotted 6Mhz space each in the crowded "airwaves." High-definition TV researchers were told by the FCC that they would have to somehow fit HDTV's much thicker stream of data into the existing 6Mhz bandwidth. The answer they came up with was: compression at the TV studio, transmission in compressed form, then decompression (expansion) in your house for display on your TV.

Now that we've got some background, let's see how to get music and video playing on the computer. For information on installing a new CD player or an audio or video card in your computer, you'll use the *Add New Hardware* feature on the Control Panel (click Start, then Settings, then Control Panel). For more on this, see Chapter 15.

The simplest multimedia is a little tune playing in the background while you read some ordinary text onscreen. A sound card is therefore essential to multimedia. If you have a CD-ROM unit, another essential, it can communicate with the sound card. You attach the output of the sound card to an amplifier. Finally, when speakers are attached to the amplifier, sound emerges. The source of the sound can be .WAV or .MID files on a disk or on a CD, or other audio formats. Some CD-ROM units also permit you to play ordinary audio CDs as well as CD-ROM.

CD-ROM

The current medium of choice for multimedia is the CD-ROM. CD's permit huge amounts (over 600 megabytes) of music or video to be stored on a convenient, durable CD. Within the next year or so, few computers will be sold without a CD-ROM unit as part of the necessary equipment.

Using a CD-ROM unit with Windows 3.1 required a 16-bit *driver*, a software program called MSCDEX.EXE (Microsoft Compact Disc extensions). This was loaded by your CONFIG.SYS or AUTOEXEC.BAT startup program when the computer was turned on. Windows 95 includes its own 32-bit version of this driver, as well as a built-in CD controller, the 32-bit "CD file system" (CDFS). This speeds things up because, among other things, the CDFS has a RAM cache.

A *cache* is some memory that's set aside to hold data. RAM is always the fastest way to get something onto your screen or to your speakers. Disk drives and CDs are slower. For example, if you're reading about Beethoven from a CD, the page you're looking at might contain a button that will play the *Moonlight Sonata*. You haven't pressed the button, but the sonata, or at least the first part of it, could be moved into RAM from the CD *while you're reading*. In other words, while it's idle, waiting for you to finish reading, the software can load into RAM the next pages of text or music or whatever. This way, they're instantly available.

Buying a CD-ROM

If you buy a CD-ROM unit, try to get one with the greatest speed, "4x" if you can afford it. (The *x* refers to how many times faster the drive runs, compared to the original CD-ROMs, which were 1x.) At a minimum, purchase a 3x drive. The speed measurement tells you how fast the CD spins inside the unit, and consequently how swiftly the sound or images stream into your computer. The original 1x drives transferred data at 150k per second; 4x drives spin it off at 600k per second. (CDs are still sluggish compared to the 3-5 megabytes per second of a typical hard drive.) By 1996, many commercial CD-ROM titles simply won't run on a 1x drive at all. And if you're interested in full-screen video with quality audio, you must have at least a 3x drive. Moral: If you want your CD-ROM unit to remain useful for more than a year or two, buy a 4x unit now.

On-board caching and average access time specs are relatively unimportant compared to speed. Caching can be handled by Windows 95 itself. Access time refers to the time the unit needs to move the laser pickup across the disc to a particular location, a different "track." But do try to find a unit with .3 seconds access time or less. (The typical hard drive has an access time of 10 *milliseconds*.)

There are two primary approaches to loading the discs—direct and "caddy." The latter, requiring you to put the disc into a special plastic holder before inserting it, has all but disappeared. It was inconvenient, though it did offer marginal protection to the disc. Most units sold today feature a drawer that slides out. You place the CD directly on it, then the drawer retracts. This is similar to the loading mechanisms found on most audio CD players.

Installing a CD-ROM

You can buy external CD-ROM units that plug into your printer port, simplifying the installation process. But they cost more and it's not that hard to remove your computer's cover and install one yourself. Be sure to unplug the computer before unscrewing the cover.

Treat the CD-ROM as if it were a hard drive—locate an empty "bay" that you can slide it into. Most computers have plastic spacers covering the empty bays; just pop off the spacer and slide the CD-ROM in from the front of the computer. The CD-ROM unit will come with instructions telling you how to secure it and where to plug it in. Some units require an interface card that you insert into an empty slot, others plug into your sound card, and yet a third type plugs into the disk-drive controller card that comes with your computer.

Windows 95 doesn't directly support all CD-ROM units. At the time of this writing, it supports some Sony, Panasonic (Matsushita) and Mitsumi drives. If your particular CD-ROM unit isn't supported, Windows 95 will use the settings in your AUTOEXEC.BAT or CONFIG.SYS files to use drivers that work with your unit. However, it shouldn't be long before most CD-ROM manufacturers provide full 32-bit Windows 95-compatible drivers for their hardware. If you buy such a unit, or if you get a Windows 95 driver for an installed unit, you can replace the current 16-bit driver by changing the settings in Control Panel. Click on Start, then Settings and Control Panel. Double-click on *Add New Hardware*. Then click on *CD-ROM Controllers* and click on *Have Disk*.

Media Player—MIDI

The easiest, most direct way to play a tune in Windows 95 is to bring up the Media Player:

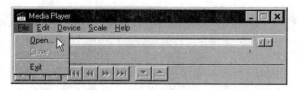

Figure 20-10: *Select Open in the Media Player's File Menu, then double-click on the filename of a .MID file.*

To open Media Player, click on Start, then Programs, then Accessories. Select MultiMedia and click on Media Player. Once you've opened the Media Player, click on the File menu and you'll see the Open window shown in Figure 20-10. Move to the Windows\Media subdirectory (folder) and click on Canyon (or Canyon.mid if you've chosen to have Explorer display file extensions like .MID, by selecting that option in Explorer's View menu, Options).

After you double-click on Canyon, Media Player knows that you want to play a MIDI file. (It can tell by the .MID extension on the end of the filename.) Media Player then changes its appearance to resemble a tape player, with a timeline dividing the duration of the piece into minutes and seconds. The duration is also displayed in a small box to the right:

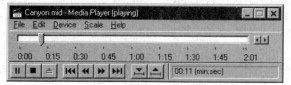

Figure 20-11: *Media Player changes itself into a tape player when you load in a MIDI file.*

You can do many things with the Media Player. You can drag the pointer along the timeline to reposition the start location anywhere within the piece. You can accomplish the same thing by clicking on the two arrows at the right of the timeline. Each click moves you one second; holding down the mouse button scrolls slowly.

The Media Player Buttons

Whether you're playing a MIDI song, a WAV sound, or an AVI video clip, or controlling an outboard device like a videotape player or CD, the buttons do pretty much the same things. Some will be unavailable in some situations (you can't "eject" a playing MIDI file), but generally, all the media are controlled the same ways.

The buttons resemble the choices you'd have on a typical tape player, with a couple of extras. The first (right triangle) button is "play." It starts the music from wherever the pointer is within the timeline. Once the music begins, the start button changes to a double line pause button. Next is the "stop" (square) button. Following that is an "eject" button, but since we're not playing an actual outboard device that could eject its media (a VCR, CD or Videodisk player), the eject button remains gray. A gray button or menu item tells you that the item is unavailable because it's inappropriate in the current context.

Next is a set of four fast-movement buttons. The first (line and two triangles) moves you to the start of the recording or to the start of a "mark." The next button is "rewind," and each time you click, it moves you 1/16th of the total duration back toward the start. Next, "fast forward" moves 1/16th toward the end. Finally, the Next Mark button (triangles and line) moves you to the end, or to the end of a selection.

The last two buttons let you set a single selection within the larger piece of music. If you click the Start Selection button, a small triangle appears in the timeline at the location of the pointer. If you want to skip to this location to start playing the music, click Start Selection once. From then on, you can just click on the Next Mark or Previous Mark buttons to go right to that location. (You can insert a start or end mark while the music is playing if you wish.)

If you want to listen to a particular zone within the music, click the End Selection button somewhere to the right of the start mark. A gray indicator will show you your selection. To cancel a selection, click the Start or End Selection buttons until the gray line disappears. (Or choose None from the Selection option on the Edit menu.) When a selection exists, clicking on the Play button begins the selection from wherever the pointer is. If you want to hear just the selection, press Alt+P.

The Media Player Menus

As with the buttons, the media player menus are fairly consistent, no matter whether you're playing a MIDI file, a video or whatever. Let's go through the menus in order, starting with File.

The File menu includes an Open option which allows you to load in a MIDI or other media file (.WAV, .AVI). You'll find sample files in the WINDOWS\MEDIA folder. There's also a Close option, but you'll never use it. Close merely empties the Media Player of content. If you want to load a different song, just click on Open. If you want to exit the Media Player program itself, click on Exit.

In the Edit menu, the Copy Object option puts the current song into the Windows Clipboard. From there, you can *embed* the song into a spreadsheet, word processor or database document, if the application containing the document is OLE-capable. You'll know if it is capable because the Edit menu of the application will have a Paste Special option. Click that option to insert the object at the current cursor position.

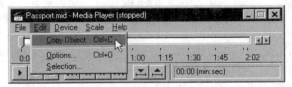

Figure 20-12: *Use this option to copy the current song to the Clipboard, from which it can be inserted into documents.*

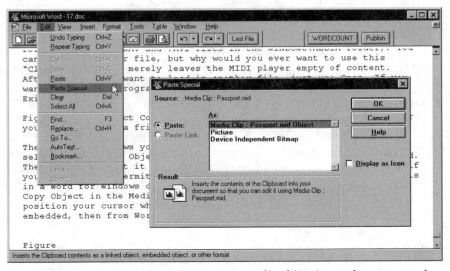

Figure 20-13: *Use Paste Special to insert a media object into a document, as here in Word for Windows.*

The first two items under Options in the Edit Menu let you reset the pointer to the start when the song ends (Auto Rewind) or to endlessly repeat the song (Auto Repeat). If you have defined a zone, a "selection" within the song, then play it by pressing Alt+P, the actions will take place within the zone rather than for the entire piece.

Figure 20-14: *The various options you can adjust in the Media Player.*

The third item allows you to change the caption under an embedded object and to determine whether an abbreviated bar of buttons (Play/Pause and Stop buttons only) appears when you double-click to play the song.

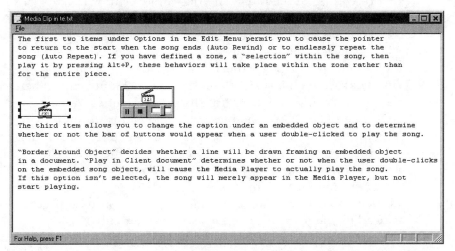

Figure 20-15: *If you choose Control Bar on Playback, you'll get the embedded object on the right. If not, you'll see the one on the left.*

Border around object determines whether a line will frame an embedded object in a document. *Play in client document* determines whether a double-click on the embedded song object will play the song. If this option isn't selected, Media Player will appear (the song loaded into it), but won't start playing.

The final item on the Edit menu, Selection, permits you to be highly specific about the start and end of a selected zone. You can use the scroll pointers to adjust either the start or end mark, but for greater precision, you can type in a mark time and specify it down to the 1000ths of a second (milliseconds).

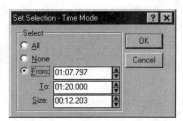

Figure 20-16: *Here you can specify a selection down to the millisecond.*

Although the Sound Recorder accessory is in some ways more flexible as a music editor, Sound Recorder cannot work with MIDI files. MIDI, you will recall, is like sheet music—a series of symbols describing music, but not a recording of the music. If you want to edit MIDI, you'll really need a MIDI sequencer (call a music store to get the names of several good MIDI software packages).

The Device menu lets you select a different medium—to load in, for example, a video clip (.AVI) file. Click on Video for Windows, then go to the Windows\Media folder. Click on the sample Skiing clip. When you open (load) this file, Media Player transforms itself into a video player instead of a MIDI song player. Two changes achieve this transformation in the Devices menu, the Configure option changes from renaming or reordering MIDI instruments to specifying the onscreen size of the video clip; in the Scale menu, a Frames option appears in addition to the Time option (Time is the only permitted measurement scale for MIDI).

When you click on the Device menu, then choose Configure, you can make adjustments to your MIDI setup—essentially reassigning instruments to different channels. MIDI permits you to play 16 different instruments at a time (more, if you add additional synthesizers to your system). By convention, the piano is on Channel 1, bass on Channel 2, drums on 10 and so on. Music can involve many instruments playing together—one or more play the melody, another might echo or supplement the melody, a string section might supply harmony underneath, and so on. The instruments you assign to the MIDI channels determine the *instrumentation*.

For instance, a MIDI song will say "play C two octaves below middle C on Channel 2 for 1/4 note duration." If you change the instrument assigned to Channel 2 from bass to, say, drums—the result will be strange indeed. If, however, you change from string bass to electric bass, you'll affect the song but perhaps in a beneficial way. Assigning different instruments to the MIDI channels is called *orchestration*. To hear most MIDI correctly orchestrated, you should probably leave the channel assignments in their default configurations. In any case, changing orchestration is often more easily accomplished using the MIDI software that came with your sound card than it is in the Media Player's Configure screen.

TIP In the early days of MIDI a few years ago, chaos reigned: someone might compose a MIDI song on one synthesizer with the horns on channel 3 and the strings on channel 4. Then you'd play it back on your synthesizer (or sound card) and your channel 3 would sound a guitar, your channel 4 a tuba or something. In other words, massive transformations of the instrumentation were the norm. Songs usually sounded pretty weird until you reassigned instruments to the correct channels. Then, happily, a standard evolved called *General MIDI*, which assigned certain instruments to specific channels. Windows 95 follows this instrumentation standard, but if you're playing an older MIDI song or just want to play around with the sound, you can change the default General MIDI channel assignments. (As shown in Figure 20–17, the instruments listed will depend on your sound card.) One thing to remember—leave channel 10 alone: it's *always* percussion, and assigning multi-pitched instruments to the drum channel will create havoc.

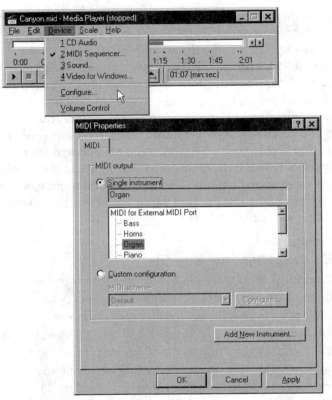

Figure 20-17: *Here's where you can find the MIDI Setup Wizard—to adjust instrumentation or to load and save custom instrument configurations.*

The Volume Control option (on the Media Player's Devices menu) displays the same simple "mixer" as you'd see if you double-clicked on the small yellow speaker symbol on the right of your taskbar at the bottom of the screen. You could also right-click on that speaker symbol, then select Volume Controls. However, once there, the mixer allows you to adjust the relative loudness and stereo balance of all your sound devices: Wave, MIDI, CD player, Line-In (an outside sound source, such as a cassette player plugged into the back of your sound card), microphone (likewise plugged into your card), or the little PC speaker. The slider at the far left of the mixer controls the overall volume of all sound sources; the remaining sliders set (or "mix") the relative volumes of the various sources. So if you're using the Sound Recorder accessory and you want to mix yourself speaking into the microphone while simultaneously recording music from a cassette tape, you can adjust the relative loudness of your voice and the music until you get the best effect.

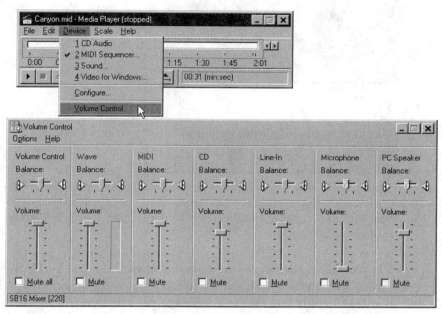

Figure 20-18: *This "mixer" allows you to adjust the relative volume of various sound sources.*

If you don't see all the devices shown in Figure 20-18, click the Volume Control's Options menu, then select Properties. Click on the devices or sources you want to adjust, so the check mark appears next to them as shown in Figure 20-19.

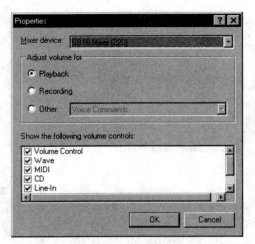

Figure 20-19: *Here you adjust the sound sources that appear on the mixer and select between recording, playback or alternative audio like "voice commands," where you speak into a microphone and the computer opens applications, or displays menus (this requires special software).*

If you select the Recording option shown in Figure 20-19, the number of sliders on the mixer will reduce to the four possible sources: MIDI, CD, Line-In and Mic, plus one on the left for the overall recording level.

Of course, to hear sounds from anything other than your PC speaker, you must have an amplifier attached to your sound card. At the very least, you need amplified speakers. Whatever the case, you can control the amps' or speakers' volume and balance. So why use the computer's internal mixer?

There are two important reasons to use the mixer. First, you can set the loudness of several sources, so they'll blend well when played together—one won't dominate another. Second, you can use the slider on the far left of the mixer to get the least noisy sound. Usually, you'll get the best results by setting the various sliders on the mixer as high (loud) as possible, while maintaining the relative mix you want. Then move the mixer's left slider all the way up. Finally, adjust the volume on your outside amplifier to a pleasant listening level.

Figure 20-20: *The last menu on the Media Player offers three ways to measure a media object.*

The final menu on the Media Player is Scale. Here you select the marks that appear along the slider—Time (any medium); Frames (video); or Tracks (CD).

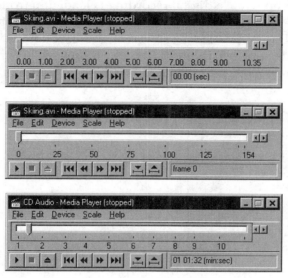

Figure 20-21: *The three kinds of Scales: Time, Frames and Tracks.*

As you can see in Figure 20-21, the scale at the top is time, measured in minutes and seconds. The middle example measures a video clip in frames. The one at the bottom displays the tracks of a music CD. (In the framed display of the current position, the 01:01:32 means: track 1, with 1 minute, 32 seconds elapsed on that track.)

Playing a CD

Although you can use the Media Player to play an audio CD (if your CD-ROM unit has this capability), you'd probably prefer to use the dedicated CD Player accessory described below. To play a CD, click on the Device menu, then select CD Audio. The Device menu's Configure option also changes—it permits you to adjust the headphone volume of the CD player.

Playing a digital recording (.WAV)

Again, you can use the Media Player to play .WAV files, but the Sound Recorder accessory described below has more features and is more fun to watch (it has a graphic display of the waveform). To play a .WAV file, click on the Devices menu, then select Sound and look in the Windows\Media

folder, where you'll find dozens of .WAV files. The Device menu's Configure option also changes—you can adjust the "buffer" size, the RAM set aside
as a temporary dump while a digital recording is loaded in from the disk.
Usually, you can leave the buffer at the default setting of 4 seconds. If you're
playing a CD-quality .WAV file on a slow disk drive, you might hear a
rough sound. If this happens, try increasing the buffer size to smooth the
sound (giving Windows 95 more room to assemble the audio in fast RAM
memory before playing it).

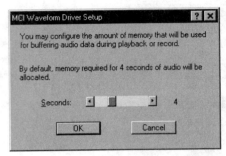

Figure 20-22: *The default "buffer" setting for playing digitized audio.*

Playing video

To play an .AVI video file, click on the Media Player's Device Menu, then
select Video for Windows. Look in the Windows\Media folder for a sample
.AVI file (or look in the \Funstuff\Video on the Companion CD-ROM) and
double-click the filename. Then click Media Player's Play button to watch (and
listen, if it has sound). The Selection apparatus works as it does for a MIDI or
.WAV file—press Alt+P to play a marked zone within the video. The Scale
menu allows two measurements of elapsed video: Time or Frames. The Device menu's Configure option lets you adjust the size of the video onscreen
from 1/16th of screen size all the way to full screen. Beware, though, that
setting a screen size bigger than your video and disk hardware can keep up
with will result in a jumpy view—frames will be skipped to keep things rolling. Also, the larger you make the screen size in relation to the video's original
size as captured, the more grainy the result will be.

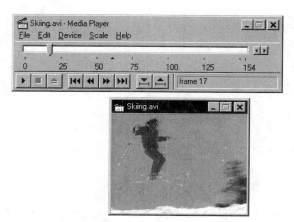

Figure 20-23: *Playing a video clip is as easy as playing audio.*

Where to Get More MIDI & .WAV Files

You can buy collections of .WAV and .MIDI files on CD in computer stores. But a much larger source is just a phone call away. The online world is awash with sound effects, Star Trek sound bites, elaborate, well-done classical, rock, country and every other kind of MIDI music.

If you want to add to your collection of .WAV or MIDI files, use your modem. Subscribe to The Microsoft Network, America Online, CompuServe or one of the other online services. Then, use their search capabilities to locate MIDI or MUSIC. You'll soon be directed to the right forum and you can then read the extensive lists of MIDI and .WAV files and *download* the ones you want (bring them over the phone from the online service to your hard drive). For more on downloading, see Chapter 16.

The CD Player Accessory

Windows comes with a full-featured audio CD controller application. If your CD-ROM unit is capable of playing audio CDs, try putting one in, then click Start, Programs, Accessories, Multimedia then CD Player.

Figure 20-24: *The CD Player gives you considerable control when playing a CD.*

Your computer can control almost everything about playing the music on a CD. As you can see in Figure 20-24, you've got a high-tech controller that can remember the name of the disc and the names of all the tracks, their durations, elapsed times and so on. You can play tracks in random order—out of order according to your own "playlist"—or sample the first few seconds of each track.

If you want the computer to remember the artist, title and track names of a CD, click on the Disc menu. You'll see the Disc Settings editor shown in Figure 20-25.

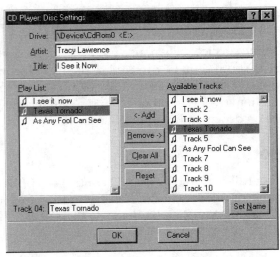

Figure 20-25: *Here's where you teach the computer the details about a CD.*

Windows detects when a music CD is placed into your CD-ROM unit. CDs are full of numbers, including an ID number. Once you've used the Disc Settings editor to describe the contents of a particular CD, the CD Player can look up the ID in a file on your hard drive and retrieve your descriptions.

To store information about a CD, type into the Artist and Title Text Boxes. Then, if you plan to type in all the track names, go to the text box at the bottom and type the title, deleting "Track 1." Click the Set Name button (or just press Enter). That will simultaneously enter the new title and put the next track into the text box at the bottom. Once you're finished, click the OK button.

If you want to create a custom playlist, look at the songs listed on the CD case and decide which ones you want to hear. Click on Clear All to remove all tracks from the Play List. In the Available Tracks list, click a track you want to hear. Then type its name in the text box at the bottom and press Enter, or click Set Name. Then click on the next track you want to hear, and continue typing all the names you want to play. Now, decide the order you want to hear them in. Click on the track you want to hear first, then click Add. Click the second one you want to hear, click Add. Continue until you've built your custom playlist. Then click the OK button.

The View Menu

In the View Menu, you can toggle among the toolbar (the set of buttons); the Disk/Track information (the boxes showing the names of the Artist, Title and Track); and the status bar (at the bottom of the CD Player, showing information about the CD's total playing time and the track's playing time. Below those options you'll see a green numeric counter. It can display the time elapsed or remaining for the current track, or the time remaining for the entire CD (or for your custom playlist, if you've created one). Finally, the Volume Control option brings up the mixer described above under "Media Player."

The Options menu gives you three styles of play; you can select any combination of them, or none of them. If you've created a playlist, the three styles will play only the tracks included in your list. Random Order lets the computer decide, by a "roll of the dice," the order that the tracks will be played in. The order will continuously change. Continuous Play means that when all the tracks on the CD or on your playlist have been played, the CD Player won't stop. It will continue to play tracks from the beginning again (or in random order, if you've selected that option). Intro Play lets you preview a few seconds from the start of each track. This feature is useful if you want to remind yourself of songs you've forgotten or to listen briefly to each track to help you decide on a playlist.

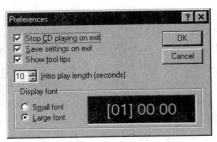

Figure 20-26: *Additional ways you can customize the CD Player are displayed in this Preferences window.*

Even though you shut down (exit) the CD Player, the CD can continue playing if you remove the check by clicking on "Stop CD playing on exit." (The CD isn't out of control. If you decide to stop it, just eject the disk manually from the CD player.) Save Settings on exit determines whether the random/continuous/intro settings, and the settings under the View menu will be recalled the next time you use the CD Player. Save Settings on exit doesn't affect any information that you typed into the Disk Settings Window (accessed from the Disk Edit Menu). The Artist, Title and playlist will be retained and will reappear whenever you insert the same CD again.

The Show Tool Tips option determines whether those helpful identification labels appear when you briefly rest your mouse pointer on a button. Just below that, you can set the length of the music that will play for each track when you're using the Intro Play feature. You can set it from 5-15 seconds. Finally, you can set the font size of the green numbers that display the elapsed (or remaining) time.

The Sound Recorder

More flexible with .WAV files (digital recordings) than the general-purpose Media Player, the Sound Recorder lets you create and edit your own digital recordings.

Figure 20-27: *In addition to recording, Sound Recorder features trimming, echo and other special effects.*

Like the other accessories we've been discussing in this chapter, Sound Recorder is in the MultiMedia folder. Click Start | Programs | Accessories | then Multimedia. Click on Sound Recorder.

What Can You Use Sound Recorder For?

Sound Recorder can clip unwanted sounds or silence from the start or end of a recording. It can add an echo and some other effects. It can also record digital audio—from a CD, from a tape player or other audio source plugged into the "line in" jacks on your sound card, even from the Media Player playing MIDI.

Of course, just because something *can* be done is not necessarily a reason to do it. Turning a MIDI file into a .WAV digital recording would be madness. A primary virtue of MIDI is its small file sizes. And the audio quality of a MIDI recording would at best be only as good as the original—perhaps worse. For example, if you use the minimal settings for recording quality music (PCM, 22.050kHz, 16-bit stereo), recording the sample MIDI file CANYON.MID would blow the 20,000 byte .MID file up into a 12-million byte .WAV file. This also assumes that Sound Recorder would let you record a song that long—it won't—and that your computer has enough RAM to do it—it doesn't.

Although you can run two copies of Sound Recorder at the same time, there's little point to it. You can't record on one what's being played back by the other.

When you first start Sound Recorder, it's set at a default recording mode of PCM 22.050kHz sampling rate and an 8-bit quantization rate, mono (one channel of sound). At 8 bits, you'll probably hear hiss if you record music. If you want a good-quality recording, do two things: change to 16 bit and stereo. This will eliminate the hiss that plagues 8-bit recordings. Of course, you can cut the resulting file size in half by choosing mono. (Also, you'll want to use the Volume Control accessory to set a good recording level, as we'll illustrate shortly.)

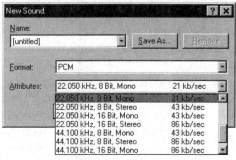

Figure 20-28: *To change the sampling or quantization rate, click on the File menu, then select New.*

To experiment with the various features of Sound Recorder, click Open in the File menu and load in one of the .WAV files in the Windows\Media folder. Try CHIMES.WAV, for example.

Notice that if you click the play button, you hear and see the sound. To play a sound, click the right-arrow button in the middle. (Unfortunately, Sound Recorder's buttons are arranged differently from the other "tape-player-style" controllers. In all other cases—Media Player and CD Player—the play button is first, on the left. Sound Recorder puts the play button in the middle, after the fast forward and rewind buttons.)

Format:	PCM		
Attributes:	22.050 kHz, 8 Bit, Mono	21 kb/sec	
	22.050 kHz, 8 Bit, Mono	21 kb/sec	
	22.050 kHz, 8 Bit, Stereo	43 kb/sec	
	22.050 kHz, 16 Bit, Mono	43 kb/sec	
	22.050 kHz, 16 Bit, Stereo	86 kb/sec	
	44.100 kHz, 8 Bit, Mono	43 kb/sec	
	44.100 kHz, 8 Bit, Stereo	86 kb/sec	
	44.100 kHz, 16 Bit, Mono	86 kb/sec	

Figure 20-29: *A close-up of the customize menu.*

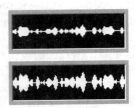

Figure 20-30: *The same sound, but the lower one has been increased in loudness by 75 percent.*

If you want a better view of the sound waves, click on the Effects menu and repeatedly click Increase Volume (by 25 percent) until you get a good view.

Any changes you've made to the original sound can be removed by clicking on Revert in the File menu. So if you want to retain the original CHIMES.WAV sound, be careful to select Revert before using the Save option. Or just avoid Save altogether.

The Properties option on the File menu allows you to change the format (quantization, sampling and codec). This is only useful just before you record a new digital sound. If you have a poor recording with little high-frequency (low sampling rate) or hissy sound (8-bit or lower quantization rate), merely adjusting the recording from, say, 8 bits to 16 bits will not remove the hiss. This would be similar to making a copy of a blurry, snowy videotape and hoping that using a better quality tape for the copy will improve the detail and eliminate the noise embedded in the original.

Making Your Own Recording

Let's make a recording. First, click Properties in the File menu and change to 16-bit at 22.050kHz. Then, either load a MIDI song into the Media Player accessory (you can use the WINDOWS\MEDIA\CANYON.MID sample MIDI file) or put a music CD in your CD-ROM unit and start the CD Player accessory.

Now that we've adjusted the Properties to 16 bit, there's one more adjustment: the incoming volume. Just as when recording on an analog recorder like a cassette recorder, making the best digital recording requires that you set a correct volume. If you record at too low a volume, you introduce noise. You'll have to boost the volume when you want to hear the playback, which will also boost noise and hum from within your amplifier as well as the recorded sound. On the other hand, if your recording volume is too high, you'll introduce distortion.

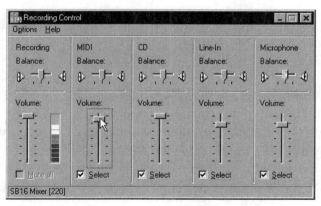

Figure 20-31: *Try to keep the bouncing gauge on the left just under the red (overload) indicator.*

So, start the Volume Control accessory and click on its Options menu. Select Properties. Then click the Recording option and click OK. Now play the source—CANYON.MID or your CD. Also, click the red Record button on the Sound Recorder to record a test we can use to adjust the levels. Leave the slider under Recording all the way up. But adjust the MIDI or CD slider until the record level gauge under Recording is as high as possible without showing red. That is, try to get the yellow bars to appear during the loudest passages, but avoid pumping the volume so high that the red bars appear at the top of the gauge. The red indicates overload, which will result in distortion.

Now stop the CD or Media Player. Stop the Sound Recorder. Your level is set. Move the slider on the Sound Recorder back to the beginning, so it says Position 0:00 sec. Click the red button to record on top of our test. Then quickly click the Play button on the Media Player or CD Player. Make your recording, and leave the sliders on the Volume Control alone.

If your recording volume is high enough above the "noise floor" (there's always some noise, but loud music tricks the brain into ignoring it), you can probably safely reduce the quantization and divide the file size in half. Let's try it. First, click the Play button on the Sound Recorder and turn the volume on your amplifier fairly high. You shouldn't hear any hiss, and the instruments should sound clean, not raspy. If you want to preserve this recording, click the File menu, then select Save As and save it as TEMP.

Now we'll reduce the quantization from 16 bit to 8 bit and listen for a noticeable hiss or buzz. Click the file menu and select Properties. Click the Convert Now button and choose 22.050kHz with *8 bit*. Then click OK.

Now play the music again. If it sounds good, you've saved some disk space. If not, you've still got the 16-bit version on disk under the name TEMP.

Here's how to make a really bad digital recording. Let's try this one final experiment. So you can hear exactly how the hissing and buzzing sounds if the bits-per-sample (quantization) setting is too low, choose Properties again under the File menu. Click the Convert Now button and change the *Format* from PCM to IMA ADPCM and change the sampling/quantization to 22.050kHz *4 bit*. This will really squeeze it. Click OK and then play the song with the amplifier's volume turned up high. You should easily hear the hissing surrounding the high sounds and a buzzing added to bass sounds. Notice that we've left the *sampling rate* at 22050. All the high frequencies are still present, but they're cluttered with spurious noise. If you want to hear the effect of too low a sampling rate, go to Properties again and convert your song to 8000kHz. Then when you play it back, you'll hear the low sounds, but the high frequencies (cymbals, snare drum hits, etc.), the "sheen," clarity and realism will have been drained from the music. Insufficient high frequencies (too low a sampling rate) make it sound like you're listening to a radio playing in someone else's apartment. The lower sounds like bass drums, the melody, and electric bass come booming through, but everything else is muffled.

The Edit Menu

Sound Recorder's Edit menu includes the usual Copy option—in this case, a copy of the recording is placed into the Windows Clipboard. From there, you can paste it into documents created by OLE-capable applications. To try it, copy a sound file, then open WordPad. Click Start | Programs | Accessories | WordPad.

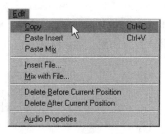

Figure 20-32: *Sound Recorder's Edit menu.*

Then, in WordPad's Edit menu, choose Paste Special. Making sure that Paste Special's window highlights Wave Sound, click OK. Your document now contains the embedded recording, symbolized by Sound Recorder's yellow speaker icon. Anyone viewing this document can either double-click the icon to play the sound, or right-click to play it, edit it, view its properties and other options.

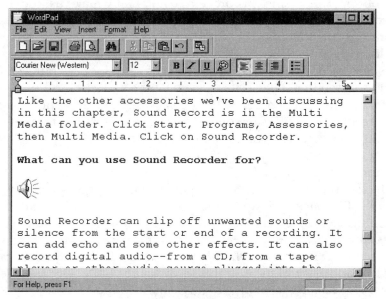

Figure 20-33: *A digital recording embedded in a WordPad document by Paste Special.*

The Edit menu's Paste Insert option makes room for whatever sound has been copied to the Clipboard (using Copy on the Edit menu). It makes room by inserting the new sound at the location of the slider. For instance, say your current sound in Sound Recorder is "Beep Beep," and you've copied the sound "Boom" (from a previously loaded sound or another instance of Sound Recorder). If your pointer is in between the Beeps, when you Paste Insert, you end up with "Beep Boom Beep." The total time of the sound will be increased by the duration of the inserted sound.

The Paste Mix option superimposes or combines the sound on the Clipboard with the sound currently in Sound Recorder. In other words, no extra space is made to absorb this new sound—it's played right along with the existing sound. The total time remains the same. The point at which the mixed sound appears within the original sound depends on the slider location.

The next two items on the Edit menu—Insert File and Mix with File— are identical to Insert Paste and Insert Mix, except that the imported sound is loaded from a file on disk, rather than a sound previously copied to the Clipboard.

The Delete Before Current Position and Delete After Current Position options are quite useful for trimming silence. Recall that when recording MIDI or from a CD, we first had to click the Recorder's red button to start recording, then move the mouse pointer to click the CD or MIDI Player's Play button. (Reversing this process would likely make us lose the start of the song.) However, a second or two of silence will appear at the start of our recording—the time it takes to move the mouse and press the Start button. To eliminate that silence, press Play and note the time when the sound actually starts, or move the slider until you see sound waves rather than a straight, green line. Then select Delete Before Current Position.

You can also use the Delete Before and Delete After options to cut and paste sections of sounds or songs—saving the pieces to disk files—then patching together new sounds by using Insert File or Mix with File to recombine your pieces.

Audio Properties, the final item on the Edit menu, allows you to customize the default devices, volume and recording settings. Normally, you'll leave the Playback and Recording Volume set at maximum, all the way to the right. Adjust the playback volume on your amplifier. Adjust the recording volume by changing the *playback* volume of the source of the sound or music (the CD Player, Line In, Microphone or Media Player). Recall that we took this approach in the example recording of CANYON.MID described above. This technique results in the cleanest sound.

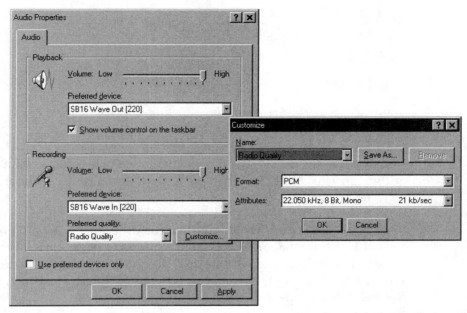

Figure 20-34: *In the Audio Properties window you can adjust default Playback and Recording modes.*

The Preferred device lists will likely show only a single device—like the SoundBlaster 16 shown in Figure 20-34. It would be unusual to have more than one audio device that could record, but here's where you could switch between them or select a default device.

The *Show volume control on the taskbar* option determines whether the volume control accessory icon appears in the lower right of your screen when the taskbar is visible. This is a quick way to change the volume of playback, but it can accomplish several things. The volume control icon on the taskbar is one of the rare three-way icons in Windows 95. Left-click it once, and an abbreviated volume control appears, with a single slider and a mute check box. Left-click it twice, and the full Volume Control accessory appears, with a separate slider for each of your playback or recording devices. Right-click it, and the Audio Properties window will appear (as shown in Figure 20-34).

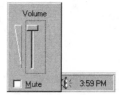

Figure 20-35: *The abbreviated Volume Control that pops up when you left-click the taskbar icon.*

As you might expect, the Effects menu lets you manipulate a sound by adding special effects. You can increase or decrease the volume in 25 percent increments. Note that increasing the volume of a poorly recorded, noisy recording increases the volume of the noise as well as of the sound. Once recorded, Windows 95 can't tell the difference between noise and music. There are elaborate professional devices (auto-correlators, de-poppers and others) that can attempt to filter out the essential randomness of noise from the abrupt, coherent transitions of music. However, the Sound Recorder doesn't include such features.

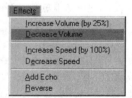

Figure 20-36: *The Effects menu of the Sound Recorder accessory.*

You can also double the speed (or halve it). Doubling results in the "Donald Duck effect"—a voice will sound as if the person has been inhaling helium.

The "Donald Duck effect" results from the way the computer increases playback speed—it merely increases the sampling rate notation. (The sound file contains a description of its sampling rate, along with other information at the beginning of the sound file. This sampling rate tag is merely doubled.) The computer then thinks that the sound was originally sampled at this higher rate; the Increase Speed by 100% option changes the tag on the sound from, for example, 22.050kHz to 44.100kHz. Sound Recorder reads this tag before playing any sound. And it now interprets the information to mean that it should play this recording faster, because it was apparently sampled at that speed—the sound file says so (even though it's lying). The *variations* in the signal, the waveform, don't really change. If you look carefully at the waveform display before and after selecting Increase Speed, you'll notice that the waves merely recede—as if you'd zoomed out from the previous view. The waves are still there and their shapes are preserved relative to each other. But now there are twice as many waves per second as before. That's why you can still understand the words, the melody and so on. However, the variations in the signal must now occur in less time than it took to record them. The waves will sound more abrupt—resulting in higher frequencies, moving the sound up a couple of octaves or so. This change both pinches and raises the sound's pitch, leading to the characteristic squawk, or, let's be honest, quack.

Adding an echo, the next option on the Effects menu, is also relatively easy for the computer. Echo repeats the original sound, somewhat delayed, and somewhat quieter. After all, the computer stores these sounds as *numbers* and it's not hard to copy, subtract and re-insert a set of numbers. The Sound Recorder uses a relatively brief delay, so the echo effect is fairly subtle. If you want to create your own echo with different loudness and delay factors, use the Decrease Volume feature and add some silence to the start of the intended echo (record silence, then splice it at the beginning of the sound using Insert File with the slider all the way to the left). Then you can save this delayed, quieted version to a disk file and paste it on top of the original sound with the Mix with File option.

 Don't confuse echo with reverb. *Reverb is* a complex series of subtle echoes that imitate the sound of a "room." The original sound bounces repeatedly off walls or is absorbed by carpets, and so on. The psychoacoustics of reverberation are sophisticated, and there are many possible reverb effects. Reverb adds a kind of depth or realism to a sound, since most music, boomboxes and stadiums excepted, is played in a room. The difference between echo and reverb is the difference between sound outdoors and sound indoors, and bouncing back once from a canyon wall between sound bouncing around within a room. Sound Recorder doesn't have a reverb effect.

The final effect, Reverse, merely flips the sound over and plays it from end to start. This isn't usually a particularly interesting or worthwhile tactic.

Moving On

Now we'll turn our attention to managing memory. It was essential in DOS and important in Windows 3. It's still important in Windows 95. It's always going to improve efficiency if you take the time to maximize the organization of the data within your computer.

Chapter 21

Optimization: Expert Memory Management

They say an elephant never forgets. But your computer has a prodigious memory that would put any pachyderm to shame. It's common these days for even home computers to sport 4 megabytes, and many business machines have at least 8 megabytes (millions of bytes—we'll explain these terms a little later).

Computers used for desktop publishing or other heavy-duty jobs can boast 32, 64 or even 128 megabytes of expensive internal memory—storage space formerly available only on less costly hard drives.

It's all too easy to confuse hard drive storage with computer memory, especially since both are measured in the same units: *bytes*. Generally, measurements are given in thousands of bytes—kilobytes (k)—or millions of bytes—megabytes (mb). And given techniques like swapping, caches, paging and other efforts to speed up data access, techniques that shift data back and forth between memory and hard drives, it's sometimes rather a blur. Sometimes you don't know, and probably don't care, exactly where your application or its documents are at any given time.

Just remember that RAM (memory chips inside the computer) is *volatile*—when the power to the computer is turned off, any documents, graphics or programs stored in RAM evaporate forever. It's like those scoreboards for football, when they flip the power switch to OFF after the game, the scores and the names of the teams disappear. By contrast, hard drives (and floppy disks, tapes, CDs and so on) are not volatile—the information they contain is stable and doesn't depend on a constant fueling from electricity.

However, both kinds of memory—volatile RAM and nonvolatile media—have been growing in size and shrinking in cost at a rate never before experienced in consumer goods. And as memory- and disk-hungry programs continue to grow in sophistication, we'll start talking about gigabytes and even terabytes. Terrifying indeed: the prospect of purchasing a trillion bytes at today's prices is daunting. At the current $40 per megabyte, a terabyte of RAM would cost $40,000,000.

To resolve the misconceptions many computer users have about memory, let's start at the beginning. (If you're already versed in these matters, skip ahead to the meat of this chapter, the section called "How Much RAM Does Windows Need?")

Under Closer Inspection

Let's examine a memory chip under an imaginary electron microscope, zooming in like a spacecraft coming down for a landing on a mysterious, sparkling silicon planet. From orbit, you see only the phosphorescent frenzy of digital energy, as electrons zip back and forth, ferrying data to and fro. As we get closer, you can make out the highway structure: a fine grid of nano-wires, more like canals than roadways. Electrons flow through these canals.

Figure 21-1: *At high imaginary magnification, a memory chip resembles a grid of lit and unlit bulbs.*

Electrons are incredibly small, among the smallest things we can detect and observe. Of course, to our unaided eye, they're invisible. But we're using an imaginary microscope after all, so we can imagine them flitting about in swarms like fireflies through these grooves. At each intersection of grid lines is a transistor, something like a tiny light bulb. If we zoom in still further, each bulb might look like a little mason jar: trapping a glowing firefly if lit, or gaping empty, waiting, if not.

Figure 21-2: *If each memory bit was a firefly, it could be stored in an imaginary glass jar. Eight jars form a byte of memory.*

Each jar can be either full or empty; there are no half-full glasses here. In numerical terms, a glowing jar could be represented by the number 1 and a lonely jar by a zero. Why ones and zeros? Computer designers are first and foremost mathematicians, and logic tables and so forth aren't exactly scientific when populated with fireflies. The digits 1 and 0 merely represent a binary state—a two-state. You could think of it as on/off, something/nothing, true/false, yes/no—there are various ways to express this smallest of possible pieces of information. But it is the very smallest way to express data that means anything.

This little piece of information, this *b*inary dig*it*, is called a *bit*. With these humble bits, when many of them are ganged together, you can store Shakespeare's works, the Mona Lisa, a powerful flight simulator, the entire oeuvre of Garcia Lorca, or anything else that's information (as opposed to something material, like a real rock or a real cow).

Eight to a Pop

Our mason jars appear to be stuffed together in eights, in little boxes, in groups of eight. To keep track of each box, a number is stamped on its side: its *address*, just like a post office box. Eight jars can fit in one box, and together these eight bits comprise a *byte*.

If you're curious about how strings of 1s and 0s could represent numbers, consider how our decimal (base ten) system works. The number 2,432 is actually "2 thousands, 4 hundreds, 3 tens, and 2 ones." In other words, each place to the left is a power of ten. The rightmost digit is the 1's zone, the next position to the left represents 10s, then 100s and so on. The decimal system operates by moving left each place and multiplying by 10 each time it moves. (Another way of saying this is that each time you move to the left one space within a decimal number, you must realize that that new number is a "power of ten" greater than the space to its right.)

Binary means "two-state" like on/off, true/false, one/zero. From right to left, binary digits increase only by a power of two, as you might expect. Therefore the binary number 10 really means 2 (when translated into decimal). Binary 10 means zero "ones" and one "twos" because the second position is the "twos" place in binary (not "tens" as it would be in our familiar decimal system).

Binary digits increase by powers of two as you move left through the digits in a binary number. The binary number 00001011 means "one 'one', one 'two', no 'four', and one 'eight'," which, when added together, makes eleven (in our familiar numbering system).

If this stuff really intrigues you, with practice you can learn to "think" in binary and avoid the constant translating process between binary and decimal. It's like learning a new language—in this case, the true language of your computer. Of course, there's little reason to try—it's regressive to deal with the computer on its terms, now that computers are reaching toward us with artificially intelligent neural nets, natural language processing, voice recognition and increasingly intuitive graphical user interfaces, soon to operate in virtual reality.

Like a dozen eggs, a six-pack of soda, a ten-number telephone keypad and other conveniently small groups, eight bits to a byte is also convenient. That's enough bits to "hold" (symbolize) any number from 0 to 255. With that amount of "data space," we can represent the entire alphabet, upper- and lowercase letters, symbols, digits, with some room to spare for punctuation marks like the comma and other miscellany. It takes at least 26 numbers to hold uppercase letters, another 26 for lowercase, 10 for the numeric digits, about 32 more for punctuation. That leaves plenty of extra, unused numbers to represent a few graphics characters, symbols and international characters with double-dots on them or accent marks.

Most of these *character sets* use only about 127 characters, but the full IBM character set uses every one of the 256 available numbers to hold all the letters, numbers and symbols. Table 21-1 shows the full IBM character set used by DOS applications and some modem software. Table 21-2 shows the

ANSI character set used by Windows, eschews the unnecessary graphics symbols in favor of additional international and typesetting symbols (although many characters, represented by small boxes, are unused). ASCII stands for American Standard Code for Information Interchange, whereas ANSI comes from the American National Standards Institute.

The DOS ASCII Character Set

32		64	@	96	⌐	128	_	160		192	╥	224	ê
33	!	65	A	97	a	129	_	161	┴	193	τ	225	ç
34	π	66	B	98	b	130	Γ	162	ó	194	σ	226	ë
35	#	67	C	99	c	131	—	163	ú	195	╠	227	ï
36	$	68	D	100	d	132	π	164	■	196	Ç	228	è
37	%	69	E	101	e	133	╟	165	┤	197	ü	229	î
38	&	70	F	102	f	134	á	166	|	198	«	230	⌐
39	⌐	71	G	103	g	135	α	167	ñ	199	é	231	ì
40	(	72	H	104	h	136	÷	168	¼	200	Θ	232	Å
41	)	73	I	105	i	137	Σ	169	┌	201	â	233	Ä
42	*	74	J	106	j	138	_	170	╗	202	μ	234	É
43	+	75	K	107	k	139	■	171	╠	203	Φ	235	æ
44	,	76	L	108	l	140	╬	172	┬	204	ø	236	ô
45	–	77	M	109	m	141	_	173	╨	205	Ω	237	Æ
46	.	78	N	110	n	142	_	174	¿	206	δ	238	ö
47	/	79	O	111	o	143	_	175	°	207	∞	239	ò
48	0	80	P	112	p	144	_	176	í	208	_	240	╢
49	1	81	Q	113	q	145	⌐	177	▓	209	ä	241	û
50	2	82	R	114	r	146	╔	178	2	210	±	242	ÿ
51	3	83	S	115	s	147	π	179	3	211	ε	243	ù
52	4	84	T	116	t	148	╜	180	½	212	∩	244	Ö
53	5	85	U	117	u	149	Ñ	181	┥	213	=	245	¢
54	6	86	V	118	v	150	╤	182	ª	214	à	246	Ü
55	7	87	W	119	w	151	╨	183	ß	215	x	247	╥
56	8	88	X	120	x	152	≈	184	Γ	216	»	248	┐
57	9	89	Y	121	y	153	¬	185	1	217	⌠	249	¥
58	:	90	Z	122	z	154	_	186	╝	218	≥	250	£
59	;	91	[	123	{	155	▌	187	╚	219	≤	251	₧
60	<	92	\	124	|	156	╧	188	_	220	å	252	ƒ
61	=	93	]	125	}	157	_	189	_	221	Y	253	y
62	>	94	^	126	~	158	_	190	_	222	_	254	_
63	?	95	_	127		159	⌐	191	└	223	°	255	╪

Table 21-1: *The DOS ASCII character set.*

The Windows ANSI Character Set

32		64	@	96	`	128	_	160		192	À	224	à
33	!	65	A	97	a	129	Ã	161	¡	193	Á	225	á
34	"	66	B	98	b	130	Ç	162	¢	194	Â	226	â
35	#	67	C	99	c	131	ƒ	163	£	195	Ã	227	ã
36	$	68	D	100	d	132	„	164	¤	196	Ä	228	ä
37	%	69	E	101	e	133	…	165	¥	197	Å	229	å
38	&	70	F	102	f	134	†	166	¦	198	Æ	230	æ
39	'	71	G	103	g	135	‡	167	§	199	Ç	231	ç
40	(	72	H	104	h	136	ˆ	168	¨	200	È	232	è
41	)	73	I	105	i	137	‰	169	©	201	É	233	é
42	*	74	J	106	j	138	_	170	ª	202	Ê	234	ê
43	+	75	K	107	k	139	‹	171	«	203	Ë	235	ë
44	,	76	L	108	l	140	Œ	172	¬	204	Ì	236	ì
45	-	77	M	109	m	141	_	173	–	205	Í	237	í
46	.	78	N	110	n	142	_	174	®	206	Î	238	î
47	/	79	O	111	o	143	_	175	¯	207	Ï	239	ï
48	0	80	P	112	p	144	_	176	°	208	_	240	
49	1	81	Q	113	q	145	'	177	±	209	Ñ	241	ñ
50	2	82	R	114	r	146	'	178	2	210	Ò	242	ò
51	3	83	S	115	s	147	"	179	3	211	Ó	243	ó
52	4	84	T	116	t	148	"	180	´	212	Ô	244	ô
53	5	85	U	117	u	149	•	181	µ	213	Õ	245	õ
54	6	86	V	118	v	150	—	182	¶	214	Ö	246	ö
55	7	87	W	119	w	151	–	183	·	215	x	247	÷
56	8	88	X	120	x	152	˜	184	,	216	Ø	248	ø
57	9	89	Y	121	y	153	™	185	1	217	Ù	249	ù
58	:	90	Z	122	z	154	_	186	º	218	Ú	250	ú
59	;	91	[	123	{	155	›	187	»	219	Û	251	û
60	<	92	\	124			156	œ	188	_	220	Ü	252	ü
61	=	93	]	125	}	157	_	189	_	221	Y	253	y
62	>	94	^	126	~	158	_	190	_	222	_	254	_
63	?	95	_	127		159	Ÿ	191	¿	223	ß	255	ÿ

Table 21-2: *The Windows ANSI character set.*

TIP You can use Windows' Charmap applet to display the characters in any font, even directly copy and paste them into any Windows program, such as Microsoft Word (which has its own built-in character mapper too). But if you already know the "code" for a special character (perhaps you have this page handy!), just hold down Alt while you type the code on the numeric keypad and then release Alt. Remember that Windows ANSI codes are always preceded by zeros. So Alt+0169 inserts the © copyright symbol into your document.

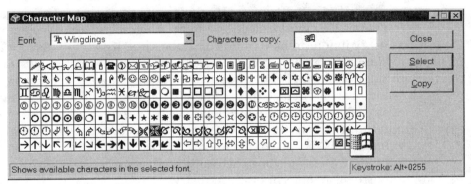

Figure 21-3: *The CharMap accessory (see Chapter 10,) is any easy way to insert special characters, such as the copyright symbol, into a document.*

Character Assignation

Instead of referring to memory cells as bytes, or boxes of jars, it's more usual to call them *characters*, and you'll often hear the terms *character* and *byte* used interchangeably.

Because an 8½- x 11-inch page can hold 60 lines of 80 columns of 10-pica (12-point) type (when printed by a laser printer), each page holds 4,800 characters, a rather low density. A typical typewritten page is even less dense, usually fewer than 2,000 characters.

The Precious Part Inside

By contrast, a computer memory chip can easily store over a million characters, about as much as fits on a floppy disk. (What we usually think of as a "chip" is really just ceramic packaging and thin wires. What we see isn't the real memory. We see the package that's guarding the precious part inside—a wafer of silicon smaller and thinner than a baby's thumbnail).

A million characters (a megabyte chip) holds over 500 typical typewritten pages.

In This Tiny World

In the works are 64 megabit memory chips, 8mb on a single chip, with tiny circuits so fine they begin to be affected by the weird rules of quantum physics: in this tiny world, electrons don't have precise locations but rather exist as fuzzy indeterminate clouds of probability. It's all too easy for an electron to "jump the track" from one wire to the next or even tunnel straight through solid silicon, instantaneously appearing on the other side of a "solid" barrier. In fact, this seemingly impossible magic trick, tunneling, is exploited by many state-of-the-art electronics devices, including the quantum tunneling electron microscope, which can be used to show us individual atoms. The tip of the microscope can even "drag and drop" individual atoms to construct vanishingly small objects, the precursor to tomorrow's nanotechnology industry.

Blurring the Line

RAM, floppy disks and hard disks have a lot in common. The differences are essentially speed and convenience (and cost). Your computer can swoop down and scoop up one of those "boxes of jars" (a byte of data) in less than 70 billionths of a second. It takes more like 10 to 20 millionths of a second to snag a byte from a hard drive (assuming the drive heads don't have to move to find the byte, which delays things even more).

But there are important practical differences between the ways you can store data in your computer. Your main memory inside the computer is called RAM, for *Random-Access Memory*, because there are no limitations to reading or writing—any byte at random can be read, without having to move to it first (whereas a disk drive head has to physically move to locate data). RAM is *solid-state memory* because there are no moving parts, other than electrons, and they move at nearly the speed of light—the fastest possible velocity in the universe, as we learned from Einstein early in this century. Electrons cause very little wear and tear (but over time, high energy electrons can actually perforate a memory chip. Nothing lasts forever). The great benefit of RAM is that any byte located anywhere on the RAM chips can be read from or written to, even randomly, with no penalty in speed or efficiency.

A tape drive (like those used for backing up) is just the opposite of RAM—highly physical and quite slow. Tape drives must fast-forward or rewind a tape to find data. And although the heads on a hard drive, floppy disk or CD-ROM drive can eventually move to any spot on their respective media, it takes time. Moving a hard drive head is relatively leisurely (the head is the "pickup" module that hovers over the drive to read or write, similar to a tone arm on an old-fashioned record player).

Better Late Than Never

Sometimes a poor substitute is better than no substitute at all. Windows uses space on your hard drive to simulate extra RAM so that programs don't squawk and die when they run out of real Random-Access Memory. Windows keeps track of how much memory programs really need, and what memory is discardable (temporarily unneeded). The least frequently used memory is dumped into this *swap file* on your hard disk to make room for a new program that decides it has a sudden, urgent need for the RAM. When the second program goes idle (you're not actively interacting with it) or is shut down, the memory in the swap file can be easily (but sluggishly) copied back into RAM.

Imagine you have a cluttered desk at work, and you suddenly need some space: you'll push all the old junk aside to make some room, but as soon as you're done, the mess mysteriously migrates back to its favorite spot—in your way.

Hard drives and floppy disks have one other advantage over RAM: they aren't erased when you turn off the power. And of course, hard drives are much larger in capacity than your computer RAM. You might have 4 or 8mb of RAM, but you'll typically have at least 200mb of hard disk space. Since the hard drive is used to permanently record the information that is originally created in RAM, it makes sense to have plenty of hard disk space, since over time you will create quite a few files. The hard drive also provides a master storage area for all the programs and program resources like graphics, digital sound, databases (like spelling dictionaries) and system software such as Windows itself.

Earlier in this chapter, we said that RAM always forgets its information when you turn off the computer (that's why you need a hard drive to store data permanently). There is a special tiny piece of RAM in your computer that is different from ordinary RAM. This RAM (called CMOS, pronounced *see-moss*) doesn't lose power when you turn off the machine. CMOS is powered by a battery, or is a special kind of nonvolatile memory (this kind of RAM is like a disk or tape—erasable but stable unless deliberately overwritten).

We need some CMOS because your computer can't afford to forget some things, such as the size and type of the hard drive, what kind of floppy drives you have, how much memory is installed, the date and time and so forth. These things are your computer's "Setup." Since the information in the CMOS is required in order to start the hard drive, the hard drive itself can't be used to store this essential setup information.

In theory, all your RAM could be made of this permanent type of memory, but it would be prohibitively expensive and slow. However, the new *flash RAM* cards, credit-card-sized modules that plug into notebook computers, are a solid-state alternative to hard drives, using nonvolatile (permanent) RAM. Even though nonvolatile RAM is slower than the *dynamic* RAM used inside your computer, it's more than fast enough as a hard drive substitute.

CMOS stands for *Complementary Metal Oxide Semiconductor,* after the kinds of low power transistors used inside them. (Most new microprocessors use complementary metal oxides too, to save power, a technology first used in battery-powered laptop computers). For more about the CMOS used to store important system Setup information, see Chapter 14, "Deep Inside the Machine."

CD-ROM is another substitute for RAM. A CD-ROM stores 640mb on a single platter, so copying a couple of CD-ROMs to even a large hard drive would quickly bankrupt it. As the name says, computer CDs are ROM—Read-Only Memory. Engineers haven't yet figured out how to make affordable rewriteable CD drives, although the first under $1,000 writeable CD-ROM drives should appear later this year. Although you'll hear these drives referred to as *Writeable CD-ROM*, it's an oxymoron; the correct terminology is *CD-R* (Compact Disc Recordable) or more generically, *WORM*, for *Write Once, Read Mostly.*

Another form of Read-Only Memory is the solid-state BIOS (Basic Input/Output System) chip that holds a tiny program. This program runs every time you turn on your computer. All it does is load and run another tiny *bootstrap* program from a floppy or hard disk that, in turn, starts up DOS or Windows.

How Much RAM Does Windows Need?

Although Windows 95 can theoretically run with as little as 2mb of RAM (4mb is actually the recommended minimum), you don't want to waste your valuable time with such a puny system: Windows itself takes up all of the RAM in a computer that ill-equipped. Running any program starts up a tug of war for precious memory, and the fight takes the form of constant disk access to the swap file (this furious disk activity is called *thrashing*). If, while running a single application, your computer spend lots of time waiting while your hard drive grinds away, you need to get more memory.

Even with 4mb of RAM, you'll still encounter thrashing and disk swapping with Windows 95, especially when you try to run more than one major application simultaneously (a major application is a word processor, database or spreadsheet as opposed to a game, fax software or utility). For best results, don't shortchange yourself: install at least 8MB of RAM, and buy the largest hard disk you can afford. You'll be amazed how fast the large programs can gobble up hard disk space. You'll also be amazed at how much better your computer works when you have more space and more memory. Your goal should probably be 16mb: Windows 95 runs nice and smooth with that amount.

More Memory = More Speed

Because it avoids thrashing, a machine with plenty of memory can seem to run twice as fast as a less endowed one. So before you upgrade your motherboard or microprocessor, consider more RAM first. Windows runs best with 8 to 16mb of RAM, although Windows 95 can put even more to good use. More RAM will further speed up disk access, for example. You typically can't use more than 16mb, unless you're using a memory-greedy application like photographic image processing or CAD.

Most computers sold at a discount (which is most computers these days) via mail order or through computer store chains contain too little memory. It's not unusual to find special sale bundles—monitor, keyboard, main machine—with only 4mb of RAM. If you can, pay the extra cost to bring that up to 16mb, or at least 8. (Each megabyte costs about $40, and prices are slowly dropping on RAM, although not nearly as dramatically as the price of other components.)

Getting a RAM boost

Installing your own memory upgrades can be as simple as plugging a tiny memory card (a SIMM module) into a slot (a SIMM socket), but it requires taking off the case of your computer. SIMM stands for Single Inline Memory Module, a tiny card that combines several RAM chips into a single unit of memory, available in sizes of 256k, 1mb, 4mb and more.

Sometimes, you have to remove your existing RAM before you can add more. For example, if your computer has only four SIMM sockets, and they are each filled with one megabyte SIMMs, you have to remove them so you can insert two 4mb SIMMs to get 8mb total memory.

If you are adding SIMMs without removing your old ones (for example, you're upgrading from two 4mb SIMMs to four 4mb SIMMs to go from 8mb to 16mb of RAM), you have to match the type and speed. In some computers, you may get unreliable results when mixing "3 chip" SIMMs with "9 chip" SIMMs. There may also be rules that govern which sockets you're allowed to use for SIMMs of various sizes. On some computers, usually 386 machines, you'll have to set some switches or rearrange jumper blocks on the motherboard.

Most of your questions about upgrading memory can be answered by reading the system manual that came with your computer or by contacting the dealer or vendor who sold you the computer. Although you can save money by upgrading yourself, most computer stores will install memory upgrades for a reasonable fee.

If you're still interested in expanding your own memory, you'll want to learn more about how to open your computer's case safely and what to look for inside the case. We discuss this topic completely in Chapter 15.

Using Memory for Faster Disk Access

Among other things, sufficient RAM allows Windows 95 to create a larger *disk cache*. A disk cache program speeds up your hard disk by storing frequently accessed data in RAM. Whenever a program needs to reread the data, it can find it in RAM instead of having to search for it on the hard disk. Since RAM is more than a thousand times faster than the hard drive, a disk cache can really speed up your computer, as long as you have enough RAM to make this trick worthwhile.

Chapter 5, "Inside The File System," delves more deeply into optimizing your disk cache and introduces the Windows 95 virtual disk cache, a great improvement over even the impressive SmartDrive. The virtual cache

(VCACHE) runs at full 32-bit speed and efficiency, and it stores entire files in its cache, not just pieces of them as SmartDrive did. (Earlier versions of Windows automatically installed the SMARTDRV (SmartDrive) disk cache, but it has now been replaced by the superior Windows 95 VCACHE.)

Flexible memory sharing

Instead of using a fixed block of memory for the cache, memory that's withheld from the use of other programs, the Windows 95 VCACHE can now exploit *all* available memory. It can use all your free memory to store frequently accessed files on hand. When another application needs some of that RAM, the cache is dynamically resized to free some up. This works quite well. Like elastic, it continually adjusts to your applications' current space requirements.

Earlier versions of Windows were dependent upon DOS to help it manage memory, but now the tables are turned—DOS relies on Windows 95 for all its needs.

The Windows 95 memory manager is a special kind of system software. It's the referee in a contentious game: mediating disputes between programs, some of which are rapacious, eager to grab all the RAM they can. The Windows 95 memory manager automatically demotes applications' RAM blocks to swap files on the hard drive when other programs need some real RAM, and it restores the data to RAM when it's needed again.

DOS Memory Management

If you want a perspective on how far Windows 95 has come in making improvements in computer performance, and to make sense of how memory was traditionally managed on DOS computers, the next several pages offer a review of the various improvements in DOS's memory management over the years. It's a sometimes amusing, sometimes dreadful history of false starts and radical underestimates of how hungry people and their applications were for sufficient memory. The struggle to make enough DOS memory available to the burgeoning needs of increasingly memory-gluttonous applications was a long and winding road. If you're not interested in these issues, or don't need this depth of understanding, skip ahead to "Memory Ecology" later in this chapter. In that section, you'll find tips and techniques to maximize the efficiency of Windows 95's memory usage.

Nonetheless, an understanding of DOS memory management is still relevant for Windows 95 users. Most of us must continue, for a while at least, to run DOS programs. For example, some DOS programs might be just more familiar to us, so we can control them and put them through their paces more quickly than we could with some new, unlearned Windows program. Many businesses also rely on custom "legacy" software written in DOS that may be too expensive to rewrite in Windows, at least in the short term. And of course, many hit games still don't require Windows and benefit from DOS memory optimization.

Chapter 22, "The Other Face: DOS 7," explains more about using DOS, when it's still necessary or preferable. For now, we'll look at the checkered history of DOS memory.

Booting Up

What happens when you turn on your computer? When you flip the power switch, DOS 7 and Windows 95 together go through a process called *booting*, as in "pull yourself up by your own bootstraps." They load the DOS extended memory manager HIMEM.SYS.

HIMEM.SYS allows DOS to make full use of all the memory in your computer. There are several types or flavors of RAM, including conventional memory, extended memory and expanded memory. We'll go into more detail on the distinction between these types during this discussion.

The "lowest" first megabyte is called *conventional memory* because it's the only memory that the old-style 8088 and 286 microprocessor can directly take advantage of. *Extended memory* (the memory governed by HIMEM.SYS) is the RAM that starts after that first megabyte of RAM.

The HIMEM.SYS memory manager also allows Windows/DOS 7 to store DOS into the *upper memory area*, a special zone of RAM within your first megabyte of extended memory. (Even Windows 95 keeps DOS around so that it can be used as the basis for DOS sessions within Windows. But Windows programs never use DOS for any purpose when you're running Windows 95, unlike Windows 3.1, which utilized DOS for many file and system services.)

Up, down, high, low?

Upper memory is so called because the higher memory addresses are usually shown at the top of most memory charts (including ours—see Figure 21-4), so the *last* 384k of memory is considered to be at the top, or upper memory. Figure 21-4 should help make these various zones of memory more clear.

HIMEM.SYS allows Windows to access the rest of your memory as well: for compatibility with older DOS programs, conventional, expanded and extended memory are still available, and we'll review these types for those of you who are joining this game in progress.

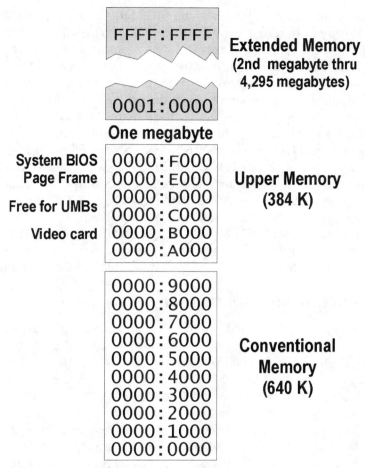

Figure 21-4: *A memory map symbolically represents how your memory addresses are laid out.*

The Good Old Bad Old Days

It helps to proceed with this explanation historically. The original Microsoft DOS was lucky to have 64k of RAM to run programs with (by contrast, a contemporary Windows word processor might want a hundred times more memory). With many other home computers often limited to 16k, the 128k IBM PCs were the Cadillac of the personal computer world in the early 1980s.

Intel designed the 8088 microprocessor to control up to one megabyte of total memory. The topmost 384k of memory bytes were never intended for use as RAM: these bytes were reserved for ROM BIOS code, including 64k for your system BIOS (remember, the BIOS lets your computer start DOS from a floppy or hard drive, and also contains some software for displaying characters on the screen and performing a memory checkout and power-on self test.). It was thought that many expansion cards would need some ROM, too, so that's why so much space (relatively speaking) was set aside.

And along the way, many video cards did use some space up there. Monochrome video cards frequently used memory at address B0000 through B7FFF (don't worry about what these hexadecimal numbers mean: just consider them labels that appear on the memory map in Figure 21-4). Early color graphic cards grabbed B8000–BFFFF, so it was possible to have both types of video cards, black-and-white and color, in the same machine. Contemporary VGA cards own A0000 through AFFFF, C0000 through C7FFF, and since they can usually simulate the early cards as well, can use areas from B0000 through BFFFF, too. (Actually, since almost nobody uses monochrome video/graphics modes anymore, the old region from B0000 through B7FFF lies fallow and is ripe for exploitation. But more on that later.)

Back to conventional memory

There's still the first 640k within that 1mb of address space (remember that each byte of memory is located by its unique address). Addresses within the first megabyte run from 00000, 00001, 00002 ... 10001, 10002, 10003 ... all the way up to FFFFC, FFFFD, FFFFE and FFFFF. The range from 0 to 640k is shown on the memory map as 00000 to 9FFFF.

The memory map in Figure 21-4 shows the zones of memory as used by IBM-PC computers. While a mere 64k of RAM may have been a little limiting, at the time, 256k of RAM was plenty, and some power users upgraded to 512k just to show off. That was back in the days of 360k floppy disk drives and 5 and 10mb hard drives, and we're talking only ten years ago. If automobiles had progressed this fast, we'd all be flying now, don't you think?

RAM Takes Off

Then something greedy came on the scene, and computing was rapidly transformed. The original Visicalc program, the mother of all spreadsheets, was such a hit that it quickly and powerfully boosted the sales of the original Apple II computer (that's the pre-Macintosh Apple). Due to what some said were unfortunate marketing blunders, VisiCorp failed to make a successful transition to the IBM PC, and a little startup company called Lotus came out with their 1-2-3 spreadsheet. And that's where the memory voracity came into the picture.

Managers around the world began creating models of their businesses, in great detail, creating spreadsheets with dozens of columns and hundreds of rows. Others saw Lotus 1-2-3 as a great new database substitute and started filling it with all their mailing labels and so forth. But the only problem was that the entire spreadsheet had to fit in RAM, and when you considered the memory already used up by DOS and Lotus 1-2-3 itself, there just wasn't enough room—even in 640k!—for these burgeoning spreadsheets people were building.

Something had to be done. It was easy enough to build larger hard drives and wide carriage printers (ideal for spreadsheets), and RAM was getting cheap enough, but DOS still had that 640k limit. Also, the 8088 microprocessor couldn't blithely step over that one megabyte fence, either.

The spreadsheet solution: expanded memory

Two things happened. In 1985, Lotus, Intel and Microsoft invented a new *expanded memory system* (EMS) board that circumvented the limitations. It allowed *paged* access to any amount of extra memory. Each "page" is only 64k of RAM, but the *page frame* (a special 64k block of RAM) can "point to" any part of the memory on the expanded memory board. Therefore, by "scrolling" through the 64k window, the EMS technique could get at any of the memory in this larger pool of RAM.

The 64k size of the page was not considered awkward either, since even "main" RAM between 0 and 1 megabytes had to be accessed in 64k chunks, due to the 16-bit constraints of the 8088. (If you shuffled a deck of cards this way, you wouldn't be able to shuffle the entire deck. Instead, you'd divide the stack into smaller stacks and shuffle each sub-stack.)

To make room for the extra 64k required for the EMS page frame, sometimes 64k was subtracted from the 640k RAM and set aside for the page frame (no great sacrifice if it lets you access megabytes of additional memory). Other times, on some computers, the page frame could locate itself in the often unused address space in the top 384k of addresses within that first megabyte.

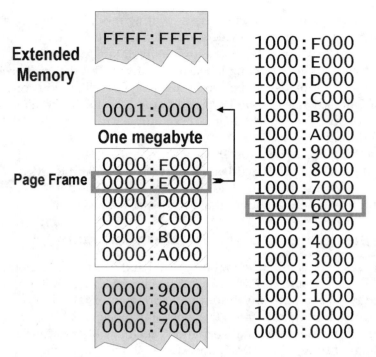

Figure 21-5: *The expanded memory page frame is like a "window" that slides across available RAM.*

Then Intel raised the stakes when it designed the 80286 microprocessor. This advanced chip was up to three times faster than the 8088, could directly address up to 16mb of RAM but still could use only 64k at a time. This so-called *segmented memory architecture* influenced all programming and resulted in less efficient programming, too. Applications were designed and programmed with this awkward restriction causing various kinds of inefficiencies. Programmers writing applications for other microprocessors, such as the Motorola 68000 used by the Apple Macintosh, could directly access all memory continuously. It was like pulling up venetian blinds—the computer could now see the whole picture, undivided and entire.

No longer limited to 1mb of address space, the 80286 PC chip could access the extended memory beyond 1mb directly, without having to resort to the page frame trick. Hardware manufacturers began to discontinue using expanded memory in favor of this new, faster, extended memory. The only problem was that DOS still couldn't make any use of all this new memory, and far too many programs continued to rely on the older expanded memory (far too many DOS program still do, even to this day).

Red-hot RAM

The PC industry came up with two solutions: In cooperation with leading developers, Microsoft developed new specifications for accessing extended memory so that multiple programs could share this bonanza, and they created a HIMEM.SYS driver to make sense of it and manage it. HIMEM.SYS turned "raw" extended memory into XMS memory, the now-preferred standard.

But what about those programs that still need expanded memory? Extended memory was cheaper to build into computers and was also a lot faster than expanded memory cards. The elegant solution came with the introduction of Intel's 80386 chip, the first Intel chip with true 32-bit-wide addressing, meaning that it can directly access up to four billion bytes of RAM (4gb; it will be awhile before we see this much RAM in our machines). Instead of reading or writing data one byte at a time, the 32-bit data pathway allowed the microprocessor to access and process four bytes at the same time.

Because the 286 couldn't take full advantage of all its memory, we had to wait for the introduction of the 80386 chip to really take advantage of large amounts of RAM memory. It wasn't until now, with the release of Windows 95, that our computers have the caught up with this 32-bit, full-memory-direct-access technology. No wonder there's a sudden burst of speed, power, and efficiency ushered in by the 32-bit *flat memory model* of Windows 95 made possible by the 386 processor. (More on this a little later.)

Another new technology of the 80386 processor allows memory to be divided into multiple regions, ideal for a multitasking operating system like Windows. A program can be given one of these zones of memory for its use, and the microprocessor can *fault* (announce a failure) when the program attempts to access memory that it has not been given permission for. An error like this means that a program is running into bugs that could potentially corrupt many programs and their data, so this new *protected mode* proved invaluable in creating a safer, more secure environment for Windows, OS/2 and other PC operating systems.

Ironically, protected mode's hair-trigger response to illegal memory access can make Windows seem unstable, since it crashes at the first sign of a protection violation. Since there is no way to know how far the damage has gone, it's usually safer to shut down the entire computer and reboot when you get a General Protection Fault (which was called an Unrecoverable Application Error in Windows 3.0).

Windows 95 goes even further than Windows 3.1 to validate a programs' procedure calls, verifying that no mistakes were made by the programmer.

Overall, this helps programming errors from cascading into more serious corruption. When you run programs designed for 32-bit mode, Windows can provide even more protection and permit you to continue using other programs even when one of them fails drastically and has to be shut down.

 TIP   If you encounter a crash or lockup, meaning that the mouse and keyboard doesn't respond and the mouse cursor remains an hourglass for a long time, you may think you have to turn off the computer or press the Reset button to reboot all over again. Instead, try pressing the Ctrl+Alt+Del keys at the same time. In many cases, Windows can "break out" of the crash and show you a list of running programs. If a program in the list is shown as "not responding," you can click on it and then on the End Task button to excise the offending program and free up your computer.

With the new protected mode of the 80386 finally working properly (unlike the limited usefulness of protected mode on the 80286), Microsoft engineered the EMM386.EXE memory manager software to emulate (simulate in software) the way expanded memory works as hardware. It could swap sections of extended memory in and out of a 64k simulated page frame, and since the EMS standard was already supported by so much software, the EMM (expanded memory manager) could fool those DOS programs that require EMS into believing they had real expanded memory.

The first EMM386-style program shipped with DOS 4.0 had an annoying problem: any memory you set aside as expanded memory was not available as extended memory anymore. Alternatives like Quarterdeck's QEMM memory management utility worked around these limitations and pioneered many tricky techniques for freeing up conventional memory (the first 640k in the first megabyte of RAM).

Expanded Memory Miracles

At the time, most people paid little attention to expanded memory and EMM386. But with the introduction of DOS 5.0, attention was paid. With DOS 5, EMM386 gained a new power: the ability to load programs into *upper memory blocks*. This trick was used to map some of the extended memory into the memory addresses within the otherwise now-rarely-used memory between 640k and 1mb. This memory is still within the 1mb limit that DOS can directly "see," so it's a fine place to store programs such as device drivers and TSRs.

RAM-resident programs

TSRs are a special breed of DOS utility programs. They Terminate, yet Stay Resident. A "normal" DOS program is resident in memory only while it's actively running and terminates when it completes, freeing up memory. By exploiting a little-known feature of DOS, a program could load into memory, then hide there, monitoring for some event, such as a special keystroke sequence, that would bring it to life. In this way, TSRs add capabilities not found in DOS itself.

All the while, a TSR runs in the background, while other, normal DOS applications do their thing. TSRs were an early, relatively restricted form of multitasking on PCs. They led to the demand for programs like Windows 1.0 that promised to let you switch between multiple DOS programs, even view many of them on the screen at the same time within "windows."

The promise & the illusion

The promise of multitasking is that you don't have to shut down (close) one program before you run another one. Not only can you switch between multiple programs (assuming you have enough memory to keep them all loaded), a true multitasking system apparently allows all the programs to run at the same time. It does this by sharing the microprocessor, dividing its time into multiple slices, and letting each program have a time slice to run for a few microseconds before it gives up its opportunity and lets another program run for a few microseconds. By rapidly switching between all these programs, the illusion of multitasking succeeds in making all the programs run "at the same time." Of course, your microprocessor still does only one thing at a time, but it's fast enough to pull off this hoax.

In Windows NT, you can actually add additional microprocessors to your computer's motherboard and achieve true *symmetrical multiprocessing*. Each microprocessor runs a different program (or subprogram—a *thread*) truly simultaneously. In a few years, expect to see this powerful multiprocessing capability even in affordable personal computers.

DOS extensions

DOS *device drivers* are somewhat like TSRs, in that they stay resident in memory to provide extended services for DOS. For example, by itself, DOS can't access a SCSI hard drive or a Novell network. (SCSI stands for Small Computer System Interface; see Chapters 14 and 15.)

Device drivers are usually loaded from the C:\CONFIG.SYS file; TSRs are usually found in C:\AUTOEXEC.BAT. As we'll see, Windows 95 actually makes most of them obsolete, since it supports most devices directly with superior 32-bit drivers, freeing up the DOS memory that would have been required for the driver software.

A network driver inserts itself into DOS like a benign parasite and fools it into thinking it has additional drives available. This driver then assists DOS in accessing the SCSI hard disk. Other device drivers support devices such as CD-ROMs, scanners, video cards, and of course, the now ubiquitous mouse.

By loading drivers and utilities "out of the way," EMM386 freed up conventional memory (the lower 640k of memory). By relocating DOS into the High Memory Area, and DOS drivers and TSRs into Upper Memory Blocks, a DOS program could have as much as 620k free RAM out of the 640k possible—a virtual miracle.

Memory Ecology

Why was it still important to conserve the first 640k of RAM, especially when it was now possible to add multiple megabytes of RAM? Many DOS programs didn't make any use of expanded or extended memory (EMS or XMS), so you still want as much free conventional RAM as possible. Also available are many desirable drivers and TSRs that enhance DOS, such as the SmartDrive disk cache; RAM disks that emulate hard drives using RAM (so are much faster); network drivers that create simulated hard drives that actually reside on network file servers; printer spoolers to capture printed output and print it "in the background" while you continue to work in your main applications; and pop-up tools like Borland's Sidekick, offering a calendar, notepad, calculator and so forth. (In fact, these types of tools are the ancestors of Windows' accessories such as Notepad and Calculator.)

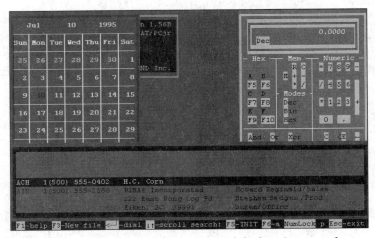

Figure 21-6: *Borland Sidekick was one of the best integrated pop-up TSRs; it foreshadowed the convenience of Windows.*

In fact, these pop-up tools helped create demand for a "DOS extender" like Windows, an advanced way to access multiple applications and tools without the disadvantages of trying to squeeze them all into limited conventional memory.

Up high

But perhaps you're still wondering why it's preferable to load TSRs and drivers into upper memory. Let's take a closer look at upper memory. Recall the 384k of memory addresses (at the top of the memory map in Figure 21-4) that often go unused, and believe it or not, don't actually contain any RAM. But these addresses are valuable because they lie within the first megabyte of RAM that older DOS applications can access.

Because EMM386 knows how to remap memory, for the sake of simulating expanded memory, it can also map some of your extended memory into these otherwise unused addresses. EMM386 makes it look like there is RAM in the upper memory space. It can then load most TSRs and drivers into these zones and magically free up conventional RAM.

Beware of upper memory conflicts

The only snafu with upper memory is that the upper memory addresses aren't always unused. Certainly, the block from F0000 through FFFFF is used for the ROM BIOS we discussed. A VGA video card (and more advanced video cards which, nonetheless, emulate VGA) uses A0000 through AFFFF and C0000 through C7FFF. EMM386 and Windows knows to avoid most areas, but it can't always detect memory used by certain cards, so you may need to manually exclude them (more on this later).

Optimizing DOS Memory

We'll return to a discussion on Windows memory management later in this chapter. But while we're still discussing DOS memory, let's see how to make the most of it, even under Windows.

When your computer first starts, it reads the contents of two special files—CONFIG.SYS and AUTOEXEC.BAT—to figure out how to proceed. It looks at each line, one a time, in order, and runs the program or command on that line. Booting starts with CONFIG.SYS and then proceeds with AUTOEXEC.BAT.

CONFIG.SYS mostly contains configuration information, as the name implies, including *device drivers* (for devices like CD-ROM drives).

AUTOEXEC.BAT is a *batch file*, a simple kind of program (written in a rudimentary programming language) that gets the computer ready to start Windows. It usually has lines to start drivers that can't go in CONFIG.SYS, such as most TSRs.

In Chapter 22, "The Other Face: DOS 7," we explain a special way to run DOS programs outside Windows, using MS-DOS mode. In MS-DOS mode, you can create custom CONFIG.SYS and AUTOEXEC.BAT files for your special DOS programs that won't run properly within Windows 95. The techniques for DOS memory optimization (described later in this chapter) would then be applied to these special-case versions of AUTOEXEC.BAT and CONFIG.SYS, not your actual (original) versions in the C:\ directory, which you use only for starting Windows 95.

 Click on the Start button and select Programs I MS-DOS Prompt to start a DOS session within Windows 95. You can also press Shift+F5 during bootup to prevent Windows from loading and access DOS 7 directly.

You can use the DOS prompt if you want to make all these changes directly using DOS commands. In DOS, type **EDIT C:\CONFIG.SYS** or **EDIT C:\AUTOEXEC.BAT**. Or you can run Notepad and then select File I Open to edit these files.

 The Windows utility SYSEDIT is stored in the WINDOWS\SYSTEM folder (see Chapter 4 to learn how to navigate through folders). SYSEDIT displays all your system files in one place for convenient access. To activate SYSEDIT, click on Start and then select Run. Type **SYSEDIT** and then press Enter. (Use the SYSEDIT's Window menu to find CONFIG.SYS or AUTOEXEC.BAT if they get buried or overlapped by the other windows.) If you use it frequently, consider creating a Shortcut to SYSEDIT for future use.

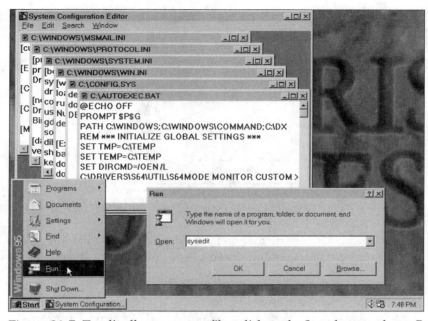

Figure 21-7: *To edit all your system files, click on the Start button, choose Run, type* **SYSEDIT** *and press Enter. You may also want to create a shortcut to SYSEDIT if you use it a lot.*

Rewiring CONFIG.SYS

Now that you've got your tools at hand, let's plunge in and see how to optimize your system files to maximize memory for running DOS programs. Since Windows does a credible job of setting up your system files for you, you can skip ahead to "Making the Most of Windows Memory" if you don't use DOS programs or require DOS device drivers.

Back up your system files first

All of this tomfoolery with boot files is enough to make even the most determined optimizing nut a little queasy. It's a good idea to make backup copies of your CONFIG.SYS and AUTOEXEC.BAT files on a floppy disk before you start adjusting them.

Figure 21-8: *Create Disk makes it easy to keep your important system files safe.*

You can also create an emergency startup disk that keeps the original files on a disk for safekeeping. Here's how:

1. Click on Start and then select Settings.
2. Click on Control Panel.
3. Double-click on the icon for Add/Remove Programs.
4. Click on the Startup Disk tab.
5. Insert a disk in the drive and click on the Create Disk button.

Another way to bypass a messed up set of system files (if things don't work well after you've made your changes to CONFIG.SYS and AUTOEXEC.BAT) is to press Shift and the F5 function key as soon as you see the message "Starting Windows 95" after you turn on your computer. This key combination dumps you rather ungracefully into DOS, skipping CONFIG.SYS and AUTOEXEC.BAT entirely.

Onward With Optimizing

Assuming you've saved a copy of CONFIG.SYS and AUTOEXEC.BAT to a disk, let's start making some changes. Since HIMEM.SYS is a prerequisite for using EMM386, it must come first in your CONFIG.SYS. Besides, it's always good to free up the roughly 45k that DOS consumes by forcing it into the Upper Memory Area (the area just above the first megabyte of RAM). So be sure to include the line DOS=HIGH. Otherwise, DOS simply ignores the Upper Memory Area and plugs itself into lower memory, eating up part of that precious resource.

If you have EMM386.EXE in your CONFIG.SYS, it will look something like this (HIMEM.SYS is always required if EMM386.EXE is used):

```
DEVICE=C:\WINDOWS\HIMEM.SYS
DOS=HIGH
DEVICE=C:\WINDOWS\EMM386.EXE RAM
```

The word *RAM* following EMM386.EXE allows EMM386 to provide expanded memory for those DOS programs that need it. **Note:** Windows programs do not need, nor can they take advantage of expanded memory. Don't use expanded memory if you don't need it for running DOS.

Here's an alternative option, NOEMS:

```
DEVICE=C:\WINDOWS\HIMEM.SYS
DOS=HIGH
DEVICE=C:\WINDOWS\EMM386.EXE NOEMS
```

The NOEMS keyword allows EMM386 to load software into upper memory but disables the EMS emulation. Using this keyword also frees up the memory block E0000 through EFFFF, which is usually reserved for the page frame. On most computers, you can add another 32k of upper memory blocks by adding the following *include switch* I=B000-B7FF:

```
DEVICE=C:\DOS\HIMEM.SYS
DOS=HIGH
DEVICE=C:\WINDOWS\EMM386.EXE NOEMS I=B000-B7FF
```

Note that we are now including the memory range B0000-B7FFF. It's common to leave off the last digit of the actual memory addresses, as shown in the memory map in Figure 24-7, so that's why we only referenced B000-B7FF.

 Windows might not work properly when you enable the use of the B0000-B7FFF memory range. It's only for those truly desperate for more DOS memory. You'll probably have to add the line DEVICE=MONOUMB.386 after the [Enhanced] keyword in SYSTEM.INI. The MONOUMB.386 driver is included with earlier versions of MS-DOS. It's also found on the Windows 95 CD-ROM (not the one in this book) in the \OTHER\OLDMSDOS folder.

Protecting your hardware

If you have a hardware card that actually does use upper memory for DMA (direct memory access) or ROM, you may need to add an *exclude switch* to the EMM386 line. For example, with a SCSI card that uses DC000 through DFFFF, you'd have the following:

```
DEVICE=C:\WINDOWS\HIMEM.SYS
DEVICE=C:\WINDOWS\EMM386.EXE NOEMS I=B000-B7FF X=DC00-DFFF
```

Again, note that we drop the last digit of the range DC0000-DFFFF when referenced by EMM386.

Now that EMM386 is purring, you're ready to transform those stodgy old drivers and TSRs. What follows is a fictional set of system files, for illustration only. It shows you how you can move the CD-ROM driver (CDDRIVER.SYS) and the DOS interface to the CD-ROM (MSCDEX.EXE) into upper memory and free a considerable amount of conventional memory. (For simplicity, we don't show other common lines in these files, such as FILES=, BUFFERS=, PATH, PROMPT and so on.)

CONFIG.SYS, Before:

```
DEVICE=C:\DRIVERS\CDDRIVER.SYS /D:MSCD001
```

CONFIG.SYS, After:

```
DEVICE=C:\WINDOWS\HIMEM.SYS
DEVICE=C:\WINDOWS\EMM386.EXE NOEMS
DOS=HIGH
DOS=UMB
DEVICEHIGH=C:\DRIVERS\CDDRIVER.SYS /D:MSCD001
```

Notice the addition of DOS=UMB. This line tells DOS to actually use the upper memory blocks that EMM386 provides. DEVICEHIGH is the substitute for DEVICE, and LOADHIGH leaves a TSR in a UMB. Also notice that we don't use DEVICEHIGH with HIMEM.SYS and EMM386. That's because EMM386 is loaded after HIMEM.SYS, so it can't be used to load HIMEM.SYS into high memory. And EMM386 already moves most of itself into upper memory, and since it provides this "load high" capability, it's kind of like putting the cart before the horse to use DEVICEHIGH=EMM386.EXE.

AUTOEXEC.BAT, Before:

C:\WINDOWS\COMMAND\MSCDEX.EXE /D:MSCD001 /M:15

AUTOEXEC.BAT, After:

LOADHIGH C:\WINDOWS\COMMAND\MSCDEX.EXE /D:MSCD001 /M:15

If you want to see how well you've done with your optimizing efforts, you can switch to the DOS command line and type **MEM /C /P** to get a detailed memory map, as shown in Table 21-3. It clearly shows which programs (modules) load in conventional memory and which go into upper memory. It also gives you a summary of total free memory, total conventional memory, free upper memory and the largest free upper memory block. (Note that Windows also leaves a "stub" of itself in DOS memory, which shows up on this table as "WIN.")

To get a true picture of your memory map, you have to run MEM /C "outside" of Windows, which you can achieve by pressing F8 during bootup, and choosing option 5 ("Command prompt only,") which lets you start your CONFIG.SYS and AUTOEXEC.BAT files without starting Windows. Otherwise, the MEM command reflects only the settings in the MS-DOS Properties for the DOS Prompt.

Typical DOS Memory Layout as reported by DOS			
Modules using memory below 1 MB:			
Name	Total	Conventional	Upper Memory
MSDOS	17,789 (17K)	17,789 (17K)	0 (0K)
HHSCAN	8,800 (9K)	8,800 (9K)	0 (0K)
HIMEM	1,168 (1K)	1,168 (1K)	0 (0K)
DBLBUFF	2,448 (2K)	2,448 (2K)	0 (0K)
IFSHLP	2,816 (3K)	2,816 (3K)	0 (0K)
SETVER	688 (1K)	688 (1K)	0 (0K)
COMMAND	32 (0K)	32 (0K)	0 (0K)
SAPI	13,568 (13K)	13,568 (13K)	0 (0K)
S64MODE	1,600 (2K)	1,600 (2K)	0 (0K)
WIN	3,424 (3K)	3,424 (3K)	0 (0K)
vmm32	3,088 (3K)	3,088 (3K)	0 (0K)
COMMAND	7,456 (7K)	7,456 (7K)	0 (0K)
Free	590,304 (576K)	590,304 (576K)	0 (0K)

```
Memory Summary:
Type of Memory          Total         Used          Free

Conventional            655,360        65,056       590,304
Upper                         0             0             0
Reserved                393,216       393,216             0
Extended (XMS)       32,505,856    11,943,936    20,561,920


Total memory         33,554,432    12,402,208    21,152,224
Total under 1MB         655,360        65,056       590,304


Total Expanded (EMS)               33,046,528 (32M)
Free Expanded (EMS)                16,777,216 (16M)
Largest executable program size      590,256 (576K)
Largest free upper memory block            0 (0K)
MS-DOS is resident in the high memory area.
```

Table 21-3: *Typical DOS memory layout.*

To get a true picture of your memory map, you have to run MEM /C outside Windows, which you can achieve by pressing F8 during bootup and choosing option 5 (Command prompt only), which lets you start your CONFIG.SYS and AUTOEXEC.BAT files without starting Windows. Otherwise, the MEM command reflects only the settings in the MS-DOS Properties for the DOS prompt.

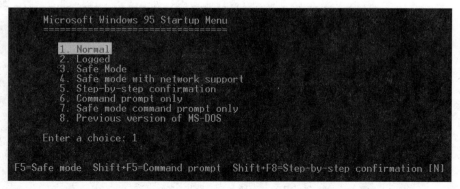

Figure 21-9: *Press F8 during startup to get this list of different ways to run DOS and Windows, useful for troubleshooting. This list may also appear if Windows did not start properly the last time you booted.*

Does DOS Really Matter?

Optimizing DOS memory won't necessarily make Windows run any better, although it does help when running DOS applications in a DOS session, since each new DOS session "inherits" the settings of the original DOS session that exists during boot time, before Windows is started. And it's that original DOS configuration that AUTOEXEC.BAT and CONFIG.SYS define.

Windows 95 actually uses some conventional memory for certain drivers, so optimizing conventional memory can be useful even if you don't use MS-DOS programs. But the techniques presented here may be overkill for this purpose; Windows 95 already frees up a great deal of conventional memory when you use Windows 95 drivers.

As we mentioned, Windows 95 now supports most hardware devices with 32-bit drivers that don't use any conventional memory, making these devices available both for Windows and DOS programs. An example is the driver for the mouse. You don't need to put MOUSE.EXE in your AUTOEXEC.BAT anymore; the Windows mouse driver provides DOS mouse support directly now.

When running DOS programs from within Windows 95, you don't need EMM386 if all you need is expanded memory support. Windows 95 can provide expanded memory emulation directly, unless you've loaded EMM386 in your CONFIG.SYS file. Note that if you use the NOEMS option of EMM386, which you might do if you're just using EMM386's ability to load TSRs into upper memory, Windows will not provide expanded memory services, since this function has been co-opted by EMM386.

Windows 95 replaces most types of TSRs and device drivers with its own software, and therefore makes it unnecessary to worry so much about optimizing DOS memory with EMM386. You may get best results by simply removing all your unnecessary drivers and getting rid of EMM386 altogether.

Getting rid of drivers

To find out which drivers or other items you really need in AUTOEXEC.BAT and CONFIG.SYS, first make a backup copy of these two system files and then try adding the word *REM* to the beginning of each line in these files. This way, you can disable the line but later reenable it just by taking out the REM. After neutering CONFIG.SYS and AUTOEXEC.BAT, start Windows 95 and see if everything still works, including your CD-ROM drive, mouse and so forth. If so, you can actually delete AUTOEXEC.BAT and CONFIG.SYS; Windows doesn't need them at all! (Otherwise, you may need to selectively reenable some lines, in case your brand of CD-ROM doesn't have Windows 95 drivers yet, for example.)

Disabled:

REM DEVICEHIGH=C:\DRIVERS\CDDRIVER.SYS /D:MSCD001

Enabled:

DEVICEHIGH=C:\DRIVERS\CDDRIVER.SYS /D:MSCD001

Making the Most of Windows Memory

Even with multiple megabytes, it's easy to use up memory in Windows 95, especially if you're trying to manage with only 4mb of RAM. For example, with that relatively small amount of RAM, the disk cache must be kept to a minimum size (but it can't be eliminated altogether, or hard drive access becomes unbearably slow).

What to do? The first thing to get rid of is Windows wallpaper. Although it's sometimes pretty, wallpaper uses memory at all times, even though it's just an adornment. It's especially inefficient to display wallpaper if you are using a high-resolution video card with lots of colors. A 1024x768, 256-color screen requires a full megabyte to store a screen of wallpaper, even if the wallpaper is covered up by a maximized application. The more typical 800x600, 256-color display mode still uses fully half a megabyte of RAM for wallpaper. You just can't afford this extravagance unless you have at least 8mb of RAM, and even then, question if you really want to spend $25 to $50 worth of memory for a pretty picture. (The extra time required to redraw the wallpaper when you move windows around can also make a slow computer feel even more sluggish.)

Of course, you could use wallpaper most of the time and get rid of it only when you run low on RAM. Run Display from the Control Panel (or right-click on the empty desktop and choose Properties); then click on the Background tab heading to change your wallpaper, as shown in Figure 21-10.

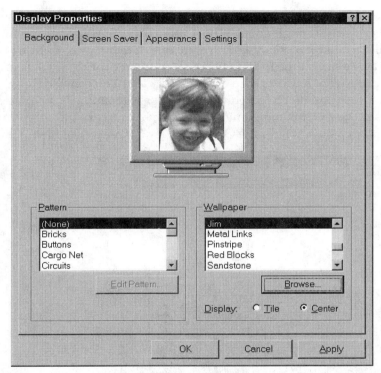

Figure 21-10: *Wallpaper can waste from 512k to a full megabyte, depending on your display settings.*

If you do want decoration, a much less memory-expensive alternative is to choose a Pattern from the same dialog box, although it's difficult to find a pleasing pattern that doesn't give you a headache eventually. Although smaller, tiled wallpaper patterns use less disk space, they still use just as much memory when active as wallpaper, since Windows has to keep the entire wallpaper image in memory for fast redrawing when you move windows around. (Read more about wallpaper in Chapter 6.)

Minimizing Multitasking

If you're running low on RAM, you'll want to close programs that you're no longer using. You can click on any program showing on the taskbar to switch to it and then click its Close button (the little X in the upper-right corner) to shut it down. Or right-click on its icon in the taskbar and choose Close to terminate it.

However, a few utility programs hide their icons and don't show up on the taskbar, and although none of these utilities come with Windows, they are usually available as shareware. To kill one of them, press the Ctrl+Alt+Del keys at the same time to see a list of all running programs. Click on the program you want to close; then choose End Task. You can use the same trick to close a program that's locked up, no longer responding to your keyboard or mouse actions. This sometimes seems to halt or freeze the entire computer. But before you reach for the Off switch, try Ctrl+Alt+Del first.

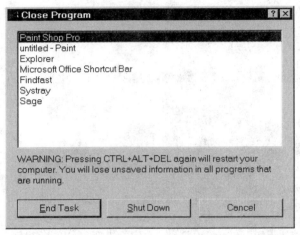

Figure 21-11: *Press Ctrl+Alt+Del to get a list of all running "tasks" (programs).*

Put Your Computer on a Diet

Another way to free up memory is to install your favorite applications fat-free. This is also necessary when installing applications on many notebook computers, which typically have considerably smaller hard drives and less memory than their desktop counterparts. Most install programs feature a Minimal Install or Compact Install option. Not only does it save disk space to forgo the spelling checker, equation editor, graph designer or art module, it also saves having to load support programming code for these modules when you're not using them.

Old programs, even those you never use anymore, can also leave traces of themselves behind. You may think you've removed them from your computer by deleting them from your hard drive, but Windows may still be loading drivers and libraries previously installed by the old software. You may want to try one of the commercial Windows uninstaller programs to root out all detitrus. (We also discuss this issue in Chapter 4.)

Windows also has an Uninstall feature. Click the Start button and then select Settings | Control Panel | Add/Remove Programs. In this dialog box, you'll find a list of any applications that, when originally installed, notified Windows of all their components. Also, you can at least free up some disk space by removing any of Windows' own accessories, such as games, that you don't use. Click on the Windows Setup tab to get rid of these accessories.

Too Many Fonts

It's also all too easy to get carried away with fonts. With TrueType fonts at an all-time low price and often included by the hundreds with applications like CorelDRAW or Microsoft Office, you may have dozens of TrueType fonts installed on your computer, even though you probably use only a handful regularly. Resist the temptation to install every font you fancy, unless you have lots of memory. Lots of fonts take a long time to load when you start Windows, and, once loaded, waste memory that your applications may need.

Select Start | Settings | Control Panel to start the Control Panel. Next, double-click on Fonts to open the Fonts folder and see the fonts you have installed. It may surprise you to see how many you have, unless you've just installed Windows 95 from scratch. Click on any font you no longer need and press the Del key to remove it if it's a shortcut to a font elsewhere on the drive. On the other hand, some fonts make themselves at home in the Fonts folder. To avoid deleting the original file from your hard drive, move the font to another folder. That way, you still have the font easily available in case you do want it later. (Remember that a shortcut is identified by the small curved arrow in the lower left of an icon.) See Chapter 12, "Personal Publishing," to learn more about using fonts in your programs.

Cut Out Cut & Paste

Watch out for the Windows Clipboard. It's possible to cut or copy huge objects (high-resolution graphics can be many megabytes in size) into the Clipboard. Even after something is pasted, it still remains in the Clipboard until something else is stored there. The easiest way to clear the Clipboard is to select and copy something trivial, like a single character or a tiny part of a picture.

OLE (Object Linking and Embedding) can also be a memory monster. If you have an object from Excel and an object from Access and an object from CorelDRAW all inserted into a Microsoft Word document, all four applications must be running in order to update or print the document. The advent of component objects, which contain only the program fragments needed to display or print an object, will help relieve this "RAM cram" in the future. You can also avoid this mess by pasting the object as a *link* to the original object, instead of embedding it. (For more on OLE, see Chapter 11, "Compound Documents.")

Finally, the best way to save memory is to choose Display as Icon, which reduces both RAM and video overhead.

 Here's another way to save memory: Instead of referencing an Access database directly in a Word mail merge operation, just export the part of the database you're using for addresses as a text file, and use the text file for the mail merge. It's less convenient, since you have to export the database table again if you've made changes to the table, but it avoids having to load both Access and Word during the mail merge.

What About Limited Resources?

You may be all too familiar with the resource depletion that plagued Windows 3.1. No matter how much total memory you had, you were still restricted to four 64k chunks of memory for many purposes. Most resources were taken from one of the three User heaps, the rest from a single 64K GDI (Graphics Device Interface) heap. The memory needed to keep track of all the icons, graphics and user interface elements (visual controls such as check boxes, edit fields and menus); they had to be acquired from one of these limited heaps of memory. When programs allocated memory for tables and documents, the user heap gradually filled up, too.

Even on a computer with eight more megabytes of RAM, it was still not uncommon to get an Out of Memory error due to overusage of these 64k heaps. Worse, when a program closed, it often left behind pieces of itself in the heaps, so as you opened and closed programs during the workday, your resources would mysteriously dwindle. (These 64k limitations are a hallmark of 16-bit code, a legacy of the original *segmented memory architecture* of the 8088, as we discussed earlier in this chapter.)

Windows 3.1 could become unstable and even lock up when resources got too low, so savvy users learned to restart their computers, sometimes several times a day if they were very busy, to forestall the problems caused by resource depletion. Rebooting clears the slate, so to speak, and frees up lost resources. You get clean heaps that way.

Thankfully, these frustrating inconveniences are just a bad memory now with Windows 95. Instead of just 64k heaps, Windows 95 can now draw upon the full amount of memory in your computer for most purposes. When you exit a 32-bit Windows application, Windows automatically frees up any leftover resources, even if the application's programmers forgot to do so. Although 16-bit Windows programs can fail to free up resources, Windows 95 can now clear them automatically, as soon as all running 16-bit programs have been closed. (It waits until they are all shut down because some older Windows programs actually depend on finding resources left behind by a previous program.)

Advanced Memory Optimization

If this book were about Windows 3.1, we could discuss additional ways to optimize memory. We'd talk about setting up a permanent swap file, carefully choosing a size for the SmartDrive disk cache, and whether to also cache floppy drives and CD-ROMs. (Caching takes place when the computer stores frequently accessed files in memory for quick reference.)

But there's almost nothing to fiddle with in Windows 95. It's all automatic. There is no fixed size for the hard disk cache. Windows can use all available memory for this purpose, and it frees up the cache dynamically, whenever necessary.

Instead of a permanent swap file, Windows uses an ordinary file on the hard disk to dump temporarily idle memory and then reclaim it when the memory pages are needed again. The virtual memory management in Windows 95 is far more sophisticated than it was in Windows 3.1. In fact, there is no advantage to choosing its size, unless you need to limit how much disk space it consumes.

While you should avoid changing your swap-file settings, since this may actually impair your performance and reduce memory, you'll still probably want to see where the "dials and knobs" are, even if you don't twiddle them. (And you shouldn't; Windows knows best in this situation.) Click on Start and then select Settings | Control Panel. Then click on the System icon. (Or right-click on My Computer from the desktop and choose Properties.) Then click on the Performance tab to see the property sheet shown in Figure 21-12.

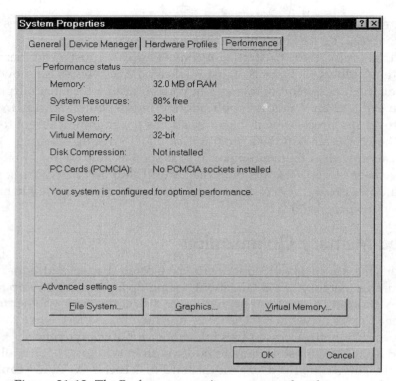

Figure 21-12: *The Performance settings property sheet lets you review your computer's free memory and related resources and observe other technical statistics, such as the type of file system in use.*

You can configure two memory-related settings from this panel. First, click on the Virtual Memory button. You then see the property sheet shown in Figure 21-13. (We'll discuss the File System choice below.)

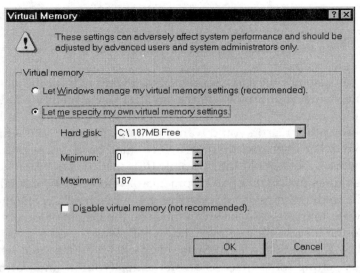

Figure 21-13: *The Virtual Memory settings let you "twiddle" the knobs and dials of the swap file, even though this isn't necessary—or even wise. It's a good idea to leave these settings alone—let Windows manage your virtual memory.*

Virtual Memory—A Closer Look

Virtual memory is a kind of substitute for RAM. Virtual memory uses your hard drive to store pages (zones) of memory that aren't currently in use, such as when a program is minimized on the taskbar. This way, Windows can pretend it has more usable RAM than you actually have as physical memory chips.

If you upgraded from Windows 3.1, you may still have a permanent swap file on your hard drive. The permanence of the Windows 3.1 swap file resulted in better performance because Windows knew precisely where on the disk to go. What's more, this huge file was contiguous—all in one place on the drive, without the fragmentation that can put pieces of a file on various locations on the drive. (Read more about fragmentation and hard drive optimization in Chapter 5, "Inside the File System.")

To avoid wasting the hard drive space, Windows 95 may reuse the permanent swap file as the basis for its virtual memory system. In this case, on the Virtual Memory settings panel, instead of the *Let Windows manage my virtual memory settings (recommended)* option, the virtual memory box shows the *Let me specify my own virtual memory settings* option. The size of the permanent swap file is shown in both the Minimum and Maximum settings. (See the "Hands-On" section to learn how to remove an old permanent swap file.")

You can also use the same settings if you want to limit the size of the swap file, using Minimum to set the smallest size (8mb is a good value for this) and Maximum for the largest size it can grow to (24 to 32mb are best).

The only other reason you'd want to change the swap file settings is if you need to move it. Perhaps you have a very small hard drive, and you rely on the network drive to hold the swap file (this tactic is best avoided, though—it slows things up too much to be practical). Windows 95 normally stores the swap file in the Windows folder. If you have two hard drives, though, you might want to make sure the swap file is on the fastest of the two.

Although it's okay to keep a Windows 95 swap file on a compressed drive created by DoubleSpace, DriveSpace or Stacker, you may get better performance by setting some space aside on the host volume and putting the swap file there. However, since this limits the maximum size of the swap file, you may in some cases notice decreased performance by moving the swap file from your large compressed drive to the smaller amount of space left over on the host volume. (You can read more about setting up DriveSpace disk compression in Chapter 5, "Inside the File System.")

Once you've chosen the *Let me specify my own swap file settings* option, you can drop down a list of drives on your computer by clicking next to Hard Disk (shown in Figure 21-13) and choose the drive to host the swap file.

If you're coming from a DOS background, you may consider creating a RAM disk and putting the swap file there for the ultimate in speed. Don't. A RAM disk wastes memory that can be much more intelligently managed by Windows (a large disk cache has almost all the advantages of a RAM disk, and is much safer, since Windows continuously transfers the RAM cache to the hard drive, whereas the entire contents of a RAM disk can be erased by a crash or power failure). And putting a swap file on a RAM disk makes no sense. Think about it: Windows discards unused memory to a swap file—a swap file on a RAM disk? That just moves memory around, it doesn't free up anything.

Why does Windows 95 need such a big swap file? One reason is that it doesn't always reuse space at the beginning of the swap file, preferring to just add to the end of the swap file, for the sake of speed. It will occasionally compact the swap file during idle times, and the swap file is reset to its minimum size whenever you restart Windows. The large size required for fast performance is one reason that you don't want to manually change these settings, hampering Windows by restricting the size of its swap file.

One exception: If you have as much as 24mb of RAM, you may actually get better performance by disabling the swap file, selecting the Disable virtual memory (not recommended) option, as shown in Figure 21-13. But think twice before you do this. If you have that much RAM, you probably need it, and having a swap file will let you open larger documents and graphics than even your large amount of RAM can manage. Since some paging always occurs, no matter how much RAM you have, disabling virtual memory may make your computer run more smoothly if you have lots of RAM.

Hands-On: Getting Rid of an Old Permanent Swap File

You may want to get rid of your permanent swap file if you no longer run Windows 3.1. Here's how:

1. Configure Explorer to show hidden files (the permanent swap file, 386spart.par, is a hidden file).
   a. In Explorer, click on View | Options.
   b. From the View Options property sheet, choose *Show All Files*.
   c. Close the View Options page by clicking on OK.
2. Open the Control Panel by selecting Start | Settings | Control Panel.
3. Double-click on the System icon.
4. Click on the Performance tab heading on the System Properties panel.
5. Click on the Virtual Memory button on the Performance property sheet.
6. Choose the *Let Windows manage my virtual memory settings* option.
7. Close the System Properties sheet and allow Windows to restart.
8. When Windows is ready again, open Explorer by selecting Start | Programs | Windows Explorer.
9. Click on the icon for your C: drive to view the root directory.
10. Look for a file named 386spart.par.
11. If you can't find it, and you're sure you have a permanent swap file, check that you've performed Step 1; then look for the swap file on a different drive.
12. Click on the 386spart.par filename and press the Delete key, or choose File | Delete.
13. Windows responds by saying, "386spart.par is a system file. Deleting this file may make your system or some programs no longer work correctly." It then asks, "Are you sure you want to remove it?"

14. If you're sure you aren't still using Windows 3.1 (which may be true if you installed Windows 95 to a new directory), click Yes.
15. You've now freed up the fixed amount of disk space used by the swap file.

Optimizing CD-ROM Caching

Even a modest CD-ROM cache can speed up these sluggish creatures. By keeping the most popular and frequently accessed files in memory, you save the time it takes to go back to the disc to retrieve them.

However, Windows 95 doesn't require that you install a separate commercial caching program to speed up your CD-ROM drive. CD-ROM caching is built into Windows now, so you'll want to jettison any third-party CD-ROM "accelerators" still cluttering up your CONFIG.SYS and AUTOEXEC.BAT files. Delete them. And be skeptical of claims that these third-party caches provide superior performance; it's not likely to improve on Windows 32-bit caching system, and most of these third-party CD utilities were designed for DOS and Windows 3.1 anyway.

But you may still need to "tweak" Windows CD-ROM settings for best performance. Open the System Properties sheet by clicking on the System icon in the Control Panel (or right-clicking on My Computer and choosing Properties.) This time, click on the File System tab heading. You'll see a page similar to Figure 21-14.

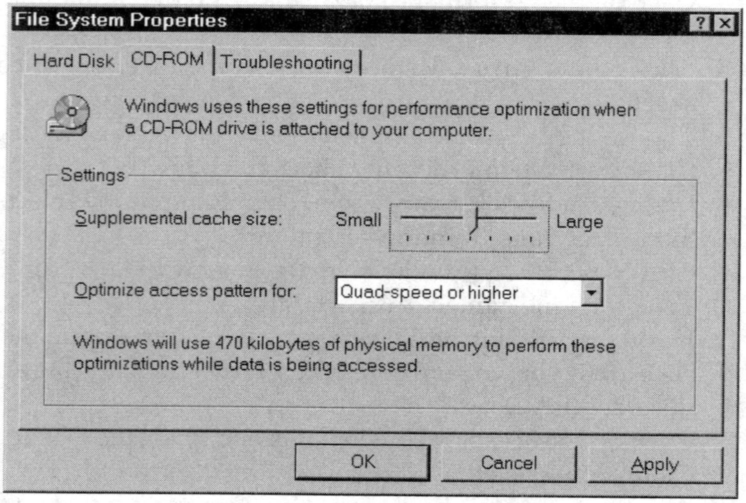

Figure 21-14: *File System Properties allow you to configure the CD-ROM cache, among other things.*

Under the section for CD-ROM, you can choose the type of drive you have (single speed, double speed, triple speed, quad speed or higher) and adjust the size of the CD-ROM cache. Unless you have only 4mb of RAM, it makes sense to choose the largest size, which occupies only a modest 676k of memory while accessing the CD-ROM (this memory is freed up when the CD-ROM isn't being used).

 TIP If video clips don't seem to play as smoothly as you like, make sure the CD-ROM settings are optimal for your system. Experiment. You might also try actually reducing the size of the CD-ROM cache, to avoid the delay caused by prereading the data into the cache. Another option is to choose No read ahead as the CD type.

Hard Drive Optimization

The File System property sheets also include a section for Hard Disk. Click it and you'll see something like Figure 21-15. Normally, you'll leave it as is. The drop-down list box contains options for *Desktop computer, Mobile or docking system,* and *Network server.* Each computer application requires a different set of optimizations, so you're telling Windows 95 which type best describes your computer. If your computer shares its hard drives with other computers on a network and gets heavy access, you'll want to choose Network server.

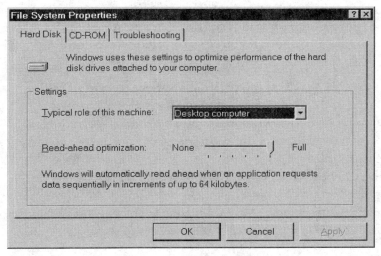

Figure 21-15: *Normally, you won't make any changes to your hard drive optimization.*

This panel also contains a slider for the size of the read-ahead cache. Windows 95 not only stores frequently accessed data in the cache, it also tries to anticipate file access by reading ahead of the current position in the file. Normally, the read-ahead cache is set to maximum, since it takes up only 64k. Change this slider only if you are extremely tight on memory or if you're directed to do so by a Microsoft support engineer to solve some specific problem.

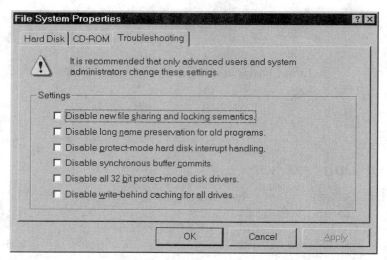

Figure 21-16: *Troubleshooting settings should also be left alone. (Normally, no settings are checked.)*

The last panel of the File System property sheets, Troubleshooting, serves no real purpose for typical Windows 95 users. Again, it should be used only to solve specific problems, if you're so directed by technical support engineers.

There is one check box on the Troubleshooting page ("Disable synchronous buffer commits") that deserves closer attention, because it can actually speed up your hard drive's performance. However, this change might cause problems in some circumstances, so a little background is in order.

MS-DOS has a file system API that allows an application to force a flushing of it's data buffers to disk. This is called a synchronous buffer commit. Most applications will ask the system to "please write this data to disk," but the data is really stored in various internal file system buffers and will be written out the next time the disk heads are in the general area of the apppropriate sectors. This usually happens within two seconds of the application requesting the disk write. However there are some applications, such as databases, that want to insure that when they say "please *really* write this data to disk" that the filesystem really does physically write the data to disk immediately. So they call this API to force the disk buffers to be flushed.

Under Windows 3.1 running on regular MS-DOS, or running with the SmartDrive disk cache, the file system would really write the data to disk immediately after the application requested a synchronous buffer commit. When Windows for Workgroups 3.11 came out with VFAT, however, this behavior changed. When an application explicitly asked for a synchronous buffer commit, the file system would lie to the application and say "yes, the data was written," but in reality it wasn't. This was a classic speed vs. reliability tradeoff that the Windows for Workgroups (WFWG) team made.

In earlier versions of Windows 95 (up until Build 474 or so), the default behavior for this synchronous buffer commit was to emulate the WFW 3.11 VFAT behavior of lying to the application. But Microsoft ultimately decided that this was more dangerous than Windows for Workgroups, because the cache could grow dynamically, whereas the WFWG cache was fixed in size. Therefore, you could have potentially more data in memory if the power failed. So Microsoft changed the behavior back to the Windows 3.1 style.

You can now control this behavior by right-clicking on My Computer, choose Properties, then Performance. Click the File System button, then the Troubleshooting tab. By default the "Disable synchronous buffer commits" option will be unchecked. This is the Windows 3.1 style. If you want the WFWG 3.11 style, then you need to check that option and restart the system. This speeds up some benchmarks, such as WinStone 95 by around 10%, at a possible reliability cost if your power happens to fail a lot. Of course, if you have a UPS or are on a laptop, then this shouldn't be an issue for you.

Moving On

In this chapter, we've learned how to take advantage of all the memory you have and how to let Windows create additional memory using virtual memory technology. We've also covered how to optimize memory for DOS applications.

Although DOS programs are fast going the way of the dinosaur, DOS isn't going to disappear overnight. In the next chapter, we'll see how to efficiently use DOS programs within the Windows 95 environment, and we'll examine the most useful DOS commands, in case you find yourself atavistically drawn to that old command line.

Chapter 22

The Other Face: DOS 7

Since it's there, retrogressive but still available under Windows—like an old record player sitting under a CD player—we have to deal with it: MS-DOS. Zillions of DOS programs and data files are still out there. Some machine has to be able to play them—if they're ever needed.

Have you been using computers for more than a couple of years? If so, you probably have these remnants of an earlier age. Like an LP record collector, maybe you even value this old, somewhat clumsy text-based style of computing. Some people used to wipe and rinse and protect their 33 1/3 vinyl record albums as if they were precious. And, to them, at that time, with nothing better available, they were.

In any case, Windows is forced to respect the fact that DOS remnants still exist in large quantities, and that this stuff still needs to be serviced. For a while anyway.

Two Faces

Windows 95 has two faces. You're probably comfortable with the friendly, colorful graphical user interface (GUI) that you control with the mouse, as you click on buttons, icons or menus to open and position and launch files and other things.

But there is another side to Windows 95—not exactly an alter ego, more primitive: the world of DOS, the original Disk Operating System of IBM PC compatible computers (*nee* circa 1981). To distinguish itself from several DOS clones such as IBM DOS, DR DOS and Novell DOS, Microsoft uses "MS-DOS" to refer to the original and "true" DOS.

In this chapter, we'll find out how to make the most of DOS programs with Windows 95, for those times it is still necessary.

Windows 95 goes a long way toward liberating itself from the limitations of DOS. These old limitations are the result of early design decisions. In the old days (the early 1980s), even the more sophisticated, forward-looking engineers couldn't imagine the speed of our current computers and the amount of memory that they would contain. DOS was designed for the capabilities of the original Intel 8088 microprocessor. It could use only one megabyte of memory at most (and a third of that memory was reserved for plug-in cards and the system BIOS).

The 640k Barrier

DOS is left with 640k of RAM, the most it can take advantage of. (This 640k of RAM is called *conventional memory*.) For the sake of compatibility with previous DOS programs, DOS continues this tradition, even though today's 386, 486 and Pentium-class microprocessors can directly support over four thousand megabytes (4 gigabytes) of RAM.

As you read in Chapter 21, "Optimization: Expert Memory Management," various techniques, such as expanded memory and extended memory, were developed to help make up for DOS's deficiencies and limitations, to help take advantage of any additional memory that your computer might have that DOS wasn't designed to recognize automatically. These techniques allowed even an 8086 to run programs that require additional memory. Compatibility with these techniques has been maintained over the years.

It's the old lowest-common-denominator problem. Do you teach a class so the slowest student understands everything? This results in total compatibility, but damages efficiency. The results aren't optimal by one standard of measurement, but are optimal by another standard. Or do you strike a happy medium, unfortunately leaving some students confused?

A Seamless Continuum

This is opposed to the *real mode* limitations of the 8086 and 286 microprocessors, which can't "see" the extra memory on their own. (The 286 has a faulty protected mode, so it's usually limited just as the 8088 is.) Instead of resorting to desperate tricks such as expanded memory, Windows 95 breaks through the old 640k ceiling and directly accesses all memory as a seamless continuum, without the fits and starts that resulted in programming for the 64k "segmented" memory architecture of earlier PCs. Windows 95 won't run on a 286; it requires at least a 386 microprocessor. A 286 is way too slow by today's standards anyway. A 286 machine just can't keep up with the demanding graphics and data transfer rate required by modern software, especially since a 286 computer is also hampered by slow hard drives and antiquated video cards.

Windows 3.1 was, truth be told, just another DOS application. (A "DOS extender" to be more technical.) Windows 3.1 was described as running "on top of DOS." Although a Windows 95 machine starts up in DOS, so that it can load any old-fashioned RAM-resident software and device drivers you might have in your outdated CONFIG.SYS and AUTOEXEC.BAT files, Windows 95 quickly discards almost all of that old DOS rubbish after it starts up. Since Windows 95 now includes advanced 32-bit protected mode drivers for almost all devices (your hardware peripherals like CD-ROM drives, printers and so on) and for most network protocols, even this brief encounter with DOS usually has no real impact on your Windows 95 configuration or behavior.

TIP   Try removing most or all of the contents of your CONFIG.SYS and AUTOEXEC.BAT files and see if everything still works while you're using Windows 95. If not, erase this retrograde stuff. Just in case, be sure to keep a backup of your old files.

The only significance of DOS to Windows 95 is that DOS's configuration matters if you run a DOS program from within Windows 95.

DOS Under Glass

You can click on the Start button and then select Programs | MS-DOS Prompt to start an MS-DOS *session*, also called a *DOS box*. The entire DOS session is in a window on the desktop and is, in a sense, like a glass box in an aquarium (see Figure 22-1). It's an exhibit, really. It's not a real Windows computer program. Windows has to maintain its environment, controlling the "temperature" of this alien environment in the same way that a museum maintains the optimal conditions for some thing that can't last in the real atmosphere of the world.

This is why there were Windows 3.1 PIF files to specify the atmosphere required by each DOS program and why in Windows 95 each DOS program has property sheets explaining those same conditions that permit it to survive in the Windows environment. But it's a faithful reproduction of the DOS environment nonetheless, and compatible with almost all DOS applications.

Figure 22-1: *An MS-DOS session is available with just three clicks of the mouse: Start, Programs, MS-DOS Prompt.*

Indeed, Microsoft has worked hard to improve the performance and compatibility of the DOS box, with the goal of being able to run almost all DOS software, including DOS games (which are probably the acid test of Windows and DOS compatibility) without having to bypass Windows 95 and start the computer up in a native DOS mode (by pressing Shift+F5 during the startup process when you first turn on the computer).

In Windows 95, parts of the original real-mode DOS programming are still used when running DOS programs. After all, if you're running DOS, it makes sense to use the actual DOS to do it. Unlike Windows 3.1, though, the DOS in Windows 95 actually relies on Windows 95 for many functions, including support for the new long filenames.

In Windows 3.1 and DOS, filenames that you gave to your documents had to be eight letters followed by a dot, followed by an *extension* that indicated what kind of document it was—for example, MYSTORY.DOC for Word files, MYSTORY.TXT for Notepad files and MYPICTUR.BMP for a graphic file. Now, in Windows 95, you can get really descriptive, using upper- and lowercase and spaces, and you can even leave off the extension; for example, you might name your file "The Story Of Alaska."

The DOS used with Windows 95 is equivalent to MS-DOS Version 7.0, the successor to DOS 6.22. At the time of this writing, Microsoft had not decided if MS-DOS 7.0 would be available as a separate product and if it would include any Windows 95 enhancements, such as long filename support. But it's not likely.

Yet the days are numbered for DOS computers, and very few companies are still releasing new DOS versions of their venerable software. Even game developers are moving toward Windows 95 with its support for the high-speed graphics required for action-packed entertainment titles.

The New Graphical DOS Toolbar

One improvement on the DOS box (compared to the DOS box in Windows 3) is the addition of a graphical toolbar (see Figure 22-2), giving you quick access to the most useful Windows gadgets for running DOS programs. From left to right, you have the options Mark, Copy, Paste, Full-Screen, Properties, Exclusive, Background and Font. We'll cover each of these options in the following sections.

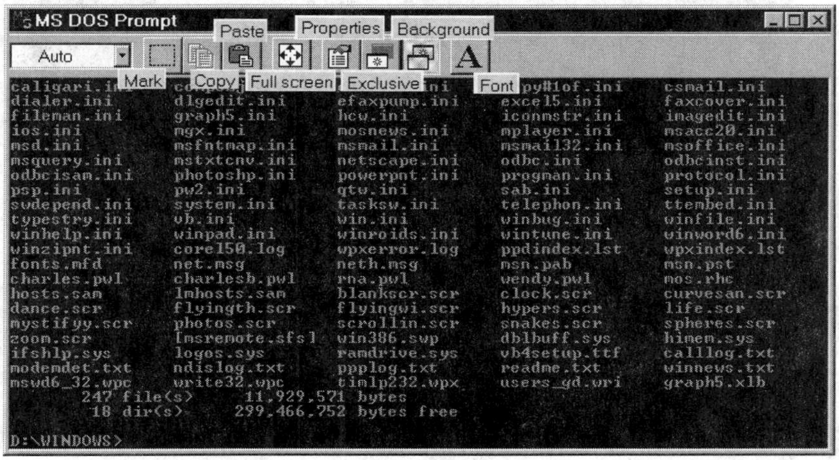

Figure 22-2: *The MS-DOS toolbar provides quick access to Windows DOS support features.*

If you don't see a toolbar with an MS-DOS program, you may be running the program full screen (in text mode). The keyboard shortcut for switching back to a window is Alt+Enter. (It's easier to remember if you think of it as "Entering the Alternate World of DOS.")

If you are running DOS in a window without a toolbar, you can turn on the toolbar by clicking the right mouse button on the title bar and choosing Toolbar. The same trick works to disable the toolbar. This right mouse button context menu also gives you quick access to the same menu that you get when you press the keyboard shortcut Alt+Spacebar, or by left-clicking on the MS-DOS icon in the upper-left corner of the window. (This icon is called the Control box, and the menu that drops down is the Control menu.)

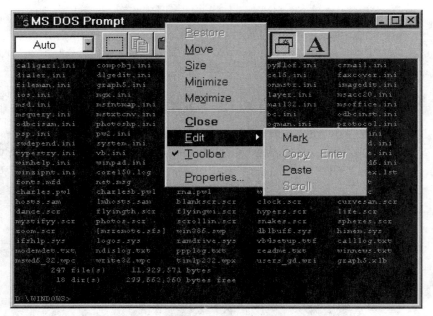

Figure 22-3: *Clicking the right mouse button pops up a handy menu for controlling the MS-DOS program.*

Mark

One advantage of a DOS box is that you can extend the metaphor of the Windows Clipboard to DOS programs. By clicking on the Mark button, you're allowed to click and drag within the text of the DOS window, highlighting a rectangular region of the screen.

It's also possible to customize a DOS application so that you don't have to choose Mark before selecting a region. Windows 95 allows a DOS program to use the mouse, if supported by the DOS program, so that you can click on entries or select text for its own purposes. You need to choose Mark to temporarily disable the DOS mouse support so that Windows can use the mouse for selecting text for the Windows Clipboard.

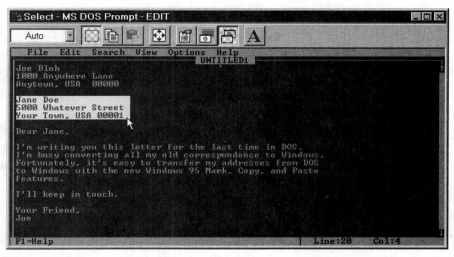

Figure 22-4: *Using Mark makes it easy to transfer screen data from DOS to Windows.*

As we mentioned in Chapter 9, you no longer need to load a DOS mouse driver in your AUTOEXEC.BAT file. Windows 95 automatically provides both Windows and DOS mouse support, without using any conventional memory.

If your DOS program doesn't use the mouse for anything, though, you can customize it for Quick Edit, which is like having Mark turned on all the time—the mouse always selects text for Windows. To do this, click on the Properties button on the toolbar (or right-click on the title bar and choose Properties from the context menu). Now choose the Misc tab of the property sheet and click on Quick Edit. All DOS properties are remembered the next time you run the same DOS program, so you have to make this change only once. If you have trouble using DOS mouse support with a DOS program, you might want to make sure Quick Edit is disabled.

Copy

After you have marked text, you can click on the Copy button to transfer it to the Windows Clipboard. (Or just press Enter to copy the highlighted region to the Clipboard.) You can then open or switch to a Windows application, such as Notepad or WordPad, and select Edit | Paste (or the keyboard Shortcut keys Ctrl+V or Shift+Insert) to paste the text you captured into the application. These Shortcut keys can be handy if you still use a DOS database program to keep your mailing list, and you want to copy an address into a letter you're typing with WordPad. You can also copy anything that you've typed at the DOS command prompt.

Instead of separately choosing Copy after using Mark, you can use the left mouse button to click and drag the selection and click the *right* mouse button to automatically end the selection and copy the highlighted region to the Clipboard.

If you're not a fan of toolbars, you can activate Mark by choosing it from the Edit submenu (shown in Figure 22-3), which appears when you click the right mouse button on the title bar of the DOS window. From the keyboard, try pressing Alt+Spacebar, E, K. You can get the Copy option from the same menu or by using the Enter key.

Paste

The Clipboard works in both directions. You can copy some text in a Windows application and paste it into a DOS program. When you choose Paste from the toolbar or from the Edit submenu of the control menu, Windows fools the DOS program into thinking that someone is typing from the keyboard. These keystrokes come from the Windows Clipboard, so if you paste the word *Evergreen* from the Clipboard, Windows quickly types E-v-e-r-g-r-e-e-n into the DOS program. For this to work, the DOS program has to accept keyboard input, as in a word processor or data entry screen.

 Another way to paste some text into a DOS prompt is to drag and drop a file from Explorer onto an open DOS window. The folder or filename is "typed into" the DOS prompt, and you can execute it by pressing Enter. Or you could drag it into a file open dialog in an MS-DOS based app in order to quickly open the file for editing. In other words, when you drag and drop a filename onto a DOS window, it has the same effect as pasting—it's as if you typed the characters in the filename that you dropped.

Full Screen

As we mentioned, you can press Alt+Enter to toggle (turn on or off) the Full Screen mode of a DOS program. Full Screen uses the text mode of your computer, which displays typewritten-style characters without graphical adornments. Full Screen is the "natural" way of using a DOS program, and by far the fastest way to run one, especially with games. But it can also be convenient to share the screen with Windows programs especially when you're using the Mark, Copy and Paste features. If you have a high-resolution video card (800x600, 1024x768 or higher), it's easy to fit a DOS screen along with all your other open windows. Unlike Windows 3.1, which had limited support for displaying DOS graphics in a windows, Windows 95 now lets you run most graphical DOS programs within a window, although it does update the screen more slowly than normal.

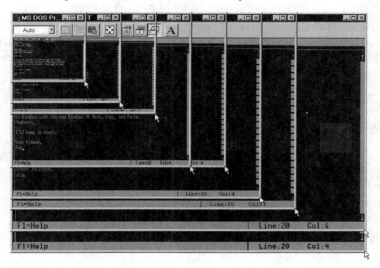

Figure 22-5: *Just drag the corner of the window to choose among several sizes and shapes of DOS windows.*

One advantage of running a DOS program in a window is that you can "capture" its screen display as a graphic and paste it into many Windows applications. While a DOS program is in a window, press Alt+PrintScrn to capture the display. Unlike Mark/Copy, this method does not put the text in the Clipboard, but rather the image of the pixels on the screen. You run the Paint accessory (see Chapter 10, "Accessories") and paste the image into it for freehand editing or into your word processor to use as a figure. Indeed, we've used this method to capture all of the DOS screens you see in this chapter, a far superior method to taking photographs of the screen. (Alt+PrintScrn can be used with any window, not just DOS programs. PrintScrn by itself copies the entire screen to the Clipboard.)

If you want PrintScrn to "print screen" to the printer as it normally does in DOS, just click the Full Screen button to switch to text mode. Now PrintScrn copies the image of the text screen to your printer. This procedure works only with DOS. If you want to print a DOS screen that's displaying graphics, use Alt+Enter to put it in a window, press Alt+PrintScrn and then paste it into Paint to print it.

Properties

When you click on the Properties button (or choose it from the right mouse button pop-up menu or after pressing Alt+Spacebar), the first property sheet, labeled Program, shows you the name and filename (or command line) for the program. It's very similar to a Windows 95 shortcut. In fact, a DOS program uses a form of a shortcut called a .PIF (for Program Information File). You may be familiar with PIFs from Windows 3, which gave you a separate PIF Editor to customize a DOS application. There is no PIF Editor in Windows 95; its functionality is incorporated into the DOS Properties settings. You can still use PIFs created for the sake of Windows 3.1, but they are converted to DOS shortcuts automatically when you put them in a folder.

 TIP If you get lost while editing the MS-DOS properties, you can move the mouse pointer over most options and press the right mouse button. This pops up the repetitive (some say totally useless) "What's This?" message. However, clicking on "What's This?" gives you a brief pop-up help description of that item. Or you can click on the question mark in the upper right-hand corner of a property sheet and then use the "help cursor" to click on items that you need help on.

Figure 22-6: *DOS Properties are divided into five headings, or panels. Programs defines the command line used to start the program.*

You can create a new DOS shortcut, just as you do with Windows shortcuts, by dragging a DOS program from Explorer (or My Computer) to a folder, or by selecting the New Shortcut command from the folder's File menu, also available from the right mouse button. After you create the shortcut, you can use Properties to customize it.

You don't need to create a shortcut to customize the properties for a program. You can simply locate the program in its original directory and right-click on it to choose Properties. If you simply double-click on the program file in Explorer (or a My Computer-style folder), it will be started with the default Properties settings.

There's a big advantage to creating a shortcut to an existing MS-
DOS application. When you create a shortcut, Windows 95
automatically checks the exe or batch filename and version
against a list that's stored in \windows\inf\apps.inf. It contains
over 400 different popular MS-DOS applications and games. It
also contains the necessary default settings to make the application work well under Windows 95 (screen settings, memory, MS-
DOS compatibility mode yes/no and so on). So if you have
some sort of a hot MS-DOS game, it's much easier to create a
shortcut to the game so that Windows 95 will automatically
create the necessary settings. Otherwise, you'll need to make
trial and error changes that could waste hours tweaking all of the
various settings. For example, here's the listing in that file for
Wing Commander 2:
    [WC2.BAT]
    LowMem=512
    Enable=dos,mse,ems,cdr
    Disable=win

Program

In the Program property sheet, the first entry is the name of the program,
which appears on the title bar when the program is running in Windows. It
has no bearing on the filename of the program. That goes in the box labeled
Cmd Line. It's called *Cmd Line* (for Command Line) because it's not only the
filename, but may also include command-line options. It is common for DOS
programs to let you customize them by adding *switches* to the command line.
Or you can put the name of another file after the filename of the program to
have it open that program.

For example, if the command line is EDIT C:\AUTOEXEC.BAT, the program will start the DOS EDIT command and open the C:\AUTOEXEC.BAT
file automatically. Or you could use a switch, like /R for read-only (prevents
changes from being made when you're just browsing.) The command line
EDIT C:\CONFIG.SYS /R opens CONFIG.SYS but won't let you change
anything.

If in doubt about the command line, open a DOS box and try typing it directly at the DOS prompt to see if it works. You can then use the Mark/ Copy feature to copy the command line right out of the DOS box and paste it into the *Cmd Line* of the Properties setting. You can often get a list of the command line switches by typing **/?** after the command name at the DOS prompt. For a complete list and description of command-line switches, you must look at a DOS application's manual.

Working Directory

DOS searches the DOS PATH to find the program listed in the command line (by default, the path is C:\WINDOWS;C:\WINDOWS\COMMAND; so Windows searches each of these directories in order to find the program you've entered). That's why you don't have to specify which directory to use when running a DOS command.

Some DOS commands are internal to DOS and aren't found on the hard drive, so you can't just put them in the *Cmd Line* box. One example is the DIR command, used to display DOS directories. To get around this, just prefix the command with the phrase **COMMAND /C**, as in COMMAND /C DIR.

Also use COMMAND /C when you use Start I Run to execute an internal DOS command. For example, say you want to delete the file C:\PROJECTS\INFO.TXT. Instead of opening Explorer and browsing for the file, just click Start I Run and enter **COMMAND / C DEL C:\PROJECTS\INFO.TXT.** Note that you don't need COMMAND /C for program files that reside on the hard drive, such as XCOPY.

While you can edit the PATH in the AUTOEXEC.BAT file (learn more about editing your system files in Chapter 23, "Expert Configuration & Optimization"), it's far better just to put the name of the directory (remember, directories and folders are the same thing) in the Working box shown in Figure 22-6. When you double-click the DOS shortcut, it first switches to the working directory (equivalent to using CHDIR or CD in DOS) and then starts the program.

Instead of using the working directory, you could just prefix the command line with the name of the working directory. So instead of using a *Cmd Line* of EDIT.COM and a Working Directory of C:\DOS, you could simply put **C:\DOS\EDIT.COM** in the *Cmd Line*.

Batch File

The line for Batch File lets you enter the name of a DOS batch file that you'd like to run before the command line listed. Of course, you could just put the name of the batch file in the *Cmd Line* and include the program's filename in the batch file itself. The intention of this batch file is to let you load any TSRs (Terminate-and-Stay-Resident programs are DOS utilities that run in the background) that the DOS program needs. When loaded from the batch file, these TSRs use up memory only during the lifespan of the program. When the program ends, the TSRs are discarded from memory. This is in contrast to TSRs that are loaded in AUTOEXEC.BAT, which use up memory in all DOS sessions, even those that don't need it.

Also on the Programs property sheet, you can use the *Shortcut key* and *Run* choices as you do with Windows shortcuts. Click in the *Shortcut key* box in the Programs panel and press any Ctrl+Alt key combination (ideally, one that's not used by any other program). For example, you could use Ctrl+Alt+E to pop up the DOS Editor, if you put EDIT.COM in the *Cmd Line*. The Run box lets you choose whether the program starts up Normal, Minimized (on the taskbar) or Maximized (the largest size for a DOS box—not necessarily the full size of the screen).

The last option on the Programs panel is *Close on exit*. It's enabled normally for a DOS prompt, so the window disappears when you type the EXIT command. This option is turned off, though, when you run a DOS program from Explorer or My Computer, since Windows wants to make sure you have a chance to view the output of the program before it closes. When the program ends, the title bar changes to show that it's "Finished," and you can then click on the Close box (the little X symbol in the upper-right corner of the toolbar). You can also click on the Close box whenever you're at the DOS prompt instead of typing **EXIT**.

On the other hand, while a DOS program is running, you usually can't just click the Close box to end it, since Windows has no way to warn the DOS program that it's about to be closed (there is no universal method for ending DOS programs. Some use Esc or Ctrl+Esc; others use Alt+X, Alt+F3 and so on, or a menu option to shut them down). If you click on the Close box anyway, Windows will warn you that it has no way to make sure you've saved your work, and you may suffer data loss. Some older DOS applications won't write out their most recent changes to open files, and these files could thus become corrupted by this sudden shutdown. For this reason, it's always best to exit the DOS program, from within that program, before clicking on the Close box. (See the "Misc" section for more information.) On the other hand, if the DOS program has locked up, your best choice is to go ahead and let Windows shut it down.

Change Icon

Windows programs include their own built-in icons, and a document, graphic or text file inherits the icon of its associated program (the one used to open or edit it). With DOS programs, you have to assign an icon or else accept the generic DOS icon, which looks like a computer screen with a blue background. From the Programs Panel, click on the Change Icon button to get a choice of icons, as shown in Figure 22-7. These icons come from the PIFMGR.DLL. (A DLL file not only contains program code, but can also hold a list of icons.) Many Windows .EXE files also contain icons. Another big group of DOS-based icons can be found in the MORICONS.DLL file (also handy when creating a DOS shortcut), and you can find additional icons in SHELL32.DLL and PROGMAN.EXE (all of these files are in the \Windows folder). Just enter one of these filenames in the Filename box and then press Tab to switch to the strip of icons. To reveal more icons, click on the arrows on the scroll bar at the bottom. To discover still more icons, choose Browse and look for files ending with .ICO, .DLL and .EXE. Many icon editors are also available as shareware; they let you create and customize your own icons.

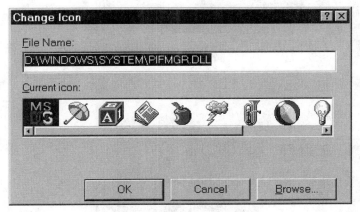

Figure 22-7: *Pick an icon from the MS-DOS icons list or use any Windows icon or icon library.*

We'll discuss it a little later, since it's a complex topic (see "Advanced DOS Mode").

Font

You can customize the size of the DOS window just by dragging the borders (for best results, drag the lower-right corner). It instantly changes to any of several TrueType or system fonts to fit the new size. You can also click on the Maximize button on the title bar to grow the DOS box to the largest size that will fit on your screen. Note that this is not the same as Full Screen, which does not run in a window at all.

Click on the toolbar's Font button to choose the specific size of the font, which also controls the size and shape of the DOS box (as shown in Figure 22-8). You can also choose the Font tab after choosing Properties to get the same dialog box.

 TIP Just use the drop-down list box at the left of the DOS toolbar to quickly choose a font size and automatically resize the DOS window. Change it back to Auto if you want to resize the window using the mouse.

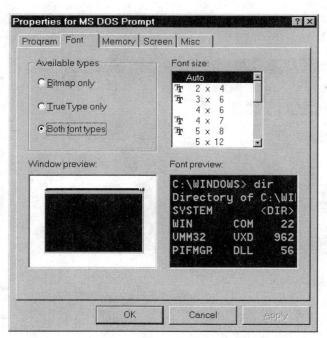

Figure 22-8: *Click on the Font button to directly choose a font and size for the DOS window.*

The TrueType font uses the Courier New typeface for several of the sizes. The only disadvantage is that Courier New uses rather thin, fine lines. If you prefer a blockier, bolder look, it's best to use Bitmap fonts (those not marked with the TT symbols). When autosizing the window, you can restrict the choice of fonts to "Bitmap only" or "TrueType only." Use the font preview display to get an idea of how the typeface looks. Some of the sizes are too large for a 640x480 display or too small for a 1024x768 display.

Microsoft Plus! for Windows 95 substitutes a more readable font for Courier New, called Lucida Console, when displaying DOS in a window.

It's possible for some DOS programs to run using a special mode that allows 43 lines with EGA or 50 lines with VGA. Full-screen, these characters are half-height, but when running in a window, the window is just twice as high. (See "Screen" later in this chapter to turn on 43/50 line mode.)

However, Windows 95 no longer supports CGA or EGA video cards; you have to have at least a minimal 16-color VGA card.

Memory

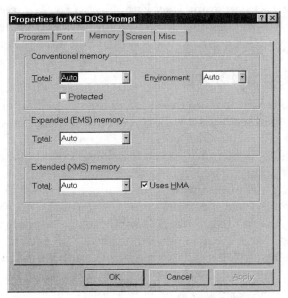

Figure 22-9: *Most DOS programs require no customization, but you can control how much memory to allocate if necessary.*

Windows 95 creates a "virtual DOS machine" (VDM) when you open a DOS prompt or double-click on a DOS program in Explorer. A VDM fools DOS into believing it has its own private 640k memory space, with access to extended and expanded memory, if required. Most DOS programs and games will run as is, but you have a lot of control over the configuration of the VDM when necessary.

By default, Windows gives a VDM all the memory it needs (up to the amount of free DOS memory, over 600k if there are no TSRs or real-mode drivers in AUTOEXEC.BAT/CONFIG.SYS). It also makes expanded memory and extended memory available, in any quantity required.

When physical memory gets taxed, Windows uses the swap file to page out inactive Windows and DOS programs, and this takes time. (Read more about this in Chapters 5 and 19.) If you know a DOS program doesn't need all available memory, you can limit its usage to speed up its load time and free up memory for other programs. Many DOS programs will run just fine with 512k or even 256k, and that makes them load more quickly, too.

You'll never need to worry about the Environment size option. This is a part of DOS that holds the DOS path and environment variables (defined with the DOS SET command). The default size is sufficient for most programs, but if you get the error message "Out of Environment Space," you can choose a larger environment for the program.

You can click on the Protected box to help prevent some crashes that are caused by bugs in a DOS program; they lead it to overwrite memory that it doesn't "own," such as the memory used by Windows programs. This safety checking slows down a program, so use it only if you have problems.

Expanded & Extended Memory

We cover the use of expanded and extended memory in Chapter 21. If you know that a program doesn't need either, you can set these choices to None to speed up program loading. Or if you have a "greedy" DOS program that tries to claim all available memory—even if it doesn't need that much—you can restrict the availability of expanded or extended memory, especially if you're multitasking DOS programs (running more than one DOS window at a time) and want to improve speed performance. (Some DOS programs use DPMI—DOS Protected Mode Interface—to acquire extended memory, and they can force Windows to create an enormous swap file on disk to satisfy the insatiable demand for "all available memory." In this case, just restrict the size of extended memory to a figure low enough to allow the program to run properly. Eight megabytes is a good choice for games.)

The *Uses HMA* button is a relic from the old PIF Editor choices in Windows 3. Since the DOS HIMEM.SYS driver loads into high memory (the region of memory just above the first megabyte of RAM), this HMA (High Memory Area) is not usually available anyway. If you have a cranky DOS program that does require using HMA, you'll have to remove HIMEM.SYS and DOS=HIGH from C:\CONFIG.SYS to free up the HMA for this program.

Screen

The Screen property sheet is related to the Font property sheet, which controls the way Windows displays the DOS session. Instead of clicking on the Full Screen button or pressing Alt+Enter, you can use the Usage section and click on Full Screen to have the program always start up full screen, or Windows to display in a window. With Convert Automatically enabled, Windows starts a DOS program in a window, and if the DOS program displays graphics, it automatically converts to full screen for best performance.

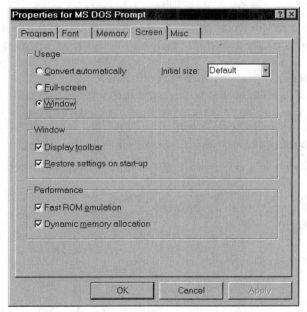

Figure 22-10: *A DOS program can start up in a window or full screen, or just remember the way it was running the last time you ran it.*

We already covered the Display toolbar option previously in this chapter. With Restore Settings turned on, Windows remembers the setting you're using when you close the program (full screen, window size, font and window position) and starts it up the same way next time, or if this option is turned off, the application is returned to the default Windows size, position and font.

The last two options for Screen are a little tricky. *Fast ROM Emulation* should be turned on normally. Instead of using the system BIOS for screen updates, faster Windows code gets substituted. You want to disable this option only if you have a DOS program that uses undocumented or specialized BIOS extensions. If the DOS program doesn't update the screen properly, try turning this option off.

The other option, *Dynamic Memory Allocation*, is actually not related to the Memory settings directly. It refers to the memory used to display screen graphics. For example, simple text mode uses only 2,048 bytes of memory, whereas a 320x200, 256-color mode uses 64,000 bytes. With Dynamic Memory Allocation turned on, Windows can detect when the program switches from text mode to graphics mode, acquire the extra memory required for graphics mode and then release this memory automatically when the program returns to text mode. However, if you run another program while the first DOS program is in text mode, there might not be enough memory left over to allow it to switch back into graphics mode. In that case, turn off the Dynamic Memory choice to make sure that enough memory is always reserved for a DOS graphic display. Usually, this only wastes memory, though.

Misc

The Misc page lets you control a bevy of miscellaneous features, including multitasking options.

Figure 22-11: *The rest of the DOS properties are grouped together in a motley fashion on the Misc page.*

Each DOS application running in its own VDM can execute simultaneously with the others, as long as it is set to run in background mode.

Background

For convenience, you can just click on the Background button on the taskbar to enable this feature, which is now the default with Windows 95, to make it easy to use multitasking with DOS applications.

When background mode is turned off, the Always suspend check box is turned on. This means that when you minimize a program—or "click away from it"—on another DOS application or on a Windows program, the DOS program is suspended, frozen in time. When you click on it again or restore it by clicking on its taskbar program, it picks up right where it left off. Turn off Always suspend to turn on (enable) background mode.

Exclusive

A program running minimized in the background will not run as fast as it can, since it is sharing the computer with other running DOS boxes and with

Windows applications. One way to improve its speed is to turn on the Exclusive mode for that application. If any application is running exclusively, other applications, even if set to run in the background, will be suspended until the Exclusive application is itself suspended (by clicking on another DOS application or minimizing it.) But if you have both Exclusive and Background set for an application, it will never get suspended and will prevent true multitasking of DOS programs.

Exclusive mode is rarely needed, except in critical DOS applications such as high-speed modem software, that can't afford to lose any time. But improvements to Windows 95's DOS support let background applications run better than ever, even without Exclusive mode.

It's convenient, though, to choose Exclusive as-needed from the toolbar. That way you don't have to use it all the time, only when you need to let a lengthy DOS application continue running while you do something else. Note that any DOS program runs nearly full speed when it is displayed full-screen, even without the Exclusive setting.

(Since it's presumed that a DOS program running in Exclusive mode can't afford to be interrupted, you have the option of disabling the screen saver while a DOS program is running exclusively. Doing so defeats the purpose of the screen saver, especially if you use it for security with password protection. For this reason, Allow screen saver is normally left turned on.)

 TIP   If you're playing a DOS game full screen and using only the joystick, Windows may turn on the screen saver even though you're still using the computer. That's because Windows monitors only the mouse and keyboard to determine if you're busy. So you'll want to disable the screen saver from the Misc property sheet for that game.

Fine-Tuning

You can "tweak" background mode in another way so that it runs a little faster, at the expense of other programs, including 16-bit Windows applications. To do this, you need to raise the priority setting of background applications. Normally, background programs run about half the time (50% priority). You can raise this setting a little (to about 60%) to give a background application more emphasis. Whereas the Windows 3 PIF Editor made you enter the percentage directly, you can now just drag the Idle Sensitivity slider directly using the mouse to accomplish the same end.

However, the slider is counterintuitive. If a program doesn't seem to run fast enough, you actually reduce its idle sensitivity. Increase the idle sensitivity if the program uses frequent keyboard input to give other programs a chance to take advantage of the idle time between each keystroke. If you set the idle sensitivity to the minimum, you slow down other background DOS applications so much that you might as well use the Exclusive mode instead.

The Other Options

We already covered most of the other features on the Misc screen, but to review: use Quick Edit to keep the Mark mode always on, disabling the DOS mouse cursor to allow you to select text to put into the Windows Clipboard. The alter ego of Quick Edit is Exclusive mode (better named "Mouse Exclusive Mode" to prevent confusion with the Exclusive multitasking option). This curious mode prevents the Windows cursor from working at all. Only the DOS mouse cursor works. This way, you can see the text symbol for the DOS mouse cursor instead of the Windows arrow, and the mouse is confined to the boundaries of the DOS box. Once you enable this option, you can't use the mouse to turn off this feature. Press Alt+Spacebar and then P to open the Properties settings. The mouse is now enabled, so you can click on the Misc tab and turn off Mouse Exclusive Mode.

As shown in Figure 22-11, Warn if Active prevents you from closing a DOS program prematurely. The consequences of closing an active DOS program were mentioned previously.

We also mentioned that pasting into a DOS program simulates typing at the keyboard. Windows sends these keystrokes at high speed, but perhaps too high for some older, slower programs. If Paste drops characters, you can turn off Allow Fast Paste for a particular program to slow down pasting into a DOS program.

The Windows shortcut keys section is used to specify which Windows shortcut keys are permitted. For example, if your DOS program uses Alt+Enter for its own purpose, then this feature is unavailable, since Alt+Enter makes Windows switch the program between full-screen and windowed display. You want to keep these boxes turned on when possible, since they activate powerful features, such as Alt+Tab for switching between running programs.

Advanced DOS Mode

Despite improvements, not all DOS programs can run from a DOS box. Some of them assume they are in control of the entire computer, believing they still live in the "good old days" of DOS-only machines. Fortunately,

Windows 95 provides an "escape hatch" for these irksome applications, in the form of *MS-DOS mode* (see Figure 22-12).

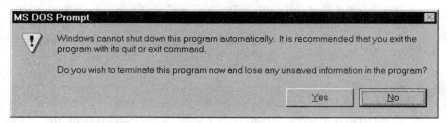

Figure 22-12: *MS-DOS mode is a way to run a program "outside" of Windows 95.*

To get started with Advanced DOS options, open the property sheet for the program. (One way to do this is to right-click on the DOS program's .EXE file and choose Properties from the pop-up menu. Or choose Properties for a shortcut to the DOS program.) When the Programs property sheet is displayed, click on the Advanced button.

A Tricky Tip

Some programs refuse to run when Windows is also running, because with Windows 3.1, those programs (usually high-performance DOS games) just don't run very well. But Windows 95 has better support for DOS games, so you can fool these programs into believing Windows is not running. You turn on the *Prevent MS-DOS based programs from detecting Windows* check box. If this trick works for you, you may not need to resort to MS-DOS mode.

MS-DOS Mode

To set up a program for MS-DOS mode, you create a shortcut to it as usual, using New Shortcut from Explorer or dragging the filename from Explorer or My Computer to a new folder. (Put the shortcut in a subfolder of \Windows\Start Menu if you want it to appear on the Start menu.) You can also configure the actual program file in its original folder, without creating a shortcut. In this case, simply right-click on the program and choose Properties.

When you know you're going to use MS-DOS mode, you don't need to use any of the other property sheets; they just aren't applicable when not running with Windows. Just choose Advanced from the Programs menu, and enable the checkbox for *MS-DOS mode*. (If you use the program frequently, you might also want to turn off the *Warn before entering MS-DOS mode* check box.)

When you double-click on a program that's been configured for MS-DOS mode, you get a warning message. Then Windows is shut down and your computer reboots. Next, MS-DOS runs without starting Windows 95, and then your application starts. When the application ends, the computer reboots again and Windows 95 is started as usual.

Since the program is running "naked," you're allowed to create a custom AUTOEXEC.BAT and CONFIG.SYS for the sake of that program, to provide the program with any TSRs or drivers it needs to run without Windows. Once you choose MS-DOS mode, you're allowed to type in the boxes marked AUTOEXEC.BAT and CONFIG.SYS. Remember, these are custom versions created only for this one program; you are not modifying your original, primary versions of these files.

Without the benefit of Windows' built-in drivers for devices like CD-ROMs and networking, you have to use the "old fashioned" DOS drivers such as MSCDEX for CD-ROM and NETX for NetWare login.

Because of the size of these drivers, a DOS application running in MS-DOS mode may actually have less memory available to it than when running under Windows 95. And all this these changes take a lot of extra time, so you don't want to set up a program for MS-DOS mode unless you really need that mode. Its only advantage is that this mode gives the DOS application full control over all the computer's resources.

Instead of creating your own AUTOEXEC.BAT and CONFIG.SYS files, you may want to use a copy of your regular AUTOEXE/CONFIG files. In that case, just turn on the checkbox for *Use current MS-DOS configuration*.

The current MS-DOS configuration probably isn't optimized for running MS-DOS and games, however. Windows 95 intentionally disables some of your old entries, such as SmartDrive or a line that loads a mouse driver, since Windows 95 replaces them with powerful drivers that don't require MS-DOS. But when you're running "pure" MS-DOS, these old-style drivers are still often necessary. So you have to go back to the "bad old days," of fiddling with CONFIG.SYS and AUTOEXEC.BAT to make DOS games run properly. Fortunately, Windows 95 games are quickly making DOS games obsolete.

Windows 95 does make it easier by offering to create a custom AUTOEXEC.BAT and CONFIG.SYS for you. After you enable MS-DOS mode, turn off the *Use current MS-DOS configuration* option. Instantly, Windows fills in the AUTOEXEC and CONFIG boxes with suggested entries. Next, click on the Configuration button. You get a screen that looks similar to Figure 22-13.

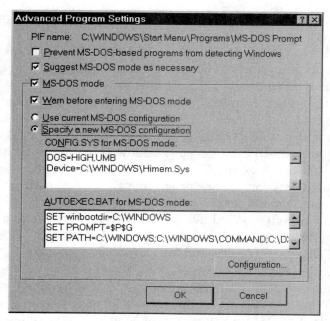

Figure 22-13: *Choose the features that your MS-DOS application needs, and Windows creates a custom set of boot files for you.*

Each feature creates a corresponding entry in the custom AUTOEXEC.BAT and CONFIG.SYS file. For example, Expanded Memory creates an entry for EMM386.EXE, the way DOS provides expanded memory services. The Disk Cache line adds an entry for SmartDrive, which is necessary for fast DOS disk access, since the virtual disk caching provided by Windows 95 is not present in MS-DOS mode. You may also want to enable the line for DosKey, since this feature makes it easy to edit your command lines using the cursor keys, but it's not needed to simply run most DOS programs.

If you're running an MS-DOS program that needs to directly modify the disk structure, such as Norton Utilities or Central Point Tools, be sure to enable Direct Disk Access. This option adds the line LOCK to AUTOEXEC.BAT, which is explained further below. (Avoid using such utilities in any case, since they can damage long filenames. Instead use utilities designed specifically for Windows 95. However, you may still need LOCK for some rare DOS programs, even if they aren't disk utilities.) After you choose OK, you can review and further edit the resulting entries in the custom version of AUTOEXEC.BAT and CONFIG.SYS. Note that Windows 95 has also transferred some DOS-specific lines from your original AUTOEXEC.BAT file, such as the PATH statement and any SET commands.

(If you upgraded from a prior version of DOS or Windows, you might want to use your old AUTOEXEC.BAT and CONFIG.SYS files for MS-DOS mode. Try opening C:\AUTOEXEC.DOS and C:\CONFIG.DOS with Notepad and copying and pasting the lines into the MS-DOS mode boxes. You can then edit them to take out anything the MS-DOS application doesn't need.)

If you change your mind about MS-DOS mode, wait until you return to Windows and then choose Properties for the program or shortcut again, and turn off MS-DOS mode. Remember, if a program is configured for MS-DOS mode, you can't edit any of its other Windows-specific properties, since it isn't run from within Windows.

 TIP If you want to run a certain program both ways, from within Windows and in MS-DOS mode, create an extra shortcut to the program and make your second set of configuration changes to that shortcut.

Long Filenames & DOS

Windows 95 now allows us to save files with long, meaningful filenames, with up to 255 characters and spaces between words. When you are running MS-DOS from within Windows 95, you also see the long filenames with several DOS commands, such as XCOPY and the DIR (directory) command. The second half of this chapter, the reference section, points out which commands support long filenames. The only DOS application that supports long filenames, at the time of this writing, is the DOS EDIT command, which has been improved for Windows 95 and DOS 7.

With earlier versions of DOS or when using Windows 3.1 software, you see only the short filenames, which are created automatically by Windows 95 from the first eight characters of the filename. If another file already exists with those same eight characters, Windows creates a unique variation. This subject is explained more fully in Chapter 5, "Inside the File System."

One conflict with long filenames occurs with Windows 3 and DOS-based backup software. Some of these programs get confused by the extra data in the directory entries for the long filenames; they may believe that the file size has been bloated beyond reason. As a result, this can cause a single file to take up a whole tape, thus ruining your attempt to back up. If your needs can be met by the Windows 95 Backup accessory (also covered in Chapter 5), it's a better alternative.

Beware of Truncation

Another problem occurs when you try to run disk management software designed for earlier versions of DOS, such as Norton Disk Doctor, and all defragmentation/optimizer programs. These programs are ignorant of the tricks Microsoft uses to support long filenames, and in the process of modifying the hard drive, will wipe out the long filenames. The data and the files are still okay, but the only filename for them is the short MS-DOS filename with eight characters and a three-character extension. The long filename is *truncated.*

Windows 95 makes most old-fashioned disk checkers and defragmentation programs obsolete, since it includes ScanDisk for Windows and Disk Defragmenter, via Start | Programs | Accessories | System Tools. These tools are covered completely in Chapter 5.

For Expert Users: Intentional Truncation

Even if you have to use older DOS backup or disk-editing tools, for some curious reason (such as the fact that the Windows 95 Backup program doesn't support DAT tape drives), both of these issues have a workaround, in the form of the LFNBK utility, found in the \Windows\Command folder. It's designed to strip out and back up the long filenames for a drive, storing them in a data file called LFNBK.DAT. It's important to strip away the long filenames for the sake of tools like older backup programs that get confused by the long filename information. But read the following sections carefully, and don't use LFNBK until you fully understand the potential dangers.

Backing up & stripping long filenames

The LFNBK utility is not installed by Windows Setup, but you can find it on the Windows 95 CD-ROM in the \ADMIN\APPTOOLS\LFNBK folder. Just copy it to your \Windows\Command directory.

You can run LFNBK only from within a Windows 95 DOS box, since MS DOS 7 doesn't understand long filenames by itself, but only when empowered by Windows 95.

The LFNBK utility strips off old file names, saving them in a separate file (LFNBK.DAT). It can also restore the long filenames using this file.

But before you start LFNBK, you have to make a strange change to Windows 95. Right-click on My Computer and choose Properties, or double-click on the System icon in Control Panel, to open the System Properties. Click on the Performance tab heading, then click on the Troubleshooting tab heading of the Performance property sheets. Now turn on the *Disable long filename preservation for old programs* check box. (When you reverse LFBNK, you should turn off the check box to restore Windows to its normal state.)

This step is required for safety's sake. You can actually bypass it by adding /FORCE to the LFNBK command. We've used /FORCE without incident, but you may rather be safe than sorry.

Once you've made the change in Troubleshooting. To get ready to use an old backup program, start Windows 95, and and then open the MS-DOS prompt. From the C:> prompt, type **LFNBK /B**

This command strips away and backs up all the long filenames for the current drive (drive C:). If you have another hard drive on your computer, you must change to it (by typing **D:** at the DOS prompt) and run LFNBK /B again on that drive. It creates another LFNBK.DAT in the root directory of that drive.

> When you strip the long filenames, your Start menu appears to be wiped out because Windows is looking for "Start Menu" and sees only the short DOS directory name of STARTM~1. Many desktop shortcuts also appear to be damaged. Don't worry, your old Start menu and icons will come back when you use LFNBK /R to restore the long filenames.

Bypassing Windows 95

You can now exit Windows 95 and restart your previous version of MS-DOS by pressing F4 as soon as you see the message "Starting Windows 95." (This only works if you installed Windows 95 to a new directory. If you upgraded an existing Windows 3.1 directory, your old version of DOS is not retained.)

Or, to start "real mode" MS-DOS 7 without Windows 95, you can press Shift+F5 during bootup. This key combination dumps you unceremoniously into DOS 7 without executing your AUTOEXEC.BAT and CONFIG.SYS files. If you need to run part of these files, you can instead press F8 during bootup. This way, you can choose several options, including running DOS without Windows or single-stepping through your system files, which allow you to verify each statement in AUTOEXEC.BAT and CONFIG.SYS.

Now that you're in "plain DOS," you can run your DOS backup program or start your previous version of Windows (if you still have it) and run your backup program. (You can also run a Windows backup program from Windows 95 if the long filenames have been previously stripped off with

LFNBK.) Although the long filenames are not backed up, if you include LFNBK.DAT in the backup, you'll be able to restore the long filenames later.

When the backup (or restore) is complete, you then restart your computer and let Windows 95 run as usual, and once again start the MS-DOS prompt, and type **LFNBK /R**

This command restores the long filenames, assuming you haven't renamed any of the files in the meantime. Be sure to also switch to any other drives on your computer and use LFNBK /R to fix those names, too. You can then restart Windows again to reset everything—a step that's probably not necessary but certainly can't hurt.

You'll rarely use the other LFNBK options. You can type **LFNBK /?** at the MS-DOS prompt to read more about them.

Direct Disk Access

Recall that Windows 95 bypasses DOS. DOS itself no longer "owns" the hard drive exclusively. Some DOS utilities attempt to directly modify the disk, such as disk sector editors. Even the DOS Label command (used to change the volume label) works by modifying the hard drive directly. Other tools such as UNDELETE and UNFORMAT also alter the disk structure.

Because Windows 95 is a multitasking operating system, several programs could be trying to use the disk at the same time. Therefore, it would be dangerous to interrupt a program that is directly modifying the drive. A special LOCK command is provided in case you do need to run one of these tools. While LOCK is active, no other program can use the hard drive, except for those running in the current DOS session. It's possible to use LOCK and run programs like the old UNDELETE command from within Windows 95, but it's not a great idea. It's far better to boot into the real-mode version of DOS by pressing Shift+F5 during bootup, and run those type of tools without Windows 95.

MS-DOS 7 Command Reference

By now you've got a handle on running DOS programs from Windows 95. And while you'll rarely need to use the DOS prompt, you may still need to use DOS for running older programs. It's helpful to understand the language of DOS, especially if you have to figure out how an old DOS batch file works or if you are assisting someone who is still stuck with DOS. It also gives you a greater appreciation for the ease of use that Windows provides. Who wouldn't rather drag and drop an icon instead of typing a cryptic line like XCOPY C:\PROJECTS\BOOK D:\BACKUP\ /S /E?

Finally, there are some tasks you can't accomplish any other way than by using DOS, such as using FDISK to prepare a new hard drive. (Actually, if you buy the full Windows 95 product instead of the upgrade, you can boot from Disk 1, and Setup will offer to FDISK and FORMAT the hard drive for you.)

Instead of just providing an alphabetical list of DOS commands, we'll group them into task-oriented solutions.

In addition to this chapter, you can also learn a great deal about DOS by using the built-in DOS help system. Just type **HELP** at the DOS prompt to get a complete list of all DOS commands (see Figure 22-14). You can also type **HELP** *command-name*, such as **HELP XCOPY**, to jump directly to the information on that command.

Figure 22-14: *The DOS Help system gives you detailed instructions for using DOS commands.*

The HELP feature for DOS isn't included with Windows 95, however. You can still run it if you have a DOS directory left over from a previous version of DOS. Or you can copy the files HELP.COM and HELP.HLP to \Windows\Command from the \OTHER\OLDMSDOS folder of the Windows 95 CD-ROM.

Another way to get "quick help" is to use the /? switch with most commands. For example, typing **DIR /?** gives you a complete reference to the DIR command, as shown in Figure 22-15.

Displays a list of files and subdirectories in a directory.
DIR [drive:][path][filename] [/P] [/W] [/A[[:]attributes]]
[/O[[:]sortorder]] [/S] [/B] [/L] [/V]

[drive:][path][filename]
    Specifies drive, directory, and/or files to list.
    (Could be enhanced file specification or multiple filespecs.)
/P   Pauses after each screenful of information.
/W   Uses wide list format.
/A   Displays files with specified attributes.
attributes D Directories   R Read-only files
    H Hidden files   A Files ready for archiving
    S System files   - Prefix meaning not
/O   List by files in sorted order.
sortorder N By name (alphabetic) S By size (smallest first)
    E By extension (alphabetic) D By date & time (earliest first)
    G Group directories first - Prefix to reverse order
    A By Last Access Date (earliest first)
/S   Displays files in specified directory and all subdirectories.
/B   Uses bare format (no heading information or summary).
/L   Uses lowercase.
/V   Verbose mode.

Switches may be preset in the DIRCMD environment variable. Override preset switches by prefixing any switch with - (hyphen)—for example, /-W.

Figure 22-15: *Type DIR /? to get a complete listing of the optional switches for DIR.*

When you're reading these descriptions, it may be helpful to know a few documentation conventions used by MS-DOS and many other programs. Anything in square brackets is an optional *command-line argument*. When more than one item is in the brackets, separated by a vertical bar, it means you can use one or the other, but not both. (Example: You can have [eggs | pancakes][juice][toast], which means "you can have eggs OR pancakes, and you can have juice, and you can have toast." Or you can have nothing at all, since all the items are optional.)

The forward slashes are actually used in the command line; they denote a special option. Don't mistake the forward slash for the backward slash used between directory names in a path specification. Sometimes a hyphen can be used interchangeably with forward slashes.

Other conventions include the use of directory and pathnames, and wildcard characters. Chapter 5, "Inside the File System," is a good starting point for learning about wildcards, filename conventions and how directories are organized. (Remember, the terms *directory* and *folder* are interchangeable in a discussion about file management.)

Since so much online help is available, we won't go into full detail in our reference but will focus on the usefulness of each command.

Most Useful Internal MS-DOS Commands

Internal commands don't exist as separate disk files but are built into DOS. The other external commands are found in the \DOS or \Windows\ Command folders. Following are the most common commands, and the ones you'll use the most in DOS.

CD, CHDIR

The *current* directory is kind of like the "current window" in Windows; it's the one that you're working with, the one that reacts when you type something on the keyboard. Similarly, the current directory is used by most DOS commands if you don't use a different drive and directory name in the DOS command line.

When you start your computer, the current directory is the root directory on your boot drive (C:\). If you wanted to "change into" the DOS directory, you would type **CD \DOS**. Note the use of the backslash before *DOS*. It makes sure you are referring to a directory that branches directly from the root directory. It also prevents confusion, since CD DOS (no backslash) could refer to a directory that branches off the current directory instead.

You can't change the *current drive* with CD or CHDIR. Instead, you just type the letter of the drive (along with its colon) and press Enter. If the current drive is C: and you want to change to D:, just type **D:** at the DOS prompt and then press Enter.

To keep track of the current directory, use the command PROMPT PG in your AUTOEXEC.BAT file (which is the Windows 95 default if you have no AUTOEXEC.BAT file). This command puts the name of the current drive and directory in the command-line prompt. Instead of just C:\ as the prompt, you'll see the name of the current directory, for example, C:\WINDOWS\SYSTEM>.

When you type in a word that's not recognized as an internal DOS command, DOS assumes you want to run a program. It first searches within the current directory for a file with that name ending in .BAT, .COM .or .EXE (in that order). Then it searches the directories specified in the PATH statement (see "PATH"), usually defined in your AUTOEXEC.BAT file.

Windows 95 honors the current directory sometimes, such as in the Open File dialog box of some programs, but it's a largely obsolete concept for Windows programs.

How to use it:

Follow CD with the name of the directory you want to make the current directory. Use CD by itself to display the name of the current directory.

Examples:

    CD \

Switches you to the root directory.

    CD \DOS

Switches you to the DOS directory.

    CD DOCS

Since there is no \ symbol, switches you to the DOCS directory within the current directory.

Variations:

    CD ..
Backs you up to the previous (parent) directory.
    CD ...
Backs you up one previous level (one period per level). (This variation is a new feature in DOS 7. Previously you had to use CD ..\.. to back up two levels.)

COPY

Creates a duplicate copy of a file.

How to use it:

After COPY, enter the name of the original file. If it's not in the current directory, prefix it with the drive and directory name where it can be found.

Then add a space and type the name of the destination file. The duplicate can have a different name, or the same name in a different directory (you can't copy a file "on top of itself" in the same directory).

Examples:

> COPY AUTOEXEC.BAT AUTOEXEC.SAV

Creates a backup copy of AUTOEXEC.BAT in the same directory.

> COPY "C:\MSOFFICE\WINWORD\Metric System Conversion Table.DOC" C:\BACKUP

Note that there is no filename in the destination, just a destination pathname. This convention is permitted if you want to copy the file using the same name.

Variations:

> COPY ROLOFILE.* ROLOSAVE.*

Creates a copy of all files beginning with "ROLOFILE" and saves them as ROLOSAVE, using the same extensions. For ROLOFILE.DB, ROLOFILE.DBS, ROLOFILE.PIX and so on, creates ROLOSAVE.DB, ROLOSAVE.DBS, ROLOSAVE.PIX and so on. See "XCOPY" in the "External MS-DOS Commands" section for a way to copy entire directories of files.

> COPY CONFIG.SYS LPT1:

Has the effect of printing CONFIG.SYS, since LPT1: is the name of the printer device. If the file is not a simple text file, add /B to the beginning of the copy command to make sure that all eight bits of each byte are transferred and that the file is not truncated when it reads an end-of-file character.

> COPY CON "New File"

CON: is the name of the *console device*. This command lets you create a text file from scratch. After typing all the lines in the new file, press Ctrl+Z or the function key F6 to end your typing and create the file.

> COPY C:\AUTOEXEC.SAV C:\AUTOEXEC.BAT /Y

If the destination file already exists, you'll be asked "Are you sure?" if the destination file would be overwritten by the new file. This new safety measure was added after DOS 6. (COPY commands in batch files still work the old way, without asking first.) Use the /Y switch to defeat this often needless safety check.

COPY FILE1.TXT + FILE2.TXT FILE3.TXT

Combines (concatenates, one after the other) FILE1.TXT and FILE2.TXT, storing the combined file in FILE3.TXT. Add the /B switch to the beginning if you are concatenating binary files.

DEL, ERASE

Both of these commands do the same thing: they delete a file from the hard drive (or whatever device the file is on). Although it is possible to undelete a file using UNDELETE (under special circumstances), consider it a permanent removal and use it carefully. Files deleted from DOS are not moved to the Recycler Bin.

 The Norton Utilities for Windows 95 converts the Recycle Bin into a "SmartCan" that tracks all deletions, even files deleted from MS-DOS or from within a program.

How to use it:

Follow DEL with the name of the file you want to delete in the current directory. You can also prefix the name of the file with a drive and directory to arbitrarily delete any file. Long filenames are supported; enclose them in quotation marks if they contain spaces.

Examples:

DEL MYFILE.TXT

ERASE "Second quarter profit and loss statement"

DEL *.TMP

Warning! Wildcards allow you to delete a range of matching files. Use wildcards with extreme caution when using the DEL command. For example, DEL *.* erases *all* files in the current directory. To be safer, use the /P switch with DEL. It asks "Are you sure" for each file that matches the wildcard. You can "preview" which files will be deleted by a wildcard by using DIR instead of DEL with the same file specification—for example, DIR W*.TXT shows you all the files that will be erased with DEL W*.TXT.

DIR

Displays the *current directory* (see CD) in the form of a list. The leftmost column shows the short filenames, and the long filenames are shown on the right. In between you see the size of the file and the date and time the file was last modified.

How to use it:

Use DIR by itself to view the current directory. You can follow DIR with the name of another directory to arbitrarily view any directory on the drive.

Example:

DIR \WINDOWS\SYSTEM

Displays the \Windows\System folder.

Most useful variations (can be combined):

DIR /L

Gives you an easy-on-the-eyes lowercase display of filenames. This command affects only the short filenames; long filenames can already be in upper- and lowercase.

DIR /W

Displays only the filenames from left to right instead of in a list, so it's the "wide" directory format.

DIR /O

Changes the order of the directory listing. Combine it with any of the following characters: N for Name, E for Extension, D for Date and S for Size. To reverse the order, prefix the character with a hyphen, such as -S to list from largest to smallest instead of the other way around.

DIR /P

Displays the message "Press any key to continue..." after each screenful of information, allowing you to read a screen before it scrolls away off the top of the screen.

DIR /V

Displays additional details, including extra date and time information on the last time the file was accessed, and shows the attributes for the files. Attributes include the status of a file, such as Read Only, Hidden and System.

You can create an entry called DIRCMD in your AUTOEXEC.BAT file to customize the DIR command. For example, add the line SET DIRCMD=/OEN /L to make the plain DIR command always sort by extension and display the entries in lowercase.

MD, MKDIR

Creates a new directory (folder) underneath the current one.

How to use it:

Follow MD with a full path specification to create an arbitrary directory. You can't create a subdirectory to a directory that hasn't been created yet; that is, you can't use MD \TEMP\OLD if a \TEMP directory doesn't already exist.

Examples:

```
MD \TEMP
MD D:\BACKUP
MKDIR D:\BACKUP
```

Variations:

None.

PATH

Specifies the search order for programs that can't be found in the current directory. Normally, you'd have PATH C:\WINDOWS;C:\WINDOWS\COMMAND;C:\DOS in your AUTOEXEC.BAT file. Some Windows programs add themselves to your path, even if it's not really necessary. An excessively long PATH statement can slow down the search for commands, and the total length of a PATH statement can't exceed 128 characters. The pidgin cousin of PATH is APPEND, and it can be used to find data files that aren't in the current directory. APPEND makes those directories always appear to be part of the current directory; APPEND doesn't work well with Windows and isn't very useful anyway.

How to use it:

Follow PATH with a list of directory names, separated by semicolons.

Example:

PATH C:\WINDOWS;C:\WINDOWS\DOS;C:\DOS;C:\EXCEL;D:\AMIPRO

Variations:

Use PATH ; by itself to clear the path; only the current directory will be searched for commands.

In a batch file, you can use a line like SET PATH %PATH%;C:\TEMP to add a new directory to the current path.

RD, RMDIR

Removes (deletes) a directory. For safety's sake, you can remove a directory only if it is empty, that is, contains no files or subdirectories. If you can't remove a seemingly empty directory, it may contain hidden files. (See "ATTRIB" in the "Most Useful External MS-DOS Commands" section.)

How to use it:

Enter the name of an existing, empty directory after the RMDIR command.

Example:

RMDIR \TEMP

Variations:

None.

REN, RENAME

Changes the name of a file.

How to use it:

After the REN command, type the original name of the file (either the long or the short name). Then type a space and type the new name you'd like. The new name can be a long filename, and it will create a new short filename if necessary. If the long filename (the original or the new one) contains spaces, enclose the filename in quotation marks. You can't RENAME a directory name; you must use MOVE (see "Most Useful MS-DOS External Commands") to change the name of a directory.

Examples:

```
REN AUTOEXEC.BAK AUTOEXEC.SAV
RENAME "This is a long filename" "This is the new filename"
REN THISISAL "This is the new filename"
RENAME C:\AUTOEXEC.BAK AUTOEXEC.SAV
```

Variation:

If you don't specify a drive and directory for the original name, you are attempting to rename a file in the current directory (see "CHDIR"). You can use a drive and directory to rename a file in another folder, and you don't need to repeat it for the new name; however, you can't use a different drive and directory for the new name, as this would imply a MOVE rather than a RENAME.

START

Unlike Windows 3.1 Window 95 now lets you start Windows programs directly from the command line. So typing **NOTEPAD** at the DOS prompt starts the Notepad accessory.

Even though you can start Windows applications by typing their name directly on the command line, the big difference between typing something like **START CALC** vs. simply **CALC** is the fact that the START command forces the command to go through Explorer. This makes things a lot friendlier. For example, **START FOO.HELP** will automatically figure out the association for that extension and bring up the Windows help engine. Simply typing **FOO.HLP** on the command line will utilize the normal MS-DOS search rules and won't launch the Windows help engine for the foo.hlp file.

Note that the usage of the START command exactly mimics what the GUI Start: Run dialog does as well.

For Advanced Users: The other big benefit of the START command is the fact that it passes through the shell code that deals with the per-process environment settings for Win32 applications. This info is stored in the registry, and the shell knows how to parse it before it's handed to kernel. If you type in the name of the Win32 application directly on the MS-DOS command line, you'll get the default global environment and path settings. If you use the START command, the shell will look up any possible per-process path settings and use those for the application in question. In addition, ISVs (Independent Software Vendors) can register the exact location of where their EXE lives, so if you don't have that directory in your default search path (because, say, you don't have an AUTOEXEC.BAT), then Windows 95 will still be able to find the EXE by looking it up in the registry.

How to use it:

Follow START with the filename of a Windows application. You can also use START with a document that is associated with a Windows application. START is optional; you can directly type the name of a Windows program if you want to start it in a normal window.

Examples:

    START WordPad

Opens the WordPad accessory.

    START Memo.sam

Opens the Ami Pro document Memo.sam with Ami Pro.

Variations:

    START MSPAINT.EXE /MAX

Opens Microsoft Paint in a maximized window.

START WINPOPUP /M

Opens the WinPopup utility, minimized on the taskbar.

START README.TXT /R

Opens Notepad, loading README.TXT, in a normal window. The /R is actually the usual behavior of START.

START READ1ST.TXT /W

In a batch file (see "Introduction to Batch Files"), you could have a number of START commands. Each one runs immediately after the other, since Windows applications can run simultaneously. But if you want to pace things and force one program to end before running the next, use the /W switch.

TYPE

Displays a file (usually a text file) to the screen.

How to use it:

After TYPE, enter the filename of the file in the current directory you'd like to view, or prefix the filename with a drive and directory name to view a file in another directory.

Examples:

TYPE AUTOEXEC.BAT
TYPE C:\TEXT\README.TXT

Variations:

TYPE README.1ST | MORE

If a file is long, it will scroll off the screen too fast to read it. Even if you try to press the Pause key, you probably don't have fast enough reflexes to keep up with the high speed of today's computers. Using a vertical bar "pipes" the contents of the TYPE command into the MORE command and displays "— MORE —" to remind you to press any key to continue, after each screenful of text. Also consider using EDIT to view long files; it's more convenient to be able to scroll up or down as you need.

Most Useful External MS-DOS Commands

The C:\WINDOWS\COMMAND directory (its usual location, your computer might start up from a different drive than C:) contains dozens of DOS commands. (You might also have some of these commands in a C:\DOS directory, if you installed Windows 95 to a new directory instead of upgrading from Windows 3.1.) In addition, just about any MS-DOS program can be considered an "external command." We'll limit our discussion here to the most popular and useful DOS commands.

ATTRIB

The status of a file can include the state of being *Read-Only* (it can't be re-written or deleted), *Archived* (was recently modified and needs to be backed up), *Hidden* (normally not visible in a DIR command or in Explorer) and *System* (a special variation on hidden, prevents changes to the attributes without first clearing the system attribute). You can accomplish the same thing with Explorer by choosing Properties for a file.

How to use it:

Follow the ATTRIB command with a filename (or use wildcard to define a range of files), followed by a + sign to set an attribute, or a hyphen to clear the attribute, followed by the first letter of the attribute (R=Read-Only, H=Hidden, S=System, A= Needs to be Archived).

To view attributes for the files in the current directory, use ATTRIB by itself. To see the attributes in a different directory, follow ATTRIB with the drive and directory, and use a wildcard (see examples) to see all the files.

Examples:

    ATTRIB MSDOS.SYS -S -H -R

Turns off the System, Hidden, and Read-Only attributes for MSDOS.SYS, allowing you to edit and change the file. Afterward, use ATTRIB MSDOS.SYS +S +H +R to restore its protected status.

    ATTRIB C:\DOS *.*

Shows the attributes for all the files in C:\DOS.

Variation:

    ATTRIB C:\BACKUP*.* +R /S

Flags all the files in C:\BACKUP and all the files in all subdirectories of C:\BACKUP as Read-Only.

DELTREE

Use with caution! Unlike RMDIR, which will remove only empty directories, DELTREE is like a pruning shear, lopping off not only the directory you specify, but all the subdirectories contained within it. DELTREE C:\ will erase *all* files on drive C:. Fortunately, the command asks "Are you sure?" first, so don't absentmindedly get in the habit of always pressing Y.

On the other hand, manually stripping out a directory used by an old program can be tedious, since you have to use CD to go to the innermost subdirectory, delete all files, back out one level, delete those files, on and on until you've backed out to the topmost level.

How to use it:

After DELTREE, type the name of the directory you want to delete, along with all its files and subdirectories.

Example:

    DELTREE C:\WP60

Deletes not only the WP60 directory, but all files and subdirectories within WP60. You might use this command if you are uninstalling an application.

Variation:

    DELTREE C:\TEMP /Y

Use the /Y switch to bypass the "Are you sure?" prompt. Actually, don't use it—DELTREE is too dangerous to risk an accident.

DISKCOPY

Use DISKCOPY to duplicate one floppy onto another. It can only copy a disk between identical drives or can be used with just one drive. If sufficient memory is available (usually the case), DISKCOPY will copy the entire disk into memory before asking you to insert the destination disk, which makes it easy to perform disk backups using just one drive.

 An easier way to copy a file, from Windows, is to right-click on the floppy drive icon in My Computer and choose Copy Disk.

Although it's possible to copy a disk by copying all the files on it to a temporary directory on the hard drive (or to a folder on the Windows desktop) and then copying those files onto a blank disk, this method does not achieve a perfect copy. DISKCOPY creates a nearly perfect copy, automatically transferring hidden files and transferring the volume label. Also, DISKCOPY formats the disk as it works, so you don't have to FORMAT the destination disk separately. Just make sure the destination disk is empty or obsolete, since DISKCOPY will completely overwrite it.

DISKCOPY can usually be defeated by disk copy protection, but very few programs use copy protection anymore. Just keep in mind that you are licensed to create one set of backup copies of any software program, but you can't transfer the software to another person unless you've destroyed all your copies. (Check your license to clarify this issue.)

How to use it:

Type **DISKCOPY**, then the name of the source drive, a space and then the name of the destination drive. (The source and destination drives can be the same drive, but both drives have to be the same type.)

Examples:

    DISKCOPY A: B:

Duplicates a disk between two identical drives (A: and B: are both 3.5-inch or are identical 5.25-inch drives). You can't DISKCOPY from a 3.5-inch drive to a 5.25-inch drive.

DISKCOPY A: A:

Duplicates a disk using the same drive. After copying the disk into memory, you insert the second disk to receive the copy.

Variations:

No useful variations.

EDIT

Opens a file into a word processor-style full-screen editor for viewing or making changes. Even though it's a DOS program, EDIT behaves like a Windows program, with full mouse support for selecting text, clicking on buttons and pulling down menus. It works much like Notepad but has additional capabilities.

How to use it:

Follow EDIT with the name of the file you want to open in the current directory, or use a drive and directory name to edit a file in a different directory. If you use a filename that isn't on the drive, it's assumed you want to create a new file with that name. You can use EDIT by itself to start the program and then use File | Open to select the file you want to edit. You can also follow EDIT with a long filename. Enclose the filename in quotation marks if it includes spaces.

EDIT is usually only useful with plain text (ASCII) documents. Other formats, such as WordPad files, usually display with some amount of gibberish, and using EDIT to change these files may damage them if you save them back out to the drive.

Examples:

EDIT README.DOC

Opens README.DOC for editing.

EDIT C:\AUTOEXEC.BAT C:\CONFIG.SYS

Opens two files for editing at the same time. You can press Alt+1 to switch to the first file and Alt+2 to switch to the second file. Opening multiple files at once is a new feature of EDIT in DOS 7 and Windows 95.

EDIT "Pinewood Derby Rules and Regulations"

You can open documents with long filenames.

Variations:

EDIT /R README.TXT

The /R switch is ideal for viewing documents that you don't want to alter, even accidentally. You can use the cursor keys only to scroll through the document. No changes are permitted.

EDIT /H README.TXT

With EGA, allows EDIT to use 43 lines; with VGA, you get a 50-line display. (However, EGA cards are not supported from within Windows 95.)

EDIT /B README.TXT

Forces EDIT into monochrome mode, useful if you have a paper-white (monochrome) VGA monitor.

EDIT /S

Prevents you from saving files with long filenames, and shows only the short versions of filenames when you open files. For backward compatibility with older programs, presumably.

EDIT COMMAND.COM /100

Opens a binary file. The numeric switch specifies the number of columns to display, since carriage returns are rendered literally on the screen instead of creating line breaks. In binary mode, each number in the file is treated as an ASCII value and displayed as the corresponding character. (ASCII is discussed in Chapter 5.) To enter a value arbitrarily, hold down Alt, type the three-digit code (000 through 255) and then release Alt. You can try some scary tricks this way, such as searching for MS-DOS and replacing it with MY-DOS or your name. However, if you change any characters, you must replace them with exactly the same number of characters, or you will ruin the binary file. Be sure you experiment only on backup copies of your original files. Some clever people have used a similar technique with the Windows 3.1 Write applet to "patch" programs in interesting ways.

FDISK

WARNING! Used improperly, this command can erase all the files on your hard drive. On the other hand, it's a necessary step in preparing a new, unformatted hard drive for use with Windows 95. FDISK is used to create *partitions* on a hard drive. In principle, you can divide a single hard drive into a number of smaller "logical" hard drives, each with a different drive letter. In practice, you will almost always use the entire hard drive as a single partition. One use, however, for a separate partition is if you want to use two or more distinctly different file systems on the same drive, such as the ordinary default DOS FAT (File Allocation System), OS/2 HPFS (High Performance File System) or Windows NT's NTFS (New Technology File System).

Hands-On: Preparing a New Hard Drive

We discussed how to add a new hard drive in Chapter 15. The next step is to prepare it for DOS, assuming DOS has not already been preloaded on your computer by the dealer (in which case you also paid for a DOS license). To prepare the hard drive, you'll need a bootable floppy disk that also contains the FDISK.EXE and FORMAT.EXE files. You'll usually find them on the first disk of an MS-DOS installation disk (press F5 while booting this disk to bypass the install program). When you first installed Windows 95, it offered to create a startup disk, which also contains these files. If you don't have a startup disk, use Add New Software from the Control Panel, and click on the startup disk tab header to create one before you remove your old hard drive (or do this on another computer running Windows 95).

1. Boot from the startup disk and then type **FDISK** at the DOS prompt. You'll then get a screen similar to the one in Figure 22-16.

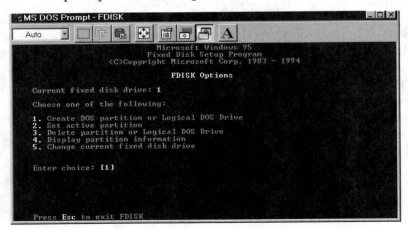

Figure 22-16: *Use FDISK to prepare a new hard drive for first use.*

2. Choose "1. Create DOS Partition or Logical Disk Drive."
3. You'll be asked, "Do you want to use the largest size available for this partition and make it active?" Type **Y** and press Enter.
4. FDISK reports the size of the partition. Don't be alarmed if it is smaller than the advertised size of the drive; the advertised size is misleading (see Chapter 15 to see why).
5. You now have to reboot the computer so that it can add the new drive letter. Boot from the startup disk again.
6. At the DOS prompt, type **FORMAT C: /S**. This command formats the new hard drive and also copies the system (boot) files onto it.
7. When FORMAT is complete, you're asked to enter a volume name for the hard drive. You can use your name or any descriptive title up to 11 characters.
8. You can now restart your computer and boot from the hard drive.
9. Finally, you can run the DOS installation program or the Windows 95 SETUP program to install Windows 95 directly.

 A special, largely unknown variation of FDISK is FDISK /MBR, which rewrites the *master boot record* of a hard drive. This command can sometimes cure a hard drive that won't boot. Just boot from your startup disk and use FDISK /MBR. You can also use FDISK /MBR to repair a boot sector damaged by a virus.

FORMAT

Except when setting up a new hard drive (see "FDISK" above), you should use FORMAT only when initializing a new floppy disk. Since packages of floppy disks are available preformatted, you may never need to format at all, although the Quick Format variation is a thorough, fast way to erase an old floppy completely. You can also format a disk from within Windows 95 by right-clicking on your floppy disk drive from My Computer or Explorer and choosing Format from the pop-up menu.

How to use it:

Follow the FORMAT command with the letter of the floppy drive containing the disk you want to erase. You'll be reminded to insert the disk (a holdover from the days people always booted from a DOS disk and kept their DOS commands on that disk—you would want to be reminded to remove your DOS disk before inserting the disk you want to format) and press Enter to begin the formatting. Afterward, you're prompted to enter a volume name, kind of like a filename for the disk, or just press Enter to use a blank volume name.

During formatting, the drive is checked for bad sectors, and if any are found, the bad sectors are "set aside" as unusable, so the final capacity of the disk may be lower than the maximum if you find problems on the drive. If you get much less than the known capacity (1,468,000 bytes on a 3.5-inch high-density floppy and 1,258,291 bytes on a 5.25-inch high-density floppy), you may have tried to format a low-density disk on the drive or just have a bad disk. Don't try to use it.

Example:

    FORMAT A:

The most basic format command, erases and formats (or reformats) a floppy in drive A:. If the disk was already formatted, DOS saves Unformat information on the drive in case you change your mind and want to get the old contents back (see "UNFORMAT").

Variations (most can be combined):

    FORMAT A: /Q

Used to wipe out a previously formatted disk. It's quicker than deleting the files from a disk, especially if the disk contains multiple directories, and it writes a new, clean FAT for the disk. By default, it also saves Unformat information on the disk, using up some space, so that you can "undo" the format if necessary (see "UNFORMAT"). Quick Format does not scan the disk for bad sectors like the usual format command, so use it only on known good disks.

    FORMAT B: /Q /U

Similar to Quick Format, but also Unconditional, which means no space is wasted to store Unformat information. You can't "undo" this type of format, so use it with confidence.

    FORMAT A: /V:label

If you add the label to the FORMAT command, you can skip the step of typing in the label after the format is complete.

FORMAT A: /S

After the format is complete, transfers the system files (IO.SYS, MSDOS.SYS, COMMAND.COM) to the disk, making it bootable.

FORMAT A: /F:720

Formats a double-sided, double-density (DSDD) 720k floppy in a 3.5-inch 1.44mb drive. By default, FORMAT tries to format a disk to the highest capacity supported by your floppy drive. You need the /F switch to format a lower capacity floppy. You can also use /F:360 for a low-density 5.25-inch disk. Don't format a floppy disk for a greater capacity than it's capable of—sometimes it almost works, but it's not reliable.

MODE

The MODE command is a jack-of-all-trades. It's used to set the screen display mode, key repeat rate, keyboard code page (international language), serial port speed, even redirect the printer port to use a serial printer. Almost all of these functions are obsolete with Windows 95, so we'll just explore a few of the options useful in a DOS window.

Variations:

MODE CO80

Switches into 80-column and color. Use MODE CO40 for 40 columns (supported only full screen), originally designed for using a television as a monitor. You can also use MODE CON COLS=40 and MODE CON COLS=80 for the same effect.

MODE CON LINES=50

Switch to 50-line VGA mode. Gives you twice as many lines, half height, for the MS-DOS CONsole. (In a window, you still get twice as many lines, but using full-size characters, so the box is twice as tall.) Use MODE CON LINES=25 to go back to the normal height.

MODE CON RATE=30 DELAY=2

Rate and Delay control the "typeamatic" or repeat speed of keys held down. Using a higher value for Rate and a lower value of Delay makes the keyboard feel "faster" and more responsive. This does not affect Windows; use the Keyboard option in Control Panel to control the keyboard speed in Windows.

MODE MONO

If you have both a monochrome video card and a color card in the same machine (some programmers use this setup so they can display debugging information on the second monitor), MODE MONO switches you to the alternate monitor, and MODE CO80 switches you back to the color screen. Or if your VGA card can emulate a monochrome video card, MODE MONO switches it in this mode.

MODE COM2: BAUD=96 PARITY=E DATA=7 STOP=1

Configures COM2: for 9600 baud, even parity, with seven data bits and one stop bit. Used to configure a serial printer, rarely used with PCs.

MODE LPT1:=COM2:

Once the serial port is configured, you can redirect LPT1: to the serial port. LPT1: is normally used by DOS for printing to the parallel port. You would put both MODE commands in your AUTOEXEC.BAT file. Neither of them is really necessary with Windows 95.

MOVE

One of the handiest DOS commands added in DOS 5, MOVE lets you copy a file to a new directory and delete it from the original directory, all in one step. It can also rename a directory (you can't do this with the REN command.)

How to use it:

Follow MOVE with the name of the file you want to move (using a drive and directory name if it's not in the current directory). Add a space and then enter the destination drive and directory to receive the file.

To rename a directory, just use the name of the directory (without a filename afterward) after MOVE, type a space, and then add the new name for that directory.

Examples:

MOVE C:\TEXT\README.TXT D:\TEXT

Relocates a file from one directory and drive to another.

MOVE "The Long Filename" C:\TEXT

Relocates the file (long filenames are allowed) from the current directory to another directory. This directory must already exist; otherwise, it names the file TEXT in the root directory C:\.

MOVE "Hamburger Recipe" "Spamburger Recipe"

Has the same effect as a rename command. It renames the file in the process of copying and then deleting the original file.

MOVE C:\TEMP C:\TEMPDIR

Renames the directory C:\TEMP to C:\TEMPDIR.

MOVE C:\TEXT C:\DOCUMENTS

Relocates the C:\TEXT directory so that it is now a subdirectory of C:\DOCUMENTS.

MOVE C:\DOCUMENTS\TEXT C:\TEXT

Relocates the TEXT directory back to the root.

SMARTDRV

Starts the 16-bit DOS caching utility. (A caching program keeps frequently accessed files in memory, which is much faster than the hard drive.) You would use this command only when running a program in MS-DOS mode to help speed up disk access, since in MS-DOS mode, no Windows 95 disk caching is available. If you had SMARTDRV in your AUTOEXEC.BAT previously, it's removed by the Windows 95 SETUP program, since it only wastes memory that can be better used for Windows 95 32-bit disk caching.

How to use it:

By itself, SMARTDRV automatically installs caching for all the hard drives and floppy drives on your computer. It does not cache network drives, but it does cache a CD-ROM drive, as long as the MSCDEX program has already started.

If you want to control which drives are cached, put their names after SMARTDRV. To disable caching, follow the drive letter with a hyphen (minus) symbol. For read-only caching, put the drive letter by itself. For write-behind caching (changes are made first to the file in memory, which is streamed out to disk during idle moments), put a + symbol after the drive letter.

SmartDrive, like most disk caches, can't directly cache a compressed drive created with Stacker, DoubleSpace or DriveSpace, but you can cache the host drive to achieve the same effect.

It automatically determines how much memory should be set aside for the cache, but you can choose this memory size yourself by putting the size of the memory buffer, in kilobytes, after the drive letters. Since you don't use SmartDrive with Windows anymore, you don't need the feature that lets you put a second number after the first, which is the size of the SmartDrive cache within Windows (which often can't afford as large a buffer as you can use in DOS).

SmartDrive requires that you use HIMEM.SYS in your CONFIG.SYS file.

Example:

```
SMARTDRV A- B- C+ D 1024
```

Starts SmartDrive, disabling the caching of floppy drives, enabling write-back caching of the hard drive and enabling caching for the CD-ROM (drive D:). The size of the cache is one megabyte (1024 kilobytes).

Variations:

```
SMARTDRV /X
```

Disables write-behind caching for all drives. This provides a smaller performance boost but is safer if you have a computer that crashes a lot, which might prevent recent changes from being transferred from the cache back to the drive.

```
SMARTDRV /C
```

Commits the contents of the write-behind cache immediately to the hard drive. You may want to make sure your changes have been written before you turn off your computer. It's not usually necessary to verify changes, since it takes only a few seconds for this to happen automatically—just wait five seconds before powering off.

```
SMARTDRV /S
```

Displays the status of SmartDrive, including its size and which drives are being cached.

SMARTDRV C+ /U

The /U switch prevents SmartDrive from caching the CD-ROM and unloads the support for this functionality, freeing up some conventional memory.

DEVICE=SMARTDRV.EXE /DOUBLEBUFFER

You may need to use this in your CONFIG.SYS file if you use a bus-mastering SCSI controller on the ISA bus, especially if you have more than 16mb of RAM. It is not necessary if your SCSI drivers are ASPI compatible.

SYS

Transfers the system files (IO.SYS, MSDOS.SYS, COMMAND.COM) onto a disk, making it bootable.

How to use it:

Follow SYS with the name of the disk or drive you want to make bootable. If you forgot to use /S while formatting a hard drive, you can use SYS to add these files. Or you can turn a regular floppy into a boot floppy, assuming there's room on the disk for the extra boot files. Also, if the boot files on your hard drive become corrupted (which happens only very rarely), you can boot from your startup disk and use SYS to rewrite the boot files on the hard drive.

Example:

SYS A:

Makes the floppy in drive A: bootable.

Variation:

SYS C: A:

If for some reason DOS can't find the original boot files, you can precede the drive letter (A:) with their location (C:\).

UNDELETE

In Windows 95, you can use the Recycler Bin to retrieve files that you have deleted. In DOS, your only recourse is the UNDELETE command. You have to use UNDELETE very soon after deleting a file, since its space can get overwritten by other programs that create files. Also, UNDELETE can't be run from within a Windows 95 DOS session; use Shift+F5 during booting to run real-mode DOS 7 directly so you can use UNDELETE. UNDELETE does not support long filenames. If you erase a file with a long filename, you need to undelete it using the short form.

How to use it:

Follow UNDELETE with the name of the file you want to retrieve. If you don't know the name of the file, use UNDELETE by itself to see all deleted files. DOS destroys the first character of the filename when it's deleted and prompts you to enter it before the file is undeleted.

Examples:

    UNDELETE VITLINFO.TXT

Restores the file in the current directory. You have to remember that the first letter is V, despite the fact that the UNDELETE command appears to provide this information already.

    UNDELETE C:\DOCS

Displays the name of each undeleted file, giving you the choice of restoring each one.

UNFORMAT

You can use UNFORMAT after formatting a disk or accidentally formatting a hard drive (heaven forbid!), as long as you didn't use the /U switch during formatting. This command must be run from real-mode DOS 7 (press Shift+F5 during booting). It won't work from within Windows 95.

How to use it:

Put the drive letter and a colon after the UNFORMAT command.

Example:

    UNFORMAT C:

Variations:

    UNFORMAT C: /TEST

Shows you a preview of how UNFORMAT will work on the drive.

UNFORMAT C: /P

This variation rebuilds a damaged partition table (originally created with FDISK). It can help you fix your hard drive if you get the message "Drive not ready error. Insert boot disk into drive A: and press any key when ready" when you turn on your computer.

XCOPY

Works just like COPY, but can also copy the files in a subdirectory and can be used as a simple backup/restore utility.

How to use it:

Follow XCOPY with the name of the original file, then a space and then the name of the new file or the new location for that file (using a drive and directory name). You can also copy all files from a directory (similar to using a filename of *.*) by just leaving off the filename and using a directory name after XCOPY.

Example:

XCOPY C:\TEMP\SAVEME.TXT C:\TEXT

Variations:

XCOPY C:\TOOLS D:\DOSTOOLS\ /S

Copies all the files in C:\TOOLS, creating a new directory called DOSTOOLS on drive D: with all the same files. It also copies all the subdirectories in C:\TOOLS as subdirectories under D:\DOSTOOLS. Using this command is similar to dragging a folder from one drive to another in Windows. Unless you add the /E switch also, XCOPY won't transfer any empty directories.

XCOPY C:\MSOFFICE\WINWORD\DOCS C:\BACKUP /A

With the /A switch, XCOPY copies only files that have the Archive attribute set (see "ATTRIB"). The Archive bit means that a file needs to be backed up, since it was modified since the last time the Archive bit was cleared. The /A switch does not clear the Archive bit, though, so you may want to use /M, it works like /A, only copying files with the Archive bit set, but it then clears the bit, marking those files as "backed up."

XCOPY C:\OLDFILES A: /D:01/01/90

Copies only those files that have changed or been created since January 1, 1990.

XCOPY C:\DOCS*.DOC C:\BACKUP /P

Allows you to decide, file by file, which .DOC files will be copied. /P lets you confirm each copy.

Commands to Avoid

Some DOS commands, such as RECOVER, are simply poisonous to Windows 95. Others aren't compatible with Windows 95. The rest we're going to mention here are also inherently dangerous but sometimes necessary. You must take precautions when you invoke them.

APPEND was used to make a specific directory appear to be "merged" with the current directory at all times. This is explained in the "PATH" discussion earlier in this reference section. It's not very useful, though, and doesn't work with Windows. So typing **DIR** would show the files in the APPEND directory to be included in every other directory. Even though this command is fascinating, it can cause problems for Windows 95 if used in AUTOEXEC.BAT. (Feel free to use it in an MS-DOS window.)

CHKDSK can damage the long filenames on a drive. It has been supplanted by SCANDISK (in DOS) and ScanDisk for Windows. In fact, if you try to use CHKDSK, Windows 95 intervenes and tells you to use its replacement, ScanDisk, instead.

FASTOPEN was used to keep track of the locations of frequently accessed files. In effect, it caches the directory structure but not the files. It doesn't work with Windows and was made obsolete by SmartDrive. Even SmartDrive has been replaced by Windows 95's 32-bit disk caching (see Chapter 5).

FDISK can be used to remove your hard drive's partition information. Use it with care.

FORMAT can erase all the files on a floppy disk, or worse, erase your entire hard drive. Be careful with FORMAT.

RECOVER was an old DOS command used to rebuild a damaged hard drive with lost directory entries. It was also just about useless, since all the files are numbered, and you'd have to examine each one individually. Much

worse, it would destroy a perfectly good hard drive if you used it accidentally, or in hopes that it would solve a minor problem. It has been removed
from DOS 6 through 7, but it may still be on your hard drive if you've upgraded from an earlier version of DOS. Recommendation: *delete RECOVER
from your DOS directory if it still exists.*

SMARTDRV is no longer necessary with Windows 95 but can be used in
MS-DOS mode (discussed earlier, see "Advanced DOS Mode"). Using it
only wastes memory that can be better deployed for Windows 95 virtual
disk caching.

SUBST was used to substitute a fake drive letter for a directory on a drive.
It's too tricky a technique to rely upon for most purposes, and it doesn't
work well with Windows. But you can still use it in an MS-DOS window if
your application requires it.

UNDELETE and UNFORMAT don't work from within Windows 95 unless used with the LOCK command.

Introduction to Batch Files

You can automate common tasks in DOS by using *batch files*. A batch file is a
text file containing a list of DOS commands (and can also include special
batch file commands).

You can use Notepad or the DOS EDIT command to create or edit a batch
file. It must be in plain ASCII text. You can't write one in a word processor
like Word and save it as a .DOC file because the formatting codes and other
stuff that gets added to a word processor file would be confusing to DOS. If
you do want to write your batch files in some word processor, use the Save
As ASCII or Text File feature.

Try this simple batch file, which is a variation on the MOVE command.
Name it MOVEIT.BAT. (You'll probably want to save it to your C:\DOS
directory so you can use it with any current directory. See "PATH" earlier in
this reference section to see why this works.)

```
COPY %1 %2
DEL %1
```

The symbols %1 and %2 are replaced by the command-line parameters that
you use with the batch file. If you type **MOVEIT C:\TEXT\README.TXT
D:\BACKUP**, then the batch file substitutes the actual command-line parameters for %1 and %2. When you run the batch file, you'll see the following:

```
MOVEIT C:\TEXT\README.TXT D:\BACKUP
COPY C:\TEXT\README.TXT D:\BACKUP
```

```
1 file(s) copied
DEL C:\TEXT\README.TXT
```

You can prevent these lines from appearing on the screen while the batch file runs by preceding them with the @ symbol. Or you can use @ECHO OFF as the first line in the batch file (most people do).

During a batch file, you might want to display messages. For example, you could add this line to the MOVEIT.BAT batch file to show the user what was done:

```
ECHO %1 was moved to %2
```

This displays the following:

```
C:\TEXT\README.TXT was moved to D:\BACKUP
```

You might also want to check and see that the parameters were supplied correctly. You can do this by using the IF command. Here is an update to the MOVEIT batch file:

```
@ECHO OFF
IF "%1"=="" GOTO SKIPIT
IF "%2"=="" GOTO SKIPIT
COPY %1 %2 > NUL
DEL %1
ECHO %1 was moved to %2
GOTO END
:SKIPIT
ECHO Use MOVEIT file1 dirname to move
ECHO file1 to directory dirname.
:END
```

This example also introduces line labels, allowing you to conditionally execute some commands and not others. The IF command checks to see if the command-line parameter is blank ("") and if so, skips over the COPY and DEL commands, since they won't work without something to work with. When the IF condition is true, the batch file skips ahead to the label SKIPIT to continue. Otherwise, it moves on to the next line. (We also added > NUL to the COPY command, a little trick that suppresses the status message "1 file(s) copied" for a cleaner look.)

A complete discussion of batch file programming is beyond the scope of this book, and batch files aren't very useful in the world of Windows 95 anyway. They work only in DOS, which is, after all, a dead-end "vestigial organ" to Windows 95.

Since you can now include Windows commands in batch files, they may actually be useful for Windows automation, but the built-in batch file language of DOS is really quite limited and requires opening an MS-DOS session. It's not very pretty.

There is, though, an equivalent of batch files within Windows. You can utilize some useful techniques, such as the macro languages built into Windows applications, that can be used like batch files to customize most anything. Make things happen the way you want them to happen. Write "scripts" that do 15 things with a click on a button. Make your applications work together, sharing data, exchanging data, even controlling each other's behavior.

Moving On

We'll explore powerful customization techniques in the next chapter. With macros and other techniques such as OLE automation, you can make your Windows applications dance to your tune. Customer customization is a Microsoft philosophy, and is one of the qualities that distinguishes their products. If you want things to work a special way, or you want to automate a complicated, frequently required task, you can probably make it happen.

Chapter 23

Automation & Programming

Clearly, it's best if tools you work with are comfortable. They should suit you. They should work the way you want them to work, should "fit your hand." Right?

One of the best ways to work more efficiently and more comfortably is to use tools that have been customized to reflect your preferences and personal style. You can modify most computer software. It's well worth customizing your Windows applications—your comfort and productivity can go *way* up—and it can be surprisingly easy to do. One way to do this is by creating *macros*, little jobs the computer remembers how to do for you.

Do you send e-mail to a certain person all the time? Well then...create a macro that types his or her Internet address for you. Do you send e-mail to a group of 14 people sometimes? Create another macro that inserts all their addresses for you.

Whenever you find yourself doing something over and over, consider that task a candidate for automation. Consider it something you should *teach the computer to do*. Teaching a computer to do something is the definition of *programming*.

Computers do many things, but primary among their skills is automation. Once taught how to do something, these thinking machines will do it flawlessly from now until doomsday. Computers, like accountants, are born to carry out repetitive tasks with great attention to detail. But unlike accountants, computers *never* vary a behavior that they've learned. When you read in the newspapers that some problem occurred because of a "computer error" or "software error," it's simply untrue. Computers and software don't make mistakes any more than knocking over a glass of milk could be called a glass error or a milk mistake.

All major Windows applications let you change "preferences" or "options." But, of necessity, the ones you can change are *general* options, common to all of us, such as whether or how often you want your work automatically saved to disk in case of a power failure. But what about the toolbar in a particular application, with its various buttons? Should you have to deal with the arrangement that ships with the application? Some programs let you edit the buttons in an "options" window; others don't. We'll show you how to do it yourself below.

You perform many repetitive tasks every time you use, say, your word processor. These particular tasks cannot, though, be part of the application's "preferences" menus because the tasks are peculiar to you and the jobs you do. For instance, if you write lots of letters, you'll likely type your name and address quite often. Obviously, the word processor can't offer your name and address as a built-in option. But you can easily *teach* your word processor to type this information whenever you press a special key combination like Ctrl+A.

It's precisely these recurring behaviors—things you do often—that you should record as macros. Then, instead of typing all those words each time, you merely click on an icon in your button bar or press a key combination like Ctrl+A, and voilà, your address is typed in automatically.

We'll demonstrate how to record macros and how to use them, and we'll also describe and implement some macros that we've found most useful over the years.

Creating Your First Macro

Word for Windows 6.0 is the most popular Windows word processor, so we'll use it as our example application. The process of recording and running macros in other applications is largely the same.

Let's make a macro that will print a letter closing, including your address. Here's how:

1. Start Word.
2. Press Alt+T, M, then type **myaddress.**
3. Press Alt+O, Enter, then click the OK button to start the recording.

You'll see two things happen. A small window will appear with a square icon (to stop the recording process) and an equal+circle icon (to pause it). Also, your cursor will have a cassette tape image attached to it. See Figure 23-1.

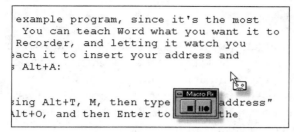

example program, since it's the most
  You can teach Word what you want it to
Recorder, and letting it watch you
ach it to insert your address and
 Alt+A:

ing Alt+T, M, then type   address"
lt+O, and then Enter to   the

Figure 23-1: *The cassette tape image and the Macro Recording window both appear while you are recording a macro.*

 TIP   Pressing the pause icon is useful if you want to type something or perform some activities that you don't want included as part of the macro.

4. Now type in your letter closing, like this:

   Yours truly,
   Richard Mansfield
   212 Tennis Court
   Pinecone, NC 27455

5. Then stop the recording by clicking on the square icon or from within the Tools menu (Alt+T, M, Alt+O, Esc).

Running a Macro

Now that you've recorded your macro, you can run it from the Tool/Macro menu like this:

1. Press Alt+T, M and type **myaddress**.
2. Double-click on *myaddress*. Or you can just press Enter, since *myaddress* will now be highlighted, and the Run button is the "active" button (its border is darker than those around the other buttons).

You should see your letter closing inserted into the active document.

Using a Shortcut Key

Of course, you can trigger your macros by going into the Tools menu, but there's a much better, faster way: shortcut keys. Once you assign the macro to a key combination, triggering it is as simple and as swift as pressing two keys at the same time. After all, you're *typing* in a word processor; your hands are on the keyboard. You don't want to reach for the mouse every time you need to accomplish a common task.

After a while, hitting a key combination becomes automatic. Let's assign our letter closing macro to Ctrl+A, so it's easy to remember ("A" for "address"):

1. Press Alt+T, C to reveal the customize menu.
2. Select Keyboard from the three cardfile dividers.
3. In the Categories list box, select Macros.
4. In the Macros list box, select myaddress (See Figure 23-2).

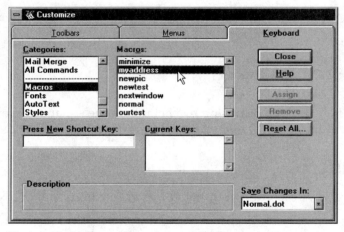

Figure 23-2: *Choose the macro to which you want to assign a key combination.*

5. Click on the Press New Shortcut Key window.
6. Press Ctrl+A.

By default, Word has pre-assigned a number of shortcut key combinations to many of its menu items. Ctrl+A is assigned to Edit/SelectAll (and so is Ctrl+5 [number keypad]). However, few people use this system of key assignments, preferring to set up their own macros and custom shortcut key assignments. What's easy for one person to remember isn't necessarily easy for another. Also, Word comes with so *many* special keys assigned to menus that few people could possibly remember them all.

 It's usually best to create a small, easily remembered set of personal shortcuts. Perhaps 10 is the maximum for most of us. For things you rarely need to do (like Select the entire document), just go through the menu process. (By the way, you can also select an entire document by holding down the Ctrl key while clicking in the left margin.)

7. Click the Assign key to make Ctrl+A trigger your *myaddress* macro.
8. Click the Close key.
9. Press Ctrl+A, and your address should be typed in for you.

Which key combinations?

You can use Alt+key, Ctrl+key or Shift+key for your shortcuts. You can also combine them for additional shortcut key combinations: Alt+Ctrl+key, Shift+Alt+key, Shift+Ctrl+key or even Shift+Alt+Ctrl+key. However, most people stick with Ctrl+key, and that gives them more combinations than they can remember, anyway.

> *WARNING: Avoid assigning Alt+key shortcuts. Using Alt will override the Alt+menu key convention that is used throughout Windows as a quick way to navigate through menus and to make selections in Input boxes. People get used to pressing Alt+F to drop the file down. It's probably best to stick with Ctrl+key combinations for macros. For a similar reason, avoid Alt+Ctrl+key combinations, because they're used by Windows 95 as desktop shortcut keys (see "Hotkeys" in Chapter 8).*

TIP You can also assign menu items to shortcut key combinations. To do that, follow essentially the same procedure as demonstrated above. Here's how to make Ctrl+F toggle full-screen view in Word:

1. Press Alt+T, C to reveal the customize menu.
2. Select Keyboard from the three cardfile dividers.
3. In the Categories list box, select View.
4. In the Commands list box, select ToggleFull (see Figure 23-3).

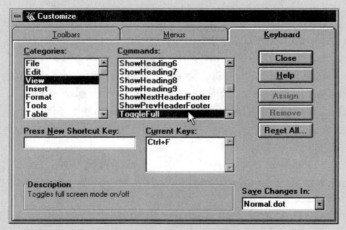

Figure 23-3: *ToggleFull is here under the View menu.*

5. Click on the Press New Shortcut Key window.
6. Press Ctrl+F.
7. Click the Assign key to make Ctrl+F trigger this menu item.
8. Click the Close key.

Assigning Macros to the Toolbar

Along the top of all Microsoft applications, and those of most other software producers, you'll see an optional, but useful, toolbar. (Some call it a button bar or toolbar.) This provides you with yet another way to access frequently used macros and menu items instantly.

Figure 23-4: *A typical Word for Windows toolbar.*

Adding a macro to a toolbar is quite similar to creating a keyboard shortcut for a macro:

1. Press Alt+T, C to reveal the customize menu.
2. Select Toolbars from the three cardfile dividers.
3. In the Categories list box, select Macros.
4. In the Macros list box, press your left mouse button on the word "myaddress" and drag it up to your toolbar (see Figure 23-5).
5. Release the left mouse button wherever on the toolbar you want to drop the new button.
6. Now you'll see the button-selection window (Figure 23-6) pop up.
7. Click on one of the available button symbols to select it.
8. If you prefer to place a text description of your macro onto the toolbar, rather than an icon, type a new name (or leave the default macro name) in the Text Box at the bottom of the button-selection window. (See Figure 23-7.)
9. Click the Assign key to make the change.
10. At this point (while the Customize window is visible) you can drag any of the buttons on the toolbar to rearrange them. Likewise, to remove a button, drag it off the toolbar onto your document.
11. If you like the way the toolbar is organized and want to make no further changes, click the Close button. (You can edit the toolbar at any time by pressing Alt+T, C.)

TIP Follow this same procedure to add Word's menu items to your toolbar. Look for them in the Categories list box shown in Figure 23-5.

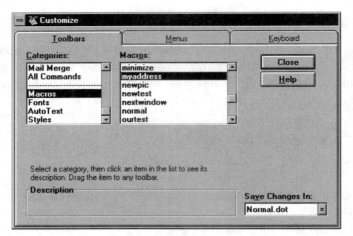

Figure 23-5: *Here's where you can add macros to your toolbar.*

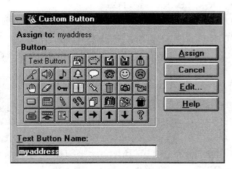

Figure 23-6: *You are offered a selection of icons to assign to your macro.*

Figure 23-7: *You can use a text caption if you prefer that to an icon symbol.*

If you don't find an icon to your liking among the 29 default symbols presented to you (see Figure 23-6), you can access hundreds more that are normally hidden. To do this, we'll directly type some brief instructions to Word (rather than having Word record this macro). Unless you've worked with WordBasic—Word's macro language—you won't understand exactly what's happening here. But go ahead anyway. We'll explain WordBasic shortly. Here's how to get to the treasure chest of 312 secret buttons in Word 6.0:

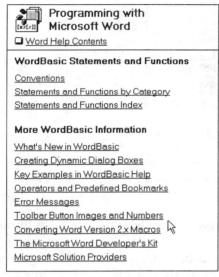

Figure 23-8: *To see the extra buttons, click on Toolbar Button Images and Numbers.*

1. First, choose which of the hidden button symbols you want to add to your toolbar (we'll replace one of your existing button symbols with one of these hidden ones).
2. Click on Word's Help (or press F1).
3. Choose Contents, then Programming with Microsoft Word.
4. Click on Toolbar Button Images and Numbers (see Figure 23-8).
5. Browse around until you find a button face that appeals to you (see Figure 23-9). Jot down its number. We're going to use number 180, which looks like a cassette tape.

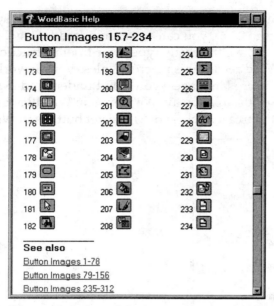

Figure 23-9: *One of the four secret sets of toolbar buttons you can use.*

6. WordBasic is a complete computer language, with hundreds of commands that you can use to make Word jump through hoops and customize it to your heart's content. We'll use just one of these commands now: ChooseButtonImage, which allows you to change an icon on the toolbar. It won't change what that button *does*—just the image on the button.

7. To directly write a WordBasic macro, press Alt+T, M, then type the name of your new macro. Let's type : **changebutton.**

8. Then click the Create button in the Macro window (or just press Enter, since Create is the default, highlighted option, anyway).

9. Now you'll see a new document window (see Figure 23-10). It looks pretty much like any document window. In fact, you type in macros just as you would type in any other document. The only difference is that you're describing to Word some behaviors that you want it to learn.

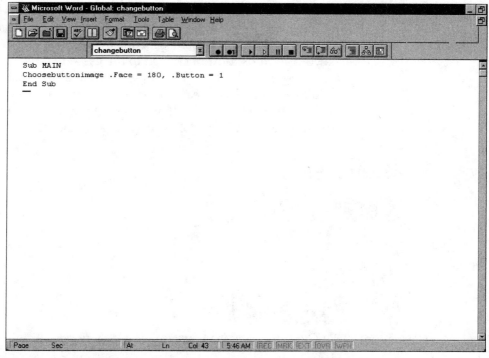

```
Sub MAIN
Choosebuttonimage  .Face = 180,  .Button = 1
End Sub
```

Figure 23-10: *Tell Word what to do in this Macro document screen.*

10. Word provides the "shell" that every macro needs:

    Sub MAIN
    End Sub

    Also, notice that Word has temporarily displayed a new set of 12 buttons (they're all related to writing, running and testing macros).

11. Within this shell, you type in your commands:

    Sub MAIN
    ChooseButtonImage .Face = 180, .Button = 1, .Toolbar = "Standard"
    End Sub

    We've told Word that when this macro runs, it should change the first button (.Button = 1) to image number 180 (.Face = 180). We've also identified the toolbar we want changed—it's the one named Standard.

12. We only need to run this macro once—the change will persist once you've made it. So, let's run it now. Click the solid triangle button (Start) on the Macro toolbar—it runs the current macro. You should see your leftmost button change to the cassette tape symbol. (If it doesn't, or if you get an error message, make sure that you've put a period (dot) in front of each of the three commands: .Face, .Button and .Toolbar. Also be sure that you've separated them with commas. In other words, proof your typing against step 11 above.)

Before

After

Figure 23-11: *Our new cassette icon replaces the old blank paper icon.*

13. Close the macro editing window just as you would close any other document window (select Close from the File menu). Word will ask whether you want to save the macro (see Figure 23-12). Click Yes, and the window will close. Save it, because now you can use it any time to change any icon on any of your toolbars.

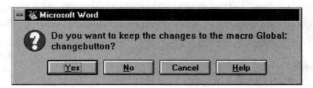

Figure 23-12: *Answer "Yes" to save your new macro.*

Now You Can Change Any Button

For example, if you decide to change the third icon into a pair of binoculars (icon #182, see Figure 23-9):

1. Press Alt+T, M.
2. Type in **changebutton**.
3. Click the Edit button, or press Alt+E, to reveal the macro editing window.
4. Change our macro to:

```
Sub MAIN
ChooseButtonImage .Face = 182, .Button = 3, .Toolbar = "Standard"
End Sub
```

5. Run the macro by clicking the solid triangle Start button on the Macro toolbar.
6. Close the macro editing document.

Restoring original icons

If you want to restore the icon that was on your first button (before we ran this macro), go back into the Tools/Customize window and select the menu item or macro that the first button represents. Now, from the group of buttons Word provides, drag the original icon up onto button one. It's likely to be among the icons Word provides by default.

Editing Macros

Using the hidden button icons *requires* that you type in the instructions—this isn't something that you can record into a macro. But you can also use macro editing as a way of modifying any of your existing macros, without having to re-record it. For example, if you move, it's easy to change your address in the *myaddress* macro described earlier in this chapter:

1. Press Alt+T, M.
2. Type in **myaddress**.
3. Click on the Edit button, or press Alt+E, to reveal the macro editing window.

4. Edit the address:

```
Sub MAIN
InsertPara
Insert "Yours truly,"
InsertPara
InsertPara
InsertPara
InsertPara
Insert "Richard Mansfield"
InsertPara
Insert "44 Diabla Drive"
InsertPara
Insert "Crowbone, NM 27455"
InsertPara
End Sub
```

"InsertPara" is WordBasic for "press the Enter key."

5. Close the macro editing document and answer Yes when asked whether you want to keep the changes.

Help with things you can't do easily

Macros also allow you to save time by carrying out tasks that are awkward to access via menus. For example, if you frequently need to find out how many words are in your document, accomplishing this by navigating the menus can be annoying. You have to remember a weird, unmemorable key combination (Alt+T, W). Also, how do you remember what menu to access? There's nothing obvious about the location of the Word Count feature in the Tools menu, rather than the Format, View or Edit menus.

Wouldn't Ctrl+W be easier to recall when you want a word count? Plus, Word displays the word count along with other things you may not be interested in. You have to look at lots of other information such as a count of pages, characters, paragraphs and lines, when all you want is a word count.

Word Count

The solution? Create a macro that displays only the word count.

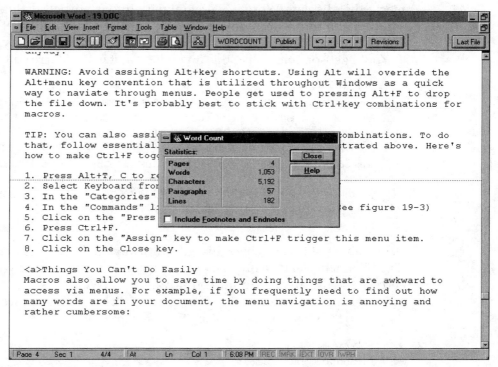

Figure 23-13: *Before: The default statistics message box may contain too many statistics.*

Figure 23-14: *After: A custom pop-up message box, crafted by you to display just want you want to see.*

This next technique allows you to capture the information displayed in *any* Word dialog box and do with it what you will. In this case, we want to display only the word count, so we'll extract that information from Word's Tools/Wordcount menu item.

Sometimes the easiest way to figure out how to *write* a macro is to first *record* something similar to what you want to do—then modify it. This is a rather advanced technique, but you can use it for any dialog box. Record a macro that displays Word's File/Summary Info (statistics) dialog boxes. Start a new macro recording (name it "words," or something), then let it record you pressing Alt+F, I, Alt+I, to display the File menu's Summary Info.

You'll get something like this if you look at it in the Macro editing window:

```
Sub MAIN
FileSummaryInfo .Title = "VGWIN/Mansfield & Brannon/8/21/94", .Subject = "",
.Author = "Richard Mansfield", .Keywords = "", .Comments = "", .FileName =
"19.DOC", .Directory = "C:\BOOKWIN", .Template =
"C:\WINWORD\TEMPLATE\NORMAL.DOT", .CreateDate = "05/23/94 7:04 AM",
.LastSavedDate = "05/25/94 10:46 AM", .LastSavedBy = "Richard Mansfield",
.RevisionNumber = "34", .EditTime = "210 Minutes", .LastPrintedDate = "",
.NumPages = "9", .NumWords = "2,588", .NumChars = "12,167", .NumParas =
"144", .NumLines = "434", .FileSize = "38,912 Bytes"
End Sub
```

But we want to customize this—throw away all the useless data about lines, characters and so on. The only commands we need from within this entire structure are: FileSummaryInfo and .NumWords.

So, open a new macro editing document (Alt+T, M, type in **wordcount**, then click the Create button). Then type this in:

```
Sub MAIN
FileSummaryInfo .Update
Dim dlg As DocumentStatistics
GetCurValues dlg   •
MsgBox "    " + dlg.Words
End Sub
```

The .Update command forces the statistics to be recalculated, so they will be current and accurate. Then we use the Dim command to create a special variable called *dlg*, into which the current values of DocumentStatistics is placed. Finally, we display the subsection of DocumentStatistics identified by .Words.

If you want to learn how to do more things with Word 6.0, you may want to order the *Microsoft Word Developer's Kit* (Microsoft Press). Some bookstores carry it, or you can order it directly from Microsoft Press, 1-800-677-7377. There's a wealth of information in Word's Help (under Contents, look for Programming with Microsoft Word, WordBasic or Macros). But books (thank goodness) remain more convenient and easier to work with than computer monitors when you're trying to learn something.

Our Best Macros

What follows is a collection of the macros we've found most useful in our collective 24 years of using word processors. Even if you don't use Word, or even if you never process words and limit your computing to, say, databases, you should find some useful ideas here for increasing your productivity.

How to enter these macros

Each of the following macros is ready to be typed into the macro editing window. In each case, press Alt+T, M, then type in whatever name you want to give the macro, and press the Create button so that Word will open a clean macro editing document. You'll see the familiar:

```
Sub MAIN
End Sub
```

Between those lines, you type in words that WordBasic will understand. When finished, close the macro editing window (press Alt+F, C) and answer Yes when asked whether you want to keep the changes. Then test the macro by pressing Alt+T, M, locating it in the list box, then clicking the Run button. If you have problems or get an error message, by far the most likely culprit is a typo, particularly punctuation. So reopen the macro for editing (Alt+T, M, find its name, and click the Edit button). Then carefully examine what you've typed to be sure that it matches the original in this book.

LastFile

This useful macro causes Word to load the document you were working on when you last closed Word. Beyond that, it moves your cursor to the precise position where you stopped writing or editing within that document. This is particularly helpful when you spend several days working on a document— you're taken directly to your last position to continue editing:

```
Sub MAIN
FileList 1
GoBack
End Sub
```

The FileList 1 command loads the most recent file, and the GoBack command places the cursor at the most recently edited position within that document. (Pressing Shift+F5 will cycle you through the three most recently edited locations within any document, at any time—a valuable tool.) This is a good one to put on your toolbar, as described earlier in this chapter. That way you can fire up Word and, if desired, go directly and automatically to the right place in the right document with a single mouse click.

Fiddling With Word Itself

Word, of course, has hundreds of internal, pre-written behaviors. They're not macros, exactly (*functions* is the usual technical term), but they carry out tasks just like macros do. For every item on a menu, there's a corresponding internal Word function. Can you change the way Format/Font works? Can you customize the File/Open behavior? You bet.

More Than DOC

Many people find it annoying that Word always displays only the .DOC files when you choose Open from the File menu. Often enough, you want to look at a .TXT file or some other format. It's exasperating to have to click on the little drop-down list box and locate .TXT or whatever, before you can see a full list of the files. If you're one of those who want to see all files right off the bat (like using DIR *.* in DOS), this macro is for you.

 TIP If you're looking for a built-in Word function, it's probably named after the Menu+Item where you would locate it in the Menus. For example, in the File menu is an Open item. The formal name of this item is, logically enough, FileOpen.

Personalizing one of Word's internal behaviors couldn't be easier. Here it is, step-by-step:

1. Open the Macro Window: Alt+T, M.
2. In the List Box titled *Macros Available In*: select Word Commands (see Figure 23-15).

Figure 23-15: *Here's how to customize one of Word's built-in features.*

3. Select (click on or move to with the arrow keys) the one named FileOpen. Don't double-click or you'll Run it.

4. With FileOpen highlighted, go back down to the *Macros Available In* list box, and select Normal.dot [Global Template].

5. At this point, you'll see FileOpen listed among your own macros (instead of among the Word commands).

6. Click the Edit button.

7. The usual macro recording window will open, *and it will be filled with the commands Word uses to perform a File Open.*

8. So here you are, presented with the appropriate commands—all you have to do is insert a few things to customize it.

9. Word's behaviors when opening a file are listed like this:

```
Sub MAIN
Dim dlg As FileOpen
GetCurValues dlg
Dialog dlg
FileOpen dlg
End Sub
```

10. Add these three lines to the existing Word lines:

```
Sub MAIN
Dim dlg As FileOpen
GetCurValues dlg
On Error Goto Exit
dlg.Name = "*.*"
Dialog dlg
FileOpen dlg
Exit:
End Sub
```

11. Now close the macro editing document and answer Yes when asked whether you want to keep the changes.

Now try it out. You'll see the results in Figure 23-16—all files will now be displayed whenever you select Open from the File menu.

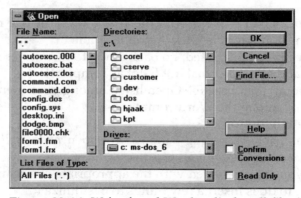

Figure 23-16: *We've forced Word to display* all *files in the Open dialog box, not just .DOC files.*

Two of the lines we added (*On Error Goto Exit* and later, *Exit:*) come into play when you press Esc or Cancel to abort the File Open dialog box. Without this exit mechanism, Word would display an error message (harmless, but exasperating).

We've now changed the pattern that is used to choose which files are displayed.

The key change we made was to tell Word that the .Name property of this dialog box will, henceforth, be *.* so that all files will be displayed. If you frequently work with .TXT files and want to put a button on your toolbar to display just .TXT files, change it to:

```
dlg.Name = "*.TXT"
```

You now have complete freedom to make Word display whatever kinds of files (through whatever "filter") you want.

Note that by adding a macro named FileOpen to our personal macros, we are *overriding* Word's built-in FileOpen feature. In other words, when you select Open from the File menu, Word first checks to see whether you have a personal macro by that name. If so, it doesn't look any further, it just carries out whatever instructions your macro contains. Word doesn't look to its interior list of features to find FileOpen.

Restoring Word's Original Behaviors. •

If you want to revert to Word's native state—that is, to have FileOpen show only .DOC files—simply remove your personal FileOpen macro and Word will then use its built-in FileOpen:

1. Open the Macro window (Alt+T, M).
2. Use the Scroll Bar to locate FileOpen in the list of macros in Normal.dot, so that FileOpen is highlighted.
3. Click on the Delete button.

That's it. It's gone. (If you try File Open, you'll still see *.* because Word retains the last filter you've used. But, trust me, .DOC will be the default filter the next time you run Word.)

Temporarily Restoring Word's Defaults

If you want to preserve your macro, but temporarily permit Word to behave in its default way—just use the macro Organizer to rename FileOpen. As long as it has some other name, Word's own FileOpen will take effect:

1. Open the Macro window (Alt+T, M).
2. Use the Scroll Bar to locate FileOpen in the list of macros in Normal.dot, so that FileOpen is highlighted.
3. Click the Organizer button.
4. Click on Rename.
5. Change the name from FileOpen to zFileOpen to keep it down at the bottom of your list of personal macros—ready to be renamed once again to FileOpen, should you want to customize Word's behavior again.

Whither .Name?

How did we know what to call the item that specifies the filter that changes
.DOC to *.*? To get a list of all the items in a dialog box, simply record a
temporary macro, then look at it in the Edit macro window. You'll be able to
pick out any items you want to modify, they're all English words.

1. Press Alt+T, M, then type **temp.**
2. Press Alt+O, Enter to start the recording.
3. Click on the File menu, then click on Open.
4. When the dialog box is displayed, double-click on a filename to
   actually open that document (otherwise the macro won't record the
   dialog items).
5. Then stop the recording by clicking on the square icon or by entering the Tools menu (Alt+T, M, Alt+O, Esc).
6. Now, to see the results, the dialog items: Press Alt+T, M then highlight *temp* in the list of macros.
7. Click on Edit.

You should see something like this:

```
Sub MAIN
FileOpen .Name = "AUTOEXEC.BAT", .ConfirmConversions = 0, .ReadOnly = 0,
.AddToMru = 0, .PasswordDoc = "", .PasswordDot = "", .Revert = 0,
.WritePasswordDoc = "", .WritePasswordDot = ""
End Sub
```

From this, we can tell that the .Name item describes to FileOpen which
file (and default filter) will be displayed in the FileOpen dialog box. If you
wanted to prevent someone from making changes to any opened file, you
could cause the opened file to be Read Only. This corresponds to clicking the
Read Only check box in the File Open dialog box. Here's how:

```
Sub MAIN
Dim dlg As FileOpen
GetCurValues dlg
On Error Goto Exit
dlg.Name = "*.*"
dlg.ReadOnly = 1
Dialog dlg
FileOpen dlg
Exit:
End Sub
```

Recall that in macros, 1 means "true" or "on."

Special Keys

Quite sensibly, Word doesn't allow you to attach macros to normal keys, like the *k* or +. After all, if *k* triggered a macro, how would you ever type? How would you type *quick* if instead of the *k* the File Open dialog box appeared because you'd told Word that k didn't mean k, it meant open a file?

Nonetheless, writers, like any other worker, want their tool, their keyboard, to be a sleek, effective instrument. And for most of us, there are a few keys (the braces [ ], the accent grave ' and the lowercase tilde ~) we never need in our documents. Wouldn't it make sense to use those keys for something? Why not have them trigger something we do often, because hitting a single key is easier than an Alt+key, Ctrl+key or other combination?

If you want to use the accent grave (the symbol under the ~) to cycle among all open documents—a good use for it—follow these steps:

1. Create a macro that toggles between open screens. Press Alt+T, M, then type in **nextdoc**.
2. Click the Create button and type:

```
Sub MAIN
NextWindow
End Sub
```

3. Close the document to save this macro.
4. Create the macro that assigns the accent grave to *nextdoc*. Press Alt+T, M and type **assignkey.**
5. Click the Create button and type:

```
Sub MAIN
ToolsCustomizeKeyboard .Category = 1, .Name = "nextdoc", .KeyCode = 192, .Add
End Sub
```

6. Click on the Start symbol in the toolbar (the solid triangle) to run this macro. It will assign the code 192 (accent grave key) to the *nextdoc* macro.
7. Now test it. Press the accent grave key a few times and you'll see Word toggle among all open documents.
8. You only need to run this *assignkey* macro once, but you might as well save it in case you want to assign other keys to other macros. So, close the macro editing window and click on Yes to keep the changes.

Here is a list of other keys that you might want to consider using as superfast macro triggers:

Key	Code
Pause	19
Scroll Lock	145
Semicolon (;)	186
Equal Sign (=)	187
Slash (/)	191
Accent grave (')	192
Left Bracket ([)	219
Backslash (\)	220
Right Bracket (])	221

Removing a Key Assignment

Let's say you suddenly have to write lots of letters to France. You'll want to get that accent grave key back to its normal state. If you find that you need to restore a specially assigned key like accent grave, just run the following macro:

1. Create a macro that restores the accent grave to its normal state. Press Alt+T, M and type **removekey.**
2. Click the Create button and type:

```
Sub MAIN
ToolsCustomizeKeyboard .Category = 1, .KeyCode = 192, .Remove
End Sub
```

3. Click on the Start symbol in the toolbar (the solid triangle) to run this macro. It will restore the accent grave key so it can now print. It will no longer trigger a macro.

Delete Word

Deleting individual words is something most writers need to do quite often. Unhappily, the key combinations to do that in Word are perversely awkward: Ctrl+Del deletes the word to the right, Ctrl+Backspace deletes the word to the left. There are several problems with this approach. First, on most keyboards, you have to be rather dexterous to hit these keys accurately while typing because they're so far apart. Second, there should be a key combination that always deletes the word to the right of the cursor (as WordPerfect used to do). Forget deleting the word to the left. Finally, using Word's approach to deletion, if you're *within* a word, rather than on a space between words, only the characters to the right or left are deleted, *not the whole word*. Most peculiar indeed. Trying to delete the word *why* with your cursor between the *w* and the *h* leaves the *w* behind!

Luckily, we can construct our own delete-word macro, then assign it to both bracket keys [ ]. This solves all our problems, and gives us two keys to slam when we want to remove a word. Even the wildest typist will be able to hit one of those keys during a furious bout of writing.

Our delete-word macro should combine *both* the Ctrl+Backspace and Ctrl+Del styles of deletion. That way, no matter where your cursor is placed within the target word, the entire word will be removed. However, if the cursor is on a space, we want to delete only the word to the right (Ctrl+Del). (Otherwise we'd delete two words at once.)

So our macro has three things to test for: 1.) Is the cursor to the left of a space? 2.) To the right of a space? 3.) Within a word? We want the macro to behave differently in each case. In effect, repeatedly triggering this macro will seem to *suck words, one by one, into the cursor*.

To create the macro:

1. Create a macro that restores the accent grave to its normal state. Press Alt+T, M and type **killword**.
2. Click the Create button and type in:

```
Sub MAIN
'If cursor is:
'to left of a space...
If Selection$() = " " Then
        CharRight() : DeleteWord : Goto Exit
EndIf
CharLeft()
'in middle of a word..
If Selection$() <> " " Then
        CharRight() : DeleteWord : DeleteBackWord
        CharRight() : Goto Exit
EndIf
'to right of a space
CharRight() : DeleteWord
Exit:
End Sub
```

3. Now close the macro editing document and answer Yes when asked whether you want to keep the changes. (Note that lines in a macro that begin with a single quote are merely comments to remind us of what were doing. Such lines are ignored by Word.)

To attach this macro to both brace keys:

1. If you created the macro called *assignkey*, open it for editing and skip step 2. (Press Alt+T, M, then locate *assignkey* and click the Edit button. Go to step 3.)
2. Or, create the macro that assigns a single key to a macro. Press Alt+T, M and type **assignkey**. Click the Create button.
3. Type this into the macro:

```
Sub MAIN
ToolsCustomizeKeyboard .Category = 1, .Name = "killword", .KeyCode = 219, .Add
End Sub
```

4. Click the Start symbol in the toolbar (the solid triangle) to run this macro. It will assign the code 219 (the left bracket key) to the *killword* macro.
5. Edit the macro again, changing the .Keycode to 221:

```
Sub MAIN
ToolsCustomizeKeyboard .Category = 1, .Name = "killword", .KeyCode = 221, .Add
End Sub
```

6. Again, click on the Start symbol in the toolbar to run the macro.

Toggling Toolbars

Toolbars are useful, but they do take up precious document space, reducing the amount of text you can read at any one time. One good solution is to create a macro that will toggle a set of toolbars. When you need the ruler, or the set of formatting buttons it's useful to have them onscreen. But otherwise, they just distract. We'll create a macro to drop a set of our favorite toolbars, then retract them when we're done.

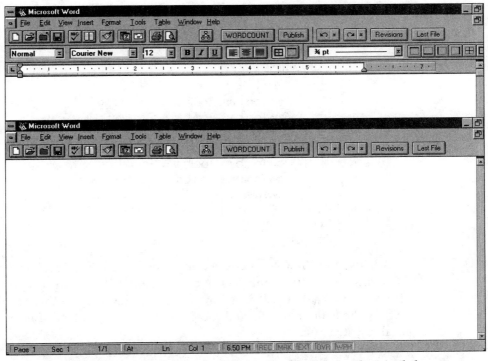

Figure 23-17: *Display or hide your favorite group of toolbars with a single keypress.*

A *toggle* remembers its current state. Like a light switch, changing it turns something on (if it's currently off) and vice versa. Therefore, our *toggletoolbars* macro has to check the current status—deciding whether we want the toolbars to appear or disappear. We don't want the mess of having one key-combination display, and a different key-combination hide, these toolbars. In older houses, you may still find light switches with two buttons—a button for "on" and another separate button for "off." Eventually, people realized that a light switch should be a single object, with two states, like a teeter-totter.

1. Decide which set of your toolbars you want to toggle. In my case, I always leave a single, main toolbar visible, but toggle the macro toolbar, the formatting toolbar and the ruler as a single group. Press Alt+V, T to find the names of the group of toolbars you would like to make optionally visible.

2. Create the macro. Press Alt+T, M then type the name **toggletools** and click the Create button.

3. Type this in:

```
Sub MAIN
On Error Goto Exit
x = ViewRuler()
If x = - 1 Then
        ViewToolbars .Toolbar = "Formatting", .Hide
        ViewToolbars .Toolbar = "Borders", .Hide
        ViewRuler
Else
        ViewToolbars .Toolbar = "Formatting", .Show
        ViewToolbars .Toolbar = "Borders", .Show
        ViewRuler
EndIf
Exit:
End Sub
```

We use the ViewRuler command to test whether the Ruler is currently showing. ViewRuler puts a -1 in the variable x if it's true, the Ruler is visible. If not, it puts a 0 in x. This is how the macro knows whether to .Hide or .Show the Ruler and selected toolbars within the If...Else...Endif decision-making structure.

If you don't want the ruler among the toolbars that drop down, then test for the visibility of one of the toolbars in the group you do want to toggle. Change this:

```
x = ViewRuler()
```

to this:

```
x = ToolbarState("Borders")
```

or one of the toolbar names that you are working with. Note that your custom toolbars might not have actual names; instead, they are called Toolbar 1, Toolbar 2, and so on. These names can also be used as the test (x = ToolbarState("Toolbar 4")).

You can now attach this macro to a key combination like Ctrl+T (for "toggle" or "toolbar") or add it as a button on your main, always-visible, toolbar. (See "Using a Shortcut Key" at the start of this chapter for more.)

Toggle Revisions

When you work with other writers or editors, you want to let them know what you've changed. So you turn on Tools | Revisions, *Mark Revisions While Editing*. But sometimes while making changes, you need to turn off Mark Revisions temporarily to make formatting adjustments and so on. A toggle works well here:

1. Press Alt+T, M then name the macro *ToggleRev*.
2. Click the Create button.
3. Type this in:

```
Sub MAIN
Dim DR As ToolsRevisions
GetCurValues DR
If DR.MarkRevisions = 0 Then
        Print "Revision Marks ON"
        ToolsRevisions .MarkRevisions = 1
Else
        Print "Revision Marks OFF"
        ToolsRevisions .MarkRevisions = 0
EndIf
End Sub
```

This toggle is similar to Toggling Toolbars above, but we're checking the status of a dialog box (Tools | Revisions). Therefore, we have to use the Dim command to create a temporary variable (DR) for the current values. Then we check the .MarkRevisions property of Revisions. If it's off (0), we turn it on, and vice versa. Note that the Print command merely displays the current state of MarkRevisions on the status bar at the bottom of the screen.

For Power Users Only

If you really want to take advantage of all the capabilities of Windows 95 and the efficiencies you can achieve under it—buy Microsoft's Visual Basic (retail $99). There is no substitute. VB gives you the tools to control and manipulate Windows 95 with little programming overhead. You get results rapidly with this most English-like of all computer languages.

Why bother? The answer is, there's much you can accomplish within the operating system (the OS) itself. Notably absent from Windows 95 is the Windows 3 Recorder. It was an admittedly crude little tool that could, in some cases, create a macro that would do something within Windows. But at least it provided a way to automate some OS behaviors.

As you know, most serious applications contain their own macro recorders and macro languages. But what about the operating system? What if you want to customize or automate the behavior of Windows itself? When you're on the desktop, you can't trigger a macro within an application (the application isn't the currently active entity—the operating system, Windows 95 itself, is active). Or what if you want to write a utility, like an icon that you click to start America Online and switch to the stock reports—all automatically?

Visual Basic also lets you interact with the new VBA language, Visual Basic for Applications, that's appearing now as the macro language in the newest versions of Excel and Project, and will doubtless soon become part of Access and Word as well.

In DOS there was the batch file. In Windows 3 there was the recorder. There is nothing like them in Windows 95. The solution: Visual Basic. If you do decide to take the plunge and add Visual Basic to Windows 95, what follows is a brief overview. If you've never worked with a computer language before, we'll get you started with Visual Basic, an extraordinary—you might say revolutionarily effective—tool.

Opening Windows

Programmers have wrestled for years with computer languages—various ways of telling the computer what to do. Visual Basic has more power than most of the older languages. What's more, many elements of a Visual Basic program—particularly the tricky visual elements—are already written for you. Visual Basic is a breakthrough.

Visual Basic (VB) provides such a full set of built-in intelligent tools that creating programs for the Windows environment can be astonishingly easy. You can just drag and drop an entire Directory List Box onto a window in your program. All the directories and subdirectories are automatically visible. If you click on one of the directories in the box, the box reacts by changing to that directory and showing you any of its subdirectories. You don't have to write a single word of programming to create this fully functional Directory list.

Visual Basic is not a toy, even though it's often fun to use. With VB, you can write efficient, polished programs that are every bit as professional as commercial applications. Yet, creating a Visual Basic program is much easier than writing in C or other computer languages.

"Designing" Instead of Writing

If you're new to programming, the first phase of writing a program in Visual Basic will seem more like designing a picture than writing out cryptic, half-mathematical instructions for a machine to follow. If you have struggled with more primitive languages, it will seem paradoxical that programming for a sophisticated environment like Windows should prove easier than programming for the more elementary world of DOS.

Visual Basic contains so many built-in features that creating the user-interface elements of a program is more like picking out a backyard deck from a catalog than building it yourself, plank by plank.

But Visual Basic's tools and custom Controls are more than simply nice-looking; they also know how to *do* things. Perhaps the quickest way to grasp what makes Visual Basic so special is to think of it as a collection of prebuilt robot parts. You just choose the parts you want on the visible surface of your program.

Visual Basic provides all the visual components necessary for computer interaction: List boxes that automatically alphabetize and arrange items in columns, Scroll Bars, resizable windows, push buttons, and more.

These Tools Come with Built-In Capabilities: A Text Box automatically wraps words around to the next line and responds to arrow, Backspace, Del, Enter, Caps Lock and Shift keys. It would take days to construct this in the C language; placing it into a window in Visual Basic takes seconds.

In addition, you can customize each tool by selecting qualities from the Properties window. For example, some of the choices for a Text Box's Properties are BackColor, BorderStyle, DragIcon, Enabled, FontBold, FontSize, ForeColor, Height and Width, Index, LinkMode, MousePointer, Name, ScrollBars, TabStop, Text and Visible.

Want to change the background color of a Text Box? Just click your mouse on BackColor and select from a palette:

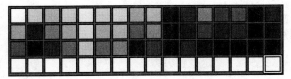

Figure 23-18: *Changing colors is as easy as clicking.*

And You Can Edit Objects Globally: Want to change the color of five Labels? Drag the mouse around them to "select them as a group." This is just the way you would group visual objects in a graphics program. (Or , you can also group them by holding down the Shift key and clicking on each Label you want to change.) VB is so intelligent that its Properties window (where the qualities of objects, such as their size or color, are adjusted) will display the Properties that the selected group of objects *have in common.* After selecting all the Labels whose colors you want to change, just double-click on the Properties window BackColor item. The Color Palette will appear. Click on the color you want and, voilà, all the selected Labels change from white to magenta.

Want to copy a group of selected objects within a given Form or from one Form to another, or cut and paste them? It's just as easy as copying and pasting text in a well-designed word processor—delete, cut, copy or paste them using the same Windows conventions that you would with words: click on an object, or if you want to manipulate a group of objects, drag the mouse around them to select them. (Remember, if you don't want to drag the mouse around them—perhaps they're not contiguous—hold down the Shift key and click the mouse. This adds an object to a selected group.)

Then, as in a word processor:

- The Del key *deletes* the object or group.
- Shift+Del *cuts* (deletes, but copies to the Clipboard for any later pasting you might want to do. This is the way you *move* objects from one window to another).
- Ctrl+Ins *copies* the selected objects to the Clipboard, from which they can be pasted as often as you want. *The Properties of the objects* (qualities such as color, width, text fonts and so forth) *will also be copied.*
- Shift+Ins *pastes* the objects.

If you're in the habit of using non-Windows conventions, you can also use a parallel set of keyboard-only commands that mimic the behavior of the Windows commands, such as Ctrl+C, which copies, and Ctrl+V, which pastes.

Drawing in the Design Phase

One very important Visual Basic breakthrough is a reversal of the normal approach to programming: instead of spending weeks writing instructions that tell the computer how to make your program respond and how it should look, you simply *draw* the program. You drag the various items you want onto a window (called a *form* in Visual Basic), select their qualities and then see how your program looks to the user.

This design stage takes very little time. You don't write a single instruction to the computer—you click, drag and drop. You can resize, reposition and delete things. And from each item's individual Properties window, you can select its qualities, adjusting aspects of behavior and appearance. This way to organize a program and achieve an interface between computer and user is both quick and intuitive. You are, in effect, describing how the program should behave, but you're describing it *visually*. And recall that many of the tools you assemble on a window come from the factory already functional, equipped to react intelligently when the user types or clicks the mouse.

This approach also helps you build the rest of the program (when you write specific commands for the computer to follow) more efficiently. In Visual Basic, you draw the goal onscreen so that the final product is there for you to see. Programming the user interface can often take up as much as 50 percent of a programmer's time. In Visual Basic, it takes maybe 3 percent of the time. What's more, you've got a visual description of the organization and features of your program, before you even write a line of program. This not only helps keep things coherent, it also assists you in keeping the goal of your program always right in front of your face. Therefore, it's hard to get lost or confused.

Figure 23-19: *Adding, resizing and positioning graphic backgrounds in a Visual Basic window is a simple mouse click and drag.*

Not the End

Of necessity, this chapter was limited to only a few examples—tantalizing, we hope—of what you can do with macros and programming. Throughout the book, however, we've tried to cover in-depth all the features, major and minor, of Windows 95 itself, and the accessories, utilities and applications bundled with it. Nevertheless, this book is not finished and likely never will be.

If you read the Introduction, you might recall our mentioning that—even after having used Windows 95 eight hours a day, every day for nearly two years—we're still discovering new shortcuts, efficiencies and interesting techniques. We expect this process of discovery will be ongoing; Windows 95 is a remarkably intricate operating system—in spite of its charming, placid and inviting surface.

Windows 95 is expected to undergo a continuing process of refinement in the coming years. This book will be frequently refined as well. Between new printings and editions of *The Windows 95 Book*, the authors will be posting revisions, additions and new tips in the book's *Online Companion*. Please drop in from time to time to see what's new, and, if you wish, leave messages with suggestions, corrections, tips and techniques that you've discovered. To access us at Ventana's *Windows 95 Online Companion*, connect via the World Wide Web to http://www.vmedia.com/win95.html.

Appendices

Appendix A

About the Online Companion

The *Windows 95 Online Companion* is an informative tool as well as an annotated software library. It aids in your exploration of Windows 95 features while at the same time offering you the online support you need to get up to speed with this new operating system. The *Windows 95 Online Companion* hyperlinks you to Windows 95 Internet resources: newsgroups, archives and sites pertaining to Microsoft's new operating system. So you can just click on the reference name and jump directly to the resources you are interested in.

Perhaps one of the most valuable features of the *Windows 95 Online Companion* is its Software Archive. Here, you'll find and be able to download the latest versions of all the software mentioned in *The Windows 95 Book* that are freely available on the Internet. Available applications range from simple icon-editing programs to powerful compression utilities, and everything in-between. Also with Ventana Online's helpful description of the software you'll know exactly what you're getting and why. So you won't download the software just to find you have no use for it.

The *Windows 95 Online Companion* also links you to the Ventana Library where you will find useful press and jacket information on a variety of Ventana Press offerings. Plus, you have access to a wide selection of exciting new releases and coming attractions. In addition, Ventana's Online Library allows you to order the books you want.

The Windows 95 Online Companion represents Ventana Online's ongoing commitment to offering the most dynamic and exciting products possible. And soon Ventana Online will be adding more services, including more multimedia supplements, searchable indexes and sections of the book reproduced and hyperlinked to the Internet resources they reference.

To access, connect via the World Wide Web to http://www.vmedia.com/win95.html

Appendix B

About the *CD-ROM*

The CD-ROM included with this book features over 40 shareware and freeware applications written specifically to take advantage of Windows 95's 32-bit environment—and enhance it as well. Also included are 100 eye-catching custom wallpaper textures, designed for quick redraw and memory efficiency, and many more bonus games, systems tools and utilities.

Shareware is intended to allow you to evaluate the software for a limited trial period. You then must either pay the author a registration fee, or discontinue use of the software. You are encouraged to share and distribute the shareware to others, although you will need to obtain permission from the original author if you are distributing the software for a fee. Shareware only works if we all participate and register the software.

To run the CD: Insert the CD in drive; double-click on the My Computer icon; double-click on *The Windows 95 Book* CD icon; then double-click on setup.exe.

The applications are contained in the following folders on our CD-ROM. Double-click on the "Read Me" file in each folder for specific installation instructions:

Folder	Name
\acts	*Somar ACTS* allows you to accurately set your computer's internal clock.
\alarm32	*Alarm* is an easy-to-use alarm clock
\anicurso	A collection of colored and animated mouse pointers (cursors)
\aclock2	*Astronomy Clock* displays the current time in local mean time, Universal Time, local sidereal time and Greenwich sidereal time.

\astrlab2	*Astronomy Lab* generates animated movies that simulate a host of astronomical events.
\bmpview	*Bitmap Viewer* allows you to view preview-sized images of bitmaps in your drive/directories.
\bog2	*Bog* is a word game similar to Boggle.
\bomb_sq2	*Bomb Squad* is a logic puzzle.
\cwptrs	*Color Wave Pointer Set* is a set of colorful mouse pointers.
\easyicon	*Easy Icons 95* is a complete Icon Management System for Windows users.
\ecopadnt	*EcopadNT* is a text editor, a super-Notepad for Windows 95 and NT.
\fracview	*FracView 2* displays the Mandelbrot set and allows you to zoom in on a region of interest.
\hangman2	*Hangman* is a computerized version of the well-known hangman game.
\insecta	*Insecta* is a basic Entomology program targeted at children ages 8 and up.
\mdb95	*Michael's Disk Benchmark* Version 1.10 allows you to run performance benchmarks on your hard drives.
\mgacur	More animated mouse pointers.
\midijuk2	*MIDI JukeBox 2* allows you to select and play multiple MIDI and or .WAV files.
\pzl82	*Puzzle-8* is a computerized version of the well-known 8 tile puzzle.
\rcalc2	*RCALC* is a Reverse Polish Notation (RPN) calculator.
\ripbar	*RipBAR Version 6.2* provides services such as application and drag-and-drop launching, memory and resource tracking, task switching, HotKey access, and so on
\ripspace	*RipSPACE Version 3.0* analyzes disk space usage.
\run25	*Run* allows you to launch an application with a single mouse click.
\st_gra	*Stereogram 2* converts monochrome bitmaps into random-dot stereograms that can be viewed onscreen or printed.
\swat2a	*GrabIt Pro 5.0* is a screen capture utility.
\sw2	*Stopwatch* is a stopwatch/clock utility.

\systip	*SysTips* is a utility that provides additional "tooltips" to new Windows users.
\task15	*Task* is a utility that shows all the tasks running on your system.
\tclock2	*Talking Clock* displays the current time and optionally announces the time every 15 minutes using a sound card.
\telpz2	*Telephone Puzzle* displays words as telephone numbers.
\tpad32	*TextPad 1.29* is an enhanced text editor that provides power and functionality to handle demanding text editing requirements.
\trackit	*TrackIt* allows you to track vital system resource information.
\trayqt	*TrayQuit* is a "fast exit" utility that includes "fast logoff" via two tray icons.
\vault	*Vault* stores information as an outline and organizes the information into categories and subcategories for easy search and retrieval.
\vidres	*VidRes* is a video resolution switching utility.
\walpaper	100 wallpaper bitmaps ideal for tiling on your desktop.
\w32ss	*Windows 95 Screen Saver Pack.*
\wf32_2	*WinFlic Version 2.0* is the AutoDesk FLI and FLC Player utility.
\winbatch	*WinBatch 32* is the Windows Batch Language you can use to write batch programs.
\winima21	*WinImage Version 2.10* is a disk image management utility.
\winjive	*WinJive* distorts bitmaps in real-time.
\winplax	*WinPlax* scrolls multiple bitmap backgrounds in real-time
\winrage	*WinRage* is the MONOLITH 3D demo that gives the user the ability to move within a futuristic 3D environment.
\winstar	*WinStar* simulates 3D starfields in real-time.
\winzip95	*WinZip for Windows Version 6.0* is an archive manager for PKZIP and much more.

Appendix C

Technical Support & Other Sources of Information

Contacting Microsoft

Before you call technical support, be at your computer and have at your fingertips all the information concerning your computer. It's a good idea to use Start | Run SYSEDIT so that all your system files are displayed for ready access. If you are reporting a bug, write down the steps necessary to reliably reproduce the symptoms, and take note of which applications you were running at the time. Write down any error messages you encounter *exactly*. Finally, make an effort to resolve your problem by reading the user manuals and of course, this book. Customer hold times are expected to be significant, and you'll help reduce the burden by reserving technical support for real emergencies. We've also provided a list of online resources for technical support and updated files, which can be a real time saver.

Telephone Support

Microsoft FastTips

From a touch-tone telephone call (800) 936-4200 to receive automated answers to common technical problems. You can also access popular articles from the Microsoft Knowledge Base, which can be delivered by fax or read to you over the phone.

TT/TDD For the Deaf/Disabled

Requires a TT/TDD device or modem
United States   (206) 635-4948
Canada   (905) 568-9641

Technical Support Lines

Free technical support is provided within the first 90 days after your first call. After 90 days, you will have to use fee-based technical support. (No free support is available for network issues.) You do pay for the toll charges.
United States   (206) 635-7000
Canada   (905) 568-4494

Toll-free, but you pay either by the minute or per incident.
United States   (900) 555-2000 $1.95 (U.S.) per minute, $35 maximum.
   Charge will appear on your telephone bill.

United States   (800) 936-5700; $35 (U.S.) per incident.
Canada   (800) 668-7975; $50 (CDN, including GST)
   You can charge the fee to your VISA, MasterCard or American Express card.
   Refer to the document C:\WINDOWS\SUPPORT.TXT for more details and international support telephone numbers.

Microsoft Files & Online Support

You can download updated files, such as additional video drivers, when they become available from the following online locations. You can also obtain the Microsoft Internet Explorer from these locations. (Note: Not all the forums listed here are staffed by Microsoft support personnel. Some are run by third parties or by the information service itself.) The Microsoft Knowledge Base, which contains thousands of articles concerning Windows and Windows 95, is available on CompuServe (GO MSKB) and on America Online (GO MICROSOFT).

The Microsoft Network

Browse the folder \Categories\Computers and software\Software\ Microsoft\Windows 95.

Internet: FTP

ftp://ftp.microsoft.com/Products/Windows/Windows95/
ftp://ftp.microsoft.com/PerOpSys/Win_News/

Internet: Gopher

gopher://gopher.microsoft.com

Internet: World Wide Web

http://www.microsoft.com/Windows

Via Modem (HyperTerminal)

(206) 936-6735

Prodigy

JUMP WINNEWS

CompuServe

GO MSL
GO WINNEWS
GO MICROSOFT
GO WINSUPPORT

Genie

Go to Microsoft Roundtable
MOVE TO PAGE 95

America Online

Keyword WINNEWS
Keyword MICROSOFT
Keyword WINDOWS

Index

Colophon

The Windows 95 Book was produced using Adobe PageMaker 5.0, Adobe Illustrator 5.5 and Adobe Photoshop 3.0 on Power Macintosh 7100 and 8100 computers with 19" and 20" Apple RGB monitors. Pages were proofed using Apple LaserWriter Pro 630 and Hewlett Packard Laserjet 4MP laser printers.

Body copy for the book is set in Adobe Palatino. Headlines, tips and sidebars are set in Adobe Futura, Computer code samples are set in ITC Kabel. Chapter numbers are set in ITC Garamond.

Ride the Windows Wave

Voodoo Windows 95

$24.95, 375 pages, illustrated

Users will need voodoo to make the move to Windows 95! Nelson is back with more secrets, shortcuts and spells than ever. Scores of tips—many never before published—on installing, customizing, editing, printing, virtual memory, Internet connections and much more. Organized by task for easy reference. The companion disk contains shareware utilities, fonts and magic!

Microsoft Network Tour Guide

$24.95, 400 pages, illustrated

In the entertaining, informative tradition of Ventana's bestselling *Tour Guides,* this new title takes readers on a pleasure cruise of Microsoft's new online service. The introduction to MSN's innovative content includes a look at customizable menus, shortcut icons and integration with Windows 95.

The Official America Online for Windows 95 Membership Kit & Tour Guide

$27.95, 350 pages, illustrated

AOL tops the charts with more than 2.5 million members, thousands of whom were introduced to AOL by "Major Tom" Lichty. Now Lichty samples AOL's newest version, providing an easy introduction to Win95 features. Along the way, readers enjoy Lichty's signature tips on saving time and money with a liberal helping of online lore. The companion disk features AOL software (Version 2.6) plus 20 hours free online time (for new members).

Microsoft Office Companion

$24.95, 650 pages, illustrated

This all-in-one reference to Microsoft's red-hot suite is a worthy sequel to Ventana's bestselling *Windows, Word & Excel Office Companion*. Covers basic commands and features, as well as dozens of tips and tricks not found in the manuals. Includes a section on using Windows 95. The companion disk contains examples, exercises, software and sample files from the book.

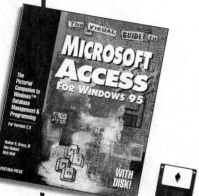

The Visual Guide to Microsoft Access for Windows 95

$34.95, 650 pages, illustrated

Updated for Windows 95, this bestseller focuses on professional database design, with tips and strategies for creating workable forms, reports and tables, plus more than 600 illustrations! The disk includes a fully functional application and all files necessary to complete the examples in the book.

America Online's Internet for Windows, Second Edition

$24.95, 315 pages, illustrated

Forget about expensive, inscrutable Internet conntections! AOL members can slide onto the Infobahn with a mere mouse-click. Same easy, graphical interface, no extra charges. This new edition adds tips on using AOL's new Web browser along with FTP newsgroups and more. Includes AOL quick-start. The companion disk includes AOL software, ready to install, and 10 hours free online time (for new members).

Books marked with this logo include a free Internet *Online Companion*™, featuring archives of free utilities plus a software archive and links to other Internet resources.

Internet Resources

The Web Server Book

$49.95, 680 pages, illustrated

The cornerstone of Internet publishing is a set of UNIX tools, which transform a computer into a "server" that can be accessed by networked "clients." This step-by-step guide to the tools also features a look at key issues—including content development, services and security. The companion CD-ROM contains Linux™, Netscape Navigator™, ready-to-run server software and more.

Walking the World Wide Web

$29.95, 360 pages, illustrated

Enough of lengthy listings! This tour features more than 300 memorable Websites, with in-depth descriptions of what's special about each. Includes international sites, exotic exhibits, entertainment, business and more. The companion CD-ROM contains Ventana Mosaic™ and a hyperlinked version of the book providing live links when you log onto the Internet.

Internet Roadside Attractions

$29.95, 376 pages, illustrated

Why take the word of one when you can get a quorum? Seven experienced Internauts—teachers and bestselling authors—share their favorite Web sites, Gophers, FTP sites, chats, games, newsgroups and mailing lists. In-depth descriptions are organized alphabetically by category for easy browsing. The companion CD-ROM contains the entire text of the book, hyperlinked for off-line browsing and Web hopping.

Acrobat Quick Tour

$14.95, 272 pages, illustrated

In the three-ring circus of electronic publishing, Adobe®
Acrobat® is turning cartwheels around the competition.
Learn the key tools and features of Acrobat's base components in this hands-on guide that includes a look at the
emerging world of document exchange.

HTML Publishing on the Internet for Windows

$49.95, 512 pages, illustrated

Successful publishing for the Internet requires an understanding of "nonlinear" presentation as well as specialized software. Both are here. Learn how HTML builds the
hot links that let readers choose their own paths—and
how to use effective design to drive your message for
them. The enclosed CD-ROM includes Ventana Mosaic,
HoTMetaL PRO, graphic viewer, templates conversion
software and more!

Netscape Quick Tour for Windows, Special Edition

$24.95, 192 pages, illustrated

The hottest browser to storm the Internet allows for fast
throughput and continuous document streaming, enabling
users to start reading a Web page as soon as it begins
to load. This jump-start for Netscape introduces its handy
toolbar, progress indicator and built-in image decompressor to everyday Net surfers. A basic Web overview is
spiced with listings of the authors' favorite sights—and

Check your local bookstore or software retailer for
these and other bestselling titles, or call toll free:

800/743-5369

STOP CHASING YOUR TAIL!

SINK YOUR TEETH INTO THE WORLD WIDE WEB

You want World Wide Web access? Want it now? You got it. The *World Wide Web Kit* has everything you need—access, tools and instructions—to make the Web your own territory.

▶ **Connect to the Web through the IBM Internet Connection** service, provided by the IBM Global Network: reliable Internet access at affordable prices.

▶ **Explore the Web using Ventana Mosaic™ 2.0**—with a convenient new toolbar, turbocharged text flow, tough security modules, built-in sound system and much more. Fully supported!

▶ **Learn more about Ventana Mosaic** with *Mosaic Quick Tour, Special Edition*—the bestselling guide to accessing and navigating the World Wide Web.

▶ **Find your way with** *Walking the World Wide Web*, the richly illustrated tour of the Web that includes an interactive CD-ROM with live links to top Web sites once you log on!

▶ **Plus! A free, one-year subscription to** the *Walking the World Wide Web Online Companion*™, a regularly updated online version of the book.

All that for only $49.95. That's something to wag your tail about!

Available in Windows and Macintosh versions.

FROM THE MAKER OF THE BESTSELLING *INTERNET MEMBERSHIP KIT*™.

TO ORDER ANY VENTANA PRESS TITLE, COMPLETE THIS ORDER FORM AND MAIL OR FAX IT TO US, WITH PAYMENT, FOR QUICK SHIPMENT.

TITLE	ISBN	QUANTITY	PRICE	TOTAL
Acrobat Quick Tour	1-56604-255-0	_____	x $14.95	= $ _____
America Online's Internet for Windows, 2nd Edition	1-56604-283-6	_____	x $24.95	= $ _____
HTML Publishing on the Internet for Windows	1-56604-229-1	_____	x $49.95	= $ _____
Internet Roadside Attractions	1-56604-193-7	_____	x $29.95	= $ _____
Looking Good in Color	1-56604-219-4	_____	x $29.95	= $ _____
Microsoft Network Tour Guide	1-56604-256-9	_____	x $24.95	= $ _____
Microsoft Office Companion	1-56604-188-0	_____	x $24.95	= $ _____
Microsoft Office for Windows 95 Power Toolkit	1-56604-290-9	_____	x $49.95	= $ _____
Netscape Quick Tour for Windows, Special Edition	1-56604-266-6	_____	x $24.95	= $ _____
The Official America Online for Windows 95 Membership Kit & Tour Guide	1-56604-253-4	_____	x $27.95	= $ _____
The Visual Guide to Microsoft Access for Windows 95	1-56604-286-0	_____	x $34.95	= $ _____
Voodoo Windows 95	1-56604-145-7	_____	x $24.95	= $ _____
Walking the World Wide Web	1-56604-208-9	_____	x $29.95	= $ _____
The Web Server Book	1-56604-317-4	_____	x $49.95	= $ _____
The Windows 95 Book	1-56604-154-6	_____	x $39.95	= $ _____
World Wide Web Kit—Macintosh, Ventana Mosaic Version	1-56604-272-0	_____	x $49.95	= $ _____
World Wide Web Kit—Windows, Ventana Mosaic Version	1-56604-271-2	_____	x $49.95	= $ _____

SHIPPING

For all standard orders, please ADD $4.50/first book, $1.35/each additional.
For *World Wide Web Kit* orders, ADD $6.50/first kit, $2.00/each additional.
For "two-day air," ADD $8.25/first book/$2.25/each additional.
For "two-day air" on the kits, ADD $10.50/first book, $4.00/each additional.
For orders to Canada, ADD $6.50/book.
For orders sent C.O.D., ADD $4.50 to your shipping rate.
North Carolina residents must ADD 6% sales tax.
International orders require additional shipping charges.

SUBTOTAL = $ _____
SHIPPING = $ _____
TOTAL = $ _____

Name _____ Daytime telephone _____

Company _____

Address (No PO Box) _____

City _____ State _____ Zip _____

Payment enclosed ____VISA ____MC ____ Acc't # _____ Exp. date _____

Signature _____ Exact name on card _____

Mail to: Ventana Press • PO Box 13964 • Research Triangle Park, NC 27709-3964 ☎ 800/743-5369 • Fax 919/544-9472

Check your local bookstore or software retailer for these and other bestselling titles, or call toll free: **800/743-5369**